D1217200

Modern Real Estate Practice in Illinois

10th Edition

Fillmore W. Galaty, Wellington J. Allaway, and Robert C. Kyle
with Martha R. Williams, JD, Consulting Editor, and Leo Schwartz, Contributing Editor

This publication is designed to provide accurate and authoritative information in regard to the subject matter covered. It is sold with the understanding that the publisher is not engaged in rendering legal, accounting, or other professional advice. If legal advice or other expert assistance is required, the services of a competent professional should be sought.

Executive Director, Real Estate Education: Toby Schifsky
Development Editor: Jody Manderfeld

MODERN REAL ESTATE PRACTICE IN ILLINOIS TENTH EDITION
©2020 Kaplan, Inc.
Published by DF Institute, Inc., d/b/a Dearborn Real Estate Education
332 Front St. S., Suite 501
La Crosse, WI 54601

All rights reserved. The text of this publication, or any part thereof, may not be reproduced in any manner whatsoever without written permission from the publisher.

10 9 8 7 6 5
ISBN: 978-1-07-880128-7 (print)

10 9 8 7 6 5 4
ISBN: 978-1-07-880514-8 (custom)

10 9 8 7 6 5 4 3 2
ISBN: 978-1-0788-0513-1 (custom)

CONTENTS

INTRODUCTION

Whether you are preparing for the Illinois real estate licensing examination, fulfilling a college or university requirement, looking for specific guidance about buying a home or investment property, or simply expanding your understanding of this fascinating field, you can rely on *Modern Real Estate Practice in Illinois* for accurate and comprehensive information in a format that is easy to use.

SPECIAL FEATURES

Illinois-Specific Content

Illinois-specific laws and topics appear throughout the text for classroom and study emphasis. Where appropriate, unit quizzes also include Illinois-specific questions. Also included are two sample licensing examinations and an Illinois-specific exam.

To access the student question bank—to create customized quizzes and exams from the hundreds of questions in the *Modern Real Estate Practice in Illinois* text—go to the website and enter your personal Student Access Code: 81304

www .modernquestion .com

Key Terms

Key terms appear at the beginning of each unit. This feature not only lets you know what important vocabulary words you should look for as you read but also helps you to study and review.

Margin Notes

Margin notes direct your attention to important vocabulary terms, concepts, and study tips. They help you move more easily through the text and locate issues for review, and they serve as memory prompts for more efficient and effective studying.

Summaries

Unit summaries provide you with a quick review of the most essential content covered in each unit.

Real Estate Mathematics

Unit 24 covers real estate mathematics, complete with common terms and equations. As an additional time-saving reference tool, the most frequently used real estate math equations are printed inside the front and back covers of the book.

Updated and Revised Unit Quizzes and Sample Examinations

These quizzes and exams have been revised with demanding fact-pattern problems that encourage you to not just memorize but also understand and apply information—important test-taking and exam-preparation skills. The questions have been carefully designed to follow the style and content of the most widely used testing services and to demonstrate the types of questions that you will likely encounter on state licensing exams.

Glossary

The glossary contains definitions for every key term in the book.

As always, the fundamental goal of *Modern Real Estate Practice in Illinois* is to help you understand the dynamics of the real estate industry, providing the critical information needed to pass the licensing examination, buy or sell property, or establish a real estate career.

Answer Key

Answers to the Unit Quizzes and Sample Examinations can be found starting on page 515.

ACKNOWLEDGMENTS

Like a real estate transaction, this book is the product of teamwork and cooperation among professionals. We would like to express our gratitude and appreciation to the instructors and other real estate professionals whose invaluable suggestions and advice help *Modern Real Estate Practice in Illinois* remain the state's leading real estate principles text. Whether they responded to instructor surveys, provided suggestions for improving the previous edition, or reviewed the content for this edition, the participation of these professionals—and their willingness to share their expertise—is greatly appreciated.

CONSULTING EDITOR

Martha Williams received her juris doctor from the University of Texas, is an author and educator, and has practiced law in Texas and California. She is author or coauthor of *Fundamentals of Real Estate Appraisal*, *The Art of Real Estate Appraisal*, *How to Use the Uniform Residential Appraisal Report*, *California Mortgage Loan Brokerage*, *California Real Estate Principles*, other textbooks, and numerous electronic courses.

CONTRIBUTING EDITOR

Leo Schwartz is Managing Broker and President of Prairie State Real Estate. As an educator, mentor, and trainer he has over 20 years of experience. He is the creator of Real Estate Exam Pro.

REVIEWERS

Reviewers for the Tenth Edition

George Biderman

Sharon L. Halperin, CDEI, SFR

Sam Martin, PhD, DREI, CDEI, MOT

Sue Miranda-Rosensteel, CDEI, GSI, One-on-One Real Estate Education

Eric Schwartz

Each new edition of *Modern Real Estate Practice in Illinois* builds on earlier editions. The authors would like to thank the following individuals for their reviews of prior editions of this book:

Jean Bartholomew, Elyse Berns, Maureen Cain, Patrick Cal, Carol Carlson-Nosfinger, William Carmody, Sandra CeCe, Michael Fair, Ron Hardgrove, Richard Ives, Kerry Kidwell, Maureen LeVanti, Deborah Lopes, Vincent Lopez, Laurie MacDougal, Rose McDonald, Derek McNeal, Clarke Marquis, Sam Martin, Lynda McKay, Robert Mocella, Francis Patrick Murphy, Wayne Paprocki, Chris Read, Karen Stefano, Joyce Bea Sterling, Dawn Svenningsen, Alan Toban, Casey Voris, Barry Ward, Terry W. Watson, Mary Wezeman.

UNIT 1

Introduction to the Real Estate Business

LEARNING OBJECTIVES

When you have completed this unit, you will be able to accomplish the following.

> Identify the various career opportunities available in real estate and the professional organizations that support them.
> Describe the five types of real property.
> Explain the operation of supply and demand in the real estate market; and distinguish the economic, political, and social factors that influence supply and demand.

KEY TERMS

brokerage	real estate licensee	supply and demand
market	sponsoring broker	

OVERVIEW

Real estate transactions take place all around us, all the time. When a commercial leasing company rents space in a shopping center or the owner of a building rents an apartment, it's a real estate transaction. If an appraiser gives an expert opinion of the value of farmland or a bank lends money to purchase an office building, it's a real estate transaction. Most common of all, when a family sells its old home to buy a new one or steps into the housing market for the first time, it's a real estate transaction. Consumers of real estate services include home buyers and sellers, tenants and landlords, investors, and developers. Nearly everyone at some time is an active participant in the real estate industry.

All of this adds up to big business—complex transactions that involve billions of dollars every year.

The services of highly trained individuals are required to support these transactions: attorneys, bankers, appraisers, abstract and title insurance agents, architects, surveyors, accountants, tax experts, home inspectors, and many others, in addition to buyers and sellers. All of these people depend on the skills, knowledge, and integrity of licensed real estate professionals.

REAL ESTATE: A BUSINESS WITH MANY SPECIALTIES

Despite the size and complexity of the real estate business, many people think of it as consisting only of brokerage. Actually, the real estate industry is much broader than that. Appraisal, property management, financing, subdivision and development, home inspection, counseling, education, and auctioning are all separate businesses within the real estate field. To succeed in this complex industry, every real estate professional must have a basic understanding of these specialties.

Brokerage

Brokerage is the business of bringing people together in a real estate transaction. A **real estate licensee** acts as a point of contact between two or more people in negotiating the sale, purchase, or rental of property. A real estate licensee may be the agent for the buyer, for the seller, or for both. The property may be residential, commercial, or industrial. Illinois license categories include broker, managing broker, and residential leasing agent. All licensees are employed by a **sponsoring broker** and conduct brokerage services on behalf of that sponsoring broker. A managing broker, who may or may not be the owner, must be designated to supervise the licensees and run the office. *Residential leasing agents* bring together tenants and prospective rental properties. The sponsoring broker is ultimately responsible for the actions of all licensees working under the umbrella of that particular firm.

Appraisal

Appraisal is the process of rendering an opinion of a property's market value based on established methods and the appraiser's professional judgment. Although real estate training will provide brokers and managing brokers some understanding of the valuation process, most lenders require that a loan package be accompanied by a professional appraisal performed by a licensed appraiser. The appraisal substantiates the sales price of the home and assists the lender in determining maximum loan amount. Appraisals are also used for refinancing and insurance purposes. Detailed expertise in all methods of valuation is required. In order to perform appraisals in Illinois, an appraiser license is required.

Property Management

A *property manager* is a person or company hired to maintain and manage property on behalf of its owner. By hiring a property manager, the owner is relieved of many day-to-day management tasks, such as finding new tenants, collecting rents, altering or constructing new space for tenants, ordering repairs, and generally maintaining the property. The scope of the manager's duties depends upon the terms of the property management agreement. Whatever tasks are specified, the property manager must protect the owner's investment and maximize the owner's return on his investment. In Illinois, property management requires a real estate license, and an individual real estate licensee must perform property management services under the supervision of his or her sponsoring broker.

Financing

Financing is the business of providing the funds that make real estate transactions possible. Most transactions are financed by means of mortgage loans or trust deed loans secured by the property. Individuals involved in financing real estate may work in commercial banks, mortgage banking, or mortgage brokerage companies. A growing number of real estate brokerage firms affiliate with mortgage brokers to provide consumers with one-stop-shopping real estate services. Mortgage brokers and the loan officers working for them must be licensed and registered in Illinois.

Subdivision and Development

Subdivision is the splitting of a single property into smaller parcels. *Development* involves the construction of improvements on the land. These improvements may be either on site or off site. Offsite improvements, such as water lines and storm sewers, are made on public lands to serve the new development. Onsite improvements are additions or enhancements within the buildings or lots being sold that increase the value of the properties within the development. Onsite improvements include roads and infrastructure or new buildings. While subdivision and development normally are related, they are independent processes that can occur separately.

Home Inspection

Home inspection is a profession that allows practitioners to combine their interest in real estate with their professional skills and training in the construction trades or in engineering. Professional home inspectors conduct a thorough visual survey of a property's structure, systems, and site conditions and prepare an analytical report that is valuable to both purchasers and homeowners. In Illinois, home inspectors must be licensed.

Professional inspections occur on other types of property as well. For example, commercial properties may undergo an environmental assessment to determine the probability of hazardous substances being present on the property. In Illinois, a home inspection license is required to perform home inspections.

Counseling

Counseling involves providing clients with competent independent advice based on sound professional judgment. A real estate counselor helps clients choose among the various alternatives involved in purchasing, using, or investing in property. A counselor's role is to furnish clients with the information needed to make informed decisions. Professional real estate counselors must have a high degree of industry expertise.

Education

Real estate education is available to both practitioners and consumers. Colleges and universities, private schools, and trade organizations all offer real estate courses and seminars, from the principles of a prelicensing program to the technical aspects of tax and real property exchange law. State licensing laws establish the minimum educational requirements for obtaining—and keeping—a real estate license. Continuing education requirements help ensure that licensees keep their skills and knowledge current.

Auctioning

Buying or selling real estate at auction uses an open and competitive bidding process to transfer property. In Illinois, as in many states, auctioneers have licensing requirements.

Other Areas

Many other real estate career options are available. Practitioners will find that real estate specialists are needed in a variety of business settings. *Lawyers* who specialize in real estate are always in demand. Large *corporations* with extensive land holdings often have their own *real estate* and *property tax departments*. Local governments must staff both *zoning boards* and *assessment offices*.

PROFESSIONAL ORGANIZATIONS

Many trade organizations serve the real estate business. The largest is the National Association of REALTORS® (NAR). NAR sponsors various affiliated organizations that offer professional designations to brokers, managing brokers, and other professionals who complete required courses in areas of special interest. Members subscribe to a Code of Ethics and are entitled to be called REALTORS® or REALTOR-ASSOCIATES®. You must be a member of NAR to use the term *REALTORS*®.

NAR has the following affiliated institutes, societies, and councils:

- Counselors of Real Estate (CRE)
- Institute of Real Estate Management (IREM)
- REALTORS® Land Institute (RLI)
- REALTORS® National Marketing Institute (RNMI)
- Real Estate Buyer's Agent Council (REBAC)
- Certified Real Estate Brokerage Manager (CRB)
- Certified Residential Specialist (CRS)
- Graduate, REALTOR® Institute (GRI)
- Council of Residential Specialists (CRS)
- Society of Industrial and Office REALTORS® (SIOR)
- Women's Council of REALTORS® (WCR)

The National Association of Real Estate Brokers (NAREB), whose members are called *Realtists*, was formed in 1947 by African-American real estate professionals out of a need to secure the right to equal housing opportunities. Today, NAREB remains dedicated to equal housing opportunity.

The National Association of Hispanic Real Estate Professionals (NAHREP) is the largest minority trade group in the real estate industry. Its mission is to advance sustainable Hispanic homeownership by educating and empowering real estate professionals who serve Hispanic home buyers and sellers.

The Asian Real Estate Association of America (AREAA) is a nonprofit professional trade organization dedicated to promoting sustainable homeownership opportunities in Asian-American communities by empowering real estate professionals who serve this dynamic market.

Other professional associations include the following:

- American Society of Appraisers (ASA)
- National Association of Independent Fee Appraisers (NAIFA)
- Real Estate Educators Association (REEA)
- National Association of Exclusive Buyer Agents (NAEBA)
- Building Owners and Managers Association International (BOMA)
- Certified Commercial Investment Managers (CCIM)
- American Society of Home Inspectors (ASHI)
- International Association of Certified Home Inspectors (InterNACHI)

Members are expected to comply with the standards of practice and code of conduct as set forth by each organization.

TYPES OF REAL PROPERTY

Five Categories of Real Property

- Residential
- Commercial
- Industrial
- Agricultural
- Special purpose

Just as there are areas of specialization within the real estate industry, there are different types of property in which to specialize. Real estate can be classified as

- *residential*—all property used for single-family or multifamily housing, whether in urban, suburban, or rural areas;
- *commercial*—business property, including office space, shopping centers, stores, theaters, hotels, and parking facilities;
- *industrial*—warehouses, factories, and land in industrial districts;
- *agricultural*—farms, timberland, ranches, and orchards; or
- *special purpose*—churches or places of worship, schools, cemeteries, and government-held lands.

The market for each of these types of property can be subdivided into the *sales market*, which involves the transfer of title and ownership rights, and the *rental market*, in which space is temporarily leased.

Most licensees choose to specialize in only one type of property, such as residential or commercial.

THE REAL ESTATE MARKET

A **market** is a place where goods can be bought and sold. A market may be a specific place, such as the village square, or it may be a vast, complex, worldwide economic system for moving goods and services. In either case, the function of a market is to provide a setting in which supply and demand can establish market value, making it advantageous for buyers and sellers to trade.

SUPPLY AND DEMAND

When supply in-
creases and demand
remains stable,
prices go down.
When demand
increases and sup-
ply remains stable,
prices go up. Price
follows demand:
High demand results
in high prices, while
low demand results
in low prices.

The forces of supply and demand in the market determine how prices for goods and services are set. Essentially, when supply increases and demand remains stable, prices go down; when demand increases and supply remains stable, prices go up. Greater supply means producers need to attract more buyers, so they lower prices. Greater demand means producers can raise their prices because buyers compete for the product.

Supply and Demand in the Real Estate Market

Two characteristics of real estate govern the way the market reacts to the pressures of supply and demand: uniqueness and immobility. *Uniqueness* means that no matter how similar two parcels of real estate may appear, they are never exactly alike. Each occupies its own unique geographic location, and two properties are never exactly the same inside. *Immobility* refers to the fact that property cannot be relocated to satisfy demand where supply is low, nor do buyers necessarily make relocation decisions based on greater housing supply in a certain locale. For these reasons, real estate markets are *local markets*. Each geographic area has different types of real estate and different conditions that drive prices.

Factors that tend to affect the supply side of the real estate market's supply and demand balance include the labor force, construction and material costs, government controls, and financial policies.

Factors Affecting Supply

Five Factors That Affect the Supply of Real Estate

■ Labor force
■ Construction costs
■ Government controls
■ Government financial policies

Labor Force and Construction Costs

A shortage of skilled labor or building materials or an increase in the cost of materials can decrease the amount of new construction. Construction permit fees and high property transfer costs can also discourage development. An attempt may be made to pass increased construction costs along to buyers and tenants in the form of higher prices and increased rents, which can further slow the market.

Government Controls and Financial Policies

The government's monetary policy can have a substantial impact on the real estate market. The Federal Reserve establishes a discount rate of interest for the money it lends to its member banks. That rate has a direct impact on the interest rates that banks charge to borrowers. These interest rates play a significant part in people's ability to buy homes. The Federal Reserve Board attempts to keep the rates at a level that will keep the market moving without leading to inflation.

Governmental agencies, such as the Federal Housing Administration (FHA) and the Department of Veterans Affairs (VA), also have impact by insuring or guaranteeing loans. They are intended to benefit the economy, the consumer, and housing purchases.

Policies on the taxation of real estate can have both significant and complex effects on the real estate market. Real estate taxation is a necessary source of revenue for local governments. High taxes may deter investors but may also be necessary to maintain continued economic growth within the community. Tax incentives can attract new business and industries. With these enterprises come increased employment and expanded residential real estate markets.

Local governments also can influence supply. Land-use controls, building codes, and zoning ordinances help shape the character of a community and control the use of land.

Factors That Affect the Demand of Real Estate

■ Population
■ Demographics
■ Employment and wage levels

Factors Affecting Demand

Factors that tend to affect the *demand* side of the real estate market include population, demographics, and employment and wage levels.

Population

Shelter is a basic human need, so the demand for housing grows with the population. Although the total population of the country continues to rise, the demand for real estate increases at a faster rate in some areas than in others. In some locations, growth has ceased altogether as the population has declined. This may be due to economic changes (e.g., high unemployment), social concerns (e.g., going green), or population changes (e.g., shifts from colder to warmer climates). The result can be a drop in demand for real estate in one area matched by an increased demand elsewhere.

Demographics

Demographics is the study and description of population. The population of a community is a major factor in determining the quantity and type of housing in that community. Family size, the ratio of adults to children, the ages of children, the number of retirees, family income, lifestyle, and the growing number of single-parent and empty-nester households are all demographic factors that contribute to the amount and type of housing needed.

IN PRACTICE

"Niche marketing "refers to a subset of the market, both in the products and the people who will buy the products. The phrase may reference a specific group in a specific geographical area or property category. It can also refer to the demographics that it is intended to impact—for example, marketing to specific demographic populations such as the baby boomers (born between 1946–1964), Gen-Xers (born between 1965–1976), and millennials (born between 1977–1998), or agents fluent in Spanish and English marketing to Hispanic consumers. By understanding the various niches, real estate licensees are better able to service buyers and sellers on their purchase and sale decisions.

Employment and Wage Levels

Decisions about whether to buy or rent and how much to spend on housing are closely related to income. When job opportunities are scarce or wage levels low, demand for real estate usually drops.

SUMMARY

The real estate market depends on a variety of economic forces, such as interest rates and employment levels. To be successful, licensees must follow economic trends and anticipate where they will lead. How people use their income depends on consumer confidence. Consumer confidence is based not only on perceived job security but also on the availability of credit, the impact of inflation, and actions of the Federal Reserve Board. General trends in the economy, such as the availability of mortgage money and the interest rate that must be paid to have it, will strongly influence an individual's decision to invest in real estate.

Although brokerage is the most widely recognized real estate activity, the industry provides many other services. These include appraisal, property management, property development, counseling, property financing, and education. Most real estate firms specialize in only one or two of these areas; however, the highly complex and competitive nature of our society requires that a real estate licensee be knowledgeable in a number of fields.

Real property can be classified by its general type as residential, commercial, industrial, agricultural, or special purpose. Although many real estate licensees deal with more than one type of real property, they usually specialize to some degree.

A market is a place where goods and services can be bought and sold and where price levels can be established based on supply and demand. Because of its unique characteristics, real estate is usually relatively slow to adjust to the forces of supply and demand.

Real estate supply and demand is affected by many factors, including changes in population and demographics, wage and employment levels, construction costs, availability of labor, and governmental monetary policy and controls. Demand influences supply. High demand, high prices; low demand, low prices.

UNIT 1 QUIZ

1. A professional opinion of a property's market value, based on established methods and using trained, professional judgment, is performed by a
   A. real estate broker.
   B. real estate counselor.
   C. real estate appraiser.
   D. home inspector.

2. In general, when the supply of a certain commodity increases,
   A. prices tend to rise.
   B. prices tend to drop.
   C. demand tends to rise.
   D. demand is unchanged.

3. Which of these factors tends to affect supply in the real estate market?
   A. Population
   B. Demographics
   C. Employment and wage levels
   D. Government controls and financial policies

4. Which factor *MOST* likely influences the demand for real estate?
   A. Labor force
   B. Construction costs
   C. Wage levels and employment opportunities
   D. Government financial policies

5. Property management, leasing, appraisal, financing, and development are all examples of
   A. specializations within the real estate industry.
   B. factors affecting demand.
   C. non–real estate professions.
   D. government regulation of the real estate industry.

6. A REALTOR® is
   A. a specially licensed real estate broker.
   B. any real estate broker who assists buyers, sellers, landlords, or tenants in any real estate transaction.
   C. a member of the National Association of Real Estate Brokers who specializes in residential properties.
   D. a real estate licensee who is a member of the National Association of REALTORS®.

7. A major manufacturer of automobiles announces that it will relocate one of its factories, along with 2,000 employees, to a small town. What effect will this announcement *MOST* likely have on the small town's housing market?
   A. Housing will become less expensive.
   B. Housing will become more expensive.
   C. The announcement involves an issue of demographics, not a supply and demand issue; housing prices will stay about the same.
   D. The announcement involves an industrial property; residential housing will not be affected.

8. A licensee who has several years of experience in the industry decided to retire from actively marketing properties. Now this licensee helps clients choose among the various alternatives involved in purchasing, using, or investing in property. What is the licensee's profession?
   A. Real estate appraiser
   B. Real estate educator
   C. Real estate counselor
   D. REALTOR®

9. The term *REALTOR®* refers to
   A. any real estate licensee.
   B. a real estate licensee specializing in residential properties.
   C. a real estate educator.
   D. a member of the National Association of REALTORS®.

10. Schools are considered part of which real estate classification?
    A. Special-purpose
    B. Industrial
    C. Commercial
    D. Government-held

11. When demand for a commodity decreases and supply remains the same,
    A. price tends to rise.
    B. price is not affected.
    C. price tends to fall.
    D. the market becomes stagnant.

12. The term *appraisal* is defined as the
    A. process of splitting a single property into smaller parcels.
    B. method of estimating a property's market value based on established methods and the appraiser's professional judgment.
    C. transfer of funds in the financing of real estate transactions.
    D. process of providing clients with competent independent advice.

13. The Federal Reserve Board
    A. monitors the Federal Housing Administration.
    B. monitors nationwide construction costs.
    C. establishes a discount rate of interest for the money it lends to its member banks.
    D. establishes real estate appraisal standards.

14. All of these are categories of the uses of real property *EXCEPT*
    A. developmental.
    B. residential.
    C. agricultural.
    D. industrial.

15. All of these would affect overall demand in the real estate market *EXCEPT*
    A. population.
    B. demographics.
    C. wage levels.
    D. zoning ordinances.

16. Local government can influence the supply of real estate by
    A. land-use controls.
    B. zoning ordinances.
    C. building codes.
    D. all of these.

17. A real estate professional who performs a visual survey of a property's structure and systems and prepares an analytical report for a purchaser or an owner is acting as
    A. an educator.
    B. a home inspector.
    C. an appraiser.
    D. a property manager.

18. When the supply of a commodity decreases while demand remains the same, price tends to
    A. drop.
    B. not be affected.
    C. rise.
    D. go in the direction of supply.

19. When responsible for maintaining a client's property and maximizing the return on the client's investment, a real estate licensee is serving as
    A. a rental agent.
    B. a property manager.
    C. a building maintenance specialist.
    D. an investment counselor.

20. Detailed information about the age, education, behavior, and other characteristics of members of a population group is called
    A. population analysis.
    B. demographics.
    C. family lifestyles.
    D. household data.

UNIT 2

Real Property and the Law

LEARNING OBJECTIVES

When you have completed this unit, you will be able to accomplish the following.

> Distinguish among the concepts of land, real estate, and real property.
> Identify the characteristics of real estate and the rights that convey with ownership of real property.
> Describe the difference between real and personal property, and the various types of personalty.
> Explain the types of laws that affect real estate.

KEY TERMS

accession	deed	Real Estate License Act of
air rights	emblements	2000 (the Act)
annexation	fixture	real property
appurtenance	improvement	severance
attachment	land	situs
bill of sale	manufactured housing	subsurface rights
bundle of legal rights	personal property	surface rights
chattel	real estate	trade fixture

OVERVIEW

Real estate is a market like any other. Real property is the product, and the real estate professional is the salesperson. Product knowledge is the key to success. The real estate professional needs to know enough about the product to be able to educate and guide clients and customers. Here you will learn about the fundamental principles of the product that is at the heart of every real estate transaction.

LAND, REAL ESTATE, AND REAL PROPERTY

MEMORY TIP

Land: no improvements

Real estate: land with improvements

Real property: land with improvements plus rights

The terms *land*, *real estate*, and *real property* often are used interchangeably. To most people, they mean the same thing. Strictly speaking, however, these terms refer to different aspects of the same idea. To fully understand the nature of real estate and the laws that affect it, licensees must be aware of these subtle yet important differences.

Land

Land is defined as the earth's surface extending downward to the center of the earth and upward to infinity. Land includes not only the surface of the earth but also the underlying soil. Land also refers to objects that are naturally attached to the earth's surface, such as boulders and plants. Land includes the minerals and substances that lie far below the earth's surface (*subsurface*). It even includes the air above the earth, all the way up into space (*airspace*) (see Figure 2.1).

Figure 2.1: Distinguishing Land, Real Estate, and Real Property

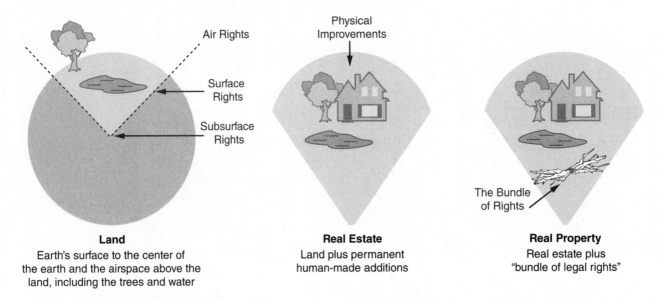

Land
Earth's surface to the center of the earth and the airspace above the land, including the trees and water

Real Estate
Land plus permanent human-made additions

Real Property
Real estate plus "bundle of legal rights"

Real Estate

Real estate is defined as land at, above, and below the earth's surface, plus all things permanently attached to it. Real estate is similar to land but means much more: Real estate includes the natural land along with all human-made improvements. An **improvement** is any artificial addition to land, such as a building or a fence (see Figure 2.1).

The term *improvement*, as used in the real estate industry, refers to any addition to the land. The word is neutral: Whether the artificial attachment makes the property better-looking, more useful, or more or less valuable, the land still is said to be improved. Land also may be improved by streets, utilities, sewers, and other additions that make it suitable for building.

Real Property

The term *real property* is the broadest of all. It includes both land and real estate. **Real property** is the interests, benefits, and rights that are automatically included in the ownership of land and real estate (see Figure 2.1).

Real property includes the surface, subsurface, airspace, any improvements, and the *bundle of legal rights*—the legal rights of ownership that attach to ownership of a parcel of real estate (see Figure 2.2).

An **appurtenance** is anything, tangible or intangible, associated with the property, although not necessarily a direct part of it. Typical appurtenances include parking spaces in multiunit buildings, septic tanks, easements, water rights, and other improvements. An appurtenance is connected to the property, and ownership of the appurtenance normally transfers to the new owner when the property is sold.

Surface and Subsurface Rights

The right to use the surface of the earth is called **surface rights**. However, real property ownership also can include **subsurface rights**, which are the rights to the natural resources lying below the earth's surface. The two rights are distinct; an owner may transfer surface rights without transferring the subsurface rights.

EXAMPLE

A landowner sells the rights to any oil and gas found beneath her farm to an oil company. Later, the same landowner sells the remaining interests (the surface, air, and limited subsurface rights) to a buyer, reserving the rights to any coal that may be found in the land. This buyer sells the remaining land to yet another buyer but retains the farmhouse, stable, and pasture. After these sales, the following four parties now have ownership interests in the same real estate:

1. The original landowner owns all the coal.
2. The oil company owns all the oil and gas.
3. The first buyer owns the farmhouse, stable, and pasture.
4. The second buyer owns the rights to the remaining real estate.

Air Rights

The rights to use the space above the earth may be sold or leased independently, provided those rights have not been preempted by law. **Air rights** can be an important part of real estate, particularly in large cities where air rights must be purchased to construct office buildings. Examples of construction based on air rights include the MetLife Building in New York City and One Prudential Plaza in Chicago. To construct such a building, the developer must purchase not only the air rights but also numerous small portions of the land's subsurface for the building's foundation supports.

Before air travel was common, a property's air rights were considered unlimited, extending upward into the farthest reaches of outer space. However, now that air travel is common, Congress and the courts have placed limits on air rights. Today, the courts permit reasonable interference with air rights, such as that necessary for aircraft, so long as the owner's right to use and occupy the land is not unduly lessened. Governments and airport authorities often purchase adjacent air rights to provide approach patterns for air traffic.

With the continuing development of solar power, air rights, solar rights, and even "view" rights are being closely examined by the courts. A proposed tall building that blocks sunlight from a smaller, existing building may be held to be interfering with the smaller building's right to sunlight, especially if the smaller building is solar-powered.

CHARACTERISTICS AND OWNERSHIP OF REAL PROPERTY

Characteristics of Real Estate

Real estate possesses seven basic characteristics that define its nature and affect its use. These characteristics fall into two broad categories—economic and physical.

Economic Characteristics

Economic Characteristics of Real Estate

- Scarcity
- Improvements
- Permanence of investment
- Location

The economic characteristics of land affect its investment value. These four characteristics are scarcity, improvements, permanence of investment, and location (situs).

Scarcity

Land is not usually considered a rare commodity, but only a quarter of the earth's surface is dry land; the rest is water. The total available supply of land is not limitless. While a considerable amount of land remains unused or uninhabited, the supply in a given location or of a particular quality is generally considered limited.

Improvements

Building an improvement on one parcel of land can affect the land's value and use, as well as that of neighboring tracts and whole communities. For example, constructing a new shopping center or selecting a nuclear power site or toxic waste dump can dramatically shift land values in a large area.

Permanence of Investment

The capital and labor used to build an improvement represent a large fixed investment. Although even a well-built structure can be razed to make way for a newer building, improvements such as drainage, electricity, water, and sewage systems often remain.

Location

This economic characteristic, sometimes called **situs**, does not directly refer to a geographic location but rather to people's preferences for given areas. It is the unique quality of these preferences that results in different values for similar units. Location is the most important economic characteristic of land.

PHYSICAL CHARACTERISTICS OF REAL ESTATE

- Immobility
- Indestructibility
- Uniqueness

Physical Characteristics

Land has three main physical characteristics: immobility, indestructibility, and uniqueness.

Immobility

It is true that some of the substances of land are removable and that topography may shift. Nevertheless, the geographic location of any given parcel of land can never be changed. It is fixed or immobile.

Indestructibility

Land is also indestructible. This permanence of land, coupled with the long-term nature of most improvements, tends to stabilize investments in real estate.

The fact that land is indestructible does not change the fact that man-made improvements on land depreciate and can become obsolete, which may dramatically reduce the land's value.

Uniqueness

No two parcels of land are ever exactly the same. The characteristics of each property, no matter how small, differ from those of every other. At a minimum, all parcels differ geographically because each parcel has its own location.

EXAMPLE

Because of the uniqueness of property, a person who contracts to buy unit 305 of a new condominium building cannot have unit 307 substituted at closing, even though the two units appear to be identical. The buyer could sue for specific performance (asking the seller to "perform" on the promise of unit 305) based on the uniqueness of real estate.

OWNERSHIP OF REAL PROPERTY

MEMORY TIP

Bundle of Legal Rights

■ Disposition
■ Enjoyment
■ Exclusion
■ Possession
■ Control

Traditionally, ownership of real property is described as carrying a **bundle of legal rights**. These rights include the

■ right of possession,

■ right to control the property (within the framework of the law),

■ right of enjoyment (that is, to use the property as the owner wishes, within the framework of the law),

■ right of exclusion (to keep others from entering or using the property), and

■ right of disposition (to sell, will, transfer, or otherwise dispose of or encumber the property).

The concept of a bundle of rights comes from old English law. In the Middle Ages, a seller transferred property by giving the purchaser a handful of earth or a bundle of bound sticks from a tree on the property, symbolizing the whole property. The purchaser, who accepted the bundle in a ceremony, became owner of the tree producing the sticks and the land to which the tree was attached. Because the rights of ownership (like the sticks) can be separated and individually transferred, the sticks became symbolic of those rights (see Figure 2.2).

Figure 2.2: The Bundle of Legal Rights

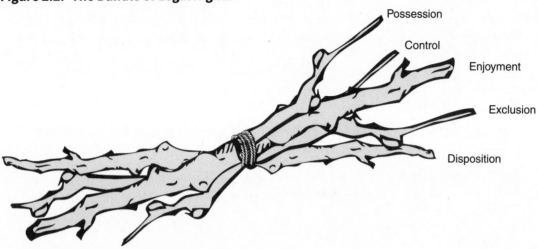

Possession
Control
Enjoyment
Exclusion
Disposition

REAL PROPERTY AND PERSONAL PROPERTY

Property may be classified as either real or personal. **Personal property** (or *personalty*) is property that is movable and not affixed to or associated with the land. Basically, personal property includes all property except real property.

Chattels are items of personal property, including such tangibles as chairs, tables, clothing, money, bonds, and bank accounts. Trade fixtures are included in this category.

Manufactured Housing

Manufactured housing is defined as dwellings that are built off site and trucked to a building lot where they are installed or assembled. Manufactured housing includes modular, panelized, precut, and mobile homes. However, the term *mobile home* usually refers to factory-built housing constructed before 1976.

The distinction between real and personal property is not always obvious. Manufactured housing, for example, is generally considered personal property until it becomes permanently affixed to the land, at which point it becomes real property.

Plants

Trees and crops generally fall into one of two of the following classes:

■ Trees, perennial shrubbery, and grasses that do not require annual cultivation are considered real estate. They attach to the land. The Latin term *fructus naturales* is often used to describe them.

■ Annually cultivated crops such as wheat, corn, vegetables, and fruit, called **emblements**, are generally considered personal property. As long as an annual crop is growing, it will stay with the real property unless other provisions are made in the sales contract. The Latin term *fructus industriales*, meaning the fruit of one's effort, is often used to describe them.

When Illinois farmland is sold, it is customary for possession to be transferred to the buyer on March 1 because it falls after the last year's crops have been harvested and before the new crops are planted. Because of this "standard" date, no special provisions are required regarding the annual crops. However, when possession is transferred to the buyer on March 1, it also is customary for the buyer to assume full payment of the current year's tax bill without proration. This is because the buyer will receive the full benefit of the new crop for that tax year.

If the sale is closed at another time during the year and before the crops are harvested, the sales contract should indicate whether the growing crops are included in the sales price. Sometimes, when the crop is included in the sale, the buyer reimburses the seller for crop-related costs already incurred, such as seed, planting, fertilizing, and spraying.

As for farm leases, if an owner wishes to break a lease with a tenant, notification must be given by November 1. This produces the least interference with the cycle of spring planting and fall harvesting.

An item of real property can become personal property by **severance**. For example, a growing tree is real estate until the owner cuts it down, severing it from the property. Similarly, an apple becomes personal property once it is picked from a tree, and a wheat crop becomes personal property once harvested.

It also is possible to change personal property into real property through a process called **annexation**. For example, a landowner buys cement, stones, and sand, mixes them into concrete, and constructs a sidewalk across her land. This landowner has effectively converted personal property (cement, stones, and sand) into real property (a sidewalk).

Licensees need to know whether property is real or personal for many reasons. An important distinction arises, for example, when the property is transferred from one owner to another. Real property is conveyed by **deed**, while personal property is conveyed by a **bill of sale**.

Classifications of Fixtures

In considering the differences between real and personal property, it is necessary to distinguish between a *fixture* and *personal property*.

Fixtures

A **fixture** is personal property that has been so affixed to land or a building that, by law, it becomes part of the real property. Examples of fixtures are heating systems, elevator equipment in highrise buildings, radiators, kitchen cabinets, attached bookcases, light fixtures, doors, and plumbing fixtures. Almost any item that has been added as a permanent part of a building is considered a fixture.

Legal Tests of a Fixture

The primary test that is used in determining whether an item is a fixture or personal property is a question of intent (see Figure 2.3). Did the person who installed the item intend for it to remain permanently on the property or for it to be removable in the future? In determining intent, courts use the following three basic tests:

- *Method of attachment.* How permanent is the method of attachment? Can the item be removed without causing damage to the surrounding property?

- *Adaptation to real estate.* Is the item being used as real property or personal property?

- *Agreement.* Have the parties agreed in writing on whether the item is real or personal property? What does the contract say?

Figure 2.3: Legal Tests of a Fixture

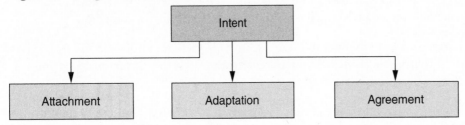

Although these tests may seem simple, court decisions have occasionally been inconsistent. Property that appears to be permanently affixed sometimes has been ruled to be personal property, while property that seems removable has been ruled a fixture. It is important that an owner clarify what is to be sold with the real estate at the very beginning of the sales process. The written sales contract between the buyer and the seller should list articles included in the sale if any doubt exists as to whether they are personal property or fixtures.

Trade Fixtures

A special category of fixture includes property used in the course of business. An article owned by a tenant and attached to a rented space or building or used in conducting a business is a **trade fixture** (or *chattel fixture*). Trade fixtures differ from other fixtures in two ways:

- Fixtures belong to the owner of the real estate, but trade fixtures are usually owned and installed by a tenant for the tenant's use.

- Fixtures are considered a permanent part of a building, but trade fixtures are removable.

Some examples of trade fixtures are bowling alleys, store shelves, bars, and restaurant equipment. Agricultural fixtures, such as chicken coops and tool sheds, also are included in this category. Trade fixtures must be removed on or before the last day of the lease term. The tenant is responsible for any damage caused by the removal of a trade fixture. Trade fixtures that are not removed become the real property of the landlord. Acquiring the property in this way is called **accession**. Personal property that "turns into" real property does so by **attachment**.

EXAMPLE

A pizza parlor leased space in a small shopping center, and the restaurateur bolted a large iron oven to the floor of the unit. When the pizza parlor goes out of business or relocates, the restaurateur will be able to remove the pizza oven if the bolt holes in the floor can be repaired. The oven is a trade fixture. On the other hand, if the pizza oven was brought into the restaurant in pieces, welded together, and set in concrete, the restaurateur might not be able to remove it without causing structural damage. In that case, the oven might become a fixture.

LAWS AFFECTING REAL ESTATE

Licensees must have a clear and accurate understanding of the laws that affect real estate.

Seven Sources of Law

- U.S. Constitution
- Laws passed by Congress
- Rules of the regulatory agencies
- State constitutions
- State statutes
- Local ordinances
- Common law

Specific areas important to the real estate practitioner include the law of contracts, general property law, law of agency, and the state's real estate license law. All of these will be discussed later in this book. Federal regulations (such as environmental laws), as well as federal, state, and local tax laws, also play an important role in real estate transactions. Finally, state and local land-use and zoning laws, as well as environmental regulations, also have a significant impact on the practice of real estate.

Laws come from seven different sources. They are the U.S. Constitution, laws passed by Congress, rules of the regulatory agencies, state constitutions, state statutes, local ordinances, and common law (court decisions). A real estate practitioner can't be an expert in all areas of real estate law. However, licensees should know and understand some basic principles. Perhaps most important is the ability to recognize which problems should be referred to a real estate attorney. Only attorneys are trained and licensed to give advice on matters of law. Under no circumstances may a real estate licensee act as an attorney unless the licensee is also a licensed attorney representing a client but only in that capacity.

The purpose of real estate license law is to protect the public from fraud, dishonesty, and incompetence in real estate transactions. All 50 states, the District of Columbia, and all Canadian provinces have passed laws that require real estate practitioners to be licensed. Although state license laws are similar in many broad respects, they may differ on key points, from the amount of education required for a license to appropriate approaches for handling agency relationships.

The practice of real estate in Illinois is governed by the **Real Estate License Act of 2000 (the Act)** (225 ILCS 454), as amended in 2020, and rules established by the Illinois Department of Financial and Professional Regulation (IDFPR). Other laws affecting real estate in Illinois may be found throughout the Illinois compiled statutes, but many of those addressing real property are in 765 ILCS. Rules and regulations that govern the industry are established by a joint committee, with procedures governed by the provisions of the Illinois Administrative Procedure Act.

SUMMARY

Although most people think of land as the surface of the earth, land actually includes the earth's surface, the mineral deposits under the earth, and the air above the earth. The term *real estate* further expands this definition to include all natural and man-made improvements attached to the land. The term *real property* is used to describe real estate plus the bundle of legal rights associated with its ownership. A buyer of real estate purchases from the seller the legal rights to use the land in certain ways, going back to the old English transfer of a "bundle of rights." The various rights to the same parcel of real estate may be owned and controlled by different parties. For example, one person may own the surface rights, one the air rights, and one the subsurface rights.

Property that does not fit the definition of real estate is classified as personal property (also called chattels). When articles of personal property are attached to real estate, they may become fixtures and as such are considered part of the real estate. However, personal property attached to real property by a tenant for business purposes is called a trade fixture, and it remains personal property, transportable by the tenant at the end of the lease. The special nature of land as an investment is apparent in both its economic and physical characteristics.

The economic characteristics are scarcity, improvements, permanence of investment, and location. The physical characteristics of land are that it is immobile, indestructible, and unique.

Even the simplest real estate transaction reflects a complex body of laws. Those laws include the U.S. Constitution, laws passed by Congress, rules of the regulatory agencies, state constitutions, state statutes, local ordinances, and common law (court decisions).

All 50 states, the District of Columbia, and all Canadian provinces have some type of licensing requirement for real estate practitioners. Real estate licensees have an obligation to be familiar with the real estate laws and licensing requirements in the states in which they practice.

UNIT 2 QUIZ

1. One defining difference between real estate (real property) and personal property is that real estate includes
   A. land and the rights and interests inherent in the ownership of land, while personal property includes only air and mineral rights.
   B. the trees and air rights, while personal property includes the house and its contents.
   C. land and all things permanently attached, while personal property includes property that is movable.
   D. annual crops, while personal property includes mineral rights.

2. A bookstore owner rents space in a commercial building. The bookstore has large tables fastened to the walls where customers are encouraged to sit and read. Shelves create aisles from the front of the store to the back. The shelves are bolted to both the ceiling and the floor. Which of these *BEST* characterizes these tables and shelves?
   A. The shelves and the tables are trade fixtures and will be sold when the owner sells the building.
   B. The shelves and the tables are trade fixtures and must be removed before the bookstore's lease expires; the tenant is responsible to the landlord for any damage that their removal causes to the premises.
   C. Because the bookstore is a tenant, the shelves and the tables are fixtures and may not be removed, except with the owner's permission.
   D. Because the shelves and tables are attached to the building, they are treated the same way as other fixtures.

3. Which of these is considered the *MOST* important characteristic of land?
   A. Air rights
   B. Permanence
   C. Subsurface rights
   D. Location

4. Another term for *personal property* is
   A. fixtures.
   B. realty.
   C. chattels.
   D. fructus naturales.

5. When an owner of real estate sells the property to someone else, which of the "sticks" in the bundle of legal rights is she using?
   A. Exclusion
   B. Legal enjoyment
   C. Control
   D. Disposition

6. A man inherited a farm from his uncle. As a new owner, the first thing he did with the vacant property was to remove all the topsoil, which he sold to a landscaping company. He then removed a thick layer of limestone and sold it to a construction company. Finally, he dug 40 feet into the bedrock and sold it for gravel. When the farm owner died, he left the farm to his daughter. Which of these statements is *TRUE*?
   A. The daughter inherits nothing because the farm no longer exists.
   B. The daughter owns the gravel, limestone, and topsoil, no matter where it is.
   C. The daughter inherits a large hole in the ground, but it is still a farm, down to the center of the earth.
   D. The man's estate must restore the land to its original condition.

7. The buyer and the seller of a home are debating whether a certain item is real or personal property. The buyer says it is real property and should convey with the house; the seller says it is personal property and would not convey without a separate bill of sale. In determining whether an item is real or personal property, a court would *NOT* consider
   A. whether its removal would cause severe damage to the real estate.
   B. whether the item is clearly adapted to the real estate.
   C. the cost of the item when it was purchased.
   D. any relevant agreement of the parties in their contract of sale.

8. Which of these *BEST* describes the economic characteristics of real estate?
    A. Scarcity, improvements, and location
    B. Location, uniqueness, and indestructibility
    C. Scarcity, immobility, and improvements
    D. Attachment, location, and improvements

9. An owner decides to sell her house and takes the antique front door with her when she moves. In the absence of any provision in the contract, is the owner allowed to remove the door?
    A. No, this act of severance is not allowed at time of selling because the door is a fixture.
    B. Yes, the owner can remove the door, and the act is called accession.
    C. No, this is conversion.
    D. Yes, the owner can remove the door, and the act is called separation.

10. When moving into a newly purchased home, the buyer discovered that the seller had taken the electric lighting units that were installed over the vanity in the bathroom. The seller had not indicated in the sales contract that these would be removed. Which of these is *TRUE*?
    A. The lighting fixtures belong to the seller because he installed them as personal property.
    B. These lighting fixtures are considered trade fixtures and could be removed.
    C. Installed lighting units normally are considered real estate fixtures.
    D. Original lighting fixtures are real property, but replacement lighting is personal property and can be taken by the seller.

11. A homeowner is building a new enclosed front porch on his home. A truckload of lumber has been left in his driveway for use in building the porch. At this point, the lumber is considered
    A. a fixture, because it will be permanently affixed to existing real property.
    B. personal property.
    C. a chattel that is real property.
    D. a trade fixture or a chattel fixture.

12. Intent of the parties, method of attachment, adaptation to real estate, and agreement between the parties are the legal tests for determining whether an item is
    A. a fixture or personal property.
    B. a trade fixture or personal property.
    C. real property or real estate.
    D. an improvement.

13. Parking spaces in multiunit buildings, water rights, and other improvements are classified as
    A. trade fixtures.
    B. emblements.
    C. subsurface rights.
    D. appurtenances.

14. A person buys a parcel of natural forest. The person then immediately cuts down all the trees and constructs a large shed out of old sheets of rusted steel for storing turpentine, varnish, and industrial waste products. Which of these statements is *TRUE* about this rusty shed?
    A. The shed is personal property.
    B. If the owner is in the business of storing toxic substances, the shed is a trade fixture.
    C. Altering the property in order to construct a shed is not included in the bundle of rights.
    D. The owner's action constitutes improvement of the property.

15. The phrase *bundle of legal rights* is properly included in
    A. the definition of real property.
    B. a legal description.
    C. real estate transactions.
    D. leases for less than one year.

16. Which of these is an example of an appurtenance?
    A. Personal property
    B. Water rights
    C. A fixture
    D. A trade fixture

17. All of these rights are included in the right to control one's property *EXCEPT*
    A. sell the property to a neighbor.
    B. erect "No Trespassing" signs.
    C. enjoy profits from its ownership.
    D. exclude utility meter readers.

18. According to law, a trade fixture is usually treated as
    A. a fixture.
    B. an easement.
    C. personalty.
    D. a license.

19. A buyer is interested in a house that fits most of her needs, but it is located in a busy area where she is not sure she wants to live. The real estate characteristic associated with her concern is
    A. physical deterioration.
    B. area preference.
    C. permanence of investment.
    D. immobility.

20. Which of these is considered personal property?
    A. Woodburning fireplace
    B. Awnings
    C. Patio furniture
    D. Bathtubs

UNIT
3

Concepts of Home Ownership

LEARNING OBJECTIVES

When you have completed this unit, you will be able to accomplish the following.

- › Identify the various types of housing choices available to homebuyers.
- › Describe the issues involved in making a home ownership decision.
- › Explain the tax benefits of home ownership.
- › Distinguish the various types of homeowners insurance policy coverage.

KEY TERMS

boot	equity	liability coverage
capital gains	homeowners insurance	PITI
coinsurance clause	policy	replacement cost

HOME OWNERSHIP

People buy homes for both psychological and financial reasons. To many, home ownership is a sign of financial stability. It is an investment that can appreciate in value and provide federal income tax deductions. Home ownership also imparts benefits that are less tangible but no less valuable: pride, security, and a sense of belonging to the community.

Types of Housing

As our society evolves, the needs of its homebuyers become more specialized. These different forms of housing respond to the demands of a diverse marketplace.

Apartment complexes are groups of apartment buildings with any number of units in each building. The buildings may be lowrise or highrise, and the amenities may include parking, security, clubhouses, swimming pools, tennis courts, and even golf courses.

The *condominium* is a popular form of residential ownership, particularly for people who want the security of owning property without the care and maintenance a house demands. Condominium owners share ownership of common facilities such as halls, elevators, swimming pools, clubhouses, tennis courts, and surrounding grounds. Management and maintenance of building exteriors and common facilities are provided by the governing association or by outside contractors, with expenses paid out of monthly assessments charged to owners.

A *cooperative* is similar to a condominium in that it also may offer units with shared common facilities. Unlike condominiums, the "owners" do not actually own the units. Instead, they buy shares of stock in the corporation that holds title to the building. Owners receive proprietary leases that entitle them to occupy particular units. Like condominium unit owners, cooperative unit owners pay their share of the building's maintenance expenses. Condominium ownership and cooperative ownership are discussed in more detail in Unit 8.

Planned unit developments (PUDs) (also called *master-planned communities*) merge such diverse land uses as housing, recreation facilities, and commercial concerns in one self-contained development. PUDs are planned under special zoning ordinances. These ordinances permit maximum use of open space by reducing lot sizes and street areas. Owners do not have direct ownership in the common areas. A community association is formed to maintain these areas with fees collected from the owners. A PUD may be a small development of just a few homes or an entire planned city.

Retirement communities (also called *active adult communities*), often are structured as PUDs. They are often located in temperate climates and may provide shopping, recreational opportunities, and health care facilities in addition to residential units.

Highrise developments (also called *mixed-use developments [MUDs]*) combine such elements as office space, stores, theaters, and apartment units into a single vertical community. MUDs are usually self-contained, offering convenient options (such as spas or exercise facilities) to those living there.

Converted-use properties are factories, warehouses, office buildings, hotels, schools, places of worship or churches, and other structures that have been converted to residential use. Developers often find renovation of such properties more aesthetically and economically appealing than demolishing a perfectly sound structure to build something new. An abandoned warehouse may be transformed into luxury loft condominium units or a closed hotel may reopen as an apartment building.

Manufactured housing, including mobile homes, was once considered useful only as temporary residences. Now, however, such homes are more often permanent principal residences or stationary vacation homes. Increased living space now available in the newer models, combined with low cost, has made such homes an attractive option for many.

Modular homes (or *prefabricated homes*) are also gaining in popularity as the price rises for newly constructed homes. Each room in a modular home is pre-assembled at a factory, driven to the building site on a truck, and then lowered onto its foundation by a crane. Later, workers finish the structure and connect plumbing and wiring. Entire developments can be built at a fraction of the time and cost of conventional construction.

Time-shares allow multiple purchasers to share ownership or use of a single property, usually a vacation home, in intervals. Each owner is entitled to use the property for a certain period of time each year, usually a specific week. In addition to the purchase price, each owner pays an annual maintenance fee.

HOUSING AFFORDABILITY

Increasing the supply of affordable housing is a key concern for many members of Congress, state legislatures, and local governments. Because more homeowners mean more business opportunities, real estate professionals have a vital interest in ensuring affordable housing for all segments of the population.

According to the U.S. Census Bureau, as of the first quarter of 2020, the home ownership rate in the United States was 65.3%. Those considering home ownership must evaluate many factors before they decide to purchase property. The purchasing decision must be weighed carefully in light of each individual's financial circumstances. The decision of whether to buy or rent property involves considering

- how long a person wants to live in a particular area,
- a person's financial situation,
- a person's credit score,
- housing affordability,
- current mortgage interest rates,
- tax consequences of owning versus renting property, and
- what may happen to home prices and tax laws in the future.

Ownership Expenses and Ability to Pay

MEMORY TIP

The basic costs of owning a home may be remembered by the acronym PITI:
- Principal
- Interest
- Taxes
- Insurance

Equity = current market value − property debt

The basic costs of owning a home include mortgage principal, interest, taxes, and insurance, known by the acronym **PITI**. Home ownership also involves many other expenses, including trash removal fees, sewer charges, and maintenance and repairs.

Investment Considerations

Purchasing a home offers several financial advantages to a buyer. First, if the property's value increases, a sale could bring in more money than the owner paid, creating a long-term gain. Second, as the total mortgage debt is reduced through monthly payments, the owner's actual ownership interest in the property increases. This increasing ownership interest is called **equity** and represents the paid-off share of the property held free of any mortgage. A tenant accumulates a good credit rating by paying the rent on time, but a homeowner's mortgage payments build equity and, thus, increase net worth. Equity also builds when the property's value rises through area appreciation. The third financial advantage of home ownership is in tax deductions available to homeowners but not to renters.

TAX BENEFITS

Tax Benefits of Home Ownership

Sales price − purchse price = gain

To encourage home ownership, the federal government allows homeowners certain income tax advantages. Homeowners may deduct from their income some or all of the mortgage interest paid up to a certain point. For mortgages taken out after December 14, 2017, an individual may deduct interest off of debt up to $750,000. Loans in existence prior to that date are not affected, as long as they are not over $1,000,000. If a loan was generated prior to that date and is refinanced, that interest is deductible as well, as long as the amount refinanced is not greater than the original loan amount. Finally, between January 1, 2018, and

December 31, 2025, the interest on a second mortgage is no longer tax deductible. State and local real estate taxes can be used as an itemized deduction up to a limit of $10,000.

In addition, in the late 1990s, the federal government enacted several federal tax reforms that significantly changed the importance of tax considerations for most homesellers. For example, $500,000 is excluded from capital gains tax for profits on the sale of a principal residence by married taxpayers who file jointly. Taxpayers who file singly are entitled to a $250,000 exclusion. The exemption is available so long as the homeowners have both owned and occupied the property as their primary residence for at least two of the past five years. The term *capital gains* refers generally to the profit made when an asset is sold.

For capital gains beyond these $500,000/$250,000 exclusions, the tax rate has varied over the past decade and depends upon what tax bracket an individual or married couple falls into. Because the capital gains taxation rate may change from year to year, a competent tax professional should be consulted.

Renters can probably make a higher mortgage payment than their current rent payment without requiring a pay increase because of the tax savings realized by home ownership. As such, tax considerations may be an important part of any decision to purchase a home.

Exchanges

Real estate investors can defer taxation of capital gains by making property exchanges. Even property that has appreciated greatly since its initial purchase may be exchanged for other property. A property owner will incur tax liability on a sale only if additional capital or property is also received; the tax is deferred, not eliminated. Whenever the investor sells the property, the capital gain will be taxed. In many states, state income taxes can also be deferred by using the exchange form of property transfer.

To qualify as a tax-deferred exchange, the properties involved must be of like kind as defined under Section 1031 of the Internal Revenue Code. (Like-kind property is property of the same nature, character or class. Quality or grade does not matter. Most real estate will be like-kind to other real estate. For example, real property that is improved with a residential rental house is like-kind to vacant land.) To avoid paying tax, the exchanged property must be real estate of equal or greater value to avoid capital gains tax. Receipt of cash gain or lessening of mortgaged debt is considered boot and that amount or value will be taxed. The IRS requires tax on the boot to be paid at the time of the exchange by the party who receives it. The value of the boot is added to the basis of the property for which it is given. Tax-deferred exchanges are governed by strict federal requirements, and competent guidance from a tax professional is essential.

Licensee's Role

While it is important for a real estate licensee to be familiar with the tax implications of purchasing or selling property, making representations about those implications to their clients opens the licensee up to a great deal of liability. It is essential to recommend that clients seek the advice of an accountant or tax professional for guidance.

HOMEOWNERS INSURANCE

A home is often the largest investment people will ever make. Most homeowners see the importance of protecting their investment by insuring it. Furthermore, lenders usually require that a homeowner obtain insurance when a debt is secured by the property. While owners can purchase individual policies that insure against destruction of property by fire or windstorm, injury to others, and theft of personal property, most buy a combined **homeowners insurance policy** to cover all of these risks.

Coverage and Claims

The most common homeowners policy is called a *basic form*. It provides property coverage against

- fire and lightning,
- glass breakage,
- windstorm and hail,
- explosion,
- riot and civil commotion,
- damage by aircraft,
- damage from vehicles,
- damage from smoke,
- vandalism and malicious mischief,
- theft, and
- loss of property removed from the premises when it is endangered by fire or other perils.

A broad form policy also is available. This type of policy covers

- falling objects;
- damage due to the weight of ice, snow, or sleet;
- collapse of all or part of the building;
- bursting, cracking, burning, or bulging of a steam or hot water heating system or of appliances used to heat water;
- accidental discharge, leakage, or overflow of water or steam from within a plumbing, heating, or air-conditioning system;
- freezing of plumbing, heating, and air-conditioning systems and domestic appliances; and
- injury to electrical appliances, devices, fixtures, and wiring from short circuits or other accidentally generated currents.

Most homeowners insurance policies contain a **coinsurance clause**. This provision usually requires the owner to maintain insurance equal to a specified percentage (usually 80%) of the **replacement cost** of the dwelling (not including the price of the land). An owner who has this type of policy may make a claim for the full cost of the repair or replacement of the damaged property without deduction for depreciation or annual wear and tear. In short, the insurance company wants to make sure that the premiums it is receiving cover at least 80% of the risk. Why should it pay to replace a $500,000 structure when the premiums are only supporting $250,000 of insurance? Hence the 80% coinsurance clause.

Special apartment and condominium policies generally provide fire and windstorm, theft, and public **liability coverage** for injuries or losses sustained within the unit. However, they do not usually cover losses or damages to the structure. The basic structure, in such cases, is insured by either the landlord or the condominium owner's association.

EXAMPLE

A homeowners insurance policy covers 80% of the replacement cost of the home, or $80,000. The structure is valued at $100,000. (Land does not figure in here.) If the homeowner sustains $30,000 in fire damage to the house, she can make a claim for the full cost of the repair or replacement of the damaged property. However, if the owner has insurance of only $70,000, the claim will be prorated by dividing the percentage actually covered (0.70) by the policy minimum coverage requirement (0.80).

0.70 ÷ 0.80 = 0.875 (0.875 is the percentage that $70,000 represents of the required minimum insurance. Therefore, the insurance company will only pay for 0.875 of the loss of $30,000.)

$$\$30,000 \times 0.875 = \$26,250$$

FEDERAL FLOOD INSURANCE

The *National Flood Insurance Act of 1968* was enacted by Congress to help owners of property in flood-prone areas by subsidizing flood insurance and by taking land-use and land-control measures to improve future management for floodplain areas. The Federal Emergency Management Agency (FEMA) administers the flood insurance program. The Army Corps of Engineers has prepared detailed maps that identify specific flood-prone areas throughout the country. To finance property with federal or federally related mortgage loans, owners in flood-prone areas called special flood hazard areas (SFHAs) are required to obtain flood insurance. The insurance agent must receive a copy of an elevation certificate, a form supplied by a licensed surveyor before determining the appropriate insurance rate. Homeowners' insurance policies in flood-prone areas always exclude floods, so flood coverage must always be purchased as a separate policy.

In designated areas, flood insurance is required on all types of buildings—residential, commercial, industrial, and agricultural—for either the value of the property or the amount of the mortgage loan, subject to the maximum limits available. Policies are written annually and can be purchased from any licensed property insurance broker, the National Flood Insurance Program (NFIP), or the designated servicing companies in each state.

Flood Insurance: What's Covered and What's Not

FEMA defines a flood as

"a general and temporary condition of partial or complete inundation of two or more acres of normally dry land or two or more properties (at least one of which is the policyholder's property) from

- overflow of inland or tidal waters;
- unusual and rapid accumulation or runoff of surface waters from any source;
- mudflow; or
- collapse or subsidence of land along the shore of a lake or similar body of water as a result of erosion or undermining caused by waves or currents of water exceeding anticipated cyclical levels that result in a flood as defined above."

The physical damage to a building or personal property directly caused by a flood is covered by flood insurance policies. For example, damage from sewer backups is covered if it results directly from flooding. Policies are of two types: replacement cost value (RCV) or actual cost value (ACV). Deductibles and premiums vary accordingly.

SUMMARY

Current trends in home ownership include cooperatives, apartment complexes, condominiums, planned unit developments (PUDs), retirement communities, highrise developments, converted-use properties, modular homes, mobile homes, time-shares/time-uses, and of course, residential housing. Prospective buyers should be aware of the advantages and disadvantages of home ownership. While a homeowner might gain financial security and pride of ownership, both the initial price and the continuing expenses and risks must be considered.

One of the tax benefits available to homeowners is the ability to deduct mortgage interest payments (with certain limitations) and property taxes from federal income taxes. Up to $250,000 (filing singly) or $500,000 (married, filing jointly) in profit can be excluded from capital gains tax. To claim the exemption, the homeowners must have occupied the property as their principal residence for at least two years out of the last five.

To protect their investment in real estate, most homeowners purchase insurance. A basic form homeowners insurance policy covers fire, theft, and liability, and it can be extended to cover other risks. Many homeowners policies contain a coinsurance clause stipulating that the policyholder maintain insurance in an amount equal to 80% of the replacement cost of the home. If this percentage is not met, the policyholder receives only partial compensation for repair costs if a loss occurs. Guaranteed replacement cost policies, with coinsurance met, offer the most security by providing full replacement coverage.

The federal government requires flood insurance for federally regulated or federally insured mortgage loans for properties located in special flood hazard areas (SFHAs).

Unit 3

UNIT 3 QUIZ

1. Which of these is *NOT* a cost or expense of owning a home?
   A. Taxes on personal property
   B. Interest paid on borrowed capital
   C. Homeowners insurance
   D. Maintenance and repairs

2. Homeowners may deduct which of the following expenses when preparing their income tax return?
   A. Interest paid on maintenance and repairs
   B. Real estate taxes
   C. Insurance premiums
   D. Flood insurance premiums

3. A couple paid $56,000 for their property 20 years ago. Today, the market value is $119,000, and they owe $5,000 on their mortgage. Regarding this situation, which of these is *TRUE*?
   A. The $114,000 difference between the market value and the amount owed on the mortgage is their equity.
   B. The $63,000 difference between the original investment and the market value is their tax basis.
   C. The $63,000 difference between the original investment and the market value will be used to compute the capital gains.
   D. The $114,000 difference between the market value and the mortgage is their replacement cost.

4. A building that is remodeled into residential units and is no longer used for the purpose for which it was originally built is an example of
   A. urban homesteading.
   B. planned unit development.
   C. a converted-use property.
   D. a modular home.

5. A highrise development that includes office space, stores, theaters, and apartment units is an example of
   A. a mixed-use development (MUD).
   B. a planned unit development (PUD).
   C. a converted-use property.
   D. special cluster zoning.

6. Each room of a house was pre-assembled at a factory, driven to the building site on a truck, and then lowered onto its foundation by a crane. Later, workers finished the structure and connected plumbing and wiring before the owners moved in. Which term *BEST* describes this type of home?
   A. Modular
   B. Mobile
   C. Manufactured
   D. Converted

7. A single woman bought a home 18 months ago and is now selling because she found a new job in another city. A married couple filing joint taxes has owned a nine-bedroom home for three years. Now, the couple wants to move to a small condominium unit. A single man owned his home for 17 years, sold it, and will use the proceeds from the sale to purchase a larger house. Based on these facts, which of these people is entitled to the $500,000 capital gains exclusion?
   A. The married couple
   B. The single woman
   C. The married couple and the single man
   D. The single woman and the single man

8. When married homeowners who file jointly realize a profit from the sale of their home that exceeds $500,000, which of these is *TRUE*?
   A. The gain exceeding $500,000 will be taxed at the current applicable capital gains rate.
   B. The homeowners will not pay capital gains tax if they are over 55.
   C. Up to $125,000 of the excess profit will be taxed as a capital gain.
   D. The excess gain will be taxed at the homeowners' income tax rate.

9. Theft, smoke damage, and damage from fire are covered under which type of homeowners insurance policy?
   A. Broad form
   B. Coinsurance
   C. National Flood Insurance Program policies
   D. Basic form

10. One result of the capital gains tax law is that *MOST* homeowners
   A. will pay capital gains tax at an 8% lower rate on their home sales.
   B. may build more equity in their primary residence.
   C. may use the $250,000 or $500,000 capital gains exclusion if they lived in the property for two out of the last five years.
   D. will be permitted to use the $125,000 over-55 exclusion more than once.

11. In determining whether a prospective buyer can afford a certain home purchase, lenders will consider
   A. ethnicity of the buyer.
   B. all of these.
   C. address of the home.
   D. credit score.

12. Tom, an art history professor owned and lived in a home in Dubuque, Iowa, for the past four years. He spends a year in Italy after which he decides to sell his home in Dubuque and live in Rome. If Tom is single, he can claim
   A. a one-time exemption of $250,000.
   B. a 1031 exchange.
   C. the $250,000 capital gains exemption.
   D. the $500,000 capital gains exemption.

13. An unmarried homeowner has $80,000 in equity in his primary residence of three years. The owner sells the residence for $135,000. The broker's commission was 5.5%, and other selling expenses amounted to $1,200. What is the owner's taxable gain on this transaction?
   A. $0
   B. $46,375
   C. $47,575
   D. $61,425

14. A man incurs the following expenses: $9,500 in interest on a mortgage loan on his residence, $800 in real estate taxes plus a $450 late payment penalty, and a $1,000 loan origination fee paid in the course of purchasing his home. How much may be deducted from his gross income?
   A. $9,800
   B. $10,500
   C. $11,750
   D. $11,300

15. A community that merges housing, recreation, and commercial units into one self-contained development is called a
   A. mixed-use development (MUD).
   B. cooperative.
   C. planned unit development (PUD).
   D. condominium.

16. Examples of policy efforts to increase home ownership include
   A. lower closing costs for first-time homebuyers.
   B. requiring higher down payments.
   C. requiring higher credit scores.
   D. penalizing first-time homebuyers for using funds from IRAs.

17. Which of the following would *NOT* be like-kind property in a 1031 exchange of a rental single family home?
   A. A condo purchased as income property
   B. Vacant land
   C. Three-unit rental building
   D. Single family home to be used as principal residence

18. Which of these is *NOT* covered in either a basic form or a broad form homeowners insurance policy?
   A. Fire and lightening
   B. Explosion
   C. Flood
   D. Windstorm and hail

19. Which clause is found in *MOST* homeowners insurance policies?
   A. Property improvement clause
   B. Coinsurance clause
   C. Co-ownership clause
   D. Property devaluation clause

20. The portion of an owners' property value that exceeds the amount of their mortgage debt is called
   A. equity.
   B. equality.
   C. escrow.
   D. surplus.

UNIT
4

Real Estate Agency

LEARNING OBJECTIVES

When you have completed this unit, you will be able to accomplish the following.

› Describe the fiduciary duties involved in an agency relationship and distinguish the duties owed by an agent to her client from those owed to customers.
› Explain the process by which agency is created and terminated and the role of disclosure in agency relationships.
› Identify the various types of agency relationships common in the real estate profession and the characteristics of each.

KEY TERMS

agency	cooperative commission	implied contract
agency coupled with an interest	customer	latent defect
	designated agent	listing agreement
agent	dual agency	material fact
brokerage agreement	express agency	negligent
buyer agency agreement	express contract	misrepresentation
client	fiduciary duties	principal
commingling	fraud	puffing
compensation	general agency	single agency
confidential information	general agent	special agent
consumer	gratuitous agency	substantive contact
conversion	implied agency	universal agent

OVERVIEW

The relationship between a real estate licensee and the parties involved in a real estate transaction is not a simple one. In addition to the parties' assumptions and expectations, the licensee is subject to a wide range of legal and ethical requirements designed to protect the seller, the buyer, and the transaction itself. The term *agency* is used to describe that special relationship. Agency is governed by two kinds of law: *statutory law*, the laws, rules, and regulations enacted by legislatures and other governing bodies; and *common law*, the rules of a society established by court decisions.

LAW OF AGENCY

Definitions

Agency refers to a strict, defined legal relationship. In real estate, agency refers to the relationship that a broker, managing broker, or residential leasing agent (representing the sponsoring broker) may have with buyers, sellers, landlords, or tenants. Those who hire are clients, or principals, and those who are hired are agents. A real estate licensee becomes an agent through a contractual agreement, whether expressed or implied, written or oral. The agent owes the client, or principal, a duty of loyalty. This duty of loyalty rises above any personal interests of the agent. The real estate licensee is regarded as an expert on whom the principal can rely for specialized professional advice.

In a broader sense than the agent-client relationship, the relationship of the broker, managing broker, or residential leasing agent with the sponsoring broker is also called a **general agency** because they represent the sponsoring broker in all daily actions. Contracts most effectively establish the agent-client relationship.

Agency relationships in Illinois are governed under statutory law. The body of law on which Illinois agency is based is Article 15 of the Real Estate License Act of 2000 and may serve as a basis for private rights of action and defenses by sellers, buyers, landlords, tenants, managing brokers, and brokers. The law of agency defines the rights and duties of the principal and the agent. Both contract law and real estate licensing laws—in addition to the law of agency— interpret the relationship between real estate licensees and their clients. In Illinois, the Real Estate License Act of 2000 is given precedence in defining legal real estate agency concepts. Insofar as real estate is considered, Illinois is a statutory agency state that has replaced common-law duties with statutory duties. In Illinois, a licensee is presumed to have an agency relationship with the principal unless there is a statement in writing articulating a different relationship.

Statutory Definitions

Key terms of the law of agency under Article 15 of the Real Estate License Act of 2000 are defined as follows:

- **Agency** means a relationship in which a real estate broker or licensee, whether directly or through an affiliated licensee, represents a consumer by the consumer's consent, whether express or implied, in a real property transaction.

- An **agent** is the individual who is authorized and consents to represent the interests of another person. In the real estate business, a firm's sponsoring broker is the agent and shares this responsibility with the licensees who work for him.

- A **brokerage agreement** is an agreement, written or oral, between a sponsoring broker and a consumer for licensed activities to be provided to a consumer in return for compensation or the right to receive compensation from another. In Illinois, any exclusive brokerage agreement must be in writing.

- A **consumer** means a person or entity seeking or receiving licensed activities.

- A **client** means a person who is being represented by a licensee.

- A **customer** means a consumer who is not being represented by the licensee.

- **Compensation** means the valuable consideration given by one person or entity to another person or entity in exchange for the performance of some activity or service. Compensation includes, without limitation: commissions, referral fees, bonuses, prizes, merchandise, finder fees, performance of services, coupons or gift certificates, discounts, rebates, a chance to win a raffle or like game of chance, retainer fee, or salary.

- **Confidential information** means information obtained by a licensee during the term of a brokerage agreement that (i) was made confidential by the written request or written instruction of the client, (ii) deals with the negotiating position of the client, or (iii) is information the disclosure of which could materially harm the negotiating position of the client. This information must not be shared unless the client gives authorization (by word or conduct) for the licensee to share the information, the disclosure is required by law , or the information becomes public from a source other than the licensee.

| An agent works for the client and with the customer. | There is a distinction between the level of services a licensee (as agent) provides to a client and the level of services a licensee may provide to a customer. The client is the **principal** to whom the agent gives advice and counsel. The agent is entrusted with certain confidential information and has fiduciary responsibilities (called *statutory responsibilities* in Illinois) to the principal. |

In contrast, the customer is entitled to factual information and honest dealings as a consumer but never receives advice and counsel or confidential information about the principal. The real estate licensee works for the client but cooperates with the customer.

Just as the agent owes certain duties to the principal, the principal has responsibilities toward the agent. The principal's primary duties are to comply with the brokerage agreement and cooperate with the agent. The principal must not hinder the agent and must deal with the agent in good faith. The principal also must compensate the agent according to the terms of the brokerage agreement.

Fiduciary/Statutory Responsibilities

MEMORY TIP

The six common-law fiduciary duties may be remembered by the acronym COLD AC:

- Care
- Obedience
- Loyalty
- Disclosure
- Accounting
- Confidentiality

The agency agreement usually authorizes the real estate licensee to act for the principal. As such, the real estate licensee owes the principal certain **fiduciary duties**. (A **fiduciary** is one who is placed in a position of trust and confidence.) These duties include the duties of care, obedience, loyalty, disclosure, accounting, and confidentiality. The obligations are summarized in Figure 4.1.

Figure 4.1: Fiduciary Responsibilities

Seller's Agent (Seller is agent's client)	Buyer's Agent (Buyer is agent's client)
Care	
• Provide seller with accurate CMA. • Advise on best pricing options as they relate to market competition. • Advise on preparing the property to be seen on the market. • Show the property and respond to inquiries promptly. • Suggest options during the negotiation process. • Follow through on all required inspections and appraisals. • Follow through on all required paperwork including mandated disclosures. • As latent physical defects and material facts become known, bring them to the attention of the seller.	• Show properties that meet the needs of the buyer. • Suggest other properties that might also fit their needs. • Provide an accurate CMA so that the buyer can make an informed decision. • Point out potential problems that may need to be addressed by inspectors, attorneys, or lenders. • As latent physical defects and material facts become known, bring them to the attention of the buyer.
Obedience	
• Follow all lawful and ethical instructions from the client. • Requests to break Fair Housing Law or the REALTOR® Code of Ethics must be denied and should be discussed with the Sponsoring Broker.	• Follow all lawful and ethical instructions from the client. • Requests to break Fair Housing Law or the REALTOR® Code of Ethics must be denied and should be discussed with the Sponsoring Broker.
Loyalty	
• Always act in the client's best interest as opposed to the agent's or anyone else's best interest. • Do not disclose confidential information to another agent just to "make the deal happen." There is no "between you and me" in the role of a fiduciary.	• Always act in the client's best interest as opposed to the agent's or anyone else's best interest. • Do not disclose confidential information to another agent just to "make the deal happen." There is no "between you and me" in the role of a fiduciary.
Disclosure	
• Disclose all known latent defects and material facts. • Require seller to complete state and federal forms relating to disclosure and provide these and any associated material to the buyer and their agent.	• Disclose all known latent defects and material facts. • Request all appropriate state and federal disclosure forms from seller's agent. Also make sure that all additional material is supplied to your buyer.
Accounting	
• Properly handle all property entrusted to you by seller. • If acting as the escrow agent, make sure the handling of the funds is done in accordance with state law.	• Properly handle all property entrusted to you by buyer. • If acting as the escrow agent, make sure the handling of the funds is done in accordance with state law.
Confidentiality	
• Do not disclose seller's reason or motive for selling, if it affects their negotiating position. • Do not disclose minimum amount seller will accept. • Do not disclose if seller is acting under duress.	• Do not disclose buyer's reason or motivation for buying, if it affects their negotiating position. • Do not disclose maximum amount buyer can afford or is willing to pay.

The Duty of Care

Agents must exercise a reasonable degree of care while transacting the business entrusted to them by the principal. Principals expect the agent's skill and expertise in real estate matters to be superior to that of the average person. The agent should know all facts pertinent to the principal's affairs, such as the physical characteristics of the property being transferred and the type of financing being used.

If the agent represents the seller, care and skill include helping the seller arrive at an appropriate listing price, discovering and disclosing facts that affect the seller, and properly presenting the contracts that the seller signs. It also means properly marketing the property and helping the seller evaluate the terms and conditions of offers to purchase.

An agent who represents the buyer is expected to help the buyer locate suitable property and evaluate property values, neighborhoods and property conditions, financing alternatives, and offers and counteroffers with the buyer's interest in mind.

The Duty of Obedience

The fiduciary relationship obligates the agent to act in good faith at all times, obeying the principal's instructions in accordance with the contract. However, that obedience is not absolute. The agent may not obey instructions that are unlawful or unethical.

EXAMPLE

A seller tells the listing agent, "I don't want you to show this house to any minorities." Because refusing to show a property to someone on the basis of race is illegal, the agent must not follow the seller's instructions and should withdraw from the agency relationship. Violating fair housing laws is illegal, and the duty of obedience never extends to illegal actions.

The Duty of Loyalty

The principal's interests come first, even above the self-interest of the agent. Agents must not consider how the result of negotiations will serve their own interests (for example, by providing them with a commission). Rather, agents must perform all services with the goal of promoting the principal's interests.

Illinois license law prohibits a licensee to serve as a dual agent in any transaction to which he or she, or an entity in which he or she has an ownership interest, is a party to the transaction. The agent must be particularly sensitive to any possible conflicts of interest.

The Duty of Disclosure

It is the agent's duty to keep the principal informed of all facts or information that could affect a transaction. Duty of disclosure includes disclosure of relevant information or material facts that the agent knows or should have known about.

The agent is obligated to disclose facts that a reasonable person would feel are important in choosing a course of action, regardless of whether those facts are favorable or unfavorable to the principal's position.

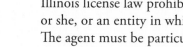

Disclosure forms are usually completed by the seller before he signs the listing agreement or at the time of signing. Regardless of the seller's completion of the disclosure form, the seller's agent is required to disclose all material defects known to her, including in cases where the agent knows that the seller has misrepresented the extent or existence of property defects or has not fully disclosed them. An agent for a buyer must disclose deficiencies of a property as well.

The Illinois Association of REALTORS® Residential Real Property Disclosure Report (see Figure 4.2) shifts the responsibility for full disclosure from the real estate agent to the seller. It requires that sellers of one- to four-unit residential properties fill out property disclosure forms revealing any material defects they are aware of in the real estate for sale. The completed forms are given to buyers before an offer is made. If the disclosure form is delivered after the offer has been accepted and if it has any negative disclosures, the buyer has three business days to cancel the contract. Furthermore, if the seller learns of a new problem after a contract is signed and up until closing, disclosure must be made in writing to the buyer. In the latter case, the buyer does not have the power to simply cancel the contract. Compensation may be negotiated or the problem remedied by the seller. Under no circumstances should a real estate licensee help the seller complete this form (either physically or by answering any questions).

The Duty of Accounting

Most states' license laws require that agents periodically report the status of all funds or property received from or on behalf of the principal. Similarly, most state license laws require that licensees give accurate copies of all documents to all affected parties and keep copies on file for a period of time.

Illinois licensees are required to deliver true copies of all executed or initialed documents to the people who signed or initialed them within 24 hours. In Illinois, all funds entrusted to a licensee must be deposited in a special escrow account by the next business day following the signing of a sales contract or lease (unless the contract terms specify a different time frame). **Commingling** such monies with the licensee's personal or general business funds is illegal. **Conversion**, the practice of using those escrow funds as the licensee's own money, is illegal as well. Licensees should be aware that records of escrow account transactions and reconciliations must be kept on file for at least five years.

Figure 4.2: Residential Real Property Disclosure Report

Illinois REALTORS®
RESIDENTIAL REAL PROPERTY DISCLOSURE REPORT
(765 ILCS 77/35)

NOTICE: THE PURPOSE OF THIS REPORT IS TO PROVIDE PROSPECTIVE BUYERS WITH INFORMATION ABOUT MATERIAL DEFECTS IN THE RESIDENTIAL REAL PROPERTY. THIS REPORT DOES NOT LIMIT THE PARTIES' RIGHT TO CONTRACT FOR THE SALE OF RESIDENTIAL REAL PROPERTY IN "AS IS" CONDITION. UNDER COMMON LAW, SELLERS WHO DISCLOSE MATERIAL DEFECTS MAY BE UNDER A CONTINUING OBLIGATION TO ADVISE THE PROSPECTIVE BUYERS ABOUT THE CONDITION OF THE RESIDENTIAL REAL PROPERTY EVEN AFTER THE REPORT IS DELIVERED TO THE PROSPECTIVE BUYER. COMPLETION OF THIS REPORT BY THE SELLER CREATES LEGAL OBLIGATIONS ON THE SELLER; THEREFORE SELLER MAY WISH TO CONSULT AN ATTORNEY PRIOR TO COMPLETION OF THIS REPORT.

Property Address: _____

City, State & Zip Code: _____

Seller's Name: _____

This Report is a disclosure of certain conditions of the residential real property listed above in compliance with the Residential Real Property Disclosure Act. This information is provided as of _____, 20___, and does not reflect any changes made or occurring after that date or information that becomes known to the seller after that date. The disclosures herein shall not be deemed warranties of any kind by the seller or any person representing any party in this transaction.

In this form, "am aware" means to have actual notice or actual knowledge without any specific investigation or inquiry. In this form, a "material defect" means a condition that would have a substantial adverse effect on the value of the residential real property or that would significantly impair the health or safety of future occupants of the residential real property unless the seller reasonably believes that the condition has been corrected.

The seller discloses the following information with the knowledge that even though the statements herein are not deemed to be warranties, prospective buyers may choose to rely on this information in deciding whether or not and on what terms to purchase the residential real property.

The seller represents that to the best of his or her actual knowledge, the following statements have been accurately noted as "yes" (correct), "no" (incorrect), or "not applicable" to the property being sold. If the seller indicates that the response to any statement, except number 1, is yes or not applicable, the seller shall provide an explanation, in the additional information area of this form.

	YES	NO	N/A	
1.	___	___	___	Seller has occupied the property within the last 12 months. (No explanation is needed.)
2.	___	___	___	I am aware of flooding or recurring leakage problems in the crawl space or basement.
3.	___	___	___	I am aware that the property is located in a flood plain or that I currently have flood hazard insurance on the property.
4.	___	___	___	I am aware of material defects in the basement or foundation (including cracks and bulges).
5.	___	___	___	I am aware of leaks or material defects in the roof, ceilings, or chimney.
6.	___	___	___	I am aware of material defects in the walls, windows, doors, or floors.
7.	___	___	___	I am aware of material defects in the electrical system.
8.	___	___	___	I am aware of material defects in the plumbing system (includes such things as water heater, sump pump, water treatment system, sprinkler system, and swimming pool).
9.	___	___	___	I am aware of material defects in the well or well equipment.
10.	___	___	___	I am aware of unsafe conditions in the drinking water.
11.	___	___	___	I am aware of material defects in the heating, air conditioning, or ventilating systems.
12.	___	___	___	I am aware of material defects in the fireplace or wood burning stove.
13.	___	___	___	I am aware of material defects in the septic, sanitary sewer, or other disposal system.
14.	___	___	___	I am aware of unsafe concentrations of radon on the premises.
15.	___	___	___	I am aware of unsafe concentrations of or unsafe conditions relating to asbestos on the premises.
16.	___	___	___	I am aware of unsafe concentrations of or unsafe conditions relating to lead paint, lead water pipes, lead plumbing pipes or lead in the soil on the premises.
17.	___	___	___	I am aware of mine subsidence, underground pits, settlement, sliding, upheaval, or other earth stability defects on the premises.
18.	___	___	___	I am aware of current infestations of termites or other wood boring insects.
19.	___	___	___	I am aware of a structural defect caused by previous infestations of termites or other wood boring insects.
20.	___	___	___	I am aware of underground fuel storage tanks on the property.
21.	___	___	___	I am aware of boundary or lot line disputes.
22.	___	___	___	I have received notice of violation of local, state or federal laws or regulations relating to this property, which violation has not been corrected.
23.	___	___	___	I am aware that this property has been used for the manufacture of methamphetamine as defined in Section 10 of the Methamphetamine Control and Community Protection Act.

Note: These disclosures are not intended to cover the common elements of a condominium, but only the actual residential real property including limited common elements allocated to the exclusive use thereof that form an integral part of the condominium unit.
Note: These disclosures are intended to reflect the current condition of the premises and do not include previous problems, if any, that the seller reasonably believes have been corrected.

FORM 108 (05/2021) COPYRIGHT ILLINOIS REALTORS®   Page 1 of 4

Copyright Illinois Association of REALTORS®, www.illinoisrealtor.org. Reprinted with permission.

Figure 4.2: Residential Real Property Disclosure Report (continued)

If any of the above are marked "not applicable" or "yes", please explain here or use additional pages, if necessary: _____
_____
_____
_____
_____
_____

Check here if additional pages used: _____

Seller certifies that seller has prepared this statement and certifies that the information provided is based on the actual notice or actual knowledge of the seller without any specific investigation or inquiry on the part of the seller. The seller hereby authorizes any person representing any principal in this transaction to provide a copy of this report, and to disclose any information in the report, to any person in connection with any actual or anticipated sale of the property.

Seller: _____Date: _____

Seller: _____Date: _____

THE PROSPECTIVE BUYER IS AWARE THAT THE PARTIES MAY CHOOSE TO NEGOTIATE AN AGREEMENT FOR THE SALE OF THE PROPERTY SUBJECT TO ANY OR ALL MATERIAL DEFECTS DISCLOSED IN THIS REPORT ("AS IS"). THIS DISCLOSURE IS NOT A SUBSTITUTE FOR ANY INSPECTIONS OR WARRANTIES THAT THE PROSPECTIVE BUYER OR SELLER MAY WISH TO OBTAIN OR NEGOTIATE. THE FACT THAT THE SELLER IS NOT AWARE OF A PARTICULAR CONDITION OR PROBLEM IS NO GUARANTEE THAT IT DOES NOT EXIST. THE PROSPECTIVE BUYER IS AWARE THAT HE MAY REQUEST AN INSPECTION OF THE PREMISES PERFORMED BY A QUALIFIED PROFESSIONAL.

Prospective Buyer: _____ Date: _____ Time: _____

Prospective Buyer: _____ Date: _____ Time: _____

A COPY OF ARTICLE 2 OF THE RESIDENTIAL REAL PROPERTY DISCLOSURE ACT IS AFFIXED HERETO AND SHOULD BE REVIEWED BY PROSPECTIVE BUYER.

Figure 4.2: Residential Real Property Disclosure Report (continued)

RESIDENTIAL REAL PROPERTY DISCLOSURE ACT
ARTICLE 2: DISCLOSURES
765 ILCS 77/5 *et seq.*

Section 5. Definitions: As used in this Act, unless the context otherwise requires the following terms have the meaning given in this section:

"Residential real property" means real property improved with not less than one nor more than four residential dwelling units: units in residential cooperatives; or, condominium units including the limited common elements allocated to the exclusive use thereof that form an integral part of the condominium unit. The term includes a manufactured home as defined in subdivision (53) of Section 9-102 of the Uniform Commercial Code that is real property as defined in the Conveyance and Encumbrance of Manufactured Homes as Real Property and Severance Act.

"Seller" means every person or entity who is an owner, beneficiary of a trust, contract purchaser or lessee of a ground lease, who has an interest (legal or equitable) in residential real property. However, "seller" shall not include any person who has both (i) never occupied the residential real property and (ii) never had the management responsibility for the residential real property nor delegated such responsibility for the residential real property to another person or entity.

"Prospective buyer" means any person or entity negotiating or offering to become an owner or lessee of residential real property by means of a transfer for value to which this Act applies.

Section 10. Applicability. Except as provided in Section 15, this Act applies to any transfer by sale, exchange, installment land sale-contract, assignment of beneficial interest, lease with an option to purchase, ground lease or assignment of ground lease of residential real property.

Section 15. Applicability; Exceptions. The provisions of this Act do not apply to the following:

(1) Transfers pursuant to court order, including, but not limited to, transfers ordered by a probate court in administration of an estate, transfers between spouses resulting from a judgment of dissolution of marriage or legal separation, transfers pursuant to an order of possession, transfers by a trustee in bankruptcy, transfers by eminent domain and transfers resulting from a decree for specific performance.

(2) Transfers from a mortgagor to a mortgagee by deed in lieu of foreclosure or consent judgment, transfer by judicial deed issued pursuant to a foreclosure sale to the successful bidder or the assignee of a certificate of sale, transfer by a collateral assignment of a beneficial interest of a land trust, or a transfer by a mortgagee or a successor in interest to the mortgagee's secured position or a beneficiary under a deed in trust who has acquired the real property by deed in lieu of foreclosure, consent judgment or judicial deed issued pursuant to a foreclosure sale.

(3) Transfers by a fiduciary in the course of the administration of a decedent's estate, guardianship, conservatorship, or trust.

(4) Transfers from one co-owner to one or more other co-owners.

(5) Transfers pursuant to testate or intestate succession.

(6) Transfers made to a spouse, or to a person or persons in the lineal line of consanguinity of one or more of the sellers.

(7) Transfers from an entity that has taken title to residential real property from a seller for the purpose of assisting in the relocation of the seller, so long as the entity makes available to all prospective buyers a copy of the disclosure form furnished to the entity by the seller.

(8) Transfers to or from any governmental entity.

(9) Transfers of newly constructed residential real property that has not been occupied.

Section 20. Disclosure Report; Completion; Time of Delivery. A seller of residential real property shall complete all applicable items in the disclosure document described in Section 35 of this Act. The seller shall deliver to the prospective buyer the written disclosure statement required by this Act before the signing of a written agreement by the seller and prospective buyer that would, subject to the satisfaction of any negotiated contingencies, require the prospective buyer to accept a transfer of the residential real property.

Section 25. Liability of seller.

(a) The seller is not liable for any error, inaccuracy, or omission of any information delivered pursuant to this Act if (i) the seller had no knowledge of the error, inaccuracy, or omission, (ii) the error, inaccuracy, or omission was based on a reasonable belief that a material defect or other matter not disclosed had been corrected, or (iii) the error, inaccuracy, or omission was based on information provided by a public agency or by a licensed engineer, land surveyor, structural pest control operator, or by a contractor about matters within the scope of the contractor's occupation and the seller had no knowledge of the error, inaccuracy, or omission.

(b) The seller shall disclose material defects of which the seller has actual knowledge.

(c) The seller is not obligated by this Act to make any specific investigation or inquiry in an effort to complete the disclosure statement.

Section 30. Disclosure supplement. If, prior to closing, any seller has actual knowledge of an error, inaccuracy, or omission in any prior disclosure document after delivery of that disclosure document to a prospective buyer, that seller shall supplement the prior disclosure document with a written supplemental disclosure.

Section 35. Disclosure report form. . . .[omitted]

Section 40. Material defect. If a material defect is disclosed in the Residential Real Property Disclosure Report, after acceptance by the prospective buyer of an offer or counter-offer made by a seller or after the execution of an offer made by a prospective buyer that is accepted by the seller for the conveyance of the residential real property, then the Prospective Buyer may, within three business days after receipt of that Report by the prospective buyer, terminate the contract or other agreement without any liability or recourse except for the return to prospective buyer of all earnest money deposits or down payments paid by prospective buyer in the transaction. If a material defect is disclosed in a supplement to this disclosure document, the prospective buyer shall not have a right to terminate unless the material defect results from an error, inaccuracy, or omission of which the seller had actual knowledge at the time the prior disclosure document was completed and signed by the seller. The right to terminate the contract, however, shall no longer exist after the conveyance of the residential real property. For purposes of this Act the termination shall be deemed to be made when written notice of termination is personally delivered to at least one of the sellers identified in the contract or other agreement or when deposited, certified or registered mail, with the United States Postal Service, addressed to one of the sellers at the address indicated in the contract or agreement, or, if there is not an address contained therein, then at the address indicated for the residential real property on the Report.

Section 45. Effect of Act on Other Statutes or Common Law. This Act is not intended to limit or modify any obligation to disclose created by any other statute or that may exist in common law in order to avoid fraud, misrepresentation, or deceit in the transaction.

Section 50. Disclosure Report; Method of Delivery. Delivery of the Residential Real Property Disclosure Report provided by this Act shall be by:

(1) personal or facsimile delivery to the prospective buyer;

(2) depositing the report with the United States Postal Service, postage prepaid, first class mail, addressed to the prospective buyer at the address provided by the prospective buyer or indicated on the contract or other agreement; or

(3) depositing the report with an alternative delivery service such as Federal Express, UPS, or Airborne, delivery charges prepaid, addressed to the prospective buyer at the address provided by the prospective buyer or indicated on the contract or other agreement.

Figure 4.2: Residential Real Property Disclosure Report (continued)

For purposes of this Act, delivery to one prospective buyer is deemed delivery to all prospective buyers. Delivery to an authorized individual acting on behalf of a prospective buyer constitutes delivery to all prospective buyers. Delivery of the Report is effective upon receipt by the prospective buyer. Receipt may be acknowledged on the Report, in an agreement for the conveyance of the residential real property, or shown in any other verifiable manner.

Section 55. Violations and damages. If the seller fails or refuses to provide the disclosure document prior to the conveyance of the residential real property, the buyer shall have the right to terminate the contract. A person who knowingly violates or fails to perform any duty prescribed by any provision of this Act or who discloses any information on the Residential Real Property Disclosure Report that he knows to be false shall be liable in the amount of actual damages and court costs, and the court may award reasonable attorney fees incurred by the prevailing party.

Section 60. Limitation of Action. No action for violation of this Act may be commenced later than one year from the earlier of the date of possession, date of occupancy or date of recording of an instrument of conveyance of the residential real property.

Section 65. Disclosure Report Form; Contents; Copy of Act. A copy of this Act, excluding Section 35, must be printed on or as a part of the Residential Real Property Disclosure Report form.

Date provided to Buyer: _____

Seller: _____

The Duty of Confidentiality

Confidentiality is a key element of fiduciary duties. Client information obtained during the term of the brokerage agreement must be kept confidential. For example, when the principal is the seller, the agent may not reveal such things as the principal's willingness to accept less than the listing price or urgency to sell, unless the principal has authorized the disclosure by word or conduct. If the principal is the buyer, the agent may not disclose that the buyer will pay a higher price, is under a tight moving schedule, or other facts that might harm the principal's bargaining position.

Although an agent may not disclose personal, confidential information about her principal, known material facts about the property's physical condition or its environs must always be disclosed. A **material fact** is any fact that, if known, might reasonably be expected to affect the course of events.

These fiduciary/statutory duties are set forth in Article 15 of the Real Estate License Act of 2000. According to this statute, the agent must

- perform the terms of the brokerage agreement between a sponsoring broker and the client;
- promote the best interests of the client by
  - seeking a transaction at the price and terms stated in the brokerage agreement or at a price and terms otherwise acceptable to the client,
  - timely presenting all offers to and from the client, unless the client has waived this duty,
  - disclosing to the client material facts concerning the transaction of which the licensee has actual knowledge, unless that information is confidential information,
  - timely accounting for all money and property received in which the client has, may have, or should have had an interest,
  - obeying specific directions of the client that are not otherwise contrary to applicable statutes, ordinances, or rules, and
  - acting in a manner consistent with promoting the client's best interests as opposed to a licensee's or any other person's self-interest;
- exercise reasonable skill and care in the performance of brokerage services;
- keep confidential all confidential information received from the client; and
- comply with all the requirements of the Act and all applicable statutes and regulations, including fair housing and civil rights.

Opinion Versus Fact

Real estate licensees and other staff members must always be careful about the statements they make. They must be sure that the consumer understands whether the statement is opinion or fact. Statements of opinion are permissible only as long as they are offered as opinions and without any intention to deceive.

Statements of fact must be accurate. Generalized, vague exaggeration of a property's benefits is called **puffing**. While puffing is not illegal, licensees must ensure that none of their statements can be interpreted as fraudulent. **Fraud** is the intentional misrepresentation of a material fact so as to harm or take advantage of another person. That includes not only making false statements about a property but also intentionally concealing or failing to disclose important facts.

The misrepresentation or omission does not have to be intentional to result in licensee liability. **Negligent misrepresentation** occurs when the licensee should have known that a statement about a material fact was false. If the consumer relies on the licensee's statement, the licensee is liable for any damages that result.

EXAMPLE

While showing a potential buyer an average-looking house, the broker described even its plainest features as "charming" and "beautiful." Because the statements were obviously the broker's personal opinions designed to encourage a positive feeling about the property (or puff it up), the truth or falsity of the statements is not an issue. In contrast, if the broker neglected to inform the buyer that the lot next to the house the buyer was considering had been sold to a waste disposal company for use as a toxic dump, fraudulent misrepresentation has more than likely occurred.

The Illinois Real Estate License Act clearly states that a licensee shall not be liable to a client for providing false information to the client if the false information was provided to the licensee by a customer unless the licensee knew or should have known the information was false. It also states that licensee shall not be liable to a customer for providing false information to the customer if the false information was provided to the licensee by the licensee's client and the licensee did not have actual knowledge that information was false. In addition, the act states that licensees shall treat all customers honestly and shall not negligently or knowingly give them false information.

Latent Defects

A structural defect that would not normally be uncovered over the course of an ordinary inspection (due to the placement or type of defect, for example) is called a **latent defect**. The seller has a duty to disclose any known latent defects that threaten structural soundness or personal safety. Buyers have been able to either rescind the sales contract or receive monetary damages when a seller fails to reveal known latent defects. The courts also have decided in favor of the buyer when the seller neglected to reveal violations of zoning or building codes.

It is the licensee's duty to disclose any material facts that may affect the property's value or desirability, whether or not they are known to or disclosed by the seller. Any such material facts discovered by the licensee must be disclosed to prospective buyers. A licensee who should have known about a substantial defect that is detected later by the buyer may be liable to the buyer for any damages resulting from that defect.

EXAMPLE

The listing broker knew that a house had been built on a landfill. A few days after the house was listed, another broker in the same real estate office noticed that the living room floor was uneven and sagging in places. In some states, both brokers have a duty to conduct further investigations into the structural soundness of the property. In other states, no such duty exists, but the listing broker would have the duty of discussing the issue with the seller and advising the buyer to have an inspection performed. They cannot simply ignore the problem or place throw rugs over particularly bad spots and hope buyers won't look underneath. If the seller refuses to disclose the problem, then the broker should refuse the listing.

Stigmatized Properties

Stigmatized properties are those properties that society has branded undesirable because of events that occurred there. Stigma is the continuing negative association with or feeling about the property. Typically, the stigma is a criminal event such as homicide, gang-related activity, or a tragedy such as suicide. Properties have even been stigmatized by rumors that they are haunted. Because of the potential liability to a licensee for inadequately researching and disclosing material facts concerning a property's condition, licensees should seek legal counsel when dealing with a stigmatized property. In Illinois, licensees have no legal duty to disclose that a property is stigmatized.

Megan's Law

Megan's Law is a general name for state and federal laws requiring law enforcement authorities to make information available to the general public regarding registered sex offenders. Federal law also requires persons convicted of sex crimes against children to notify local law enforcement of any change of address or employment after release from custody.

Listing agents have no legal duty to disclose that a registered sex offender lives near a listed home. Buyer's agents should refer their buyer clients to publicly available sex-offender-location lists if asked.

Article 15 of the Real Estate License Act of 2000 states that

- "no cause of action shall arise against a licensee for the failure to disclose a fact situation on property that is not the subject of the transaction" and

- "no cause of action shall arise against a licensee for the failure to disclose physical conditions, located on property that is not the subject of the transaction, that do not have a substantial adverse effect on the value of the real estate that is the subject of the transaction."

Article 15 further states that, in dealing with specific situations related to disclosure, "no cause of action shall arise against a licensee for the failure to disclose that an occupant of that property was afflicted with HIV or any other medical condition or that the property was the site of an act or occurrence which had no effect on the physical condition of the property or its environment or the structures located thereon."

Any action brought under Article 15 must commence within two years after the person bringing the action knew or should have known of such act or omission. In no event can the action be brought more than five years after the date on which the act or omission occurred.

CUSTOMER-LEVEL SERVICES

Even though an agent's primary responsibility is to the principal, the agent also has duties to third parties. Anytime a licensee works with a third party or a customer, the licensee is responsible for adhering to state and federal consumer protection laws as well as to the ethical requirements imposed by professional associations and state regulators.

An agent owes a customer the duties of reasonable care and skill, honest and fair dealing, and disclosure of known facts.

An agent's primary responsibility is to the principal, and Illinois courts have long held that the contractual principal-agent relationship as defined in a listing agreement or buyer agency agreement gives the seller or the buyer a cause of action against the licensee who breaches her fiduciary duties to the client. The courts have not demanded fiduciary duties to third parties. However, Illinois license law does set forth the duties that licensees owe to third-party customers (buyers or sellers). Licensees are to treat all customers honestly. They cannot negligently or knowingly give customers false information.

Finally, licensees must disclose all adverse material facts about the physical condition of the property to the customer that are actually known by the licensee and that could not be discovered by a reasonably diligent inspection of the property by the customer.

In Illinois, a licensee may be held liable to a seller or a buyer if the licensee misrepresents material facts about a property and if the seller or the buyer suffers monetary loss through reliance on these statements. The licensee's loyalty to the principal is no defense, even though the principal may have ordered the agent to misrepresent. Licensees have a duty to prospective sellers and buyers to disclose all material information within their knowledge. If the licensee knowingly makes untrue statements, Illinois courts will have no difficulty in finding the licensee liable to the appropriate party.

Furthermore, liability may be imposed when the licensee is aware of facts that tend to indicate she is making a false statement. For example, if the seller tells his agent/licensee that "the roof was replaced last year," and the agent has good reason to believe that statement is untrue, the licensee should attempt to ascertain the truth and pass the correct information on to the buyer. However, if the client provided the false information and the licensee did not have knowledge that the information was false or the licensee has not acted negligently, the licensee will not be held liable to the customer.

Licensees who attempt to avoid liability to buyers through the use of a waiver or an exculpatory clause in the sales contract will probably be unsuccessful. Illinois courts have ruled that a contract cannot eliminate the rights given to a consumer via the law.

CREATION AND TERMINATION OF AGENCY

Creation of Agency

An agency relationship may be based on a formal agreement between the parties (**express agency**) or it may result from the parties' behavior (**implied agency**).

Express Agency

The principal and agent may enter into an **express contract** (also called an *express agreement*) in which the parties formally express their intention to establish an agency relationship and state its terms and conditions. The agreement may be either oral or written. An agency relationship between a seller and a sponsoring broker is generally created by a written employment contract, commonly called a **listing agreement**, which authorizes the sponsoring broker (or designated licensees) to find a buyer or a tenant for the owner's property. An express agency relationship between a buyer and a sponsoring broker is created by a **buyer agency agreement**. Similar to a listing agreement, it stipulates the activities and responsibilities the buyer expects from the sponsoring broker (or designated licensees) in finding the appropriate property for purchase or rent.

Implied Agency

An agency also may be created by **implied contract**. This occurs when the actions of the licensee indicate that the licensee has formed an agency relationship with a party. Even though the licensee may not have consciously planned to create an agency relationship, the parties can create one unintentionally, inadvertently, or accidentally by their actions.

EXAMPLE

Buyers enter a real estate office asking to see a property listed with another brokerage. A real estate licensee immediately calls the sellers' agent and makes an appointment to show the property. Without discussing the available agency options or having the customers sign a written agency agreement, the licensee drives them to the house. Through the actions of the licensee, the customers think they are being represented.

Licensees shall be considered to be representing the consumer they are working with as a designated agent for the consumer unless there is a written agreement between the consumer and the sponsoring broker stating otherwise. Agency disclosure is crucial to the consumer's understanding of their relationship to the licensee.

Compensation

The source of compensation does not determine agency. A real estate agent does not necessarily represent the person who pays her commission. In fact, agency can exist even if no fee is involved; it is called a **gratuitous agency**.

In Illinois, compensation does not determine the agency relationship. Both the buyer's and the seller's real estate agents are often paid by the seller in a **cooperative commission** arrangement. The seller first pays the listing sponsoring broker, and the listing sponsoring broker cuts a check to the cooperating sponsoring broker or directs commission to be paid out of proceeds at the closing. Sometimes the seller pays only the listing sponsoring broker and the buyer pays the buyer's sponsoring broker. Regardless of the particular arrangement, the licensee is required to disclose to a client the sponsoring broker's compensation and policy with regard to cooperating with brokers who represent other parties in a transaction.

Termination of Agency

An agency may be terminated for any of the following reasons:

- Death or incapacity of either party
- Destruction or condemnation of the property
- Expiration of the term of the agency
- Mutual agreement by all parties to the contract
- Breach by one of the parties, in which case the breaching party might be liable for damages
- By operation of law, as in bankruptcy of the principal (bankruptcy terminates the agency contract, and title to the property transfers to a court-appointed receiver)
- Completion, performance, or fulfillment of the purpose for which the agency was created

Licensees are not allowed to obtain a written brokerage agreement that does not expire automatically within a certain time period or provide the client the right to terminate the agreement annually by giving no more than 30 days' advance written notice.

In **agency coupled with an interest**, the agent has an interest in the subject of the agency, such as the property being sold. An agency coupled with an interest cannot be revoked by the principal or be terminated on the principal's death.

EXAMPLE

A broker agrees to provide the financing for a condominium building being constructed by a developer in exchange for the exclusive right to sell the units once the building is completed. The developer may not revoke the listing agreement once the broker has provided the financing because this is an agency coupled with an interest.

TYPES OF AGENCY RELATIONSHIPS

What an agent may do as the principal's representative depends solely on what the principal authorizes the agent to do.

Limitations on an Agent's Authority

A **universal agent** is a person empowered to do anything the principal could do personally. The universal agent's authority to act on behalf of the principal is virtually unlimited.

In Illinois, a written power of attorney is required to create a universal agency.

A **general agent** may represent the principal in a broad range of matters related to a particular business or activity. The general agent may, for example, bind the principal to any contract within the scope of the agent's authority. A property manager is typically considered a general agent to the property owner. Brokers and managing brokers are general agents to their sponsoring broker.

A general agent represents the principal generally.

A special agent represents the principal only for a specific act, such as the sale of a house.

A **special agent** is authorized to represent the principal in one specific act or business transaction only, under detailed instructions. A real estate licensee usually is a "special" agent to a client. If hired by a seller, the licensee is limited to finding a ready, willing, and able buyer for the property. A special agent for a buyer (buyer's agent) has the limited responsibility of finding a property that fits the buyer's criteria.

As a special agent, the licensee may not bind the principal to a contract. The principal makes all contractually related decisions and will sign on her own. A *special power of attorney* is another legal means of authorizing an agent to carry out only a specified act or acts.

Finally, a **designated agent** is a person authorized by the sponsoring broker to act as the agent of a specific principal. A designated agent is the only licensee in the company who has a fiduciary responsibility toward that principal. When one licensee in the company is a designated agent, the others are free to act as agents for the other party in a transaction. In this way, two licensees from the same real estate company may represent opposite sides in a property sale without entering dual agency.

Designated agency is recognized in Illinois. A sponsoring broker entering into a brokerage agreement must specifically designate those licensees employed by or affiliated with the sponsoring broker to act as legal agents of that client to the exclusion of all other licensees employed by or affiliated with the sponsoring broker. The sponsoring broker will not be considered to be acting for more than one party in a transaction if the licensees specifically designated as legal agents of a person are not representing more than one party in a transaction (see Figure 4.3 and Figure 4.4). Also, a licensee shall advise a consumer in writing, before acting as their designated agent, that a designated agency relationship exists and disclose the name(s) of the consumer's designated agent(s).

Figure 4.3: Disclosure of Buyer's Designated Agent

ILLINOIS REALTORS®
DISCLOSURE OF BUYER'S DESIGNATED AGENT

_____ (Sponsoring Brokerage Company, hereinafter referred to as "Broker") designates _____ ("Designated Agent") as the legal agent(s) of _____ (hereinafter referred to as "Buyer") for the purpose of representing Buyer in the acquisition of real estate by Buyer. Buyer understands and agrees that neither Broker nor any other licensees affiliated with Broker (except as provided for herein) will be acting as legal agent of the Buyer. Broker shall have the discretion to appoint a substitute or additional designated agent for Buyer as Broker determines necessary. Buyer shall be advised within a reasonable time of any such substitution or addition.

Broker acknowledges and agrees that Buyer has no current exclusive Buyer representation agreement with any other real estate licensee or firm. Buyer represents that if Buyer previously entered into any exclusive Buyer representation agreements that they have expired and/or have been terminated. Further, Buyer agrees to immediately inform Designated Agent if Designated Agent is showing Buyer a property previously shown to Buyer.

Buyer, by continuing to work with Buyer's Designated Agent, acknowledges that the representations and agreements made above are true and correct.

BUYER REPRESENTATION OPTIONS
Check the box that applies

☐ Use **IR Terms of Non-Exclusive Buyer Representation,** if Buyer does not choose to enter a buyer brokerage representation agreement.
  • Use form number 341.

NOTE: If Buyer consents to Dual Agency, use form number 335, Disclosure and Consent to Dual Agency, together with form number 341.

☐ Use **IR Non–Exclusive Buyer Representation Contract,** if Buyer does not want an exclusive agency relationship with Broker, but will sign a non-exclusive agreement.
  • Use form number 339 with Disclosure and Consent to Dual Agency
  • Use form number 339a if Broker's office policy does not allow disclosed dual agency or if Buyer does not consent to dual agency.

☐ Use **IR Exclusive Buyer Representation/Exclusive Right to Purchase Contract,** if Buyer will enter exclusive agency relationship with Broker.
  • Use form number 338 with Disclosure and Consent to Dual Agency
  • Use form number 338a if Broker's office policy does not allow disclosed dual agency or if Buyer does not consent to dual agency.

Date copy furnished to Buyer: _____   By: _____

_____   _____
Buyer's Signature **(OPTIONAL)**   Buyer's Signature **(OPTIONAL)**

(NOTE: Give copy to Buyer and retain copy for Brokerage company file.)

FORM 349 (05/2021) COPYRIGHT ILLINOIS REALTORS®   1/1

Figure 4.4: Additional Agent Designation

ILLINOIS REALTORS®
ADDITIONAL AGENT DESIGNATION

*(Use this form when naming an additional designated legal agent
to represent a seller-client, buyer-client or tenant/lessee client)*

_____ ("Sponsoring Broker") is designating the licensee named below as an additional designated agent for the client named below.

Additional Designated Agent: _____
(print or type name)

Additional Designated Agent shall serve you as one of your agents until such time as (check all that apply)

☐   terminated by the client or Sponsoring Broker
☐   for the time period beginning _____, 20____ until _____, 20____.

Sponsoring Broker:

By: _____   Date: _____
      Authorized Signer

Client Name: _____
                        (print or type)

Property Address (if listing): _____

The sponsoring broker must take care to protect confidential information disclosed by a client to the designated agent. A designated agent may disclose to the sponsoring broker or persons specified by the sponsoring broker confidential information of a client for the purpose of seeking advice or assistance for the benefit of the client in regard to a possible transaction. The sponsoring broker cannot disclose confidential information unless otherwise required by Illinois law or requested or permitted by the client who originally disclosed the confidential information.

Single Agency

When an agent or firm represents only one party (buyer, seller, landlord, or tenant) exclusively in a real estate transaction, this relationship is called **single agency**. The agent and firm's fiduciary and statutory duties are provided only to that one party (the principal).

While a single agency licensee may represent both sellers and buyers, that licensee cannot represent both in the same transaction. This avoids conflict and results in client-based service and loyalty to only one client. On the other hand, it traditionally rules out the sale of in-house listings to represented buyers.

Buyer Agency

Many licensees involved with residential property are discovering opportunities for buyer representation. Some licensees have become specialists in the emerging field of buyer agency, even representing buyers exclusively.

A buyer agency relationship is established in the same way as any other agency relationship: by contract, agreement, or implication. The buyer's agent may receive a fee from the buyer or share in the seller-paid commission to the listing sponsoring broker or both, depending on the terms of the agency agreement.

In Illinois, though not required by law, it is common for the listing sponsoring brokerage to share the listing commission with the buyer's sponsoring brokerage.

Property Management Agency

An owner may employ a sponsoring broker to market, lease, maintain, or manage the owner's property. Such an arrangement is called *property management.* The sponsoring broker is made the agent of the property owner through a property management agreement. As in any other agency relationship, the sponsoring broker has a fiduciary responsibility to the client-owner.

Dual Agency

In **dual agency**, the agent represents two principals in the same transaction. Dual agency requires equal loyalty to two separate principals at the same time. The challenge is to fulfill the fiduciary obligations to one principal without compromising the interests of the other, especially when the parties' interests may not only be separate but even opposite.

Disclosed Dual Agency

Real estate licensing laws permit dual agency only if the buyer and the seller are informed and consent to the licensee's representation of both in the same transaction. Although the possibility of conflict of interest still exists, disclosure is intended to minimize the risk for the licensee by ensuring that both principals are aware of the effect of dual agency on their respective interests. The disclosure alerts the principals that they may have to assume greater responsibility for protecting their interests than they would if each had independent representation. Because the duties of disclosure and confidentiality are limited by mutual agreement, they must be carefully explained to the parties in order to establish informed consent (see Figure 4.5 and Figure 4.6).

Confirmation of Consent to Dual Agency

In Illinois, all parties must give consent and confirmation to the arrangement, in writing.

Undisclosed Dual Agency

A licensee may not intend to create a dual agency. For example, a licensee representing the seller might tell a buyer that the seller will accept less than the listing price to entice the buyer into making an offer, or the listing licensee might try to persuade the seller to accept an offer that is really in the buyer's interest. Giving a buyer any specific advice on how much to offer can lead the buyer to believe that the licensee represents the buyer's interests and is acting as the buyer's advocate.

Any of these actions creates an implied agency with the buyer and violates the duties of loyalty and confidentiality to the principal-seller. Because neither party has been informed of that situation and been given the opportunity to seek separate representation, the interests of both are jeopardized.

EXAMPLE

A real estate licensee is the agent for the owner of a large mansion. A prospective buyer comes into the licensee's office and asks her to represent him in a search for a modest home. After several weeks of activity, including low offers unsuccessfully negotiated by the licensee, the prospective buyer spots the For Sale sign in front of the mansion. He tells the licensee that he wants to make an offer and asks for the licensee's advice on a likely price range. The licensee is now in the difficult position of being a dual agent. She represents the seller, who naturally is interested in receiving the highest possible price, and the buyer, who is interested in making a successful low offer.

Figure 4.5: Disclosure and Consent to Dual Agency

ILLINOIS REALTORS®
DISCLOSURE AND CONSENT TO DUAL AGENCY
(DESIGNATED AGENCY)

NOTE TO CONSUMER: THIS DOCUMENT SERVES THREE PURPOSES. FIRST, IT DISCLOSES THAT A REAL ESTATE LICENSEE MAY POTENTIALLY ACT AS A DUAL AGENT, THAT IS, REPRESENT MORE THAN ONE PARTY TO THE TRANSACTION. SECOND, THIS DOCUMENT EXPLAINS THE CONCEPT OF DUAL AGENCY. THIRD, THIS DOCUMENT SEEKS YOUR CONSENT TO ALLOW THE REAL ESTATE LICENSEE TO ACT AS A DUAL AGENT. A LICENSEE MAY LEGALLY ACT AS A DUAL AGENT ONLY WITH YOUR CONSENT. BY CHOOSING TO SIGN THIS DOCUMENT, YOU ARE CONSENTING TO DUAL AGENCY REPRESENTATION.

The undersigned _____, ("Licensee"), (insert name(s) of Licensee undertaking dual representation) may undertake a dual representation (represent both the seller or landlord and the buyer or tenant) for the sale or lease of property. The undersigned acknowledge they were informed of the possibility of this type of representation. Before signing this document please read the following:

Representing more than one party to a transaction presents a conflict of interest since both clients may rely upon Licensee's advice and the client's respective interests may be adverse to each other. Licensee will undertake this representation only with the written consent of ALL clients in the transaction.

Any agreement between the clients as to a final contract price and other terms is a result of negotiations between the clients acting in their own best interests and on their own behalf. You acknowledge that Licensee has explained the implications of dual representation, including the risks involved, and understand that you have been advised to seek independent advice from your advisors or attorneys before signing any documents in this transaction.

WHAT A LICENSEE CAN DO FOR CLIENTS WHEN ACTING AS A DUAL AGENT

1. Treat all clients honestly.
2. Provide information about the property to the buyer or tenant.
3. Disclose all latent material defects in the property that are known to the Licensee.
4. Disclose financial qualification of the buyer or tenant to the seller or landlord.
5. Explain real estate terms.
6. Help the buyer or tenant to arrange for property inspections.
7. Explain closing costs and procedures.
8. Help the buyer compare financing alternatives.
9. Provide information about comparable properties that have sold so both clients may make educated decisions on what price to accept or offer.

WHAT LICENSEE CANNOT DISCLOSE TO CLIENTS WHEN ACTING AS A DUAL AGENT

1. Confidential information that Licensee may know about a client, without that client's permission.
2. The price or terms the seller or landlord will take other than the listing price without permission of the seller or landlord.
3. The price or terms the buyer or tenant is willing to pay without permission of the buyer or tenant.
4. A recommended or suggested price or terms the buyer or tenant should offer.
5. A recommended or suggested price or terms the seller or landlord should counter with or accept.

If either client is uncomfortable with this disclosure and dual representation, please let Licensee know. You are not required to sign this document unless you want to allow the Licensee to proceed as a Dual Agent in this transaction.

By signing below, you acknowledge that you have read and understand this form and voluntarily consent to the Licensee acting as a Dual Agent (that is, to represent BOTH the seller or landlord and the buyer or tenant) should that become necessary.

CLIENT:_____ **CLIENT:**_____

Date:_____ Date:_____

Document presented on _____, 20____
By: _____
(Broker/Licensee Initials)

LICENSEE:_____

Date:_____

FORM 335 (05/2021) COPYRIGHT ILLINOIS REALTORS®   1/1

Figure 4.6: Confirmation of Consent to Dual Agency

ILLINOIS REALTORS

ILLINOIS REALTORS®
CONFIRMATION OF CONSENT TO DUAL AGENCY

The undersigned confirm that they have previously consented to_____,
(insert Licensee's name(s))

("Licensee"), acting as a Dual Agent in providing brokerage services on their behalf and specifically consent to Licensee acting as a Dual Agent in regard to the transaction for the property located at

_____.
(insert address)

Signature of client(s):   _____   Date:_____

_____   Date:_____

_____   Date:_____

_____   Date:_____

Dual Agency Consent

Dual agency is when one licensee represents the interests of both buyer and seller or lessor and lessee in a transaction. In Illinois, dual agency is legal, as long as all parties give their consent and confirmation in writing. The licensee must receive the written consent before acting as a dual agent for the parties. When acting as a dual agent, the licensee may assist in the ways spelled out in article 15-45 of the Act. But at the same time, the licensee must not disclose confidential information or influence the negotiation in any fashion. When acting as a dual agent, the licensee is the designated agent of both parties.

If a client refuses dual agency representation, then the licensee may not offer dual agency representation to another consumer interested in engaging in a transaction with the licensee's client. If the client does approve dual agency but the interested consumer does not wish to allow it, then that consumer may represent their own interests or may consult with another licensee.

A third option for the licensee being refused dual agency is to refer the consumer to another licensee for representation and, as a result, collect a referral fee, as long as that fee is disclosed in writing to the remaining client as per article 10-10 of the Act, which states: "A licensee must disclose to a client all sources of compensation related to the transaction received by the licensee from a third party."

Designated agency describes a business model where licensees in an office may represent both buyers and sellers. Under designated agency, the sponsoring broker designates one agent to represent the seller and one agent to represent the buyer. Designated agency is legal in Illinois and constitutes a business model that is commonly chosen and described in a real estate company's written policies. License law requires the licensee to disclose that a designated agency relationship exists and to put in writing the name of the designated agent. The purpose of this requirement is to ensure that a client knows to whom their secrets are told and to ensure that all other licensees sponsored within the same company do not obtain confidential information.

Disclosure of Agency

Real estate licensees are required to disclose the parties they represent. Understanding the scope of the service a party can expect from the agent allows consumers to make an informed decision about whether to seek their own representation.

Licensees are considered to be representing the consumer they are working with as the consumer's designated agent, unless there is a written agreement between the sponsoring broker and the consumer providing that there is a different relationship.

Figure 4.7: Notice of No Agency Relationship

ILLINOIS REALTORS®
NOTICE OF NO AGENCY RELATIONSHIP

Name of Licensee: _____

Name of Sponsoring Brokerage Company: _____

Property Address: _____

☐ **NOTICE OF NO AGENCY RELATIONSHIP**
(Check here if you represent either seller or buyer)

Thank you for giving Licensee the opportunity to (Insert description of work, i.e. showing property of a FSBO)

_____

in regard to the above mentioned property.

Licensee's Sponsoring Broker has previously entered into an agreement with a client to provide certain real estate brokerage services through Licensee who acts as that client's designated agent. As a result, Licensee will not be acting as your agent.

THIS NOTICE OF NO AGENCY IS BEING PROVIDED AS REQUIRED BY STATE LAW.

_____   Date_____
Licensee's Signature

_____
Print Customer's Name (OPTIONAL)

_____   Date_____
Customer Signature (OPTIONAL)

_____
Print Customer's Name (OPTIONAL)

_____   Date_____
Customer Signature (OPTIONAL)

Article 15, Section 15-35, of the Real Estate License Act of 2000 discusses agency relationship disclosure. It requires that a consumer be advised in writing that a designated agency relationship exists, unless there is a written agreement between the sponsoring broker and the consumer providing for a different brokerage relationship. This must occur no later than beginning to work as a designated agent on behalf of the consumer. The name or names of the designated agent or agents must be in writing, and the sponsoring broker's compensation and policy regarding cooperating with sponsoring brokers who represent other parties in a transaction must be disclosed.

A licensee must also disclose in writing to a customer that the licensee is not acting as the agent of the customer at a time intended to prevent disclosure of confidential information from a customer to a licensee, but in no event later than the preparation of an offer to purchase or lease real property. This is known as the Disclosure of No Agency (See Figure 4.7) and is required at first **substantive contact**. *Substantive contact* is when the dialogue between a licensee and consumer moves from casual conversation to the consumer's motives, objectives, financial qualifications, and other confidential information that, if disclosed, could harm the consumer's bargaining position.

SUMMARY

The common law of agency has historically governed the principal-agent relationship. Agency relationships may be expressed either by the words of the parties or by written agreement or they may be implied by the parties' actions. In single agency relationships, the licensee or agent represents one party, either the buyer or the seller, in the transaction. In some states, if the agent elicits the assistance of other licensees who cooperate in the transaction, the other licensees may become *subagents* of the principal. Any blanket offering of subagency by a multiple listing service (MLS) in Illinois is illegal.

Many states, including Illinois, are dominated by non-single-agency firms. These firms work with both buyers and sellers, including buyers and sellers in the same transaction. They will consider dual agency in the event it develops or will assign designated agents to each of the two parties (usually a seller and a buyer). Many states, including Illinois, have adopted statutes that replace the common law of agency and amplify it.

Representing two opposing parties in the same transaction constitutes dual agency. Licensees must be careful not to create dual agency when none was intended. This unintentional or inadvertent dual agency can result in the sales contract being rescinded and the commission being forfeited or in a lawsuit. Disclosed dual agency requires that both principals give consent to and confirmation of in writing to the licensee's multiple representation. In any case, the prospective parties in any transaction should be informed about agency alternatives and the ways in which client-level versus customer-level services differ. Many states, including Illinois, have mandatory agency disclosure laws. The source of compensation for the client services does not determine which party is represented.

Licensees have certain duties and obligations to their customers as well. Consumers are entitled to fair and honest dealings and to the information necessary for them to make informed decisions. This includes accurate information about the property. Some states, including Illinois, have mandatory property disclosure laws.

Real estate license laws and regulations govern the professional conduct of brokers, managing brokers, and residential leasing agents. The license laws are enacted to protect the public by ensuring a standard of competence and professionalism in the real estate industry.

Stigmatized properties are those properties that society has branded undesirable because of events that occurred there. Stigma is the continuing negative association with or feeling about the property.

Article 15 of the Real Estate License Act of 2000, as amended in 2020, supersedes any previous agency law. Illinois agency law currently presumes that a broker or managing broker who is working with a seller represents the seller (client relationship). A licensee working with a buyer is presumed to represent the buyer. However, before a customer discloses confidential information, the licensee shall provide them with a written disclosure of "No-Agency." Before a licensee can act as a designated agent, the consumer shall receive a written disclosure of designated agency. An express written agreement, with either seller or buyer, is most protective of everyone's interests.

The Real Estate License Act of 2000, along with the rules governing permitted dual agency, stipulate that consent and confirmation of dual agency must be obtained in writing to be legal. Merely designating one licensee to represent sellers and another to represent buyers does not by itself constitute dual agency. Licensees operate as designated agents most of the time. Agency relationship disclosures require written notice to the consumer of the name or names of the designated agent; that a designated agency relationship exists, unless there is a written agreement providing otherwise; and the sponsoring broker's compensation and policy regarding compensation cooperation with other sponsoring brokers. Dual agency, however, occurs if the same agent represents both parties in a transaction. Then additional designated agents sometimes need to be made so that two licensees are involved (each representing only one party) unless a disclosed dual agency is agreed to in writing.

UNIT 4 QUIZ

1. Which of these *BEST* describes an agent?
   A. A person who gives someone else the legal power to act on her behalf
   B. A person who is in a customer-agent relationship
   C. Two agents who work for the same brokerage firm
   D. A person who is placed in a position of trust and confidence

2. A seller listed his property with a brokerage company. The agency relationship between the seller and the sponsoring broker is what type of agency?
   A. Special
   B. General
   C. Implied
   D. Universal

3. Which of these statements is *TRUE* of a real estate broker acting as the agent of the seller?
   A. The broker can disclose personal information to a buyer if it increases the likelihood of a sale.
   B. The broker is obligated to render faithful service to the seller.
   C. The broker can agree to a change in price without the seller's approval.
   D. The broker can accept a commission from the buyer without notifying the seller.

4. A seller lists his home with a real estate broker for $289,500 and has given written permission for dual agency. Later the same day, a potential buyer comes into the broker's office and asks for general information about homes for sale in the $250,000–$300,000 price range. Based on these facts, which of these statements is *TRUE*?
   A. The seller and potential buyer are both the broker's customers.
   B. The broker owes fiduciary duties to both the seller and the potential buyer.
   C. The seller is the broker's client; the broker must obtain written consent for dual agency from the buyer if intending to show his own listing.
   D. If the potential buyer asks the broker to be his buyer representative, the broker must decline because of the pre-existing agreement with the seller.

5. A licensee who has contracted with an apartment building owner to manage a highrise apartment is probably
   A. a general agent.
   B. a transactional broker.
   C. a buyer's agent.
   D. a special agent.

6. Which of these events will terminate an agency in a broker-seller relationship?
   A. The owner declares personal bankruptcy.
   B. The broker discovers that the market value of the property is such that she will not make an adequate commission.
   C. The owner abandons the property.
   D. The broker appoints other brokers to help sell the property.

7. In Illinois, a real estate broker hired by an owner to sell a parcel of real estate must comply with the
   A. federal common law of compensation.
   B. Illinois statute called the Real Estate License Act of 2000, as amended in 2020.
   C. concept of market value as codified in Illinois law.
   D. concept of caveat emptor as codified in Illinois law.

8. The six common law fiduciary duties are
   A. care, obedience, loyalty, disclosure, accounting, and confidentiality.
   B. accounting, appraisal, negotiation, confidentiality, obedience, and loyalty.
   C. obedience, negotiation, care, accounting, loyalty, and efficiency.
   D. care, obedience, loyalty, disclosure, accounting, and efficiency.

9. A broker lists a residence. The owner of the residence must sell the house quickly. To expedite the sale, the broker tells a prospective purchaser that the seller will accept at least $5,000 less than the asking price for the property. Based on these facts, which of these statements is *TRUE*?
   A. The broker has not violated his agency responsibilities to the seller.
   B. Unless given written permission from the seller to do so, the disclosure was improper, regardless of the broker's motive.
   C. The broker should have disclosed this information, regardless of its accuracy.
   D. The relationship between the broker and the seller is called a general agency relationship.

10. A buyer who is a client of the broker wants to purchase a house that the broker has listed for sale. Which of these statements is *TRUE*?
    A. Illinois law no longer regulates this situation.
    B. The broker should refer the buyer to another broker to negotiate the sale.
    C. The seller and the buyer must give written consent for the broker to represent them both.
    D. The buyer should not have been shown a house listed by the broker.

11. A buyer comes into a real estate broker's office and asks the broker to represent her while searching for a home in the $190,000–$200,000 price range. The broker recalls a house for sale by an owner listed at $198,000. The broker calls the owner of the house, asking for permission for his client to see the house. Based on these facts, which of these statements is *TRUE*?
    A. The for-sale-by-owner seller is the broker's customer; the buyer is a client.
    B. Both the buyer and for-sale-by-owner seller are customers of the broker.
    C. The buyer is the broker's customer; the for-sale-by-owner seller is the broker's client.
    D. The broker is now a dual agent.

12. A real estate licensee was representing a buyer. At their first meeting, the buyer explained that he planned to operate a dog grooming business out of any house he bought. The licensee did not check the local zoning ordinances to determine in which parts of town such a business could be conducted. Which agency duty did the licensee violate?
    A. Obedience
    B. Care
    C. Loyalty
    D. Accountability

13. Broker A tells a prospective buyer, "This property has the most beautiful view." In fact, the view includes the back of a shopping center. In a separate transaction, broker B fails to mention to some enthusiastic potential buyers that a six-lane highway is planned for construction within 10 feet of a house the buyers think is perfect. Based on these facts, which of these statements is *TRUE*?
    A. Broker A has committed fraud.
    B. Broker B has committed puffing.
    C. Both brokers are guilty of intentional misrepresentation.
    D. Broker A is merely puffing; broker B has misrepresented the property.

14. Under Illinois agency law, which of these is *TRUE*?
    A. Sponsoring brokers may designate which sponsored licensee represents the client.
    B. The law codifies the common-law concept of caveat emptor by eliminating any assumption of a buyer's right to representation or disclosure.
    C. Sellers are not legally obligated to make any disclosures regarding the known physical condition of the property.
    D. Dual agency is illegal.

15. A sponsoring broker listed and sold a home. The seller had told the sponsoring broker that the home was structurally sound. This information was passed on to a prospective buyer by one of the licensee's sponsored by the broker. If the sponsoring broker has no way of knowing that this information is false, who will likely be held liable if a latent defect is later discovered?
    A. The sponsored licensee
    B. The seller and the sponsored licensee
    C. The seller
    D. The buyer

16. In real estate transactions, the term *fiduciary* typically refers to the
    A. sale of real property.
    B. person who gives someone else the legal power to act on her behalf.
    C. person who has legal power to act on behalf of another.
    D. agent's relationship to the principal.

17. A real estate licensee's responsibility to keep the principal informed of all the facts that could affect a transaction is the duty of
    A. disclosure.
    B. care.
    C. obedience.
    D. accounting.

18. Which of these is considered dual agency?
    A. A licensee acting for both the buyer and the seller in the same transaction
    B. Two brokerage companies cooperating with each other
    C. A licensee representing two or more sellers at the same time
    D. A licensee listing and then selling the same property

19. In a dual agency situation, a licensee may represent both the seller and the buyer if
    A. the licensee informs either the buyer or the seller of this fact.
    B. both parties give their informed consent, in writing, to the dual agency.
    C. the buyer and the seller are related by blood or marriage.
    D. both parties are represented by attorneys.

20. In Illinois, which of these is *TRUE* concerning designated agency?
    A. Designated agency is always illegal.
    B. Designated agency is the same as creating an implied agency.
    C. License law requires the licensee to disclose, in writing, that a designated agency relationship exists.
    D. License law requires that the seller and the buyer be represented by different companies.

UNIT
5

Real Estate Brokerage

LEARNING OBJECTIVES

When you have completed this unit, you will be able to accomplish the following.

> Identify the role of technologies, personnel, and license laws in the operation of a real estate business and explain the importance of distinguishing employees from independent contractors.
> Explain how a licensee's compensation is usually determined.
> Describe the various types of antitrust violations common in the real estate industry and the penalties involved with each.

KEY TERMS

antitrust laws	errors and omissions	price-fixing
broker	(E&O) insurance	procuring cause
CAN-SPAM Act of 2003	fiduciary standard	ready, willing, and able
commission	group boycotting	buyer
cooperative commission	independent contractor	regular employee
designated managing	Junk Fax Prevention Act	sponsoring broker
broker	of 2005	tie-in agreement
employee	National Do Not Call	
	Registry	

REAL ESTATE BROKERAGE

Brokerage is simply the business of bringing parties together. A real estate license is required to exchange, purchase, or lease real property for others and to charge a fee for these services.

A brokerage business may take many forms. It may be a sole proprietorship (single-owner company), corporation, or partnership. The office may be independent or part of a regional or national franchise. The business may consist of a single office or multiple branches. A typical real estate brokerage may specialize in one kind of transaction or service, or it may offer a variety of services.

A **sponsoring broker** faces the same challenges as an entrepreneur in any other industry. In addition to mastering the complexities of real estate transactions, she must be able to handle the day-to-day details of running a business and to set effective policies for every aspect of the brokerage operation. This includes maintaining space and equipment, hiring employees and real estate licensees, determining compensation, directing staff and sales activities, and implementing procedures to follow in carrying out agency duties.

Brokerage firms vary widely in size and style. Much of the business's success hinges on the relationship between sponsoring brokers and their sponsored licenses. The three types of real estate licenses for individuals in Illinois are

- broker,
- managing broker, and
- residential leasing agent.

The managing broker license was created to increase accountability and awareness of the statutory duties of supervision. Section 1450.700 of the Real Estate License Act of 2000 defines the roles and responsibilities of sponsoring brokers, designated managing brokers, and brokers. Every real estate office must have a sponsoring or designated managing broker of record, neither of which is required to be the owner of the business. All licensees acting as a designated managing broker or a self-sponsored broker must have a managing broker's license or acquire one within 90 days after being named designated managing broker.

Sponsoring Brokers

A sponsoring broker means the broker who certifies to the Department his, her, or its sponsorship of a licensed managing broker, a broker, or a residential leasing agent. The sponsoring broker entity must be licensed and may be self-sponsored. There may be only one sponsoring broker for any one real estate company. A sponsoring broker may authorize a designated managing broker to register sponsored licensees with the Department.

Likewise, the sponsoring broker may assign escrow account bookkeeping duties to a qualified company employee or an independent contractor and may delegate authorized individuals to sign on behalf of the sponsoring broker. The sponsoring broker may authorize company personnel to sign contracts entered into by the sponsoring broker, according to the sponsoring broker's company policy. Even though the sponsoring broker may delegate authority, the sponsoring broker is ultimately responsible for all activities.

Designated Managing Brokers

A managing broker's license is obtained by taking additional courses and receiving a managing broker license. The sponsoring broker assigns the designated managing broker with supervisory duties and legally appoints that individual to oversee the office. A sponsoring broker may also be the designated managing broker of an office or may appoint a designated managing broker to serve for several branch offices. Different designated managing brokers may be responsible for individual branch offices. In any event, the designated managing broker is responsible for the supervision of all real estate activities performed by affiliated licensees.

Additionally, pursuant to Section 1450.705, each designated managing broker is responsible for recordkeeping, maintenance of the employment agreements entered into with each sponsored licensee, and maintenance of escrow monies.

IRS Tax Considerations: Independent Contractor vs. Regular Employee

One of the most important decisions a sponsoring broker needs to make is how to classify workers for tax purposes. Determining employee classification should always be discussed with a tax professional. This section is not intended to provide tax advice; it is only to provide information to help a business owner better use a tax professional.

Every sponsoring broker who hires licensees or has an independent contractor relationship with a licensee must have a *written employment or independent contractor agreement* with each licensee. The agreement defines the employment or independent contractor relationship, including supervision, duties, compensation, and termination. The employment agreement must be dated and signed by both parties. An executed copy of the employment agreement must be provided in physical or electronic format to the sponsored licensees. Employment or independent contractor agreements must be maintained for five years after the broker licensee is no longer with the sponsoring broker (1450.755(a)(4)).

With **employees**, a sponsoring broker is required by federal law to withhold Social Security tax and income tax from wages paid to those employees. The sponsoring broker must also pay unemployment compensation tax on wages paid to one or more employees as defined by state and federal laws. In addition, employees might receive benefits such as health insurance, profit-sharing plans, or workers' compensation.

The Real Estate License Act of 2000 makes the following distinctions between an "Employee" and a "Regular Employee":

- "Employee" or other derivative of the word "employee," when used to refer to, describe, or delineate the relationship between a sponsoring broker and a managing broker, broker, or a residential leasing agent, shall be construed to include an independent contractor relationship, provided that a written agreement exists that clearly establishes and states the relationship. All responsibilities of a broker shall remain.

- "Regular Employee" means a person working an average of 20 hours per week for a person or entity who would be considered as an employee under the Internal Revenue Service rules for classifying workers.

A sponsoring broker's relationship with a sponsored licensee who is an **independent contractor** can be very different from the relationship with an employee.

In order to be treated as an independent contractor for federal tax purposes, a licensee must meet three specific criteria set out by the Internal Revenue Service:

- The individual must hold an active real estate license.

- The individual must agree in writing not to be treated as an employee for federal tax purposes.

- At least 90% of the individual's income as a licensee must be based on sales production rather than hours worked.

IN PRACTICE

The sponsoring broker must have a written employment or independent contractor agreement for all sponsored licensees both for independent contractors and for employees. No matter the position, all licensees must have an employment agreement with the sponsoring broker.

Independent contractors are responsible for paying their own income taxes and Social Security taxes.

Designated Managing Broker Responsibilities

The **designated managing broker** has supervisory responsibilities for all licensees in the sponsoring broker's office(s). Sometimes, in the case of a sole proprietorship, the designated managing broker and the sponsoring broker are one and the same. If they are not the same, the sponsoring broker can delegate to the designated manager broker the responsibility of registering the sponsorship of licensees with the Department.

Working With New Licensees

The designated managing broker has the responsibility for handling all earnest money, escrows, and contract negotiations for all transactions where the designated agent for the transaction has not completed the 45 hours of postlicense education. This includes the approval of all advertisements involving a licensee who has not completed the 45 hours of postlicense education. Licensees who have not completed their 45 hours of postlicense education cannot bind the sponsoring broker to contracts.

Maintenance of Licenses

Sponsoring brokers are required to notify the Illinois Department of Financial Professional Regulation (IDFPR) of the names and license numbers of all designated managing brokers employed by the sponsoring broker and the office or branch offices for which each designated managing broker is responsible. The designated managing broker must have a current active managing broker's license.

Unexpected Loss of Designated Managing Broker

Upon the loss of a designated managing broker who is not replaced by the sponsoring broker or in the event of the death or adjudicated disability of the sole proprietor of an office, a written request for authorization allowing the continued operation of the office may be submitted to the Department within 15 days of the loss. The extension may be granted for up to 60 days. In the case of an owner's death, a representative of the estate could operate the office for up to 60 days. In most cases of loss of a sponsoring or designated managing broker, a licensed managing broker temporarily assumes the management of the office. The appointed licensee must sign a written promise to personally supervise the office operations and accept responsibility for the office until a permanent replacement is located.

Death of Self-Sponsored Broker

IDFPR will honor the order of a court of competent jurisdiction appointing a legal representative for the sole purpose of closing out the brokerage affairs of a deceased or disabled broker who was a sole proprietor.

New Licenses and Renewals

Though the initial license and renewal used to be mailed to the sponsoring/managing broker, IDFPR now generates the license online. Licensees can print their own license and deliver it to the office where it will be held. The IDFPR now requires licensees to carry on themselves either a physical or an electronic copy of their license.

Change of Business Address

All designated managing brokers must notify IDFPR through the website or in a manner prescribed by the Department of any change of business address for any of the offices they manage within 24 hours of any change. Change-of-address filing is required for all offices. Licensees must provide the Division notice of change of physical office location or virtual office website or digital platform (1450.150).

Advertising

All licensees who are named as designated managing brokers with the IDFPR must indicate this status on all advertising that includes their name (with the exception of property signs). Those who hold a managing broker license but are not named as the designated managing broker with the IDFPR may not represent or indicate that they are a designated managing broker. They may identify themselves as managing brokers.

Supervision

A designated managing broker must exercise reasonable supervision over the activities of licensees and anyone else working in those offices managed by the designated managing broker. These supervisory duties include the following:

- Implementation of office policies and procedures established by the sponsoring broker
- Training of licensees or other employees on the company's policies, as well as on relevant provisions of the Act
- Providing assistance to all licensees in real estate transactions
- Supervising escrow accounts over which the sponsoring broker has delegated responsibility to the designated managing broker in order to ensure compliance with the escrow account provisions of the Real Estate License Act of 2000
- Supervising all advertising of any service for which a license is required
- Familiarizing sponsored licensees with the requirements of federal and state laws relating to the practice of real estate
- Compliance with the rules for licensees and offices under his supervision

The sponsoring broker is ultimately responsible for the actions of all sponsored licensees, including those of designated managing brokers.

Termination of Sponsorship

If a broker, designated managing broker, or residential leasing agent terminates employment with the sponsoring broker for any reason, the licensee must notify the Division within 24 hours, and immediately notify the sponsoring broker. The licensee's license is inactive until a new valid sponsorship is registered. Upon termination of a sponsorship by a sponsoring broker, the sponsoring broker must immediately notify the terminated licensee, and notify the Division within 24 hours (1450.115).

Unit 5

Planning

Planning is the most fundamental management activity. Almost every business decision is guided by a *business plan*. Planning takes time and money; however, the resources devoted to planning are relatively small in comparison to the benefits of a sound plan that is followed and reviewed often. It is useful for building credibility with others outside your company. An effective plan must be flexible, measurable, and, most importantly, achievable.

The development of a business plan begins with creating a mission statement. This statement identifies the company's purpose for being in business and sets the organization's course, purpose, and tone. The mission statement provides the focus for the company. Everything else in the business plan supports the mission statement.

The mission statement identifies specific objectives or goals for accomplishing the mission. These are the end results to be achieved. Goals must be translated into specific words that tell exactly how to focus the company's resources. Goals have several characteristics. They must

- be specific or identifiable,
- be measurable,
- be attainable, and
- have beginning and ending dates.

Each goal is supported by strategies that prescribe the methodology used in accomplishing that specific goal. Strategies include things needing to be done to overcome any obstacles or enhancement of resources. They also help to eliminate nonproductive activities. Finally, day-to-day activities or tasks must be designed to carry out the strategies to accomplish the goal.

The Policy and Procedures Manual

A policy and procedures manual should be written and should serve as a risk management tool for the company. The Illinois Association of REALTORS® (IAR) provides the *IAR Sample Office Policy Manual* that can serve as a general guideline in developing your policy manual.

Policies and procedures are extremely beneficial for

- establishing a clear understanding of the relationship between broker and sponsored licensees, as well as administrative functions versus staff functions;
- working to resolve conflicts before they come up;
- helping everyone understand the rules and how the company is supposed to operate; and
- giving guidance for many of the situations licensees face on a day-to-day basis.

Keep in mind that the policy and procedures manual is not a sales training manual. Obviously, the policy manual cannot become the complete solution to every policy issue. When a decision cannot be made easily about a specific problem, the manual should state how it is to be interpreted and who will do the interpretation.

To stay on top of changes in the real estate industry and practice, as well as keeping up with emerging technologies, brokers should regularly review and update their policy manuals. Every licensee should have access to the manual.

The Real Estate License Act of 2000 Section 10-40 requires that "every brokerage company or entity, other than a sole proprietorship with no other sponsored licensees, shall adopt a company or office policy dealing with topics" such as

- the agency policy of the entity;

- fair housing, nondiscrimination, and harassment;

- confidentiality of client information;

- advertising;

- training and supervision of sponsored licensees;

- required disclosures and use of forms;

- handling of risk management matters; and

- handling of earnest monies and escrows.

Licensee Safety

While real estate has historically been a safe profession, recent trends have seen agents robbed, raped, and murdered while showing homes and other properties. Many real estate firms now include safety procedures in their policy and procedures manual. The following suggestions may minimize licensee risk:

- Ask the customer for work, home, and cell phone numbers and a physical address. Verify the information by calling the customer at one or more of the numbers.

- Give someone in your office an itinerary of properties you plan to show and then check back in often by cell phone.

- Do not meet unknown customers at a property; require that they meet you at your office. Make sure someone writes down their license plate number and the type of car they are driving.

- Never get into a car with someone you don't know. Use your vehicle for showings or ask your customer to follow you in another car.

- Program your cell phone to dial 911 at the touch of a button.

- Never work at a public open house by yourself.

- Do not show vacant properties by yourself unless you know your customers, and never show properties after dark.

- Keep pepper spray handy.

- Always follow the customers into the property and let them enter while you stay by the door.

- Be aware of exits.

- Ask someone else to accompany you to show or list property if you feel uncomfortable about the people with whom you are working. Don't assume that women are safer customers than men; women are as just as capable of armed robbery and sometimes work with a partner who waits at the house for the two of you to arrive.

For offices that don't have office safety policies, the National Association of REALTORS® and other state and local associations have developed safety guidelines that will aid licensees when showing or listing properties and holding open houses.

Errors and Omissions Insurance

A real estate licensee needs insurance protection from claims made by clients, customers, and consumers related to the provision of real estate activities, called professional services by the insurance industry. This protection can be obtained through an **errors and omissions (E&O) insurance** policy.

Sponsoring or designated managing brokers have an array of issues and options to consider when deciding what form of E&O policy to obtain. In general, they need to determine what level of protection to seek in the policy and how to tailor the coverage to their sponsoring/ managing practice. Because insurance policies and practices vary from company to company, the sponsoring or designated managing broker must be careful to review any specific policy intended for the office and should discuss coverage with more than one insurance provider before obtaining coverage.

Brokers are licensed professionals who are held to fiduciary standards. A **fiduciary standard** is a legal standard that holds a licensee to the highest ethical standards that the law provides. Licensees have the duties of advice and counsel to the represented client and must be fair, honest, and accurate in dealing with consumers and customers whom they do not represent. In this regard, the broker is treated no differently than a doctor, a lawyer, or other licensed professional acting in a confidential environment. However, unlike a doctor or a lawyer, the broker is expected to engage in sales activities that can conflict with the duties owed by a fiduciary. This conflict can create significant professional liability exposure for the real estate licensee.

The classes of services performed by licensees shape the types of liability claims most often filed against real estate licensees. Real estate licensees may represent buyers, sellers, lessors, and lessees. They coordinate a variety of services, such as insurance, title, loan origination, and home inspection. In addition, they often function as independent professionals managing their own offices, advertising campaigns, and other related business functions. In providing these services, licensees become vulnerable to potential legal liabilities.

Licensees earn a specified **commission** or negotiated fee (typically based on some percentage of the final sale price or annual rental cost) because they help secure buyers or tenants for various kinds of real property usually owned by third parties. Because earnings are a function of commission for each transaction, increasing the number of transactions increases the annual earnings. Dual agency also increases the total compensation through representation of both parties in the transaction but can also increase the possibility of conflicts of interest. In order to prevent a breach of fiduciary duty, licensees must know how to balance a client's specific requirements with the duties owed to third parties.

Liability claims can also arise from a number of related services provided occasionally for a separate fee basis or which are incidental to the transaction. These include property appraisal, property management, auctioneering, consulting, and handling earnest monies or security deposits. The real estate licensee needs to be aware that not all these activities are covered by standard real estate broker's liability coverage forms. Some real estate licensee services require a special endorsement to the insurance policy for an additional premium; other services require the purchase of a separate insurance policy.

The most common E&O claims against real estate licensees include

- mishandling monies (earnest money or security deposits) during transactions;
- making misstatements about material facts regarding the property, such as the presence of lead-based paint, asbestos, or radon;

- misrepresenting the property dimensions or failure to measure property dimensions accurately;
- disclosure of confidential information without authorization from the client;
- undisclosed dual agency;
- failure to identify the real or personal property correctly in the contract;
- mistakes regarding the property index number (PIN) for the subject property or failure to provide an adequate legal description of the property;
- misrepresentations about financing arrangements;
- failure to disclose a financial interest in the customer who is negotiating with the client;
- failure to disclose financial relationships compensating the licensee in the transaction;
- violations of the federal Fair Housing Act and the Illinois Human Rights Act; and
- breaching the terms of the listing or buyer agreement or the property management agreement.

The sponsoring/designated managing broker must determine whether the errors and omissions policy adequately addresses what

- services are covered,
- person(s) is(are) covered,
- damages are covered,
- defenses are covered, and
- territory is covered.

Real estate licensees should know whether the services they provide constitute professional services and are, thus, insurable under the policy. They should also be aware that professional services are defined differently in each insurer's policy.

The phrase *professional real estate services* typically refers to services that require a person to have an Illinois real estate license in order to perform those services on behalf of clients, customers, and consumers. As a prerequisite for coverage, the licensee must possess all valid necessary licenses or certifications at the time of the act or omission giving rise to the claim and must be acting within the scope of the employment agreement, either written or oral. Sometimes insurance companies will include coverage for ancillary professional real estate services rendered by the insured for others, such as a notary public's duties.

Covered Defense Costs

E&O policies may sometimes pay the costs involved in investigating, defending, and settling claims. These costs primarily involve attorney's fees but also include related expenses required by the claim settlement process. The sponsoring broker should determine whether defense costs are covered by the policy or in addition to the policy limits. If defense costs are covered within the policy limits, then as the legal fees increase, the limits of the coverage of the policy are proportionately reduced.

Excluded Coverage

Most E&O policies exclude certain ancillary real estate–related activities. These exclusions include a licensee's involvement in areas that do not require an Illinois real estate license, such as property development and insurance agency operations.

Depending on the insurer, coverage for such services may be bought back for an additional premium, if an insured's operations require such coverage. A real estate licensee who wants coverage for such services may obtain it by paying an additional premium or, depending on the limitations of the policy, by obtaining a separate policy. The sponsoring or designated managing broker should also be aware that violations of fair housing laws, some civil sanctions, and criminal acts are not covered by E&O policies. Some policies will cover the legal defense for certain issues, such as discrimination, but not the damages awarded.

Other possible exclusions from coverage under E&O policies include

- bankruptcy of the insured;
- violation of securities law;
- wrongful termination;
- Employee Retirement Income Security Act (ERISA) violations;
- workers' compensation claims;
- personal injury claims;
- claims arising from usage of vehicles, aircraft, and watercraft;
- environmental issues, such as mold and asbestos;
- real estate owned by the insured; and
- commission disputes.

Because there can be coverage gaps between E&O policies and commercial general liability (CGL) policies, the sponsoring/designated managing broker should ensure that excluded coverage for bodily injury, property damage, and personal injury are covered by CGL policies or by special endorsement. Potential gap coverage between E&O policies and CGL policies should be discussed by the sponsoring broker with the insurer to best customize the coverage to the brokerage firm.

Covered Persons

E&O policies are intended to cover those licensees whose licenses are held by the sponsoring broker, as well as office staff and unlicensed assistants. Where the sponsoring broker is a business entity, such as a partnership, corporation, or limited liability company (LLC), these policies can include coverage for past and present partners, officers, directors, and regular employees. Because the nature of the claims against the policies can survive the death or incapacity of the insured, coverage should be structured to include the heirs, executors, administrators, and trustees in bankruptcy of the insured.

Independent Contractors

Most real estate offices that sell residential real estate will sponsor licensees who are treated as independent contractors. Therefore, it is important that the E&O policies cover those independent contractors. A sponsoring broker must also address liability arising from predecessor firm issues. For example, brokerage firm A acquires brokerage firm B, with at least 50% of brokerage firm B's licensees joining brokerage firm A or where brokerage firm A assumes at least 50% of brokerage firm B's assets and/or liabilities. Under these circumstances, a claim against a brokerage firm B licensee (for an incident before the acquisition) who currently works with brokerage firm A could become the obligation of brokerage firm A.

Covered Territory

Most E&O policies cover claims resulting from anywhere in the world, provided the claim and concomitant litigation is brought in the United States, its territories or possessions, or Canada. Actions conducted outside these areas will likely require additional coverage or a separate policy. The licensee should be aware that use of websites with their worldwide exposure may lead to claims and litigation outside the United States; a licensee would need a policy with unrestricted territorial coverage to address this issue.

Other Policy Issues

The sponsoring or designated managing broker should be aware of additional issues that might affect E&O coverage. The insurance claims process varies from insurer to insurer. Therefore, licensees need to understand the procedures of their provider. Some policy issues to be aware of include the following:

- Most E&O policies have liability caps that set a payment limit per claim and an aggregate payment limit; the licensee should obtain coverage that matches the licensee's liability exposure.

- There are two basic types of deductible provisions. One type of deductible applies to each error committed, and the other type applies to each claim filed. Limits per error are found in a nonaccumulation clause. For example, if a licensee represents a condo developer whose units have a series of claims filed for multiple coverage periods, the policy will restrict coverage to the monetary limit of the first coverage period. Also, most policies permit the insurer to assess the deductible even if the claim does not lead to a liability against the licensee if the insurer pays for the successful legal defense.

- Most E&O policies have provisions that limit payment to the amount offered in a settlement offer. If the licensee refuses the settlement and the subsequent trial judgment is higher than the settlement offer, then the licensee will be liable for the payment amount in excess of the settlement offer, as well as the defenses costs of the trial.

- All E&O policies have some additional conditions that are essential elements of the policy's coverage. All policies have subrogation provisions that allow the insurer the right to initiate litigation where the insurer has paid on claims against the policy. Insurers require the insured to cooperate with the claims process and subsequent litigation and prohibit the insured from making voluntary settlements.

- Problems may arise when one insured sues another insured. This can occur when one licensee sues another licensee in the sponsoring broker's office resulting from a claim arising from professional services provided (e.g., one agent selling another agent's property) in that office. The policy should include a special clause that ensures coverage for that type of claim.

- Although most insurers limit coverage to the inception date of the policy, some insurers will consider providing first-time insurance buyers coverage for prior acts (for an additional premium). Generally, prior acts coverage is limited to retroactive claims for no more than five years. If the policy expires or is canceled and is not replaced with a new policy with prior acts coverage, then the licensee must have an extended-reporting-period clause that allows a claim that occurred during the coverage period to be processed against the expired policy. This type of coverage is usually limited to no more than one to three years after expiration of the policy.

It is the duty of the sponsoring broker to determine what level of E&O insurance is necessary to meet the needs of the brokerage office.

Unit 5

Personal Assistants

Though no longer identified in the Act, a licensee can hire another licensee to aid in the business. The same rules for the licensee also apply to any "assistants": they need an employment agreement with the sponsoring broker, may only be compensated by the sponsoring broker, and must abide by all provisions of the law.

Legal Rights and Obligations

As each contract is prepared for signature during a real estate transaction, the licensee should advise the parties of the desirability of securing legal counsel to protect their interests. Only a lawyer can offer legal advice. Licensees are prohibited from practicing law.

Technology and Brokerage of the Future

The internet has brought tremendous change to the real estate industry. Real estate practitioners and consumers rely heavily on the internet for a variety of services. Practitioners use videos, photos, and *virtual staging* to target out-of-area consumers looking for properties. Virtual staging allows consumers to see what a vacant property can look like to make it more appealing to sell. Social media is also increasingly useful in business—and the real estate industry is no different.

Sponsoring brokers should set clear guidelines in policy manuals and brokerage agreements to permit and guide the use of these technologies by licensees. Sponsoring brokers must also learn about the potential risks and liabilities of these sites—for example, recognizing that communication through these sites establishes a permanent record of sorts—and establish appropriate policies and guidelines. They must also work to ensure that clients understand the helpful role these technologies can play in real estate transactions and consent to their use.

The Real Estate License Act of 2000 deals specifically with internet and related advertising. Licensees intending to sell or share consumer information gathered from or through the internet or other electronic communication media must disclose that intention to consumers in a timely and readily apparent manner. A licensee using the internet cannot

- use a URL or domain name that is deceptive or misleading;
- deceptively or without authorization frame another real estate brokerage or MLS website; or
- engage in the deceptive use of keywords or other devices to direct, drive, or divert internet traffic or mislead consumers.

In addition, the Code of Ethics and Standards of Practice of the National Association of REALTORS® requires REALTORS® to present an accurate picture in their advertising, marketing, and other representations, including URLs and domain names. The obligation to present an accurate picture in representations to the public includes information presented, provided, or displayed on websites and that the information be current.

Real estate licensees must make careful decisions about which technologies best suit their needs and invest in them to have a cutting edge on today's market.

COMPENSATION

Broker Compensation

The sponsoring broker's compensation is specified in the contract with the client.

Real estate license laws may stipulate that a written agreement must establish compensation to be paid. Compensation can be in the form of a commission (computed as a percentage of the total sales price), a flat fee, or an hourly rate. The amount of a broker's commission is negotiable in every case. A sponsoring broker, however, may set the minimum commission rate acceptable for her own company. The important point is that the broker and the client agree on a rate before the agency relationship is established.

Only a sponsoring broker may collect a commission in Illinois; the sponsoring broker then may share it with any licensees who are directly involved in or responsible for a given transaction. To collect a commission on a real estate transaction, the agent must have been "hired" by way of an agreement in which the principal (seller or buyer) agreed to pay a specified commission for services. The percentage of sales price or dollar amount of commission must have been expressed clearly in the agreement. If another real estate office "brought in" the buyer, the concept of **cooperative commission** allows the listing brokerage (working with the seller) to pay the buyer's brokerage (working with the buyer) the amount of cooperative commission advertised in advance on the multiple listing service (MLS) listing. This check is issued by the listing broker's office to the buyer broker's office, and checks then are cut by each of these sponsoring brokers to any respective licensees who were directly involved in the transaction.

A commission is usually considered earned when the work for which the real estate broker was hired has been accomplished. Most sales commissions are payable when the sale is consummated by delivery of the seller's deed. This provision is generally included in the listing agreement. When the sales or listing agreement specifies no time for the payment of the broker's commission, the commission is usually earned when

- a completed sales contract has been executed by a ready, willing, and able buyer;
- the contract has been accepted and executed by the seller; and
- copies of the contract are in possession by all parties.

To be entitled to a sales commission, an individual must be

- a licensed real estate broker,
- the procuring cause of the sale, and
- employed by the buyer or the seller under a valid contract.

To be considered the **procuring cause** of a sale, the broker must have started or caused a chain of events that resulted in the sale. A broker who causes or completes such an action without a contract or without having been promised payment is a volunteer and may not legally claim compensation.

 IN PRACTICE

Procuring cause disputes between brokers are usually settled through an arbitration hearing conducted by the local real estate board or association. Disputes between a broker and a client may be settled through an arbitration hearing, or they may go to court. They may not be taken to IDFPR.

Unit 5

A **ready, willing, and able buyer** is one who is prepared to buy on the seller's terms and ready to take positive steps toward consummation of the transaction. Once a seller accepts an offer from a ready, willing, and able buyer, the real estate broker is entitled to a commission. Courts may prevent the real estate broker from receiving a commission if the real estate broker knew the buyer was unable to perform. If the transaction is not consummated, the real estate broker may still be entitled to a commission if the seller

- had a change of mind and refused to sell,
- has a spouse who refused to sign the deed,
- had a title with uncorrected defects,
- committed fraud with respect to the transaction,
- was unable to deliver possession within a reasonable time,
- insisted on terms not in the listing (e.g., the right to restrict the use of the property), or
- had a mutual agreement with the buyer to cancel the transaction.

In Illinois, the closing of the sale is the usual proof in a court of law that the broker has produced a buyer and earned a commission.

Sales Force Compensation

The amount of compensation a licensee receives from a sale is set by mutual agreement between the affiliated licensees and their sponsoring brokers. This compensation agreement is included in the employment agreement. A sponsoring broker may agree to pay a fixed salary or a predetermined percentage based on transactions originated by a specific licensee. Some sponsoring brokers require that sales staff pay all or part of the expenses of advertising listed properties; this may be subtracted from commissions by agreement or be billed separately to the licensee.

In many states, including Illinois, it is illegal for a sponsoring broker to pay a commission to anyone other than

- licensees under that same sponsoring broker, or
- another firm's sponsoring broker (cooperative commission) who then pays his own sponsored licensees involved.

Fees, commissions, or other compensation cannot be paid to unlicensed persons for services that legally require a real estate license. "Other compensation" includes certain items of personal property, such as a new television, or other premiums, such as vacations, given to nonlicensed persons to perhaps acquire names of "leads." This is not to be confused with referral fees paid between designated managing brokers or sponsoring brokers for "leads," which are legal as long as the individuals are licensed.

Sponsoring brokers may pay their sponsored licensees their commissions directly, or under the Act, a licensee may form an entity (corporation, LLC, LLP, etc.) for the purpose of receiving compensation. This entity can be solely owned or owned together with the licensee's spouse, as long as both are licensed and sponsored by the same sponsoring broker or the spouse is not also licensed. Though receiving compensation, this business entity is not required to be licensed under the Act. However, the licensee must file a copy of the certificate of incorporation issued by the secretary of state with IDFPR. The entity can receive compensation earned by that licensee only, both from real estate– and non-real estate–related activities. This entity cannot be licensed and cannot be used by the licensee to perform real estate activities, sponsor or employ other licensees, or advertise itself to the public in the corporation's name. An entity will not be given a license if a non-participating owner, member, manager, partner, or officer has a suspended or revoked license (1450.600).

IN PRACTICE

All monies going in and out of real estate offices are handled by the sponsoring broker. This includes, but is not limited to, incentive prizes for selling agents, earnest money deposits, escrows, commissions, referral fees, licensee's wages, bonuses, and other monies or awards.

Commissions and Disclosures

The sponsoring broker's compensation and policy with cooperating brokers who represent other parties in a transaction must always be disclosed. If there is compensation from two parties to a transaction—from both the buyer and the seller—that needs to be disclosed in writing as well. If a licensee refers the client to another source for services related to the transaction and the licensee has an interest greater than 1% in that source, it must be disclosed. In addition, a licensee must disclose in writing to a client all sources of compensation related to the transaction received by the licensee from a third party.

Commission Structures

Commission "splits" earned by sponsored licensees vary. Some firms have adopted a 100% commission plan, wherein sponsored licensees pay a monthly service charge or desk fee to their sponsoring brokers to cover the costs of office space, telephones, and supervision in return for keeping 100% of the commissions from the sales they negotiate. The 100% commission sponsored licensee pays all of his own expenses.

Other companies offer graduated commission splits based on a sponsored licensee's achieving specified production goals. For example, a sponsoring broker might agree to split commissions 50/50 with a certain sponsored licensee until the sponsoring broker has earnings of $25,000 for the year from that sponsored licensee, or 60/40 until the sponsoring broker's tally reaches $50,000. Past that point, the sponsored licensee's portion of the split might go to 70%, 80%, or even 100%. Commission splits of 80/20 or 90/10 are not uncommon for high producers. No matter how the licensee's compensation package is structured, only the sponsoring broker can pay it.

In cooperating transactions (usually stated as "co-op: X%" on the MLS sheet), the commission is paid by the sponsoring broker of the "list side" to the sponsoring broker of the "buy side," and then paid to the sponsored licensee who worked for or with the buyer. The listing sponsored licensee is similarly paid by the listing sponsoring broker.

If the commission is from a listing that has sold, the sponsoring broker of the listing firm is first paid by the seller. Then the sponsoring broker pays the sponsored licensee involved at the listing office and also pays the cooperating sponsoring broker at any other firm involved in the transaction. The cooperating sponsoring broker in turn issues the appropriate amount to the sponsored licensee involved at his office, based on their agreed-upon split. Sometimes a commission or fee does not involve a seller. It might come from a buyer who has agreed to a buyer agent fee. The same procedure applies: incoming funds always go to the sponsoring broker first; from there, they are dispersed to others involved.

If a sponsored licensee had earned a commission but his employment had been terminated before the payment of the commission, the former sponsoring broker may pay the commission directly to the former associate, even if that former associate has a new sponsoring broker.

Unit 5

MATH CONCEPTS Sharing Commissions

A commission might be shared by many people: the listing sponsoring broker, the listing broker, the buyer's sponsoring broker, and the buyer's broker.

For example, while working for sponsoring broker Harry, licensee Ed took a listing on a $73,000 house at a 6% commission rate. Licensee Tom, who works for sponsoring broker Matt, found the buyer for the property. The two brokerages split the commission equally. Matt's brokerage kept 45% of the commission that his brokerage received. How much did his licensee Tom receive?

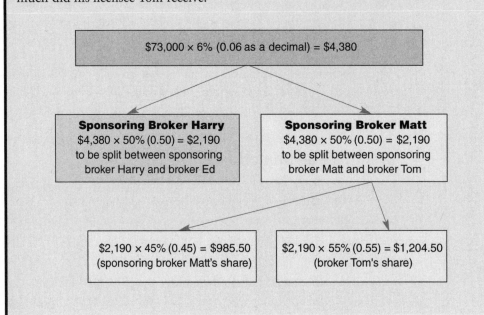

ANTITRUST LAWS

Antitrust violations include

■ price-fixing,

■ group boycotting,

■ allocation of customers,

■ allocation of markets, and

■ tie-in agreements.

The real estate industry is subject to federal and state Antitrust laws. These laws prohibit monopolies, collusion, and any contracts, combinations, and conspiracies that unreasonably restrain trade—that is, acts that interfere with the free flow of goods and services in a competitive marketplace. The most common antitrust violations are price-fixing, group boycotting, allocation of customers or markets, tie-in agreements, and disparaging the competition.

Price-Fixing

Price-fixing is the practice of setting prices for products or services rather than letting competition in the open market establish those prices. In real estate, price-fixing occurs when competing real estate companies agree to set standard sales commissions, fees, or management rates or if they attempt illegal tying arrangements. Price-fixing is illegal. Real estate companies must independently determine any minimum commission rates or minimum fees. These decisions must be based on a company's business judgment and revenue requirements without input from competitors.

MLSs, REALTORS® associations, and other professional organizations may not set fees or commission splits, nor can they deny membership to licensees based on the fees the licensees charge. Either practice could lead the public to believe that the industry encourages the illegal practice of restricting open-market competition.

Group Boycotting

Group boycotting occurs when two or more businesses conspire against another business, or agree to withhold their patronage, in order to reduce competition. Group boycotting is illegal.

Allocation of Customers or Markets

Allocation of customers or markets involves an agreement among real estate companies to divide their markets and refrain from competing for each other's business. Allocations might be made on a geographic basis, with real estate companies agreeing to specific territories within which they will operate exclusively. The division also might occur by markets, such as by price range or category of housing. These agreements result in reduced competition and are illegal.

Tie-in Agreements

Tie-in agreements (or *tying agreements*) are agreements to sell one product only if the buyer purchases another product as well. The sale of the first (desired) product is "tied" to the purchase of a second, less desirable, product. Tie-in agreements are illegal when they restrict competition without benefit to the consumer.

EXAMPLE

A sponsoring broker owns a vacant lot in a popular area of town. A builder wants to buy the lot and build three new homes on it. The sponsoring broker refuses to sell the lot to the builder unless the builder also agrees to purchase three other less desirable lots further east. This sort of tie-in arrangement may violate antitrust laws.

Disparaging the Competition

Saying or writing derogatory or dismissive content about a competitor can easily be construed as trying to drive them out of business. When done between businesses, it quickly rises to the point of collusion and group boycotting. Not only does it become a potential antitrust violation, it can also open up one for a lawsuit of commercial disparagement involving derogatory or false statements.

Penalties

The penalties for violating antitrust laws are severe. For example, under the Sherman Antitrust Act, people who fix prices or allocate markets may be subject to a maximum $1 million fine and up to 10 years in prison. For corporations, the penalty may be as high as $100 million. An individual who has suffered a loss because of an antitrust activity may sue for threefold the damages sustained. This is known as treble-damages. In addition, the injured party may recover the cost of the suit, including reasonable attorney fees.

OTHER CONSUMER PROTECTION MEASURES

Phishing and Electronic Media Scams

Licensees need to be cautious in the transfer of their client's confidential information via email and text. One should always verify the sender or recipient before responding. For instance, there have been numerous cases of thieves, while impersonating attorneys, title companies, or lenders, emailing escrow agents and requesting the transfer of the earnest money into a bank account in anticipation of closing. Savvy licensees will pick up the phone and verify, using the phone numbers from their files.

Emails requesting confidential information, Social Security numbers, or bank account numbers are also not uncommon. Fraud is a reality from which licensees must protect their clients and themselves.

National Do Not Call Registry

The **National Do Not Call Registry** is a list of phone numbers of consumers who do not want to be contacted by commercial telemarketers. It is managed by the Federal Trade Commission (FTC) and is enforced by the FTC, the Federal Communications Commission (FCC), and state officials. The registry applies to any plan, program, or campaign to sell goods or services through interstate phone calls. The registry does not limit calls by political organizations, charities, collection agencies, or telephone surveyors.

The law establishes specific guidelines for when licensees may contact consumers, even when they are listed in the registry. Licensees are permitted to call consumers with whom they have an established business relationship up to 18 months after the consumer's last payment, purchase, or delivery. With consumers on the registry who have submitted applications or made inquiries, licensees are allowed additional contact for up to three months after the fact.

For example, it is permissible for a real estate licensee to call expired listings for the purpose of listing the property because the established business relationship exception permits the listing licensee and the listing real estate company to contact the seller for up to 18 months after the listing expiration date.

Accessing the National Do Not Call Registry

Sellers, telemarketers, and other service providers must register to access the registry. The registry may not be used for any purpose other than preventing telemarketing calls to the telephone numbers on the registry.

Regulators say that brokerage companies must have a do-not-call policy even if they do not engage in cold calling. A company that is a seller or a telemarketer could be in violation of the law for placing any telemarketing calls (even to numbers not on the registry) if the company does not have a policy governing access to the registry. Violators may be subject to fines for each call placed.

To successfully avoid penalties, the seller or the telemarketer must demonstrate that

- it has written procedures to comply with the do-not-call requirements,
- it trains its personnel in those procedures,
- it monitors and enforces compliance with these procedures,
- it maintains a company-specific list of telephone numbers it may not call,
- it accesses the national registry every 31 days before calling any consumer and maintains records documenting this process, and
- demonstrates that any call made in violation of the do-not-call rules was the result of an error.

The CAN-SPAM Act

The Controlling the Assault of Non-Solicited Pornography and Marketing Act of 2003 (**CAN-SPAM Act of 2003**) established requirements for sending commercial email; establishes penalties for noncompliance; and gives consumers the right to have emailers (not just "spammers") stop emailing them.

The CAN-SPAM Act targets email used to promote or advertise products and services (including online products and services) offered for commercial purposes. The act does not apply to "transactional or relationship content," that is, those messages meant to facilitate or alter existing customer agreements (for example, by giving a customer additional information about an existing agreement or conducting business as part of an existing agreement). However, these emails must not explicitly or implicitly operate for the purposes of advertising or promotion, as this is in violation of the law.

The CAN-SPAM Act is enforced by the FTC and other federal and state agencies, which have jurisdiction over the company or companies in question. In addition, companies that violate the CAN-SPAM Act can be sued by internet service providers. Criminal sanctions can be brought against violators by the Department of Justice.

Briefly, the CAN-SPAM Act requires the following:

- False or misleading header information is banned. An email's "From," "To," and routing information—including the original domain name and email address—must be accurate and identify the person who initiated the email.

- Deceptive subject lines are prohibited. The subject line cannot mislead the recipient about the contents or subject matter of the message.

- Email recipients must have an opt-out method. You must provide a return email address or another internet-based response mechanism that allows a recipient to ask you not to send future email messages to that email address, and requests must be honored.

- Commercial email must be identified as an advertisement and include the sender's valid physical postal address.

Each violation is subject to fines. Deceptive commercial emails are also subject to laws banning false or misleading advertising. Additional fines are provided for commercial emailers who violate the rules and do any of the following:

- "Harvest" email addresses from websites or online services that have published a notice prohibiting the transfer of email addresses for the purpose of sending email

- Generate email addresses using a "dictionary attack" (combining names, letters, or numbers into multiple permutations)

- Use scripts or other automated ways to register for multiple email or user accounts to send commercial email

- Relay emails through a computer or network without permission—for example, taking advantage of open relays or open proxies without notification.

The Electronic Mail Act imposes additional regulations on use of commercial email in Illinois. The use of email communication and web advertising is also restricted as laid out in Rules Section 1450.720.

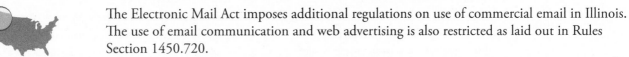

The Junk Fax Prevention Act

The **Junk Fax Prevention Act of 2005** does not legalize unsolicited fax advertisements or solicitations but does allow for an established business relationship exception. As a rule, a real estate licensee may not legally send an unsolicited commercial fax message without express written consent or without an established business relationship with the recipient.

The Junk Fax Prevention Act does the following:

- It sets out guidelines for what constitutes an established business relationship (EBR).

- It does not place time limitations on EBRs.

- It requires companies to offer a free method by which fax recipients may opt out of receiving future fax communications. The opt-out method must be available at any time of day, every day; and the opt-out information must be made available on the first page of the fax.

- It permits businesses to send faxes to numbers that they had access to via an EBR before July 9, 2005, when the act became law.

- It requires businesses to receive direct consent from EBR customers for whom they did not already have fax numbers before the effective date of the legislation, or to obtain these numbers via some other source to which the EBR customer willingly provided them with permission for such use by other parties (including the sender).

In 2008, the FCC added the following clarifications to the law:

- Senders have met the consent requirement if they buy the fax number(s) from companies who have obtained the information from published sources; however, if there are errors in the list, the sender could be held liable.

- Senders must make a reasonable effort to ascertain whether recipients have given consent.

- Senders are permitted to provide a website, which must be easily accessible and usable, through which recipients may opt out of receiving fax communications.

State laws regarding unsolicited fax advertising have not been replaced or preempted by the federal law. Under Illinois law, for example, sending unsolicited fundraising and advertising emails without the recipients' permission may be punishable by a $500 fine.

SUMMARY

Real estate brokerage is the act of bringing people together, for a fee or commission, for the purpose of buying, selling, exchanging, or leasing real estate. New technologies are changing the way that brokerage offices are managed and operated. Social media is changing the way properties are marketed. To avoid liability and as a means of risk management, office policy manuals should contain language under which sponsored licensees may employ these social networking methods in their real estate practices.

The licensee's compensation in a real estate sale may take the form of a percentage commission, a flat fee, or an hourly rate. The licensee is considered to have earned a commission when he procures a ready, willing, and able buyer for a seller. Sponsored licensees who work under a sponsoring broker do so either as an employee or as an independent contractor. Either way, there must be a written employment agreement signed by both parties.

Federal and state antitrust laws prohibit licensees from conspiring to fix prices, engage in boycotts designed to reduce competition, allocate customers or markets, or establish tie-in agreements.

The National Do Not Call Registry is a list of consumer telephone numbers that do not want to be contacted by businesses who sell goods or services. Violators are subject to fines for each illegal call placed.

The CAN-SPAM Act establishes requirements for commercial email, spells out penalties for email senders who violate the Act, and gives consumers the right to have emailers stop sending emails to them. The Act is enforced by the FTC and the Department of Justice with fines levied per transgression.

The Junk Fax Prevention Act prohibits faxing unsolicited fax advertisements or solicitations, but does allow for an established business relationship exception.

In Illinois, the Real Estate License Act of 2000, as amended in 2020, provides the guidelines for compliance in handling real estate activities.

The Electronic Mail Act imposes additional requirements over and above federal CAN-SPAM rules on senders of commercial email messages.

UNIT 5 QUIZ

1. "To recover a commission for brokerage services, a sponsoring broker must be employed as the agent of the seller." Which of these statements *BEST* explains this sentence?
   A. The seller must have made an express or implied written agreement to pay a commission to the sponsoring broker for selling the property.
   B. The sponsoring broker must work in a real estate office.
   C. The sponsoring broker must have asked the seller the price of the property and then found a ready, willing, and able buyer.
   D. The sponsoring broker must have one or more sponsored licensees employed in the office.

2. An Illinois real estate licensee who is engaged as an independent contractor
   A. is considered an employee by the IRS for tax purposes.
   B. must be covered by workers' compensation.
   C. must have a employment contract with the sponsoring broker.
   D. may work as an independent contractor for two or more sponsoring brokers.

3. In Illinois, the usual "proof" that the listing broker has earned commission is the
   A. closing of the sale.
   B. submission to the seller of a signed offer from a ready, willing, and able buyer.
   C. signing of an exclusive listing contract.
   D. deposit of the buyer's earnest money into escrow.

4. A broker listed the seller's home for $300,000. Before the listing contract expired, the broker brought the seller a full-price offer on the seller's terms, containing no contingencies. The seller then decided not to sell. Which of these statements is *TRUE*?
   A. The broker has no reason to collect a commission in this case.
   B. The broker must immediately file suit against the seller.
   C. The seller's only liability is to the buyer.
   D. The seller probably is liable for the commission.

5. Which of the following is an example of price-fixing?
   A. "We have an agreement with ABC Brokerage to not practice real estate in our neighborhood."
   B. "In order to buy this new construction home, you must use us as your listing brokerage should you sell it within the next 10 years."
   C. "I'm going to tell every real estate agent I know not to refer "Acme Property Inspectors" to their clients.
   D. "This is the same commission that every other real estate company in town charges."

6. According to the Illinois license law, a sponsored real estate licensee may *NOT*
   A. represent both buyer and seller.
   B. buy or sell real estate for himself.
   C. accept a commission from another sponsoring broker unless previously earned at that sponsoring brokerage.
   D. engage in dual agency.

7. A sponsoring broker must have a written employment agreement with
   A. all of these.
   B. a non-practicing licensee.
   C. a licensed managing broker.
   D. sponsored brokers.

8. Two real estate companies agreed to boycott the services of a title company so that a new title company can take over the corresponding market share. The two real estate companies are violating the
   A. Antiboycotting Act.
   B. Sherman Antitrust Act.
   C. Illinois Lincoln Antitrust Act.
   D. Lincoln Fair Trade Act.

9. The broker's commission was $8,200. If the commission rate was 6%, what was the selling price of the property?
   A. $132,666.67
   B. $136,666.67
   C. $154,232.50
   D. $175,452.48

10. A broker received $2,520 as the firm's 50% share of a commission. If the property sold for $72,000, what was the commission rate?
    A. 6%
    B. 7%
    C. 6.5%
    D. 8%

11. One general rule of the National Do Not Call Registry is
    A. states must maintain separate do-not-call lists.
    B. the national registry must be updated once a year.
    C. Unless there is an established business relationship, it is illegal to make an unsolicited phone call to a number listed on the national registry.
    D. real estate offices are exempt from the laws because they are not considered telemarketers.

12. Federal regulations on unsolicited email
    A. require prior permission of recipients in order to send email to them.
    B. require that email lists be scrubbed every 31 days.
    C. exempt phone calls to individuals with whom the real estate office has a prior business relationship.
    D. require commercial emails to include a physical address, among other things, for the sender.

13. Which statement is *TRUE* regarding the National Do Not Call Registry?
    A. Real estate licensees are not required to search the national registry before making telemarketing calls to solicit listings or to solicit potential buyers.
    B. Real estate licensees are exempt from telemarketing laws.
    C. Real estate licensees may phone any visitors to an open house for up to three months after that open house.
    D. Real estate licensees may not call their current listings for leads.

14. Real estate licensees who are paid in a lump sum and who are personally responsible for paying their own taxes are probably
    A. independent contractors.
    B. nonexempt.
    C. buyer's brokers.
    D. employees.

15. An active licensee entered into a contract with her sponsoring broker, specifying that she is not an employee. In the past year, 90% of the licensee's income comes from real estate sales commissions. The IRS would *MOST* likely classify the licensee as
    A. self-employed.
    B. an independent contractor.
    C. a part-time real estate licensee.
    D. an employee.

16. Which of these may a sponsoring broker dictate to an independent contractor?
    A. Number of hours the person would have to work
    B. Work schedule that the person would need to follow
    C. Number of vacation days the person would receive
    D. Compensation the person would receive

17. After a particularly challenging transaction finally closes, the client gives the sponsored broker representing the client a check for $500 "for all your extra work." Which statement is *TRUE*?
    A. The sponsored broker may receive compensation only from the sponsoring broker.
    B. While such compensation is irregular, it is appropriate for the sponsored broker to accept the check.
    C. The sponsored broker should accept the check and deposit it immediately in a special escrow account.
    D. The sponsoring broker is entitled to 80% of the check.

18. The amount of commission paid to a sponsored licensee is determined by
    A. Illinois law.
    B. mutual agreement with the sponsoring broker.
    C. the local real estate board.
    D. mutual agreement with the client.

19. A sponsored licensee wants to receive a lump-sum payment at the end of each transaction. The sponsored licensee must meet all these requirements *EXCEPT*
    A. receive 90% of income from the brokerage based on production, not time worked.
    B. be free from supervision by the sponsoring broker and/or office manager.
    C. hold a current real estate license.
    D. have a written agreement with the sponsoring broker stating that the sponsored licensee will not be treated as an employee for federal tax purposes.

20. A new sponsored real estate licensee wants to find new business among the firm's expired listings. Under the National Do Not Call Registry, for how long after the listing has expired may the licensee solicit business from the firm's previous listings?
    A. 30 days
    B. 18 months
    C. 90 days
    D. 6 months

UNIT
6

Brokerage Agreements

LEARNING OBJECTIVES

When you have completed this unit, you will be able to accomplish the following.

> Identify the different types of listing and buyer representation agreements and their terms.
> Explain the listing process and the parts of the listing agreement.
> Distinguish among the characteristics of the various types of listing and buyer representation agreements.
> Describe the ways in which a listing may be terminated.

KEY TERMS

buyer agency agreement	exclusive right-to-sell	net listing
comparative market	listing	open listing
analysis (CMA)	market value	option listing
contemporaneous offers	minimum services	statute of frauds
exclusive-agency listing	multiple listing service	
	(MLS)	

OVERVIEW

Brokerage agreements are employment contracts for the personal professional services of the sponsoring broker, not for the transfer of real estate. The various types of brokerage agreements establish the basic relationship between the parties and provide different levels of rights and responsibilities for the sponsoring broker. Perhaps most important, brokerage agreements address the essential questions of exclusivity and compensation.

A listing agreement is an employment contract between a sponsoring broker and a seller; a buyer representation agreement is an employment contract as well because it establishes the rights and responsibilities of the sponsoring broker as agent for the buyer. A management contract sets up the relationship between the sponsoring broker and the owner of a rental property.

For most real estate licensees, listing and buyer representation agreements are the fundamental, bedrock documents of the real estate profession.

In most states, either by **statutes of frauds** or by specific rules from real estate licensing authorities, exclusive brokerage agreements must be in writing to be enforceable in court. Oral agreements are not illegal, but they are not recommended because they cannot be enforced in court.

In Illinois, according to the Illinois Real Estate License Act, all exclusive brokerage agreements must be in writing and must indicate the required minimum services to be provided to the consumer in return for compensation or the right to receive compensation from another.

Each brokerage agreement must also clearly state that it is illegal for either the owner or the sponsoring broker to refuse to display or sell to any person because of one's membership in a protected class (e.g., race, color, religion, national origin, sex, ancestry, age, marital status, physical or mental handicap, familial status, or any other class protected by Article 3 of the Illinois Human Rights Act).

TYPES OF LISTING AGREEMENTS

Exclusive Right-to-Sell Listing

One authorized broker receives a commission regardless of who sells the property.

Several types of listing agreements exist. The type of listing agreement determines the specific rights and obligations of the broker and seller.

Exclusive Right-to-Sell Listing Agreement

In an **exclusive right-to-sell listing**, one broker is appointed as the seller's sole agent. The listing broker is given the exclusive right, or *authorization*, to market the seller's property. If the property is sold while the listing is in effect, the seller must pay the broker a commission regardless of who sells the property: the listing broker, another broker, or even if the seller finds a buyer without the broker's assistance. Sellers benefit from this form of agreement because the broker feels freer to spend time and money actively marketing the property, making a timely and profitable sale more likely. From the broker's perspective, an exclusive right-to-sell listing offers the greatest opportunity to receive a commission. Most residential listing agreements in Illinois are exclusive right-to-sell listing agreements.

Exclusive-Agency Listing Agreement

In an **exclusive-agency listing**, one broker is authorized to act as the exclusive agent of the seller-principal. However, the seller retains the right to sell the property without obligation to the broker. The seller is obligated to pay a commission to the broker only if the listing broker or a cooperating broker has been the procuring cause of a sale. The seller retains the right to sell the property without financial obligation to the listing broker.

In Illinois, exclusive listing agreements must be in writing. All written exclusive listing agreements must include

- the list price of the property,
- the agreed-upon amount of commission and the time of payment,
- the duration of the agreement,
- the names of the broker and seller,
- the identification of the property involved (address or legal description),
- the duties of the listing broker,

- minimum services language,
- a statement of nondiscrimination, and
- a statement regarding antitrust.

Licensees may not obtain written listings that contain blank spaces to be filled in later.

Open Listing Agreement

Open Listing

- There are multiple brokers.
- Only the selling broker is entitled to a commission.
- Seller retains the right to sell independently without obligation.

In an **open listing** (called a *nonexclusive listing* in some areas), the seller retains the right to employ any number of brokers as agents. The brokers can act simultaneously, and the seller is financially obligated only to that broker who successfully produces a ready, willing, and able buyer. If the seller personally sells the property without the aid of any of the brokers, the seller is not obligated to pay a commission.

Negotiated terms of an open listing agreement should be in writing to protect the broker's ability to collect an agreed-on fee from the seller. Written terms may be in the form of a listing agreement (if the broker represents the seller) or a fee agreement (if the broker represents the buyer or the seller does not wish to be represented).

Net Listing

Net Listing

The broker is entitled to any amount exceeding the seller's stated net.

A **net listing** provision specifies that the seller will receive a net amount of money from any sale, with the excess going to the listing broker as commission. The broker is free to offer the property at any price greater than the net amount the seller wants; the difference is the broker's fee. Because a net listing can create a clear conflict of interest between the broker's fiduciary responsibility to the seller and the broker's profit motive, net listings are illegal in many states and are discouraged in others.

In Illinois, net listings are legal but not recommended because of the potential for fraud.

In a net listing, actual sale price minus the seller-required net equals broker profit.

Option Listing

Option Listing

The broker has the right to purchase the property.

An **option listing** provision gives the broker the right to purchase the listed property at some point in the future. The specific length of the time period is by agreement and usually matches the length of the listing. Use of an option listing may open the broker to charges of fraud unless the broker is scrupulous in fulfilling all obligations to the property owner.

Note that an option listing differs from an option contract, the latter involving a consumer's option to purchase a given property.

Sometimes, brokers and sellers enter into guaranteed sale agreements, in which the broker agrees to buy the listed property if it fails to sell before the end of the listing period. Typically, these guarantees are made to the seller as an inducement to list the property with the broker.

Multiple Listing Services

A *multiple listing* clause may be included in an exclusive listing. It is used by licensees who are members of a **multiple listing service (MLS)**. An MLS is a marketing organization whose members make their listings available for showing and sale through all the other member licensees.

An MLS offers advantages to licensees, sellers, and buyers. Licensees develop a sizable inventory of properties to be sold and are assured a portion of the commission if they list property or participate in the sale of another licensee's listing. Sellers gain because the property is exposed to a much larger market. Buyers gain because of the variety of properties on the market.

The contractual obligations among the member licensees of an MLS vary widely. Most MLSs require that licensees turn over new listings to the service within a specific, fairly short time after the licensee obtains the listing. The length of time during which the listing licensee can offer a property to the public on her own without involving the MLS varies. Of course, sellers must be informed and give their written consent for any delay in notifying the MLS. This gives the listing company a strong chance to sell its own listing.

Under the provisions of most MLSs, a participating licensee makes a unilateral offer of cooperation and compensation to other member licensees when the listing enters the MLS. The licensee must have the written consent of the seller to include the property in an MLS.

IN PRACTICE

Technology has enhanced the benefits of MLS membership. In addition to providing instant access to information about the status of listed properties, MLSs often offer a broad range of other useful information about mortgage loans, real estate taxes and assessments, municipalities, and school districts. They are equally helpful to licensees who need to make a comparative market analysis (CMA) to determine the value of a particular property before suggesting an appropriate range of prices. Computer-assisted searches also help buyers select properties that best meet their needs.

While a few buyers choose to remain as customers without representation, even that lack of agency is now subject to disclosure. By statute, a notice of no agency should be provided. If nothing is said about agency, licensees are considered to be representing the consumer with whom they are working, as a designated agent for the consumer (unless there is a written agreement to the contrary). However, the Designated Agency Relationship must be disclosed in writing to the client.

In spite of these relatively clear lines regarding whose agent is whose, sellers often still pay the fees for both agents in a transaction. These fees are called *cooperative commissions*. In an Illinois MLS listing data sheet, this is typically stated as "co-op: X% or as a flat fee." Paying someone a commission does not create agency in Illinois.

THE LISTING PROCESS

Before signing a contract, the broker and the seller must discuss a variety of issues. The seller's most critical concerns typically are the selling price of the property and the net amount the seller can expect to receive from the sale. The broker has several professional tools available to provide information about a property's value and to calculate the proceeds from a sale.

An important safeguard is to check title records to see who has an interest in the property so that all the appropriate parties are involved. Are there homestead rights? Are there any other holders of title who need to be involved? Is it a qualified estate? Should an attorney be consulted to ensure proper execution of all documents?

Listing Appointment

The backbone of the real estate practice is the listing appointment, the meeting of the licensee with the potential client, the seller. Every licensee has their own approach and style, but in general, listing appointments should cover some standard fare.

It's important to prepare an accurate comparative market analysis and these require the collection of data on other properties, also known as comparables or "comps." They generally fall into three categories: solds, actives, and expireds. Sold properties inform the agent as to what prices are attractive to buyers and what the average neighborhood market time is. Actives show an agent what the competition is and if there are any "price points," which are the high or low ends of a range of prices for similar properties. An expired comp usually indicates a price that did not attract a buyer. More often than not, it's an indication of overpricing.

Remember, the eventual price of the property is determined by the seller with the input and advice of the licensee, but it is the seller's final decision. A licensee violates the Act by promoting a price other than the one the seller agreed to.

Sellers will often need help determining what their equity is and what their net will be. The licensee should be familiar with how to calculate these figures. However, because there may be many variables as the transaction progresses, it should be stressed to the seller that these calculations are estimates only.

Ongoing Communication

It is good at these initial appointments with either sellers or buyers to set up an agreed mode of communication. Licensees, especially new ones, should keep in mind that success in the real estate business depends on good customer relations and interpersonal skills, including communication. It is imperative to communicate with clients throughout the entire real estate transaction, as well as afterward.

Not everyone likes to communicate in the same fashion. Whether it be by text, email, or phone, recordkeeping is an important part of making sure your client's wishes are met and that your liability is protected. Here are some tips to keep in mind regarding communication: (1) after oral conversations, make notes with dates and times; (2) save texts and emails; and (3) follow laws and regulations regarding electronic communication.

Remember that though social media may be a convenient way of conversing with customers and clients, it can lack privacy and confidentiality. Another drawback is that social media can be challenging to log for recordkeeping. A real estate professional can establish a presence on social media, but should always be mindful that information available to the public imposes a level of restraint on comments and photos posted to avoid embarrassment or even potential liability.

Ongoing communication, no matter the format, can help build and maintain a relationship with clients who may then provide repeat business or referrals.

Pricing the Property

While it is the responsibility of the broker to advise and assist, it is the seller who must determine the listing price for the property. Because the average seller does not have the skills needed to determine a market-based listing price, brokers must be prepared to offer their knowledge and expertise.

Brokers can help sellers determine a listing price for the property by using a **comparative market analysis (CMA)**. A CMA analyzes properties similar to the subject property in size, location, and amenities. Though appraisals are more in depth than a CMA, a CMA still requires an amount of skill and consideration.

In Illinois, the License Act now requires a CMA to be of a certain form, in writing, and with statutorily prescribed language as per 225 ILCS 454/10-45. The requirements and restrictions are lengthy and should be reviewed before creating a CMA.

A broker price opinion or comparative market analysis shall be in writing either on paper or electronically and shall include the following provisions:

(1) A statement of the intended purpose of the broker price opinion or comparative market analysis

(2) A brief description of the interest in real estate that is the subject of the broker price opinion or comparative market analysis

(3) A brief description of the methodology used to develop the broker price opinion or comparative market analysis

(4) Any assumptions or limiting conditions

(5) A disclosure of any existing or contemplated interest of the broker or managing broker in the interest in real estate that is the subject of the broker price opinion or comparative market analysis

(6) The name, license number, and signature of the broker or managing broker that developed the broker price opinion or comparative market analysis

(7) A statement in substantially the following form: "This is a broker price opinion/comparative market analysis, not an appraisal of the market value of the real estate, and was prepared by a licensed real estate broker or managing broker, not by a State certified real estate appraiser."

(8) Such other items as the broker or managing broker may deem appropriate

The CMA is based on

■ recently closed (sold) properties,
■ properties currently on the market (properties in competition with the subject property), and
■ properties that did not sell (expired listings in the area).

Licensees should keep in mind the importance of historical and expired sales and use them as supporting data when they present their CMA to a client or potential client.

Sold prices represent what buyers have been willing to pay for similar properties in the neighborhood. Very often, the expired listing prices are those prices that buyers have not been willing to pay for a property similar to the subject property. Current asking prices of current, similar properties on the market indicate the trend: asking prices lower than the "solds" indicate a slow or declining market. An optimistic market is indicated when the asking prices are higher than the "solds."

Although a CMA is not viewed as a formal appraisal, the broker uses many of the appraiser's methods and techniques. Data generally falls into two basic categories: (1) general (secondary) data—information about the social, economic, governmental, and environmental influences on value, which is typically not collected by the appraiser; and (2) specific (primary) data—details about the subject, comparables, and local market conditions, which is collected by the appraiser.

Data can also be viewed as qualitative versus quantitative. Qualitative data describes things like amenities, style, or location that cannot be expressed with a numerical value. Quantitative data includes information that can be expressed as a numerical value, such as square feet, room count, marketing time, or lot size.

When presenting information and statistics to clients or consumers, keep it simple and be prepared to back up a CMA or price opinion with supporting details.

The figure sought in both CMAs and appraisals is the property's market value. **Market value** is the most probable price a property would bring in an arm's-length transaction under normal conditions on the open market. A CMA estimates market value as likely to fall within a range of values (e.g., $335,000 to $350,000). A formal appraisal indicates a specific value rather than a range. In both cases, the seller/principal must make the final decision on the asking price.

While it is the property owner's privilege to set whatever listing price the owner chooses, a broker should consider rejecting any listing in which the price is substantially exaggerated or severely out of line with the indications of the CMA or appraisal. These tools provide the best indications of what a buyer will likely pay for the property. An unrealistic listing price will make it difficult for the broker to properly market the seller's property within the agreed upon listing period. Furthermore, a buyer may have difficulty obtaining financing because the property will not appraise for the sale price.

 IN PRACTICE

When helping a seller determine an appropriate listing price, the broker must give an estimate of value that is reasonable and as accurate as possible. Overpriced listings cost the broker time and money in wasted marketing and advertising and give sellers false hopes of riches to come. Additionally, some research suggests that listings priced too high in the beginning sell for less in the end than if they had been more moderately priced at the outset.

Information Needed for Listing Agreements

Once the broker and the owner agree on a listing price, the broker must obtain specific, detailed information about the property. Obtaining as many facts as possible ensures that most contingencies can be anticipated. This is particularly important when the listing will be shared with other licensees through an MLS, and the other licensees must rely on the information taken by the listing broker.

Measuring Structures and Room Count

In determining the size and scope of a property, guidelines vary. According to the American Measurement Standard (AMS), in a single-family detached dwelling, square footage is defined as the sum of all connected, finished, and usable areas. The square footage is determined by the measurements of the exterior dimensions. When the parallel sides of a home have the same measurement, the house is said to be "square." Levels of the dwelling are counted individually. Any space above grade (above ground level) is then combined to arrive at one total square footage.

Equally as important is what characteristics determine a bedroom. In practice, multiple listing guidelines are in accordance with appraisal guidelines, while variations from local ordinances will prevail even further. For instance, the Midwest Real Estate Data (MRED) states that a bedroom is a private room that is closed off from other living spaces and does not have its only entrance from another bedroom, a configuration that would make it a tandem room. Bedrooms are not required to have a closet and/or a window.

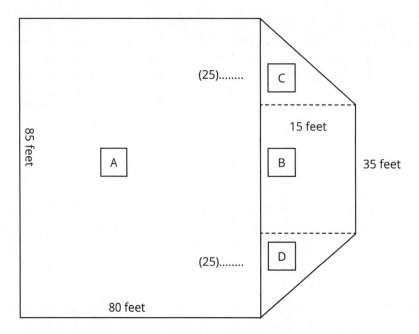

This diagram can be broken into the following components to figure out the square footage. If one were to flip the right triangles on top of each other (C & D), one could eliminate a step and figure the combined areas as a rectangle.

A: 85' × 80' = 6,800 sq. ft.

B: 15' × 35' = 525 sq. ft.

C: (25' × 15') ÷ 2 = 187.5 sq. ft.

D: (25' × 15') ÷ 2 = 187.5 sq. ft.

6,800 + 525 + 187.50 + 187.50 = 7,700 sq. ft.

MATH CONCEPTS Calculating Sales Prices, Commissions, And Nets To Seller

When a property sells, the sales price equals 100% of the money being transferred. Therefore, if a broker is to receive a 6% commission, 94% will remain for the seller's other expenses and equity. To calculate a commission using a sales price of $225,000 and a commission rate of 6%, multiply the sales price by the commission rate:

$225,000 × 6% = $225,000 × 0.06 = $13,500 commission

To calculate a sales price using a commission of $13,500 and a commission rate of 7%, divide the commission by the commission rate:

$13,500 ÷ 7% = $13,500 ÷ 0.07 = $192,857 sales price

To calculate a commission rate using a commission of $8,200 and a sales price of $164,000, divide the commission by the sales price:

$8,200 ÷ $164,000 = 0.05, or 5% commission rate

To calculate the net to the seller using a sales price of $125,000 and a commission rate of 8%, multiply the sales price by 100% minus the commission rate:

$125,000 × (100% − 8%) = $125,000 × (92%) = $125,000 × 0.92 = $115,000

The same result can be achieved by calculating the commission ($125,000 × 0.08 = $10,000) and deducting it from the sales price ($125,000 − $10,000 = $115,000); however, this involves unnecessary extra calculations.

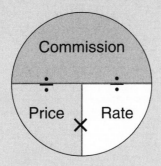

In summary:

Sales price × commission rate = commission

Commission ÷ commission rate = sales price

Commission ÷ sales price = commission rate

Sales price × (100% − commission rate) = net to seller

Disclosures

Disclosure of agency relationships and property conditions has become the focus of consumer safeguards in recent years. Property condition disclosures normally cover a wide range of structural, mechanical, and other conditions that a prospective purchaser should know about to make an informed decision. Brokers should caution sellers to make truthful, careful disclosures to avoid litigation arising from fraudulent or careless misrepresentations. It is the broker's responsibility to ensure that the seller is aware of these mandatory disclosures.

By using the Disclosure of No Agency, Illinois agents are required to disclose whose interests they legally represent to a customer. It is important that the seller be informed of the brokerage company's policies about cooperating with other brokers. Seller disclosure of property conditions is also required by Illinois law.

THE LISTING AGREEMENT

A wide variety of listing agreement forms are available. Some brokers have attorneys draft contracts, some use forms prepared by local associations of REALTORS®, and some use forms produced by state real estate licensing authorities. Some brokers use a separate information sheet (or *profile or data sheet*) for recording property features. That sheet is wed to a second form containing the contractual obligations between the seller and the broker: listing price, duration of the agreement, signatures of the parties, and so forth. Other brokers use a single form. A sample listing agreement appears in Figure 6.1.

Once a long-lasting agreement has been finalized and signed by the broker and seller, Illinois law prohibits the broker from making any addition to, deletion from, or alteration of the written listing without the written consent of the principal. The broker must return a true copy of the listing agreement, signed by the seller and by the broker, to all parties within 24 hours of execution.

Figure 6.1: Exclusive Seller Representation Contract

ILLINOIS REALTORS®
EXCLUSIVE RIGHT TO SELL CONTRACT
(DUAL AGENCY DISCLOSURE AND CONSENT INCLUDED)

1. In consideration of the services to be performed by _____, (Brokerage Company, hereinafter referred to as "Sponsoring Broker") and the commissions to be paid by _____, ("Seller"), the parties agree that Sponsoring Broker shall have the exclusive right to market and sell Seller's property upon the following terms and conditions:

   Property Address: _____

   City: _____, Illinois   Zip: _____

   Marketing Price: $_____

   Marketing Period (Choose One)

   ☐ From _____ 20_____ through 11:59 p.m. on _____, 20_____; OR

   ☐ This Contract shall automatically renew on _____, 20_____, and on _____ of each succeeding year (each date to be known herein as "Renewal Date") unless Seller provides Sponsoring Broker with written notice of Seller's intention to not renew this contract no more than thirty (30) days and no less than _____ (_____) days prior to the Renewal Date.

2. Sponsoring Broker agrees to provide those brokerage services set forth in Section 15-75 of the Illinois Real Estate License Act.

3. If during the term of this Contract Sponsoring Broker obtains an offer to purchase the property from a ready, willing, and able buyer at the marketing price, or if Seller enters into a contract or receives an offer that results in a contract for the sale or exchange of the property at any price and upon any terms to which Seller consents, Seller shall be obligated to pay Sponsoring Broker a total commission of _____ percent (___%) of the purchase price of the sale or exchange. Generally, Sponsoring Broker will offer to pay a participating cooperating broker who brings the buyer, and who is the procuring cause in a successful transaction, _____% of the total commission set forth herein. The total commission is to be paid at closing, which in the case of a sale on contract for deed shall be at the time buyer and Seller execute the initial contract or agreement for deed.

4. Seller agrees that such a commission shall be paid if the property is sold or exchanged by Seller within a protection period of _____ (__) days following the term of this Contract or any extensions thereof to anyone to whom the property was presented during the term of this Contract. However, this provision shall not apply if Seller has entered into a valid, written listing agreement with another licensed real estate broker during the protection period.

5. In the event a purchase contract is entered into and buyer defaults without fault on the Seller's part, Sponsoring Broker will waive the commission, and this agreement shall be continued from the date of default through the date provided in paragraph 1. Should Seller default on any contract for the purchase or exchange of the property, any commission owed under this agreement shall become payable immediately.

6. When a contract to purchase is entered into for the purchase of Seller's property, the buyer may deposit earnest money with Sponsoring Broker. If Sponsoring Broker is holding the earnest money as escrow agent, Sponsoring Broker will hold any such earnest money in a special, non-interest-bearing escrow account on behalf of the buyer and Seller. At closing, the earnest money will be disbursed according to the terms of the contract to purchase. If the transaction fails to close:

   (a) Due to fault of the Seller, as determined by the parties to the purchase contract or a court, the earnest money shall be returned to the buyer.

   [AS TO (b) THROUGH (d) BELOW, THE PARTIES SHOULD CHECK THE ONE PARAGRAPH WHICH APPLIES].

   ☐ (b) Due to fault of the buyer, as determined by the parties to the purchase contract or a court, the earnest money shall first go toward paying the commission Sponsoring Broker would have earned in the sale, and the balance, if any, shall go to Seller.

   ☐ (c) Due to the fault of the buyer, as determined by the parties to the purchase contract or a court, the earnest money shall be distributed to the Seller, less any cost of advertising or reasonable expenses incurred by Sponsoring Broker.

   ☐ (d) Due to fault of the buyer, as determined by the parties to the purchase contract or a court, the earnest money shall be distributed to the Seller.

7. Seller agrees that for the purpose of marketing Seller's property, Sponsoring Broker shall place Seller's property in the Multiple Listing Service(s) in which Sponsoring Broker is a member.

Figure 6.1: Exclusive Seller Representation Contract (continued)

8. Seller makes the following elections with regard to having Seller's property displayed on any Internet site:

    (circle YES or NO to all that apply)

    - Display listing on any Internet site, including social media such as Facebook, etc.:   YES   NO

    - Display Seller's property address on Internet: YES   NO

    > **Seller understands and acknowledges that if Seller circles "NO" for the above two options, consumers who conduct searches for listings on the Internet will not see the corresponding information about Seller's property in response to their searches.**
    >
    > _____   _____   _____
    > **Seller's Initials**   **Seller's Initials**   **Date**

    - Allow for automatic valuation tools to be used for Seller's listing: YES   NO

    - Allow for blogging or comments to be used or made regarding Seller's listing: YES   NO

9. Seller(s) acknowledge(s) that they have been informed of the responsibilities imposed upon sellers under the Residential Real Property Disclosure Act. Seller agrees to comply with the requirements of this Act to the best of Seller's ability and to not knowingly give any false or inaccurate information regarding the disclosures required by that Act. Seller also acknowledges compliance with any other applicable disclosure laws.

10. Sponsoring Broker designates _____, ("Seller's Designated Agent"), a licensee(s) affiliated with Sponsoring Broker as the only legal agent(s) of the Seller. Sponsoring Broker reserves the right to name additional designated agents when in Sponsoring Broker's discretion it is necessary. If additional designated agents are named, Seller shall be informed in writing within a reasonable time. (ADD IF DESIRED: Seller acknowledges that Seller's Designated Agent may from time to time have another licensee, who is not an agent of Seller, sit an open house of Seller's property or provide similar support in the marketing of Seller's property.) Seller understands and agrees that this agreement is a contract for Sponsoring Broker to market Seller's property and that Seller's Designated Agent(s) is (are) the only legal agent(s) of Seller. Seller's Designated Agent will be primarily responsible for the direct marketing and sale of Seller's property.

11. Seller has been informed that potential buyers may elect to employ the services of a licensed real estate broker or licensee as their own agent (buyer's agent).

12. **DISCLOSURE AND CONSENT TO DUAL AGENCY**

    NOTE TO CONSUMER: THIS SECTION SERVES THREE PURPOSES. FIRST, IT DISCLOSES THAT A REAL ESTATE LICENSEE MAY POTENTIALLY ACT AS A DUAL AGENT, THAT IS, REPRESENT MORE THAN ONE PARTY TO THE TRANSACTION. SECOND, THIS SECTION EXPLAINS THE CONCEPT OF DUAL AGENCY. THIRD, THIS SECTION SEEKS YOUR CONSENT TO ALLOW THE REAL ESTATE LICENSEE TO ACT AS A DUAL AGENT. A LICENSEE MAY LEGALLY ACT AS A DUAL AGENT ONLY WITH YOUR CONSENT. BY CHOOSING TO SIGN THIS SECTION, YOU ARE CONSENTING TO DUAL AGENCY REPRESENTATION.

    The undersigned _____, ("Licensee" / "Seller's Designated Agent"), may
    (insert name(s) of Licensee undertaking dual representation)

    undertake a dual representation (represent both the seller or landlord and the buyer or tenant) for the sale or lease of property. The undersigned acknowledge they were informed of the possibility of this type of representation. Before signing this document please read the following:

    Representing more than one party to a transaction presents a conflict of interest since both clients may rely upon Licensee's advice and the client's respective interests may be adverse to each other. Licensee will undertake this representation only with the written consent of ALL clients in the transaction.

    Any agreement between the clients as to a final contract price and other terms is a result of negotiations between the clients acting in their own best interests and on their own behalf. You acknowledge that Licensee has explained the implications of dual representation, including the risks involved, and understand that you have been advised to seek independent advice from your advisors or attorneys before signing any documents in this transaction.

    WHAT A LICENSEE CAN DO FOR CLIENTS WHEN ACTING AS A DUAL AGENT

    1. Treat all clients honestly.
    2. Provide information about the property to the buyer or tenant.
    3. Disclose all latent material defects in the property that are known to the Licensee.
    4. Disclose financial qualification of the buyer or tenant to the seller or landlord.
    5. Explain real estate terms.
    6. Help the buyer or tenant to arrange for property inspections.

Figure 6.1: Exclusive Seller Representation Contract (continued)

7. Explain closing costs and procedures.

8. Help the buyer compare financing alternatives.

9. Provide information about comparable properties that have sold so both clients may make educated decisions on what price to accept or offer.

WHAT LICENSEE CANNOT DISCLOSE TO CLIENTS WHEN ACTING AS A DUAL AGENT

1. Confidential information that Licensee may know about a client, without that client's permission.

2. The price or terms the seller or landlord will take other than the listing price without permission of the seller or landlord.

3. The price or terms the buyer or tenant is willing to pay without permission of the buyer or tenant.

4. A recommended or suggested price or terms the buyer or tenant should offer.

5. A recommended or suggested price or terms the seller or landlord should counter with or accept.

If either client is uncomfortable with this disclosure and dual representation, please let Licensee know. You are not required to sign this section unless you want to allow the Licensee to proceed as a Dual Agent in this transaction.

By initialing here and signing below, you acknowledge that you have read and understand this form and voluntarily consent to the Licensee acting as a Dual Agent (that is, to represent BOTH the seller or landlord and the buyer or tenant) should that become necessary.

_____   _____   _____
Seller's initials   Seller's initials   Date

13. Sponsoring Broker is authorized to show the property to prospective buyers represented by buyer's agents, and Sponsoring Broker, in its sole discretion, may pay a part of the above commission to buyer's agent or other cooperating agents. Sponsoring Broker is authorized in its sole discretion to determine with which brokers it will cooperate, and the amount of compensation that it will offer cooperating brokers in the sale of Seller's property. Seller acknowledges that the compensation offered to such cooperating brokers may vary from broker to broker.

14. Seller understands that Sponsoring Broker and/or Designated Agent may have previously represented a buyer who is interested in your property. During that representation, Sponsoring Broker and/or Designated Agent may have learned material information about the buyer that is considered confidential. Under the law, neither Sponsoring Broker nor Designated Agent may disclose any such confidential information to Seller.

15. Seller understands and agrees that other licensees affiliated with Sponsoring Broker, other than Seller's Designated Agent(s), may represent the actual or prospective buyer of Seller's property. Further, Seller understands and agrees that if the property is sold through the efforts of a licensee affiliated with Sponsoring Broker who represents the Buyer, the other licensee affiliated with Sponsoring Broker will be acting as a buyer's designated agent.

16. Seller agrees to immediately refer to Seller's Designated Agent all prospective buyers or brokers who contact Seller for any reason and to provide Seller's Designated Agent with their names and addresses.

17. Sponsoring Broker and Seller's Designated Agent are authorized in their sole discretion, to place a for sale sign on the property, if permitted by law, to remove all other such signs, to place a lockbox on the property, to have access to the property at all reasonable times for the purpose of showing it to prospective buyers, to cooperate with other brokers and to use pictures of the property and to expose property information and/or images to the Internet for marketing purposes.

18. Seller agrees to provide a limited home warranty program from _____ at a charge of $_____ plus options, if any. Seller acknowledges that the home warranty program is a limited warranty with a deductible. Seller acknowledges receipt of the application for such home warranty program. [STRIKE THROUGH IF NOT OFFERED].

19. Items such as wall-to-wall carpeting, solar panels, garage door openers, smoke detectors, built-in appliances, light fixtures, landscaping and many indoor and outdoor decorative items may legally be "fixtures" and if so, they must remain with the house unless specifically excluded in the Purchase Agreement. (Discuss this matter with Seller's Designated Agent to avoid uncertainty for all parties regarding what you may take and what should remain with the house, and make specific provisions for these items in the Purchase Agreement.)

20. Seller understands that the information which Seller provides to Seller's Designated Agent as listing information will be used to advertise Seller's property to the public, and it is essential that this information be accurate. SELLER HAS EITHER REVIEWED THE MLS LISTING INPUT SHEET AND REPRESENTS THAT THE INFORMATION CONTAINED IN IT IS TRUE AND ACCURATE TO THE BEST OF SELLER'S KNOWLEDGE, OR SELLER UNDERSTANDS THAT THEY HAVE AN OBLIGATION TO PROVIDE ACCURATE, TRUTHFUL INFORMATION TO BE PUT IN THE MLS INPUT SHEET AND HEREBY PROMISES TO FULFILL THIS OBLIGATION. Although Seller is listing Seller's property in its present physical condition ("as is" condition), Seller understands that Seller may be held responsible by a buyer for any latent or hidden, undisclosed defects or concealed defects in the property which are known to Seller but which are not disclosed to the buyer.

21. Notice to Seller regarding recordings within the property

Figure 6.1: Exclusive Seller Representation Contract (continued)

a. In the event Seller has a recording system in the Seller's property which records or transmits audio, Seller understands that recording or transmitting of audio may result in violation of state and/or federal wiretapping laws. Seller hereby releases and indemnifies Sponsoring Broker, Sponsoring Broker's Designated Agent(s) and employees from any liability which may result from any recording or transmitting in the property.

b. Seller understands that while potential buyers viewing the property should not engage in photography, videography, or videotelephony in the property without prior written permission, such recordings or transmissions may occur. Seller should remove any items of a personal nature Seller does not wish to have recorded or transmitted. Seller hereby releases Sponsoring Broker, Sponsoring Broker's Designated Agent(s) and employees from any liability which may result from any recording or transmission in the property.

22. Seller agrees to save and hold Sponsoring Broker harmless from all claims, disputes, litigation, judgments, and costs (including reasonable attorney's fees) arising from Seller's breach of this agreement, from any incorrect information or misrepresentation supplied by Seller or from any material facts, including latent defects, that are known to Seller that Seller fails to disclose.

23. This contract shall be binding upon and inure to the benefit of the heirs, administrators, successors, and assigns of the parties hereto. This contract can only be amended by a writing signed by the parties.

24. The parties agree that electronic signature on this Contract and facsimile of PDF copies of the same shall have the same legal force and effect as original signatures.

25. THE PARTIES UNDERSTAND AND AGREE THAT IT IS ILLEGAL FOR EITHER OF THE PARTIES TO REFUSE TO DISPLAY OR SELL SELLER'S PROPERTY TO ANY PERSON ON THE BASIS OF RACE, COLOR, RELIGION, SEX, NATIONAL ORIGIN, ANCESTRY, AGE, ORDER OF PROTECTION STATUS, MARITAL STATUS, PHYSICAL OR MENTAL HANDICAP, MILITARY STATUS, SEXUAL ORIENTATION, GENDER IDENTITY, UNFAVORABLE DISCHARGE FROM MILITARY SERVICE, FAMILIAL STATUS, ARREST RECORD, OR ANY OTHER CLASS PROTECTED BY ARTICLE 3 OF THE ILLINOIS HUMAN RIGHTS ACT. THE PARTIES AGREE TO COMPLY WITH ALL APPLICABLE FEDERAL, STATE AND LOCAL FAIR HOUSING LAWS.

Seller hereby acknowledges receipt of a signed copy of this agreement and all attachments. The attachments include the following: [HERE LIST ALL ATTACHMENTS]._____
_____.

(If seller is married or in a civil union both signatures are required)

SELLER:_____   _____, Sponsoring Broker

SELLER:_____   BY:_____

ADDRESS:_____   _____ DATE: _____
                                      Authorized Signer

_____

DATE:_____   PHONE:_____ OFFICE:_____

The undersigned seller(s) agree(s) that _____, Sponsoring Brokerage Company hereinafter referred to as "Sponsoring Broker" and any authorized representative or agent of Sponsoring Broker are hereby given express consent to contact the undersigned by telephone by means of calls and/or text messages, facsimile transmission or electronic mail at the following locations, addresses and/or telephone numbers.

_____   _____
Print Name   Signature

_____   _____
Print Name   Signature

_____   _____
Telephone Number(s)   Facsimile Number(s)

_____
E-mail Address(es)

Disclosures

Illinois law requires that the following disclosures be included with listing contracts.

Disclosure of Material Facts

A broker must not withhold material facts concerning a property of which she has knowledge from any purchaser, prospective purchaser, seller, lessee, lessor, or other party to the transaction. Material facts are any facts on which a reasonable person would base a contractual decision.

Disclosure of Interest

A broker must disclose in writing to the parties to the transaction her status as a broker and any direct or indirect interest she has or may have in the subject property. For example, if the buyer or the seller is a licensed broker, this must be clearly stated in the contract.

Disclosure of Special Compensation

A broker is prohibited from accepting "any finder fees, commissions, discounts, kickbacks, or other compensation from any financial institution, title insurance company, or any other person other than another licensee, without full disclosure in writing of such receipt to all parties to the transaction." Sponsored licensees receive any such compensation only through their respective sponsoring brokers. Such fees may also be in violation of federal law.

Earnest Money and Purchaser Default

When any written listing includes provision that the seller will not receive the earnest money deposit if the purchaser defaults, this fact must appear emphasized in letters larger than those otherwise used in the listing agreement.

Disclosure of Property Condition

Seller disclosure of property conditions is required by law in Illinois. These disclosures normally cover a wide range of structural, mechanical, and other conditions that a prospective purchaser should know about to make an informed decision. Brokers should caution sellers to make truthful disclosures to avoid litigation arising from fraudulent or careless misrepresentations. A property disclosure statement must be given to the buyer before an offer is made and accepted or the buyer will have three business days in which to rescind the contract, based on any negative disclosures.

In Illinois, many listing brokers choose to leave the disclosure statement on display with their sellers and available in the home itself for all showings or it may be included with the other required disclosures as an attachment on the MLS.

In addition, a lead paint disclosure is required on any property built before 1978, and a radon disclosure may also be required of the seller.

Listing Agreement Issues

In addition to the foregoing, there are several other issues to address in the listing agreement.

Broker's Authority and Responsibilities

The contract should specify details such as whether the broker may place a sign on the property or advertise and market the property through social media. Another major consideration is whether the broker is permitted to notify buyers' brokers of the listing through an MLS and the internet. It should also address whether or not the broker may accept earnest money on behalf of the seller and the responsibilities for holding such funds.

Names of All Parties to the Contract

Anyone who has an ownership interest in the property must be identified and must sign the listing to validate it. If the property is owned under some form of co-ownership, that fact must be clearly established.

If the property is the principal residence of a married couple, both spouses must sign the listing agreement, even if only one is on title, in order to release homestead rights. If the property is in the possession of a tenant, that should be disclosed and instructions given on how the property is to be shown to a prospective buyer.

Brokerage Firm

The brokerage company name, the sponsoring broker, and the designated agent of the sponsoring broker must all be identified.

Listing Price

This is the proposed gross sales price. The seller's proceeds will be reduced by unpaid real estate taxes, special assessments, mortgage or trust deed debts, and any other outstanding obligations.

Real Property and Personal Property

The listing agreement must note that certain items on the property may be fixtures and if so they must remain with the property unless explicitly identified in the subsequent purchase contract between the seller and buyer.

Leased Equipment

It must be determined whether leased equipment—security systems, cable television boxes, water softeners, special antennas—will be left with the property. If so, the seller is responsible for notifying the equipment's lessor of the change of property ownership.

Description of the Premises

In addition to the street address, the legal description, lot size, and tax parcel number (property index number or PIN) may be required for future insertion into a purchase offer.

The street address of the property is sufficient for listing agreements to be valid and enforceable under Illinois law. However, it is advisable to include the parcel number or Property Index Number (PIN), and most listing agreements include a blank for it. This number can be acquired from the county tax database.

Evidence of Ownership

A warranty deed, title insurance policy, or abstract of title with an attorney's opinion can be used for proof of title.

Encumbrances

All liens must be paid by the seller or be assumed by the buyer at the closing. Identify as much information as possible about existing loans, such as the name and address of each lender, the type of loan, the loan number, the loan balance, the interest rate, the monthly payment, and if the loan can be prepaid without penalty. Determine whether the buyer can assume the present loan, and if so, under what circumstances and if there is any possibility of seller financing.

Physical encroachments on the property (such as a fence) and their legal implications are questions best referred to an attorney, even if they were noted in the listing file.

Zoning

Identify current zoning for the property.

Property Taxes

Ask about current (or most recent year's) property taxes and determine the amount of any outstanding special assessments and whether they will be paid by the seller or assumed by the buyer.

Home Warranty Program

In some situations, it may be advisable to offer a *home warranty* with the property. These warranties often benefit both the seller and the buyer. Most real estate offices have information about various home warranty programs available to homeowners. Brokers must disclose in writing any monies sent to them by a home warranty company.

Commission

The circumstances under which a commission will be paid must be specifically stated in the contract. The fee can be either a percentage or a flat rate and is usually paid at closing directly by the seller or the party handling the closing. Negotiation of commission is a key discussion point in creating a listing contract. The commission amount is fully negotiable between the parties. The contract should indicate that all commissions have been negotiated between the seller and the broker. It is illegal for commissions to be set by any regulatory agency, trade association, or other industry organization.

 By law, written listing agreements in Illinois must state that no change in the amount of the commission or time of payment will be valid or binding unless the change is made in writing and signed by all parties.

Warranties by the Owner

The owner is responsible for certain assurances and disclosures that are vital to the agent's ability to market the property successfully. Is the property suitable for its intended purpose?

Does it comply with the appropriate zoning and building codes? Will it be transferred to the buyer in essentially the same condition as it was originally presented, considering repairs or alterations to be made as provided for in a purchase contract? Are there any known defects?

Indemnification ("Hold Harmless") Wording

The seller and the broker may agree to hold each other harmless (i.e., not to sue one another) for any incorrect information supplied by one to the other.

A client is not vicariously liable for the acts or omissions of a licensee in providing brokerage services for or on behalf of the client.

Nondiscrimination (Equal Opportunity) Wording

Federal, state, and local fair housing laws protect a variety of different groups and individuals. The seller must understand that the property will be shown and offered without regard to the race, color, creed, or religious preference, national origin, family status, sex, age, or disability of the prospective buyer.

Minimum Services

All exclusive brokerage agreements must specify that the sponsoring broker, through its sponsored licensees, will provide the following required **minimum services**:

- Accept delivery of and present to the client all offers and counteroffers to buy, sell, or lease the client's property or the property the client seeks to purchase or lease
- Assist the client in developing, communicating, negotiating, and presenting offers, counteroffers, and notices that relate to the offers and counteroffers until a lease or purchase agreement is signed and all contingencies are satisfied or waived
- Answer the client's questions relating to the offers, counteroffers, notices, and contingencies

The Signatures of the Parties

All parties identified in the listing contract must sign the contract, including all individuals who have a legal interest in the property.

The Date the Contract is Signed

This date may differ from the date the contract actually becomes effective (e.g., if a sponsored licensee takes the listing and then must have the sponsoring broker sign the contract to accept employment under its terms).

Additional Information

Although not required on the listing agreement, the listing broker should also obtain any additional information that would make the property more appealing and marketable, such as neighborhood amenities. Such amenities might include information about schools, parks and recreational areas, places of worship, and public transportation.

Any written brokerage agreement must provide either an automatic expiration within a definite period of time or provide the client with a right to terminate the agreement annually by giving no more than 30 days' prior written notice.

Broker Protection

The *broker protection clause* provides that the property owner will pay the listing broker a commission if, within a specified time period after the listing agreement expires, the owner transfers property title to someone who saw the property while it was listed with the broker. The protection clause protects brokers from losing a commission on a sale involving buyers who saw the property while it was listed and to discourage others from trying to reach private arrangements with sellers.

The length of time for a protection clause is set by agreement. Any new buyers the sellers might procure on their own after expiration of the listing are not affected.

Each brokerage agreement for a residential property of four units or less that provides for a protection period subsequent to its termination date must also provide that no commission or fee will be due and owing pursuant to the terms of the brokerage agreement if, during the protection period, a valid, written brokerage agreement is entered into with another licensed real estate broker.

BUYER AGENCY AGREEMENTS

Like a listing agreement, a **buyer agency agreement** is an employment contract. In this case, the broker is employed as the buyer's agent. The buyer, rather than the seller, is the principal. The purpose of the agreement is to find a suitable property. A buyer agency agreement gives the buyer a degree of representation possible only in a fiduciary relationship. A buyer's broker must protect the buyer's interests at all points in the transaction.

Types of Buyer Agency Agreements

The following three basic types of buyer agency agreements exist:

- *Exclusive buyer agency agreement.* Also called an exclusive right to represent, this is a true exclusive agency agreement. The buyer is legally bound to compensate the broker whenever the buyer purchases a property of the type described in the contract. The broker is entitled to payment regardless of whether she locates the property. Even if the buyer finds the property independently, the broker is entitled to payment. A sample exclusive buyer agency contract appears in Figure 6.2.

- *Exclusive-agency buyer agency agreement.* Like an exclusive buyer agency agreement, this is an exclusive contract between the buyer and the broker. However, this agreement limits the broker's right to payment. Brokers are only entitled to payment if they locate the property the buyer ultimately purchases. The buyer retains the right to locate and buy property without financial obligation to the broker. Under this type of agreement, brokers risk "educating" buyers about the purchase process and showing many homes only to find that the buyers avoid compensating the broker by working directly with the owners of an unlisted property.

- *Open buyer agency agreement.* This agreement is a nonexclusive buyer representation agreement between a broker and a buyer. It permits the buyer to enter into similar agreements with an unlimited number of brokers. The buyer is obligated to compensate only the broker who locates the property the buyer ultimately purchases.

Buyer Representation Issues

A broker and a buyer must discuss a number of issues before entering into a written buyer agency agreement. The broker should conduct a counseling session with the buyer to determine the buyer's needs and goals, financial capabilities, and motivation. This session gives the broker the ability to educate the buyer on the buying process and market conditions and to formulate a strategy for finding the right property. In addition, compensation needs to be addressed and negotiated in the event there is no offer of cooperative compensation from the listing broker to the buyer's broker.

The broker should make the same disclosures to the buyer that the broker would make in a listing agreement. The broker should explain the forms of agency available and the parties' rights and responsibilities under each type of agreement. The specific scope of services provided to a buyer-client need to be clearly explained.

In Illinois, it is common for the listing broker to share the listing fee with the buyer's broker. Note that this is a clear case where commission does not equate to agency or representation. Discussions regarding a commission or fee provided by the buyer may still take place. A broker is free to negotiate for compensation from any buyer for whom service was provided in an agency capacity. However, if the broker receives compensation from more than one source in a transaction, it always needs to be disclosed in writing to the client.

QUALIFYING BUYER SERVICES

The buyer's broker provides the following services throughout the real estate transaction:

- *Needs assessment.* Determine and evaluate the needs, wants, and financial capacity of the buyer.

- *Property selection.* Locate the best property for the buyer by notifying buyers of new listings and for-sale-by-owner properties.

- *Viewing properties.* Provide an objective evaluation of the property and show buyers how to compare properties. Disclose material facts that are pertinent to the property.

- *Negotiate.* Strategize with the buyer, suggesting techniques that strengthen the buyer's position. Then, implement those strategies on the buyer's behalf. Provide price counseling and prepare a comparative market analysis (CMA) on the property the buyer is considering.

- *Follow-up.* Resolve any issues that could prevent a closing from occurring. Provide ongoing communications with the client, preferably by email for maintaining records.

Figure 6.2: Exclusive Buyer Representation/Exclusive Right to Purchase Contract

ILLINOIS REALTORS®
EXCLUSIVE BUYER REPRESENTATION/
EXCLUSIVE RIGHT TO PURCHASE CONTRACT
(DUAL AGENCY DISCLOSURE AND CONSENT INCLUDED)

In consideration of _____'s (Brokerage Company hereinafter referred to as "Sponsoring Broker") agreement to designate a licensee affiliated with Sponsoring Broker to act as an agent of the Buyer for the purpose of identifying and negotiating to acquire real estate for _____ ("Buyer"), the Buyer hereby grants to Sponsoring Broker the relationship as marked in Section 1 of the Contract.

SECTION 1: TYPE OF REPRESENTATION
(Instruction: check the box next to desired choice – choose one):

☐ **Exclusive Representation**. Buyer understands that this exclusive right to represent Buyer (Exclusive Representation) means that if the Buyer makes an acquisition of property, whether through the efforts of Sponsoring Broker and their agents or through the efforts of another real estate office or agent, Buyer will be obligated to compensate Sponsoring Broker pursuant to Section 8 of this Contract. This Exclusive Agency shall be effective for the following area: _____. The term "acquisition" shall include the purchase, lease, exchange or option of real estate. Buyer reserves the right to purchase on Buyer's own without assistance of the Sponsoring Broker or any other broker.

☐ **Exclusive Right to Acquire**. Buyer understands that this "exclusive right to purchase" means that if Buyer acquires any property, whether through the efforts of the Buyer, Sponsoring Broker and their agents, another real estate agency besides Sponsoring Broker's, or other third party, Buyer will be obligated to compensate Sponsoring Broker pursuant to Section 8 of this Contract. This exclusive right to acquire shall be effective for the following area:_____. "Acquisition" shall include the purchase, lease, exchange or option of real estate.

Sponsoring Broker designates and Buyer accepts_____ ("Buyer's Designated Agent") as the legal agent(s) of Buyer for the purpose of representing Buyer in the acquisition of real estate by Buyer. Buyer understands and agrees that neither Sponsoring Broker nor any other licensees affiliated with Sponsoring Broker (except as provided for herein) will be acting as legal agent of the Buyer. Sponsoring Broker shall have the discretion to appoint a substitute designated agent for Buyer as Sponsoring Broker determines necessary. Buyer shall be advised within a reasonable time of any such substitution.

SECTION 2: TERM (Check One)
☐ This Contract shall be effective until 11:59 p.m. on _____, 20____, when it shall then terminate. This Contract is irrevocable and can be terminated prior to the termination date only by written agreement of the parties. If within ____ days after the termination of this Contract (i.e. the protection period), Buyer purchases any property to which Buyer was introduced by Buyer's Designated Agent, then Buyer agrees to pay Sponsoring Broker the compensation provided for in Section 8. However, no compensation will be due to Sponsoring Broker if, during this protection period, Buyer enters into a separate buyer representation agreement with another broker.
☐ This Contract shall automatically renew on _____, 20____, and on _____ of each succeeding year (each date to be known herein as "Renewal Date") unless Buyer provides Sponsoring Broker written notice of Buyer's intention to not renew this contract no more than thirty (30) days and no less than _____ (____) days prior to the Renewal Date.

SECTION 3: BUYER'S DESIGNATED AGENT'S DUTIES
(a)   To use Buyer's Designated Agent's best efforts to identify properties listed in the multiple listing service that meet the Buyer's specifications relating to location, price, features and amenities, as identified on the attached Buyer's Information Checklist.
    • List here any sources for properties other than the multiple listing service Buyer would like Buyer's Designated Agent to research: _____.
(b)   To arrange for inspections of properties identified by the Buyer as potentially appropriate for acquisition.
(c)   To advise Buyer as to the pricing of comparable properties.
(d)   To assist Buyer in the negotiation of a contract acceptable to the Buyer for the acquisition of property.
(e)   To provide reasonable safeguards for confidential information that the Buyer discloses to Buyer's Designated Agent.
(f)   Other services: _____.

SECTION 4: SPONSORING BROKER'S DUTIES
(a)   To provide through Buyer's Designated Agent, those brokerage services set forth in Section 15-75 of the Illinois Real Estate License Act.
(b)   To provide Buyer's Designated Agent with assistance and advice as necessary in Buyer's Designated Agent's work on Buyer's behalf.
(c)   To make the managing broker affiliated with Sponsoring Broker, or his /her designated representative, available to consult with Buyer's Designated Agent as to Buyer's negotiations for the acquisition of real estate, who will maintain the confidence of Buyer's confidential information.
(d)   To make other licensees affiliated with licensees aware of Buyer's general specifications for real property.
(e)   As needed, to designate one or more licensees as Designated Agent(s) of Buyer.

SECTION 5: BUYER'S DUTIES
(a)   To complete the Buyer's checklist which will provide Buyer's specifications for the real estate Buyer is seeking.
(b)   To work exclusively with Buyer's Designated Agent to identify and acquire real estate during the time that this Contract is in

Figure 6.2: Exclusive Buyer Representation/Exclusive Right to Purchase Contract (continued)

force.

(c) To supply relevant financial information that may be necessary to permit Buyer's Designated Agent to fulfill Agent's obligations under this Contract.

(d) To be available upon reasonable notice and at reasonable hours to inspect properties that seem to meet Buyer's specifications.

(e) To pay Sponsoring Broker according to the terms specified in Section 8 of this Contract.

SECTION 6: REPRESENTING OTHER BUYER

Buyer understands that Buyer's Designated Agent has **no** duty to represent only Buyer, and that Buyer's Designated Agent may represent other prospective buyers who may be interested in acquiring the same property or properties that Buyer is interested in acquiring, subject to Section 15-15(b) of the Illinois Real Estate License Act regarding contemporaneous offers.

SECTION 7: DISCLOSURE AND CONSENT TO DUAL AGENCY

NOTE TO CONSUMER: THIS SECTION SERVES THREE PURPOSES. FIRST, IT DISCLOSES THAT A REAL ESTATE LICENSEE MAY POTENTIALLY ACT AS A DUAL AGENT, THAT IS, REPRESENT MORE THAN ONE PARTY TO THE TRANSACTION. SECOND, THIS SECTION EXPLAINS THE CONCEPT OF DUAL AGENCY. THIRD, THIS SECTION SEEKS YOUR CONSENT TO ALLOW THE REAL ESTATE LICENSEE TO ACT AS A DUAL AGENT. A LICENSEE MAY LEGALLY ACT AS A DUAL AGENT ONLY WITH YOUR CONSENT. BY CHOOSING TO SIGN THIS SECTION, YOU ARE CONSENTING TO DUAL AGENCY REPRESENTATION.

The undersigned, _____,("Licensee"/"Buyer's
　　　　　　　　　　　　　　　　　　insert name(s) of licensee(s)

Designated Agent") may undertake a dual representation (represent both the seller or landlord and the buyer or tenant) for the sale or lease of property. The undersigned acknowledge they were informed of the possibility of this type of representation. Before signing this document please read the following:

Representing more than one party to a transaction presents a conflict of interest since both clients may rely upon Licensee's advice and the client's respective interests may be adverse to each other. Licensee will undertake this representation only with the written consent of ALL clients in the transaction.

Any agreement between the clients as to a final contract price and other terms is a result of negotiations between the clients acting in their own best interests and on their own behalf. You acknowledge that Licensee has explained the implications of dual representation, including the risks involved, and understand that you have been advised to seek independent advice from your advisors or attorneys before signing any documents in this transaction.

WHAT A LICENSEE CAN DO FOR CLIENTS WHEN ACTING AS A DUAL AGENT

1. Treat all clients honestly.
2. Provide information about the property to the buyer or tenant.
3. Disclose all latent material defects in the property that are known to the Licensee.
4. Disclose financial qualification of the buyer or tenant to the seller or landlord.
5. Explain real estate terms.
6. Help the buyer or tenant to arrange for property inspections.
7. Explain closing costs and procedures.
8. Help the buyer compare financing alternatives.
9. Provide information about comparable properties that have sold so both clients may make educated decisions on what price to accept or offer.

WHAT LICENSEE CANNOT DISCLOSE TO CLIENTS WHEN ACTING AS A DUAL AGENT

1. Confidential information that Licensee may know about a client, without that client's permission.
2. The price or terms the seller or landlord will take other than the listing price without permission of the seller or landlord.
3. The price or terms the buyer or tenant is willing to pay without permission of the buyer or tenant.
4. A recommended or suggested price or terms the buyer or tenant should offer.
5. A recommended or suggested price or terms the seller or landlord should counter with or accept.

If either client is uncomfortable with this disclosure and dual representation, please let Licensee know. You are not required to sign this section unless you want to allow the Licensee to proceed as a Dual Agent in this transaction.

By initialing here and signing below, you acknowledge that you have read and understand this form and voluntarily consent to the Licensee acting as a Dual Agent (that is, to represent BOTH the seller or landlord and the buyer or tenant) should that become necessary.

_____   _____   _____
Buyer's initials   　　　　　　 Buyer's initials   　　　　　　　 Date

SECTION 8: COMPENSATION

Sponsoring Broker and Buyer expect that Sponsoring Broker's commission will be paid by the seller or seller's broker for Sponsoring

Figure 6.2: Exclusive Buyer Representation/Exclusive Right to Purchase Contract (continued)

Broker's acting as a cooperating agent. However, if Sponsoring Broker is not compensated by seller or seller's broker, or if the amount of compensation paid by seller or seller's broker is not at least _____% of the purchase price (as defined in the local/regional MLS), then Buyer agrees to pay Sponsoring Broker the difference between _____% of the purchase price and what seller or seller's broker actually paid to Sponsoring Broker. This Section applies if the Buyer enters into a contract to acquire real estate during the term of this Contract or the protection period, and such contract results in a closed transaction. Any modification to this Section, including the commission to be paid to Sponsoring Broker, shall be by a separate written agreement to this Contract.

SECTION 9: PREVIOUS REPRESENTATION
Buyer understands that Sponsoring Broker and/or Designated Agent may have previously represented the seller from whom Buyer wishes to purchase property. During that representation, Sponsoring Broker and/or Designated Agent may have learned material information about the seller that is considered confidential. Under the law, neither Sponsoring Broker nor Designated Agent may disclose any such confidential information to Buyer.

SECTION 10: FAILURE TO CLOSE
If a seller or lessor in an agreement made on behalf of Buyer fails to close such agreement, with no fault on the part of Buyer, the Buyer shall have no obligation to pay the commission provided for in Section 8. If such transaction fails to close because of any fault on the part of Buyer, such commission will not be waived, but will be due and payable immediately. In no case shall Sponsoring Broker or Buyer's Designated Agent be obligated to advance funds for the benefit of Buyer in order to complete a closing.

SECTION 11: DISCLAIMER
The Buyer acknowledges that Sponsoring Broker and Buyer's Designated Agent are being retained solely as real estate professionals, and not as attorneys, tax advisors, surveyors, structural engineers, home inspectors, environmental consultants, architects, contractors, or other professional service providers. The Buyer understands that such other professional service providers are available to render advice or services to the Buyer, if desired, at Buyer's expense.

SECTION 12: COSTS OF THIRD-PARTY SERVICES OR PRODUCTS
Buyer agrees to reimburse Sponsoring Broker the cost of any products or services such as surveys, soil tests, title reports and engineering studies, furnished by outside sources immediately when payment is due.

SECTION 13: INDEMNIFICATION OF SPONSORING BROKER
Buyer agrees to indemnify Sponsoring Broker and Buyer's Designated Agent and to hold Sponsoring Broker and Buyer's Designated Agent harmless on account of any and all loss, damage, cost or expense, including attorneys' fees incurred by Sponsoring Broker or Buyer's Designated Agent, arising out of this Contract, or the collection of fees or commission due Sponsoring Broker pursuant to the terms and conditions of this Contract, provided the loss damage, cost, expense or attorneys' fees do not result because of Sponsoring Broker's or Buyer's Designated Agent's own negligence or willful and wanton misconduct.

SECTION 14: ASSIGNMENT BY BUYERS
No assignment of Buyer's interest under this Contract and no assignment of rights in real property obtained for Buyer pursuant to this Contract shall operate to defeat any of Sponsoring Broker's rights under this exclusive representation contract.

SECTION 15: NONDISCRIMINATION
THE PARTIES UNDERSTAND AND AGREE THAT IT IS ILLEGAL FOR EITHER OF THE PARTIES TO REFUSE TO DISPLAY OR SELL SELLER'S PROPERTY TO ANY PERSON ON THE BASIS OF RACE, COLOR, RELIGION, SEX, NATIONAL ORIGIN, ANCESTRY, AGE, ORDER OF PROTECTION STATUS, MARITAL STATUS, PHYSICAL OR MENTAL HANDICAP, MILITARY STATUS, SEXUAL ORIENTATION, GENDER IDENTITY, UNFAVORABLE DISCHARGE FROM MILITARY SERVICE, FAMILIAL STATUS, ARREST RECORD OR ANY OTHER CLASS PROTECTED BY ARTICLE 3 OF THE ILLINOIS HUMAN RIGHTS ACT. THE PARTIES AGREE TO COMPLY WITH ALL APPLICABLE FEDERAL, STATE AND LOCAL FAIR HOUSING LAWS.

SECTION 16: MODIFICATION OF THIS CONTRACT
No modification of any of the terms of this Contract shall be valid and binding upon the parties or entitled to enforcement unless such modification has first been reduced to writing and signed by the parties.

SECTION 17: ELECTRONIC SIGNATURES
The parties agree that electronic signatures on this Contract and facsimile or PDF copies of the same shall have the same legal force and effect as original signatures.

SECTION 18: RECORDINGS WITHIN THE PROPERTY
Prior to photographing, videographing or videotelephoning the property without prior written permission of the seller, Buyer should speak with an attorney.

Also, Buyer should be aware that the seller may have a security system that records or allows for remote monitoring of the property, including recording or broadcasting audio. Sellers may be able to listen to conversations in their properties and Buyer should be aware that any discussions of negotiation strategies held in the property may not be confidential. [Buyer hereby releases Sponsoring Broker, Buyer's Designated Agent and employees from any liability which may result from any recording in the property.]

SECTION 19: ENTIRE AGREEMENT
This Contract constitutes the entire agreement between the parties relating to the subject thereof, and any prior agreements pertaining hereto, whether oral or written have been merged and integrated into this Contract.

Figure 6.2: Exclusive Buyer Representation/Exclusive Right to Purchase Contract (continued)

Unit 6

This Contract may be executed in multiple copies and signature of Buyer(s) hereon acknowledge(s) that Buyer(s) has(ve) received a signed copy.

_____   Accepted by:

Buyer   _____, Sponsoring Broker

_____

Buyer   BY:_____

Buyer's Address: _____ DATE: _____

_____   Authorized Signer

_____   PHONE:_____ OFFICE:_____

Date:_____

The undersigned buyer(s) agree(s) that _____, Sponsoring Brokerage Company hereinafter referred to as "Sponsoring Broker" and any authorized representative or agent of Sponsoring Broker are hereby given express consent to contact the undersigned by telephone by means of calls and/or text messages, facsimile transmission or electronic mail at the following locations, addresses and/or telephone numbers.

_____   _____

Print Name   Signature

_____   _____

Print Name   Signature

_____   _____

Telephone Number(s)   Facsimile Number(s)

_____

E-mail Address(es)

SAMPLE

THE BUYING PROCESS

When the buyers have found the right property, the next step is to prepare and negotiate an offer that will lead to a signed sales contract between the seller and the buyer. The buyer's broker should prepare a CMA to establish a price for the buyer to offer. Factors to take into consideration include the following:

- *Property condition.* Does the property need a lot of repairs?

- *Length of time on the market.* This indicates the selling pace of the market, the level of inventory, or a potential problem with the property.

- *Supply and demand.* Essentially, when supply increases and demand remains stable, prices go down; when demand increases and supply remains stable, prices go up. Greater supply means sellers need to attract more buyers, so they lower prices. Greater demand means sellers can raise their prices because buyers compete for the product.

- *Seller's motivation.* Is the property in distress, pre-foreclosure, or requiring a short sale?

- *Terms and contingencies.* The fewer the contingencies, the stronger the offer, making it more attractive to the seller or bank (if property is bank owned or requires bank approval for a short sale).

The buyer's broker is obligated to keep confidential all confidential information received from the client.

When buyer brokers are working with two or more clients who are seeking similar properties in the same price range, the buyer's broker is permitted to show alternative properties to prospective buyers or tenants. Specifically, the buyer's broker does not breach a duty or obligation to the client by showing alternative properties to prospective buyers or tenants, by showing properties in which the client is interested to other prospective buyers or tenants, or by making or preparing **contemporaneous offers** or contracts to purchase or lease the same property.

However, brokers must provide written disclosure to all clients for whom the licensee is preparing or making contemporaneous offers or contracts to purchase or lease the same property and must refer to another designated agent any client that requests such referral (see Figure 6.3).

Figure 6.3: Contemporaneous Offers

ILLINOIS REALTORS®
DISCLOSURE OF CONTEMPORANEOUS OFFERS

_____, an agent (hereinafter referred to as "Designated Agent") with _____ (Brokerage Company, hereinafter referred to as "Sponsoring Broker"), is acting as Designated Agent for more than one prospective buyer or tenant whom the Designated Agent has reason to believe are making or preparing to make contemporaneous offers to purchase or lease the property located at

_____
_____.
(street address or description of property)

At this time, prospective buyers/tenants have the option of being referred to another designated agent who will serve as the agent for buyer/tenant.

Signed by: _____ Dated _____
           (Designated Agent)

BUYER/TENANT ELECTS:
(choose one of the following)

☐ to remain with Designated Agent identified above notwithstanding that another client of Designated Agent may be making a contemporaneous offer to purchase or lease the real property identified above.

☐ to be referred to another designated agent who will act as agent for buyer/tenant in the making of an offer to purchase or lease the real property identified above.

Signed by: _____ Dated _____
           (Buyer or Tenant)

Signed by: _____ Dated _____
           (Buyer or Tenant)

(Note: Give a copy to prospective buyers/tenants and retain a copy for the Sponsoring Broker's file.)

TERMINATION OF BROKER EMPLOYMENT AGREEMENTS

A broker employment agreement is a contract between a broker and a seller or a buyer. Its success depends on the broker's personal and professional efforts. Because broker services are unique, a broker cannot turn over the contract to another broker without the principal's written consent. The client cannot force the broker to perform, but the broker's failure to work diligently toward fulfilling the contract's terms constitutes abandonment of the contract. In the event the contract is abandoned or revoked by the broker, the principal is entitled to sue the broker for damages.

On the other hand, the principal might fail to fulfill the terms of the agreement. For example, a property owner who refuses to cooperate with the broker's reasonable requests, such as allowing the broker to show the property to prospective buyers or refusing to proceed with a completed sales contract, could be liable for damages to the broker. If either party cancels the contract, one party may be liable for damages to the other.

An employment agreement may be canceled for the following reasons:

- When the agreement's purpose is fulfilled
- When the agreement's term expires without a successful transfer
- If the property is destroyed or its use is changed by some force outside the client's control, such as a zoning change or condemnation by eminent domain
- If title to the property is transferred by operation of law, as in the case of the client's bankruptcy or foreclosure
- If the sponsoring broker and the client mutually agree to end the agreement
- If either the sponsoring broker or the client dies or becomes incapacitated
- If either the sponsoring broker or the client breaches the contract, the agreement is terminated and the breaching or canceling party may be liable to the other for damages.

Except as may be provided in a written agreement between the broker and the client, neither a sponsoring broker nor any licensee affiliated with the sponsoring broker owes any further duties to the client after termination, expiration, or completion of performance of the brokerage agreement except

- to account for all monies and property relating to the transaction, and
- to keep confidential all confidential information received during the course of the brokerage agreement.

Expiration of Brokerage Agreement

No licensee may obtain any written brokerage agreement that does not either provide for automatic expiration within a definite period of time or provide the client with a right to terminate the agreement annually by giving no more than 30 days' prior written notice.

SUMMARY

To acquire an inventory of property to sell, brokers must obtain listings. Types of listings include exclusive right-to-sell, exclusive-agency, and open listings. With an exclusive right-to-sell listing, the seller employs only one broker and must pay that broker a commission regardless of whether it is the broker or the seller who finds a buyer, provided the buyer is found within the listing period.

Under exclusive agency, the broker is given the exclusive right to represent the seller, but the seller can avoid paying the broker a commission by selling the property to someone not procured by the broker.

With an open listing, to obtain a commission, the broker must find a ready, willing, and able buyer on the seller's terms before the property is sold by the seller or another broker.

A multiple listing service (MLS) provision may appear in an exclusive right-to-sell or an exclusive-agency listing. It gives the broker the additional authority and obligation to distribute the listing to other members of the broker's multiple listing organization, which enhances the odds of the property selling.

A net listing, which is illegal in some states and considered unethical in most areas, is based on the net price the seller will receive if the property is sold. The broker is free to offer the property for sale at the highest available price and will receive as commission any amount exceeding the seller's stipulated net. Net listings are legal in Illinois but not recommended.

An option listing, which also must be handled with caution, gives the broker the option to purchase the listed property if it does not sell in a specified amount of time.

When listing a property for sale, the seller is concerned about the selling price and the net amount due from the sale. A comparative market analysis (CMA) compares the prices of recently sold properties that are similar to the seller's property. The CMA or a formal appraisal report can be used to help the seller determine a reasonable listing price. The approximate amount the seller will net from the sale is calculated by subtracting the broker's commission, any other seller expenses (attorney, title search), and any existing liens (such as the mortgage) from the approximate sales price.

Listing contracts typically are preprinted forms that include such information as the type of listing agreement, the broker's authority and responsibility under the listing, the listing price, the duration of the listing, information about the property, terms for the payment of commission, details regarding the buyer's possession, and nondiscrimination and antitrust laws. Detailed information about the property may be included in the listing contract or on a separate property data sheet. Disclosure of the broker's agency relationships and agency policies are required. The seller will be expected to comply honestly with legally required disclosures of property conditions.

A buyer agency agreement ensures that a buyer's interest will be represented. Different forms of buyer agency agreements exist—an exclusive buyer agency, an exclusive-agency buyer agency, and open buyer agency. In an exclusive buyer agency, the broker is compensated regardless of whether the broker locates the property. In an exclusive-agency buyer agency, the broker is compensated only if the broker locates the property the buyer purchases. In open buyer agency, the buyer is obligated to compensate only the broker who locates the property the buyer purchases.

A buyer's broker is obligated to find a suitable property for the client, who is owed fiduciary or statutory duties of agency. Buyer agency is regulated by Illinois agency laws.

A buyer agent's duties include providing best efforts to identify properties listed in the MLS that meet the buyer's criteria, arranging for property inspections identified by the buyer as potentially appropriate for purchase, advising the buyer about the pricing of comparable properties, assisting the buyer in the negotiation of a sales contract that is acceptable to the buyer, and preserving confidentiality on all information that buyer discloses to the agent.

A best practice is for the broker to conduct a counseling session with the buyer to determine the buyer's needs and goals, financial capabilities, and motivation. This gives the broker the ability to educate the buyer on the buying process and market conditions and to formulate a strategy for finding the right property.

Qualifying buyer services include needs/financial capabilities assessment, property selection, and viewing properties. The buying process also includes the agent preparing a CMA for the buyer on the selected property and then preparing and negotiating the offer that ultimately leads to a contract between the buyer and seller.

Listings and buyer agency agreements may be terminated for the same reasons as any other agency relationship.

In Illinois, a written exclusive or exclusive-right-to-sell listing agreement must include the list price, the basis for and time of payment of the commission, the term of the listing, the names and signatures of the listing broker and seller, and the address or legal description of the property.

All exclusive brokerage agreements must be in writing according to the Real Estate License Act of 2000. In addition, under the Act, all exclusive brokerage agreements must provide for minimum services.

Detailed information about a property should be included for the record in the listing contract or on a separate property data sheet. Full disclosure of the broker's agency relationship, any interest the broker has in the subject property, material facts pertaining to the property, any guaranteed sales agreement, or any special bonus or fee provided to an agent is required by Illinois law.

A broker who represents a seller may show alternative properties to prospective buyers or tenants. Likewise, a buyer's broker may show the same property to other buyers. However, when the broker is making or preparing offers on the same property, called contemporaneous offers, the broker must provide written disclosure to the other clients, and if requested, must refer a buyer to another designated agent.

UNIT 6 QUIZ

1. A listing taken by a real estate licensee is an agreement between the seller and the
   A. local multiple listing service.
   B. sponsoring broker.
   C. sponsored licensee associated with the firm.
   D. local association of REALTORS®.

2. Which of these is a similarity between an exclusive-agency listing and an exclusive right-to-sell listing?
   A. Under both, the seller retains the right to sell the real estate without the broker's help and without paying the broker a commission.
   B. Under both, the seller authorizes only one particular broker to show the property.
   C. Both types of listings give the responsibility of representing the seller to one broker only.
   D. Both types of listings are open listings.

3. A listing agreement expires on May 2. The seller's house is destroyed by fire on April 25. Which of the following is *TRUE*?
   A. The agreement may be canceled due to the destruction of the property.
   B. The agreement automatically renews after May 2.
   C. The agreement remains active until the property sells.
   D. Listing agreements do not have expiration dates.

4. The seller has listed his property under an exclusive-agency listing with the broker. If the seller sells the property himself during the term of the listing to someone introduced to the property by the seller, he will owe the broker
   A. the full commission.
   B. a partial commission.
   C. no commission.
   D. only reimbursement for the broker's costs.

5. A broker sold a residence for $235,000 and received $12,925 as her commission in accordance with the terms of the listing. What was the broker's commission rate?
   A. 5.7%
   B. 6.25%
   C. 5.5%
   D. 6.5%

6. Under a listing agreement, the broker is entitled to sell the property for any price, as long as the seller receives $185,000. The broker may keep any amount over what the seller needs to net. This type of listing is called
   A. a net listing.
   B. an exclusive right-to-sell listing.
   C. an exclusive-agency listing.
   D. an open listing.

7. Which of these is a similarity between an open listing and an exclusive-agency listing?
   A. Under both, the seller avoids paying the broker a commission if the seller sells the property to someone the broker did not procure.
   B. Both grant a commission to any broker who procures a buyer for the seller's property.
   C. Under both, the broker earns a commission regardless of who sells the property as long as it is sold within the listing period.
   D. Both grant an exclusive right to sell to whatever broker procures a buyer for the seller's property.

8. The final decision on a property's listed price should be determined by the
   A. broker based on information from the local MLS.
   B. broker and the appraiser.
   C. broker and seller equally.
   D. seller based on the broker's CMAs and advice.

9. Which of these statements is *TRUE* of a listing contract?
   A. It is an employment contract for the professional services of the broker.
   B. It obligates the seller to convey the property if the broker procures a ready, willing, and able buyer.
   C. It obligates the broker to work diligently for both the seller and the buyer.
   D. It automatically binds the owner, broker, and MLS to the agreed provisions.

10. A real estate company received a 6.5% commission on the sale of a property. The listing broker in the company received 40% of the commission, or $9,750. What was the selling price of the property?
    A. $55,000
    B. $375,000
    C. $150,000
    D. $250,000

11. A seller listed her residence with a broker. The broker brought an offer at full price and satisfying terms of the listing from buyers who were ready, willing, and able to pay cash for the property. However, the seller changed her mind and rejected the buyers' offer. In this situation, the seller
    A. must sell her property.
    B. is liable to the buyers for specific performance.
    C. owes a commission to the broker.
    D. is liable to the buyers for compensatory damages.

12. A comparative market analysis
    A. is the same as an appraisal.
    B. by law must be completed for each listing taken.
    C. can help the seller price the property.
    D. should not be retained in the property's listing file.

13. A property was listed with a broker who belonged to a multiple listing service and was sold by another member broker for $153,500. The total commission was 6% of the sales price. The selling broker received 60% of the commission, and the listing broker kept the balance. What was the listing broker's commission?
    A. $3,684
    B. $4,464
    C. $5,526
    D. $36,840

14. A seller signs a listing agreement with a broker to sell his home. The agreement states that the broker will receive a 5.5% commission. The home sells for $387,000. What is the net amount that the seller will receive from the sale?
    A. $4,785
    B. $21,285
    C. $365,715
    D. $369,585

15. A real estate broker and a seller enter into a listing agreement that contains the following language: "Seller will receive $100,000 from the sale of the subject property. Any amount greater than $100,000 will constitute Broker's sole and complete compensation." Which of these statements is *TRUE*?
    A. This agreement is an example of an option listing.
    B. The broker may offer the property for any price over $100,000, but the agreement may be unethical.
    C. If the seller's home sells for exactly $100,000, the broker still will be entitled to receive the standard commission in the area.
    D. This type of listing is called an open listing because the selling price is left open.

16. A broker enters into an agreement with a client. The agreement states, "In return for the compensation agreed upon, Broker will assist Client in locating and purchasing a suitable property. Broker will receive the agreed compensation regardless of whether Broker, Client, or some other party locates the property ultimately purchased by Client." What kind of agreement is this?
    A. Exclusive-agency listing
    B. Exclusive-agency buyer agency agreement
    C. Exclusive buyer agency agreement
    D. Open buyer agency agreement

17. Illinois licensees may
    A. refuse to show a property to racial minorities if their sellers so instruct them.
    B. advertise in their own name as long as they hold independent contractor status.
    C. submit a listing to the local MLS.
    D. never take open listings.

18. Under what conditions is a disclosure of contemporaneous offers required?
    A. When a seller's agent is also representing the buyer on the same transaction
    B. When a buyer's agent does not want to engage in dual agency
    C. When a buyer wants the agent to also represent the seller on the sale of her property
    D. When a buyer's agent is acting as designated agent for more than one buyer interested in buying the same property

19. Illinois requires that listing agreements contain
    A. a multiple listing service (MLS) clause.
    B. an automatic extension clause.
    C. an automatic expiration date or statement of client's right to terminate.
    D. a broker protection clause.

20. In Illinois, what brokerage agreements must be in writing?
    A. Exclusive brokerage agreements
    B. Any brokerage agreement
    C. Only listing agreements
    D. Those listed with a REALTOR®

UNIT 7

Interests in Real Estate

LEARNING OBJECTIVES

When you have completed this unit, you will be able to accomplish the following.

› Identify the kinds of limitations on ownership rights that are imposed by government action and the form of conveyance of property.
› Describe the various estates in land and the rights and limitations they convey.
› Explain concepts related to encumbrances and water rights.

KEY TERMS

accretion	encroachment	life estate
appurtenant easement	encumbrance	life tenant
avulsion	Equity in Eminent Domain	littoral rights
condemnation	Act	party wall
conventional life estate	erosion	police power
deed restrictions	escheat	pur autre vie
doctrine of prior	estate in land	quick-take
appropriation	fee simple absolute	reliction
dominant tenement	fee simple defeasible	remainder interest
easement	fee simple determinable	reversionary interest
easement by	freehold estate	riparian rights
condemnation	future interest	servient tenement
easement by necessity	homestead	tacking
easement by prescription	leasehold estate	taxation
easement in gross	license	Uniform Probate Code
eminent domain	lien	waste

OVERVIEW

Ownership of a parcel of real estate is not absolute; that is, it is dependent on the type of interest a person holds in the property. Keep in mind that the power to control one's own property relates to having title of the property and the bundle of legal rights that accompanies the title. Even the most complete ownership the law allows is limited by public and private restrictions. These restrictions are intended to ensure that one owner's use or enjoyment of her property does not interfere with others' use or enjoyment of their property, or with the welfare of the general public. Real estate licensees should have a working knowledge of the restrictions that might limit current or future owners. For example, a zoning ordinance that will not allow a doctor's office to coexist with a residence, a condo association bylaw prohibiting resale without board approval, or an easement allowing the neighbors to use the private beach may not only burden today's purchaser but also deter a future buyer.

GOVERNMENTAL POWERS

MEMORY TIP

Remember the four government powers as PETE:

■ Police power

■ Eminent domain

■ Taxation

■ Escheatment

Individual ownership rights are subject to certain powers, or rights, held by federal, state, and local governments. These limitations on the ownership of real estate are imposed for the general welfare of the community and, therefore, supersede the rights or interests of the individual. Government powers include police power, eminent domain, taxation, and escheatment.

Police Power

Every state has the power to enact legislation to preserve order, protect the public health and safety, and promote the general welfare of its citizens. That authority is called a state's **police power**. The state's authority is passed on to municipalities and counties through legislation called *enabling acts*. What is identified as being in the public interest can vary considerably from state to state and region to region. For example, police power is used to enact environmental protection laws, zoning ordinances, and building codes. Regulations that govern the use, occupancy, size, location, and construction of real estate also fall within government police powers.

MEMORY TIP

Eminent domain is the government's right to acquire property for public use.

Condemnation is the actual process of taking the property.

Eminent Domain

Eminent domain is the right of the government to acquire privately owned real estate for public use, private or economic development purposes. **Condemnation** is the process by which the government exercises this right, by either judicial or administrative proceedings. In the taking of property, just compensation must be paid to the owner, and the rights of the property owner must be protected by due process of law. In short, eminent domain is the right; condemnation is the process.

Ideally, the public agency and the owner of the property in question agree on compensation through direct negotiation, and the government purchases the property for a price considered fair by the owner. In some cases, the owner may simply dedicate the property to the government as a site for a school, park, or another beneficial use. Sometimes, however, in cases where the owner's consent cannot be obtained, the government agency can initiate condemnation proceedings to acquire the property.

Local units of government and quasi-governmental bodies are given the power of eminent domain by the Illinois Constitution and by the Illinois Code of Civil Procedure. In certain situations, Illinois law permits a summary proceeding in which a plaintiff/condemnor may obtain immediate fee simple title to real property, including the rights of possession and use. Such a proceeding in Illinois is called a **quick-take**.

In a quick-take, the plaintiff must deposit a sum with the county treasurer that is preliminarily considered by the court to be just compensation; this can be litigated later. A quick-take might be appropriate, for example, in the following circumstances:

- The state of Illinois or the Illinois Toll Highway Authority takes property to construct, maintain, and operate highways.

- A sanitary district takes property to remove obstructions in a river, such as the Des Plaines River or Illinois River.

- An airport authority takes property to provide additional land for airport purposes.

Generally, states delegate their power of eminent domain to quasi-public bodies and publicly held companies responsible for various facets of public service. For example, a public housing authority might take privately owned land to build low-income housing, or the state's land-clearance commission or redevelopment authority could use the power of eminent domain to make way for urban renewal. If there were no other feasible way to accomplish its aims, a railway, utility company, or highway department might acquire farmland or residential properties to extend railroad tracks, bring electricity to a remote new development, or build a new highway.

In the past, the proposed use for taking property was to be for the public good. However, in June 2005, the U.S. Supreme Court in *Kelo v. City of New London*, significantly changed the definition of public use. The court held that local governments can condemn homes and businesses for private or economic development purposes.

Illinois enacted the **Equity in Eminent Domain Act**. This law places the obligation on the government to prove that an area is blighted before forcing property owners to sell their property for private development projects. In addition, the act helps owners receive fair market value for their property, requires relocation costs for displaced residents and businesses, and pays attorneys' fees when property owners successfully sue to keep their property.

Taxation

Taxation is a charge on real estate to raise funds to meet the public needs of a government. Taxes on real estate include annual real estate taxes assessed by local governmental entities, including school districts; taxes on income realized by individuals and corporations on the sale of property; and special fees that may be levied for special projects. Nonpayment of taxes may give government the power to claim an interest in the subject property.

Escheat

Escheatment is a process by which the state may acquire privately owned real or personal property. State laws provide for ownership to transfer, or **escheat**, to the state when an owner dies and leaves no heirs and also leaves no will or living trust instrument that directs how the real estate is to be distributed. In some states, real property escheats to the county where the land is located. In other states, it becomes the property of the state. Escheatment is intended to prevent property from being ownerless or abandoned.

In Illinois, real property will escheat to the county in which it is located rather than to the state.

ESTATES IN LAND

An **estate in land** is the degree, quantity, nature, and extent of an owner's interest in real property. Many types of estates exist, but not all interests in real estate are estates. To be an estate in land, an interest must allow possession, meaning the holding and enjoyment of the property either now or in the future, and must be measured according to time. Historically, estates in land have been classified primarily by their length of time of possession (i.e., as freehold estates and leasehold estates).

Freehold estates last for an indeterminate length of time, such as for a lifetime or forever. They include *fee simple* (or *indefeasible fee*), *defeasible fee*, and *life estates*. The first two of these estates continue for an indefinite period and may be passed along to the owner's heirs. A life estate is based on the lifetime of a person and ends when that individual dies. For an illustration, see Figure 7.1.

Figure 7.1: Freehold Estates

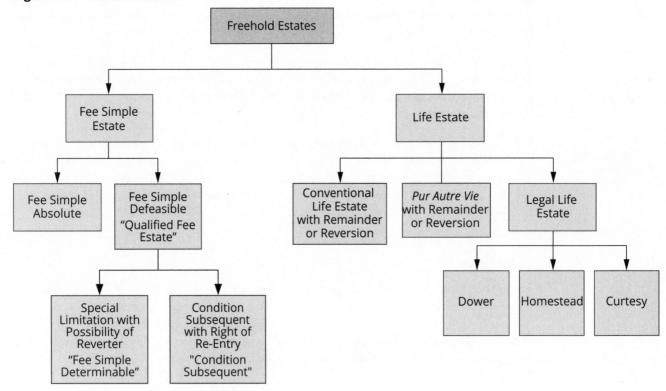

Leasehold estates last for a fixed period of time. They include estates for years and estates from period to period. Estates at will and estates at sufferance also are leaseholds, though by their operation, they are not generally viewed as being for fixed terms.

The traditional freehold and leasehold estates found in most states are also recognized under Illinois law.

Fee Simple Estate

Because fee simple estates are of unlimited duration, they are said to run "forever." Upon the death of the owner, a fee simple passes to the owner's heirs or as provided by will. A fee simple estate is also called an *estate of inheritance* (because that is how it passes unless the owner chooses to sell the property) or *fee ownership*. There are two major divisions of fee ownership: fee simple absolute and fee simple defeasible.

Fee Simple Absolute

A **fee simple absolute** estate is the highest interest in real estate recognized by law. Fee simple ownership is absolute ownership; the holder is entitled to all rights to the property. It is limited only by certain public and private restrictions, such as zoning laws and restrictive covenants.

Fee Simple Defeasible

A **fee simple defeasible** (also called *defeasible fee*) estate is a qualified estate—that is, it is subject to the occurrence or nonoccurrence of some specified event. Two categories of defeasible estates exist: those subject to a *condition subsequent or by a fee simple determinable* (qualified by a special limitation). These qualified, defeasible estates are created using specific language in the deed. A "condition subsequent" is only created by using the words "on the condition that." (See example below.) To create a "fee simple determinable," the words "as long as," "while," or "during" might be used.

A fee simple estate may be qualified by a condition subsequent. This means that the new owner must not perform some action or activity. The former owner retains a right of reentry so that if the condition is broken, the former owner can retake possession of the property through legal action. Conditions in a deed under "condition subsequent" are different from restrictions or covenants because of the grantor's right to reclaim ownership. Possible reclamation of ownership does not exist under private restrictions made by builders or homeowner associations.

EXAMPLE

An owner grants some land to her church "on the condition that no alcohol is consumed on the premises." This is a fee simple subject to a condition subsequent. If alcohol is consumed on the property, the former owner has the right to reacquire full ownership. It will be necessary for the grantor (or the grantor's heirs or successors) to go to court to assert that right.

A **fee simple determinable** is a fee simple defeasible estate that may be inherited. This estate is qualified by a special limitation (which is an occurrence or event). The language used to distinguish a special limitation—words such as *so long as*, *while*, or *during*—is the key to creating this special limitation. The former owner retains a *possibility of reverter*. If the limitation is violated, the former owner (or heirs or successors) can reacquire full ownership with no need to go the court. The deed is automatically returned to the former owner.

The right of reentry and possibility of reverter may never take effect. If they do, it will be only at some time in the future. Therefore, each of these rights is considered a **future interest**.

EXAMPLE

When an owner gives land to a church, "so long as the land is used for only religious purposes," it is called a fee simple determinable. The church had the full bundle of rights possessed by a property owner, but in this case one of the "sticks" in the bundle is a control "stick." If the church ever decides to use the land for a nonreligious purpose, the original owner has the right to reacquire the land without going to court. In Illinois

Because the right of reentry and possibility of reverter can happen only in the future, they are considered future interests. While the condition passes from owner to owner forever, Illinois allows the original grantor's right of reverter to continue for only 40 years. After that time, the condition still may be enforced but no longer by the threat of losing the property.

Life Estate

A **life estate** is a freehold estate limited in duration to the life of the owner or the life of some other designated person or persons. Unlike other freehold estates, a life estate is not inheritable. It passes to future owners according to the prearranged provisions of the life estate. Two of the life estates, conventional and pur autre vie, are created through grant or conveyance to another. The third, a legal life estate, is created by statute or law. All three avoid the probate process.

A **life tenant** is entitled to the rights and benefits of ownership from both possession and ordinary use and profits just as if the individual held a fee simple interest. The life tenant's ownership may be sold, mortgaged, or leased, but it is always subject to the limitation of the life estate, and under those conditions, the life estate must always be disclosed.

A life tenant's ownership rights are not absolute. The life tenant may not injure the property, such as by destroying a building or allowing it to deteriorate. In legal terms, such injury is called **waste**. Those who eventually will own the property could seek an injunction against the life tenant or sue for damages if waste occurs.

Because the ownership will terminate on the death of the person against whose life the estate is measured, a purchaser, lessee, or lender can be affected if the life tenant has sold his rights. Because the interest is less desirable than a fee simple estate, the life tenant's limited rights must be disclosed if the property is sold. The new purchaser will lose the property at whatever point in time the original life tenant would have lost it.

Assisting a client with life estates, determinable fees, or fees with conditions subsequent should be the job of a skilled real estate attorney. Noting such situations in a sales transaction is, however, a responsibility of careful listing agents. In day-to-day practice, however, basic fee simple absolute—the simplest to understand form of ownership—will dominate.

Conventional Life Estate

A *conventional life estate* is created intentionally by the owner. It may be established either by deed at the time the ownership is transferred during the owner's life or by a provision of the owner's will after the owner's death. The estate is conveyed to an individual who is called the life tenant. The life tenant has full enjoyment of the ownership for the duration of his life. When the life tenant dies, the estate ends and its ownership passes, often as a fee simple to another designated individual, or returns to the previous owner.

EXAMPLE

A woman, who has a fee simple estate in a property, conveys a life estate to a man for his lifetime. The man is the life tenant. On his death, the life estate terminates, and the woman once again owns the property. If the man's life estate had been created by the woman's will, however, subsequent ownership of the property would be determined by the provisions of the will.

Pur Autre Vie

A life estate also may be based on the lifetime of a person other than the life tenant. This is called a life estate *pur autre vie* ("for the life of another"). Although a life estate is not considered an estate of inheritance, a life estate pur autre vie provides for the life tenant's "ownership" only until the death of the person against whose life the estate is measured.

EXAMPLE

A man often does not pay his apartment rent. He is set to inherit his family home after his father dies. In the meantime, a woman sets up a life estate pur autre vie giving the man the rights of a life tenant to a cottage she owns. The man's life tenancy terminates at the moment of his father's death, at which time ownership of the cottage will revert to the woman, her heirs, or pass to a designated remainderman.

Remainder and Reversion

The fee simple owner who creates a conventional life estate must plan for future ownership. When the life estate ends, it is replaced by a fee simple estate. The future owner of the fee simple estate may be designated in one of two ways:

1. In **remainder interest**, the creator of the life estate may name a remainderman as the person to whom the property will pass when the life estate ends (see Figure 7.2). Note that "remainderman" is the legal term; neither the term *remainderperson* nor the term *remainderwoman* is used legally.

Figure 7.2: Remainder Interest

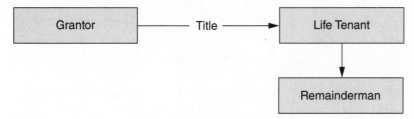

2. In **reversionary interest**, the creator of the life estate may choose not to name a remainderman. In that case, the creator will recapture ownership when the life estate ends. The ownership is said to "revert to the original owner" (see Figure 7.3).

Figure 7.3: Reversionary Interest

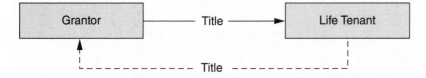

EXAMPLE

Craig conveys a ranch to Jean for Jean's lifetime and designates James to be the remainderman. While Jean is still alive, James owns a remainder interest, which is a nonpossessory estate; that is, James does not possess the property but has an interest in it nonetheless. This is a future interest in the fee simple estate. If Jean should die, James automatically becomes the fee simple owner.

Alternatively, Craig may convey a life estate in the ranch to Jean during and based on Jean's life. On Jean's death, ownership of the ranch reverts to Craig. In this scenario, Craig has retained a reversionary interest (or nonpossessory estate). Craig has a future interest in the ownership and may reclaim the fee simple estate when Jean dies. If Craig dies before Jean, Craig's heirs (or other individuals specified in Craig's will) will assume ownership of the ranch whenever Jean dies.

Legal Life Estate

A *legal life estate* is not created voluntarily by an owner. Rather, it is a form of life estate established by state law. Dower, curtesy, and homestead are the legal life estates currently used in many states.

Dower is the life estate that a wife has in the real estate of her deceased husband. *Curtesy* is the identical interest that a husband has in the real estate of his deceased wife.

Most *separate* or marital property states, including Illinois, have abolished the common-law concepts of dower and curtesy in favor of the **Uniform Probate Code**. This gives the surviving spouse the right to take an elective share on the death of the other spouse.

Illinois has **homestead**, a legal life estate in real estate occupied as the family home. In effect, the home is protected from unsecured creditors during the occupant's lifetime. In states that have homestead exemption laws, a portion of the area or value of the property occupied as the family home is exempt from certain judgments for debts such as credit card balances. The homestead is not protected from real estate taxes levied against the property or from a mortgage for the purchase or cost of improvements. In other words, if the debt is secured by the property, the property cannot be exempt from a judgment on that debt.

In practice, the homestead merely reserves a certain amount of money for the family in the event of a court sale of the property. On such a sale, any debts secured by the home, such as a mortgage, unpaid taxes, or mechanics' liens are paid from the sale proceeds first. The family then receives the amount reserved by the homestead exemption. Finally, whatever amount remains from the sale proceeds is applied to the family's unsecured debts, such as credit card debts.

Every homeowner in Illinois is entitled to a homestead exemption up to a value of $15,000 per head of household, $30,000 for two heads of household (maximum amount). The exemption continues after the death of an individual for the benefit of the survivor as long as he or she continues to occupy the homestead residence. It also extends for the benefit of all children living there until the youngest reaches 18 years of age. The estate extends to all types of residential property, including condominiums and cooperatives. A family can have only one homestead at any one time.

No notice has to be recorded or filed to establish a homestead in Illinois. Therefore, prospective purchasers, lienholders, and other concerned parties are charged with inspecting a property to see if it serves as the residence of the potential debtor and if homestead estate rights can be claimed by that debtor.

To release possible homestead rights, even if the property in question is owned solely by either spouse, the signatures of both are always required on residential sales contracts, listing agreements, notes, mortgages, deeds, and other conveyances.

EXAMPLE

A man has a homestead in Illinois. In Illinois, the homestead exemption is $15,000. At a court-ordered sale, the property is purchased for $60,000. First, the man's remaining $15,000 mortgage balance is paid, and then he receives a $15,000 homestead exemption. The remaining $30,000 is applied to his unsecured debts (those debts not encumbered with a lien).

ENCUMBRANCES AND WATER RIGHTS

Encumbrances

An **encumbrance** is a claim, charge, or liability that attaches to real estate. An encumbrance does not give a possessory interest in real property; it is not an estate. In essence, an encumbrance is a right or an interest held by someone other than the property owner that affects title to the real estate but does not necessarily prevent a transfer of title. As such, an encumbrance may decrease the value or obstruct the use of the property.

Encumbrances may be divided into the following two classifications:

1. Liens (usually monetary charges)
2. Physical encumbrances (restrictions, easements, licenses, and encroachments)

Liens

A **lien** is a charge against property that provides security for a debt or an obligation of the property owner. If the obligation is not repaid, the lienholder is entitled to have the debt satisfied from the proceeds of a court-ordered or forced sale of the debtor's property. Real estate taxes, mortgages and trust deeds, judgments, and mechanics' liens all represent possible liens against an owner's real estate.

Deed Restrictions

Deed restrictions are private agreements that affect land use. Once placed in the deed by a previous owner, they "run with the land," limiting the use of the property and binding to all grantees. Deed restrictions are enforced by an owner of real estate and are included in the seller's deed to the buyer.

Covenants, conditions, and restrictions (CC&Rs) are private agreements that affect land use and are typically imposed by a developer or subdivider to maintain specific standards in a subdivision. CC&Rs are listed in the original development plans for the subdivision filed in the public record. They may be enforced by the original owner or developer, or by a homeowners association.

MEMORY TIP

The servient tenement is the land that serves the other party.

The dominant tenement is the dominating party benefitted by the easement.

Easements

An **easement** is the right to use the land of another for a particular purpose. It may exist in any portion of the real estate, including the airspace above or a right-of-way across the land. Easements are by agreement at any time or created by a seller when a property is conveyed.

An appurtenant easement is attached to the ownership of one parcel and allows the owner the use of a neighbor's land. For an appurtenant easement to exist, two adjacent parcels of land must be owned by two different parties. The parcel over which the easement runs is called the **servient tenement**; the neighboring parcel that benefits is called the **dominant tenement** (see Figure 7.4 and Figure 7.5).

Figure 7.4: Easement Appurtenant

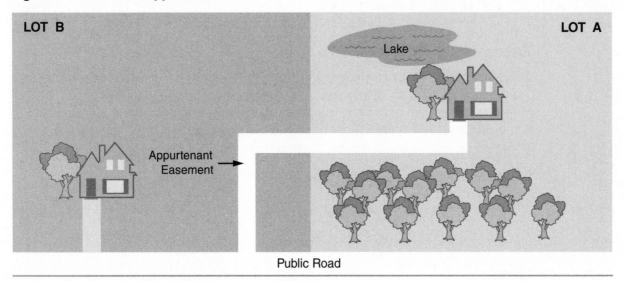

The owner of Lot A has an appurtenant easement across Lot B to gain access to his property from the paved road. Lot A is dominant and Lot B is servient.

Figure 7.5: Easement Appurtenant and Easement in Gross

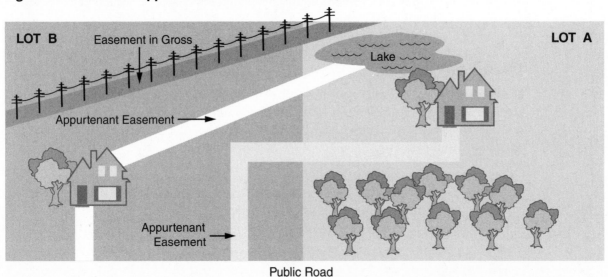

The owner of Lot B has an appurtenant easement across Lot A to gain access to the lake. Lot B is dominant and Lot A is servient. The utility company has an easement in gross across both parcels of land for its power lines. Note that Lot A also has an appurtenant easement across Lot B for its driveway. Lot A is dominant and Lot B is servient.

An **appurtenant easement** is part of the dominant tenement. If the dominant tenement is conveyed to another party, the beneficial easement transfers with the title, or "runs with the land." It will transfer with the deed of the dominant tenement forever unless the holder of the dominant tenement releases that right. Easements are considered encumbrances for disclosure, especially so for the servient tenement whose land is being used. While the easement must also be mentioned for a dominant tenement, the fact that it exists is often a marketing plus (such as an easement accessing a beach).

A **party wall** can be an exterior wall of a building that straddles the boundary line between two lots, or it can be a commonly shared partition wall between two connected properties. Each lot owner owns the half of the wall on his lot, and each lot owner has an appurtenant easement in the other half of the wall. A written party wall agreement must be used to create the easement rights. Expenses to build and maintain the wall are usually shared. A fence built on the lot line is treated the same as a wall. A party driveway shared by and partly on the land of adjoining owners must also be created by written agreement, specifying responsibility for expenses.

An **easement in gross** is an individual or company interest in or right to use someone else's land (see Figure 7.5). A railroad's right-of-way is an easement in gross, as are the rights-of-way of utility easements (such as for a pipeline or high-tension power line). Commercial easements in gross may be assigned, conveyed, and inherited. Personal easements in gross are usually not assignable. Generally, a personal easement in gross terminates on the death of the easement owner. An easement in gross is often confused with the similar but less formal *personal right of license*.

Creating an Easement

An easement is commonly created by a written agreement between parties that establishes the easement right. It may be created by the grantor in a deed of conveyance, in which the grantor either reserves an easement over the sold land or grants the new owner an easement over the grantor's remaining land. Two other ways for an easement to be created are *easement by necessity* and *easement by prescription*.

Easement by Necessity

An easement that is created when an owner sells a parcel of land that has no access to a street or public way except over the seller's remaining land is an **easement by necessity**. An easement by necessity is created by court order based on the principle that owners must have the right to enter and exit their land—the right of ingress (enter) and egress (exit); they cannot be landlocked.

Easement by Prescription

Prescriptive Use (NACHO):

Notorious
Adverse
Continuous
Hostile
Open

If the claimant has made use of another's land for a certain period of time as defined by state law, an **easement by prescription** (also called *prescriptive easement*) may be created. To create a prescriptive easement, the claimant's use must have been continuous, exclusive, and without the owner's approval ("adverse"). The use must be visible, open, and notorious; that is, the owner must have been able to learn of it. A visible fence, continuous gardening on the back lot, or driving over property so often that ruts are visible are all examples.

To establish an easement by prescription in Illinois, the use must be adverse, exclusive, under claim of right, and continuous and uninterrupted for a period of 20 years. To block the establishment of a prescriptive easement, the owner of any property must display signs or send a certified letter stating that access to or use of the property is by permission (and thus not adverse).

The concept of *tacking* provides that successive periods of continuous occupation by different parties may be combined (tacked) to reach the required total number of years necessary to establish a claim for a prescriptive easement. To tack on one person's possession to that of another, the parties must have been "successors in interest," such as an ancestor and his heir, a landlord and tenant, or a seller and buyer.

EXAMPLE

Jana's property is located in a state with a prescriptive period of 20 years. For the past 22 years, Frank has driven his car across Jana's front yard every day to reach his garage with ease. Frank has created an easement by prescription.

For 25 years, Linda has driven across Jana's front yard two or three times a year to reach her property when she's in a hurry. Linda has not created an easement by prescription because her use has not been continuous.

Easement by Condemnation

An **easement by condemnation** is acquired for a public purpose, through the right of *eminent domain*. The owner of the servient tenement must be compensated for any loss in property value.

Terminating an Easement

An easement terminates

- when the need no longer exists,

- when the owner of either the dominant or the servient tenement becomes the owner of both properties (or *termination by merger*),

- by release of the right of easement to the owner of the servient tenement,

- by abandonment of the easement (the intention of the parties is the determining factor),

- by destruction of the servient tenement (e.g., the demolition of a party wall), or

- by lawsuit ("action to quiet title") against someone claiming an easement.

License

A **license** is a personal privilege (not a right) to enter the land of another for a specific purpose. A license differs from an easement in that it can be terminated or canceled by the licensor (the person who granted the license) at any time. If the use of another's property is given orally or informally, it generally is considered to be a license rather than a personal easement. A license ends on the death of either party or by the sale of the land by the licensor.

EXAMPLE

A man asks a woman for permission to park a boat in her driveway. The woman says, "Sure, go ahead!" The man now has a license to park in the driveway, but the driveway owner may tell the man to move the boat at any time. Similarly, a ticket to a theater or sporting event is a license: the holder is permitted to enter the facility and is entitled to a seat. However, if the ticketholder becomes rowdy or abusive, he may be asked to leave at any time.

Encroachments

An **encroachment** occurs when all or part of a structure (such as a building, fence, or driveway) illegally extends beyond the land of its owner. An encroachment usually is disclosed by either a physical inspection of the property or a spot survey. A *spot survey* shows the location of all improvements located on a property and whether they extend over the lot or building lines. A spot survey is more informational and useful than a simple *survey sketch* with only the lot dimensions. If a spot survey and physical inspection show that a building encroaches on adjoining land, the neighbor may be able to either recover damages or secure removal of the portion of the building that encroaches. Unchallenged encroachments that last beyond a state's prescriptive period, however, may give rise to easements by prescription.

IN PRACTICE

Because an undisclosed encroachment could create a serious situation if discovered late in a transaction, any known encroachments should be noted in a listing agreement and in the sales contract. Spot surveys provide evidence of encroachments. However, the new survey may only become available fairly late in the transaction process. For this reason, listing agents often encourage sellers to attach an existent survey to listing materials if one is available.

NATURE AND WATER: RIGHTS AND RESTRICTIONS

MEMORY TIP

Riparian refers to rivers, streams, and similar waterways.

Littoral refers to lakes, oceans, and similar bodies of water.

Whether for agricultural, recreational, or other purposes, waterfront real estate has always been desirable. Each state has strict laws that govern the ownership and use of water, as well as the adjacent land. The laws vary among the states, but all are closely linked to climatic and topographic conditions. Where water is plentiful, for example, many states rely on the simple parameters set by the common-law doctrines of riparian and littoral rights. Where water is scarce, a state may control all but limited domestic use of water according to the doctrine of prior appropriation.

Riparian Rights

Riparian rights are common-law rights granted to owners of land along the course of a river, stream, or similar body of flowing water and generally include the unrestricted right to use the water. As a rule, the only limitation on the owner's use is that it cannot interrupt or alter the flow of the water or contaminate it in any way. In addition, an owner of land that borders a nonnavigable waterway (that is, a body of water unsuitable for commercial boat traffic) owns the land under the water to the exact center of the waterway.

Land adjoining commercially navigable rivers, on the other hand, is usually owned to the water's edge, with the state holding title to the submerged land (see Figure 7.6). Navigable waters are considered public waterways on which the public has an easement or right to travel.

Figure 7.6: Riparian Rights Illustration

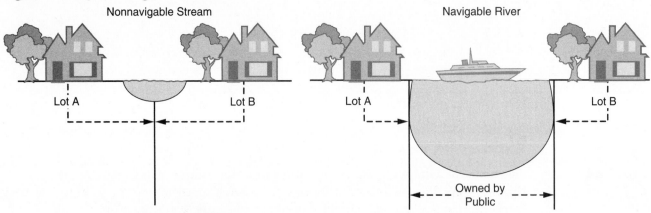

Littoral Rights

Closely related to riparian rights are the **littoral rights** of owners whose land borders commercially navigable lakes, seas, and oceans. Owners with littoral rights enjoy unrestricted use of available waters but own the land adjacent to the water only up to the mean high-water mark (see Figure 7.7). All land below this point is owned by the public.

Figure 7.7: Littoral Rights Illustration

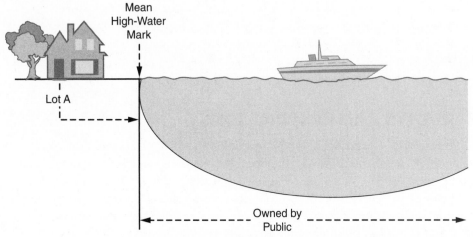

Riparian and littoral rights are appurtenant to (attached to) the land. The right to use the water belongs to whoever owns the bordering land and cannot be retained by a former owner after the land is sold.

Accretion, Erosion, and Avulsion

The amount of land an individual owns may be affected by the natural action of water. An owner is entitled to all land created through **accretion**—increases in the land resulting from the deposit of soil by the water's action (such deposits are called *alluvion* or *alluvium*). If a property's boundary extends to "the water's edge" and the water recedes, the new land is acquired by *reliction*.

On the other hand, an owner may lose land through **erosion**—the gradual and imperceptible wearing away of the land by natural forces such as wind, rain, and flowing water. Fortunately, erosion usually takes hundreds of years to have any noticeable effect on a person's property. Flash floods or heavy winds may increase the speed of erosion.

Avulsion is the sudden removal of soil by an act of nature. It is an event that causes the loss of land much less subtly than erosion. A major earthquake or a mudslide, for example, can cause an individual's land holdings to become much smaller very quickly.

SUMMARY

Ownership of real estate is not absolute because a landowner's power to control that property is subject to public controls and private restrictions. Individual ownership rights are subject to certain powers held by federal, state, and local governments. Government powers include police power, eminent domain, taxation, and escheatment.

An estate is the degree, quantity, nature, and extent of interest a person holds in land. Freehold estates are estates of indeterminate length and last until they are sold or the owner dies, and then they pass freely by will to stated parties. Less-than-freehold estates are called leasehold estates, and they involve landlords and rent rather than sales contracts and owners.

A freehold estate may be a fee simple estate or a life estate. A fee simple estate can be absolute (sometimes just called a fee) or defeasible (rights affected by the happening of some event). A fee simple absolute is the highest form of real estate ownership and comes with the most rights attached.

One type of defeasible fee, the fee simple determinable, is especially restrictive: The property automatically reverts to the original owner if a given promise or restriction is broken. Defeasible fees with condition subsequent must go to court for the original owner to gain right of reentry over similar issues. Illinois limits right of reverter or reentry by the original owner to a maximum length of 40 years. After that, the restrictions may still be enforced, but the original owner may not take back the property.

A conventional life estate is created by the owner of a fee estate and involves measuring limited ownership rights by the life of the owner, the life tenant, or a third party. On the death of this individual, ownership shifts based on the original owner's instructions in the life estate.

Legal life estates are created by law and are quite different from other life estates: these life estates involve long-lived (for the life of the property) monetary rights granted to homeowners and spouses of homeowners. Common legal life estates in the United States include dower and curtesy and homestead rights.

 In Illinois, dower and curtesy has been replaced by spousal elective shares based on the Uniform Probate Code. Illinois offers homestead rights of $15,000 per head of household to a maximum of two ($30,000). This amount is protected from unsecured creditors.

Encumbrances against real estate can be legal or physical: liens, deed restrictions, easements such as driveways, licenses to use a property for a stated purpose, and physical encroachments such as fences or sheds built over a property line are all examples of various forms of encumbrances.

An easement is a right to use another's real estate. Easements are classified as interests in real estate but are not large enough in concept to be estates in land. There are two types of easements. Appurtenant easements involve two separately owned tracts. The tract benefited is called the dominant tenement; the tract over which the easement is found is called the servient tenement. An easement in gross is an individual or company interest in or right to use someone else's land, such as the right granted to utility companies to maintain poles, wires, and pipelines. Easements may be created by agreement, express grant or reservation in a deed, by necessity, by prescription, or by condemnation. An easement can be terminated when the purpose of the easement no longer exists, by merger of both interests, or by release or abandonment of the easement.

A license is permission to enter another's property for a specific purpose. A license usually is created orally and is temporary; it can easily be ended by the property owner. Ownership of land encompasses not only the land but also the right to use the water on or adjacent to it. Many states subscribe to the common-law doctrine of riparian rights, which allows ownership of nonnavigable streams to their midpoint. Littoral rights are held by owners of land next to lakes and oceans; land rights here go to the mean high-water mark.

Local units of government and quasi-governmental bodies are granted the power of eminent domain by the Illinois Constitution and Illinois Code of Civil Procedure. A quick-take in Illinois is a fast proceeding to obtain title, such as for highway construction.

The Equity in Eminent Domain Act places the obligation on government to prove that an area is blighted before forcing property owners to sell their property for private development projects.

Real property escheats to the county in which it is located if no will was left and no heirs are found.

The period for an easement by prescription in Illinois is 20 years.

UNIT 7 QUIZ

1. A city decides to build a new library. Which of these terms *BEST* describes the action taken by the city to acquire the land for the new library?
   A. Zoning allows the city to take the land by granting a variance for the library.
   B. The city has the right to take the land by eminent domain as long as just compensation is paid the property owners.
   C. County laws permit the city to take the land by escheatment so long as the property owners are paid just compensation.
   D. The sheriff sells the property at a public sale and pays the owners just compensation, and then the city could build the library.

2. A purchaser of real estate learned that his ownership rights could continue forever and that no other person could claim to be the owner or exert any ownership control over the property. This person owns a
   A. life estate.
   B. determinable fee estate.
   C. fee simple absolute interest.
   D. fee simple on condition.

3. A person owned the fee simple title to a vacant lot adjacent to a hospital and was persuaded to make a gift of the lot. She wanted to have some control over its use, so her attorney prepared her deed to convey ownership of the lot to the hospital "so long as it is used for hospital purposes." After completion of the gift, the hospital will own a
   A. fee simple absolute estate.
   B. license.
   C. leasehold estate.
   D. fee simple determinable.

4. Your neighbors regularly use your driveway to reach their garage, which is on their property. Your attorney explains that ownership of the neighbor's real estate includes an easement appurtenant giving them the right to do this. Your property is the
   A. dominant tenement.
   B. servient tenement.
   C. license property.
   D. a leasehold interest.

5. A tenant who rents an apartment from the owner of the property holds
   A. an easement.
   B. a license.
   C. a leasehold interest.
   D. a freehold interest.

6. If the owner of real estate does not take action against a persistent trespasser before the statutory period has passed, the trespasser may acquire
   A. an easement by necessity.
   B. an easement by prescription.
   C. a license.
   D. title by eminent domain.

7. A property owner wants to use water from a river that runs through his property to irrigate a potato field. To do so, the owner is required by his state's law to submit an application to the Department of Water Resources describing in detail the beneficial use he plans for the water. If the department approves the property owner's application, it will issue a permit allowing a limited amount of river water to be diverted onto the property. Based on these facts, what doctrine of law is the state likely relying upon in requiring the property owner to submit this application?
   A. Doctrine of prior appropriation
   B. Common-law riparian rights
   C. Common-law littoral rights
   D. Doctrine of highest and best use

8. Which of these is *NOT* a governmental power?
   A. Easement in gross
   B. Police power
   C. Eminent domain
   D. Taxation

9. Property deeded to a town "on the condition that it is used for recreational purposes" conveys a
   A. fee simple absolute.
   B. condition subsequent.
   C. fee simple on condition precedent.
   D. leasehold interest.

10. A property owner has the legal right to pass over the land owned by her neighbor. This is
    A. an easement.
    B. an estate in land.
    C. a police power.
    D. an encroachment.

11. Which of these is a legal life estate?
    A. Leasehold
    B. Homestead
    C. Fee simple absolute
    D. Determinable fee

12. A father conveys ownership of his residence to his daughter to last for the length of his life. The interest the daughter owns during her father's lifetime is
    A. pur autre vie.
    B. a reversion.
    C. a remainder.
    D. a leasehold.

13. An owner has a fence on her property. By mistake, the fence extends one foot onto the property of a neighbor. The fence is an example of
    A. a license.
    B. an easement by necessity.
    C. an easement by prescription.
    D. an encroachment.

14. Encumbrances on real estate
    A. make it impossible to sell the encumbered property.
    B. must all be removed before the title can be transferred.
    C. are established by condition subsequent.
    D. include easements and encroachments.

15. A person has permission from a property owner to hike on the owner's property during the autumn months. The hiker has
    A. an easement by necessity.
    B. a license.
    C. an easement by prescription.
    D. a determinable freehold interest.

16. In Illinois, the homestead exemption
    A. must be recorded with the county recorder to be in effect.
    B. can never be released.
    C. is limited to $15,000 per head of household.
    D. is limited to littoral rights of $15,000 per residence.

17. What can terminate an easement?
    A. Continued use of the easement
    B. Owner of either property becomes sole owner of both
    C. Release of the easement by the servient tenement
    D. Maintenance of the easement

18. In Illinois, a prescriptive easement may be
    A. established by 15 years of continuous, uninterrupted use without the owner's approval or permission.
    B. prevented by posting a "No Trespassing" sign in a prominent place on or near the boundary of the property.
    C. established by 20 years of continuous, uninterrupted, exclusive use under claim of right and without the owner's permission.
    D. defeated by showing that the adverse possession was not exercised by a single individual for the requisite period but by successive parties in interest.

19. In Illinois, which of these is *TRUE* when a decedent's real property escheats?
    A. Ownership of the property goes to the county in which it is located.
    B. The decedent's heirs must receive just compensation for the property's fair market value, measured at the time of the decedent's death.
    C. The state laws of eminent domain apply.
    D. Ownership of the property goes to the state.

20. The type of easement that is a right-of-way for a utility company's power lines is
    A. an easement by necessity.
    B. an easement by prescription.
    C. a nonassignable easement.
    D. an easement in gross.

UNIT
8

Forms of Real Estate Ownership

LEARNING OBJECTIVES

When you have completed this unit, you will be able to accomplish the following.

› Explain the distinction between ownership in severalty and co-ownership and describe the various forms of co-ownership.
› Describe the ways in which various business organizations may own property.
› Distinguish cooperative ownership from condominium ownership.

KEY TERMS

common elements	limited liability company	severalty
condominium	(LLC)	syndicate
cooperative	limited partnership	tenancy by the entirety
co-ownership	marital property	tenancy in common
corporation	partition	time-share
general partnership	partnership	town house
joint tenancy	proprietary lease	trust
joint venture	right of survivorship	

OVERVIEW

Real estate licensees will find that buyers will need to determine the type of ownership that best fit their needs. The choice of ownership will affect the ability to transfer the real estate, has tax implications, and decides rights to future claims. Because of this, it's in the best interest of the client that they consult with an attorney about what best matches their needs.

Although the forms of ownership available are controlled by state laws, a fee simple estate may be held in the following three basic ways:

■ In severalty, where title is held by one individual or entity

- In co-ownership, where title is held by two or more individuals or entities
- In trust, where a third individual holds title for the benefit of another

FORMS OF REAL ESTATE OWNERSHIP

Ownership in Severalty

Ownership in **severalty** occurs when property is owned by one individual or corporation. The term comes from the fact that this sole owner is "severed" or "cut off" from other owners. The severalty owner has sole rights to the ownership and sole discretion to sell, will, lease, or otherwise transfer part or all of the ownerships rights to another person or entity. When a husband or wife owns property in severalty, state law may affect how ownership is held.

Sole ownership of property is quite common in Illinois, and title held in severalty presents no unique legal problems. However, when either a husband or a wife owns property in severalty, lenders, grantees, and title insurers in Illinois usually require that the spouse sign in order to release any potential homestead rights. This is true for both listing and sales contracts.

CO-OWNERSHIP

When title to one parcel of real estate is held by two or more individuals, those parties are called *co-owners* or *concurrent owners*. Most states commonly recognize various forms of **co-ownership**. Individuals may co-own property as tenants in common, joint tenants, or tenants by the entirety, or they may co-own *community property* in states recognizing community property.

Illinois recognizes co-ownership and most traditional forms of co-ownership except for community property (Illinois is a marital property state). Illinois also recognizes ownership in trust, in partnership, and by commercial entities such as corporations and limited liability companies.

Tenancy in Common

A parcel of real estate may be owned by two or more people as tenants in common. In a **tenancy in common**, each tenant holds an *undivided fractional interest* in the property. A tenant in common may hold, for example, a one-half or one-third interest in a property. The physical property, however, is not divided into a specific half or third. Hence, it is called an undivided fractional interest. The co-owners have *unity of possession*, meaning they are entitled to possession of the whole property. It is the ownership interest, not the property, that is divided.

The deed creating a tenancy in common may or may not state the fractional interest held by each co-owner. If no fractions are stated, the tenants are presumed to hold equal shares. For example, if five people hold title, each would own an undivided one-fifth interest.

Because the co-owners own separate interests, they can sell, convey, mortgage, or transfer their individual interests without the consent of the other co-owners. However, no individual tenant may transfer the ownership of the entire property. When one co-owner dies, the tenant's undivided interest passes according to the co-owner's will or living trust.

In Illinois, a single deed may show the proportional interests of each tenant in common, or a separate deed issued to each tenant may show her individual proportional interest. When a single deed is used, lack of a description of each tenant's share means all tenants hold equal, undivided shares.

Tenants in common also hold their ownership interests in severalty. In other words, because the co-owners own separate interests, each can sell, convey, mortgage, or transfer their interest. The consent of the other co-owners is not needed. When one co-owner dies, the tenant's undivided interest passes according to the person's will (see Figure 8.1).

In Illinois, the law presumes that two or more owners hold title as tenants in common if the deed does not state specifically how title is to be held.

Figure 8.1: Tenancy in Common Illustration

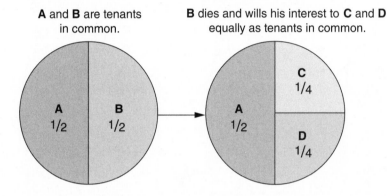

Joint Tenancy

Typical wording in a deed creating a joint tenancy is "To A and B as joint tenants and not as tenants in common."

Most states recognize some form of **joint tenancy** in property owned by two or more people. The feature that distinguishes a joint tenancy from a tenancy in common is *unity of interest*. Title is held as though all the owners, collectively, constitute one unit. Joint tenancy includes the **right of survivorship**: Upon the death of a joint tenant, the deceased's interest transfers directly to the surviving joint tenant(s). A will has no effect of the transfer of property. Essentially, there is one less owner. The joint tenancy continues until only one owner remains.

The last survivor then takes title in severalty and has all the rights of sole ownership, including the right to pass the property to any heirs (see Figure 8.2).

Creating Joint Tenancies

MEMORY TIP

The four unities necessary to create a joint tenancy may be remembered by the acronym PITT:

■ Possession
■ Interest
■ Time
■ Title

A joint tenancy can be created only by the intentional act of conveying a deed or giving the property by will. It cannot be implied or created by operation of law. The deed must specifically state the parties' intention to create a joint tenancy, and the parties must be explicitly identified as joint tenants.

The following four "unities" are required to create a joint tenancy:

1. *Unity of possession.* All joint tenants hold an undivided right to possession of the property.
2. *Unity of interest.* All joint tenants hold equal ownership interests in the property.
3. *Unity of time.* All joint tenants acquire their interests at the same time.
4. *Unity of title.* All joint tenants acquire their interests by the same deed.

Illinois allows a sole owner to execute a deed to herself and others "as joint tenants and not as tenants in common" in order to create a valid joint tenancy.

Figure 8.2: Joint Tenancy With Right of Survivorship

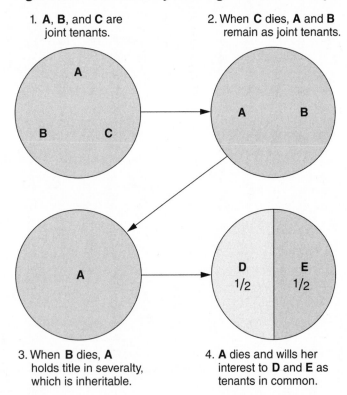

1. **A**, **B**, and **C** are joint tenants.

2. When **C** dies, **A** and **B** remain as joint tenants.

3. When **B** dies, **A** holds title in severalty, which is inheritable.

4. **A** dies and wills her interest to **D** and **E** as tenants in common.

Terminating Joint Tenancies

A joint tenancy is destroyed when any one of the four unities of joint tenancy is terminated. Joint tenants are free to convey their interest in the jointly held property, but doing so destroys the unities of time and title. The new owner cannot become a joint tenant in the original joint tenancy and will hold interest as a tenant in common. Rights of other joint tenants, however, are unaffected.

EXAMPLE

A, B, and C hold title to a ranch as joint tenants (see Figure 8.3). A sells her interest to D. D now owns a fractional interest in the ranch as a tenant in common with B and C, who continue to own their undivided interest as joint tenants. D is presumed to have a one-third interest, which may be reconveyed or left to D's heirs.

Figure 8.3: Combination of Tenancies

A, B, and **C** are joint tenants.   **A** sells her interest to **D**.

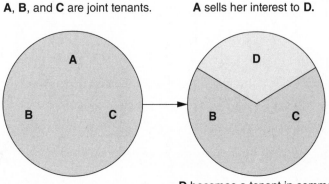

D becomes a tenant in common with **B** and **C** as remaining joint tenants.

In the 1983 Illinois Supreme Court case *Minonk State Bank v. Gassman*, the court held that a joint tenant may unilaterally sever the tenancy by conveying her interest to herself as a tenant in common, even without the consent of her co-owners. As a result, any owner holding property in a joint tenancy may elect, at any time, to become a tenant in common. At such time, that particular owner may will her interest to heirs or sell it. Any joint tenancy may also be severed by mutual agreement of all cotenants, by conveyance to third parties, or through a partition suit in the courts.

Termination of Co-Ownership by Partition Suit

Co-owners who wish to terminate their co-ownership may file an action in court (called a *partition suit* or *suit to partition*) to partition the property. **Partition** is a legal way to dissolve the relationship when the parties do not voluntarily agree to its termination. If the court determines that the land cannot be divided physically into separate parcels without destroying its value, the court will order the real estate sold. The proceeds of the sale will then be divided among the co-owners according to their fractional interests.

An Illinois partition suit may be filed by one or more of the owners in the circuit court of the county in which the subject parcel is located. The court appoints commissioners who must, if possible, divide the property by legal description among the owners in title. If such division cannot be made without harming the rights of the co-owners, the commissioners must report a valuation of the property. The property is then offered for public sale at a price not less than two-thirds of the value as set by the commissioners.

All defendants to the suit (the co-owners who object to the partition) are required to pay their proportionate share of court costs and the lawyer fees of the plaintiff (the co-owner who is seeking partition). However, this requirement may be waived if the defendants have a sound and substantial defense. Upon completion of the sale, confirmation of the sale by the court, and delivery of a proper conveyance to the purchaser at the sale, the proceeds of the sale are delivered to the former cotenants according to the court order. Generally, the proceeds of the sale are divided among the former owners according to their fractional interests.

Tenancy by the Entirety

Some states, including Illinois, allow spouses to use a special form of co-ownership called **tenancy by the entirety** for their personal residence. The term *entirety* refers to the fact that the owners are considered one indivisible unit: Under early common law, a married couple was viewed as one "legal person." In this form of ownership, each spouse has an equal, undivided interest in the property. Spouses who are tenants by the entirety have rights of survivorship. During their lives, they can convey title only by a deed signed by both parties. One party cannot convey a one-half interest, and generally they have no right to partition or divide.

The main reason married couples own property by the entirety is that a lawsuit against one of the spouses will not result in a lien against the house. A married couple owning property by the entirety would be eligible for homestead protection in the event of a judgment against either the husband or the wife. In addition, on the death of one spouse, the survivor automatically becomes the sole owner. Married couples often take title to property as tenants by the entirety so the surviving spouse can enjoy the benefits of ownership without the delay of probate proceedings.

MEMORY TIP

The methods of terminating a tenancy by the entirety may be remembered by the acronym JSDAD:
- Judgment Sale
- Death
- Agreement
- Divorce

Tenancy by the entirety is recognized in Illinois. To create a tenancy by the entirety, the deed must indicate that the property is to be owned "not as joint tenants or tenants in common, but as tenants by the entirety."

A tenancy by the entirety may be terminated by

- a court-ordered sale of the property to satisfy a judgment against the husband and the wife as joint debtors (the tenancy is dissolved so that the property can be sold to pay the judgment);
- the death of either spouse (the surviving spouse becomes sole owner in severalty);
- agreement between both parties through the execution of a new deed; or
- divorce, which leaves the parties as tenants in common.

Community Property

Community property laws, in use in nine states but not Illinois, recognize two kinds of property: separate property and community property.

Separate property is real or personal property that was owned solely by either spouse before the marriage. It also includes property acquired by gift or inheritance during the marriage, as well as any property purchased with separate funds during the marriage.

Community property consists of all other property, both real and personal, acquired by either spouse during the marriage. Any conveyance or encumbrance of community property requires the signatures of both spouses. When one spouse dies, the survivor automatically owns one-half of the community property. The other half is distributed according to the deceased spouse's will.

Illinois is not a community property state. However, as a **marital property** state, Illinois has certain similarities to community property states but with important differences. Illinois, too, breaks property down into two major categories based on marital status: marital property and nonmarital property. Illinois law recognizes that the spouses acquire joint rights in all property acquired after the date of marriage for the duration of the marriage. Illinois labels such property *marital property*, all of which will be divided between the two parties in the event of a divorce.

Nonmarital property is property that was acquired before the marriage or by gift or inheritance at any time, even during the marriage. If nonmarital property is exchanged for other property, if it increases in value, or if it returns income, the exchange, increase, or income also would be considered nonmarital property (i.e., property belonging to the individual). If nonmarital property is commingled with marital property, however, a presumption of transmutation is created, the resulting "mixed" property is presumed to be marital property. The spouses may execute an express contract agreeing to exclude certain property from being classified as marital property.

The Illinois Marriage and Dissolution of Marriage Act gives the courts flexibility in determining the precise division of marital property.

Figure 8.4 briefly describes the forms of co-ownership.

Figure 8.4: Forms of Co-Ownership Details

	Property Held	Property Conveyed
Tenancy in common	Each tenant holds an undivided fractional interest.	Each tenant can convey or devise his or her interest, but not entire interest.
Joint tenancy	Unity of ownership. Created by intentional act; unities of possession, interest, time, title.	Right of survivorship; cannot be conveyed to heirs.
Tenancy by the entirety	Husband and wife have equal undivided interest in their personal residence.	Right of survivorship; convey by deed signed by both parties. One party can't convey one-half interest.

TRUSTS

Living and Testamentary Trusts

A **trust** is a device by which one person transfers ownership of property to someone else to hold or manage for the benefit of a third party.

A property owner may provide for her own financial care or for that of the owner's family by establishing a trust.

The person who creates the trust conveys real or personal property to a trustee, with the understanding that the trustee will assume certain duties. These duties may include the care and investment of the trust assets to produce an income. After paying the trust's operating expenses and trustee's fees, the income is paid to or used for the benefit of the beneficiary. The trust may continue for the beneficiary's lifetime, or the assets may be distributed when the beneficiary reaches a certain age or when other conditions are met.

Perhaps a grandfather who wishes to ensure the college education of his granddaughter transfers his oil field to the grandchild's mother. He instructs the mother to use income from the trust to pay for the grandchild's college tuition. In this case, the grandfather is the *trustor*—the person who creates the trust. The granddaughter is the *beneficiary*—the person who benefits from the trust. The mother is the *trustee*—the party who holds legal title to the property and is entrusted with carrying out the trustor's instructions regarding the purpose of the trust. The trustee is a *fiduciary*, who acts in confidence or trust and has a special legal relationship with the beneficiary. The trustee's power and authority are limited by the terms of the trust agreement, will, or deed in trust.

IN PRACTICE

The legal and tax implications of setting up a trust are complex and vary widely from state to state. Attorneys and tax experts should always be consulted on the subject of trusts.

Illinois permits real estate to be held in trust as part of a living or testamentary trust or as the sole asset in a land trust.

Land Trusts

A few states, including Illinois, permit the creation of land trusts, in which real estate is the only asset. As in all trusts, the title to the property is conveyed to a trustee, and the beneficial interest belongs to the beneficiary. In the case of land trusts, however, the beneficiary usually is also the trustor. While the beneficial interest is personal property, the beneficiary retains management and control of the real property and has the right of possession and the right to any income or proceeds from its sale. Land trusts are frequently created for the conservation of farmland, forests, coastal land, and scenic vistas.

One of the distinguishing characteristics of a land trust is that the public records usually do not name the beneficiary. A land trust may be used for secrecy when assembling separate parcels. There are other benefits as well. A beneficial interest in a land trust is personal property and can be transferred by assignment, making the formalities of a deed unnecessary. The beneficial interest in property can be pledged as security for a loan without having a mortgage recorded. Because the beneficiary's interest is personal, it passes at the beneficiary's death under the laws of the state in which the beneficiary lived. If the deceased owned property in several states, additional probate costs and inheritance taxes can be avoided.

A land trust ordinarily continues for a definite term, such as 20 years. If the beneficiary does not extend the trust term when it expires, the trustee is usually obligated to sell the real estate and return the net proceeds to the beneficiary.

Land trusts are used in Illinois. However, Illinois law requires that the trustee disclose the beneficiary's name to certain parties under specific circumstances.

The beneficiary's name must be revealed

- to the concerned housing authority within 10 days after receiving a complaint of a violation of a building ordinance or law;

- when applying to any state of Illinois agency for a license or permit affecting the entrusted real estate;

- if selling the entrusted property by land contract (seller financing);

- if the trustee is named as a defendant in a private lawsuit or criminal complaint regarding the subject real estate (the beneficiary's identity can then be "discovered" by the plaintiff); or

- if a fire inspector or another officer is investigating arson.

IN PRACTICE

Licensees should be cautious in using the term *trust deed*. It can mean both a *deed in trust* (which relates to the creation of a living, testamentary, or land trust) and a *deed of trust* (a financing document similar to a mortgage). These documents are not interchangeable. Using an inaccurate term can trigger serious legal consequences.

OWNERSHIP OF REAL ESTATE BY BUSINESS ORGANIZATIONS

A business organization is a legal entity that exists independently of its members. Ownership by a business organization makes it possible for many people to hold an interest in the same parcel of real estate. Investors may be organized to finance a real estate project in various ways. Some provide for the real estate to be owned by the entity; others provide for direct ownership by the investors.

Partnerships

A **partnership** is an association of two or more persons who carry on a business for profit as co-owners. In a **general partnership**, all the partners participate in the operation and management of the business and share full liability for business losses and obligations. A **limited partnership**, on the other hand, consists of one or more general partners as well as limited partners. The business is run by the general partner or partners. The limited partners are not legally permitted to participate, and each can be held liable for business losses only to the extent of his or her investment. The limited partnership is a popular method of organizing investors because it permits investors with small amounts of capital to participate in large real estate projects with a minimum of personal risk.

Illinois has adopted the federal Uniform Partnership Act (UPA), which permits real estate to be held in the partnership name. The Uniform Limited Partnership Act (ULPA) also has been widely adopted. It establishes the legality of the limited partnership entity and provides that realty may be held in the limited partnership's name. Profits and losses are passed through the partnership to each partner, whose individual tax situation determines the tax consequences.

Corporations

A **corporation** is a legal entity created under the authority of the laws of the state from which it receives its charter. A corporation is managed and operated by its *board of directors*. The *charter* sets forth the powers of the corporation, including its right to buy and sell real estate (based on a resolution by the board of directors). Because the corporation is a legal entity, it can own real estate in severalty or as a tenant in common. Some corporations are permitted by their charters to purchase real estate for any purpose; others are limited to purchasing only the land necessary to fulfill the entity's stated corporate purposes.

As a legal entity, a corporation continues to exist until it is formally dissolved. The death of one of the officers or directors does not affect title to property owned by the corporation.

Individuals participate, or invest, in a corporation by purchasing stock. Because stock is personal property, shareholders do not have direct ownership interest in real estate owned by a corporation. Each shareholder's liability for the corporation's losses is usually limited to the amount of her investment.

One of the main disadvantages of corporate ownership of income property is that the profits are subject to double taxation. As a legal entity, a corporation must file an income tax return and pay tax on its profits. The portion of the remaining profits distributed to shareholders as dividends is taxed again as part of the shareholders' individual incomes.

An alternative form of business ownership that provides the benefit of a corporation as a legal entity but avoids double taxation is called an *S corporation*. Only the shares of the profits that are passed to the shareholders are taxed. The profits of the S corporation are not taxed. S corporations are subject to strict requirements regulating their structure, membership, and operation. If the IRS determines that an S corporation has failed to comply with these detailed rules, the entity will be redefined as some other form of business organization, and its favorable tax treatment will be lost.

Limited Liability Companies

The **limited liability company (LLC)** combines the most attractive features of limited partnerships and corporations. The members of an LLC enjoy the limited liability offered by a corporate form of ownership and the tax advantages of a partnership. In addition, the LLC offers flexible management structures without the complicated requirements of S corporations or the restrictions of limited partnerships. The structure and methods of establishing a new LLC or of converting an existing entity to the LLC form vary from state to state.

With passage of the Limited Liability Company Act in 1994, Illinois joined the majority of states that recognize LLCs as legitimate business organizations.

Syndicates and Joint Ventures

Generally speaking, a **syndicate** is two or more people or firms joined together to make and operate a real estate investment. A syndicate is not in itself a legal entity; however, it may be organized into a number of ownership forms, including co-ownership (tenancy in common and joint tenancy), partnership, trust, or corporation. A **joint venture** is a form of partnership in which two or more people or firms carry out a single business project. The joint venture is characterized by a time limitation resulting from the fact that the joint venturers do not intend to establish a permanent relationship.

Real Estate Investment Trust

By directing their funds into a *real estate investment trust (REIT)*, real estate investors take advantage of the same tax benefits as do mutual fund investors. A real estate investment trust does not have to pay corporate income tax as long as 90% of its income is distributed to its shareholders. Certain other conditions also must be met. To qualify as a REIT, at least 75% of the trust's income must come from real estate. Investors purchase certificates in the trust, which in turn invests in real estate or mortgages (or both). Profits are distributed to investors.

Some advantages of the REIT are avoidance of corporate tax, centralized management, continuity of operation, transferability of interests, diversification of investment, and the benefit of skilled real estate advice. Some of the disadvantages are that investments are passive in nature and usually restricted to very large real estate transactions. Losses cannot be passed through to the investor to offset her income, and usually the trust must be registered with the Securities and Exchange Commission.

Other rules have been eased for when a sale constitutes a prohibited transaction, the amount of capital gain dividends a REIT may pay, penalties on distributions of deficiency dividends, definitions of rents and interest, treatment of shared appreciation mortgage income, and distribution requirements relating to income not accompanied by the receipt of cash.

CONDOMINIUMS, COOPERATIVES, TOWN HOUSES, AND TIME-SHARES

A growing urban population, diverse lifestyles, changing family structures, and heightened mobility have created a demand for a variety of types of housing. Condominiums, cooperatives, town houses, and time-share arrangements are four types of properties that address our society's diverse real estate needs.

Condominium Ownership

Condominiums are popular throughout the United States. Condominium owners hold as fee simple title to their unit and are a tenant in common in the **common elements** of the building. The individual unit owners also own a specified share of the undivided interest in the remainder of the building and land, called the common elements. Common elements typically include such items as land, courtyards, lobbies, the exterior structure, hallways, elevators, stairways, and the roof, as well as recreational facilities such as swimming pools, tennis courts, and golf courses (see Figure 8.5). As has been stated about tenancy in common, each unit owns a fractional interest in these common elements. State law usually provides, however, that unit owners do not have the same right to partition that other tenants in common have.

Figure 8.5: Condominium Ownership

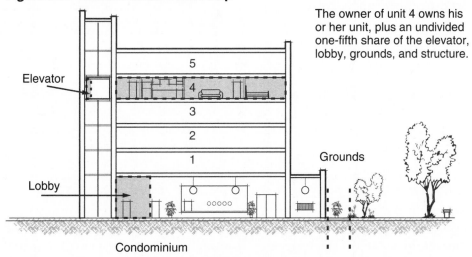

The owner of unit 4 owns his or her unit, plus an undivided one-fifth share of the elevator, lobby, grounds, and structure.

A condominium unit may be mortgaged like any other parcel of real estate. The unit can usually be sold or transferred to whomever the owner chooses unless the condominium association provides for a right of first refusal. In such a case, the owner is required to offer the unit at the same price to the other owners in the condominium or the association before accepting an outside purchase offer.

Real estate taxes are assessed and collected on each unit as an individual property. Default in the payment of taxes or a mortgage loan by one unit owner may result in a foreclosure sale of that owner's unit. One owner's default, however, does not affect the other unit owners.

Condominium ownership is not restricted to highrise buildings. Lowrises and detached structures can all be legally structured as condominiums.

Creation of a Condominium

In Illinois, creation of condominiums is governed by the Condominium Property Act (765 ILCS 605). Under this law, an owner/developer may elect to submit a parcel of real estate as a condominium project by recording a declaration to which is attached a three-dimensional plat of survey of the parcel showing the location and size of all units in the building. A building built on leased land may not be submitted for condominium designation in Illinois. Every unit purchaser acquires the fee simple title to the unit purchased, together with the percentage of ownership of the common elements that is set forth in the declaration and that belongs to that unit. This percentage is computed on the basis of the initial sales prices of each unit.

The survey required with each declaration of condominium ownership must indicate the dimensions of each unit. This survey will show the outlines of the lot, the size and shape of each unit, and the elevation or height above base datum for the upper surface of the floor level and the lower surface of the ceiling level. The difference between these two levels represents the airspace owned in fee simple by the unit owner.

Many Illinois municipalities have adopted *conversion ordinances* to protect tenants in rental buildings whose owners wish to convert to condominiums. These laws typically allow tenants an opportunity to extend their leases and often guarantee first purchase rights. Additional protections often include disclosure of all material information, structural soundness of the building, adequacy of parking, and a variety of other concerns.

Operation and Administration

The condominium property is administered by an association of unit owners, called a *homeowners association (HOA)*. The HOA may be governed by a board of directors or another official entity, and it may manage the property on its own or hire a property manager.

The HOA must enforce any rules it adopts regarding the operation and use of the property. The HOA is responsible for the maintenance, repair, cleaning, and sanitation of the common areas and structural portions of the property. It also must maintain fire, extended-coverage, and liability insurance.

The expenses of maintaining and operating the building are paid by the unit owners in the form of HOA fees. The fees often are due monthly, but the schedule may be quarterly, semiannually, or annually, depending on the provisions of the bylaws. The size of an individual owner's fee is generally determined by the size of the owner's unit. For example, the owner of a three-bedroom unit would pay a larger share of the total expense than the owner of a one-bedroom unit. If the fees are not paid, the HOA may seek a court-ordered judgment to have the delinquent owner's unit sold to cover the outstanding amount.

Special assessments are special payments required of unit owners to address some specific expense, such as a new roof. Assessments are structured in the same way as condo fees: owners of larger units pay proportionately higher assessments.

Cooperative Ownership

In a **cooperative**, a corporation holds title to the land and building and then offers shares of stock to prospective purchasers. The purchaser becomes a shareholder in the corporation by virtue of this stock ownership and receives a **proprietary lease** to a designated apartment for the life of the corporation. Because stock is personal property, the cooperative tenant-owners do not own real estate. Instead, they own an interest in a corporation that has only one asset: the building.

Operation and Management

The operation and management of a cooperative are determined by the corporation's bylaws. Through their control of the corporation, the shareholders of a cooperative control the property and its operation. They elect officers and directors who are responsible for operating the corporation and its real estate assets. Individual shareholders are obligated to abide by the corporation's bylaws.

An important issue in most cooperatives is the method by which shares in the corporation may be transferred to new owners. The bylaws may require that the board of directors approve any prospective shareholders. In some cooperatives, a tenant-owner must sell the stock back to the corporation at the original purchase price so that the corporation realizes any profits when the shares are resold. In others, if the stock is sold for the latest "going price" on the unit, stock profits may go to the departing tenant or at least be shared.

The corporation incurs costs in the operation and maintenance of the entire parcel, including both the common property and the individual apartments. These costs include real estate taxes and any mortgage payments the corporation may have. The corporation also budgets funds for such expenses as insurance, utilities, repairs and maintenance, janitorial and other services, replacement of equipment, and reserves for capital expenditures. Funds for the budget are assessed to individual shareholders, generally in the form of monthly fees similar to those charged by a homeowners' association in a condominium.

Unlike in a condominium association, which has the authority to impose a lien on the title held by a unit owner who defaults on maintenance payments, the burden of any defaulted payment in a cooperative falls on the remaining shareholders. Each shareholder is affected by the financial ability of the others. For this reason, approval of prospective tenants by the board of directors frequently involves financial evaluation. If the corporation is unable to make mortgage and tax payments because of shareholder defaults, the property might be sold by court order in a foreclosure suit. This could destroy the interests of all shareholders, including those who have paid their assessments.

Advantages

The IRS treats cooperatives as it does fee simple interest in single homes or condominiums in regard to deductibility of loan interest, property taxes, and homesellers' tax exclusions.

Illinois real estate licensees are permitted to list and sell cooperative units and interests without obtaining a securities license.

Town House Ownership

A **town house** is another popular form of housing in urban areas. The term *town house* is generally used to describe a type of housing connected by common walls. Typically, each town house has two floors and is located on a small lot. Title to each unit and lot is vested in the individual owner. Each owner also has a fractional interest in the common areas and is proportionately financially responsible. Common areas may include open spaces, recreational facilities, driveways, and sidewalks. The owner may sell, lease, will, or otherwise transfer the unit. The rights to the use of the common areas pass with title.

Time-Share Ownership

Time-share ownership permits multiple purchasers to buy interests in the same piece of real estate, usually a resort property. Each purchaser receives the right to use the facilities for a certain period. A *time-share estate* is a fee simple interest. The owner's occupancy and use of the property are limited to the contractual period purchased. The owner is assessed for maintenance and common-area expenses based on the ratio of the ownership period to the total number of ownership periods in the property. Time-share estates theoretically never end because they are real property interests. However, the physical life of the improvements is limited and must be looked at carefully when considering such a purchase.

The main difference between a time-share estate and a time-share use lies in the interest transferred to an owner by the developer of the project. A *time-share use* consists of the right to occupy and use the facilities for a certain number of years. At the end of that time, the owner's rights in the property terminate. In effect, the developer has sold only a right of occupancy and use to the owner, not a fee simple interest.

IN PRACTICE

The laws governing the development and sale of time-share properties are complex. In many states, time-share properties are now subject to subdivision requirements. In addition, the sale of time-share properties may be subject to federal securities laws. Real estate licensees providing assistance on time-shares need to be well-versed in the laws, benefits, and risks of such ownership and should counsel their clients to seek legal advice before purchasing.

Timeshare sales in Illinois were previously regulated by the Illinois Real Estate Timeshare Act. This act was repealed in 2018.

SUMMARY

Sole ownership, or ownership in severalty, means that title is held by one natural person or legal entity. Under co-ownership, title can be held concurrently by more than one person or legal entity in several ways.

Tenancy in common provides that each party holds separate title but shares possession of the whole property with the other owners, each of whom has separate interests. Upon the death of a tenant in common, her interest passes to any legal heirs. When two or more parties hold title to real estate in Illinois, they do so as tenants in common by default unless they express another intention.

Joint tenancy indicates two or more owners with the right of survivorship. The intention of the parties to establish a joint tenancy must be stated clearly. The four unities of possession, interest, time, and title (PITT) must be present.

Tenancy by the entirety, in those states where it is recognized (including Illinois), is a type of joint tenancy between spouses and applied only to the principal residence on a property held in this way if such liens are the result of one spouse's legal problems.

Real estate ownership may also be held in trust. All trusts involve three conceptual parts: trustor, trustee, and beneficiary. In a land trust (common in Illinois), the trustor and the beneficiary are typically the same party. To create any trust, the trustor conveys title and control to a third-party trustee, for the benefit of the beneficiary. Names of the owners of a land trust are not generally available except in specific circumstances.

Various types of business organizations may own real estate. A corporation is a legal entity and can hold title to real estate in severalty. A limited liability company (LLC) combines the limited liability offered by a corporate form with the tax advantages of a partnership without the complicated requirements of S corporations or the restrictions of limited partnerships. A syndicate is an association of two or more people or firms that invest in real estate. Many syndicates are joint ventures assembled for only a single project.

Cooperatives are a form of ownership in which actual title is held by one entity (a corporation or trust) that pays taxes, mortgage interest, and principal, as well as all operating expenses. Shareholders occupy the units, buy initial stock, and/or also pay monthly assessments in order to do so. They sometimes share in stock profits when they depart the building and their "shares" are sold.

In a condominium setting, each owner-occupant holds fee simple title to a unit, plus a share of the common areas. Each unit owner receives an individual tax bill and may mortgage the unit. One owner's bankruptcy or default does not affect other building occupants. Expenses for operating the building are collected by a homeowners association through monthly fees and periodic special assessments.

A town house is a popular form of housing in urban areas. Normally, each town house has two floors and is located on a small lot.

Time-shares enable multiple purchasers to own estates or "use interests" in the same piece of real estate. Each purchaser gains the right to use the property for a specified part of each year. The Illinois Real Estate Timeshare Act was repealed in 2018.

Illinois is a marital property state. Any property acquired during the marriage is likely to be viewed as marital, shared property unless it is by gift or inheritance to only one spouse. This is true even for real estate set up as ownership in severalty during the marriage. If nonmarital inherited property or gift monies are commingled, transmutation can legally transform them into marital property. Divorce laws in Illinois give courts flexibility in distributing marital property.

UNIT 8 QUIZ

1. The four unities of possession, interest, time, and title are associated with
   A. community property.
   B. joint tenancy.
   C. severalty ownership.
   D. tenants in common.

2. What is the difference between tenancy in common and joint tenancy?
   A. Tenancy in common is characterized by right of survivorship; joint tenancy is characterized by unity of possession.
   B. Tenancy in common ownership must contain specific wording; joint tenancy is presumed by the law when two or more people own property unless the deed states otherwise.
   C. Tenancy in common is an inheritable estate; joint tenancy is characterized by the right of survivorship.
   D. Under tenancy in common ownership, each owner has the right to sell, mortgage, or lease her interest without the consent of the other owners; joint tenancy can be implied or created by operation of law.

3. Three women were concurrent owners of a parcel of real estate. When one woman died, her interest, according to her will, became part of her estate. The deceased was a
   A. tenant in common.
   B. joint tenant.
   C. tenant by the entirety.
   D. severalty owner.

4. A legal arrangement under which the title to real property is held to protect the interests of a beneficiary is a
   A. corporation.
   B. limited partnership.
   C. general partnership.
   D. trust.

5. Which statement is *TRU* regarding a cooperative?
   A. Title to the land and building are held by different owners.
   B. Unit owners hold real property interests.
   C. Maintaining and operating a cooperative is paid for by the corporation from charges assessed to unit owners, generally in the form of monthly fees.
   D. Because their proprietary leases are real property, unit owners are exempt from the fees or assessments condominium owners are often required to pay for building maintenance and operation.

6. A man purchases an interest in a house. He is entitled to the right of possession only between July 10 and August 4 of each year. Which of these is *MOST* likely the type of ownership the man purchased?
   A. Time-share estate
   B. Cooperative
   C. Condominium
   D. Life estate

7. Because a corporation is a legal entity, real estate owned by it is owned in
   A. trust.
   B. partnership.
   C. survivorship tenancy.
   D. severalty.

8. Which of these is a form of co-ownership?
   A. Joint tenancy
   B. Severalty
   C. Sole owner
   D. Tenancy at will

9. A married couple owns a mansion with a right of survivorship. Theirs is *MOST* likely
   A. severalty ownership.
   B. community property.
   C. an estate by the entirety.
   D. a tenancy in common.

10. Two people are co-owners of a small office building with the right of survivorship. One of the co-owners dies intestate and leaves nothing to be distributed to his heirs. Which of these would explain why the second co-owner acquired the deceased's interest?
    A. Joint tenancy
    B. Adverse possession
    C. Law of escheat
    D. Reversionary interest

11. Which of these *BEST* proves one's right to live in a cooperative?
    A. Tax bill for the individual unit
    B. Existence of a reverter clause
    C. Proprietary lease
    D. Right of first refusal

12. Which of these statements applies to both joint tenancy and tenancy by the entirety?
    A. There is no right to file a partition suit.
    B. The survivor becomes a severalty owner.
    C. A deed signed by one owner will convey a fractional interest.
    D. A deed will not convey any interest unless signed by both spouses.

13. If property is held by two or more owners as tenants with survivorship rights, the interest of a deceased cotenant will be passed to the
    A. surviving owner(s).
    B. heirs of the deceased.
    C. state under the law of escheat.
    D. trust under which the property was owned.

14. Which of the following would NOT require special deed language to create in Illinois?
    A. Tenancy in common
    B. Life estate pur autre vie
    C. Joint tenancy
    D. Tenancy by the entireties

15. The names of the beneficiaries of a land trust must be revealed by the trustee to
    A. any member of the public who is interested in the beneficiary's identity.
    B. any unsecured creditor of the beneficiary.
    C. a licensed real estate broker if the broker is assisting in the sale or rental of the entrusted property.
    D. any Illinois agency when applying for a license or permit affecting the entrusted real estate.

16. Every co-owner of real estate in Illinois has the right to file a suit for partition when the property is held in which of these ways?
    A. Joint tenancy or tenancy in common
    B. Land trust
    C. Condominium or cooperative
    D. Time-share use or estate

17. Title to land in Illinois may be held and conveyed in which of these ways?
    A. As joint tenants only if the property is owned by a husband and wife as their principal residence
    B. As tenants in common with rights of survivorship
    C. In the name of a partnership
    D. All of these

18. If the deed of conveyance to Illinois land transfers title to two or more co-owners without defining the character of the co-ownership, which of these statements is *TRUE*?
    A. The property is construed as being held in joint tenancy.
    B. The co-owners are tenants in common.
    C. While proper in some states, such a deed would be an invalid conveyance under Illinois law.
    D. By statute, such co-owners would have the right of survivorship.

19. A and B held title to an apartment building in Illinois as joint tenants with rights of survivorship. A and B had an argument, and A didn't like the possibility that B would acquire total ownership of the building if A died. Therefore, A executed a deed to himself as a tenant in common and later willed his interest to C. Which of these statements accurately describes A's action?

    A. A's action is illegal under Illinois law.

    B. While not necessarily illegal, A's action has no effect on the joint tenancy.

    C. A's action legally severs the joint tenancy.

    D. A's goal of severing the joint tenancy can be accomplished only by a partition suit.

20. Which of these is necessary to convert an apartment building to condominium ownership in Illinois?

    A. The owner must record a certificate stating that the current tenants have been duly surveyed and that a majority of all tenants are in favor of the conversion.

    B. The owner records a condominium declaration with a three-dimensional plat.

    C. The existing tenants elect a board of directors having the power to act as legal administrator for the property, and the board petitions the state under the Condominium Property Act for certification as a condominium.

    D. The owner must execute and record a declaration of condominium under the Uniform Condominium Act as adopted in Illinois.

UNIT
9

Legal Descriptions

LEARNING OBJECTIVES

When you have completed this unit, you will be able to accomplish the following.

› Identify the three methods used to describe real estate.
› Describe how a survey is prepared.

KEY TERMS

air lot	legal description	range
base line	lot-and-block system	rectangular survey system
benchmark	metes-and-bounds	section
correction line	method	survey
datum	monument	township
fractional section	plat map	township line
government check	point of beginning (POB)	township tier
government lot	principal meridian	

OVERVIEW

A **legal description** is a detailed way of describing a parcel of land for documents such as deeds and mortgages that will be accepted in a court of law. The description is based on information collected through a **survey**—the process by which boundaries are measured by calculating the dimensions and area to determine the exact location of a piece of land. Courts have stated that a description is legally sufficient if it allows a surveyor to locate the parcel. In this context, *locate* means that the surveyor must be able to define the exact boundaries of the property. A street address will not tell a surveyor how large the property is or indicate its boundaries. Several alternative systems of identification have been developed to express a legal description of real estate.

METHODS OF DESCRIBING REAL ESTATE

The following three basic methods are used to describe real estate:

- Metes and bounds
- Rectangular (or government) survey
- Lot and block (recorded plat)

Metes-and-Bounds Method

The **metes-and-bounds method** is the oldest type of legal description (*metes* means distance and *bounds* means compass directions or angles). Used in the original 13 colonies, this method relies on a property's physical features to determine the boundaries and measurements of the parcel. A metes-and-bounds description always starts at a designated place on the parcel, called the **point of beginning (POB)**. From there, the surveyor proceeds around the property's boundaries. The boundaries are recorded by referring to linear measurements, natural and artificial landmarks (called *monuments*), and directions. A metes-and-bounds description always ends back at the POB so that the tract being described is completely enclosed.

Monuments are fixed objects used to identify the POB, the ends of boundary segments, or the location of intersecting boundaries. A monument may be a natural object, such as a large tree, lake, or stream. It may also be a man-made object, such as a street, highway, fence, canal, or markers (iron pins or concrete posts) placed by surveyors. Measurements often include the words "more or less" because the location of the monuments is more important than the distances given in the wording. In other words, the actual distance between monuments takes precedence over any linear measurements in the description.

An example of a metes-and-bounds description of the parcel of land pictured in Figure 9.1 follows:

> A tract of land located in Old Town, Liberty County, Virginia, is described as follows: Beginning at the intersection of the east line of Jones Road and the south line of Old Road; then east along the south line of Old Road 200 feet; then south 15° east 216.5 feet, more or less, to the center thread of Town Creek; then northwesterly along the center line of said creek to its intersection with the east line of Jones Road; then north 105 feet, more or less, along the east line of Jones Road to the point of beginning.

Figure 9.1: Metes-and-Bounds Tract

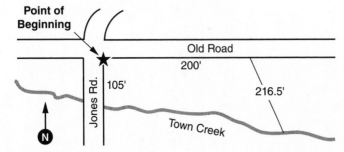

When used to describe property within a town or city, a metes-and-bounds description may begin as follows:

> Beginning at a point on the southerly side of Kent Street, 100 feet easterly from the corner formed by the intersection of the southerly side of Kent Street and the easterly side of Broadway; then...

In this description, the POB is given by reference to the corner intersection. Again, the description must eventually close by returning to the POB.

Metes-and-bounds descriptions are used in Illinois when describing irregular tracts, portions of a recorded lot, or fractions of a section. Such descriptions always incorporate the rectangular survey method and refer to the section, township, range, and principal meridian of the land. These elements are described in the following section.

IN PRACTICE

Metes-and-bounds descriptions can be complex and should be handled with extreme care. When they include detailed compass directions or concave and convex lines, these descriptions can be hard to understand. Natural deterioration or destruction of the monuments in a description can make boundaries difficult to identify. For example, "Raney's Oak" may have died long ago, and "Hunter's Rock" may no longer exist. Software programs are available that convert the data of the compass directions and dimensions to a drawing that verifies that the description represents a closed figure. Professional surveyors should be consulted for definitive interpretations of any legal description.

Rectangular Survey System

The Public Land Survey System (PLSS) (also called the **rectangular survey system**) was established by Congress in 1785 to standardize the description of land acquired by the newly formed federal government. This system is based on two sets of intersecting lines: principal meridians and base lines. The **principal meridians** run north and south, and the **base lines** run east and west. Both are located by reference to degrees of longitude and latitude. Each principal meridian has a name or number and is crossed by a base line. Each principal meridian and its corresponding base line are used to survey a definite area of land, indicated on the map by boundary lines. There are 37 principal meridians in the United States.

Each principal meridian describes only specific areas of land by boundaries. No parcel of land is described by reference to more than one principal meridian. The meridian used is not necessarily the nearest one.

Locations in Illinois are described by their relation to one of the three meridians shown in Figure 9.2. Note that only two of these three meridians actually run through Illinois, but nevertheless all are sometimes referenced in legal descriptions for Illinois properties.

Unit 9

Figure 9.2: Rectangular Survey System Map

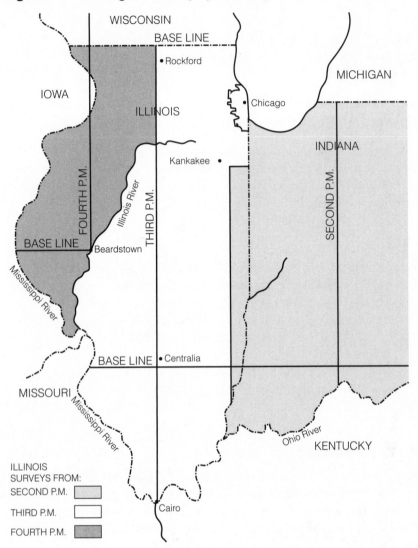

The Second Principal Meridian is located in Indiana and controls that portion of Illinois lying south and east of Kankakee. The Third Principal Meridian begins at Cairo, at the junction of the Ohio and Mississippi rivers, and extends northward toward Wisconsin and near Rockford to the Illinois-Wisconsin border. The Fourth Principal Meridian begins near Beardstown and extends northward to the Canadian border. Surveys of land located in the western portion of Illinois use a base line for the Fourth Principal Meridian at Beardstown. Surveys of land in Wisconsin and eastern Minnesota are made from the Fourth Principal Meridian using a base line that is on the Illinois-Wisconsin border.

Not all property is described by reference to the nearest principal meridian. Notice in Figure 9.2, a property on the western border of the Third Principal Meridian and just west of Rockford will be described by reference to the Fourth Principal Meridian. There are no options regarding the meridians and base lines used to describe a particular property; once made, a legal description is not changed.

Further divisions are used in the same way as monuments in the metes-and-bounds method. They are

■ townships,

- ranges,
- sections, and
- quarter-section lines.

Township Tiers

Lines running east and west, parallel to the base line and six miles apart, are called **township lines** (see Figure 9.3). They form strips of land called **township tiers**. These township tiers are designated by consecutive numbers north or south of the base line. For example, the strip of land between 6 and 12 miles north of a base line is Township 2 North.

Figure 9.3: Townships in the Rectangular Survey System

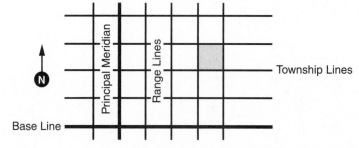

Ranges

The land on either side of a principal meridian is divided into six-mile-wide strips by lines running north and south, parallel to the meridian. These north-south strips of land are called **ranges** (see Figure 9.3). They are designated by consecutive numbers east or west of the principal meridian. For example, Range 3 East would be a strip of land between 12 and 18 miles east of its principal meridian.

Township Squares

MEMORY TIP

Note that although a town-ship square is part of a township tier, the two terms do not refer to the same thing. Township tiers are the very long strips of six-mile-wide land running east and west. For this discussion, the word township used by itself refers only to the township squares formed by the vertical range lines intersecting the tiers.

When the horizontal township lines and the vertical range lines intersect, they form squares. These township squares are the basic units of the rectangular survey system (see Figure 9.3). **Townships** are six miles square and contain 36 square miles (23,040 acres).

Each township is given a legal description. The township's description includes the following:

- Designation of the township tier in which the township is located
- Designation of the range strip
- Name or number of the principal meridian for that area

EXAMPLE

In Figure 9.3, the shaded township is described as Township 3 North, Range 4 East of the Principal Meridian (an Illinois legal description would name the 2nd, 3rd, or 4th principal meridian, naming the meridian specifically). This township is the third strip, or tier, north of the base line, and it designates the township number and direction. The township is also located in the fourth range strip (those running north and south) east of the principal meridian. Finally, reference is made to the principal meridian because the land being described is within the boundary of land surveyed from that meridian. An actual description, then, might be abbreviated as T3N, R4E 4th Principal Meridian.

Sections

Each township contains 36 sections. Each **section** is one square mile, or 640 acres. Sections are numbered 1 through 36, as shown in Figure 9.4. Section 1 is always in the northeast, or upper right-hand, corner. The numbering proceeds right to left (backward), beginning in the upper right-hand corner. From there, the numbers drop down to the next tier and continue from left to right, then back from right again to left. By law, each section number 16 is set aside for school purposes. The sale or rental proceeds from section 16 were originally available for township school use. The schoolhouse was often located in this section so it would be centrally located for all of the students in the township. As a result, Section 16 is always referred to as the school section.

Figure 9.4: Sections in a Township

N

W

6	5	4	3	2	1
7	8	9	10	11	12
18	17	16	15	14	13
19	20	21	22	23	24
30	29	28	27	26	25
31	32	33	34	35	36

E

S

As shown in Figure 9.5, sections are divided into halves (320 acres) and quarters (160 acres). In turn, each of those parts may be further divided into halves and quarters. The southeast quarter of a section, which is a 160-acre tract, is abbreviated SE¼. The SE¼ of the SE¼ of the SE¼ of Section 1 would be a 10-acre square in the lower right-hand corner of Section 1.

Figure 9.5: A Section

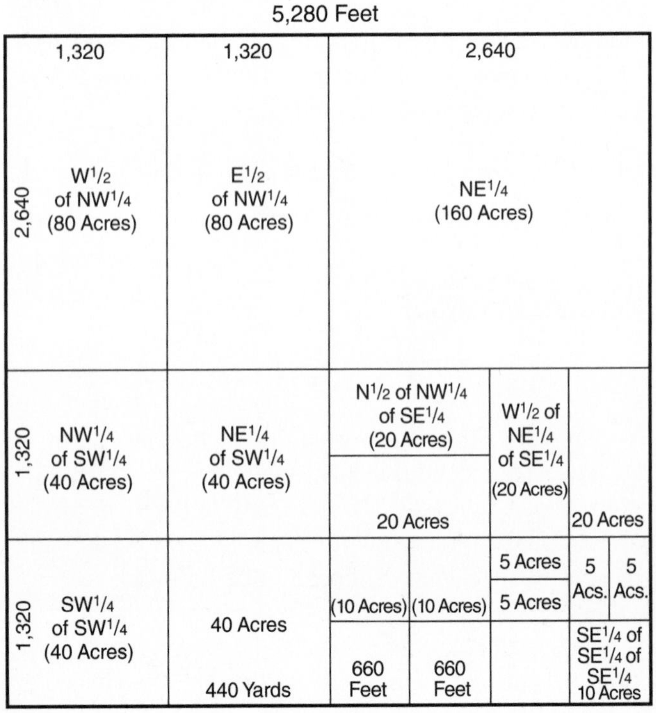

The rectangular survey system sometimes uses a shorthand method in its descriptions. For example, a comma may be used in place of the word *of:* SE¼, SE¼, SE¼, Section 1. It is possible to combine portions of a section, such as NE¼ of SW¼ and N½ of NW¼ of SE¼ of Section 1, which could also be written NE¼, SW¼; N½, NW¼, SE¼ of Section 1. A semicolon means *and.* Because of the word *and* in this description, tallying first the total amount of land on each side of *and* (or the semicolon), then adding those two numbers together for area, gives 60 acres.

Correction Lines

Range lines are parallel only in theory. Due to the curvature of the earth, range lines gradually approach each other. If they are extended northward, they eventually meet at the North Pole. The fact that the earth is not flat, combined with the crude instruments used in early days, means that few townships are exactly six-mile squares or contain exactly 36 square miles. The system compensates for this "round earth problem" with correction lines. Every fourth township line, both north and south of the base line, is designated a **correction line**. On each correction line, the range lines are measured to the full distance of six miles apart. Guide meridians run north and south at 24-mile intervals from the principal meridian. A **government check** is the irregular area created by these corrections; such an area is about 24 miles square.

Must Know Measurements

■ Sections are smaller than townships

■ Township = 6 miles × 6 miles = 36 sections per township

■ 640 acres in a section

■ Section = 1 mile × 1 mile = 1 square mile

■ 43,560 = square feet per acre

■ 5,280 feet in a mile (one side of a section)

Because most townships do not contain exactly 36 square miles, surveyors follow well-established rules of adjustment. These rules provide that any irregularity in a township must be adjusted in those sections adjacent to its north and west boundaries (Sections 1, 2, 3, 4, 5, 6, 7, 18, 19, 30, and 31). These are called *fractional sections*. All other sections are exactly one square mile and are called *standard sections*. These provisions for making corrections explain some of the variations in township and section acreage under the rectangular survey system of legal description.

Fractional Sections and Government Lots

Undersized or oversized sections are called **fractional sections**. Fractional sections may occur for a number of reasons. In some areas, for example, the rectangular survey may have been made by separate crews, and gaps less than a section wide remained when the surveys met. Other errors may have resulted from the physical difficulties encountered in the actual survey. For example, part of a section may be submerged in water.

Areas smaller than full quarter-sections were numbered and designated as **government lots** by surveyors. These lots can be created by the curvature of the earth, by land bordering or surrounding large bodies of water, or by artificial state borders. An overage or a shortage was corrected whenever possible by placing the government lots in the north or west portions of the fractional sections. For example, a government lot might be described as follows:

> Government Lot 2 in the northwest quarter of fractional Section 18, Township 2 North, Range 4 East of the Salt Lake Meridian

Reading a Rectangular Survey Description

To determine the location and size of a property described in the rectangular survey style, start at the end and work backward to the beginning. In other words, analyze the legal description right to left. It is similar to finding a location using a mailing address: John Smith, 430 N.

Unit 9

Michigan, Chicago IL, USA, North America. The largest parcel is at the end; the smallest, John, is at the beginning. Therefore, consider the following description:

> The S½ of the NW¼ of the SE¼ of Section 11, Township 8 North, Range 6 West of the Fourth Principal Meridian

To locate this tract of land from the citation alone, first search for the Fourth Principal Meridian on a map of the United States. Then, on a regional map, find the township in which the property is located by counting six range strips west of the Fourth Principal Meridian and eight townships north of its corresponding base line. After locating Section 11, divide the section into quarters. Then divide the SE¼ into quarters, and then the NW¼ of that into halves. The S½ of that NW¼ contains the property in question.

In computing the size of this tract of land, know that a section contains 640 acres. Now divide 640 by the denominators (the lower number of the fractions). You can take them in any order that you like. For instance, 640 / 2 / 4 / 4 = 20, just as 640 / 4 / 4 / 2 = 20. The property in question contains 20 acres.

If there are two or more parcels listed, such as the NE¼ of the NW¼ and the NW¼ of the NE¼, the "and" signifies that one restarts the calculation for that second parcel with 640. In other words. 640 / 4 / 4 = 40 acres PLUS 640 / 4 / 4 = 40 acres. The two individual parcels add up to an 80 acre parcel. 40 acres + 40 acres = 80 acres.

In general, if a rectangular survey description does not use the conjunction *and* or a semicolon (indicating two or more parcels are combined), the longer the description, the smaller the tract of land it describes.

Legal descriptions should always include the name of the county and state in which the land is located because meridians often relate to more than one state and occasionally relate to two base lines.

Metes-and-Bounds Descriptions Within the Rectangular Survey System

Land in states that use the rectangular survey system also may require a metes-and-bounds description. This usually occurs in one of three situations: when describing an irregular tract; when a tract is too small to be described by quarter-sections; or when a tract does not follow the lot or block lines of a recorded subdivision or section, quarter-section lines, or other fractional section lines. The following is an example of a combined metes-and-bounds and rectangular survey system description (see Figure 9.6):

> That part of the northwest quarter of Section 12, Township 10 North, Range 7 West of the Third Principal Meridian, bounded by a line described as follows: Commencing at the southeast corner of the northwest quarter of said Section 12 then north 500 feet; then west parallel with the south line of said section 1,000 feet; then south parallel with the east line of said section 500 feet to the south line of said northwest quarter; then east along said south line to the point of beginning.

Figure 9.6: Metes and Bounds With Rectangular Survey

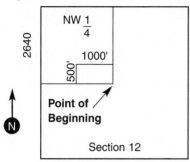

"Section 12, T10N, R7W,
Third Principal Meridian"

Metes-and-bounds descriptions may be included in the rectangular survey system used in Illinois when describing irregular or small tracts.

Lot-and-Block System

The third method of legal description is the **lot-and-block system** (also called the *recorded plat system*). This system uses lot-and-block numbers referred to in a **plat map** filed in the public records of the county where the land is located. The lot-and-block system is often used to describe property in subdivisions and urban areas.

A lot-and-block survey is performed in two steps. First, a large parcel of land is described either by metes and bounds or by rectangular survey. Once this large parcel is surveyed, it is broken into smaller parcels. As a result, a lot-and-block legal description is always a smaller part of a metes-and-bounds or rectangular survey description. For each parcel described under the lot-and-block system, the lot refers to the numerical designation of any particular parcel. The block refers to the name of the subdivision under which the map is recorded. The block reference is drawn from the early 1900s, when a city block was the most common type of subdivided property.

The lot-and-block system starts with the preparation of a *subdivision plat* by a licensed surveyor or an engineer (see Figure 9.7). On this plat, the land is divided into numbered or lettered lots and blocks, and streets or access roads for public use are indicated. Lot sizes and street details must be described completely and must comply with all local ordinances and requirements. When properly signed and approved, the subdivision plat is recorded in the county in which the land is located.

Figure 9.7: Subdivision Plat Map of Prairie Acres Estates

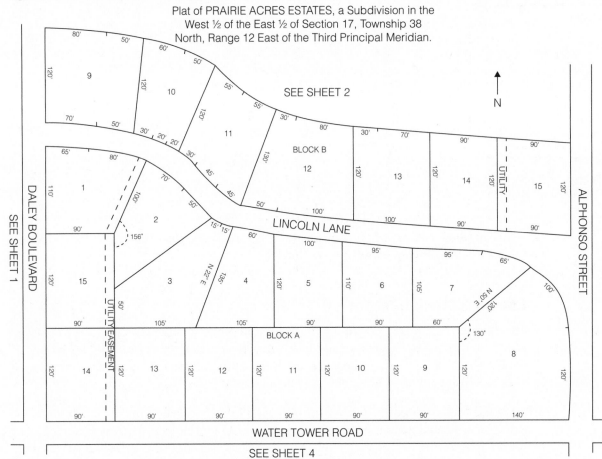

Plat of PRAIRIE ACRES ESTATES, a Subdivision in the
West ½ of the East ½ of Section 17, Township 38
North, Range 12 East of the Third Principal Meridian.

Recorded January 14, 1969, in Book 275, Page 1346, in Prairie County, Illinois.

The plat becomes part of the legal description. In describing a lot from a recorded subdivision plat, the following three identifiers are used:

1. Lot-and-block number

2. Name or number of the subdivision plat

3. Name of the county and state

The following is an example of a lot-and-block description:

> Lot 71, Happy Valley Estates 2, located in a portion of the southeast quarter of Section 23, Township 7 North, Range 4 East of the Seward Principal Meridian in _____ County, State of _____.

Anyone who wants to locate this parcel would start with the map of the Seward Principal Meridian to identify the township and range reference. Then he would consult the township map of Township 7 North, Range 4 East, and the section map of Section 23. From there, he would look at the quarter-section map of the southeast quarter. The quarter-section map would refer to the plat map for the subdivision known as the second unit (second parcel subdivided) under the name of Happy Valley Estates.

Some subdivided lands are further divided by a later resubdivision. In the following example, one developer (Western View) purchased a large parcel from a second developer (Homewood). Western View and then resubdivided the property into parcels of differing sizes:

> Lot 4, Western View Resubdivision of the Homewood Subdivision, located in a portion of the west half of Section 19, Township 10 North, Range 13 East of the Black Hills Principal Meridian, _____ County, State of _____.

The lot-and-block system is used in Illinois. Subdivision descriptions are the predominant method of describing developed land in this state. A subdivision map is illustrated in Figure 9.7.

Under the Plat Act (765 ILCS 205), when an owner divides a parcel of land into two or more parts, any of which is less than five acres, the parts must be surveyed and a plat of subdivision recorded. An exception to this would be the division of lots or blocks of less than one acre in any recorded subdivision that does not involve the creation of any new streets or easements of access. When a conveyance is made, the county recorder may require an affidavit that an exception exists.

The provisions of the Plat Act are complicated and subject to interpretation by each county recorder. Anyone attempting to record a document conveying land should consult a lawyer and the county recorder about the requirements involved.

PREPARING A SURVEY

Legal descriptions should not be altered or combined without adequate information from a surveyor or title attorney. A licensed surveyor is trained and authorized to locate and determine the legal description of any parcel of land. The surveyor does this by preparing two documents: a survey and a survey sketch. The *survey* states the property's legal description. The *survey sketch* shows the location and dimensions of the parcel. When a survey also shows the location, size, and shape of buildings on the lot, it is called a *spot survey*.

IN PRACTICE

Because legal descriptions, once recorded, affect title to real estate, they should be prepared only by a professional surveyor.

Legal descriptions should be copied with extreme care. An incorrectly worded legal description in a sales contract may result in a conveyance of more or less land than the parties intended. An incorrect legal description will likely create title problems for the buyer who seeks to convey the property at a future date. A real estate licensee risks losing a commission and may be held liable for damages suffered by an injured party because of an improperly worded legal description.

It is very important for real estate licensees to be aware of various surveys and their uses. Not all surveys include surveyor liability and warranties of accuracy. Some surveys, such as an improvement location certificate (ILC), are not full surveys. ILCs are prepared in a shorter time frame and at a lower cost, providing only the location of the structures and improvements as related to property boundaries.

Unit 9

MEASURING ELEVATIONS

Just as surface rights must be identified, surveyed, and described, so must rights to the property above the earth's surface. Elevations are measured to determine the legal descriptions of air rights and condominium apartments. As discussed earlier, land includes the space above the ground. In the same way land may be measured and divided into parcels, the air itself may be divided. An owner may subdivide the air above his or her land into air lots. **Air lots** are composed of the airspace within specific boundaries located over a parcel of land.

Because condominiums are usually air lots, condominium laws passed in all states require that a registered land surveyor prepare a plat map that shows the elevations of floor and ceiling surfaces and the vertical boundaries of each unit with reference to an official datum (discussed as follows). A unit's floor, for example, might be 60 feet above the datum, and its ceiling, 69 feet. Typically, a separate plat is prepared for each floor in the condominium building.

Subsurface rights can be legally described in the same manner as air rights. They are measured below the datum rather than above it. Subsurface rights are used not only for coal mining, petroleum drilling, and utility line location but also for multistory condominiums—both residential and commercial—that have several floors below ground level.

Datum

A **datum** is a point, line, or surface from which elevations are measured or indicated. A surveyor would use a datum in determining the height of a structure or establishing the grade of a street.

IN PRACTICE

While there are established national and international datums, virtually all large cities instead use official local datums. For example, the official datum for Chicago is called the *Chicago City Datum*.

The general datum used by Illinois surveyors is the North American Vertical Datum of 1988 (NAVD88).

Benchmarks

Monuments traditionally are used to mark surface measurements between points. A monument could be a marker set in concrete, a piece of steel-reinforcing bar (rebar), a metal pipe driven into the soil, or simply a wooden stake stuck in the dirt. Because such items are subject to the whims of nature and vandals, their accuracy is sometimes suspect. As a result, surveyors instead rely heavily on benchmarks to mark their work accurately and permanently.

Benchmarks are permanent reference points that have been established throughout the United States. They are usually embossed brass markers set into solid concrete or asphalt bases. While used to some degree for surface measurements, their principal use is for marking datums.

Cities with local datums have designated official local benchmarks, which are assigned permanent identifying numbers. Local benchmarks simplify surveyors' work because the basic benchmarks may be miles away. A major benchmark in Chicago is located at State and Madison streets. It references non-city addresses extending far west of Cook County. County addresses beginning with 33 West or 25 West refer to number of miles west of State Street. Numbers 1 North or 4 South refer to miles north or south of Madison Street.

SUMMARY

A legal description is a precise method of identifying a parcel of land. Three methods of legal description can be used: metes-and-bounds method, rectangular survey system, and lot-and-block (plat map) system. A property's description should always be noted by the same method as the one used in previous documents.

The metes-and-bounds method uses direction and distance measurement to establish precise boundaries for a parcel. Monuments are fixed objects that establish these boundaries. Their physical location takes precedence over the written linear measurement in a document. When property is described by metes and bounds, the description begins and ends at the point of beginning (POB).

The rectangular survey system is used in most states. Illinois legal descriptions refer to three principal meridians, one of which is in Indiana (the second). Meridians in and near Illinois number from east to west. A given property is not necessarily referenced by the closest meridian. Once a legal description has been made, it is permanent. With rectangular survey, each principal meridian and its corresponding base line are the primary reference points. Any parcel of land is surveyed from only one principal meridian and one base line.

East and west lines parallel with the base line form six-mile-wide strips called township tiers. North and south lines parallel with the principal meridian form six-mile-wide range strips. The resulting squares are 36 square miles in area and are called townships.

A sample legal description might partially read, "Township 3 North, Range 4 East of the 2nd Principal Meridian." Townships are divided into 36 sections, one square mile each. Each section has 640 acres, and each acre has 43,560 square feet. Section 16 is traditionally the school section; all other sections are numbered off in the township backward in S-curves, starting with Section 1 in the upper right-hand corner.

Irregularities in using a square system to match a round planet are adjusted in the rectangular system by correction lines, which in turn form pockets of land called government checks.

When a tract of land is irregular, a surveyor can prepare a combination of methods: for example, rectangular survey and metes-and-bounds description. Lot-and-block combined with rectangular survey is even more frequently used in describing suburban America.

Land in every state can be subdivided into lots and blocks by means of a plat map. An approved plat of survey is filed for record in the recorder's office of the county in which the land is located. A plat of subdivision gives the legal description of a building site in a town or city by lot, block, and subdivision in a section, township, and range of a principal meridian in a county and state. Lot and block, section, and township also comprise the essentials given in a property identification number (PIN), which also appears on tax information, surveys, and contracts.

Air lots, condominium descriptions, and other measurements of vertical elevations may be computed from national datums. Most large cities have established local survey datums for surveying within the areas. The elevations from these datums are further supplemented by reference points, called benchmarks, placed at fixed intervals from the datums. Benchmarks are used for vertical reference points but often supplement surface measurements.

UNIT 9 QUIZ

Questions 1 through 2 refer to the following illustration.

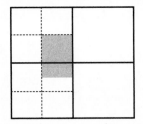

1. What is the proper description of the shaded area of a section?
    A. SW¼ of the NE¼ and the N½ of the SE¼ of the SW¼
    B. SW¼ of the SE¼ of the NW¼ and the N½ of the NE¼ of the SW¼
    C. N½ of the NE¼ of the SW¼ and the SE¼ of the NW¼
    D. S½ of the SW¼ of the NE¼ and the NE¼ of the NW¼ of the SE¼

2. What is the acreage for the shaded parcel?
    A. 60
    B. 80
    C. 15
    D. 30

3. In describing real estate, the system that uses feet, degrees, and natural and artificial markers as monuments is
    A. metes and bounds.
    B. rectangular survey.
    C. government survey.
    D. lot and block.

Questions 4 through 7 refer to the following illustration of a whole township and parts of the adjacent townships.

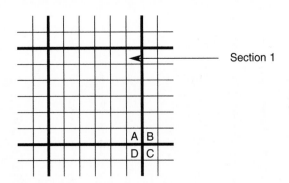

4. The section marked A is
    A. a school section.
    B. Section 36.
    C. Section 31.
    D. a government lot.

5. Which of these is Section 6?
    A. A
    B. B
    C. D
    D. C

6. The section directly below C is
    A. Section 7.
    B. Section 12.
    C. Section 25.
    D. Section 30.

7. Which of these is Section D?
    A. Section 6
    B. Section 31
    C. Section 36
    D. Section 1

8. A buyer purchased a one-acre parcel for $2.15 per square foot. What is the selling price of the parcel?
   A. $344
   B. $1,376
   C. $93,654
   D. $46,827

9. The legal description "the NW¼ of the SW¼ of Section 6, Township 4 North, Range 7 West" is defective because there is no reference to
   A. a principal meridian.
   B. lot numbers.
   C. boundary lines.
   D. a record of survey.

10. To keep the principal meridian and range lines as near to six miles apart as possible, a correction called a government check is made. How large is a government check?
    A. 1 square mile
    B. 20 square miles
    C. 24 miles square
    D. 6 miles square

11. Fractional sections in the rectangular survey system along the northern or western borders of a check that are less than a quarter-section in area are called
    A. fractional parcels.
    B. portional sections.
    C. fractional townships.
    D. government lots.

12. A woman purchased 4.5 acres of land for $78,400. A man who owns adjoining property wants to purchase a strip of the woman's land measuring 150 feet by 100 feet. What should this strip cost the man if the woman sells it for the same price per square foot she originally paid for the property?
    A. $6,000
    B. $3,000
    C. $7,800
    D. $9,400

13. A property contains 10 acres. How many lots of not less than 50 feet by 100 feet can be subdivided from the property if 26,000 square feet are dedicated for roads?
    A. 80
    B. 81
    C. 82
    D. 83

14. A parcel of land is 400 feet by 640 feet. The parcel is cut in half diagonally by a stream. How many acres are there in each half of the parcel?
    A. 2.75
    B. 5.51
    C. 2.94
    D. 5.88

15. The section due west of Section 18, Township 5 North, Range 8 West, is
    A. Section 19, T5N, R8W.
    B. Section 17, T5N, R8W.
    C. Section 12, T5N, R7W.
    D. Section 13, T5N, R9W.

16. In Illinois, legal descriptions of land are usually based on the
    A. Third, Fourth, and Fifth Principal Meridians.
    B. rectangular survey system.
    C. three base lines running through the central part of the state.
    D. nearest principal meridian.

17. Land in the northwest corner of Illinois is described with reference to which principal meridian?
    A. Fourth
    B. Second
    C. Third
    D. Fifth

Answer questions 18 through 20 using the information given on the plat of Prairie Acres Estates in Figure 9.7.

18. How many lots have easements?
    A. 3
    B. 6
    C. 4
    D. 7

19. Which of these lots has the *MOST* frontage on Lincoln Lane?
    A. Lot 10, block B
    B. Lot 11, block B
    C. Lot 8, block A
    D. Lot 7, block A

20. "Beginning at the intersection of the east line of Daley Boulevard and the south line of Lincoln Lane and running south along the east line of Daley Boulevard a distance of 230 feet; then easterly parallel to the north line of Water Tower Road a distance of 195 feet; then northeasterly on a course of N22°E a distance of 135 feet; and then northwesterly along the south line of Lincoln Lane to the point of beginning." Which lots are described here?
    A. Lots 1, 2, 3, and 15, block A
    B. Lots 7, 8, and 9, block A
    C. Lots 9, 10, and 11, block B
    D. Lots 13, 14, and 15, block A

UNIT
10

Real Estate Taxes and Other Liens

LEARNING OBJECTIVES

When you have completed this unit, you will be able to accomplish the following.

› Identify the various classifications of liens.
› Describe how real estate taxes are applied through assessments, tax liens, and the use of equalization ratios.
› Describe how non-property tax liens are applied and enforced.

KEY TERMS

appropriation	involuntary lien	statutory lien
collateral	judgment	subordination agreement
encumbrance	lien	tax deed
equalization factor	lien waiver	tax lien
equitable lien	lis pendens	tax sale
estate taxes	mechanic's lien	voluntary lien
general lien	mortgage lien	writ of attachment
general real estate tax	special assessment	
inheritance taxes	specific lien	

LIENS

All liens are encumbrances, but not all encumbrances are liens.

A **lien** is a charge or claim against property that is made to enforce the payment of money. Whenever someone borrows money, the lender generally requires some form of security. *Security* (also called **collateral**) is something of value that the borrower promises to give the lender if the borrower fails to repay the debt. When the lender's security is in the form of real estate, the security is called a lien.

Liens are not limited to security for borrowed money (such as *mortgage liens*). Liens can be enforced against property by a government agency to recover taxes owed by the owner (*tax liens*). A lien can be used to compel the payment of an assessment or other special charge as well. A *mechanic's lien* represents an effort to recover payment for work performed.

A lien represents only an interest in property; it does not constitute actual ownership of the property. It is an encumbrance on the owner's title. An **encumbrance** is any charge or claim that attaches to real property and lessens its value or impairs its use. An encumbrance does not necessarily prevent the transfer or conveyance of the property, but because it is "attached" to the property, it transfers along with it. Liens differ from other encumbrances; however, because they are financial or monetary in nature and attach to the property because of a debt.

Types of Liens

There are many different types of liens. One way that liens are classified is by how they are created. A **voluntary lien** is created intentionally by the property owner's action, such as when someone takes out a mortgage loan. An **involuntary lien**, on the other hand, is not a matter of choice; it is created by law or a court. It may be either statutory or equitable. A **statutory lien** is created by statute. A real estate tax lien, then, is an involuntary, statutory lien. It is created by statute without the property owner taking it on voluntarily. An **equitable lien** is created by a court to ensure the payment of a judgment as well as by agreement.

Liens also may be classified according to the type of property involved. **General liens** affect all the property, both real and personal, of a debtor. This includes judgments, estate and inheritance taxes, decedent's debts, corporate franchise taxes, and Internal Revenue Service taxes. A lien on real estate differs from a lien on personal property. A lien attaches to real property at the moment it is filed. In contrast, a lien does not attach to personal property until the personal property actually is levied on or seized by the sheriff.

Specific liens are secured by specific property and affect only that particular property. Specific liens on real estate include mechanics' liens, mortgage liens, real estate tax liens, and liens for special assessments and utilities. Specific liens can also secure personal property, as when a lien is placed on a car to secure payment of a car loan.

Effects of Liens on Title

The existence of a lien does not necessarily prevent a property owner from conveying title to someone else. The lien might reduce the value of the real estate, however, because few buyers will take on the risk of a property that has a lien on it.

Because the lien attaches to the property, not the property owner, a new owner could lose the property if the creditors take court action to enforce payment. Once properly established, a lien runs with the land and will bind all successive owners until the lien is paid in full.

IN PRACTICE

A buyer should insist on a title search before closing a real estate transaction so that any recorded liens are revealed. If liens are present, the buyer may decide to purchase at a lower price or at better terms, require the liens be paid, or refuse to purchase.

Priority of Liens

Priority of liens refers to the order in which claims against the property will be satisfied. In general, the rule for priority of liens is "first to record, first in right"—liens take priority from the date they are recorded in the public records of the county in which the property is located.

There are some notable exceptions to this rule. For example, real estate taxes and special assessments generally take priority over all other liens, regardless of the order in which the liens are recorded. This means that outstanding real estate taxes and special assessments are paid from the proceeds of a court-ordered sale first. The remainder of the proceeds is used to pay other outstanding liens in the order of their priority. Mechanics' liens take priority as provided by state law but never over tax and special assessment liens.

EXAMPLE

A mansion is ordered sold by the court to satisfy the owner's debts. The property is subject to a $50,000 judgment lien, incurred as a result of a mechanic's lien suit. Principal and interest totaling $295,000 remains to be paid on the mansion's mortgage. This year's unpaid real estate taxes amount to $5,000. The judgment lien was entered in the public record on February 7, 2014, and the mortgage lien was recorded January 22, 2012. If the mansion is sold at the tax sale for $375,000, the proceeds of the sale will be distributed in the following order:

1. $5,000 to the taxing bodies for this year's real estate taxes
2. $295,000 to the mortgage lender (the entire amount of the mortgage loan outstanding as of the date of sale)
3. $50,000 to the creditor named in the judgment lien
4. $25,000 to the owner (the proceeds remaining after paying the first three items)

However, if the mansion sold for $325,000, the proceeds would be distributed as follows:

1. $5,000 to the taxing bodies for this year's real estate taxes
2. $295,000 to the mortgage lender (the entire amount of the mortgage loan outstanding as of the date of sale)
3. $25,000 to the creditor named in the judgment lien
4. $0 to the owner

Although the creditor is not repaid in full, this outcome is considered fair for two reasons:

■ The creditor's interest arose later than the others, so the other interests took priority.

■ The creditor knew (or should have known) about priority creditors when credit was extended to the mansion owner, so the risk involved was clear (or should have been clear).

Subordination agreements are written agreements between lienholders to change the priority of mortgage, judgment, and other liens. Under a subordination agreement, the holder of a superior or prior lien agrees to permit a junior lienholder's interest to move ahead of her lien.

REAL ESTATE TAX LIENS

The ownership of real estate is always subject to certain government powers. One of these is the right of state and local governments to impose (levy) taxes to pay for their functions. Because the location of real estate is permanently fixed, the government can levy taxes with a high degree of certainty that the taxes will be collected. The annual taxes levied on real estate usually have priority over previously recorded liens, so they may be enforced by a court-ordered sale.

There are two types of real estate taxes: *general real estate taxes* and *special assessments*. Both are levied against specific parcels of property and automatically become **tax liens** on those properties.

General Real Estate Taxes

General real estate taxes (also called *ad valorem taxes*) are based on the value of the property being taxed (*ad valorem* is Latin for "according to value"). They are specific, involuntary, statutory liens. They are charged by various government agencies and municipalities, including

- states;
- counties;
- cities, towns, and villages;
- school districts (local elementary and high schools, publicly funded junior colleges and community colleges);
- drainage districts;
- water districts;
- sanitary districts; and
- parks, forest preserves, recreation, and other public-use districts.

Real estate property taxes are a favored source of revenue for local governments because real estate cannot be hidden and is relatively easy to value. Property taxes pay for a wide range of government services and programs.

Exemptions From General Taxes

Most state laws exempt certain real estate from taxation. Such property must be used for tax-exempt purposes, as defined in the statutes. The most common exempt properties are owned by

- various municipal organizations (such as schools, parks, and playgrounds),
- cities and counties,
- state and federal governments,
- religious and charitable organizations,
- hospitals, and
- educational institutions.

Properties in Illinois that are totally exempt from paying general real estate taxes include schools, religious institutions, cemeteries, and charitable institutions, as well as those owned by federal, state, county, and local governments. Taxing districts may elect to exempt certain other properties (within limits), such as commercial and industrial properties.

Illinois property taxes are adjusted to reflect certain concessions given on owner-occupied residences. These properties are designated as *homesteads*. A *homestead exemption* (not to be confused with a *homestead estate*) reduces the assessed value of a property subject to taxes. Here are the basic exemptions (which may vary from county to county):

- The homeowner exemption applies to owners of single-family homes, condominiums, cooperatives, and one- to six-unit apartment buildings. In some counties, owners must apply to the assessor for the exemption each year; in others, the exemption is automatically applied. The amount of exemption is currently $6,000 ($7,000 in Cook County).

- The senior citizen homestead exemption is available to homeowners over the age of 65. Seniors must prove age and ownership to the county assessor by December 31 of the assessment year for which the application is made. These exemption amounts are subtracted from the property's equalized assessed value before the tax rate is applied. This exemption reduces the equalized assessed value of a senior's home by $5,000.

- The Senior Citizen Assessment Freeze Homestead Exemption program allows Illinois seniors to freeze their assessed valuation for the remainder of their lifetime once they have turned 65 if household income does not exceed $55,000. Annual application and proof of income must be filed with the county assessor.

- The home improvement exemption allows any Illinois homeowner who has recently improved her home (by adding a new family room, for example) to forestall an increase in the home's overall assessed value for up to four years. This exemption is available up to an improvement value of $75,000.

Property owners may qualify for other tax concessions based on their status as disabled veterans or by virtue of improvements to the property, certain maintenance and repair expenses, solar heating, airport land, farmland, rehabilitation of historic buildings, and location within enterprise zones or tax concession districts.

IN PRACTICE

If there is a new addition or remodeling, the buyers' real estate agent should be aware of mechanics' liens and four-year homestead improvement exemptions.

Assessment

Real estate is valued for tax purposes by county or township assessors or appraisers. This official valuation process is called *assessment*. A property's *assessed value* generally is based on the sales prices of comparable properties; although practices may vary. Land values may be assessed separately from buildings or other improvements, and different valuation methods may be used for different types of property. State laws may provide for property to be periodically reassessed.

Depending on how the property is classified, real property in Cook County is assessed based on a sliding scale of percentages of fair market value, from 10% to 25%. In all other counties, real property is assessed at 331/3% of fair market value. Real property is defined by Illinois property tax code as the land itself and all buildings, structures, improvements, and other permanent fixtures attached to the land.

To Determine Taxes

■ Locate assessed value (usually one-third of market value)

■ Always "equalize" assessed value first

■ Subtract any exemptions

■ Tax rate × adjusted assessed value = real estate taxes

Taxpayers who believe that errors were made in their property's assessment may file a complaint directly with the county assessor. If the taxpayer's complaint is denied, the decision may be appealed to an administrative board of review (in Cook County, the Board of Appeals). Alternatively, the taxpayer can bypass the county official and go directly to the board of review. A taxpayer who is dissatisfied with the board's decision may appeal to the Illinois Property Tax Appeal Board or to the circuit court of the county in which the property is located.

Equalization

In some jurisdictions, when it is necessary to correct inequalities in statewide tax assessments, an equalization factor is used to achieve uniformity. An **equalization factor** may be applied to raise or lower assessments in a particular district or county. The basic assessed value of each property in the area is multiplied by the equalization factor to acquire an "equalized assessment," then any exemptions are subtracted, and last, the tax rate is applied.

Math Concepts: Calculating Real Estate Taxes

Assessed value × equalization factor − exemptions × tax rate = annual tax

The assessments in one county are 20% lower than the average assessments throughout the rest of the state. This underassessment can be corrected by requiring the application of an equalization factor of 125% (1.25) to each assessment in that county. Therefore, a parcel of land assessed for tax purposes at $98,000 would be taxed on an equalized value of $122,500 ($98,000 × 1.25 = $122,500). At this point, the $6,000 homestead exemption would be subtracted. Then, if there were a $5,000 senior exemption, it would be subtracted next ($122,500 − $6,000 − $5,000 = $111,500 adjusted assessed value). Using this final equalized, adjusted assessed value, taxes would then be computed by multiplying by the proper tax rate. Tax rates are often expressed in one of two ways: dollars per hundred dollars of value or in millage, also known as mills. For example, they can be either $5 per $100 of value or, as in the case of mills, 50 mills. Each can be converted to a decimal figure to use in the tax calculation. $5 per $100 of value converts to 0.05 and 50 mils converts to 0.05.

The assessed valuation of real estate is adjusted yearly in each county by applying an equalization factor determined by the Illinois Department of Revenue. Assessed values are compared with selling prices to arrive at the equalization factor, and each county is assigned a multiplier to be used for equalization purposes. The equalizer is always applied first (equalizer × basic value) before applicable homeowners' exemptions (if any) are subtracted from value. From the final equalized, adjusted assessed value, taxes are computed. Any given parcel receives a full reassessment on a quadrennial (four-year) basis, as mandated by the state, though in Cook county this reassessment is triennial (every three years).

Budgets and Tax Rates

The process of arriving at a real estate tax rate begins with the adoption of a *budget* by each taxing district. Each budget covers the financial requirements of the taxing body for the coming fiscal year. The fiscal year may be the January through December calendar year or some other 12-month period designated by statute. The budget must include an estimate of all expenditures needed for the year. In addition, the budget must indicate the amount of income expected from all fees, revenue sharing, and other sources. The net amount remaining to be raised from real estate taxes is then determined by the difference between these figures.

The next step is to spread out the needed monies among all the homeowners proportionately (based on values). The total monies needed for the coming fiscal year are divided by the total valuations of all real estate located within the taxing body's jurisdiction.

Proposed expense ÷ total assessed property values = tax rate

EXAMPLE

A taxing district's budget indicates that $800,000 must be acquired from real estate taxes to pay for needed expenditures. The assessment roll (assessor's record) of all taxable real estate within the district equals $10 million. The tax rate is computed as follows:

$800,000 ÷ $10,000,000 = 0.080 or 8%

Appropriation

Formal **appropriation** is the way a taxing body actually authorizes the expenditure of funds and provides for the sources of the funding. Appropriation generally involves the adoption of an ordinance or the passage of a law that states the specific terms of the proposed taxation. The amount to be raised from the general real estate tax is then imposed on property owners through a tax levy. A *tax levy* is the formal action taken to impose the tax, usually by way of a vote of the taxing district's governing body.

Creating the Tax Bills

After appropriation, a property owner's tax bill is computed by applying the tax rate to the assessed valuation of the property.

Generally, one tax bill that incorporates all real estate taxes levied by the various taxing districts is prepared for each property. Some tax purposes or tax targets (like the park district) are split out and easily identifiable on most bills. In some areas, however, separate bills are prepared by each taxing body.

The county collector prepares and issues only one combined tax bill to each parcel of property.

EXAMPLE

If a property is assessed for tax purposes at $160,000 and the tax rate is 3%, the tax will be $4,800 ($160,000 × 0.03) (this assumes no equalization factor).

Let's say the equalization factor is 120%. Thus, the equalized, assessed value is $192,000 ($160,000 × 1.20). From there, apply the tax rate of 3% (0.03) to arrive at taxes of $5,760 ($192,000 × 0.03).

General real estate taxes are levied annually for the calendar year and become a prior first lien, superior to all other liens, on January 1 of that tax year. However, they are not due and payable until the following year.

General real estate taxes are payable in two equal installments in the year after they are levied: one-half by June 1 and the second half by September 1 (except in Cook County, as noted later). Taxes in Illinois, then, are said to be *paid in arrears*. The payment due dates are also called *penalty dates*, after which a penalty of 1.5% per month is added to any unpaid amount. Because bills must be issued 30 days before a penalty date, the penalty date for an installment may be delayed if the county collector is late in preparing the bills.

In Cook County, the due date for the first installment of real estate taxes is the first business day in March. The second installment due date varies because the bill relies on the delivery of various sets of data by other state and county agencies. Unlike the first installment bill, the second installment bill reflects the new assessed values, assessment appeals, exemptions, the state equalization factor, and taxing district tax rates. The Cook County Treasurer's Office projects the second due date as soon as the process reaches the calculation of the tax rates.

Additional information on the Illinois tax code and specific tax situations can be found in Unit 35 of the Illinois Compiled Statutes.

Enforcement of Tax Liens

Real estate taxes must be valid to be enforceable. That means they must be levied properly, used for a legal purpose, and applied equitably to all property. Real estate taxes that have remained delinquent for the statutory period can be collected through a **tax sale**.

The statutory requirements for enforcement of tax liens are complex. When a property owner fails to pay taxes on real estate in Illinois, the property ultimately may be sold in one of the following three ways:

- At an *annual tax sale*
- At a *forfeiture sale*
- At a *scavenger sale*

Annual Sale

If the taxes on a property have not been paid by the due date of the second installment, the county collector can enforce the tax lien and request that the circuit court order a tax sale. The county has notification requirements that are prescribed by statute. The court order allows only the sale of the tax lien, not the property itself.

Before the time of sale, the owner and any other party with a legal interest (except undisclosed beneficiaries of a land trust) may redeem the property and stop the sale by paying the delinquent taxes, applicable interest, and publication costs. Successful purchasers at the sale are those who offer to pay all outstanding taxes, interest, publication costs, processing charges, and the county treasurer's indemnity fund fee.

If competitive bidding results, the bid is for the lowest rate of interest that will be accepted by the bidder in case of redemption during the first six months of the redemption period. The only persons not allowed to bid at the sale are owners, persons with legal interest, and/or their agents. The successful bidder must pay with cash, cashier's check, or certified check. Upon payment, the purchaser receives a certificate of purchase. The certificate will ripen into a **tax deed** if no redemption is made within the statutorily prescribed period. That tax deed must be recorded within one year after the expiration of the redemption period or else it is void with no right of reimbursement.

The statutory period allowed for redemption on properties with six or fewer units is 2½ years from the date of sale. If the property is not redeemed by the owner within the period allowed, the tax sale purchaser is required to give notice to the delinquent owner and other parties who hold any interest in the property before applying for a tax deed.

Forfeiture Sale

If there are no bids on a property at the annual tax sale, the property is forfeited to the state; although title does not really change. The owner still may redeem the property after forfeiture by paying delinquencies, publication costs, and interest. On the other hand, anyone who wants to purchase the property for the outstanding taxes may make application to the county. If this happens and the owner does not claim the property within 30 days of notification, the applicant will be issued a certificate of purchase after paying the outstanding taxes, interest, and other fees. If redemption is later made by the original owner, the certificate holder must be compensated based on 12% interest for each six months the certificate was held.

Scavenger Sale

If the taxes have not been paid on a property for two years or more, the property may be sold at a *scavenger sale*. The county must go through the same court process as for a tax sale and receive an order of sale. The property is sold to the highest bidder. The buyer is not required to pay the tax lien but must pay current taxes. In this case, former owners may not bid on their delinquent properties, either in person or through an agent, nor may individuals who are delinquent on their taxes by two or more years.

As noted earlier, redemption rights apply. However, the redemption period is only six months for vacant nonfarm real estate, commercial or industrial property, or property improved with seven or more residential units. For redemption to occur, all past-due taxes plus interest and penalties must be paid by the redeemer. In addition, the owner of the certificate of purchase must be repaid the bid price plus interest.

Special Assessments

Special assessments (also called *improvement taxes*) are taxes levied on real estate to fund public improvements to the property. Property owners living nearest to the improvements are required to pay for them because their properties benefit directly from the improvements. Examples of improvements include the installation of paved streets, curbs, gutters, sidewalks, storm sewers, or street lighting. The owners, in effect, reimburse the levying authority.

Special assessments are always specific and statutory, but they can be either involuntary or voluntary liens. Improvements initiated by a public agency create involuntary liens, depending on whether the government levied them or the owner requested the improvement.

Whether the lien is voluntary or involuntary, each property in the improvement district is charged a prorated share of the total amount of the assessment. The share is determined either on a fractional basis (four houses may equally share the cost of one streetlight) or on a cost-per-front-foot basis (wider lots incur a greater cost than narrower lots for street paving and curb and sidewalk installation).

Special assessments usually are due in equal annual installments, plus interest, over a period of 5 to 10 years, with the first installment usually due during the year following the public authority's approval of the assessment. The first bill includes one year's interest on the property owner's share of the entire assessment; subsequent bills include one year's interest on the unpaid balance. Property owners have the right to prepay any or all installments to avoid future interest charges. The annual due date for assessment payments in Illinois is generally January 2.

OTHER LIENS ON REAL PROPERTY

In addition to real estate tax and special assessment liens, a variety of other liens may be charged against real property.

Mortgage Liens

A **mortgage lien** (also called a *deed of trust lien*) is a voluntary lien on real estate given to a lender by a borrower as security for a real estate loan.

Mechanics' Liens

A **mechanic's lien** is a specific, involuntary lien that gives security to persons or companies that perform labor or furnish material to improve real property. A mechanic's lien is available to contractors, subcontractors, architects, equipment lessors, surveyors, laborers, and other providers. This type of lien is filed when the owner has not fully paid for the work or when the general contractor has been compensated but has not paid the subcontractors or material suppliers. In Illinois, mechanics' liens are statutory as per the Illinois Mechanics Lien Act.

To be entitled to a mechanic's lien, the person who did the work must have had a contract with the owner or the owner's authorized representative. Releases of lien or lien waivers should be sought by the seller once work is paid, with signatures from the general contractor and the subcontractors. If improvements that were not ordered by the property owner have commenced, the property owner may execute a document called a *notice of nonresponsibility* to attempt to relieve herself from possible mechanics' liens. By posting this notice in some conspicuous place on the property and recording a verified copy of it in the public record, the owner gives notice that she is not responsible for the work done.

Contractors with unpaid bills who wish to enforce their lien rights against an owner must file their lien notices within four months after the work is completed. Subcontractors have the right in Illinois to file for their unpaid claims as well, even when the general contractor has been paid in full.

Under the Illinois Mechanic's Lien Act notice requirements, a contractor who makes improvements to an owner-occupied, single-family residence must give the owner written notice within 10 days after recording a lien against any property of the owner. If timely notice is not given and, as a result, the owner suffers damages before notice is given, the lien is extinguished to the extent of the damages. The mere recording of the lien claim is not considered damages. The amendment specifically applies to contractors and not to subcontractors.

Mechanics' liens can take priority over a previously recorded lien if the work done has enhanced the value of the property. The lien attaches as of the date when the work was ordered or the contract was signed by the owner. The date of attachment establishes the lien's priority over other liens. From the point of view of the public or a prospective purchaser, an unpaid contractor has a "secret lien" until the notice is recorded.

Waiver and Disclaimer

The names of all subcontractors must be listed by the general contractor in a sworn statement. This list is presented to the landowner who ordered the work. **Lien waivers** (also called *waivers of lien*) should be collected by the landowner from each contractor and subcontractor to create a continuing record that all lien claimants have released their lien rights. Materials suppliers and property managers should also be approached for releases.

Expiration of Lien Right and Commencement of Suit

In Illinois, the contractor's lien right will expire two years after completion of that contractor's work, unless he files suit within that time to foreclose the lien. Suits to enforce mechanics' liens must be filed within two years after the last labor and/or materials were supplied. Under the Mechanics Lien Act (770 ILCS 60), a property owner can demand that the suit be commenced in 30 days. This suit can force the sale of the real estate through a court order to provide funds to pay the claimant's lien.

Judgments

A **judgment** is an order issued by a court that settles and defines the rights and obligations of the parties to a lawsuit. When the judgment establishes the amount a debtor owes and provides for money to be awarded, it is called a *money judgment.* A judgment is a general, involuntary, equitable lien on both real and personal property owned by the debtor.

A judgment becomes a general lien on all the defendant's real property in a county at the time the judgment is recorded in the county recorder's office. For the lien to be effective in another county, a memorandum of judgment must be recorded in that county.

Judgment liens are effective in Illinois for seven years and may be renewed for another seven-year term.

To enforce an actual judgment, the creditor must obtain a *writ of execution* from the court. A writ of execution directs the sheriff to seize and sell as much of the debtor's property as is necessary to pay both the debt and the expenses of the sale. A judgment does not become a lien against *personal property* (as opposed to real property) of a debtor until the creditor orders the sheriff to levy the property and the levy actually is made. When property is sold, the debtor should demand a *satisfaction of judgment* (also called a *satisfaction piece*) to clear the record.

Lis Pendens

There is often a considerable delay between the time a lawsuit is filed and the time final judgment is rendered. When any suit is filed that affects title to real estate, a special notice called a **lis pendens** (Latin for "litigation pending") is recorded. A lis pendens is not itself a lien but rather notice of a possible future lien. Recording a lis pendens notifies prospective purchasers and lenders that there is a potential claim against the property. It also establishes a priority for any later lien arising from the lawsuit: the lien is backdated to the recording date of the lis pendens.

Attachments

Special rules apply to realty that is not mortgaged or similarly encumbered. To prevent a debtor from conveying title to such previously unsecured real estate while a court suit is being decided, a creditor may seek a **writ of attachment**. By this writ, the court retains custody of the property until the suit concludes. First, the creditor must post a surety bond or deposit with the court. The bond must be sufficient to cover any possible loss or damage the debtor may suffer while the court has custody of the property. In the event the judgment is not awarded to the creditor, the debtor will be reimbursed from the bond.

Estate and Inheritance Tax Liens

Federal **estate taxes** and state **inheritance taxes** (as well as the debts of decedents) are general, statutory, involuntary liens that encumber a deceased person's real and personal property. These are normally paid or cleared in probate court proceedings.

Liens for Municipal Utilities

Municipalities often have the right to impose a specific, equitable, involuntary lien on the property of an owner who refuses to pay bills for municipal utility services.

Bail Bond Liens

A real estate owner who is charged with a crime for which he or she must face trial may post bail in the form of real estate rather than cash. The execution and recording of such a bail bond creates a specific, statutory, voluntary lien against the owner's real estate. If the accused fails to appear in court, the lien may be enforced by the court.

Corporation Franchise Tax Liens

State governments generally levy a corporation franchise tax on corporations as a condition of allowing them to do business in the state. Such a tax is a general, statutory, involuntary lien on all real and personal property owned by the corporation.

Federal Tax Liens

A *federal tax lien* (also called an *IRS tax lien*) results from a person's failure to pay any portion of federal taxes, such as income and withholding taxes. A federal tax lien is a general, statutory, involuntary lien on all real and personal property held by the delinquent taxpayer. Its priority, however, is based on the date of filing or recording; it does not supersede previously recorded liens.

The Commercial Real Estate Broker Lien Act (770 ILCS 15) permits commercial sponsoring brokers to place a lien on property in the amount of the commission they are entitled to receive for leasing, as well as for a sale under a written brokerage agreement in the event they are not paid for their services. The lien applies to commercial property only, and it must be recorded before closing to be enforceable.

A summary of the real estate–related liens appears in Figure 10.1.

Figure 10.1: Real Estate–Related Liens

	General	Specific	Voluntary	Involuntary
General real estate tax (ad valorem tax) lien		■		■
Special assessment (improvement tax) lien		■	■ or	■
Mortgage lien		■	■	
Deed of trust lien		■	■	
Mechanic's lien		■		■
Judgment lien	■			■
Estate tax lien	■			■
Inheritance tax lien	■			■
Debts of a decedent	■			■
Municipal utilities lien		■		■
Bail bond lien		■	■	
Corporation franchise tax lien	■			■
Federal tax lien	■			■

SUMMARY

Liens are claims of creditors or taxing authorities against the real and personal property of a debtor. A lien is a type of encumbrance. Liens are either general, covering all real and personal property of a debtor-owner, or specific, covering only identified property. They also are either voluntary, arising from an action of the debtor, or involuntary, created by statute (statutory) or based on the concept of fairness (equitable).

With the exception of tax liens and special assessment liens, which are always paid first, the priority of liens is generally determined by the order in which they are placed into the public record. The statutory requirements for enforcement of liens in Illinois are complex, vary from county to county, and depend on the type of property involved.

Real estate taxes are levied annually by local taxing authorities and are generally given priority over other liens when they are not paid.

Taxes are determined by first determining total cost of public needs, then dividing the cost for these needs into the sum value of taxable property (equalized and adjusted) to determine a tax rate.

Payments for property taxes are required in each county before stated dates, after which penalties accrue. An owner may lose title to property for nonpayment of taxes because such tax-delinquent property can be sold at a tax sale. Some states allow a period during which defaulted owners can use right of redemption to save their real estate from tax sale.

Special assessments are levied to allocate the cost of public improvements to the specific parcels of real estate that benefit from them. Assessments usually are payable annually over a 5- or 10-year period with interest due on the balance of the assessment.

Mortgage liens (also called deed of trust liens) are voluntary, specific liens given to lenders to secure payment for real estate loans.

Mechanics' liens protect general contractors, subcontractors, and material suppliers whose work enhances the value of real estate.

Lien waivers protect property owners when these debts have been paid.

A judgment is a court decree obtained by a creditor, usually for a monetary award from a debtor. A judgment lien can be enforced by court issuance of a writ of execution and sale by the sheriff to pay the judgment amount and costs.

Attachment is a means of preventing a defendant from conveying property before completion of a suit in which a judgment is sought.

Lis pendens is a recorded notice of a lawsuit that is pending in court and that may result in a judgment affecting title to a parcel of real estate.

Federal estate taxes and state inheritance taxes are general liens against a deceased owner's property.

Liens for water charges or other municipal utilities and bail bond liens are specific liens, while corporation franchise tax liens are general liens.

IRS tax liens are general liens against the property of a person who is delinquent in paying IRS taxes.

The homeowner exemption is an annual concession that reduces the assessed value of a property. The basic homeowner exemption in many counties must be applied for every year. The senior citizen homestead exemption is available to a homeowner over age 65 and renews automatically. The Seniors Citizen Assessment Freeze Exemption, an even stronger alternative, freezes assessed valuation for the rest of a senior citizen's life if she applies and is over age 65. The home improvement exemption gives any homeowner improving her home a four-year delay before the increased home value affects taxes.

General real estate taxes are payable in two equal installments in the year after they are levied—June 1 and September 1. Full reassessments for tax purposes take place every four years in Illinois.

When a property owner fails to pay taxes on her real estate, the property may be sold at an annual tax sale, a forfeiture sale, or a scavenger sale.

Mechanics' liens must be filed by contractors, electricians, plumbers, or other hired home improvement personnel within four months after work was completed. However, such liens are retroactive (making mechanics' liens the so-called secret liens). These liens attach (become legal and enforceable based on date) as of the time the work was ordered or when the contract was first signed by the owner.

Under the Mechanics Lien Act notice requirements, a contractor who makes improvements to an owner-occupied, single-family residence must give the owner written notice within 10 days after recording a lien against any property of the owner. If timely notice is not given and, as a result, the owner suffers damages before notice is given, the lien is extinguished to the extent of the damages. The mere recording of the lien claim is not considered damages. The amendment specifically applies to contractors and not to subcontractors.

A judgment becomes a general lien on all the defendant's real and personal property located in the county at the time the judgment was recorded. A judgment lien stays in effect in Illinois for seven years and is renewable for another seven. During such time, if the property is sold, the lien amount is usually paid from the proceeds.

UNIT 10 QUIZ

1. Which lien affects all real and personal property of a debtor?
   A. Specific
   B. Voluntary
   C. General
   D. Statutory

2. Priority of liens refers to the
   A. order in which a debtor assumes responsibility for payment of obligations.
   B. dates liens are filed for record.
   C. order in which liens will be paid if property is sold to satisfy a debt.
   D. fact that specific liens have greater priority than general liens.

3. Which of these is a lien on real estate made to secure payment for a specific municipal improvement project?
   A. Mechanic's lien
   B. Ad valorem
   C. Utility lien
   D. Special assessment

4. Which of these is classified as a general lien?
   A. Mechanic's lien
   B. Bail bond lien
   C. Real estate taxes
   D. Judgment

5. Which of these liens would usually be given highest priority in disbursing funds from a foreclosure sale?
   A. Mortgage dated last year
   B. Mechanic's lien for work started before the mortgage was made
   C. Real estate taxes due
   D. Judgment rendered yesterday

6. A specific parcel of real estate has a market value of $160,000 and is assessed for tax purposes at 75% of market value. The tax rate for the county in which the property is located is 4%. The tax bill will be
   A. $4,800.
   B. $5,000.
   C. $5,200.
   D. $6,400.

7. Which of these taxes targets homeowners in particular?
   A. Personal property tax
   B. Sales tax
   C. Real property tax
   D. Luxury tax

8. A homeowner decided to add a family room onto his house. An electrician was hired to wire the room but has not been paid. The electrician has the right to
   A. record a notice of the mechanic's lien and file a court suit within the time required by state law.
   B. tear out his work.
   C. record a notice of the mechanic's lien.
   D. have personal property of the owner sold to satisfy the lien.

9. What is the annual real estate tax on a property valued at $135,000 and assessed for tax purposes at $47,250, with an equalization factor of 125%, when the tax rate is 2.5%?
   A. $945
   B. $1,181
   C. $1,418
   D. $1,477

10. Which of these is a voluntary, specific lien?
    A. IRS tax lien
    B. Mechanic's lien
    C. Mortgage lien
    D. Special assessment

11. In two weeks, a general contractor will file a suit against a homeowner for nonpayment. The contractor just learned that the homeowner has listed the property for sale with a real estate broker. In this situation, which of the following will the contractor's attorney use to protect the contractor's interest?
    A. Lis pendens
    B. Seller's lien
    C. Buyer's lien
    D. Assessment

12. Which of these statements *BEST* describes special assessment liens?
    A. They are general liens.
    B. They take priority over mechanics' liens.
    C. They are paid on a monthly basis.
    D. They cannot be prepaid in full without penalty.

13. Which of these creates a lien on real estate?
    A. Unpaid mortgage loan
    B. Easement running with the land
    C. License
    D. Encroachment

14. A mechanic's lien would be available to a
    A. seller's real estate agent.
    B. buyer's real estate agent.
    C. taxing authority.
    D. contractor.

15. A person owns a primary residence and two apartment buildings. She pays property taxes on two of the three properties. The delinquent taxes will result in a lien on
    A. all three properties.
    B. all real and personal property that she owns.
    C. the property on which she has not paid the taxes.
    D. only her primary residence.

16. General real estate taxes levied for the operation of the government are called
    A. ad valorem taxes.
    B. assessment taxes.
    C. special taxes.
    D. improvement taxes.

17. The equalization factor used in Illinois taxation is designed to
    A. increase the tax revenues of the state.
    B. correct discrepancies between the assessed values of similar parcels of land in various counties.
    C. correct inequities in taxes for senior citizens and disabled persons.
    D. decrease taxes for the poor and unemployed.

18. A man owns a condominium town house in Cook County and a weekend retreat in Sangamon County, both in Illinois. He also owns investment property in Montana. If one of his creditors sues him in a Cook County court and a judgment is issued against him and is recorded in both Cook and Sangamon counties, which of these is *TRUE*?
    A. The judgment becomes a lien on the weekend retreat, the man's speedboat, and all other items of real and personal property in Sangamon County.
    B. The judgment becomes a lien on the property located in both Cook and Sangamon counties.
    C. The judgment becomes a lien on all of the man's real and personal property, wherever located.
    D. The judgment becomes a lien on the Cook County town house only.

19. Which of these statements is *TRUE* of the successful bidder on property offered at an annual tax sale?
    A. She may obtain a tax deed if the property is not redeemed within the redemption period.
    B. She owns the property after paying the outstanding taxes.
    C. She bids the highest percentage of interest she will accept if the property is redeemed.
    D. She receives a tax deed at the time of the sale.

20. The first installment of the tax bill for all counties except Cook is due on
    A. September 1.
    B. June 1.
    C. the first business day in March.
    D. the day after the actual amount of the current year's tax is determined.

UNIT
11

Real Estate Contracts

LEARNING OBJECTIVES

When you have completed this unit, you will be able to accomplish the following.

> Identify the requirements for a valid contract and the distinguishing features of bilateral and unilateral, executed and executory, and valid, void, and voidable contracts.
> Explain how contracts may be discharged.
> Describe the various types of contracts used in the real estate business.

KEY TERMS

assignment	equitable title	specific performance
bilateral contract	executed contract	statute of frauds
breach of contract	executory contract	time is of the essence
commingling	express contract	unenforceable contract
consideration	implied contract	unilateral contract
contingency	land contract	valid contract
contract	liquidated damages	void contract
conversion	novation	voidable contract
counteroffer	offer and acceptance	
earnest money	option	

CONTRACT LAW

A **contract** is a voluntary agreement or promise between legally competent parties, supported by legal consideration, to perform (or refrain from performing) some legal act. That definition may be easier to understand if its various parts are examined separately. A contract must

- be voluntary—no one may be forced into a contract;

- be an agreement or a promise—a contract is essentially a legally enforceable promise;

- be made by legally competent parties—the parties must be viewed by the law as capable of making a legally binding promise;

- be supported by legal consideration—a contract must be supported by something of value that induces a party to enter into the contract, and that something must be legally sufficient to support a contract; and

- have to do with a legal act—no one may legally contract to do something illegal.

Licensees use many types of contracts and agreements to carry out their responsibilities to sellers, buyers, and the general public. The general body of law that governs such agreements is called *contract law*.

 IN PRACTICE

Real estate licensees should use preprinted and preapproved forms provided by their sponsoring brokers or associations. Both the buyer and the seller have the option of seeking legal counsel for form preparation.

Express and Implied Contracts

Depending on how a contract is created, it is either express or implied. An **express contract** (also called an *express agreement*) exists when the parties state the terms and show their intentions in words. An express contract may be oral or written. Under the **statute of frauds**, certain types of contracts (including those for the sale of real property) must be in writing to be enforceable in a court of law (*enforceable* means that the parties may be forced to comply with the contract's terms and conditions). In an **implied contract**, the agreement of the parties is demonstrated by their acts and conduct.

 EXAMPLE

When a buyer signs an offer to purchase a house for $350,000, and the seller signs the contract in agreement, this is an express contract. When a diner orders a meal in a restaurant, the diner has entered an implied contract with the restaurant to pay for the meal, even though payment was not mentioned before the meal was ordered.

 The Illinois Frauds Act requires that any contracts for the sale of land, or for leases that will not be fulfilled within one year from the date they are entered into, must be in writing to be enforceable in court. The Real Estate License Act of 2000 also indicates that certain contracts must be in writing, such as employment agreements between sponsoring brokers and their sponsored licensees.

Bilateral and Unilateral Contracts

Bilateral contract: Bi means two—must have two promises.

Unilateral contract: Uni means one—has only one promise.

Contracts may be classified as either bilateral or unilateral. In a **bilateral contract**, both parties promise to do something; one promise is given in exchange for another. A real estate sales contract is a bilateral contract because the seller promises to sell a parcel of real estate and convey property title to the buyer, who in turn promises to pay a certain sum of money for the property.

A **unilateral contract**, on the other hand, is a one-sided agreement. One party makes a promise to induce a second party to do something. The second party is not legally obligated to act. However, if the second party does comply, the first party is then obligated to keep the promise. An option contract to retain one's option to possibly make a purchase later is an example of a unilateral contract.

In Illinois, an exclusive right-to-sell listing agreement is considered a bilateral contract. An open listing agreement is a unilateral contract.

Executed and Executory Contracts

A contract may be classified as either executed or executory, depending on whether the agreement is performed. An **executed contract** is one in which all parties have fulfilled their promises: the contract has been performed. This sometimes can be confused with the word *execute*, which refers to the act of signing a contract. An **executory contract** exists when one or both parties still have an act to perform. A sales contract is an executory contract from the time it is signed until closing: ownership has not yet changed hands, and the seller has not received the sales price. At closing, the sales contract is executed.

Figure 11.1 highlights the formation of a contract.

Figure 11.1: Contract Formation

Preformation	Formation	Postformation
Essential Elements	**Classification**	**Discharge**
Offer, acceptance, consideration, legal purpose, legal capacity	Valid, void, voidable, enforceable, unenforceable, express, implied, unilateral, bilateral, executory, executed	Performance, breach, remedies (damages, specific performance, rescission)

Essential Elements of a Valid Contract

Elements of a Contract

■ Offer and acceptance
■ Consideration
■ Legally competent parties
■ Consent
■ Legal purpose

A contract must meet certain minimum requirements to be considered legally valid. The following are the basic essential elements of a contract.

Offer and Acceptance (Mutual Assent)

There must be an offer by one party that is accepted by the other. The person who makes the offer is the *offeror*. The person who accepts the offer is the *offeree*. This requirement also is called *mutual assent*. It means that there must be a *meeting of the minds*, or complete agreement about the purpose and terms of the contract. Courts look to the objective intent of the parties to determine whether there was intent to enter into a binding agreement. In cases where the statute of frauds applies, the **offer and acceptance** must be in writing. The wording of the contract must express all the agreed-on terms and must be clearly understood by the parties.

An *offer* is a promise made by one party, requesting something in exchange for that promise. The offer is made with the intention that the offeror will be bound to the terms if the offer is accepted. The terms of the offer must be definite and specific and must be communicated to the offeree.

Proposing any deviation from the terms of the offer constitutes a rejection of the original offer and creates a new offer. The original offer ceases to exist because the seller has rejected it. The buyer may accept or reject the seller's **counteroffer**. If the buyer desires, the buyer can also make another counteroffer. Any change in the last offer may result in a counteroffer, and the counteroffer process might continue until the parties reach an agreement or one party walks away.

Any offer or counteroffer may be withdrawn at any time before it has been accepted.

Acceptance

If the seller agrees to the original offer or a later counteroffer exactly as it is made and signs the document, the offer has been accepted and a contract is formed. An offer is not considered accepted until the person making the offer has been notified of the other party's acceptance.

Multiple Offers

Presenting and negotiating multiple offers on the same property has the potential for misunderstanding and legal issues for real estate licensees. Licensees must be careful that the seller accepts only one offer. It is the duty of the licensee to protect the client while treating all parties honestly.

The Illinois Real Estate Licensing Act requires licensees to act in the best interest of the client. This means timely presenting all offers to the client unless the client waived that duty. A licensee should have a conversation with a buyer or seller about how they would want to handle a multiple offer situation should one arise. Then, the licensee will act on the instructions of the client in a multiple offer situation because, ultimately, decisions about how offers are presented, negotiated, and accepted are made by the buyer or seller, not the licensee.

 IN PRACTICE

The process of negotiating usually follows the same basic pattern and protocol. First, the buyer makes an offer. The seller then has three options: accept the offer, reject it, or make a counteroffer. If the seller accepts or rejects the offer, the process is over; either there is a contract or there is not. If the seller makes a counteroffer, the seller is essentially starting the process over again.

Besides being terminated by a counteroffer, an offer may be terminated by the offeree's outright rejection of it. Alternatively, an offeree may fail to accept the offer before it expires if a time frame was attached to the offer. The offeror may revoke the offer at any time before receiving the acceptance. This revocation must be communicated to the offeree by the offeror, either directly or through the licensees who are the parties' agents. The offer also is considered revoked if the offeree learns of the revocation and observes the offeror acting in a manner that indicates that the offer no longer exists (see Figure 11.2).

Figure 11.2: The Negotiation Process

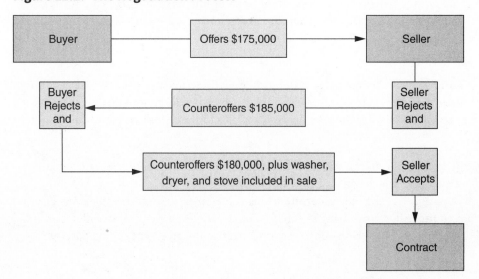

IN PRACTICE

The licensee must transmit all offers, acceptances, or other responses as soon as possible to avoid charges of deliberate delay and possible communication problems. Such speed can be critical to the client's interests. Until a final offer is accepted, the property remains on the market, available to other buyers.

There are a variety of approaches to presenting and negotiating offers, and most licensees have an approach that they feel works best for the clients and themselves. Still, there are some basics that all should follow.

Keep good records, whether handwritten or electronic. Throughout the negotiation process, changes will be made and the final contract must reflect those changes and the agreement of all parties to those changes.

As the standard contracts state, "time is of the essence." Quick response time is important in order to take full advantage of the process. Delays in responding can lead to missed opportunities, "cold feet," and multiple offers that only benefit one party. It's best to perform with all due haste.

Should the buyers find themselves in a dual offer situation, they will undoubtedly hear the phrase, "highest and best." The most expensive course of action for them to take is to bid so high that they ensure they get the property. The drawback to this approach is that the buyer may end up paying more for the property then they needed to. There is also danger that the appraisal will not support that dollar amount. Another approach is for the buyer to make a high enough offer that, should it be accepted, the buyer can own the property without concern about paying the mortgage. On the other hand, should they not succeed in obtaining the property, they know that they gave it their best effort and can move on to the next property without regret. Finally, an "escalator clause," where the buyer offers to pay a set amount on top of the highest amount, is another option, but again, it can lead to paying more than the property is worth.

Consideration

The contract must be based on **consideration**—something of legal value offered by one party and accepted by another as an inducement to perform or to refrain from performing some act. There must be a definite statement of consideration in a contract to show that something of value was given (or promised) in exchange for the other party's promise.

Consideration must be *good and valuable* between the parties, but what is "good and valuable" under the law of contracts spans a broad range. Adequate consideration ranges from as little as a promise of "love and affection," to payment of a substantial sum of money. Anything that has been bargained for and exchanged is legally sufficient to satisfy the requirement for consideration. The only requirements are that the parties agree to the consideration and that no undue influence or fraud occurred.

Legally Competent Parties

All parties to the contract must have legal capacity. That is, they must be of legal age and have enough mental capacity to understand the nature or consequences of their actions in the contract. In most states, including Illinois, 18 is the age of contractual capacity.

Reality of Consent

Under the doctrine of *reality of consent*, a contract must be entered into as the free and voluntary act of each party. Each party must be able to make a prudent and knowledgeable decision without undue influence. A mistake, misrepresentation, fraud, undue influence, or duress deprives a person of that ability. If any of these circumstances is present, the contract is voidable by the injured party. If the other party were to sue for breach of contract, the injured party could argue as a defense that the agreement lacked reality of consent.

Legal Purpose

A contract must be for a legal purpose. A contract for an illegal purpose or an act against public policies is not a valid contract.

Validity of Contracts

A contract can be described as *valid, void, voidable,* or *unenforceable,* depending on the circumstances.

A **valid contract** meets all the essential elements that make it legally sufficient or enforceable and is binding in a court of law.

A **void contract** has no legal force or effect because it lacks some or all of the essential elements of a contract. A void contract was never a legal contract.

A **voidable contract** appears on the surface to be valid but may be rescinded or disaffirmed by one or both parties based on some legal principle. If it is not disaffirmed, a voidable contract may nevertheless end up being executed. A voidable contract is considered by the courts to be valid if the party who has the option to disaffirm the agreement does not do so within a period of time prescribed by state law. A contract entered into under duress or intoxication or as a result of fraud, mistake, or misrepresentation is always voidable by the compelled or defrauded party. A contract with a minor is also voidable; minors are permitted to disaffirm real estate contracts at any time while underage and for a certain period of time after reaching majority age. Finally, a contract entered into by a mentally ill person usually is voidable during the mental illness and for a reasonable period after recovery. On the other hand, a contract made by a person who has been adjudicated insane (that is, found to be insane by a court) is void at the outset based on insanity judgments being a matter of public record.

Illinois law provides that all persons come of legal age on their 18th birthday. Most contracts entered into by a minor in Illinois are voidable until the minor reaches majority and for a reasonable time afterward. There is no statutory period within which a person may void a contract after reaching majority in Illinois. What is considered "reasonable" depends on the circumstances of each case; although the courts tend to allow a maximum of six months.

Contracts made by a minor for what the law terms necessaries are generally enforceable. "Necessaries" include items such as food, clothing, shelter, and medical expenses. While a real estate purchase contract with a minor probably would not be enforceable in Illinois, leases or rental agreements signed by minors generally are enforceable because short-term housing is usually considered a necessity.

An **unenforceable contract** may seem on the surface to be valid; however, neither party can sue the other to force performance. A contract may be unenforceable because it is not in writing, as may be required under the statute of frauds.

IN PRACTICE

If a contract contains any ambiguity, the courts generally interpret the agreement against the party who prepared it.

DISCHARGE OF CONTRACTS

A contract is discharged when the agreement is terminated. The most desirable case is when a contract terminates because it has been completely performed, with all its terms carried out. However, a contract may be terminated for other reasons, such as a party's breach or a default.

Performance of a Contract

Each party has certain rights and duties to fulfill. The question of when a contract must be performed is an important factor. Many contracts call for a specific time by which the agreed-on acts must be completely performed. In addition, many contracts provide that **time is of the essence**. This means that the contract must be performed within the time limit specified. A party who fails to perform on time is liable for breach of contract.

When a contract does not specify a date for performance, the acts it requires should be performed within a reasonable time. The interpretation of what constitutes a reasonable time depends on the situation. Generally, unless the parties agree otherwise, if the act can be done immediately, it should be performed immediately. Courts sometimes have declared contracts to be invalid because they did not contain a time or date for performance.

In Illinois, a deed or contract executed on a Sunday or legal holiday is valid and enforceable. However, when the last day on which a deed or contract must be executed is a holiday or a Sunday, the deed or contract may be executed on the next regular business day.

Assignment

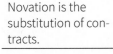
Assignment is the substitution of parties.

Novation is the substitution of contracts.

Assignment is a transfer of rights or duties under a contract. Rights may be assigned to a third party (called the *assignee*) unless the contract forbids it. Obligations also may be assigned (or *delegated*), but the original party remains primarily liable unless specifically released. An assignment may be made without the consent of the other party unless the contract includes a clause that permits or forbids assignment.

EXAMPLE

An elderly widower wants to move closer to his children. His house has been on the market for some time. The widower is in the hospital at the time a buyer makes an offer to purchase, so he assigns his contract rights to his son. This allows the property to be sold in a real estate closing transaction without him being present or signing documents.

Novation

Substitution of a new contract for an existing contract is called **novation**. The new agreement may be between the same parties, or a new party may be substituted for either (this is *novation of the parties*). The parties' intent must be to discharge the old obligation. For example, when a real estate purchaser assumes the seller's existing mortgage loan, the lender may choose to release the seller and substitute the buyer as the party primarily liable for the mortgage debt.

Breach of Contract

Buyer Remedies
- Suit for specific performance
- Suit for damages
- Rescind contract

Seller Remedies
- Suit for specific performance
- Suit for damages
- Declare contract forfeited

A contract may be terminated if it is breached by one of the parties. A **breach of contract** is a violation of any of the terms or conditions of a contract without legal excuse. For example, a seller who fails to deliver title to the buyer breaches a sales contract. The breaching or defaulting party assumes certain burdens, and the nondefaulting party has certain remedies.

If either the seller or the buyer breaches a real estate sales contract, the nonbreaching party may sue for **specific performance** unless the contract specifically states otherwise. In a suit for specific performance, the buyer asks the court to force the seller to go through with the sale and convey the property as previously agreed. Alternatively, the buyer may choose to sue for damages, in which case the buyer seeks to hold the seller liable for any costs and hardships suffered by the buyer as a result of the seller's breach. Alternatively, the buyer may *rescind* (cancel) the contract and the seller must return any earnest money deposit.

If the buyer defaults, the seller can sue for damages or sue for the purchase price. A suit for the purchase price is essentially a suit for specific performance: The seller tenders the deed and asks that the buyer be compelled to pay the agreed price, or the seller may declare the contract forfeited. In this case, the contract usually permits the seller to retain the buyer's earnest money as *liquidated damages*. In addition, the seller may sue for *compensatory damages* if the buyer's breach resulted in further financial losses for the seller.

The contract may limit the remedies available to the parties. A *liquidated damages clause* permits the seller to keep the earnest money deposit and any other payments received from the buyer as the seller's sole remedy. The clause may limit the buyer's remedy to a return of the earnest money and other payments should the seller default.

Statute of Limitations

In Illinois, the statute of limitations for oral contracts is five years; it is 10 years for written contracts. Any rights not enforced within the applicable period are lost.

Other Reasons for Termination

Contracts may also be discharged or terminated when any of the following occurs:

- *Partial performance* of the terms, along with a written acceptance by the other party

- *Substantial performance*, in which one party has substantially performed on the contract but does not complete all the details exactly as the contract requires (Such performance may be enough to force payment, with certain adjustments for any damages suffered by the other party.) For example, if a newly constructed addition to a home were finished except for polishing the brass doorknobs, the contractor would be entitled to the final payment.

- *Impossibility of performance*, in which an act required by the contract cannot be legally accomplished

- *Mutual agreement* of the parties to cancel

- *Operation of law*, such as in the voiding of a contract as a result of fraud, due to the expiration of the statute of limitations, or because a contract was altered without the written consent of all parties involved

- *Rescission*, in which one party may cancel or terminate the contract as though it had never been made. Cancellation terminates a contract without a return to the original position. Rescission, however, returns the parties to their original positions before the contract, so any monies that have been exchanged must be returned. Rescission is normally a contractual remedy for a breach, but a contract may also be rescinded by the mutual agreement of the parties.

CONTRACTS USED IN THE REAL ESTATE BUSINESS

The written agreements most commonly used by brokers and managing brokers are

- listing agreements and buyer agency agreements,
- real estate sales contracts,
- options agreements,
- escrow agreements,
- leases, and
- land contracts or contracts for deed.

IN PRACTICE

The practice of law is generally interpreted as preparing legal documents, such as deeds and mortgages, and offering advice on legal matters. To avoid charges of unauthorized practice of law, real estate licensees should avoid offering legal advice and follow the guidelines created by state real estate officials, court decisions, or statutes in their states. Generally, licensees are permitted to fill in the blanks on certain approved preprinted documents, such as sales contracts, as directed by the client. No separate fee may be charged for completing the forms.

Contract Forms

Because so many real estate transactions are similar in nature, preprinted forms are available for most kinds of contracts. The use of preprinted forms raises three problems: (1) what to write in the blanks, (2) what words and phrases should be deleted by drawing lines through them because they don't apply, and (3) what additional clauses or agreements (called *riders* or *addenda*) should be added to the forms. All changes and additions are usually initialed in the margin or on the rider by both parties when a contract is signed.

IN PRACTICE

It is essential that both parties to a contract understand exactly what they are agreeing to. Poorly drafted documents, especially those containing extensive legal language, may be subject to various interpretations and lead to litigation. The parties in a real estate transaction should be advised to have sales contracts and other legal documents examined by their lawyers before they sign to ensure that the agreements accurately reflect their intentions. When preprinted forms do not sufficiently address the unique provisions of a transaction, the parties should have an attorney draft an appropriate contract.

The Illinois Supreme Court decision in the case of *Chicago Bar Association, et al. v. Quinlan and Tyson, Inc.* placed certain limitations on real estate licensees in drafting a contract of sale. The court ruled that licensees are authorized only to fill in blanks on printed form contracts that are customarily used in the real estate community. Real estate sales contracts that fit the "customarily used" requirement typically have been drafted by local bar associations and approved by local associations of REALTORS®.

All insertions and deletions must be at the direction of the principals, based on the negotiations. Advising a buyer or a seller of the legal significance of any part of the contract or writing any change to the form language constitutes the unauthorized practice of law.

A licensee may not request or encourage a party to sign a contract or document that contains blank spaces to be "filled in later," nor can the licensee make changes to a signed contract without the written consent of the parties. If changes are made by the agreement of all the principals, the buyers and sellers must initial any changes they agree to add. All licensees are required to give each person signing or initialing the contract an original "true copy" within 24 hours of the time of signing.

A licensee also must not prepare or complete any document subsequent to the sales contract or related to its implementation, such as a deed, bill of sale, affidavit of title, note, mortgage, or other legal instrument.

Listing and Buyer Agency Agreements

Listing and buyer agency agreements are employment contracts. A *listing agreement* establishes the rights and obligations of the sponsoring broker as agent and the seller as principal. A buyer agency agreement establishes the relationship between a buyer as principal and sponsoring broker as agent.

Customary Terms of Real Estate Sales Contracts

A real estate sales contract contains the complete agreement between the buyer of a parcel of real estate and the seller. Depending on the area, this agreement may be called an *offer to purchase*, *contract of purchase and sale*, *purchase agreement*, *earnest money agreement*, *deposit receipt*, or *sales contract*.

In Illinois, a licensee should not use any form titled "Offer to Purchase" if the form is intended to become a binding real estate contract. Illinois law requires that sales contracts indicate "**Real Estate Sales Contract**" at the top in bold type.

Whatever the contract is called, it is an offer to purchase real estate as soon as it has been prepared and signed by the purchaser. If the document is accepted and signed by the seller, it becomes a contract of sale. This transformation is called *ripening* the contract.

The *contract of sale* is the most important document in the sale of real estate. It establishes the legal rights and obligations of the buyer and the seller.

Parts of a Sales Contract

Most sales contracts include the following information:

- The purchaser's name and a statement of the purchaser's obligation to purchase the property, including how the purchaser intends to take title
- An adequate description of the property, such as the street address (note that while a street address may be adequate for a sales contract, it is not legally sufficient as a description of the real property being conveyed)
- The seller's name and a statement of the type of deed a seller agrees to give, including any covenants, conditions, and restrictions that apply to the deed

- The purchase price and how the purchaser intends to pay for the property, including earnest money deposits, additional cash from the purchaser, and the conditions of any mortgage financing the purchaser intends to obtain or assume

- The amount and form of the down payment or earnest money deposit and whether it will be in the form of a check or promissory note

- A provision for the closing of the transaction and the transfer of possession of the property to the purchaser by a specific date

- A provision for title evidence (abstract and legal opinion, certificate of title, or title insurance policy)

- The method by which real estate taxes, rents, fuel costs, and other expenses are to be prorated

- A provision for the completion of the contract should the property be damaged or destroyed between the time of signing and the closing date

- A liquidated damages clause, a right-to-sue provision, or another statement of remedies available in the event of default

- Contingency clauses (such as the buyer's obtaining financing or selling a currently owned property or the seller's acquisition of another desired property or clearing of the title; attorney approval and home inspection are other commonly included contingencies)

- The appointment of a closing or settlement agent

- Closing or settlement instructions

- The transfer of any impound or escrow account funds

- The transfer or payment of any outstanding special assessments

- The purchaser's right to inspect the property shortly before the closing or settlement (often called the walk-through)

- The agreement as to what documents will be provided by each party and when and where they will be delivered

- The dated signatures of all parties. When sellers are co-owners, all must sign if the entire ownership is being transferred.

- In most states, an agency disclosure statement

Additional Provisions

Many sales contracts also provide for the following:

- Any personal property to be left with the premises for the purchaser (such as major appliances or lawn and garden equipment)

- Any real property to be removed by the seller before the closing (such as a storage shed)

- The transfer of any applicable warranties on items such as heating and cooling systems or built-in appliances

- Addition of home or construction warranties

- The identification of any leased equipment that must be transferred to the purchaser or returned to the lessor (such as security systems or cable television boxes)

The sale of a residence often includes personal property, such as drapes, as well as items that are fixtures, such as screens and storm windows or a built-in range. In Illinois, any fixtures that might be questioned as fixtures are listed in the sales contract. This can help eliminate possible arguments at the time of the final walk-through. Even attached bookcases and sometimes shrubbery have managed to disappear if they are not listed. Title to personal property usually is transferred by a *bill of sale*, prepared by the attorney. See Figure 11.3.

Home and Construction Warranties

A home warranty covers the cost to fix or replace an item in the home. Common coverage is for issues relating to air-conditioning, kitchen appliances, washers/dryers, doorbells, furnace/heating, water heaters, ductwork, garbage disposals, inside plumbing issues, ceiling fans, and electrical systems. Each warranty will be slightly different in terms of coverage and cost, but most cover large ticket items and run from $300–$600. The warranty lasts for a year and can be renewed.

It's not unusual for a seller to purchase a transferable home warranty in anticipation of selling because it makes for an attractive benefit to the buyer of the home.

Construction warranties refer to warranties for construction that are supplied by the seller or the building contractor of a new house or building. These warranties will state that the structure is free of structural, electrical, plumbing, and other defects and is fit for the intended purpose.

Generally, construction warranties last from six months to two years. The items covered in the warranty will vary from builder to builder, but they usually cover dry basement, clapboard and shingles, landscaping, carpentry, thermal and moisture cover, waterproofing, insulation, roofing and siding, doors and windows, glass, garage doors, paint, plumbing, electrical, heating and cooling, and the septic system.

Earnest Money Deposits

It is customary (although not legally required) for a purchaser to provide a deposit when making an offer to purchase real estate. This deposit, usually in the form of a check, is called **earnest money**. The earnest money deposit is evidence of the buyer's intention to carry out the terms of the contract in good faith. The check should not be delivered to the listing sponsoring broker until there is a sales contract.

The amount of the deposit is a matter to be agreed on by the parties. The amount of earnest money is determined by the buyer and the seller in the sales contract. This amount should be sufficient to

- discourage the buyer from defaulting,
- help the seller feel comfortable in taking the property off the market, and
- cover any expenses the seller might incur if the buyer defaults.

Many contracts provide that the deposit become the seller's property as liquidated damages if the buyer defaults. To release earnest money in Illinois for any reason, signatures of both parties are required. If one or more parties doesn't sign, the release can be negotiated by the parties' attorneys or either party can file a civil lawsuit for the disbursement of the earnest money. If no agreement is reached, the funds are released to the state treasurer.

Figure 11.3: Multi-Board Residential Real Estate Contract

MULTI-BOARD RESIDENTIAL REAL ESTATE CONTRACT 7.0

1 **1. THE PARTIES:** Buyer and Seller are hereinafter referred to as the "Parties."

2 Buyer Name(s) *[PLEASE PRINT]* _____

3 Seller Name(s) *[PLEASE PRINT]* _____

4 **If Dual Agency applies, check here ❑ and complete Optional Paragraph 29.**

5 **2. THE REAL ESTATE:** Real Estate is defined as the property, all improvements, the fixtures and Personal Property

6 included therein. Seller agrees to convey to Buyer or to Buyer's designated grantee, the Real Estate with

7 approximate lot size or acreage of _____ commonly known as:

8 _____

9 Address   Unit # (If applicable)   City   State   Zip   County

10 Permanent Index Number(s):_____ ❑ Single Family Attached ❑ Single Family Detached ❑ Multi-Unit

11 **If Designated Parking is Included:** # of space(s) _____; identified as space(s) # _____; location _____

12 *[CHECK TYPE]* ❑ deeded space, PIN: _____ ❑ limited common element ❑ assigned space.

13 **If Designated Storage is Included:** # of space(s) _____; identified as space(s) # _____; location _____

14 *[CHECK TYPE]* ❑ deeded space, PIN: _____ ❑ limited common element ❑ assigned space.

15 **3. FIXTURES AND PERSONAL PROPERTY AT NO ADDED VALUE:** All of the fixtures and included Personal Property

16 are owned by Seller and to Seller's knowledge are in operating condition on Date of Acceptance, unless otherwise

17 stated herein. Seller agrees to transfer to Buyer all fixtures, all heating, electrical, plumbing, and well systems

18 together with the following items at no added value by Bill of Sale at Closing *[CHECK OR ENUMERATE APPLICABLE ITEMS]*:

19 __ Refrigerator	__ Wine/Beverage Refrigerator	__ Light Fixtures, as they exist	__ Fireplace Gas Log(s)
20 __ Oven/Range/Stove	__ Sump Pump(s)	__ Built-in or attached shelving	__ Smoke Detectors
21 __ Microwave	__ Water Softener (unless rented)	__ All Window Treatments & Hardware	__ Carbon Monoxide Detectors
22 __ Dishwasher	__ Central Air Conditioning	__ Satellite Dish	__ Invisible Fence System, Collar & Box
23 __ Garbage Disposal	__ Central Humidifier	__ Wall Mounted Brackets (AV/TV)	__ Garage Door Opener(s)
24 __ Trash Compactor	__ Central Vac & Equipment	__ Security System(s) (unless rented)	with all Transmitters
25 __ Washer	__ All Tacked Down Carpeting	__ Intercom System	__ Outdoor Shed
26 __ Dryer	__ Existing Storms & Screens	__ Electronic or Media Air Filter(s)	__ Outdoor Playset(s)
27 __ Attached Gas Grill	__ Window Air Conditioner(s)	__ Backup Generator System	__ Planted Vegetation
28 __ Water Heater	__ Ceiling Fan(s)	__ Fireplace Screens/Doors/Grates	__ Hardscape

29 **Other Items Included at No Added Value:** _____

30 **Items Not Included:** _____

31 Seller warrants to Buyer that all fixtures, systems and Personal Property included in this Contract shall be in

32 operating condition at Possession except: _____.

33 A system or item shall be deemed to be in operating condition if it performs the function for which it is intended,

34 regardless of age, and does not constitute a threat to health or safety.

35 **If Home Warranty applies, check here ❑ and complete Optional Paragraph 32.**

36 **4. PURCHASE PRICE AND PAYMENT:** The Purchase Price is $ _____. After the payment of Earnest

37 Money as provided below, the balance of the Purchase Price, as adjusted by prorations, shall be paid at Closing in

38 "Good Funds" as defined by law.

39 a) **CREDIT AT CLOSING:** *[IF APPLICABLE]* Provided Buyer's lender permits such credit to show on the final

40 settlement statement or lender's closing disclosure, **and if not, such lesser amount as the lender permits,** Seller

41 agrees to credit $ _____ to Buyer at Closing to be applied to prepaid expenses, closing costs or both.

42 b) **EARNEST MONEY:** Earnest Money of $ _____ shall be tendered to Escrowee on or before ____

43 Business Days after Date of Acceptance. Additional Earnest Money, if any, of $ _____ shall be tendered

44 by _____, 20 ___. Earnest Money shall be held in trust for the mutual benefit of the Parties by

Buyer Initial _____ *Buyer Initial* _____   *Seller Initial* _____ *Seller Initial* _____

Address: _____ *v7.0*

Page 1 of 13

© Copyright 2018 by the Illinois Real Estate Lawyers Association. All rights reserved.

Figure 11.3: Multi-Board Residential Real Estate Contract (continued)

45   *[CHECK ONE]*: ❏ Seller's Brokerage; ❏ Buyer's Brokerage; ❏ As otherwise agreed by the Parties, as "Escrowee."
46   **In the event the Contract is declared null and void or is terminated, Earnest Money shall be disbursed pursuant to Paragraph 26.**
47   c) **BALANCE DUE AT CLOSING:** The Balance Due at Closing shall be the Purchase Price, plus or minus
48   prorations, less Earnest Money paid, less any credits at Closing, and shall be payable in Good Funds at Closing.

49   **5. CLOSING:** Closing shall be on _____, 20 ____ or at such time as mutually agreed by the Parties in
50   writing. Closing shall take place at the escrow office of the title insurance company, its underwriter, or its issuing
51   agent that will issue the Owner's Policy of Title Insurance, whichever is situated nearest the Real Estate.

52   **6. POSSESSION:** Unless otherwise provided in Optional Paragraph 35, Seller shall deliver possession to Buyer at
53   Closing. Possession shall be deemed to have been delivered when Seller and all occupants (if any) have vacated
54   the Real Estate and delivered keys to the Real Estate to Buyer or to the office of the Seller's Brokerage.

55   **7. FINANCING:** *[INITIAL ONLY ONE OF THE FOLLOWING SUBPARAGRAPHS a, b, or c]*
56   ___ ___ ___ ___ a) **LOAN CONTINGENCY:** Not later than **forty-five (45) days after Date of Acceptance or five**
57   **(5) Business Days prior to the date of Closing**, whichever is earlier, ("Loan Contingency Date") Buyer shall
58   provide written evidence from Buyer's licensed lending institution confirming that Buyer has received loan
59   approval subject only to "at close" conditions, matters of title, survey, and matters within Buyer's control for a loan
60   as follows: *[CHECK ONE]* ❏ fixed; ❏ adjustable; *[CHECK ONE]* ❏ conventional; ❏ FHA; ❏ VA; ❏ USDA;
61   ❏ other _____ loan for ____ % of the Purchase Price, plus private mortgage insurance (PMI),
62   if required, with an interest rate (initial rate if an adjustable rate mortgage used) not to exceed ____ % per annum,
63   amortized over not less than ____ years. Buyer shall pay discount points not to exceed ____ % of the loan amount.
64   Buyer shall pay origination fee(s), closing costs charged by lender, and title company escrow closing fees.
65   If Buyer, having applied for the loan specified above, is unable to provide such loan approval and serves Notice to
66   Seller not later than the Loan Contingency Date, this Contract shall be null and void. If Buyer is unable to provide
67   such written evidence not later than the date specified herein or by any extension date agreed to by the Parties,
68   Seller shall have the option of declaring this Contract terminated by giving Notice to Buyer. If prior to the Seller
69   serving such Notice to terminate, Buyer provides written evidence of such loan approval, this Contract shall remain
70   in full force and effect.
71   Upon the expiration of ten (10) Business Days after Date of Acceptance, if Buyer has failed to make a loan
72   application and pay all fees required for such application to proceed and the appraisal to be performed, Seller shall
73   have the option to declare this Contract terminated by giving Notice to Buyer not later than five (5) Business Days
74   thereafter or any extension thereof agreed to by the Parties in writing.
75   **A Party causing delay in the loan approval process shall not have the right to terminate under this**
76   **subparagraph. In the event neither Party elects to declare this Contract terminated as specified above, or as**
77   **otherwise agreed, then this Contract shall continue in full force and effect without any loan contingencies.**
78   **Unless otherwise provided in Paragraph 30, this Contract is not contingent upon the sale and/or closing of**
79   **Buyer's existing real estate.** Buyer shall be deemed to have satisfied the financing conditions of this subparagraph
80   if Buyer obtains a loan approval in accordance with the terms of this subparagraph even though the loan is
81   conditioned on the sale and/or closing of Buyer's existing real estate.
82   If Buyer is seeking FHA, VA, or USDA financing, **required amendments and disclosures shall be attached to this**
83   **Contract.** If VA, the Funding Fee, or if FHA, the Mortgage Insurance Premium (MIP), shall be paid by Buyer.
84   ___ ___ ___ ___ b) **CASH TRANSACTION WITH NO MORTGAGE:** *[ALL CASH]* If this selection is made, Buyer will pay
85   at Closing, in the form of "Good Funds," the Balance Due at Closing. Buyer represents to Seller, as of the Date of Offer,
86   that Buyer has sufficient funds available to satisfy the provisions of this subparagraph. Buyer agrees to verify the above
87   representation upon the reasonable request of Seller and to authorize the disclosure of such financial information to
88   Seller, Seller's attorney or Seller's broker that may be reasonably necessary to prove the availability of sufficient funds

Buyer Initial _____ *Buyer Initial* _____   *Seller Initial* _____ *Seller Initial* _____
Address: _____ *v7.0*
Page 2 of 13

Figure 11.3: Multi-Board Residential Real Estate Contract (continued)

89 to close. Buyer understands and agrees that, so long as Seller has fully complied with Seller's obligations under this
90 Contract, any act or omission outside of the control of Seller, whether intentional or not, that prevents Buyer from
91 satisfying the Balance Due at Closing, shall constitute a material breach of this Contract by Buyer. The Parties shall
92 share the title company escrow closing fee equally. **Unless otherwise provided in Paragraph 30, this Contract shall**
93 **not be contingent upon the sale and/or closing of Buyer's existing real estate.**

94 ___ ___ ___ ___ c) **CASH TRANSACTION, MORTGAGE ALLOWED:** If this selection is made, Buyer will pay at closing,
95 in the form of "Good Funds," the Balance Due at Closing. Buyer represents to Seller, as of the Date of Offer, that Buyer
96 has sufficient funds available to satisfy the provisions of this subparagraph. Buyer agrees to verify the above
97 representation upon the reasonable request of Seller and to authorize the disclosure of such financial information to
98 Seller, Seller's attorney or Seller's broker that may be reasonably necessary to prove the availability of sufficient funds
99 to close. Notwithstanding such representation, Seller agrees to reasonably and promptly cooperate with Buyer so that
100 Buyer may apply for and obtain a mortgage loan or loans including but not limited to providing access to the Real
101 Estate to satisfy Buyer's obligations to pay the Balance Due at Closing. Such cooperation shall include the performance
102 in a timely manner of all of Seller's pre-closing obligations under this Contract. **This Contract shall NOT be contingent**
103 **upon Buyer obtaining financing.** Buyer understands and agrees that, so long as Seller has fully complied with Seller's
104 obligations under this Contract, any act or omission outside of the control of Seller, whether intentional or not, that
105 prevents Buyer from satisfying the Balance Due at Closing shall constitute a material breach of this Contract by Buyer.
106 Buyer shall pay the title company escrow closing fee if Buyer obtains a mortgage; provided however, if Buyer elects
107 to close without a mortgage loan, the Parties shall share the title company escrow closing fee equally. **Unless otherwise**
108 **provided in Paragraph 30, this Contract shall not be contingent upon the sale and/or closing of Buyer's existing**
109 **real estate.**

110 **8. STATUTORY DISCLOSURES:** If applicable, prior to signing this Contract, Buyer:
111 *[CHECK ONE]* ❏ has ❏ has not received a completed Illinois Residential Real Property Disclosure;
112 *[CHECK ONE]* ❏ has ❏ has not received the EPA Pamphlet, "Protect Your Family From Lead In Your Home;"
113 *[CHECK ONE]* ❏ has ❏ has not received a Lead-Based Paint Disclosure;
114 *[CHECK ONE]* ❏ has ❏ has not received the IEMA, "Radon Testing Guidelines for Real Estate Transactions;"
115 *[CHECK ONE]* ❏ has ❏ has not received the Disclosure of Information on Radon Hazards.

116 **9. PRORATIONS:** The requirements contained in this paragraph shall survive the Closing. Proratable items shall
117 be prorated to and including the Date of Closing and shall include without limitation, general real estate taxes,
118 rents and deposits (if any) from tenants; Special Service Area or Special Assessment Area tax for the year of Closing
119 only; utilities, water and sewer, pre-purchased fuel; and Homeowner or Condominium Association fees (and
120 Master/Umbrella Association fees, if applicable). Accumulated reserves of a Homeowner/Condominium
121 Association(s) are not a proratable item.

122 a) The general real estate taxes shall be prorated to and including the date of Closing based on _____ % of
123   the most recent ascertainable full year tax bill. All general real estate tax prorations shall be final as of Closing,
124   except as provided in Paragraph 23. If the amount of the most recent ascertainable full year tax bill reflects a
125   homeowner, senior citizen, disabled veteran or other exemption, a senior freeze or senior deferral, then Seller
126   has submitted or will submit in a timely manner all necessary documentation to the appropriate governmental
127   entity, before or after Closing, to preserve said exemption(s). **The proration shall not include exemptions to**
128   **which the Seller is not lawfully entitled.**

129 b) Seller represents, if applicable, that as of Date of Acceptance Homeowner/Condominium Association(s)
130   fees are $ _____ per _____ (and, if applicable, Master/Umbrella Association fees are
131      $ _____ per _____). Seller agrees to pay prior to or at Closing the remaining balance of any
132   special assessments by the Association(s) confirmed prior to Date of Acceptance.

Buyer Initial _____ *Buyer Initial* _____   *Seller Initial* _____ *Seller Initial* _____
Address: _____ *v7.0*
Page 3 of 13

Figure 11.3: Multi-Board Residential Real Estate Contract (continued)

133   c) Special Assessment Area or Special Service Area installments due after the year of Closing shall not be
134   proratable items and shall be paid by Buyer, unless otherwise provided by ordinance or statute.

135 **10. ATTORNEY REVIEW:** Within five (5) Business Days after Date of Acceptance, the attorneys for the respective
136 Parties, by Notice, may:

137   a) Approve this Contract; or

138   b) Disapprove this Contract, which disapproval shall not be based solely upon the Purchase Price; or

139   c) Propose modifications to this Contract, except for the Purchase Price, which proposal shall be conclusively
140   deemed a counteroffer notwithstanding any language contained in any such proposal purporting to state the
141   proposal is not a counteroffer. If after expiration of ten (10) Business Days after Date of Acceptance written
142   agreement has not been reached by the Parties with respect to resolution of all proposed modifications, either
143   Party may terminate this Contract by serving Notice, whereupon this Contract shall be immediately deemed
144   terminated; or

145   d) Offer proposals specifically referring to this subparagraph d) which shall not be considered a counteroffer.
146   Any proposal not specifically referencing this subparagraph d) shall be deemed made pursuant to
147   subparagraph c) as a modification. If proposals made with specific reference to this subparagraph d) are not
148   agreed upon, **neither** Buyer nor Seller may declare this contract null and void, and this contract shall remain
149   in full force and effect.

150 **If Notice of disapproval or proposed modifications is not served within the time specified herein, the**
151 **provisions of this paragraph shall be deemed waived by the Parties and this Contract shall remain in full force**
152 **and effect. If Notice of termination is given, said termination shall be absolute and the Contract rendered null**
153 **and void upon the giving of Notice, notwithstanding any language proffered by any Party purporting to permit**
154 **unilateral reinstatement by withdrawal of any proposal(s).**

155 **11. WAIVER OF PROFESSIONAL INSPECTIONS:** *[INITIAL IF APPLICABLE]* ___ ___ ___ ___ Buyer acknowledges
156 the right to conduct inspections of the Real Estate and hereby waives the right to conduct any such inspections of
157 the Real Estate, and further agrees that the provisions of Paragraph 12 shall not apply.

158 **12. PROFESSIONAL INSPECTIONS AND INSPECTION NOTICES:** *[NOT APPLICABLE IF PARAGRAPH 11 IS INITIALED]*
159 Buyer may conduct at Buyer's expense (unless payment for such expense is otherwise required by governmental
160 regulation) any or all of the following inspections of the Real Estate by one or more licensed or certified inspection
161 services: home, radon, environmental, lead-based paint, lead-based paint hazards or wood-destroying insect
162 infestation, or any other inspections desired by Buyer in the exercise of reasonable due diligence. Seller agrees to
163 make all areas of the Real Estate accessible for inspection(s) upon reasonable notice and to have all utilities turned
164 on during the time of such inspections. Buyer shall indemnify Seller and hold Seller harmless from and against
165 any loss or damage caused by any acts of Buyer or any person performing any inspection on behalf of Buyer.

166   a) The request for repairs shall cover only the major components of the Real Estate, limited to central heating
167   and cooling system(s), plumbing and well system, electrical system, roof, walls, windows, doors, ceilings,
168   floors, appliances and foundation. A major component shall be deemed to be in operating condition, and
169   therefore not defective within the meaning of this paragraph, if it does not constitute a current threat to health
170   or safety, and performs the function for which it is intended, regardless of age or if it is near or at the end of its
171   useful life. Minor repairs, routine maintenance items and painting, decorating or other items of a cosmetic
172   nature, no matter the cost to remedy same, do not constitute defects, are not a part of this contingency and shall
173   not be a basis for the Buyer to cancel this Contract. **A request by Buyer for credits or repairs in violation of**
174   **the terms of this subparagraph shall allow Seller to declare this Contract terminated and direct the return**
175   **of Buyer's Earnest Money.** If radon mitigation is performed, Seller shall pay for any retest.

Buyer Initial _____ *Buyer Initial* _____   *Seller Initial* _____ *Seller Initial* _____
Address: _____*v7.0*

Figure 11.3: Multi-Board Residential Real Estate Contract (continued)

176   b)   Buyer shall serve Notice upon Seller or Seller's attorney of any major component defects disclosed by any
177   inspection for which Buyer requests resolution by Seller within five (5) Business Days (ten (10) calendar days
178   for a lead-based paint or lead-based paint hazard inspection) after Date of Acceptance. **Buyer shall not send**
179   **any portion of the inspection report with the Notice provided under this subparagraph unless such**
180   **inspection report, or any part thereof, is specifically requested in writing by Seller or Seller's attorney.** If
181   after expiration of ten (10) Business Days after Date of Acceptance written agreement has not been reached by
182   the Parties with respect to resolution of all inspection issues, either Party may terminate this Contract by
183   serving Notice to the other Party, whereupon this Contract shall be immediately deemed terminated.

184   c)   Notwithstanding anything to the contrary set forth above in this paragraph, in the event the inspection
185   reveals that the condition of the Real Estate is unacceptable to Buyer and Buyer serves Notice to Seller within
186   five (5) Business Days after Date of Acceptance, this Contract shall be null and void. Said Notice shall not
187   include any portion of the inspection reports unless requested by Seller.

188   d)   **Failure of Buyer to conduct said inspection(s) and notify Seller within the time specified operates as a**
189   **waiver of Buyer's rights to terminate this Contract under this Paragraph 12 and this Contract shall remain**
190   **in full force and effect.**

191   **13. HOMEOWNER INSURANCE:** This Contract is contingent upon Buyer obtaining evidence of insurability for an
192   Insurance Service Organization HO-3 or equivalent policy at standard premium rates within ten (10) Business
193   Days after Date of Acceptance. **If Buyer is unable to obtain evidence of insurability and serves Notice with proof**
194   **of same to Seller within the time specified, this Contract shall be null and void. If Notice is not served within**
195   **the time specified, Buyer shall be deemed to have waived this contingency and this Contract shall remain in**
196   **full force and effect.**

197   **14. FLOOD INSURANCE:** Buyer shall have the option to declare this Contract null and void if the Real Estate is
198   located in a special flood hazard area. **If Notice of the option to declare contract null and void is not given to**
199   **Seller within ten (10) Business Days after Date of Acceptance or by the Loan Contingency Date, whichever is**
200   **later, Buyer shall be deemed to have waived such option and this Contract shall remain in full force and effect.**
201   Nothing herein shall be deemed to affect any rights afforded by the Residential Real Property Disclosure Act.

202   **15.   CONDOMINIUM/COMMON INTEREST ASSOCIATIONS:** *[IF APPLICABLE]* The Parties agree that the terms
203   contained in this paragraph, which may be contrary to other terms of this Contract, shall supersede any conflicting
204   terms, and shall apply to property subject to the Illinois Condominium Property Act and the Common Interest
205   Community Association Act or other applicable state association law ("Governing Law").

206   a)   Title when conveyed shall be good and merchantable, subject to terms and provisions of the Declaration of
207   Condominium/Covenants, Conditions and Restrictions ("Declaration/CCRs") and all amendments; public and
208   utility easements including any easements established by or implied from the Declaration/CCRs or
209   amendments thereto; party wall rights and agreements; limitations and conditions imposed by the Governing
210   Law; installments due after the date of Closing of general assessments established pursuant to the Declaration/CCRs.

211   b)   Seller shall be responsible for payment of all regular assessments due and levied prior to Closing and for
212   all special assessments confirmed prior to Date of Acceptance.

213   c)   Seller shall notify Buyer of any proposed special assessment or increase in any regular assessment between
214   Date of Acceptance and Closing. The Parties shall have three (3) Business Days to reach agreement relative to
215   payment thereof. Absent such agreement either Party may declare the Contract null and void.

216   d)   Seller shall, within ten (10) Business Days from Date of Acceptance, apply for those items of disclosure
217   upon sale as described in the Governing Law, and provide same in a timely manner, but no later than the time
218   period provided for by law. This Contract is subject to the condition that Seller be able to procure and provide
219   to Buyer a release or waiver of any right of first refusal or other pre-emptive rights to purchase created by the

Buyer Initial _____ Buyer Initial _____   Seller Initial _____ Seller Initial _____
Address: _____v7.0
Page 5 of 13

Figure 11.3: Multi-Board Residential Real Estate Contract (continued)

220 Declaration/CCRs. In the event the Condominium Association requires the personal appearance of Buyer or
221 additional documentation, Buyer agrees to comply with same.

222 e) In the event the documents and information provided by Seller to Buyer disclose that the existing
223 improvements are in violation of existing rules, regulations or other restrictions or that the terms and
224 conditions contained within the documents would unreasonably restrict Buyer's use of the Real Estate or
225 would result in financial obligations unacceptable to Buyer in connection with owning the Real Estate, then
226 Buyer may declare this Contract null and void by giving Notice to Seller within five (5) Business Days after the
227 receipt of the documents and information required by this paragraph, listing those deficiencies which are
228 unacceptable to Buyer. If Notice is not served within the time specified, Buyer shall be deemed to have waived
229 this contingency, and this Contract shall remain in full force and effect.

230 f) Seller shall provide a certificate of insurance showing Buyer and Buyer's mortgagee, if any, as an insured.

231 **16. THE DEED:** Seller shall convey or cause to be conveyed to Buyer or Buyer's designated grantee good and
232 merchantable title to the Real Estate by recordable Warranty Deed, with release of homestead rights, (or the
233 appropriate deed if title is in trust or in an estate), and with real estate transfer stamps to be paid by Seller (unless
234 otherwise designated by local ordinance). Title when conveyed will be good and merchantable, subject only to:
235 covenants, conditions and restrictions of record and building lines and easements, if any, provided they do not
236 interfere with the current use and enjoyment of the Real Estate; and general real estate taxes not due and payable
237 at the time of Closing.

238 **17. MUNICIPAL ORDINANCE, TRANSFER TAX, AND GOVERNMENTAL COMPLIANCE:**
239 a) The Parties are cautioned that the Real Estate may be situated in a municipality that has adopted a pre-
240 closing inspection or disclosure requirement, municipal Transfer Tax or other similar ordinances. Cost of
241 transfer taxes, inspection fees, and any repairs required by an inspection pursuant to municipal ordinance shall
242 be paid by the Party designated in such ordinance unless otherwise agreed to by the Parties.

243 b) The Parties agree to comply with the reporting requirements of the applicable sections of the Internal
244 Revenue Code, the Foreign Investment in Real Property Tax Act (FIRPTA), and the Real Estate Settlement
245 Procedures Act of 1974, as amended.

246 **18. TITLE:** At Seller's expense, Seller will deliver or cause to be delivered to Buyer or Buyer's attorney within
247 customary time limitations and sufficiently in advance of Closing, as evidence of title in Seller or Grantor, a title
248 commitment for an ALTA title insurance policy in the amount of the Purchase Price with extended coverage by a
249 title company licensed to operate in the State of Illinois, issued on or subsequent to Date of Acceptance, subject
250 only to items listed in Paragraph 16 and shall cause a title policy to be issued with an effective date as of Closing.
251 The requirement to provide extended coverage shall not apply if the Real Estate is vacant land. The commitment
252 for title insurance furnished by Seller will be presumptive evidence of good and merchantable title as therein
253 shown, subject only to the exceptions therein stated. **If the title commitment discloses any unpermitted**
254 **exceptions or if the Plat of Survey shows any encroachments or other survey matters that are not acceptable to**
255 **Buyer, then Seller shall have said exceptions, survey matters or encroachments removed, or have the title**
256 **insurer commit to either insure against loss or damage that may result from such exceptions or survey matters**
257 **or insure against any court-ordered removal of the encroachments.** If Seller fails to have such exceptions waived
258 or insured over prior to Closing, Buyer may elect to take title as it then is with the right to deduct from the Purchase
259 Price prior encumbrances of a definite or ascertainable amount. Seller shall furnish to Buyer at Closing an Affidavit
260 of Title covering the date of Closing, and shall sign any other customary forms required for issuance of an ALTA
261 Insurance Policy.

262 **19. PLAT OF SURVEY:** Not less than one (1) Business Day prior to Closing, except where the Real Estate is a
263 condominium, Seller shall, at Seller's expense, furnish to Buyer or Buyer's attorney a Plat of Survey that conforms

Figure 11.3: Multi-Board Residential Real Estate Contract (continued)

264 to the current Minimum Standard of Practice for boundary surveys, is dated not more than six (6) months prior to
265 the date of Closing, and is prepared by a professional land surveyor licensed to practice land surveying under the
266 laws of the State of Illinois. The Plat of Survey shall show visible evidence of improvements, rights of way,
267 easements, use and measurements of all parcel lines. The land surveyor shall set monuments or witness corners at
268 all accessible corners of the land. **All such corners shall also be visibly staked or flagged**. The Plat of Survey shall
269 include the following statement placed near the professional land surveyor's seal and signature: "This professional
270 service conforms to the current Illinois Minimum Standards for a boundary survey." A Mortgage Inspection, as
271 defined, is not a boundary survey and is not acceptable.

272 **20. DAMAGE TO REAL ESTATE OR CONDEMNATION PRIOR TO CLOSING:** If prior to delivery of the deed the Real
273 Estate shall be destroyed or materially damaged by fire or other casualty, or the Real Estate is taken by
274 condemnation, then Buyer shall have the option of either terminating this Contract (and receiving a refund of
275 Earnest Money) or accepting the Real Estate as damaged or destroyed, together with the proceeds of the
276 condemnation award or any insurance payable as a result of the destruction or damage, which gross proceeds
277 Seller agrees to assign to Buyer and deliver to Buyer at Closing. Seller shall not be obligated to repair or replace
278 damaged improvements. The provisions of the Uniform Vendor and Purchaser Risk Act of the State of Illinois shall
279 be applicable to this Contract, except as modified by this paragraph.

280 **21. CONDITION OF REAL ESTATE AND INSPECTION:** Seller agrees to leave the Real Estate in broom clean condition.
281 All refuse and personal property that is not to be conveyed to Buyer shall be removed from the Real Estate at
282 Seller's expense prior to delivery of Possession. Buyer shall have the right to inspect the Real Estate, fixtures and
283 included Personal Property prior to Possession to verify that the Real Estate, improvements and included Personal
284 Property are in substantially the same condition as of Date of Acceptance, normal wear and tear excepted.

285 **22. SELLER REPRESENTATIONS:** Seller's representations contained in this paragraph shall survive the Closing.
286 Seller represents that with respect to the Real Estate, Seller has no knowledge of, nor has Seller received any written
287 notice from any association or governmental entity regarding:

288   a) zoning, building, fire or health code violations that have not been corrected;
289   b) any pending rezoning;
290   c) boundary line disputes;
291   d) any pending condemnation or Eminent Domain proceeding;
292   e) easements or claims of easements not shown on the public records;
293   f) any hazardous waste on the Real Estate;
294   g) real estate tax exemption(s) to which Seller is not lawfully entitled; or
295   h) any improvements to the Real Estate for which the required initial and final permits were not obtained.

296 Seller further represents that:

297 *[INITIALS]* ____ ____ ____ ____ There *[CHECK ONE]* ❑ are ❑ are not improvements to the Real Estate which are not
298 included in full in the determination of the most recent tax assessment.

299 *[INITIALS]* ____ ____ ____ ____ There *[CHECK ONE]* ❑ are ❑ are not improvements to the Real Estate which are eligible
300 for the home improvement tax exemption.

301 *[INITIALS]* ____ ____ ____ ____ There *[CHECK ONE]* ❑ is ❑ is not an unconfirmed pending special assessment affecting
302 the Real Estate by any association or governmental entity payable by Buyer after the date of Closing.

303 *[INITIALS]* ____ ____ ____ ____ The Real Estate *[CHECK ONE]* ❑ is ❑ is not located within a Special Assessment Area or
304 Special Service Area, payments for which will not be the obligation of Seller after the year in which the Closing occurs.
305 All Seller representations shall be deemed re-made as of Closing. If prior to Closing Seller becomes aware of
306 matters that require modification of the representations previously made in this Paragraph 22, Seller shall

Buyer Initial _____ *Buyer Initial* _____   *Seller Initial* _____ *Seller Initial* _____
Address: _____*v7.0*
Page 7 of 13

Figure 11.3: Multi-Board Residential Real Estate Contract (continued)

307 promptly notify Buyer. If the matters specified in such Notice are not resolved prior to Closing, Buyer may
308 terminate this Contract by Notice to Seller and this Contract shall be null and void.

309 **23. REAL ESTATE TAX ESCROW:** In the event the Real Estate is improved, but has not been previously taxed for
310 the entire year as currently improved, the sum of three percent (3%) of the Purchase Price shall be deposited in
311 escrow with the title company with the cost of the escrow to be divided equally by Buyer and Seller and paid at
312 Closing. When the exact amount of the taxes to be prorated under this Contract can be ascertained, the taxes shall
313 be prorated by Seller's attorney at the request of either Party and Seller's share of such tax liability after proration
314 shall be paid to Buyer from the escrow funds and the balance, if any, shall be paid to Seller. If Seller's obligation
315 after such proration exceeds the amount of the escrow funds, Seller agrees to pay such excess promptly upon
316 demand.

317 **24. BUSINESS DAYS/HOURS:** Business Days are defined as Monday through Friday, excluding Federal holidays.
318 Business Hours are defined as 8 a.m. to 6 p.m. Chicago time. In the event the Closing or Loan Contingency Date
319 described in this Contract does not fall on a Business Day, such date shall be the next Business Day.

320 **25. ELECTRONIC OR DIGITAL SIGNATURES:** Facsimile or digital signatures shall be sufficient for purposes of
321 executing, negotiating, finalizing, and amending this Contract, and delivery thereof by one of the following
322 methods shall be deemed delivery of this Contract containing original signature(s). An acceptable facsimile
323 signature may be produced by scanning an original, hand-signed document and transmitting same by electronic
324 means. An acceptable digital signature may be produced by use of a qualified, established electronic security
325 procedure mutually agreed upon by the Parties. Transmissions of a digitally signed copy hereof shall be by an
326 established, mutually acceptable electronic method, such as creating a PDF ("Portable Document Format")
327 document incorporating the digital signature and sending same by electronic mail.

328 **26. DIRECTION TO ESCROWEE:** In every instance where this Contract shall be deemed null and void or if this
329 Contract may be terminated by either Party, the following shall be deemed incorporated: "and Earnest Money
330 refunded upon the joint written direction by the Parties to Escrowee or upon an entry of an order by a court of
331 competent jurisdiction."

332 In the event either Party has declared the Contract null and void or the transaction has failed to close as provided
333 for in this Contract and if Escrowee has not received joint written direction by the Parties or such court order, the
334 Escrowee may elect to proceed as follows:

335   a) Escrowee shall give written Notice to the Parties as provided for in this Contract at least fourteen (14) days
336   prior to the date of intended disbursement of Earnest Money indicating the manner in which Escrowee intends
337   to disburse in the absence of any written objection. If no written objection is received by the date indicated in
338   the Notice then Escrowee shall distribute the Earnest Money as indicated in the written Notice to the Parties.
339   **If any Party objects in writing** to the intended disbursement of Earnest Money then Earnest Money shall be
340   held until receipt of joint written direction from all Parties or until receipt of an order of a court of competent jurisdiction.

341   b) Escrowee may file a Suit for Interpleader and deposit any funds held into the Court for distribution after
342   resolution of the dispute between Seller and Buyer by the Court. Escrowee may retain from the funds deposited
343   with the Court the amount necessary to reimburse Escrowee for court costs and reasonable attorney's fees
344   incurred due to the filing of the Interpleader. If the amount held in escrow is inadequate to reimburse Escrowee
345   for the costs and attorney's fees, Buyer and Seller shall jointly and severally indemnify Escrowee for additional
346   costs and fees incurred in filing the Interpleader action.

347 **27. NOTICE:** Except as provided in Paragraph 30 c) 2) regarding the manner of service for "kick-out" Notices, all
348 Notices shall be in writing and shall be served by one Party or attorney to the other Party or attorney. Notice to
349 any one of the multiple person Party shall be sufficient Notice to all. Notice shall be given in the following manner:

350   a) By personal delivery; or

Buyer Initial _____ Buyer Initial _____   Seller Initial _____ Seller Initial _____
Address: _____v7.0
Page 8 of 13

Figure 11.3: Multi-Board Residential Real Estate Contract (continued)

351 b) By mailing to the addresses recited herein on Page 13 by regular mail and by certified mail, return receipt
352 requested. Except as otherwise provided herein, Notice served by certified mail shall be effective on the date of mailing; or

353 c) By facsimile transmission. Notice shall be effective as of date and time of the transmission, provided that the
354 Notice transmitted shall be sent on Business Days during Business Hours. In the event Notice is transmitted during
355 non-business hours, the effective date and time of Notice is the first hour of the next Business Day after transmission; or

356 d) By e-mail transmission if an e-mail address has been furnished by the recipient Party or the recipient Party's
357 attorney to the sending Party or is shown in this Contract. Notice shall be effective as of date and time of e-mail
358 transmission, provided that, in the event e-mail Notice is transmitted during non-business hours, the effective date
359 and time of Notice is the first hour of the next Business Day after transmission. An attorney or Party may opt out
360 of future e-mail Notice by any form of Notice provided by this Contract; or

361 e) By commercial overnight delivery (e.g., FedEx). Such Notice shall be effective on the next Business Day
362 following deposit with the overnight delivery company.

363 f) If a Party fails to provide contact information herein, as required, Notice may be served upon the Party's
364 Designated Agent in any of the manners provided above.

365 g) The Party serving a Notice shall provide courtesy copies to the Parties' Designated Agents. Failure to provide
366 such courtesy copies shall not render Notice invalid.

367 **28. PERFORMANCE: Time is of the essence of this Contract.** In any action with respect to this Contract, the Parties
368 are free to pursue any legal remedies at law or in equity and the prevailing party in litigation shall be entitled to collect
369 reasonable attorney fees and costs from the non-prevailing party as ordered by a court of competent jurisdiction.

370 **THE FOLLOWING NUMBERED PARAGRAPHS ARE A PART OF THIS CONTRACT ONLY IF INITIALED BY THE PARTIES.**

371 *[INITIALS]* ____ ____ ____ ____ **29. CONFIRMATION OF DUAL AGENCY:** The Parties confirm that they have previously
372 consented to _____*[LICENSEE]* acting as a Dual Agent in providing brokerage services on
373 their behalf and specifically consent to Licensee acting as a Dual Agent with regard to the transaction referred to in
374 this Contract.

375 ____ ____ ____ ____ **30. SALE OF BUYER'S REAL ESTATE:**

376 a) **REPRESENTATIONS ABOUT BUYER'S REAL ESTATE:** Buyer represents to Seller as follows:

377 1) Buyer owns real estate (hereinafter referred to as "Buyer's real estate") with the address of:
378 _____.
379 Address   City   State   Zip

380 2) Buyer *[CHECK ONE]* ❑ has ❑ has not entered into a contract to sell Buyer's real estate.
381 If Buyer has entered into a contract to sell Buyer's real estate, that contract:
382 a) *[CHECK ONE]* ❑ is ❑ is not subject to a mortgage contingency.
383 b) *[CHECK ONE]* ❑ is ❑ is not subject to a real estate sale contingency.
384 c) *[CHECK ONE]* ❑ is ❑ is not subject to a real estate closing contingency.

385 3) Buyer *[CHECK ONE]* ❑ has ❑ has not publicly listed Buyer's real estate for sale with a licensed real estate broker
386 and in a local multiple listing service.

387 4) If Buyer's real estate is not publicly listed for sale with a licensed real estate broker and in a local multiple
388 listing service, Buyer *[CHECK ONE]*:
389 a) ❑ Shall publicly list real estate for sale with a licensed real estate broker who will place it in a local
390 multiple listing service within five (5) Business Days after Date of Acceptance.
391 *[FOR INFORMATION ONLY]* Broker: _____
392 Broker's Address: _____ Phone: _____
393 b) ❑ Does not intend to list said real estate for sale.

Buyer Initial _____ *Buyer Initial* _____   *Seller Initial* _____ *Seller Initial* _____
Address: _____*v7.0*
Page 9 of 13

Figure 11.3: Multi-Board Residential Real Estate Contract (continued)

394   b)   **CONTINGENCIES BASED UPON SALE AND/OR CLOSING OF REAL ESTATE:**

395   1)   This Contract is contingent upon Buyer having entered into a contract for the sale of Buyer's real estate that is
396   in full force and effect as of _____, 20 ____. Such contract should provide for a closing date not
397   later than the Closing Date set forth in this Contract. **If Notice is served on or before the date set forth in this**
398   **subparagraph that Buyer has not procured a contract for the sale of Buyer's real estate, this Contract shall**
399   **be null and void. If Notice that Buyer has not procured a contract for the sale of Buyer's real estate is not**
400   **served on or before the close of business on the date set forth in this subparagraph, Buyer shall be deemed**
401   **to have waived all contingencies contained in this Paragraph 30, and this Contract shall remain in full force**
402   **and effect.** (If this paragraph is used, then the following paragraph **must** be completed.)

403   2)   In the event Buyer has entered into a contract for the sale of Buyer's real estate as set forth in Paragraph 30 b)
404   1) and that contract is in full force and effect, or has entered into a contract for the sale of Buyer's real estate
405   prior to the execution of this Contract, this Contract is contingent upon Buyer closing the sale of Buyer's real
406   estate on or before _____, 20 ____. **If Notice that Buyer has not closed the sale of Buyer's real**
407   **estate is served before the close of business on the next Business Day after the date set forth in the preceding**
408   **sentence, this Contract shall be null and void. If Notice is not served as described in the preceding sentence,**
409   **Buyer shall have deemed to have waived all contingencies contained in this Paragraph 30, and this Contract**
410   **shall remain in full force and effect.**

411   3)   If the contract for the sale of Buyer's real estate is terminated for any reason after the date set forth in Paragraph
412   30 b) 1) (or after the date of this Contract if no date is set forth in Paragraph 30 b) 1)), Buyer shall, within three
413   (3) Business Days of such termination, notify Seller of said termination. **Unless Buyer, as part of said Notice,**
414   **waives all contingencies in Paragraph 30 and complies with Paragraph 30 d), this Contract shall be null and**
415   **void as of the date of Notice. If Notice as required by this subparagraph is not served within the time**
416   **specified, Buyer shall be in default under the terms of this Contract.**

417   c)   **SELLER'S RIGHT TO CONTINUE TO OFFER REAL ESTATE FOR SALE:** During the time of this contingency,
418   Seller has the right to continue to show the Real Estate and offer it for sale subject to the following:

419   1)   If Seller accepts another bona fide offer to purchase the Real Estate while contingencies expressed in Paragraph
420   30 b) are in effect, Seller shall notify Buyer in writing of same. Buyer shall then have ____ hours after Seller
421   gives such Notice to waive the contingencies set forth in Paragraph 30 b), subject to Paragraph 30 d).

422   2)   Seller's Notice to Buyer (commonly referred to as a "kick-out" Notice) shall be in writing and shall be served
423   on Buyer, not Buyer's attorney or Buyer's real estate agent. Courtesy copies of such "kick-out" Notice should
424   be sent to Buyer's attorney and Buyer's real estate agent, if known. Failure to provide such courtesy copies
425   shall not render Notice invalid. Notice to any one of a multiple-person Buyer shall be sufficient Notice to all
426   Buyers. Notice for the purpose of this subparagraph only shall be served upon Buyer in the following manner:
427   a) By personal delivery effective at the time and date of personal delivery; or
428   b) By mailing to the address recited herein for Buyer by regular mail and by certified mail. Notice shall be
429   effective at 10 a.m. on the morning of the second day following deposit of Notice in the U.S. Mail; or
430   c) By commercial delivery overnight (e.g., FedEx). Notice shall be effective upon delivery or at 4 p.m. Chicago
431   time on the next delivery day following deposit with the overnight delivery company, whichever first occurs.

432   3)   If Buyer complies with the provisions of Paragraph 30 d) then this Contract shall remain in full force and effect.

433   4)   If the contingencies set forth in Paragraph 30 b) are NOT waived in writing within said time period by Buyer,
434   this Contract shall be null and void.

435   5)   Except as provided in Paragraph 30 c) 2) above, all Notices shall be made in the manner provided by Paragraph
436   27 of this Contract.

437   6)   Buyer waives any ethical objection to the delivery of Notice under this paragraph by Seller's attorney or representative.

Buyer Initial _____ *Buyer Initial* _____   *Seller Initial* _____ *Seller Initial* _____

Address: _____ *v7.0*

Figure 11.3: Multi-Board Residential Real Estate Contract (continued)

438   d) **WAIVER OF PARAGRAPH 30 CONTINGENCIES:** Buyer shall be deemed to have waived the contingencies in
439   Paragraph 30 b) when Buyer has delivered written waiver and deposited with the Escrowee additional earnest
440   money in the amount of $ _____ in the form of a cashier's or certified check within the time specified.
441   **If Buyer fails to deposit the additional earnest money within the time specified, the waiver shall be deemed**
442   **ineffective and this Contract shall be null and void.**

443   e) **BUYER COOPERATION REQUIRED:** Buyer authorizes Seller or Seller's agent to verify representations
444   contained in Paragraph 30 at any time, and Buyer agrees to cooperate in providing relevant information.

445   ____ ____ ____ ____ **31. CANCELLATION OF PRIOR REAL ESTATE CONTRACT:** In the event either Party has entered
446   into a prior real estate contract, this Contract shall be subject to written cancellation of the prior contract on or before
447   _____, 20 ____. **In the event the prior contract is not cancelled within the time specified, this Contract**
448   **shall be null and void. If prior contract is subject to Paragraph 30 contingencies, Seller's notice to the purchaser**
449   **under the prior contract should not be served until after Attorney Review and Professional Inspections provisions**
450   **of this Contract have expired, been satisfied or waived.**

451   ____ ____ ____ ____ **32. HOME WARRANTY:** Seller shall provide at no expense to Buyer a Home Warranty at a cost of
452   $ _____. Evidence of a fully pre-paid policy shall be delivered at Closing.

453   ____ ____ ____ ____ **33. WELL OR SANITARY SYSTEM INSPECTIONS:** Seller shall obtain at Seller's expense a well
454   water test stating that the well delivers not less than five (5) gallons of water per minute and including a bacteria and
455   nitrate test and/or a septic report from the applicable County Health Department, a Licensed Environmental Health
456   Practitioner, or a licensed well and septic inspector, each dated not more than ninety (90) days prior to Closing, stating
457   that the well and water supply and the private sanitary system are in operating condition with no defects noted. Seller
458   shall remedy any defect or deficiency disclosed by said report(s) prior to Closing, provided that if the cost of
459   remedying a defect or deficiency and the cost of landscaping together exceed $3,000, and if the Parties cannot reach
460   agreement regarding payment of such additional cost, this Contract may be terminated by either Party. Additional
461   testing recommended by the report shall be obtained at the Seller's expense. If the report recommends additional
462   testing after Closing, the Parties shall have the option of establishing an escrow with a mutual cost allocation for
463   necessary repairs or replacements, or either Party may terminate this Contract prior to Closing. Seller shall deliver a
464   copy of such evaluation(s) to Buyer not less than ten (10) Business Days prior to Closing.

465   ____ ____ ____ ____ **34. WOOD DESTROYING INFESTATION:** Notwithstanding the provisions of Paragraph 12, within
466   ten (10) Business Days after Date of Acceptance, Seller at Seller's expense shall deliver to Buyer a written report, dated
467   not more than six (6) months prior to the Date of Closing, by a licensed inspector certified by the appropriate state
468   regulatory authority in the subcategory of termites, stating that there is no visible evidence of active infestation by
469   termites or other wood destroying insects. Unless otherwise agreed between the Parties, if the report discloses
470   evidence of active infestation or structural damage, Buyer has the option within five (5) Business Days of receipt of the
471   report to proceed with the purchase or to declare this Contract null and void.

472   ____ ____ ____ ____ **35. POSSESSION AFTER CLOSING:** Possession shall be delivered no later than 11:59 p.m. on the
473   date that is *[CHECK ONE]* ❑ ____ days after the date of Closing or ❑ _____, 20 ___ ("the Possession Date").
474   Seller shall be responsible for all utilities, contents and liability insurance, and home maintenance expenses until
475   delivery of possession. Seller shall deposit in escrow at Closing with an escrowee as agreed, the sum of $ _____
476   (if left blank, two percent (2%) of the Purchase Price) and disbursed as follows:

477   a) The sum of $ _____ per day for use and occupancy from and including the day after Closing to
478   and including the day of delivery of Possession if on or before the Possession Date;

479   b) The amount per day equal to three (3) times the daily amount set forth herein shall be paid for each day after
480   the Possession Date specified in this paragraph that Seller remains in possession of the Real Estate; and

Figure 11.3: Multi-Board Residential Real Estate Contract (continued)

481   c)   The balance, if any, to Seller after delivery of Possession and provided that the terms of Paragraph 21 have
482   been satisfied. Seller's liability under this paragraph shall not be limited to the amount of the possession escrow
483   deposit referred to above. Nothing herein shall be deemed to create a Landlord/Tenant relationship between the Parties.

484 ____ ____ ____ ____ **36. "AS IS" CONDITION:** This Contract is for the sale and purchase of the Real Estate in its "As Is"
485 condition as of the Date of Offer. Buyer acknowledges that no representations, warranties or guarantees with respect
486 to the condition of the Real Estate have been made by Seller or Seller's Designated Agent other than those known
487 defects, if any, disclosed by Seller. Buyer may conduct at Buyer's expense such inspections as Buyer desires. In that
488 event, Seller shall make the Real Estate available to Buyer's inspector at reasonable times. Buyer shall indemnify Seller
489 and hold Seller harmless from and against any loss or damage caused by the acts of negligence of Buyer or any person
490 performing any inspection. **In the event the inspection reveals that the condition of the Real Estate is unacceptable**
491 **to Buyer and Buyer so notifies Seller within five (5) Business Days after Date of Acceptance, this Contract shall be**
492 **null and void. Buyer's notice SHALL NOT include a copy of the inspection report, and Buyer shall not be obligated**
493 **to send the inspection report to Seller absent Seller's written request for same. Failure of Buyer to notify Seller or**
494 **to conduct said inspection operates as a waiver of Buyer's right to terminate this Contract under this paragraph and**
495 **this Contract shall remain in full force and effect.** Buyer acknowledges that the provisions of Paragraph 12 and the
496 warranty provisions of Paragraph 3 do not apply to this Contract. Nothing in this paragraph shall prohibit the exercise
497 of rights by Buyer in Paragraph 33, if applicable.

498 ____ ____ ____ ____ **37. SPECIFIED PARTY APPROVAL:** This Contract is contingent upon the approval of the Real
499 Estate by _____ Buyer's Specified Party, within five (5) Business Days after Date
500 of Acceptance. In the event Buyer's Specified Party does not approve of the Real Estate and Notice is given to Seller
501 within the time specified, this Contract shall be null and void. If Notice is not served within the time specified, this
502 provision shall be deemed waived by the Parties and this Contract shall remain in full force and effect.

503 ____ ____ ____ ____ **38. ATTACHMENTS:** The following attachments, if any, are hereby incorporated into this Contract
504 *[IDENTIFY BY TITLE]:* _____
505 _____.

506 ____ ____ ____ ____ **39. MISCELLANEOUS PROVISIONS:** Buyer's and Seller's obligations are contingent upon the
507 Parties entering into a separate written agreement consistent with the terms and conditions set forth herein, and with
508 such additional terms as either Party may deem necessary, providing for one or more of the following *[CHECK APPLICABLE BOXES]:*

509 ❑ Articles of Agreement for Deed   ❑ Assumption of Seller's Mortgage   ❑ Commercial/Investment
510   or Purchase Money Mortgage   ❑ Cooperative Apartment   ❑ New Construction
511 ❑ Short Sale   ❑ Tax-Deferred Exchange   ❑ Vacant Land
512 ❑ Multi-Unit (4 Units or fewer)   ❑ Interest Bearing Account   ❑ Lease Purchase

Figure 11.3: Multi-Board Residential Real Estate Contract (continued)

513   THE PARTIES ACKNOWLEDGE THAT THIS CONTRACT SHALL BE GOVERNED BY THE LAWS OF THE STATE OF ILLINOIS AND IS SUBJECT TO THE
514   COVENANT OF GOOD FAITH AND FAIR DEALING IMPLIED IN ALL ILLINOIS CONTRACTS.

515   THIS DOCUMENT WILL BECOME A LEGALLY BINDING CONTRACT WHEN SIGNED BY ALL PARTIES AND DELIVERED TO THE PARTIES OR THEIR AGENTS.

516   THE PARTIES REPRESENT THAT THE TEXT OF THIS COPYRIGHTED FORM HAS NOT BEEN ALTERED AND IS IDENTICAL TO THE OFFICIAL MULTI-
517   BOARD RESIDENTIAL REAL ESTATE CONTRACT 7.0.

518
519   Date of Offer   DATE OF ACCEPTANCE

520
521   Buyer Signature   Seller Signature

522
523   Buyer Signature   Seller Signature

524
525   Print Buyer(s) Name(s) *[REQUIRED]*   Print Seller(s) Name(s) *[REQUIRED]*

526
527   Address *[REQUIRED]*   Address *[REQUIRED]*

528
529   City, State, Zip *[REQUIRED]*   City, State, Zip *[REQUIRED]*

530
531   Phone   E-mail   Phone   E-mail

532   *FOR INFORMATION ONLY*

533
534   Buyer's Brokerage   MLS #   State License #   Seller's Brokerage   MLS #   State License #

535
536   Address   City   Zip   Address   City   Zip

537
538   Buyer's Designated Agent MLS #   State License #   Seller's Designated Agent MLS #   State License #

539
540   Phone   Fax   Phone   Fax

541
542   E-mail   E-mail

543
544   Buyer's Attorney   E-mail   Seller's Attorney   E-mail

545
546   Address   City   State   Zip   Address   City   State   Zip

547
548   Phone   Fax   Phone   Fax

549
550   Mortgage Company   Phone   Homeowner's/Condo Association (if any) Phone

551
552   Loan Officer   Phone/Fax   Management Co./Other Contact   Phone

553
554   Loan Officer E-mail   Management Co./Other Contact E-mail

555 | **Illinois Real Estate License Law** requires all offers be presented in a timely manner; Buyer requests verification that this offer was presented.
556 | **Seller rejection:** This offer was presented to Seller on _____, 20 _____ at ___:___ a.m./p.m. and rejected on _____
557 | _____, 20 _____ at ___:___ a.m./p.m. _____ _____ *[SELLER INITIALS]*

558   © *2018 Illinois Real Estate Lawyers Association. All rights reserved.* **Unauthorized duplication or alteration of this form or any portion thereof is prohibited.** *Official form available at www.irela.org*
559   *(website of Illinois Real Estate Lawyers Association). Approved by the following organizations, December 2018: Belvidere Board of REALTORS® · Chicago Association of REALTORS® · Chicago Bar Association*
560   *· DuPage County Bar Association · Heartland REALTOR® Organization · Grundy County Bar Association · Hometown Association of REALTORS® · Illinois Real Estate Lawyers Association · Illini Valley*
561   *Association of REALTORS® · Kane County Bar Association · Kankakee-Iroquois-Ford County Association of REALTORS® · Mainstreet Organization of REALTORS® · McHenry County Bar Association ·*
562   *North Shore-Barrington Association of REALTORS® · North Suburban Bar Association · Northwest Suburban Bar Association · Oak Park Area Association of REALTORS® · REALTOR® Association of*
563   *the Fox Valley, Inc. · Three Rivers Association of REALTORS · Will County Bar Association ·*

Address: _____   *v7.0*

Sponsoring brokers who are holding earnest money deposits in sales and security deposits in leasing must establish special trust accounts (also called escrow accounts) for the deposit of funds entrusted to them in connection with real estate transactions. A sponsoring broker need not open a special escrow account for each earnest money deposit received, however, but may deposit all earnest money funds in one account. This escrow account is non-interest-bearing, unless both parties agree in writing. If interest is paid on the deposit, the disposition of any accrued interest must be designated by the parties in writing, and a separate interest bearing account must be set up for that deposit.

Each sponsoring broker must maintain a complete journal and ledger of all earnest money transactions and notify IDFPR of the name of the federally insured institution where the money is deposited. All funds must be deposited to that account no later than the end of the next business day following the acceptance of the real estate contract or lease agreement, unless the contract specifies a different time frame. Both the account itself and sponsoring broker records are subject to inspection at any time. Sponsoring broker records need to be produced within 24 hours upon official request. Escrow reconciliations must be completed within 10 days after receipt of the monthly bank statement and must be kept for a minimum of five years.

Only the sponsoring broker or an authorized agent may withdraw funds from the account. Fees and/or commissions earned by the sponsoring broker that are to be paid from the funds in this account are to be disbursed by the sponsoring broker from the account no earlier than the day the transaction is consummated or terminated and no later than the next business day after consummation or termination of the transaction.

Sponsoring brokers are strictly prohibited from **commingling**, that is, mixing their own funds with funds in special escrow accounts except for the purpose of maintaining a minimum running balance required by the depository. If a sponsoring broker uses his own funds to avoid incurring service charges, scrupulous records must be kept. Sponsoring brokers may never use escrow funds for personal use; this illegal act is called **conversion**.

Equitable Title

When a buyer signs a contract to purchase real estate, the buyer does not receive legal title to the land. Legal title transfers only on delivery and acceptance of a deed. However, after both buyer and seller have executed a sales contract, the buyer acquires an interest in the land. This interest is called **equitable title**. Equitable title may give the buyer an insurable interest in the property.

Destruction of the Premises

Illinois's *Uniform Vendor and Purchaser Risk Act* (765 ILCS 65) states that the seller bears any loss that occurs before the title passes or the buyer takes possession. If the entire premises or a material part of it is destroyed, the seller cannot enforce the contract against the buyer. Any earnest money must be returned. On the other hand, if title or possession has been transferred to the buyer, he must pay the full contract price, even in the event of partially or totally destroyed premises (e.g., the house burns down while both parties are at the closing).

Liquidated Damages

To avoid a lawsuit if one party breaches the contract, the parties may agree on a certain amount of money that will compensate the nonbreaching party. That money is called **liquidated damages**. If a sales contract specifies that the earnest money deposit is to serve as liquidated damages in case the buyer defaults, the seller will be entitled to keep the deposit if the buyer refuses to perform without good reason. The seller who keeps the deposit as liquidated damages may not sue for any further damages if the contract provides that the deposit is the seller's sole remedy.

Contingencies

Additional conditions that must be satisfied before a sales contract is fully enforceable are called **contingencies**. A contingency includes the following three elements:

- The specific actions necessary to satisfy the contingency
- The time frame within which the actions must occur
- Who is responsible for paying any costs involved

The most common contingencies include the following:

- *Mortgage contingency.* Should the buyer be unable to secure financing, the contract will be rescinded. (This is sometimes called a financing contingency.)
- *Inspection contingency.* A sales contract may be contingent on the buyer obtaining certain inspections of the property within a set time frame. Inspections may include a basic home inspection or special inspections for radon, wood-boring insects, lead-based paint, structural and mechanical systems, sewage facilities, or various toxic materials.
- *Attorney contingency.* Both parties have the option of having the contract reviewed with changes made by their attorney, including cancelling the contract.
- *Property sale contingency.* Buyers may make the sales contract contingent on the sale of their current home by a certain date. This protects the buyer from owning two homes at the same time and also helps ensure the availability of cash for the purchase.
- *Escape clause.* A seller may insist on an escape clause, which permits the seller to continue to market the property until all the buyer's contingencies have been satisfied or removed. The buyer may retain the right to eliminate the contingencies if the seller receives a more favorable offer.

Note that contingencies create a voidable contract; if the contingencies are rejected or not satisfied, the contract is void.

Amendments and Addendums

An *amendment* is a change to an existing contract. For example, the parties may agree to change a closing date or alter a list of personal property items included in the sale. Anytime words or provisions are added to or deleted from the body of the contract, the contract has been amended. Amendments must be signed or initialed by all parties.

On the other hand, an *addendum* is any provision added to an existing contract without altering the content of the original. An addendum is essentially a new contract between the parties that includes the original contract's provisions "by reference"; that is, the addendum mentions the original contract. An addendum must be signed by both parties. For example, an addendum might be an agreement to split the cost of repairing certain flaws discovered in a home inspection.

Illinois requires that dual agency confirmation be included in the sales contract.

Options

An **option** is a contract by which an optionor (generally an owner) gives an optionee (a prospective purchaser or lessee) the right to buy or lease the owner's property at a fixed price within a certain period. The optionee pays a fee (agreed-on consideration) for this option right. The optionee has no other obligation until he decides to either exercise the option right or allow the option to expire. An option is enforceable by only one party—the optionee.

Options must contain all the terms and provisions required for a valid contract.

The optionee cannot recover the consideration paid for the option right should they not purchase. The contract may state whether the money paid for the option is to be applied to the purchase price of the real estate if the option is exercised.

Land Contracts

A real estate sale can be made by a **land contract**, also called a *contract for deed*, an *installment contract*, or *articles of agreement for warranty deed*. Under a typical land contract, the seller (or *vendor*) retains legal title. The buyer (or *vendee*) takes possession and gets equitable title to the property. The buyer agrees to give the seller a down payment and pay regular monthly installments of principal and interest over a number of years. The buyer also agrees to pay real estate taxes, insurance premiums, repairs, and upkeep on the property.

Land contracts (also called *installment contracts*) are seldom used today in Illinois; although they may pose an option if a seller is in a position to offer financing and a buyer needs time to procure regular lender financing. While a real estate licensee may assist in negotiating basic terms, in Illinois, the actual articles of agreement must be drawn up by an attorney owing to the legal complexities involved.

Any provision in an installment contract or land contract is void if the document

- forbids the contract buyer to record the contract,
- provides that recording does not constitute notice, or
- provides any penalty for recording.

Electronic Signatures and Paperless Transactions

The Illinois Electronic Commerce Security Act allows for certain documents, such as disclosures, offers, and contracts, to be signed electronically. As with the federal acts—the United States Electronic Signatures in Global and National Commerce (ESIGN) Act, and the Uniform Electronic Transactions Act (UETA)—the party or parties signing the documents must agree to the use of electronic signatures.

Certain documents, however, usually may not be signed by electronic signature. Included in these are wills and codicils, any documents that transfer title, and negotiable instruments.

In Illinois, the responsibility of brokerages to maintain records of transactions for five years is not waived with electronic documents. However, storage in the cloud is permissible as long as the documents can be retrieved in a timely fashion, as dictated by the Act.

Letters of Intent

Due to the unique and often complex nature of commercial real estate transactions, many commercial contracts start off as an exchange of letters of intent (LOI). While, in residential real estate, the business normally uses preprinted contracts on which agents are allowed to fill in the blanks, commercial deals often begin with a series of these letters of intent that will hopefully lead to the formation of a contract by attorneys. The attorneys then create the contract out of the fabric of the deal contained in the letters of intent.

The Illinois Supreme Court case *Quake Const., Inc., v. American Airlines, Inc.*, 141 Ill. 2d 281, 289 (1990), outlined several factors used to determine whether a letter of intent will be binding:

1. Whether the agreement is of a type usually put into writing

2. How much detail is in the agreement

3. How much amount money is involved

4. Whether a formal writing is required

5. Whether the parties contemplate a formal written document at the end of negotiations

Typically, letters of intent are not meant to be binding agreements but are only the starting place for a future contract. To that end, to ensure that the letter is not construed or interpreted as a binding agreement, it is best to include language stating that the negotiations are not binding unless and until a formal contract is actually executed. The Illinois Supreme Court has indicated that such a clause can ensure that a letter of intent is nonbinding and intended simply for purposes of negotiation.

In all such legal matters, it is always best to consult with an attorney to receive direction on a proper course of action.

SUMMARY

A contract is a legally enforceable promise or set of promises that must be performed. If a breach occurs, the law provides a remedy for this breach.

Contracts may be classified according to whether the parties' intentions are express (i.e., expressed, stated) or merely implied by their actions. They may also be classified as bilateral (when both parties have obligated themselves to act) or unilateral (when one party is obligated to perform only if the other party acts). In addition, contracts may be classified according to their legal enforceability as valid, void, voidable, or unenforceable.

Many contracts specify a time for performance. In any case, all contracts must be performed within a reasonable time. An executed contract is one that has been fully performed. An executory contract is one in which some act remains to be performed.

The essentials of a valid contract are legally competent parties, offer and acceptance, consent, consideration, and a legal purpose. A valid real estate contract must include a description of the property. It must be in writing and signed by all parties to be enforceable in court.

In many types of contracts, either party may transfer his rights and obligations under the agreement by assignment or novation (substitution of a new contract).

Contracts usually provide that the seller has the right to declare a sale canceled if the buyer defaults. If either party suffers a loss because of the other's default, he may sue for damages to cover the loss. If one party insists on completing the transaction, he may sue the defaulting party for specific performance of the terms of the contract. A court can then order the other party to comply with the agreement if it was in writing.

Contracts frequently used in the real estate business include listing agreements, sales contracts, options, land contracts (often called installment contracts or articles of agreement), and leases.

A real estate sales contract binds a buyer and a seller to a definite transaction as described in detail within the contract. The buyer is bound to purchase the property for the amount stated in the agreement and to perform by the various dates stipulated (e.g., financing, closing). The seller is bound to deliver title free from liens and encumbrances (except those identified and agreed to in the contract).

Under an option agreement, the optionee purchases from the optionor, for a limited time, the exclusive right to purchase or lease the optionor's property. A land contract or installment contract (articles of agreement for deed) is a seller financing agreement under which a buyer purchases a seller's real estate over time. The buyer takes possession of and responsibility for the property but does not receive the deed until all payments have been made in full. Instead, she receives equitable title.

The Illinois Frauds Act requires that all contracts for the sale of land and rental agreements that will not be fulfilled within one year be in writing so that they are enforceable in court. Additionally, under the Real Estate License Act of 2000, any exclusive brokerage agreement must be in writing.

Real estate contracts undertaken before the legal age of 18 are usually voidable; however, leases by minors in Illinois are often enforceable if they may be classified as "necessaries" (food, water, shelter). Contracts made under duress or undertaken while intoxicated are also voidable. Those with mistakes, misrepresentations, or fraud are voidable by the damaged party. Contracts by legally adjudicated insane persons are void.

Brokers and managing brokers may only fill in blanks on preprinted contract forms that are customarily used in the real estate industry. They may not write addendums or qualifying clauses (as per *Chicago Bar Association, et al. v. Quinlan and Tyson, Inc.*).

Land contracts and options may be used to facilitate transactions that might not otherwise occur. Licensees may negotiate basic terms in a land contract, but attorneys must prepare the articles of agreement.

Earnest money must be deposited in a special escrow or trust account, which bears interest only if all parties agree in writing. It is assumed this money will go to the seller as liquidated damages in the event of a buyer default unless some other arrangement is indicated in a typeface larger than the rest of the contract.

UNIT 11 QUIZ

1. A legally enforceable agreement under which two parties agree to do something for each other is called
   A. an escrow agreement.
   B. a valid contract.
   C. a legal promise.
   D. an option agreement.

2. A buyer approaches a seller and says, "I'd like to buy your house." The seller says, "Sure," and they agree on a price. What kind of contract is this?
   A. Implied
   B. Void
   C. Unenforceable
   D. None of these

3. A contract is said to be bilateral if
   A. one of the parties is a minor.
   B. the contract has yet to be fully performed.
   C. only one party to the agreement is bound to act.
   D. all parties to the contract are bound to act.

4. During the period of time after a real estate sales contract is signed but before title actually passes, the status of the contract is
   A. voidable.
   B. unilateral.
   C. implied.
   D. executory.

5. A man and a woman sign a contract under which the man will convey his property to the woman. The man changes his mind, and the woman sues for specific performance. What is the woman seeking in this lawsuit?
   A. Conveyance of the property
   B. Money damages
   C. New contract
   D. Deficiency judgment

6. In a standard sales contract, several words were crossed out and others were inserted. To eliminate future controversy as to whether the changes were made before or after the contract was signed, the usual procedure is to
   A. write a letter to each party listing the changes.
   B. have each party write a letter to the other approving the changes.
   C. redraw the entire contract.
   D. have both parties initial or sign in the margin, along with date, near each change.

7. A buyer makes an offer on a seller's house, and the seller accepts. Both parties sign the sales contract. At this point, the buyer has what type of title to the property?
   A. Voidable
   B. Equitable
   C. Escrow
   D. Contract

8. The sales contract says a man will purchase only if his wife approves the sale by the following Saturday. His wife's approval is a
   A. reservation.
   B. warranty.
   C. consideration.
   D. contingency.

9. Which of these statements is *TRUE* with respect to an earnest money deposit?
   A. It is generally provided with the closing or settlement instructions.
   B. It is evidence of the buyer's intention to carry out the terms of the contract in good faith.
   C. It may never exceed $25,000.
   D. It is always required if the contract provides that "time is of the essence."

10. A man and a woman enter into a real estate sales contract. Under the contract's terms, the man will pay the woman $500 a month for 10 years. The woman will continue to hold legal title to the property. The man will live on the property and pay all real estate taxes, insurance premiums, and regular upkeep costs. What kind of contract do these two people have?
    A. Land or installment contract
    B. Option contract
    C. Contract for mortgage
    D. Unilateral contract

11. Under the statute of frauds, all contracts for the sale of real estate must be
    A. originated by a real estate broker.
    B. on preprinted forms.
    C. in writing to be enforceable.
    D. accompanied by earnest money deposits.

12. A buyer makes an offer in writing to purchase a house for $220,000, including its draperies, with the offer set to expire on Saturday at noon. The seller replies in writing on Thursday, accepting the $220,000 offer, but excluding the draperies. On Friday while the buyer considers this counteroffer, the seller decides to accept the original offer, draperies included, and states that in writing. At this point, which of these statements is *TRUE*?
    A. The buyer is legally bound to buy the house; although the buyer has the right to insist that the draperies be included.
    B. The buyer must buy the house and is not entitled to the draperies.
    C. The buyer is not bound to buy.
    D. The buyer must buy the house but may deduct the value of the draperies from the $220,000.

13. A broker has found a buyer for a seller's home. The buyer has indicated in writing his willingness to buy the property for $1,000 less than the asking price and has deposited $5,000 in earnest money with the broker. The seller is out of town for the weekend, and the broker has been unable to inform him of the signed document. At this point, the buyer has signed
    A. a voidable contract.
    B. an executory agreement.
    C. an implied contract.
    D. an offer.

14. A buyer and a seller agree to the purchase of a house for $200,000. The contract states that closing will occur on April 30, 2014, and contains a clause stating that "time is of the essence." Which of these statements is *TRUE*?
    A. If the specified April 30, 2014, closing date passes and no closing takes place, the contract may have been breached.
    B. The closing must occur within three business days of execution of the contract.
    C. A "time is of the essence" clause is not binding on either party.
    D. The closing date cannot be stated as a particular calendar date.

15. A buyer signs a contract allowing her to purchase the property for $230,000 anytime in the next three months. The buyer pays the owner $5,000 at the time the contract is signed. Which of these *BEST* describes this contract?
    A. Contingency
    B. Option
    C. Installment
    D. Sales

16. In preparing a sales contract, an Illinois licensee may
    A. fill in factual and business details in the blank spaces of a customary preprinted form.
    B. draft riders to alter a preprinted contract to fit the transaction.
    C. fill out and sign an offer to purchase for the customer.
    D. advise a buyer or a seller of the legal significance of certain parts of the contract.

17. On Tuesday, a sponsoring broker received $1,750 in earnest money from a buyer. The seller accepted the offer on Thursday. Where and when must the sponsoring broker deposit the buyer's money?
    A. In the sponsoring broker's personal checking account by Wednesday
    B. In a special trust account no later than midnight on Thursday
    C. In a special non-interest-bearing trust account by the end of business on Friday
    D. In a special non-interest-bearing trust account by Wednesday

18. An Illinois broker does *NOT* need written consent of both parties to a transaction to
    A. charge a fee for her services.
    B. disburse interest accrued on an earnest money account.
    C. fill in the blanks on a sales offer as directed by the buyer.
    D. make changes in the terms of a signed sales contract.

19. The unauthorized practice of law was dealt with in which Illinois Supreme Court case?
    A. *Illinois State Bar Association v. Illinois Board of REALTORS*
    B. *Attorney Registration and Disciplinary Commission v. Illinois State Department of Professional Regulation*
    C. *Quinlan Associates, Inc. v. Illinois Real Estate Commission*
    D. *Chicago Bar Association, et al. v. Quinlan and Tyson, Inc.*

20. Which provision could legally be placed in an Illinois installment contract?
    A. "Seller will retain legal title."
    B. "Buyer may not record this contract."
    C. "Recording does not constitute notice."
    D. "Buyer will forfeit $1,000 for recording."

Transfer of Title

LEARNING OBJECTIVES

When you have completed this unit, you will be able to accomplish the following.

› Explain how property may be transferred through voluntary alienation.
› Describe the seven fundamental types of deeds.
› Explain how property may be transferred through involuntary alienation.
› Distinguish transfers of title by will from transfers by intestacy.

KEY TERMS

acknowledgment	general warranty deed	special warranty deed
adverse possession	grantee	testate
bargain and sale deed	granting clause	testator
beneficiary	grantor	title
bequest	intestate	transfer tax
deed	involuntary alienation	trustee's deed
deed in trust	probate	voluntary alienation
devise	quitclaim deed	will

OVERVIEW

Transfer of title is an aspect of the real estate transaction generally handled by lawyers and title companies, rarely by real estate licensees. Nonetheless, as with other legal aspects of the transaction, a licensee who is aware of the fundamentals of deeds and title issues will know what kind of questions to ask. An informed licensee will know how to direct consumers to the appropriate professionals and thereby avoid potential title problems.

The term *title* has two meanings. **Title** to real estate means the right to ownership or actual ownership of the land; it represents the owner's bundle of rights. Title also serves as evidence of that ownership. A person who holds the title would, if challenged in court, be able to recover or retain ownership or possession of a parcel of real estate. Title is a way of referring to ownership; it is not an actual printed document. The document by which the owner transfers the title to another is the **deed**. The deed must be recorded to give public notice of new ownership.

Real estate may be transferred *voluntarily* by sale or gift. Alternatively, it may be transferred *involuntarily* by operation of law. Real estate may be transferred at any time while the owner lives or by will or descent after the owner dies. Title transfers or passes as a symbol of ownership.

TRANSFER OF TITLE

Voluntary Alienation

A grantor conveys property to a grantee.

A grantee receives property from a grantor.

A deed is the instrument that conveys property from a grantor to a grantee.

Voluntary alienation is the legal term for the voluntary transfer of title. The owner may voluntarily transfer title by either making a gift or selling the property. To transfer during one's lifetime, the owner must use some form of deed of conveyance.

A deed is the written instrument by which an owner of real estate intentionally conveys the right, title, or interest in a parcel of real estate to someone else. The statute of frauds requires that all deeds be in writing. The owner who transfers the title is called the **grantor**. The person who acquires the title is called the **grantee**. A deed is executed only by the grantor, or seller.

The formal requirements for a deed are established by state law and vary from state to state.

Requirements for a Valid Deed

The following are the minimum requirements for a valid deed in Illinois:

- Grantor, who has the legal capacity to execute (sign) the deed
- Grantee named with reasonable certainty to be identified
- Recital of consideration
- Granting clause (words of conveyance, together with any words of limitation)
- Accurate legal description of the property conveyed
- Any relevant exceptions or reservations
- Signature of the grantor, sometimes with a seal, witness, or acknowledgment
- Delivery of the deed and acceptance by the grantee to pass title

Grantor

A grantor must be of lawful age, at least 18 years old. A deed executed by a minor is usually voidable.

A grantor also must be of sound mind. Generally, any grantor who can understand the action is viewed as mentally capable of executing a valid deed. Real estate owned by someone who is legally incompetent can be conveyed only with a court's approval.

The grantor's name must be spelled correctly and consistently throughout the deed. If the grantor's name has been changed since the title was acquired, as when a person changes her name by marriage, both names should be shown—for example, "Mary Smith, formerly Mary Jones." The grantor signs the deed.

Grantee

To be valid, a deed must name a grantee. The grantee must be specifically named so that the person to whom the property is being conveyed can be readily identified from the deed itself. However, the grantee does not sign the deed.

EXAMPLE

Phil wanted to convey Napa Ranch to his nephew, James Christian. In the deed, Phil wrote the following words of conveyance: "I, Phil, hereby convey to nephew James Christian all my interests in Napa Ranch."

If more than one grantee is involved, the granting clause should specify their rights in the property. The clause might state, for example, that the grantees will take title as "joint tenants," "tenants in common," or "tenants by the entirety." This is especially important when specific wording is necessary to create a joint tenancy or tenancy by the entirety.

The purchaser's or grantee's present address is required in Illinois as an element of a valid deed. Also, if no specific form of ownership is selected, tenancy in common is assumed in Illinois. One can determine, then, how ownership is held by consulting the deed language.

Consideration

A valid deed must contain a clause acknowledging that the grantor has received *consideration*. Generally, the amount of consideration is stated in dollars. When a deed conveys real estate as a gift to a relative, "love and affection" may be sufficient consideration. In most states, however, it is customary to recite at least a *nominal consideration*, such as "$10 and other good and valuable consideration."

Granting Clause

A deed must contain a **granting clause** (also called *words of conveyance*) that states the grantor's intention to convey the property. Depending on the type of deed and the obligations agreed to by the grantor, the wording would be similar to one of the following:

- ◼ "I, Kent Long, *convey and warrant...*" creates a warranty deed.
- ◼ "I, Kent Long, *remise, release, alienate, and convey...*" creates a special warranty deed.
- ◼ "I, Kent Long, *grant, bargain, and sell...*" creates a bargain and sale deed.
- ◼ "I, Kent Long, *remise, release, and quitclaim...*" creates a quitclaim deed.

A deed that conveys the grantor's entire fee simple absolute interest usually contains wording such as "to ABC and to her heirs and assigns forever." If the grantor conveys less than her complete interest, such as a life estate, the wording must indicate this limitation—for example, "to ABC for the duration of her natural life."

Legal Description of Real Estate

To be valid, a deed must contain an accurate *legal description* of the real estate conveyed. Land is considered adequately described if a competent surveyor can locate the property using the description.

Exceptions and Reservations

A valid deed must specifically note any encumbrances, reservations, or limitations that affect the title being conveyed. This might include such things as restrictions and easements that run with the land. In addition to citing existing encumbrances, a grantor may reserve some right to the land, such as an easement, for the grantor's use. A grantor may also place certain restrictions on a grantee's use of the property. Developers often restrict the number of houses that may be built on each lot in a subdivision. Such private restrictions must be stated in the deed or contained in a previously recorded document, such as the subdivider's master deed, that is expressly referred to in the deed. Many of these deed restrictions have time limits and often include renewal clauses.

Signature of Grantor

To be valid, a deed must be signed by all grantors named in the deed.

In Illinois, an attorney-in-fact can sign for a grantor. The attorney-in-fact must act under a *power of attorney*—the specific written authority to execute and sign one or more legal instruments for another person. Usually, the power of attorney is recorded in the county where the property is located.

In Illinois, a grantor's spouse is expected to sign any deed of conveyance to waive homestead rights.

Seals are not required in Illinois for individual grantor's signatures. Also, corporations need not affix their official corporate seals to validate a deed when they are grantors.

Acknowledgment/Notarization

An **acknowledgment** (also called *notarization*) is a formal declaration made before a notary public, that the person who signs a written document does so voluntarily and that her signature is genuine. The declaration is made before a notary public or some other person as prescribed by state law.

In Illinois, acknowledgment is not essential to the validity of the deed. However, unless the deed is acknowledged, it may not be introduced as evidence in a court of law without some further proof of its execution. As a result, it is customary that virtually all documents conveying title are acknowledged/notarized. Recording offices, as a rule, also expect deeds to be notarized before they will record them. Most title insurance companies require acknowledgment/notarization for deeds covered by their policies.

Delivery and Acceptance

A title is not considered transferred until the deed is actually delivered to and accepted by the grantee. The grantor may deliver the deed to the grantee either personally or through a third party. The third party (called a *settlement agent* or *escrow agent*) will deliver the deed to the grantee as soon as certain requirements have been satisfied. In an arm's-length transaction, the title must be delivered during the grantor's lifetime and accepted during the grantee's lifetime. The effective date of the transfer of title from the grantor to the grantee is the date of delivery of the deed itself. When a deed is delivered in escrow, the date of delivery generally relates back to the date of deposit with the escrow agent.

Execution of Corporate Deeds

The laws governing a corporation's right to convey real estate vary from state to state. However, two basic rules must be followed:

■ A corporation can convey real estate only by authority granted in its bylaws or upon resolution passed by its board of directors. If all or a substantial portion of a corporation's real estate is being conveyed, a resolution authorizing the sale must usually be secured from the shareholders.

■ Deeds to corporate real estate can be signed only by an *authorized officer*.

Rules pertaining to religious corporations and not-for-profit corporations are complex and vary even more widely. Because the legal requirements must be followed exactly, an attorney should be consulted for all corporate conveyances.

TYPES OF DEEDS

General Warranty Deed

Five covenants:
■ Covenant of seisin
■ Covenant against encumbrances
■ Covenant of quiet enjoyment
■ Covenant of further assurance
■ Covenant of warranty forever

The most common deed forms are the

■ general warranty deed,
■ special warranty deed,
■ bargain and sale deed,
■ quitclaim deed,
■ deed in trust,
■ trustee's deed, and
■ deed executed pursuant to a court order.

General Warranty Deed

A **general warranty deed** provides the greatest protection of any deed. It is called a general warranty deed because the grantor is legally bound by certain covenants or warranties (promises). In most states, the warranties are implied by the use of certain words specified by statute. The basic warranties are as follows:

■ *Covenant of seisin.* The grantor warrants that she owns the property and has the right to convey title to it. (Seisin simply means "possession.") The grantee may recover damages up to the full purchase price if this covenant is broken.

■ *Covenant against encumbrances.* The grantor warrants that the property is free from liens or encumbrances, except for any specifically stated in the deed. Encumbrances generally include mortgages, mechanics' liens, and easements. If this covenant is breached, the grantee may sue for the cost of removing the encumbrances.

■ *Covenant of quiet enjoyment.* The grantor guarantees that the grantee's title will be good against third parties who might bring court actions to establish superior title to the property. If the grantee's title is found to be inferior, the grantor is liable for damages.

■ *Covenant of further assurance.* The grantor promises to obtain and deliver any instrument needed to make the title good. For example, if the grantor's spouse has failed to sign away dower rights, the grantor must deliver a quitclaim deed (discussed later) to clear the title.

■ *Covenant of warranty forever.* The grantor promises to compensate the grantee for the loss sustained if the title fails at any time in the future.

Illinois law provides that a deed using the words *convey and warrant* implies and includes all covenants of general warranty, which are as binding on the grantor, her heirs, and personal representatives as if written at length in the deed. These covenants in a general warranty deed are not limited to matters that occurred during the time the grantor owned the property; they extend back to its origins. The grantor defends the title against herself and against all others as predecessors in title.

In addition, it is sufficient for a general warranty deed to recite only nominal consideration.

Special Warranty Deed

A **special warranty deed** contains the following two basic warranties:

- Warranty that the grantor received title

- Warranty that the property was not encumbered during the time the grantor held title, except as otherwise noted in the deed

In effect, the grantor defends the title against herself but not against previous encumbrances. The granting clause generally contains the words "grantor remises, releases, alienates, and conveys." The grantor may include additional warranties, but they must be specifically stated in the deed. In areas where a special warranty deed is more commonly used, the purchase of title insurance is viewed as providing adequate protection to the grantee.

A special warranty deed may be used by fiduciaries such as trustees, executors, and corporations. A special warranty deed is appropriate for a fiduciary because she lacks the authority to warrant against acts of predecessors in title. A fiduciary may hold title for a limited time without having a personal interest in the proceeds. Sometimes a special warranty deed may be used by a grantor who has acquired title at a tax sale.

Bargain and Sale Deed

In some states, a **bargain and sale deed** contains no express warranties against encumbrances. It does, however, imply that the grantor holds title and possession of the property.

According to the Illinois Conveyances Act, the words in the granting clause "grant, bargain, and sell" create a bargain and sale deed which conveys a simple title with the following covenants: (1) the grantor holds a fee simple estate, (2) the title is free from encumbrances made by the grantor except those listed in the deed, and (3) the grantor warrants quiet enjoyment. Because an Illinois bargain and sale deed is less complete in its warranties, the buyer should purchase title insurance for protection.

Quitclaim Deed

A **quitclaim deed** provides the grantee with the least protection of any deed. It carries no covenants or warranties and generally conveys only whatever interest the grantor may have when the deed is delivered. If the grantor has no interest, the grantee will acquire nothing, nor will the grantee acquire any right of warranty claim against the grantor. A quitclaim deed can convey title as effectively as a warranty deed if the grantor has good title when she delivers the deed, but it provides none of the guarantees that a warranty deed does. Through a quitclaim deed, the grantor only "remises, releases, and quitclaims" her interest in the property, if any.

Special Warranty Deed

Two warranties:
- Warranty that grantor received title
- Warranty that property was unencumbered by grantor

Bargain and Sale Deed

No express warranties:

Implication that grantor holds title and possession

Quitclaim Deed

No express or implied covenants or warranties:

Used primarily to convey less than fee simple or to cure a title defect

A quitclaim deed frequently is used to cure a defect, called a *cloud on the title*. For example, if the name of the grantee is misspelled on a warranty deed filed in the public record, a quitclaim deed with the correct spelling may be executed to the grantee to perfect the title.

A quitclaim deed also is used when a grantor allegedly inherits property but is not certain that the decedent's title was valid. A warranty deed in such an instance could carry with it obligations of warranty, while a quitclaim deed would convey only the grantor's interest.

A quitclaim deed uses the words "convey and quit claim," and conveys in fee all the grantor's existing legal and equitable rights held at the time of delivery.

Deed in Trust

Deed in Trust

Conveyance from trustor to trustee

A **deed in trust** is the means by which a trustor conveys real estate to a trustee for the benefit of a beneficiary. The real estate is held by the trustee to fulfill the purpose of the trust.

Trustee's Deed

Trustee's Deed

Conveyance from trustee to third party

A deed executed by a trustee is a **trustee's deed**. It is used when a trustee conveys real estate held in the trust to the beneficiary. The trustee's deed must state that the trustee is executing the instrument in accordance with the powers and authority granted by the trust instrument.

Deed Executed Pursuant to Court Order

Executors' and administrators' deeds, masters' deeds, sheriffs' deeds, and many other types are all deeds executed pursuant to a court order. These deeds are established by state statute and are used to convey title to property that is transferred by court order or by will. The form of such a deed must conform to the laws of the state in which the property is located.

Transfer Tax Stamps

Many states have enacted laws providing for a state transfer tax on conveyances of real estate. Many municipalities have local transfer stamps as well.

The Illinois Real Estate Transfer Tax Law (35 ILCS 200) imposes a tax on conveying title to real estate in the amount of $0.50 per $500 or part thereof, and in all Illinois counties, there is an additional transfer tax of $0.25 per $500 or part thereof. Total transfer tax to state and county combined is $0.75 per $500 or fraction thereof. The seller generally pays the state and county transfer tax. (The Illinois portion of the tax is divided up between three funds: 50% to the Affordable Housing Fund, 35% to the Open Space Lands Acquisition and Development Fund, and 15% to the Natural Areas Acquisition Fund.)

The **transfer tax** must be paid before the recording of the deed (or before transferring the beneficial interest in a land trust). This is done by purchasing *tax stamps* from the county recorder or the city offices if there are local stamps required. These stamps are literally affixed to the deed.

 IN PRACTICE

Real estate professionals have an important role to play in letting buyers or sellers know about transfer taxes early on. For the sellers, this comes at listing presentation time when an approximate estimate of total selling costs is usually given—commission cost, mortgage payoff, attorney fees, survey, title insurance, and transfer tax (if payable by seller). For the buyers' real estate agents, it may mean mentioning transfer taxes anytime the agent notes that the buyer has an interest in homes located where buyer-paid taxes apply.

Tax Formula

The formula used in Illinois to determine the exact taxable consideration is as follows:

Full actual consideration (sales price)	$ _____
Less value of personal property included in purchase	− _____
Less amount of mortgage to which property remains subject (for example, an assumption)	− _____
Equals net TOTAL taxable consideration to be covered by stamps	= _____
Amount of Illinois state tax stamps ($0.50 per $500 or part thereof)	$ _____
Amount of county tax ($0.25 per $500 or part thereof)	+ $ _____
Total transfer tax	= $ _____

EXAMPLE

A parcel of real estate sold for $350,000. The purchaser agreed to assume the seller's existing mortgage of $128,000 and to pay $222,000 in cash upon receipt of the seller's deed. The purchase price includes $25,000 of personal property. What amount of county and state stamps must the seller affix to the deed?

The total transfer tax would be computed as follows:

Sales price	$350,000
Less personal property	− $25,000
Less assumable mortgage	− $128,000
Equals net total taxable consideration	$197,000

To be covered by stamps:

$197,000 ÷ $500 = 394 stamps × $0.50 (state) = $197.00

$197,000 ÷ $500 = 394 stamps × $0.25 (county) = $98.50

$197.00 + $98.50 = $295.50 total transfer tax

Local Transfer Tax

Many local municipalities have their own tax as well. Charts indicating these local transfer tax amounts are available from counties and individual municipalities. Local transfer tax can be paid by either buyer or seller, so it is important to check each municipality.

Real Estate Transfer Declaration

The amount of consideration used for determining transfer taxes must be shown on the Real Estate Transfer Declaration form. The form must be signed by the buyer and the seller or their agents, and it provides for the inclusion of the property description, manner of conveyance, and type of financing used.

A completed declaration must accompany every deed presented to the recorder for recording (the Cook County recorder of deeds' office has its own separate transfer form, which also must be presented with every deed).

Exempted from the transfer tax are deeds such as those conveying real estate from or between any governmental bodies; those held by charitable, religious, or educational institutions; those securing debts or releasing property as security for a debt; partitions; tax deeds; deeds pursuant to mergers of corporations; deeds from subsidiary to parent corporations for cancellation of stock; and deeds subject to federal documentary stamp tax. When the actual consideration for conveyance is less than $100, the transfer is considered a gift and is exempt from tax. An exemption statement is usually typed on an exempted deed and signed before the deed is recorded.

INVOLUNTARY ALIENATION

Title to property may be transferred without the owner's consent by **involuntary alienation** (see Figure 12.1). Involuntary transfers are usually carried out by operation of law—such as by condemnation or a sale to satisfy delinquent tax or mortgage liens. When a person dies intestate and leaves no heirs, the title to the real estate passes to the county (in Illinois) by the state's power of escheatment. Additional land may be acquired through the process of accretion or lost through erosion and other acts of nature such as earthquakes, hurricanes, sinkholes, and mudslides.

Figure 12.1: Involuntary Alienation Illustration

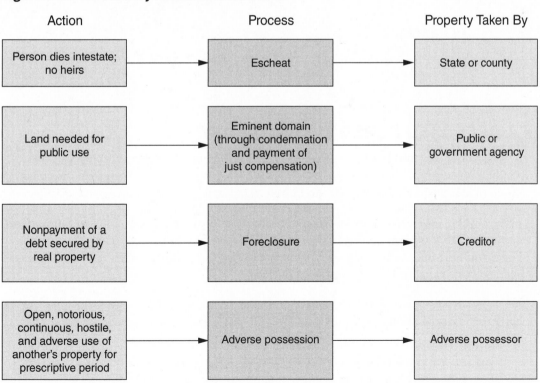

Transfer by Adverse Possession

Adverse possession (also called *squatter's rights*) is another means of involuntary transfer. The law recognizes that the use of land is an important function of its ownership. As such, an individual who makes a claim to certain property, takes possession of it, and uses it may take title away from an owner who fails to use or inspect the property for a period of years. Usually, the possession by the claimant must be

- open,
- notorious,
- continuous and uninterrupted,
- hostile, and
- adverse to the true owner's possession.

The period of uninterrupted possession required to claim title by adverse possession is 20 years. However, if the party whose property is being claimed has *color of title* (that is, if her apparently good title actually is invalidated by some flaw) and if the real estate taxes on the property are paid while satisfying the other statutory requirements, the possessory period may be shortened to seven years.

Through the principle of *tacking*, successive periods of different adverse possession by different adverse possessors can be combined, enabling a person who is not in possession for the entire required time to establish a claim. For example, if a woman held a property in adverse possession for 5 years, then the woman's daughter held the same property for 10 years, then the woman's son held the property for 5 more years, the son would be able to claim the property by adverse possession even though she had not personally possessed the property for the full statutory 20 years.

IN PRACTICE

The right of adverse possession is a statutory right. State requirements must be followed carefully to ensure the successful transfer of title. The parties to a transaction that might involve adverse possession should seek legal counsel.

TRANSFER OF A DECEASED PERSON'S PROPERTY

A person who dies **testate** has prepared a will indicating how the person's property should be handled. In contrast, when a person dies **intestate** (without a will), real estate and personal property pass to the decedent's heirs according to the state's statute of *descent and distribution*.

Legally, when a person dies, ownership of real estate immediately passes either to the heirs by descent or to the persons named in the will. Before these individuals can take full title and possession of the property, however, the estate must go through the judicial process of *probate*, and any claims against the estate must be satisfied.

When the owner of real estate dies, how title to the property was held (rather than the laws of descent and distribution or the presence of a will) may dictate who the new owners will be:

- If the property was owned by a husband and wife in *tenancy by the entirety* or was held in *joint tenancy*, the surviving spouse (or other owner) will automatically be the new owner. If the property was held as a *life estate*, it automatically reverts to the former owner or passes to a remainderman. In any case, no probate is required.

- If the property was not held in joint tenancy, tenancy by the entirety, or as a life estate, and the owner died testate, the devisees named in the will own the real estate.

- If the owner died intestate, relatives will inherit the property according to the Illinois Probate Act of 1975 (755 ILCS 5). In effect, the state makes a will for such decedents.

- If the owner died intestate and left no heirs, the real property will *escheat* to the Illinois county it lies in.

Transfer of Title by Will

A **will** is an instrument made by an owner to convey title to real or personal property after the owner's death. A will is a testamentary instrument; that is, it takes effect only after death. This differs from a deed, which must be delivered during the lifetime of the grantor and conveys a present interest in property. While the **testator** (the person who makes a will) is alive, any property included in the will can still be conveyed by the owner. The parties named in a will have no rights or interests as long as the party who made the will lives; they acquire interest or title only after the owner's death.

Only property owned by the testator at the time of death may be transferred by will. The gift of real property by will is called a **devise**, and a person who receives property by will is called a *devisee*. The gift of personal property by will is called a **bequest** (also called a *legacy*), and a person who receives the personal property by will is called a **beneficiary** (also called a *legatee*).

For title to pass to the devisee(s), state laws require that upon the death of a testator, the will must be filed with the court and probated. Probate is a legal procedure for verifying the validity of a will and accounting for the decedent's assets. The process can take several months to complete.

Legal Requirements for Making a Will

Any person 18 or older, who is of sound mind and memory, may make a will. A will must be in writing and signed and declared by the maker (the *testator*) in the presence of two or more witnesses to be her last will and testament. Witnesses cannot be beneficiaries under the will because their gifts will likely be voided by the probate court.

Transfer of Title by Descent

When a person dies intestate (without a valid will), the person's state's law of descent governs how and to whom her property will be distributed.

In Illinois, the law that governs intestate distribution is the Illinois Law of Descent and Distribution.

Probate Proceedings

Probate is a formal judicial process that

- proves or confirms the validity of a will,

- determines the precise assets of the deceased person, and

- identifies the persons to whom the assets are to pass.

The purpose of probate is to see that the assets are distributed correctly. All assets must be accounted for and the decedent's debts satisfied before any property is distributed to the heirs. In addition, estate taxes must be paid before any distribution. The laws of each state govern the probate proceedings in that state and the functions of the individuals appointed to administer the decedent's affairs.

Assets distributed through probate are those that do not otherwise distribute themselves. For example, property held in joint tenancy or tenancy by the entirety passes immediately. Any probate proceedings will take place in the county in which the decedent resided. If the decedent owned real estate in another county, probate would occur in that county as well.

The person who has possession of the will—normally the person designated in the will as *executor*—presents it for filing with the court. The court is responsible for determining that the will meets the statutory requirements for its form and execution. If a codicil or more than one will exists, the court will decide how these documents should be probated.

The court must rule on a challenge if a will is contested. Once the will is upheld, the assets can be distributed according to its provisions. Probate courts distribute assets according to statute only when no other reasonable alternative exists.

When a person dies intestate, the court determines who inherits the assets by reviewing proof from relatives of the decedent and their entitlement under the statute of descent and distribution. Once the heirs have been determined, the court appoints an *administrator* or a personal representative to administer the affairs of the estate—the role usually taken by an executor.

Whether or not a will is involved, the administrator or executor is responsible for having the estate's assets appraised and for ensuring that all the decedent's debts are satisfied. The administrator or executor is also responsible for paying federal estate taxes and state inheritance taxes out of the assets. Once all obligations have been satisfied, the representative distributes the remaining property according to the terms of the will or the state's law of descent.

SUMMARY

Title to real estate is the right to and evidence of ownership of the land. It may be transferred by voluntary alienation, involuntary alienation, will, and descent.

The voluntary transfer of an owner's title is made by a deed executed (signed) by the owner (the grantor) to the purchaser/recipient as grantee.

Among the most common requirements for a valid deed are a grantor with legal capacity to contract, a readily identifiable grantee, a granting clause, a legal description of the property, a recital of consideration, exceptions and reservations on the title, and the signature of the grantor. In addition, the deed should be properly witnessed, acknowledged, and notarized before a notary public to provide evidence of a genuine signature and to facilitate recording. Title to the property passes when the grantor delivers a deed to the grantee and it is accepted. The level of guarantee a grantor offers is determined by the form of the deed.

A general warranty deed provides the greatest protection of any deed by binding the grantor to certain covenants or warranties. A special warranty deed warrants only that the real estate is not encumbered except as stated in the deed. A bargain and sale deed carries with it no warranties but implies that the grantor holds title to the property. A quitclaim deed carries with it no warranties whatsoever and conveys only the interest, if any, the grantor possesses in the property. The granting clause of each deed is a key as to its type.

An owner's title may be transferred with or without the owner's permission by a court action or by death. The real estate of an owner who makes a valid will (who dies testate) passes to the devisees through the probating of the will. The title of an owner who dies without a will (intestate) passes according to the provisions of the laws of descent and distribution of the state in which the real estate is located.

In Illinois, the requirements for a valid deed are a grantor with legal capacity to contract, a readily identifiable grantee, a granting clause, a legal description of the property, a recital of consideration, and the signature of the grantor. Title to the property passes when the grantor delivers a deed to the grantee and it is accepted. The obligation of a grantor is determined by the form of the deed. The specific words of conveyance in the granting clause are critical in determining the form of deed.

Acknowledgment and notarization are standard in county recorders' offices. Recording is required for tax deeds and if a deed is to be used as evidence in a court of law.

In Illinois, a bargain and sale deed includes covenants that make it similar to a special warranty deed yet less complete. A quitclaim deed carries with it no warranties whatsoever and conveys only the interest, if any, the grantor possesses in the property.

Generally, state and county transfer tax stamps are paid for by the seller. This money goes to the state and county for affordable housing and land preservation. Many municipalities have their own transfer tax as well, which can be paid by either the seller or the buyer.

UNIT 12 QUIZ

1. The basic requirements for a valid conveyance are governed by
   A. local custom.
   B. state law.
   C. national law.
   D. the law of descent.

2. Every deed must be signed by the
   A. grantor.
   B. grantee.
   C. grantor and grantee.
   D. devisee.

3. A 15-year-old boy inherited many parcels of real estate from his late father and decided to sell one of the parcels. If the boy enters into a deed conveying his interest in the property to a purchaser, such a conveyance will be
   A. valid.
   B. void.
   C. voidable.
   D. invalid.

4. A husband who works for an international corporation has already moved out of the country. To authorize his wife to act on his behalf in his absence, he signed
   A. a release deed.
   B. a quitclaim deed.
   C. an acknowledgment.
   D. a power of attorney.

5. What is the major difference between a general warranty deed and a quitclaim deed?
   A. A general warranty deed provides the least protection for the buyer; a quitclaim deed provides the most protection for the buyer.
   B. A general warranty deed provides the most protection for the buyer; a quitclaim deed provides the least protection for the buyer.
   C. A general warranty deed can be used only in foreclosure sales; a quitclaim deed is used only in residential sales.
   D. A general warranty deed creates an indefeasible title; a quitclaim deed creates a defeasible title.

6. Under the covenant of quiet enjoyment, the grantor
   A. promises to obtain and deliver any instrument needed to make the title good.
   B. guarantees that if the title fails in the future, she will compensate the grantee.
   C. guarantees that the title will be good against the title claims of third parties.
   D. warrants that she is the owner and has the right to convey title to the property.

7. Which of these types of deeds merely implies, but does not specifically warrant, that the grantor holds good title to the property?
   A. Special warranty
   B. Quitclaim
   C. Trustee's
   D. Bargain and sale

8. Step 1: A man decided to convey his property to a woman. Step 2: The man signed a deed transferring title to the woman. Step 3: The man gave the signed deed to the woman, who accepted it. Step 4: The woman took the deed to the county recorder's office and had it recorded. At which step did title to the property actually transfer or pass to the woman?
   A. Step 1
   B. Step 2
   C. Step 3
   D. Step 4

9. A woman signed a deed transferring ownership of her property to a man. To provide evidence that the woman's signature was genuine, she executed a declaration before a notary. This declaration is called an
   A. affidavit.
   B. acknowledgment.
   C. affirmation.
   D. estoppel.

10. A woman bought acreage in a distant county, never went to see the acreage, and did not use the land. A man moved his mobile home onto the land, had a well drilled for water, and lived there for 22 years. The man may become the owner of the land if he has complied with the state law regarding
    A. requirements for a valid conveyance.
    B. avulsion.
    C. voluntary alienation.
    D. adverse possession.

11. What do the terms *condemnation* and *escheat* have in common?
    A. They are examples of involuntary alienation.
    B. They are examples of voluntary alienation.
    C. They are processes used in adverse possession claims.
    D. They are methods of transferring title by descent.

12. A deed contains a guarantee that the grantor will compensate the grantee for any loss resulting from the title's failure in the future. This is an example of
    A. warranty forever.
    B. further assurance.
    C. quiet enjoyment.
    D. seisin.

13. Which of these documents transfers title to real estate at the death of the owner?
    A. Warranty deed
    B. Will
    C. Special warranty deed
    D. Trustee's deed

14. For Illinois courts to recognize a will, the will must
    A. be handwritten.
    B. have no amendments.
    C. be modified by codicil.
    D. have two witnesses.

15. In Illinois, how many years are required to acquire title by adverse possession?
    A. 5
    B. 20
    C. 7
    D. 30

16. Which of these statements is *TRUE* regarding the execution of a valid will in Illinois?
    A. The testator must be at least 21 years old and of sound mind.
    B. The will must be witnessed by three people.
    C. The will must be in writing, signed, and witnessed by two people.
    D. The will must be notarized.

17. In Illinois, the state transfer tax is
    A. customarily paid by the buyer.
    B. computed on the sales price less the amount of any existing mortgage to which the property remains subject.
    C. not required if the actual total consideration is less than $500.
    D. assessed at the rate of $1 per $1,000 of sales price.

18. Which deed requires the Illinois transfer tax?
    A. Deeds between relatives
    B. A deed conveying a property owned by a charitable institution
    C. A deed conveying a property owned by a government body
    D. Deeds for property valued at less than $100

19. In Illinois, when a person dies without a valid will and with no heirs, what happens to the property?
    A. It is sold at auction
    B. It escheats to the state
    C. It escheats to the Illinois county it lies in
    D. It is foreclosed

20. The gift of real property by will is called
    A. a devise.
    B. a testate.
    C. an implied estate.
    D. a descent.

UNIT 13

Title Records

LEARNING OBJECTIVES

When you have completed this unit, you will be able to accomplish the following.

> Describe recording, notice, and chain of title issues.
> Identify the various proofs of ownership.
> Explain the process and purpose of a title search.

KEY TERMS

abstract of title	constructive notice	subrogation
actual notice	marketable title	suit to quiet title
certificate of title	priority	title insurance
chain of title	recording	title search

PUBLIC RECORDS

Public records contain detailed information about each parcel of real estate in a city or a county. These records are crucial in establishing ownership, giving notice of encumbrances, and establishing priority of liens. They protect the interests of real estate owners, taxing bodies, creditors, and the general public. The real estate recording system includes written documents that affect title, such as deeds and mortgages. Public records regarding taxes, judgments, probate, and marriage also may offer important information about the title to a particular property. In most states, written documents must be recorded in the county where the land is located.

Public records are maintained by

■ recorders of deeds,

■ county clerks,

■ county treasurers,

- city clerks,

- collectors, and

- clerks of court.

The recorder of deeds, county clerk, county treasurer, city clerk and collector, and clerks of various courts maintain these records. In Illinois, a recorder of deeds must be elected in each county with a population of 60,000 or more. In counties with a population of fewer than 60,000, the county clerk serves as the recorder of deeds.

Public records are just that: open to the public. This means that anyone interested in a particular property can review the records to learn about the documents, claims, and other issues that affect its ownership. A prospective purchaser, for example, needs to be sure that the seller can lawfully convey title to the property. If the property is subject to any liens or other encumbrances, a prospective buyer or lender will want to know.

Recording

Recording is the act of placing documents in the public record. The specific rules for recording documents are a matter of state law. However, although the details may vary, recording essentially provides that any written document that affects any estate, right, title, or interest in land must be recorded in the county where the land is located to serve as public notice. That way, anyone interested in the title to a parcel of property will know where to look to discover the various interests of all other parties. The act of recording also generally gives legal priority to those interests recorded first—the *first in time, first in right* or *first come, first served principle.*

To be eligible for recording, a document must be drawn and executed as stipulated in the recording acts of the state in which the real estate is located.

Illinois law does not require that most documents be filed or recorded within a specified period of time. However, when creditors and subsequent purchasers do not actually know the content of the documents affecting certain real estate interests, the courts will hold these creditors and purchasers responsible for "discovering" (knowing) that information only as of the date on which the documents are recorded. No instrument affecting title to real property may include any provision prohibiting recording. Any such prohibiting provision is void as a matter of law.

In most states, written documents that affect land must be recorded in the county where the land is located.

The original document must be filed with the county recorder of deeds and must meet the following specific requirements (in addition to the nine requirements of a valid deed):

- Grantor's name typed or printed below his or her signature

- Full address of the grantee

- Name and address of the person who prepared the deed

- Permanent tax index number (required only in some counties)

- Common address of the property (required only in some counties)

- 3½-inch-by-5-inch blank space for use by the recorder

- Completed real estate transfer declaration

- Proof of payment of the state and county transfer taxes or indication of an applicable exemption

- Proof of payment of the municipal transfer tax (if applicable)

When the parcel of land being transferred is a division of a larger parcel and smaller than five acres, the recording provisions of the Plat Act (765 ILCS 205) apply. If the conveyance is exempt, an affidavit stating the reason for the exemption may be required by the recorder.

In some municipalities, the water department must declare, by way of an endorsement stamp on the municipal transfer declaration, that all outstanding water bills have been paid.

A deed in any language other than English, although valid between the parties, does not give constructive notice unless an official English translation of the document is attached at the time of recording. The translation must be prepared by a credible source, such as the local consulate of a country in which the language is used.

Notice

Anyone who has an interest in a parcel of real estate can take certain steps, called *giving notice*, to ensure that others know about the individual's interest. There are two basic types of notice: *constructive notice* and *actual notice*.

Constructive notice:
Could or should
know with reason-
able inquiry

Actual notice:
Knows for certain by
personal service

Constructive notice is the legal presumption that information may be obtained by an individual through due diligence. Properly recording documents in the public record serves as constructive notice to the world of an individual's rights or interest, as does the physical possession of a property. Because the information or evidence is readily available to the world, a prospective purchaser or lender is responsible for discovering the interest.

Actual notice (also called *direct knowledge*) means not only that the information is available but also that someone has been given the information and actually knows it. An individual who has searched the public records and inspected the property has actual notice. If it can be proved that an individual has had actual notice of information, that person cannot use a lack of constructive notice (such as an unrecorded deed) to justify a claim.

Priority

Priority refers to the order of rights in time. Many complicated situations can affect the priority of rights in a parcel of real estate—who recorded first, which party was in possession first, who had actual or constructive notice. How the courts rule in any situation depends, of course, on the specific facts of the case. These are strictly legal questions that should be referred to the parties' attorneys.

Unrecorded Documents

Certain types of liens are not recorded. Real estate taxes and special assessments are liens on specific parcels of real estate and usually are not recorded until sometime after the taxes or assessments are past due. Inheritance taxes and franchise taxes are statutory liens. They are placed against all real estate owned by a decedent at the time of death or by a corporation at the time the franchise taxes became a lien. Like real estate taxes, they are not recorded.

Notice of these liens must be gained from sources other than the recorder's office. Evidence of the payment of real estate taxes, special assessments, municipal utilities, and other taxes can be gathered from paid tax receipts and letters from municipalities. Creative measures are often required to get information about these "off the record" liens.

A mechanic's lien that has not been recorded may nonetheless still have priority over other liens that have been recorded.

Chain of Title

A **chain of title** is the record of a property's ownership. Beginning with the earliest owner, each owner is linked to the next so that a chain is formed. An unbroken chain of title can be traced through linking conveyances from the present owner back to the earliest recorded owner. Chain of title does not include liens and encumbrances or any other document not directly related to ownership.

If ownership cannot be traced through an unbroken chain, a gap or cloud in the chain of title is said to exist. In these cases, the cloud on the title makes it necessary to establish ownership by a court action called a **suit to quiet title**. For example, a suit might be required when a grantor acquired title under one name and conveyed it under another name, or there may be a forged deed in the chain, after which no subsequent grantee acquired legal title. All possible claimants are allowed to present evidence during a court proceeding; then the court's judgment is filed. Often, the simple procedure of obtaining any relevant quitclaim deeds is used to clear title and establish ownership.

TITLE SEARCH AND ABSTRACT OF TITLE

A **title search** is an examination of all the public records to determine whether any defects exist in the chain of title. The records of the conveyances of ownership are examined, beginning with the present owner. Then the title is traced backward to its origin.

For normal title searches in Illinois, the search goes back 40 years under the Illinois Marketable Title Act (735 ILCS 5/13-118). When the possibility of litigation exists, the search must go back 75 years. Title searches in Cook and Du Page counties cannot go back before 1871; in that year, most records were destroyed in the Great Chicago Fire.

Other public records are examined to identify wills, judicial proceedings, and other encumbrances that may affect title. These include a variety of taxes, special assessments, and other recorded liens.

A title search usually is not ordered until after the major contingencies in a sales contract have been cleared—for example, after a loan commitment has been secured. Before providing money for a loan, a lender or the attorney orders a title search to ensure that no lien is superior to its mortgage lien. In most cases, the cost of the title search in Illinois is paid by the seller.

An **abstract of title** is a summary report of what the title search found in the public record. The person who prepares this report is called an *abstractor*. The abstractor searches all the public records and then summarizes the various events and proceedings that affected the title throughout its history. The report begins with the original grant (or root) and then provides a chronological list of recorded instruments. All recorded liens and encumbrances are included, along with their current statuses. A list of all of the public records examined is also provided as evidence of the scope of the search.

IN PRACTICE

An abstract of title is a condensed history of those items that can be found in public records. It does not reveal such items as encroachments, forgeries, or any interests or conveyances that have not been recorded.

Marketable Title

Under the terms of the typical real estate sales contract, the seller is required to deliver **marketable title** to the buyer at the closing. To be marketable, a title must

- disclose no serious defects and not depend on doubtful questions of law or fact to prove its validity;

- not expose a purchaser to the hazard of litigation or threaten the quiet enjoyment of the property; and

- convince a reasonably well-informed and prudent purchaser, acting on business principles and with knowledge of the facts and their legal significance, that he could sell or mortgage the property at a later time.

Marketable Title vs. Insurable Title

Marketable title means that the chain of ownership is free and clear of defects and should any problem arise, the title insurer will cover the issue as per the insurance policy. In Illinois, a title insurance policy for marketable title is the most common way of assuring a lender and a purchaser that the property has marketable title.

Insurable title, which is often offered by banks in a foreclosure sale, means that the title insurance company knows that there are defects on the title, but it believes that the risk of those defects becoming problematic is low. The standard for what actually constitutes insurable title is specific to each individual title company.

Though, on the surface, both marketable title and insurable title seem the same, there are potentially stark differences when the purchaser sells the property in the future. If the subsequent buyer and lender want a marketable title and the seller only received insurable title with its acknowledgment of known defects, the seller will then have to cure those defects before the title company will be willing to issue a marketable title policy.

Potential Title Issues and Remedies

Before the issuance of a title insurance policy, the insurer will check the title by doing a title search. Common issues that can hinder a clear title are errors in public records, unknown liens, illegal deeds, missing heirs, forgeries, undiscovered encumbrances, unknown easements, boundary/survey disputes, undiscovered wills, and false impersonation of previous owner.

However, the title company's search occurs only after the property has been put under contract, before closing. Should there be an issue with the title, a title search ordered by the seller before putting the property on the market may help ward off trouble that might pop up at or before closing.

PROOF OF OWNERSHIP

A deed by itself is not considered sufficient evidence of ownership in Illinois. Even though a warranty deed conveys the grantor's interest, it contains no proof of the condition of the grantor's title at the time of the conveyance. The grantee needs some assurance that he actually is acquiring ownership and that the title is marketable. A certificate of title or title insurance is commonly used to prove ownership.

Certificate of Title

A **certificate of title** is a statement of opinion regarding title status on the date the certificate is issued. A certificate of title is not a full guarantee of ownership. Rather, it certifies the condition of the title's history based on an actual examination of the public records—a title search. The certificate may be prepared by a title company, a licensed abstractor, or an attorney. An owner, a mortgage lender, or a buyer may request the certificate.

Although a certificate of title is used as evidence of ownership, it is not perfect. Unrecorded liens or rights of parties in possession cannot be discovered by a search of the public records. Hidden defects, such as transfers involving forged documents, incorrect marital information, incompetent parties, minors, or fraud cannot be detected. A certificate offers no defense against these defects because they are unknown. The person who prepares the certificate is liable only for negligence in preparing the certificate.

Abstract and Attorney's Opinion of Title

An abstract and attorney's opinion of title are used in some areas, including Illinois, as evidence of title. This is an opinion of title status based on a review of the abstract by an attorney. Similar to a certificate of title, the opinion of title does not protect against defects that cannot be discovered from the public records. Many buyers purchase title insurance to defend the title from these defects.

Title Insurance

Title insurance is a contract under which the policyholder is protected from losses arising from defects in the title. A title insurance company determines whether the title is insurable based on a review of the public records. If so, a policy is issued. Unlike other insurance policies that insure against future losses, title insurance protects the insured from an event that occurred before the policy was issued. Title insurance is considered the best defense of title; the title insurance company will defend any lawsuit based on an insurable defect and pay claims if the title proves to be defective.

After examining the public records, the title company usually issues a *preliminary report of title* (also called a *commitment to issue a title policy*). This describes the type of policy that will be issued and includes

- the name of the insured party;
- the legal description of the real estate;
- the estate or interest covered;
- conditions and stipulations under which the policy is issued; and
- a schedule of all exceptions, including encumbrances and defects found in the public records and any known unrecorded defects.

The *premium* for the policy is paid once, at closing. The maximum loss for which the company may be liable cannot exceed the face amount of the policy. When a title company makes a payment to settle a claim covered by a policy, the company generally acquires the right to any remedy or damages available to the insured. This right is called **subrogation**. An exception or defect noted in the title commitment may be waived or endorsed by the title company with the submission of credible supporting evidence. The title company may charge additional fees for the waiver or endorsement.

A title insurance policy is the most commonly used evidence that an owner of Illinois real property tenders to a prospective purchaser or lender as proof of good title.

Coverage

Exactly which defects the title company will defend depends on the type of policy (see Figure 13.1). A *standard coverage policy* normally insures the title as it is known from the public records. In addition, the standard policy insures against such hidden defects as forged documents, conveyances by incompetent grantors, incorrect marital statements, and improperly delivered deeds.

Figure 13.1: Owner's Title Insurance Policy

Standard Coverage	Extended Coverage	Not Covered by Either Policy
■ Defects found in public records ■ Forged documents ■ Incompetent grantors ■ Incorrect marital statements ■ Improperly delivered deeds	Standard coverage plus defects discoverable through the following: ■ Property inspection, including unrecorded rights of persons in possession ■ Examination of survey ■ Unrecorded liens not known by policy-holder	■ Defects and liens listed in policy ■ Defects known to buyer ■ Changes in land use brought about by zoning ordinances

Extended coverage, as provided by an American Land Title Association (ALTA) policy, includes the protections of a standard policy plus additional protections. An extended or ALTA policy protects a homeowner against defects that may be discovered by inspection of the property (i.e., rights of parties in possession, examination of a survey, and certain unrecorded liens). Most lenders require extended coverage title policies.

Title insurance does not offer guaranteed protection against all defects. A title company will not insure a bad title or offer protection against defects that clearly appear in a title search. The policy generally names certain uninsurable losses, called *exclusions*. These include zoning ordinances, restrictive covenants, easements, certain water rights, and current taxes and special assessments.

Types of Policies

The different types of policies depend on who is named as the insured. An owner's policy is issued for the benefit of the owner (new buyer) and the owner's heirs or devisees. This policy is almost always paid for by the seller at the closing. A lender's policy is issued for the benefit of the mortgage company. This policy is usually paid for by the buyer at the closing. The amount of the coverage depends on the amount of the mortgage loan. As the loan balance is reduced, the coverage decreases.

A lessee's interest can be insured with a leasehold policy. Certificate of sale policies are available to insure the title to property purchased in a court sale.

SUMMARY

The purpose of the recording acts is to give legal, public, and constructive notice to the world of parties' interests in real estate. The recording provisions have been adopted to create an orderly system for real estate transfer. Without them, it would be virtually impossible to transfer real estate from one party to another. The interests and rights of the various parties in a particular parcel of land must be recorded so that such rights are legally effective against third parties who do not have knowledge or notice of the rights. If a transfer of real estate title is taking place, any provision in the transfer documents intended to prevent recording is void.

Recording is generally interpreted as constructive notice. Actual notice is knowledge acquired through personal service or by visiting the property.

Title evidence shows whether a seller conveys marketable title. A deed of conveyance is evidence that a grantor has conveyed his interest in land, but it is not evidence of the title's kind or condition. A marketable title is generally one that is so free from significant defects that the purchaser can be insured against having to defend the title.

Three forms of providing title evidence are commonly used throughout the United States: abstract and attorney's opinion of title, certificate of title, and title insurance policy. Each form reveals the history of a title. Title evidence must be revisited or dated as a continuation whenever title evidence is reissued.

Title searches before closing are done in some detail to assure the new homeowner that the title was clear at the time of conveyance. A deed shows that the previous owner's interest was conveyed, but it does not by itself provide assurance of the condition of the title.

In Illinois, the title insurance policy is the most commonly used indication of marketable title.

UNIT 13 QUIZ

1. A title search in the public records may be conducted by
   A. attorneys and abstractors only.
   B. attorneys, abstractors, and real estate licensees only.
   C. anyone.
   D. anyone who obtains a court order under the Freedom of Information Act.

2. Which of these statements *BEST* explains why instruments affecting real estate are recorded?
   A. Failing to record will void the transfer.
   B. The instruments must be recorded to comply with the terms of the statute of frauds.
   C. Recording proves the execution of the instrument.
   D. Recording gives constructive notice to the world of the rights and interests of a party in a particular parcel of real estate.

3. A purchaser went to the county building to check the recorder's records. She found that the seller was the grantee in the last recorded deed, and no mortgage was on record against the property. The purchaser may assume that
   A. all taxes are paid, and no judgments are outstanding.
   B. the seller did not mortgage the property.
   C. the seller has good title.
   D. no one else is occupying the property.

4. The date and time a document was recorded establishes
   A. abstract of title.
   B. subrogation.
   C. priority.
   D. marketable title.

5. Mary sold her home to Lynn. Lynn moved into the home but did not record the deed. A few weeks later, Mary died. Her heirs in another city were unaware that she had sold the home. The heirs conveyed title to David, who actually recorded the deed. Who owns the property?
   A. David
   B. Mary's heirs
   C. Both Lynn and David
   D. Lynn

6. If a property has encumbrances that will outlast the closing, the property
   A. can be sold if a buyer agrees to take it subject to the encumbrances.
   B. cannot be sold.
   C. can be sold only if title insurance is provided.
   D. cannot have a deed recorded without a survey.

7. Which of these constitutes acceptable proof of ownership?
   A. A subrogation agreement
   B. Physical possession
   C. A deed signed by the last seller
   D. An abstract and attorney's opinion

8. Chain of title refers to
   A. a summary or history of all documents and legal proceedings affecting a specific parcel of land.
   B. a record of a property's ownership.
   C. a report of the contents of the public record regarding a particular property.
   D. an instrument or document that protects the insured parties (subject to specific exceptions) against defects in the examination of the record and hidden risks such as forgeries, undisclosed heirs, and errors in the public records.

9. A seller delivered a deed to a buyer at the closing. A title search disclosed no serious defects, and the title did not appear to be based on doubtful questions of law or fact nor did it appear to expose the buyer to possible litigation. The seller's title did not appear to present a threat to the buyer's quiet enjoyment, and the title policy was sufficient to convince a reasonably well-informed person that the property could be resold. The title conveyed would commonly be called
   A. a marketable title.
   B. a certificate of title.
   C. an abstract of title.
   D. an attorney's opinion of title.

10. The person who prepares an abstract of title for a parcel of real estate
    A. insures the condition of the title.
    B. inspects the property.
    C. searches the public records and then summarizes the events and proceedings that affect title.
    D. issues a certificate of title.

11. A homeowner wants to sell her property but cannot find her deed. In this situation, she
    A. may need a suit to quiet title.
    B. does not need the deed to sell if it was recorded.
    C. must buy title insurance.
    D. should execute a replacement deed to herself.

12. Mortgage title policies protect which parties from loss?
    A. Mortgagees
    B. Buyers
    C. Sellers
    D. Buyers and lenders

13. Which statement is *TRUE* regarding the lender's title insurance?
    A. The lender's protection increases with each principal payment that is made.
    B. The seller is usually required to purchase the lender's policy.
    C. The mortgagee's premium is paid monthly with the mortgage payment.
    D. The mortgagee's policy covers only the mortgagee.

14. Which of these are traditionally covered by a standard title insurance policy?
    A. Unrecorded rights of persons in possession
    B. Changes in land use due to zoning ordinances
    C. Improperly delivered deeds
    D. Unrecorded liens not known of by the policyholder

15. The documents called title evidence include
    A. warranty deeds.
    B. security agreements.
    C. a deed.
    D. title insurance.

16. The legal presumption that information can be obtained through diligent inquiry is called
    A. actual notice.
    B. constructive notice.
    C. priority.
    D. subrogation.

17. What is necessary for a deed to be recorded in Illinois?
    A. The full address of the grantee
    B. The names of the grantor and grantee typed or printed below their signatures
    C. An escrow exemption statement
    D. Permanent tax index number

18. The act of recording gives legal priority to those interests recorded
    A. at the federal level.
    B. last.
    C. first.
    D. by a licensee.

19. A Chicago resident purchases farmland in southern Illinois as an investment. The deed to the Chicago resident should be recorded in the
    A. recorder's office of the county in which the farmland is located.
    B. county recorder's office of Cook County, where the individual's permanent residence is located.
    C. statewide land registry located in Springfield.
    D. tax records of the city of Chicago.

20. The population of Outlet County is 54,000. In Outlet County, the recorder of deeds
    A. is the county clerk.
    B. must be elected.
    C. is the county treasurer.
    D. is appointed by the secretary of state.

UNIT 14

Illinois Real Estate License Law

LEARNING OBJECTIVES

When you have completed this unit, you will be able to accomplish the following.

> Explain the purpose of the Real Estate License Act of 2000.
> Identify the various categories of licensure.
> Distinguish the processes involved in sponsoring and terminating a license.
> Explain the statutory duties of the agency relationship.
> Describe the actions that result in discipline against a licensee.

KEY TERMS

blind ad	Illinois Department	Real Estate Administration
broker	of Financial and	and Disciplinary Board
designated agency	Professional Regulation	Real Estate Recovery Fund
designated managing	(IDFPR)	Real Estate Research and
broker	informed written consent	Education Fund
Division of Real Estate	license	residential leasing agent
	managing broker	sponsoring broker

NOTE: The Administrative Code ("The Rules") which amplifies and works in conjunction with the Illinois Real Estate License Act is anticipated to be effective by July 1, 2020.

OVERVIEW

Illinois has had a real estate license law since 1921. This body of law is intended to evaluate the competency of persons engaged in the real estate profession and to regulate their activities for the protection of the public. Today, the law is called the Real Estate License Act of 2000 (as amended in 2020). The real estate industry in Illinois is regulated by the Division of Real Estate, a branch of the **Illinois Department of Financial and Professional Regulation (IDFPR)** (also sometimes called the *Department*), which is charged with protecting and improving the lives of Illinois consumers. The Secretary of the IDFPR is appointed by the

Governor and oversees the Division of Real Estate. The Division of Real Estate by law is overseen by a Director of the Real Estate Division and a Real Estate Coordinator.

IDFPR is responsible for administering and enforcing the Real Estate License Act of 2000. In addition, IDFPR administers all licenses for Illinois real estate brokers, managing brokers, residential leasing agents, real estate corporations, partnerships, limited liability companies, real estate branch offices, licensed education providers, and real estate instructors.

IDFPR promulgates rules for the Act's implementation and enforcement. These are often called "the rules," and they supply explanatory detail and guidelines for the Act. The Act, rules, and other significant legislation are available online at https://www.idfpr.com/profs/REALEST.asp.

References to article and section numbers in the Act will be provided throughout so that you can reference the Act itself for more detail on any topic.

ADMINISTRATION OF THE REAL ESTATE LICENSE ACT OF 2000

The four major funds administered through IDFPR are

- the *Real Estate License Administration Fund*, to which license fees and other funds initially go;
- the *Real Estate Research and Education Fund*, for research and scholarships;
- the *Real Estate Recovery Fund*, a consumer-oriented fund for compensating consumers harmed by licensees' actions; and
- the *Real Estate Audit Fund*, for conducting audits of special accounts.

Secretary of the IDFPR

The secretary of the IDFPR is appointed by the governor and oversees the Division of Banking, the Division of Financial Institutions, the Division of Professional Regulation, and the Division of Real Estate.

Division of Real Estate

IDFPR gives the **Division of Real Estate** (the Division) the primary authority to administer the Real Estate License Act of 2000. The Division is also empowered to issue rules and regulations that implement and interpret the Act. The rules accompanying the Act are important to a full understanding of the Act's implications and applications. IDFPR has the authority to contract with third parties for any services deemed necessary for proper administration of the Act.

IDFPR is responsible for administrative activities such as

- conducting license examinations;
- issuing and renewing licenses;
- preparing all forms, including applications and licenses; and
- collecting fees from applicants and licensees.

IDFPR has the following additional functions, which may be exercised only on the initiative and approval of the Real Estate Administration and Disciplinary Board:

- Conducting hearings that may result in the revocation or suspension of licenses or in the refusal to issue or renew licenses

- Imposing penalties for violations of the Act
- Restoring suspended or revoked licenses

Real Estate Coordinator (225 ILCS 454/25-15)

A licensed broker is appointed to the position of real estate coordinator by the IDFPR secretary after the recommendations of real estate professionals and organizations are considered. This individual's license is transferred to inactive status during the appointment.

The real estate coordinator's duties include

- acting as ex officio chairperson of the Real Estate Administration and Disciplinary Board without a vote;
- being the direct liaison between IDFPR, the real estate profession, and real estate organizations and associations;
- preparing and circulating educational and informational material for licensees;
- appointing any committees necessary to assist IDFPR in carrying out its duties; and
- supervising real estate activities.

Real Estate Administration and Disciplinary Board (225 ILCS 454/25-10)

The **Real Estate Administration and Disciplinary Board** (also called *the Board*) acts in an advisory capacity to the real estate coordinator regarding matters involving standards of professional conduct, discipline, and examination. In addition to its advisory functions, the Board conducts hearings on disciplinary actions against persons accused of violating the Act or the rules.

The real estate coordinator is the nonvoting, ex officio board chairperson.

Composition of the Board

The Board is composed of 15 members appointed by the governor. Members will be appointed subject to the following conditions:

1. All members must have been residents and citizens of this state for at least six years prior to the date of appointment.

2. Twelve members must have been actively engaged as managing brokers, brokers, or both for at least the 10 years prior to the appointment, and two must possess an active prelicense instructor

3. Three members of the Board must be public members who represent consumer interests.

   Members are chosen in a manner such that all areas of the state are reasonably represented.

Members' terms are for four years and the expiration of those terms are staggered. No member is reappointed to the Board for a term that would cause his or her cumulative service to exceed 10 years. The governor may terminate a member's appointment due to cause.

The Real Estate Research and Education Fund (225 ILCS 454/25-25)

The Act created the **Real Estate Research and Education Fund**, which is held in trust in the state Treasury and administered by IDFPR. Annually, on September 15, the state treasurer transfers $125,000 to this fund from the Real Estate License Administration Fund. These funds are used for research and for education at state institutions of higher education or other organizations for research and for the advancement of education in the real estate industry. Of the $125,000 annual allocation, $15,000 is used to fund a scholarship program to support the real estate education of minority real estate professionals.

OBTAINING AND KEEPING A REAL ESTATE LICENSE

Determining who can obtain a real estate license, the purposes of a license, and the types of licenses available are all covered in Article 5 of the Real Estate License Act of 2000, with supportive definitions found in Article 1. Educational requirements such as the prelicensing coursework needed, testing requirements, and continuing education requirements for all Illinois licenses are also covered in Article 5.

Who Needs to Be Licensed? (225 ILCS 454/1-10)

It is illegal for anyone to act as a broker, managing broker, or residential leasing agent without a real estate **license** issued by IDFPR. According to 225 ILCS 454/1-10 "Broker" means an individual, partnership, limited liability company, corporation, or registered limited liability partnership other than a residential leasing agent who, whether in person or through any media or technology, for another and for compensation, or with the intention or expectation of receiving compensation, either directly or indirectly does the following:

- Sells, exchanges, purchases, rents, or leases real estate
- Offers to sell, exchange, purchase, rent, or lease real estate
- Negotiates, offers, attempts, or agrees to negotiate the sale, exchange, purchase, rental, or leasing of real estate
- Lists, offers, attempts, or agrees to list real estate for sale, lease, or exchange
- Buys, sells, offers to buy or sell, or otherwise deals in options on real estate or improvements thereon
- Whether for another or themselves, engages in a pattern of business of buying, selling, offering to buy or sell, marketing for sale, exchanging, or otherwise dealing in contracts, including assignable contracts for the purchase or sale of, or options on real estate or improvements thereon. For purposes of this definition, an individual or entity will be found to have engaged in a pattern of business if the individual or entity by itself or with any combination of other individuals or entities, whether as partners or common owners in another entity, has engaged in one or more of these practices on 2 or more occasions in any 12-month period.
- Supervises the collection, offer, attempt, or agreement to collect rent for the use of real estate
- Advertises or represents herself as being engaged in the business of buying, selling, exchanging, renting, or leasing real estate
- Assists or directs in the procuring or referring of leads or prospects intended to result in the sale, exchange, lease, or rental of real estate

- Assists or directs in the negotiation of any transaction intended to result in the sale, exchange, lease, or rental of real estate
- Opens real estate to the public for marketing purposes
- Sells, leases, or offers for sale or lease real estate at auction

Other Definitions (225 ILCS 454/1-10)

"**Designated managing broker**" means a broker who has supervisory responsibilities for licensees in one or, in the case of a multi-office company, more than one office and who has been appointed as such by the sponsoring broker registered with the Department.

"Inactive" means a status of licensure where the licensee holds a current license under the Act, but the licensee is prohibited from engaging in licensed activities because the licensee is unsponsored or the license of the sponsoring broker with whom the licensee is associated or by whom the licensee is employed is currently expired, revoked, suspended, or otherwise rendered invalid under the Act. The license of any business entity that is not in good standing with the Illinois Secretary of State, or is not authorized to conduct business in Illinois, will immediately become inactive and that entity will be prohibited from engaging in any licensed activities.

"Person" means and includes individuals, entities, corporations, limited liability companies, registered limited liability partnerships, foreign and domestic partnerships, and other business entities, except that when the context otherwise requires, the term may refer to a single individual or other described entity.

"Renewal period" means the period beginning 90 days before the expiration date of a license.

"Residential leasing agent" means a person who is employed by a broker to engage in licensed activities limited to leasing residential real estate who has obtained a license as provided by the Act.

"Sponsoring broker" means the broker who certifies to the Department the sponsorship of a licensed managing broker, broker, or a residential leasing agent.

License Requirement Exemptions (225 ILCS 454/5-20)

According to 225 ILCS 454/5-20, the requirement for holding a broker, managing broker, or residential leasing agent license does not apply to the following:

- Any person, as defined in Section 1-10, that as owner or lessor performs any of the acts described in the definition of "broker" under Section 1-10 of this Act with reference to property owned or leased by it, or to the regular employees thereof with respect to the property so owned or leased, where such acts are performed in the regular course of or as an incident to the management, sale, or other disposition of such property and the investment therein, if such regular employees do not perform any of the acts described in the definition of "broker" under Section 1-10 of this Act in connection with a vocation of selling or leasing any real estate or the improvements thereon not so owned or leased
- An attorney-in-fact acting under a duly executed and recorded power of attorney to convey real estate from the owner or lessor or the services rendered by an attorney at law in the performance of the attorney's duty as an attorney at law
- Any person acting as receiver, trustee in bankruptcy, administrator, executor, or guardian or while acting under a court order or under the authority of a will or testamentary trust

- Any person acting as a resident manager for the owner or any employee acting as the resident manager for a broker managing an apartment building, duplex, or apartment complex, when the resident manager resides on the premises, the premises is his or her primary residence, and the resident manager is engaged in the leasing of the property of which he or she is the resident manager

- Any officer or employee of a federal agency in the conduct of official duties

- Any officer or employee of the State government or any political subdivision thereof performing official duties

- Any multiple listing service or other similar information exchange that is engaged in the collection and dissemination of information concerning real estate available for sale, purchase, lease, or exchange for the purpose of providing licensees with a system by which licensees may cooperatively share information along with which no other licensed activities, as defined in Section 1-10 of this Act, are provided

- Railroads and other public utilities regulated by the State of Illinois, or the officers or full time employees thereof, unless the performance of any licensed activities is in connection with the sale, purchase, lease, or other disposition of real estate or investment therein that does not require approval of the appropriate State regulatory authority

- Any medium of advertising in the routine course of selling or publishing advertising along with which no other licensed activities, as defined in Section 1-10 of this Act, are provided

- Any resident lessee of a residential dwelling unit who refers for compensation to the owner of the dwelling unit, or to the owner's agent, prospective lessees of dwelling units in the same building or complex as the resident lessee's unit, but only if the resident lessee (i) refers no more than 3 prospective lessees in any 12-month period, (ii) receives compensation of no more than $5,000 or the equivalent of two months' rent, whichever is less, in any 12-month period, and (iii) limits his or her activities to referring prospective lessees to the owner, or the owner's agent, and does not show a residential dwelling unit to a prospective lessee, discuss terms or conditions of leasing a dwelling unit with a prospective lessee, or otherwise participate in the negotiation of the leasing of a dwelling unit

- The purchase, sale, or transfer of a time-share or similar vacation item or interest, vacation club membership, or other activity formerly regulated under the Real Estate Timeshare Act of 1999 (repealed)

- An existing time-share owner who, for compensation, refers prospective purchasers, but only if the existing time-share owner (i) refers no more than 20 prospective purchasers in any calendar year, (ii) receives no more than $1,000, or its equivalent, for referrals in any calendar year and (iii) limits his or her activities to referring prospective purchasers of time-share interests to the developer or the developer's employees or agents, and does not show, discuss terms or conditions of purchase or otherwise participate in negotiations with regard to time-share interests

- Any person who is licensed without examination under Section 10-25 (now repealed) of the Auction License Act and who is therefore exempt from holding a broker's license under this Act for the limited purpose of selling or leasing real estate at auction, so long as

  - that person has made application for said exemption by July 1, 2000;

  - that person verifies to the Department that he or she has sold real estate at auction for a period of 5 years prior to licensure as an auctioneer;

- that person has had no lapse in his or her license as an auctioneer; and

- the license issued under the Auction License Act has not been disciplined for violation of those provisions of Article 20 of the Auction License Act dealing with or related to the sale or lease of real estate at auction

■ A person who holds a valid license under the Auction License Act and a valid real estate auction certification and conducts auctions for the sale of real estate under Section 5-32 of this Act

■ A hotel operator who is registered with the Illinois Department of Revenue and pays taxes under the Hotel Operators' Occupation Tax Act and rents a room or rooms in a hotel as defined in the Hotel Operators' Occupation Tax Act for a period of not more than 30 consecutive days and not more than 60 days in a calendar year or a person who participates in an online marketplace enabling persons to rent out all or part of the person's owner residence

■ Notwithstanding any provisions to the contrary, the Department and its employee are exempt from education, course, provider, instructor, and course license requirements and fees while acting in an official capacity on behalf of the Department. Courses offered by the Department are eligible for continuing education credit.

Civil Penalty for the Unlicensed Practice of Real Estate (225 ILCS 454/20-10)

In Illinois, it is illegal for any person to practice, offer, attempt to practice, or to hold oneself out to practice as a real estate broker, managing broker, or residential leasing agent without being licensed. Anyone who does so is subject to a civil fine (in addition to any other penalties provided by law) of up to $25,000 for each offense as determined by IDFPR. The civil fine is assessed by and payable to IDFPR after a disciplinary hearing. IDFPR has the authority to investigate any and all unlicensed activity. The civil fine must be paid within 60 days after the effective date of the order. The order constitutes a judgment and may be filed and execution had thereon in the same manner from any court of record.

LICENSE CATEGORIES AND REQUIREMENTS (225 ILCS 454/5)

The Real Estate License Act of 2000 designates three categories of real estate licensees: broker, managing broker, and residential leasing agent. The law provides requirements and limitations specific to each type of licensee.

General Requirements

All individual license applicants must pass a written examination administered by an independent testing service, which currently is PSI. Anyone who wishes to take the exam must apply to PSI. PSI acts as the agent of IDFPR and is empowered to screen potential license candidates to ensure that they meet the statutory requirements as established in the Act.

An applicant for a broker's or managing broker's license who is currently an attorney admitted to practice law by the Illinois Supreme Court is exempt from the education requirements outlined as follows. The attorney still must take and pass the state exam (225 ILCS 454/5-27 and 225 ILCS 454/5-28).

The broker's or managing broker's license must be applied for within one year of passing the state test. Failure to do so means retaking the test. Failing the state test four consecutive times requires that the applicant retake the educational coursework, if they wish to obtain a license. Approved education for licensure as a managing broker, broker, or residential leasing agent is valid for two years after the date of completing of the education. (225 ILCS 454/5-35).

Each application for a license (new or renewal) must include the applicant's Social Security number or Tax Identification Number, in addition to the other required information (225 ILCS 454/5-6).

IDFPR maintains a list of all active licensees. Should a sponsoring broker's license be revoked or rendered inactive, all licensees under that sponsoring broker will be considered inactive until such time as the sponsoring broker's license is reinstated or renewed or the licensee changes employment. Expiration dates and renewal periods for each license are set by rule, and licenses can be renewed within 90 days before expiration upon completion of CE and payment of the required fees.

Broker's License (225 ILCS 454/5)

A **broker** is any individual, partnership, limited liability company (LLC), corporation, or registered limited liability partnership other than a residential leasing agent who, for another and for compensation, whether in person or through any media or technology, or with the intention or expectation of receiving compensation, either directly or indirectly, performs any of the services for which a real estate license is required (225 ILCS 454/1-10).

Broker Requirements

Applicants for a broker's license must meet the following requirements, as outlined in 225 ILCS 454/5-27:

- Be at least 18 years of age
- Be of good moral character
- Provide a Social Security number or an identification number supplied by the state
- Successfully complete a 4-year course of study in a high school or secondary school approved by the state in which the school is located, or possess a high school equivalency certificate
- Complete 120 hours of prelicensing and postlicensing education. Prelicensing includes 75 hours of instruction, 15 hours of which must consist of situational and case studies presented in the classroom or by live interactive webinar or online distance education courses. Postlicensing includes 45 hours of instruction.
- Pass an IDFPR-authorized written examination
- Submit a valid application for a broker license along with the required fees

An applicant must meet all required criteria to receive a license before they can get an active license. To have an active license, the applicant must then have a valid sponsorship.

No applicant may engage in any of the activities covered by the Act until a valid sponsorship has been registered with the Department.

Managing Broker's License (225 ILCS 454/5)

A **managing broker** is a licensee who may be authorized to assume responsibilities as a designated managing broker for licensees in one or, in the case of a multi-office company, more than one office, upon appointment by the sponsoring broker and registration with the Department. A managing broker may act as his or her own sponsor.

Managing Broker Requirements

Applicants for a managing broker's license must meet the following requirements, as outlined in 225 ILCS 454/5-28:

- Be at least 20 years of age
- Be of good moral character
- Provide a Social Security number or an identification number supplied by the state
- Have been licensed as a broker for at least two consecutive years out of the preceding three years
- Successfully complete a 4-year course of study in a high school or secondary school approved by the state in which the school is located, or possess a high school equivalency certificate
- Complete 165 hours of instruction, 120 of which must be those hours required pre-licensure and post-licensure to obtain a broker's license, and 45 additional hours completed within the year immediately preceding the filing of an application for a managing broker's license (these 45 hours should focus on brokerage administration and management and residential leasing agent management and include at least 15 hours in the classroom or by live, interactive webinar or online distance education courses)
- Pass an IDFPR-authorized written examination
- Submit a valid application for a license along with the required fees

An applicant who is authorized to practice law by the Supreme Court of Illinois and is in active standing is exempt from the 165-course-hour requirements.

Corporations, Limited Liability Companies, and Partnerships (Section 5-15)

An amendment (effective January 1, 2019) to the Real Estate License Act of 2000 makes uniform the application process for real estate business entities.

A corporation, partnership, or limited liability company (LLC) may receive a broker's license under the following conditions:

- Every officer of the entity who actively participates in the real estate activities of the entity must hold a license as a managing broker or broker.
- Provide a tax identification number.
- Every employee who acts as a managing broker, broker, or residential leasing agent for the entity must hold a license as a managing broker, broker, or residential leasing agent.
- Nonparticipating owners or officers of a corporation, partners of a partnership, limited liability partners of a limited liability partnership, or members or managers of a limited liability company must submit affidavits of nonparticipation to the Department of Real Estate.

Residential Leasing Agent's License (225 ILCS 454/5)

The Real Estate License Act of 2000 provides for a limited-scope residential leasing agent license for persons who wish to engage only in activities limited to the leasing of residential real property in which a license is required. A **residential leasing agent** is limited to "leasing or renting residential real property, or attempting, offering, or negotiating to lease or rent residential real property, or supervising the collection, offer, attempt, or agreement to collect rent for the use of residential real property" (225 ILCS 454/5-5). However, "a residential leasing agent may not engage in any activity that would otherwise require a broker's license, including, but not limited to, selling, offering for sale, negotiating for sale, listing or showing for sale, or referring for sale or commercial lease real estate." Licensed brokers and managing brokers do not need a residential leasing agent license for these activities.

A residential leasing agent license applicant must meet the following requirements:

- Be 18 years old or older
- Be of good moral character
- Provide a Social Security number or an identification number supplied by the state
- Successfully complete a 4-year course of study in a high school or secondary school approved by the state in which the school is located, or possess a high school equivalency certificate verified under oath by the applicant
- Complete a 15-hour residential leasing agent prelicense course
- Pass an IDFPR-authorized written examination

Persons who hold residential leasing agent licenses must comply with qualification requirements, standards of practice, and disciplinary guidelines established and enforced by IDFPR. A residential leasing agent must be sponsored by a licensed real estate broker.

A person may engage in residential leasing activities for 120 days without being licensed if they first obtain a residential leasing agent permit. A sponsoring broker associating with a residential leasing agent must submit to the department all required information and must also certify that the residential leasing agent will not work for more than 120 days without a license. A person can only practice under a permit one time (1450.240).

All education, examination, and fee requirements must be met during the 120-day period. IDFPR may establish additional criteria to ensure that no unlicensed person is permitted to repeatedly or continually carry out any activities that, by law, require a license.

Restrictions on Licensure (225 ILCS 454/5-15)

No person, partnership, or business entity may be granted a license if any owner, officer, director, partner, limited liability partner, member, or manager has been denied a real estate license in the previous five years or is currently barred from practice by the Department.

No corporation, partnership, or limited liability company (LLC) may be granted a license if any nonparticipating owner, officer, partner, member, or manager is currently barred from real estate practice by the Department.

THE LICENSING EXAMINATION

Applicants are eligible to take the licensing examination only after they have met the education and age requirements; they must also be able to demonstrate that they have met the other requirements set out by the Real Estate License Act of 2000 and any associated rules. The content of the licensing examinations relate directly to the skills and knowledge required of a qualified licensee and may be administered only at times and places approved by IDFPR. Each candidate must pay the required fee to the appropriate testing center but will forfeit the fee if failing to appear at the scheduled time, date, and place to take the exam following receipt and acknowledgment of one's application by IDFPR or the testing center.

Candidates must register with the testing service in advance of the test and pay any fees to reserve a spot at one of many convenient locations throughout Illinois on a day that is convenient to them.

To gain admission to the testing center, candidates must provide two forms of identification and a fingerprint scan. The first form of identification must be a driver's license with photograph, a passport or military identification with photograph, or an official state identification card with photograph. The second form of identification must display the name and signature of the candidate for signature verification.

All examinations are given on a computer that displays all the test questions on a monitor and records all the answers. No special knowledge of computers is necessary.

After completing the test, candidates are immediately informed whether they passed or failed. Passing candidates will be given a *score report*, which will let them know they passed, but they will not be given an actual score unless they fail. The score report contains instructions for applying for a license at the IDFPR Online Services Portal at https://ilesonline.idfpr.illinois .gov/DFPR/Default.aspx. Passing candidates have one year in which to apply for a license, after which time a new examination will be required.

Candidates who fail the examination will be told their score and be given diagnostic information, in addition to directions on how to apply for a future test. Candidates who fail only one portion (either the state or national portion) of the exam are required to retake only the failed portion. The candidate is required to retake that portion within one year of failing.

After four failures, the applicant must successfully repeat all prelicense education before further testing. The fifth attempt to pass the exam is then treated by IDFPR as though it were a first attempt (225 ILCS 454/5-35(c)).

THE REAL ESTATE LICENSE

Applicants will receive a score report containing the instructions to apply for their license via the Online Services Portal located at IDFPR.com.

The IDFPR portal may not immediately be updated as to the applicant's passing of the test, because PSI uploads the passing information about every 72 hours. Once uploaded, emails are sent to applicants notifying them that they may then apply.

During the application process, the state requires applicants to upload their score report and their education transcripts.

Though applicants can apply without a sponsoring broker, no license will be issued until the sponsoring broker approves the sponsorship.

Once the sponsoring broker approves the sponsorship of an applicant, the applicant may practice real estate.

A short time later, the applicant will be sent an email with a link to the IDFPR site where the license can be downloaded and printed. The license will specify whether the individual is authorized to act as a broker, a managing broker, or a residential leasing agent. The state maintains a searchable database so that the public may confirm whether an individual has an active and valid license.

Licensees must deliver a copy of their license to their sponsoring broker and carry on their person a physical or electronic copy of their license.

What Happens to Your License When You Change or Leave Firms? (225 ILCS 454/5-40)

When a licensee or the sponsoring broker terminates employment with the sponsoring broker or a managing broker for any reason, the licensee must log into the IDFPR Online Services Portal and click on the online services link. There, under "License Application, the licensee should click on "licensure options" and continue to follow the instructions on the screen to "leave current brokerage" and "select new sponsoring brokerage." A "transaction review" and a screen where the licensee pays the $25 transfer fee follows.

Both the terminating sponsoring broker and the terminating licensee have 24 hours to notify the state of the termination via the portal. When terminated, the license goes to inactive status.

Change of Address, Name, or Business Information (225 ILCS 454/5-41)

It is the licensee's responsibility to inform the Department of any change of address, email address, telephone number, or office location with 24 hours after any such change. The notification must be done through the Department's website or by any other means prescribed by the Department. Sponsoring brokers are required to notify the Department via the website of any change in designated managing brokers within 15 days of the change.

Expiration and Renewal

License expiration and renewal dates are established by rule, consistent with the Act. Licenses may be renewed—by paying required fees and meeting CE requirements—within the 90 days before expiration of the license.

Prior to the first renewal of their broker's license, a newly licensed broker must complete 45 hours of postlicense education in courses recommended by the Board and approved by the IDFPR. This 45-hour course is divided into three 15-hour classes individually covering applied brokerage principles, risk management and discipline, and transactional issues. Each course requires its own 50-question final exam. Those individuals receiving their first broker license within 180 days preceding the next broker renewal deadline are allowed to complete the 45 hours prior to the second broker renewal deadline following the receipt of their license.

A designated managing broker's responsibilities include directly handling all earnest money, escrows, and contract negotiations for all transactions in which the designated agent for the transaction has not completed 45 hours of postlicense education, as well as the approval of all advertisements involving a licensee who has not completed 45 hours of postlicense education. Licensees that have not completed their 45 hours of postlicense education have no authority to bind the sponsoring broker.

Brokers, managing brokers, and residential leasing agents may renew their licenses (provided they pay the necessary fees and meet the continuing education and other requirements) for up to two years following license expiration. A managing broker licensee, broker, or residential leasing agent whose license has been expired for more than 2 years but less than 5 years may have it restored by applying to the Department, paying the required fee, completing the continuing education requirements for the most recent pre-renewal period that ended prior to the date of the application for reinstatement, and filing acceptable proof of fitness to have his or her license restored, as set by rule.

Nonresidents and License by Reciprocity (225 ILCS 454/5-60)

A managing broker or broker who lives in a state that has a reciprocal licensing agreement with Illinois may be issued an Illinois license if the following conditions are met. For a reciprocal broker or managing broker's license, the following conditions must be met:

- The broker or managing broker holds a *broker* or *managing broker's license* in her home state

- The licensing standards of that state are substantially equivalent to or greater than the minimum standards required in Illinois

- The managing broker or broker has been actively practicing as a managing broker or broker for at least two years immediately before the application date

- The managing broker or broker furnishes IDFPR with an official statement, under seal, from her home state's licensing authority that the managing broker or broker has an active managing broker's or broker's license, is in good standing, and has no complaints pending

- The managing broker's or broker's home state grants reciprocal privileges to Illinois licensees

- The managing broker or broker passes a test on Illinois-specific real estate brokerage laws

Currently, Illinois has reciprocity with the following states under the Real Estate License Act of 2000: Colorado, Connecticut, Florida, Georgia, Indiana (broker only), Iowa, Nebraska, and Wisconsin. Always check the IDFPR website for the latest updates on reciprocal states.

Before a nonresident managing broker or broker will be issued a license, the applicant must file a designation in a manner prescribed by the Department that appoints the secretary to act as her agent upon whom all judicial or other process or legal notices directed to the nonresident may be served. Service upon the agent so designated is equivalent to personal service on the nonresident licensee.

Nonresidents applying for an Illinois license must furnish IDFPR with proof of active licensure in their home state. They also must pay the same license fees that are required of resident brokers and managing brokers. Prospective nonresident licensees must agree in writing to abide by all provisions of the Act and to submit to IDFPR's jurisdiction.

However, once acquired, the reciprocal license allows a new resident who has recently been working under a nonresident license to obtain a valid resident's license without examination. Licenses previously granted under reciprocal agreements with other states remain in force so long as IDFPR has a reciprocal agreement with that state.

Renewal Without Fee (225 ILCS 454/5-50)

Licensees whose licenses have expired may renew without paying any lapsed renewal or reinstatement fees if the license expired within two years after the termination of the service, training, or education while the licensee was performing any of the following functions:

- On active duty with the U.S. armed services or called into the service or training by the state militia

- Engaged in training or education under supervision of the United States before induction into military service
- Serving as the coordinator of real estate in Illinois or as an IDFPR employee

The licensee must request a waiver from the Department.

LICENSE FEES

Applicants for real estate licenses are subject to appropriate fees in addition to the testing fee paid to PSI when applying for the examination. The Real Estate License Act of 2000 provides for predetermined licensing fees.

The initial fee for a residential leasing agent license is $75. When applying for a broker license, the applicant must submit an initial license fee of $125. The initial broker's license fee for a partnership, LLC, or corporation is $125. Other licensing fees are indicated in the rules and are set according to actual cost incurred by IDFPR and may vary.

Failure to Pay (225 ILCS 454/20-25)

If the licensee fails to make full payment of all fees and fines owed within 30 calendar days of the notification that payment is due, IDFPR will automatically revoke the license or deny the application without a hearing. The licensee may apply for restoration or issuance of the license and pay all fees and fines due to IDFPR.

Expiration and Renewal of Licenses

Broker's licenses expire on April 30 of every even-numbered year, and managing broker's licenses expire on April 30 of every odd-numbered year. Brokers may renew their licenses before the expiration date by paying a renewal fee of $150; managing brokers must pay a renewal fee of $200. Sponsoring brokers will also submit a completed "consent to audit and examine special accounts" form.

Every residential leasing agent license expires on July 31 of each even-numbered year. A residential leasing agent license is renewable by paying the renewal fee of $100. Licenses issued to business entities or branch offices expire on October 31 of every even-numbered year.

CONTINUING EDUCATION

Residential leasing agents are required to complete no less than eight hours of core curriculum of continuing education for each two-year renewal period. The curriculum must, at a minimum, consist of a single course or courses on the subjects of fair housing and human rights issues related to residential leasing, advertising and marketing issues, leases, applications, credit reports, criminal history, the handling of funds, owner-tenant relationships and laws, and environmental issues relating to residential real estate.

Each broker and managing broker who applies for license renewal must successfully complete 12 hours during the current term of the license of real estate continuing education (CE) courses recommended by the Board and approved by the Department. The 12 hours include 4 hours of mandatory core and 8 hours of elective education (the elective education must include 1 hour of sexual harassment prevention training).

In addition, managing brokers seeking to renew their licenses must complete a 12-hour IDFPR-approved CE course on broker management during the current term of the license.

The course must be delivered in a classroom or through a live, interactive webinar or online distance education format.

All brokers and managing brokers must complete the required courses or the equivalent before their licenses may be renewed. Exceptions to this rule include

- licensees who have had the requirements waived for good cause by the Secretary as recommended by the Board (the waiver is not automatic and must be requested by the licensee prior to renewal);
- licensees who serve in the U.S. armed services;
- licensees who serve as elected state or federal officials;
- licensees who are employed full time by IDFPR; and
- licensees who, by Illinois Supreme Court rule, are authorized to practice law in the state.

A person who receives her initial broker or managing broker license less than 90 days before the renewal date is exempt from the CE course requirement for this first renewal.

Only education providers approved by the Board may provide real estate CE courses. Instructors and course materials also must be approved. The license law includes strict criteria for obtaining and renewing approvals.

Course Content

The continuing education requirement for brokers and managing brokers must consist of a single core curriculum and an elective curriculum. The core curriculum consists of four hours and is not to be further divided into subcategories. The core curriculum must consist of subjects that may include, but not be limited to

- advertising,
- agency,
- disclosures,
- escrow,
- fair housing,
- residential leasing agent management, and
- license law.

Regarding the elective curriculum of eight hours, the Board considers subjects that cover the various aspects of the practice of real estate that are covered under the scope of the act. One of the eight hours of elective education must include a sexual harassment prevention training course.

In general, the subject matter for CE courses is chosen to protect the professionalism of the industry, the consumer, and the public and prevent violations of the act. Subject matter may include without limitation

- license law and escrow;
- antitrust;
- fair housing;
- agency;
- appraisal;
- property management;
- residential brokerage;

- farm property management;
- transaction management rights and duties of parties in a transaction;
- commercial brokerage and leasing;
- real estate financing;
- disclosures;
- residential leasing management;
- advertising;
- broker supervision and managing broker responsibility;
- professional conduct; and
- use of technology.

All subject areas must be recommended by the Board and then approved by the IDFPR.

Credit Hours May Be Earned for Self-Study Programs Approved by the Department

A broker or managing broker may earn credit for a specific CE course only once during the current term of the license.

No More Than Twelve Hours of Courses May Be Taken in Any One Day

Pre- and postlicensing course hours may not be counted toward the CE credit-hour requirements unless specifically permitted by the Real Estate License Act of 2000. The 45-hour postlicense course for brokers satisfies the continuing education requirement for the period in which the course is taken. The 45-hour brokerage administration and management prelicense course for managing broker licensees satisfies the 12-hour broker management CE requirement for the license term in which the course was taken. However, the remaining 12 hours of regular CE still must be taken.

Exempt from the CE requirement are licensees who, during the pre-renewal period, served in the armed services of the United States, served as elected state or federal officials, served as a full-time employee of IDFPR, and licensees who are licensed attorneys admitted to practice law in Illinois.

If a renewal applicant has earned CE hours in another state, the Department may approve the credit at its discretion based upon whether the course is one that would be approved under the Act. The licensee must reach out to the Department before taking the out-of-state course to ensure the course will be accepted.

YOUR REAL ESTATE BUSINESS AND THE ACT

Ownership of a Real Estate Business (225 ILCS 454/5-15 & Administrative Code 1450.600)

As per the definition of "broker," real estate may be practiced by licensed individuals, corporations, partnerships, and limited liability companies. In regards to the organized entities, every officer, general partner, or manager, respectively, who engages in the business, directly or indirectly, must hold a license as a managing broker or broker.

Unlicensed officers, partners, or managers must file an affidavit of non-participation with the Division.

No partnership, limited liability company, or corporation shall be licensed to conduct a brokerage business where an individual residential leasing agent, or group of residential leasing agents owns or directly or indirectly controls more than 49% of the shares of stock or other ownership in the partnership, limited liability company, or corporation.

Place of Business (225 ILCS 454/5-45 & Administrative Code 1450.730)

Proof of licensure for all sponsored licensees must be readily available to the public in the sponsoring broker's physical office or available through electronic means. For virtual offices, this requires prominently displaying a registry of all sponsored licensees on a website or digital platform.

Offices and Virtual Offices

To operate a virtual office, the sponsoring broker must be able to demonstrate licensees are engaged in licensed activities; offering real estate services; holding out to the public they are engaging in licensed activities; and following requirements for electronic file maintenance and recordkeeping set by rule. Virtual offices must comply with all advertising requirements under Sections 1450.715 and 1450.720. The sponsoring broker must notify the Department, in a manner prescribed by the Department, of the name of all designated managing brokers of the sponsoring broker and the office or offices they manage. The designated managing broker, who must be a licensed Illinois managing broker, oversees the office's operations. The brokerage license must be displayed in each office.

The name of each office must be the same as the primary real estate office or closely linked to it. IDFPR must be notified immediately, in a manner prescribed by the Department, of any change of an office location and within 15 days of a change of a designated managing broker.

Exceptions to Required Place of Business

A broker licensed in Illinois by reciprocity with another state may be exempt from the requirement of maintaining a definite place of business in Illinois if the broker

- maintains an active broker's license in the home state;
- maintains an office in the home state; and
- has filed a written statement with IDFPR appointing the secretary to act as the broker's agent for service of process and other legal notices, agreeing to abide by all the provisions of the Real Estate License Act of 2000 and submitting to IDFPR's jurisdiction.

Loss of an Office Manager (225 ILCS 454/5-29)

Upon the loss of a designated managing broker who is not replaced by the sponsoring broker or in the event of the death or adjudicated disability of the sole proprietor of an office, a written request for authorization allowing the continued operation of the office may be submitted to the Department within 15 days of the loss. The Department may issue a written authorization allowing the continued operation, provided that a licensed managing broker, or in the case of the death or adjudicated disability of a sole proprietor, the representative of the estate, assumes responsibility, in writing, for the operation of the office and agrees to personally supervise the operation of the office. This authorization will not be valid for more than 60 days unless extended by the Department for good cause shown and upon written request by the broker or representative.

Employment or Independent Contractor Agreements (225 ILCS 454/10-20)

Who needs a written agreement with a sponsoring broker?
■ All brokers or residential leasing agents

A licensee must have only one sponsoring broker at any given time and may perform real estate activities only for that sponsoring broker. In turn, a sponsoring broker must have a written employment or independent contractor agreement with each licensee the broker employs. The agreement must describe the significant aspects of their professional relationship, such as supervision, duties, compensation, and grounds for termination, and must address the employment or independent contractor relationship terms.

Recordkeeping (225 ILCS 454/5-45 (d))

Any record required by this Act to be created or maintained must be, in the case of a physical record, securely stored and accessible for inspection by the Department at the sponsoring broker's principal office and, in the case of an electronic record, securely stored in the format in which it was originally generated, sent, or received and accessible for inspection by the Department by secure electronic access to the record. Any record relating to a transaction of a special account must be maintained for a minimum of five years, and any electronic record must be backed up at least monthly.

AGENCY RELATIONSHIPS (225 ILCS 454/15)

Once a relationship has been formed between a licensee and a sponsoring broker, Article 15 addresses the licensee's relationships with the public. The article specifies that licensees are held to the law of agency in their relationships with the public, not to common law. Note that Article 15 is the only section of the Real Estate License Act of 2000 that has private right of action.

Section 15-10 establishes the basic relationship with consumers by stating that licensees shall be considered to be representing the consumer they are working with as a designated agent for the consumer unless there is a written agreement between the sponsoring broker and the consumer providing that there is a different relationship.

In replacing common law, Section 15-15 notes the statutory duties a licensee has toward her client. The statutory duties are fulfilled by

■ performing the terms of the brokerage agreement between a sponsoring broker and a client;

■ promoting the best interest of the client (e.g., timely offer presentation, material facts disclosure, best interests of the client prevail over any self-interest);

■ obeying any directions that are not contrary to public policy or law;

■ timely accounting for all money and property received in which the client has, may have, or should have had an interest;

- exercising skill and care in performing brokerage services;
- keeping confidential information confidential; and
- complying with the Act and all applicable statutes.

The Act also clarifies certain often-misunderstood situations that occur in agency relationships. Under the Act, the following apply:

- It is considered reasonable to show available properties to various prospects without being viewed as breaching duty to a given client. However, a licensee must provide written disclosure to all clients for whom the licensee is preparing or making contemporaneous offers or contract to purchase or lease the same property and must refer any client that requests a referral to another designated agent.

- It is not considered a conflict for a buyer's agent to show homes wherein the commission is based on the ultimate sales price (in other words, where a higher price results in a higher commission).

- Unless a licensee "knew or should have known the information was false," a licensee is not considered responsible or liable for false information passed on to the client from a customer via the licensee, or vice versa.

- The licensee remains responsible under common law "as to negligent or fraudulent misrepresentation of material information."

Section 15-25 deals with a licensee's treatment of customers. A licensee must "treat all customers honestly and shall not negligently or knowingly give them false information."

Section 15-40 clearly states that compensation does not determine agency.

Informed written consent and confirmation is required of both buyer and seller (or landlord and tenant) for dual agency under Section 15-45. An individual licensee may act as a dual agent, or a sponsoring broker may permit one or more of its sponsored licensees to act as dual agents in the same transaction. Also, a licensee may not serve as dual agent in any transaction in which she has an ownership interest, whether direct or indirect.

Designated agency is highlighted in Section 15-50. This allows the sponsoring broker to appoint or designate one agent for the buyer and one agent for the seller, even within the same firm, without legally being construed a dual agent. The broker is obligated to protect any confidential information. Because of this, a designated agent may disclose to his or her sponsoring broker or persons specified by the sponsoring broker confidential information of a client for the purpose of seeking advice or assistance for the benefit of the client in regard to a possible transaction.

Article 15 also clearly notes the following:

- Offers of subagency through a multiple listing service (MLS) are not permitted in Illinois.
- A consumer cannot be held "vicariously liable" for the acts or omissions of a licensee in providing licensed activities for or on behalf of the consumer.
- IDFPR may further amplify anything in Article 15 by way of promulgating additional rules at any time.
- There is a time limit on legal actions. Legal actions under Article 15 may be "forever barred unless commenced within two years after the person bringing the action knew or should reasonably have known of such act or omission." In no case may actions be brought after more than five years.

Unit 14

Disclosure

What Must Be Disclosed

- Material facts of a property
- Known latent physical defects
- Agency relationships
- Designated agency
- Dual agency
- No-Agency
- Compensation sources
- Contemporaneous Offers

Disclosure issues go hand in hand with agency, and consequently, they are heavily addressed in Article 15. Real estate disclosure means an acknowledgment, stated clearly and usually in writing, of certain key facts that the law holds might, if left unknown or if unclear, unfairly influence the course of events. Disclosures have to do with who has clear and full representation in a transaction and who does not. They may have to do with one's interest as a licensee in a property that one is selling. Matters of structure, surroundings, client representation, dual agency, previous agency, or agent interest in a property all may demand disclosure. Failure to disclose is an increasingly serious issue in a consumer-based society and under consumer-driven laws.

Material Facts

A licensee must disclose to the client "material facts concerning the transaction of which the licensee has actual knowledge, unless that information is confidential information." Material facts must also be disclosed to customers. A listing agent must disclose to prospective buyer customers "all latent material adverse facts pertaining to the physical condition of the property that are actually known by the licensee and that could not be discovered by a reasonably diligent inspection of the property by the customer." A licensee shall not be liable to a customer for providing false information to the customer if the false information was provided to the licensee by the licensee's client and the licensee did not have actual knowledge that the information was false. (225 ILCS 454/15-25a).

According to Section 15-20, no cause of action shall arise against a licensee for the failure to disclose

- that an occupant of the property was afflicted with Human Immunodeficiency Virus (HIV) or any other medical condition;
- that the property was the site of an act or occurrence that had no effect on the physical condition of the property or its environment or the structures located thereon;
- fact situations on property that is not the subject of the transaction; or
- physical conditions located on property that is not the subject of the transaction that do not have a substantial adverse effect on the value of the real estate that is the subject of the transaction.

It is illegal under federal law to disclose that a property's occupant has or had HIV or AIDS.

Agency Relationship (225 ILCS 454/15-35)

Before a listing agreement, buyer agency agreement, or any other brokerage agreement may be created, a consumer must be informed in writing no later than when beginning to work as a designated agent on behalf of the consumer

- that a designated agency exists and
- the name or names of designated agent(s).

The licensee must discuss with the consumer the sponsoring broker's compensation policy insofar as cooperating with brokers who represent other parties in a transaction. The licensee must also disclose in writing that the licensee is not acting as the agent of the customer at a time intended to prevent disclosure of confidential information.

Compensation (225 ILCS 454/10-5)

The Act holds that clients must be made aware of compensation, source of compensation, and the sponsoring broker's policy on sharing commission with cooperating brokers.

Handling Client Funds (225 ILCS 454/20-20)

A critical area of the real estate business involves handling the funds of others. The purchase contract dictates when and with whom earnest money is to be deposited. Licensees should immediately provide any earnest money checks to their sponsoring broker for proper deposit in a special account. The Act states that the sponsoring broker's escrow account is to be a non-interest-bearing account, "unless the character of the deposit is such that payment of interest thereon is otherwise required by law or unless the principals to the transaction specifically require, in writing, that the deposit be placed in an interest-bearing account."

The sponsoring broker must maintain and deposit in a special account, separate and apart from personal and other business accounts, all escrow moneys belonging to others entrusted to a licensee while acting as a real estate broker, escrow agent, or temporary custodian of the funds of others.

Receipts must be made, and a duplicate kept by the sponsoring broker for any escrow monies received. Earnest money and security deposits must be deposited within one business day of contract or lease acceptance unless the contract dictates a different timeframe. The escrow must be in a federally insured depository. The Act does not limit the number of escrow accounts one sponsoring broker may maintain. Commingling of personal and business funds is prohibited.

If there should be disputes between parties regarding escrow money, the sponsoring broker "shall continue to hold the deposit" (68 Ill. Adm. Code 1450.750(h)(1)) / (225 ILCS 454/20(a)(17)(B)(iii)). The sponsoring broker must wait for all parties to signal agreement on the escrow disposition by signing a definite agreement; otherwise, the sponsoring broker should not disburse funds until such an agreement or a court decision is reached or deemed abandoned and transferred to the Illinois Treasurer's Office to be handled as unclaimed pursuant to the Uniform Disposition of Unclaimed Property Act. Sponsoring brokers who accept earnest money must maintain, in their office or place of business, a bookkeeping system in accordance with sound accounting principles.

The sponsoring broker must always be able to account for client or escrow funds and any pertinent documents. If IDFPR asks to view or audit escrow records, such records must be supplied within 24 hours of the request to the IDFPR personnel. Escrow records must be maintained for five years. The escrow records for the immediate prior two years must be maintained in the office location, and the balance of the records can be maintained at another location. The sponsoring broker must report loss or destruction of escrow records to the Department within 48 hours by mail or email.

Advertising Regulations (225 ILCS 454/10-30)

Teams

A team is any two or more licensees who work together to provide real estate brokerage services, who represent themselves to the public as being part of a team or group, who are identified by a team name that is different than their sponsoring broker's name, and who together are supervised by the same designated managing broker and sponsored by the same sponsoring broker. "Team" does not mean a separately organized, incorporated, or legal entity

Licensees must

■ never advertise in only their name,

■ always include the firm's name,

■ never advertise another sponsoring broker's listings without permission, and

■ always keep advertisements up to date and clear.

(225 ILCS 454/1-10). Team names may not include misleading terms, such as "company," "realty," "real estate," "agency," "associates," "brokers," "properties," or "property" (225 ILCS 454/10-30 (a)). However, if these terms are followed by the word "team" they could be used (1450.715).

All ads prepared by licensees, whether print, online, or via some other electronic media, must contain all the information necessary to communicate to the public in an accurate, direct, and readily comprehensible manner. At the very least, all ads should include

■ the licensee's name,

■ the sponsoring broker's business name in a size equal to or larger than the individual licensee's or team's name and location (city and state), and

■ the city or area of the advertised property.

Blind ads are those not indicating the brokerage firm's name; not indicating that the advertiser is a licensee; and/or offering only a box number, street address, or telephone number for responses. Blind ads are prohibited by law and may not be used to sell or lease any real estate, in the hiring of other licensees, or in any other real estate activities.

A licensee must

■ always disclose "agent-owned," and

■ place "agent-owned" on the sign if FSBO.

Licensees performing the duties of a designated managing broker must advertise as a "designated managing broker." Sponsoring brokers must include their business name and franchise affiliation in all advertisements.

Licensees must disclose to consumers their intent to share or sell consumer information that has been collected via the internet or any other means of electronic communication. This disclosure must be conspicuous and timely.

According to 68 Ill. Adm. Code 1450.751(a), the following are prohibited:

■ Advertising a property that is subject to an exclusive listing agreement with a sponsoring broker other than the licensee's own without the permission of and identifying that listing broker

■ Failing to remove advertising of a listed property within a reasonable time, given the nature of the advertising, the licensee's control over the removal or stopping of the advertising, the ease of removing or stopping the advertising, knowledge that the advertising was continuing and any other pertinent criteria after the earlier of the closing of a sale on the listed property or the expiration or termination of the listing agreement

Note that all electronic advertising has added language that requires posting the city and state of a physical office or a direct link to a virtual office website or digital platform. A URL or domain name is not considered advertising, but it must not be used for improper purposes to mislead consumers (1450.720).

Online Advertising

Online advertising includes business websites, social media, and email. In addition to general advertising rules, online ads must adhere to the following:

■ An online ad must include proper identification—licensee name, company name, company location, and geographic location of property.

■ In the case of electronic advertisements, the ad must provide a direct link to a display with all the required disclosures.

■ The licensee's name, company name, and company location are required on all e-correspondence, bulletin boards, and e-commerce discussion groups.

■ Online ads may not employ deceptive or misleading URLs or domain names, frame the website of another sponsoring broker's or multiple listing service without permission or with the intent or effect of deceiving the consumer, or engage in phishing or the deceptive use of meta tags, keywords or other devices and methods to direct, drive, or divert internet traffic, or otherwise mislead consumers.

- Links to listing information from other websites are permitted without approval unless the website's owner requires approval for links to be added. Any such link must not mislead or deceive the public as to the ownership of any listing information.

- As with other advertising, websites are to be updated periodically and kept current.

Selling Your Own Property

Selling or leasing your own property or a property in which you have an interest means you, as a licensee, must use the term "broker-owned" or "agent-owned" in all advertising and on listing sheets. If the real estate firm's sign is used in the yard and the firm's services are being used, then having the "agent-owned" or "broker-owned" notation on the sign itself is deemed not necessary. However, all written materials (listing sheets, print ads, and online ads) still must carry the "broker-owned" or "agent-owned" notation. The Real Estate License Act of 2000 provides that no matter how one lists an agent-owned property—by owner or through a real estate firm—the agent must take care not to confuse the public.

It is possible and permitted by IDFPR to list your own personal real estate with a firm other than the one at which you work if you so desire and if your sponsoring broker approves.

If a licensee advertises to personally purchase or lease real estate, disclosure of licensee status is required before initiating a transaction.

Required Identification of Sponsoring Broker

Licensees may not list their name or otherwise advertise in their name to the general public through any medium of advertising as being in the real estate business without also listing their sponsoring broker's business name. This rule is consistent throughout any and all advertising media.

Compensation and Business Practice (225 ILCS 454/10)

According to Section 10-5, a licensee may not receive compensation from anyone other than the sponsoring broker. In turn, brokers may compensate only licensees whom they personally sponsor. The one exception is a former licensee now working for another sponsoring broker but who is due a commission from work completed while still at the first firm.

Sponsoring brokers may directly compensate other sponsoring brokers (as in a cooperative commission arrangement for the listing broker to pay commission to the firm with the buyer). Disclosure of compensation is a significant issue—the Act holds that clients must be made aware of compensation, source of compensation, and the sponsoring broker's policy on sharing commission with cooperating sponsoring brokers (225 ILCS 454/10-10).

Compensation issued to an agent from both buyer and seller in one transaction must be disclosed. Any third-party compensation must also be disclosed. If a licensee refers a client to a service in which the licensee has greater than 1% ownership interest (i.e., title, legal, or mortgage), the interest must be disclosed.

It is illegal to compensate unlicensed persons or anyone being held in violation of the Act (225 ILCS 454/10-15). To sue for commission in Illinois, one must be a licensed real estate sponsoring broker.

Unit 14

Funds from sellers or buyers always pass through the sponsoring broker. Only a sponsoring broker may issue compensation to the brokers, managing brokers, or residential leasing agents working under the sponsoring broker. This means that the check at closing will be in the sponsoring broker's name only.

No licensee may pay a referral fee to an unlicensed person who is not a principal to the transaction. A licensee may not request a referral fee unless reasonable cause for payment of the fee exists (a contractual referral fee arrangement).

Section 10-15 also states that a licensee "may offer cash, gifts, prizes, awards, coupons, merchandise, rebates or chances to win a game of chance, if not prohibited by any other law" to consumers as a legitimate approach to garnering business. Additionally, it is perfectly legal to share commission compensation with a principal to a given transaction.

A licensee may not pay compensation to an unlicensed person who is not or will not become a party to a real estate transaction in exchange for a referral of real estate services.

Any payment of referral fees or compensation must also be in strict accordance with the Real Estate Settlement Procedures Act (RESPA).

It is legal for a sponsoring broker to pay an entity set up by the licensee, rather than the licensee directly, if desired. The entity is not be required to be licensed and must either be owned solely by the licensee or by the licensee together with the licensee's spouse, but only if the spouse and the licensee are both licensed and sponsored by the same sponsoring broker or the spouse is not also licensed.

Guaranteed Sales Plans (225 ILCS 454/10-50)

A "guaranteed sales plan" means a real estate purchase or sales plan whereby a licensee enters into one or more conditional or unconditional written contracts with a seller, one of which is a brokerage agreement, and wherein the person agrees to purchase the seller's property within a specified period of time, at a specific price, in the event the property is not sold in accordance with the terms of a brokerage agreement to be entered into between the sponsoring broker and the seller.

Any person who offers a guaranteed sales plan in compliance with the Act must

- be licensed;

- provide the details, including the purchase price, and conditions of the plan in writing to the seller before entering the brokerage agreement;

- offer evidence of sufficient financial resources to satisfy the agreement's purchase commitment;

- market the listing in the same manner in which the sponsoring broker would market any other property, unless the agreement with the seller provides otherwise; and

- not purchase the seller's property until the brokerage agreement has ended or is otherwise terminated.

A licensee who fails to perform on a guaranteed sales plan in strict accordance with its terms is subject to all the penalties for violating the Act, plus a civil penalty of up to $25,000, payable to the injured party.

DISCIPLINARY PROVISIONS AND LOSS OF LICENSE

The Real Estate License Act of 2000 lists specific violations for which licensees may be subject to discipline. IDFPR is authorized to impose the following disciplinary penalties:

- Refuse to issue or renew any license
- Suspend or revoke any license
- Censure or reprimand a licensee
- Place a licensee on probation
- Impose a civil penalty of not more than $25,000 per offense

Causes for Discipline

According to Section 20-20, a licensee is subject to IDFPR disciplinary action if the licensee is found guilty of any of the following activities:

- Making a false or fraudulent representation in attempting to obtain or renew a license
- Being convicted of a felony or of a crime involving dishonesty, fraud, larceny, embezzlement, or obtaining money, property, or credit by false pretenses or by means of a confidence game
- Being unable to practice the profession with reasonable judgment, skill, or safety as a result of a physical illness
- Practicing as a licensee in a retail sales establishment from an office, desk, or space that is not separated from the main retail business and located within a separate and distinct area
- Being subjected to disciplinary action by another state, the District of Columbia, a territory, a foreign nation, a government agency, or any other entity authorized to impose discipline if at least one of the grounds for that discipline is the same as or equivalent to a cause for discipline in Illinois
- Engaging in real estate brokerage without a license or with a license that is inactive, revoked, or suspended or after the licensee's temporary permit has expired
- Attempting to subvert or cheat on the licensing exam or assists someone else in doing so
- Using advertising that is inaccurate, misleading, or contrary to provisions of the Act
- Making any substantial misrepresentation or untruthful advertising
- Making any false promises to influence, persuade, or induce
- Pursuing a continued and flagrant course of misrepresentation or making false promises through licensee, employees, agents, advertising, or otherwise
- Using any misleading or untruthful advertising
- Using any trade name or insignia of membership in any real estate organization of which the licensee is not a member
- Acting for more than one party in a transaction without providing written agency disclosure
- Representing or attempting to represent, or performing licensed activities for, a broker other than the sponsoring broker
- Failing to account for or remit any monies or documents belonging to others that come into the licensee's possession
- Failing to properly maintain and deposit escrow monies in a separate account

- Failing to make all escrow records maintained in connection with the practice of real estate available during normal business hours and within 24 hours of submitted request

- Failing to furnish, on request, copies of all documents relating to a real estate transaction to all parties executing them

- Failure of the sponsoring broker or licensee to timely provide sponsorship or termination of sponsorship information to the Department

- Engaging in dishonorable, unethical, or unprofessional conduct of a character likely to deceive, defraud, or harm the public, including but not limited to conduct set forth in rules adopted by the Department

- Commingling the money or property of others with one's own

- Employing any person on a purely temporary or single-deal basis as a means of evading the law regarding illegal payment of fees to nonlicensees

- Permitting the use of the licensee's license as a broker to enable a residential leasing agent or unlicensed person to operate a real estate business without actual participation therein and control thereof by the broker

- Engaging in any dishonest dealing, whether specifically mentioned by the act or not

- Displaying a For Rent or For Sale sign on any property, or advertising in any fashion, without the written consent of the owner

- Failing to provide information requested within 30 days of the request as related to audits or complaints made against the licensee based on the Act

- Using blind advertising

- Offering an improperly constructed guaranteed sales plan, one that does not meet the Act's requirements for such plans (225 ILCS 454/10-50)

- Intending to promote racial or religious segregation by use of actions or words or behaving or speaking in such a way as to discourage integration

- Violating the Illinois Human Rights Act

- Inducing any individual to break out of an existing contract to enter into a new one, whether a sales contract or a listing contract

- Negotiating directly with the client of another agent

- Acting as an attorney in the same transaction in which one acts as a real estate licensee

- If merchandise or services are advertised for free, any conditions or obligations necessary for receiving the merchandise or services must appear in the same ad or offer

- Violating a disciplinary order

- Paying or failing to disclose compensation that violates the Act

- Disregarding or violating any provision of this act or the published rules or any regulations promulgated to enforce the Act

- Failing to provide the minimum services required under an exclusive brokerage agreement

- Violating the terms of a disciplinary order issued by IDFPR

- Forcing any party to a transaction to compensate the licensee as a requirement for releasing earnest money

- Habitual use or addiction to alcohol, narcotics, stimulants, or any other chemical agent that results in the licensee's inability to practice with skill and safety

- Failing to notify the Department of any criminal conviction that occurs during the licensee's term of licensure within 30 days after the conviction

- A designated managing broker's failure to provide an appropriate written company policy or failure to perform any of the duties set forth in Section 10-55

Nonpayment of Income Tax, Student Loans, and Child Support (225 ILCS 454/20-20)

Anyone who fails to file a tax return or to pay any tax, penalty, interest, or final assessment required by the Illinois Department of Revenue may have her license withheld or suspended until any such tax requirements are met.

If student loans were provided or guaranteed by the Illinois Student Assistance Commission or any governmental agency of the state, and not paid back, IDFPR will not grant a real estate license to that individual. For an existing licensee, a hearing is made available, after which, if no satisfactory repayment plan has been made, the license may be suspended or revoked.

IDFPR will refuse to issue or renew (or may revoke or suspend) the licenses of individuals who are more than 30 days delinquent in child support payments.

Discrimination (225 ILCS 454/20-50)

If there has been a civil or criminal trial in which a licensee has been found to have engaged in illegal discrimination in the course of a licensed activity, IDFPR must suspend or revoke the licensee's license unless the adjudication is in appeal.

Unlawful Actions by Associates if No Sponsoring Broker Knowledge

A sponsoring broker will not have her license revoked because of an unlawful act or violation by a managing broker or broker employed by or associated with the sponsoring broker, or by any unlicensed employee, unless the sponsoring broker had knowledge of the unlawful act or violation.

Procedure for Discipline

Any person providing or offering to provide real estate services, or who is licensed or claims to be licensed under the Act, may be investigated by IDFPR. After interviewing all parties involved in a complaint, an investigator recommends either closing the complaint or sending the complaint for prosecution. When a complaint is forwarded for prosecution, depending upon the nature of the complaint, an informal hearing process may be used to educate and discipline a licensee and the licensee thereby avoids a formal hearing procedure.

If the matter proceeds to a formal hearing, then at least 30 days before the hearing, and before taking any disciplinary action (including but not limited to reprimand, probation, or revocation or suspension of license), IDFPR will do the following:

- In writing, inform the person under investigation of the charges being brought against her and the location and time of the hearing

- Instruct the accused individual to respond to the charges, under oath and in writing, within 20 days of being informed of the charges

- Notify the individual that unless she responds as instructed, default will be taken against her and disciplinary action, such as imposition of a fine or license suspension, revocation, or probation, may be instituted

- Department may notify the individual's designated managing and sponsoring broker of the pending investigation

At the hearing, the charges will be presented to the Board, and the accused individual (applicant, licensee, or unlicensed person) and her counsel will be allowed to offer a defense via statements, arguments, testimony, and evidence.

IDFPR is required to keep a record of all formal hearing proceedings. According to the same guidelines provided for civil cases in state court, IDFPR is empowered to subpoena materials, such as books, documents, and records, and to bring people before it to testify.

IDFPR will present the accused individual with a copy of the Board's report following the conclusion of the hearing. The individual may request a rehearing, via a motion in writing, which indicates the reasons justifying a new hearing. This request must be made within 20 days after the licensee has been served with IDFPR's report. If the motion for rehearing is denied, the secretary is empowered to enter an order as recommended by the Board.

If the secretary determines that emergency action is required to protect the public interest, welfare, or safety, she may move to suspend the accused individual's license without a hearing first. However, a hearing must be scheduled for within 30 days of the suspension. The licensee may seek a continuance to postpone the hearing, but in such a case, the suspension will remain in effect.

In any action intended to discipline a license holder or to refuse to issue, restore, or renew a license, the secretary may appoint an Illinois-licensed attorney to serve in her place as the hearing officer, with complete authority to direct the proceedings. The officer must establish findings pertaining to the allegations, the individual's conduct, and the law, and present these conclusions to the Board, along with her recommendations. Board members may attend hearings, if they wish, and are required to review the hearing officer's report and then present the board findings to the secretary and all parties to the hearing. The secretary is permitted to enter an order that is inconsistent with the board or hearing officer's recommendations if she disagrees with either party.

Once the order to suspend or revoke a license has been put through, the licensee is required to immediately hand over her license. The department's notice must also be delivered to the licensee's managing broker and sponsoring broker. If the licensee fails to surrender her license, IDFPR is empowered to seize it. The secretary may order that another hearing be held (before the same examiners or a different set) in the event that she believes that the disciplinary action taken was unjust.

Administrative Review (225 ILCS 454/20-75)

All final administrative decisions are subject to judicial review under the provisions of the Administrative Review Law and its rules. The accused may request a judicial review by petitioning the circuit court of the county of her residence. If the party is not a resident of Illinois, the venue will be in Cook County.

Good Moral Character (225 ILCS 454/5-25)

The Board may revoke licenses or refuse to grant licenses to applicants who make false statements on their licensure applications. In evaluating an applicant's moral character and deciding whether to grant a license, the Board may take into account facts and events from the applicant's past, including prior conduct; revocation of license; conviction for a felony that involved moral turpitude; or a conviction or plea of guilty or nolo contendere in cases involving forgery, embezzlement, obtaining money under false pretenses, larceny, extortion, or conspiracy to defraud.

In its consideration of the prior revocation, conduct, or conviction, the Board will take into account the nature of the conduct, any aggravating or extenuating circumstances, the time elapsed since the revocation, conduct, or conviction, the rehabilitation or restitution performed by the applicant, mitigating factors, and any other factors that the Board deems relevant, including, but not limited to

- the lack of direct relation of the offense for which the applicant was previously convicted to the duties, functions, and responsibilities of the position for which a license is sought;

- unless otherwise specified, whether five years since a felony conviction or three years since release from confinement for the conviction, whichever is later, have passed without a subsequent conviction;

- if the applicant was previously licensed or employed in this State or other states or jurisdictions, the lack of prior misconduct arising from or related to the licensed position or position of employment;

- the age of the person at the time of the criminal offense;

- if, due to the applicant's criminal conviction history, the applicant would be explicitly prohibited by federal rules or regulations from working in the position for which a license is sought;

- successful completion of sentence and, for applicants serving a term of parole or probation, a progress report provided by the applicant's probation or parole officer that documents the applicant's compliance with conditions of supervision;

- evidence of the applicant's present fitness and professional character;

- evidence of rehabilitation or rehabilitative effort during or after incarceration, or during or after a term of supervision, including, but not limited to, a certificate of good conduct under Section 5-5.5-25 of the Unified Code of Corrections or a certificate of relief from disabilities under Section 5-5.5-10 of the Unified Code of Corrections; and

- any other mitigating factors that contribute to the person's potential and current ability to perform the job duties.

The Department may not require applicants to report the following information and may not consider the following criminal history records in connection with an application for licensure or registration:

- Juvenile adjudications of delinquent minors as defined in Section 5-105 of the Juvenile Court Act of 1987 subject to the restrictions set forth in Section 5-130 of that Act

- Law enforcement records, court records, and conviction records of an individual who was 17 years old at the time of the offense and before January 1, 2014, unless the nature of the offense required the individual to be tried as an adult

- Records of arrests not followed by a charge or conviction

Unit 14

- Records of arrests where the charges were dismissed unless related to the practice of the profession; however, applicants may not be asked to report any arrests, and an arrest not followed by a conviction may not be the basis of a denial and may be used only to assess an applicant's rehabilitation.
- Convictions overturned by a higher court
- Convictions or arrests that have been sealed or expunged

If an applicant makes a false statement of material fact on the application, the false statement may in itself be sufficient grounds to revoke or refuse to issue a license.

A licensee must report to the Department, in a manner adopted by rule, any plea of guilty, or nolo contendere to forgery, embezzlement, obtaining money under false pretenses, larceny, extortion, conspiracy to defraud, or any similar offense or offenses or any conviction of a felony involving moral turpitude that occurs during the licensee's term of licensure.

Violations (225 ILCS 454/20-22)

Any person who works or acts as a managing broker, a broker, or a residential leasing agent without being issued a valid existing license is guilty of a Class A misdemeanor and, on conviction of a second or subsequent offense, is guilty of a Class 4 felony.

Citations (225 ILCS 454/20-20.1)

The Department may adopt rules to permit the issuance of citations to any licensee for failure to comply with the continuing education requirements set forth in the Act or as adopted by rule. The citation will be issued to the licensee, and a copy will be sent to the licensee's designated managing broker and sponsoring broker. The citation must contain the licensee's name and address, the licensee's license number, the number of required hours of continuing education that have not been successfully completed by the licensee within the renewal period, and the penalty imposed, which may not exceed $2,000. The issuance of any such citation will not excuse the licensee from completing all continuing education required for that renewal period.

Service of a citation must be made in person, electronically, or by mail to the licensee at the licensee's address of record or email address of record, and it must clearly state that if the cited licensee wishes to dispute the citation, the licensee may make a written request, within 30 days after the citation is served, for a hearing before the Department. If the cited licensee does not request a hearing within 30 days after the citation is served, then the citation will become a final, nondisciplinary order, and any fine imposed is due and payable within 60 days after that final order. If the cited licensee requests a hearing within 30 days after the citation is served, the Department will afford the cited licensee a hearing conducted in the same manner as a hearing provided for in the Act for any violation of the Act and will determine whether the cited licensee committed the violation as charged and whether the fine as levied is warranted. If the violation is found, any fine will constitute nonpublic discipline and be due and payable within 30 days after the order of the Secretary, which will constitute a final order of the Department. No change in license status may be made by the Department until such time as a final order of the Department has been issued.

Payment of a fine that has been assessed pursuant to this Section does not constitute disciplinary action reportable on the Department's website or elsewhere unless a licensee has previously received two or more citations and paid two or more fines.

Nothing in Section 20-20.1 prohibits or limits the Department from taking further action pursuant to the Act and rules for additional, repeated, or continuing violations.

Injunctions (225 ILCS 454/20-21)

In addition to criminal prosecutions, IDFPR has the duty and authority to originate an injunction to prevent or stop a violation or to prevent an unlicensed person from acting as a broker, managing broker, or residential leasing agent.

A violation of the Real Estate License Act of 2000 is specifically declared to be harmful to the public welfare and a public nuisance. The attorney general of Illinois, a county state's attorney, IDFPR, and even private citizens may seek an injunction to stop or prevent a violation.

Disciplinary Statute of Limitations (225 ILCS 454/20-115)

IDFPR may only take action against persons for violation of the terms of the Act within five years after the occurrence of the alleged violation.

Index of Decisions (225 ILCS 454/20-5)

IDFPR is required to maintain an index of all its licensee-related formal decisions. This includes all refusals to issue, all renewals or refusals to renew, all revocations or suspensions of licenses, and all probationary and other disciplinary actions. The index is available online at IDFPR's website.

THE REAL ESTATE RECOVERY FUND

The **Real Estate Recovery Fund** provides a means of compensation for actual monetary losses (as opposed to losses in market value) suffered by any person as a result of

- a violation of the Real Estate License Act of 2000, including its rules and regulations; or
- act of embezzlement of money or property, obtaining money or property by false pretenses, artifice, trickery, forgery, fraud, misrepresentation, deceit, or discrimination by a licensee or a licensee's unlicensed employee.

People who have been harmed through certain actions, statements, or other behavior of a licensee or a licensee's employee may recover damages from the Real Estate Recovery Fund, which is maintained by IDFPR. This applies in instances where these actions and statements violated the Act or the accompanying rules, amounted to embezzling money or property, or resulted in the acquisition of money from someone through tricks, forgery, lies, misrepresentations, fraud, discrimination, or the like, causing cash losses (rather than the loss of market value) to the harmed party.

The fund may pay out not more than an amount adopted by rule to the wronged person, as ordered by the relevant county's circuit court. This amount can include payment for legal costs and attorneys' fees. Interest is not paid on the recovery amount. Licensees can receive payments from the fund only in cases of intentional misconduct that resulted in losses. The maximum fund liability shall be adopted by rule. Recovery sums will only be paid out in cases where valid judgments have been made. Licensees who wish to have their licenses reinstated must reimburse the fund all fees plus interest. The interest rate is established by state statute.

Unit 14

Collection from the Real Estate Recovery Fund (225 ILCS 454/20-90)

When a lawsuit might result in a claim against the Real Estate Recovery Fund, IDFPR must be notified in writing by the aggrieved person at the time the action is commenced—specifically, within seven days of filing. Failure to notify IDFPR of the potential liability precludes any recovery from the fund. If the plaintiff is unable to serve the defendant with a summons, the secretary may be served instead, and this service will be valid and binding on the defendant. Additionally, legal action must have commenced no later than two years after the aggrieved person knew of the acts or omissions that gave rise to possible right of recovery from the fund.

If a claimant recovers a valid judgment in any court against any licensee or unlicensed employee for damages resulting from an act or omission qualifying for coverage under the fund, IDFPR must receive written notice of the judgment within 30 days. IDFPR is also entitled to 20 days' written notice of any supplementary proceedings, in order to permit IDFPR to participate in all efforts to collect on the judgment.

For a claimant to obtain recovery from the fund, aggrieved individuals must show that they are not a spouse of the debtor or debtors or the personal representative of such spouse, have complied with all the requirements of the Act, and have obtained a judgment stating the amount thereof and the amount owing thereon, not including interest thereon, at the date of the application. The names of all licensees and other parties that are in any way responsible for the loss must have been named in the suit. If they were not, it may preclude recovery from the fund. Finally, the claimant must show that the amount of attorney's fees being sought is reasonable.

When a judgment amount is paid from the Real Estate Recovery Fund, IDFPR takes over the rights of the aggrieved party on this issue. This party is required to assign all right, title, and interest in judgment to IDFPR. By this subrogation, any funds recovered on the judgment will be deposited back in the Real Estate Recovery Fund.

Fund Losses Held Against the Licensee (225 ILCS 454/20-90)

When payment is made from the Real Estate Recovery Fund to settle a claim or satisfy a judgment against a licensed broker, managing broker, or unlicensed employee, the license of the offending broker or managing broker is automatically terminated. Before petitioning for license restoration, the broker, or managing broker, must first fully repay to the recovery fund all awards made because of the broker's actions, plus interest at the statutory annual rate. A discharge in bankruptcy does not relieve a person from the liabilities and penalties provided for in the Real Estate License Act of 2000.

Statute of Limitations (225 ILCS 454/20-90 and 225 ILCS 454/20-115)

A suit that may ultimately result in collection from the Real Estate Recovery Fund must be commenced within two years after the date the alleged violation occurred. IDFPR must initiate any action it plans to take against an individual licensee within five years of the violation.

Financing the Real Estate Recovery Fund (225 ILCS 454/25-35)

If at any time during the year, the Real Estate Recovery Fund slips below $750,000, the Real Estate License Administration Fund is used to upgrade the level to a minimum balance of $800,000.

All Real Estate Recovery Fund monies received from applications, renewals, and fines and penalties are deposited into the Real Estate Recovery Fund, and its sums may be invested and reinvested. Any interest or dividends returned from the investment efforts are deposited into the Real Estate Research and Education Fund.

SUMMARY

The Illinois Department of Financial and Professional Regulation (IDFPR) is the key governing authority for real estate activity in Illinois. IDFPR, through the Division of Real Estate, is responsible for administering and enforcing the Real Estate License Act of 2000 and its rules.

It is vital that all licensees and prospective licensees have a clear understanding of all facets of the Act and rules to ensure that their activities are ethical, legal, and responsible. No summary of reasonable length could do justice to the critical details of the Act. The Act also lists a long series of specific definitions designed to give a clear understanding of real estate as it is practiced in Illinois and as legally defined by the Act (225 ILCS 454/1).

UNIT 14 QUIZ

1. In Illinois, which of these needs to hold a real estate license?
    A. A licensed attorney acting under a power of attorney to convey real estate
    B. A person who employs fewer than three apartment residential leasing agents
    C. A resident apartment manager working for an owner, if the manager's primary residence is the apartment building being managed
    D. A partnership selling a building owned by the partners

2. An unlicensed man has been twice found to be engaging in activities for which a real estate license is required. He is subject to a
    A. fine not to exceed $1,000.
    B. fine not to exceed $5,000 and one-year imprisonment.
    C. civil penalty not to exceed $25,000 per violation.
    D. civil penalty not to exceed $25,000 per violation and a mandatory prison term not to exceed five years.

3. The initial broker's license fee for a partnership, LLC, or corporation is
    A. $55.
    B. $100, so long as no more than 50% of the shares of the company are held by brokers.
    C. $250.
    D. $125.

4. After the first renewal period, to meet the continuing education requirement in Illinois, brokers must obtain how many hours of continuing education during the current term of the license?
    A. 4
    B. 6
    C. 12
    D. 18

5. Should the Department issue a citation against a licensee for failure to comply with the continuing education requirements, the maximum fine allowable is
    A. $2,000.
    B. $1,000.
    C. $500.
    D. $25 per delinquent credit hour.

6. If an aggrieved person is awarded a judgment against a real estate licensee for violations of the Real Estate License Act of 2000, under the license law, the aggrieved party has the right to
    A. immediately apply for payment from the recovery fund for the full judgment amount, plus court costs and attorney's fees.
    B. a maximum award amount of $100,000 from the recovery fund, including court costs and attorney's fees.
    C. an amount adopted by rule, together with costs of suit and attorney's fees.
    D. seek satisfaction from the licensee in a private civil action after being compensated from the recovery fund.

7. Under what conditions may a sponsoring broker who lives in a state that has a reciprocal licensing agreement with Illinois be issued an Illinois license?
    A. The sponsoring broker's home state has a reciprocal licensing agreement with Illinois.
    B. The sponsoring broker maintains an office in Illinois.
    C. The sponsoring broker passes the Illinois managing broker's license exam.
    D. The sponsoring broker's sponsored licensees have reciprocal licenses in Illinois.

8. Which of the following is an acceptable name for a real estate team?
    A. Tom Carson Specialty Properties
    B. The Tom Carson Realty Team
    C. Tom Carson Associates
    D. The Tom Carson Team

9. A sponsoring broker licensed in Illinois by reciprocity with another state must
   A. appoint the secretary, in writing, to act as the agent of notice for all judicial and legal notices.
   B. employ no sponsored licensees.
   C. have been licensed for at least 10 years.
   D. not plan on engaging in any real estate activities.

10. If a sponsored broker is found guilty of violating the Real Estate License Act of 2000, her sponsoring broker also may be disciplined if the
    A. sponsored broker was a convicted criminal.
    B. sponsoring broker failed to conduct the four-step, pre-employment investigation of the sponsored broker's background and character required by the license law.
    C. sponsoring broker had prior knowledge of the violation.
    D. sponsoring broker failed to keep all local business licenses current.

11. Which of these activities requires a real estate license?
    A. An individual or entity that engages in the sale of assignable contracts on 2 or more transactions in any 12-month period
    B. A resident manager who collects rent on behalf of a building owner
    C. A multiple listing service providing listing information to members
    D. An executor selling a decedent's building

12. An Illinois real estate broker's license can be revoked for
    A. agreeing with a seller to accept a listing for more than the normal commission rate.
    B. disclosing her agency relationship.
    C. showing buyers with the same specifications the same properties.
    D. depositing escrow money in her personal checking account.

13. A broker has violated the license law, resulting in monetary damages to a consumer. What is the latest date on which the injured party may file a lawsuit that may result in a collection from the Real Estate Recovery Fund?
    A. Two years after the alleged violation occurred
    B. One year after the alleged violation occurred
    C. Three years after the alleged violation occurred
    D. Three years after the date on which a professional relationship of trust and accountability commenced

14. A sponsoring broker offers the seller the following inducement to sign his listing agreement: "I'll buy your property if it doesn't sell in 90 days." Under these facts, the sponsoring broker may *NOT*
    A. market the property as if no special agreement existed.
    B. buy the property at the agreed figure at any time during the 90 days without the agreement of the seller.
    C. show the seller evidence of the sponsoring broker's financial ability to buy the property.
    D. show the seller written details of the plan before any contract of guaranty is executed.

15. Which action is legal under Illinois law?
    A. Encouraging a seller to reject an offer because the prospective buyer is a Methodist
    B. Advertising that individuals who attend a promotional presentation will receive a prize without mentioning that they will also have to take a day trip to a new subdivision site
    C. Standing in the hallway outside the testing room and offering employment to new licensees as soon as they receive their passing score at the testing center
    D. Placing a For Sale sign in front of a house after asking the seller's permission and receiving written permission to do so

16. All advertising by an affiliated licensee must include the
    A. name of the licensee's sponsoring broker.
    B. licensee's license number.
    C. expiration date of the license.
    D. licensee's home address.

17. In Illinois, all real estate brokers' licenses expire on
    A. January 31 of every odd-numbered year.
    B. January 31 of every even-numbered year.
    C. April 30 of every even-numbered year.
    D. March 31 of every even-numbered year.

18. In Illinois, an individual who wishes to engage only in activities related to the leasing of residential real property
    A. must obtain a broker's license and associate with a sponsoring broker who specializes in residential leases.
    B. may obtain a certified residential leasing agent designation by completing a 20-hour training course and passing a written examination.
    C. may obtain a residential leasing agent license by completing 15 hours of instruction and passing a written examination.
    D. may engage in residential leasing activities without obtaining a license or other certification.

19. What is the purpose of the Real Estate Recovery Fund?
    A. To provide a means of compensation for actual monetary losses suffered by individuals as a result of the acts of a licensee who violated the license law or committed other illegal acts related to a real estate transaction
    B. To ensure that Illinois real estate licensees have adequate funds available to pay their licensing and continuing education fees
    C. To protect IDFPR from claims by individuals that they have suffered a monetary loss as the result of the action of a licensee who violated the license law or committed other illegal acts related to a real estate transaction
    D. To provide an interest-generating source of revenue to fund IDFPR's activities

20. Which of the following is a legal real estate advertisement?
    A. "Julia Wonders, 312-867-5309"
    B. "Frank Jacobs Realty, We charge 1% less than the standard area commissions."
    C. "Frontage Road Brokerage, we pay $500 for every client referral."
    D. "Addison Smith, Broker, ABC Real Estate"

UNIT 15

Real Estate Financing: Principles

LEARNING OBJECTIVES

When you have completed this unit, you will be able to accomplish the following.

> Distinguish between lien, title, and intermediate theories.
> Identify the basic provisions of security and debt instruments: promissory notes, mortgage documents, deeds of trust, and land contracts.
> Explain the procedures involved in a foreclosure.

KEY TERMS

acceleration clause	hypothecation	prepayment penalty
alienation clause	interest	promissory note
beneficiary	intermediate mortgage	release deed
certificate of sale	theory	satisfaction of mortgage
deed in lieu of foreclosure	judicial foreclosure	sheriff's deed
deed of trust	land contract	sheriff's sale
defeasance clause	lien theory	statutory right of
deficiency judgment	loan origination fee	redemption
discount point	mortgage	statutory right of
equitable right of	mortgagee	reinstatement
redemption	mortgagor	strict foreclosure
equitable title	negotiable instrument	title theory
escrow account	nonjudicial foreclosure	usury
foreclosure	novation	

OVERVIEW

Perhaps the most important investment decision your clients will ever make is the one you help them with: buying a home. In the United States, relatively few homes are purchased for cash. Most homes are bought with borrowed money, and a huge lending industry has been built to service the financial requirements of homebuyers. Knowing how real estate financing works is especially important to becoming a successful licensee. If a buyer can't get funding to purchase the property, there can be no transaction.

A borrower and a lender can tailor financing instruments to suit the type of transaction and the financial needs of both parties.

 IN PRACTICE

Because of the ever-changing requirements of the secondary market, it is best for licensees to refer consumers to a lender to be preapproved for a loan before writing a real estate sales contract. However, it is important for the licensee to be knowledgeable about real estate financing programs and products in order to provide quality service, especially when serving buyers.

MORTGAGE BASICS

A **mortgage** is a *voluntary lien* on real estate. The person who borrows money to buy a piece of property voluntarily gives the lender the right to take that property if the borrower fails to repay the loan. The borrower, or **mortgagor**, pledges the land to the lender, or **mortgagee**, as security for the debt.

The debt is created through a promissory note, which is a negotiable instrument. Promissory notes are considered a "personal promise to pay" and "evidence of a debt." The mortgage itself is basically a contract that secures the repayment of the debt by stating the terms under which the debt is to be repaid and what could happen should the mortgagor not repay that debt.

SECURITY AND DEBT

A basic principle of property law is that no one can convey more than he actually owns. This principle also applies to mortgages. The owner of a fee simple estate can mortgage the fee simple interest. The owner of a leasehold or subleasehold can mortgage that leasehold interest. The owner of a condominium unit can mortgage the fee interest in the condominium.

Mortgage Loans

A mortgage loan, like all loans, creates a relationship between a debtor and a creditor. In the relationship, the creditor loans the debtor money for some purpose, and the debtor agrees to pay or pledges to pay the principal and interest according to an agreed schedule. The debtor agrees to offer some property or collateral to the creditor if the loan is not repaid.

Mortgage loans are secured loans. Mortgage loans have two parts: the debt itself and the security for the debt. When a property is mortgaged, the owner must *execute* or sign two separate instruments—a promissory note stating the amount owed and a security document.

Hypothecation

In mortgage lending practice, a borrower is required to pledge specific real property as security (collateral) for the loan. The debtor retains the right of possession and control, while the creditor receives an underlying equitable right in the pledged property. This type of pledging is called **hypothecation**. The right to foreclose on the pledged property in the event a borrower defaults is contained in a security agreement, such as a mortgage or a deed of trust.

PROMISSORY NOTES

The **promissory note** (also called a *note* or *financing instrument*) is the borrower's personal promise to repay a debt according to agreed terms. The note exposes all the borrower's assets to claims by secured creditors. The mortgagor executes one or more promissory notes to total the amount of the debt.

A promissory note executed by a borrower (or *maker* or *payor*) is a contract complete in itself. It generally states the amount of the debt, the time and method of payment, and the rate of interest. When signed by the borrowers and other necessary parties, the note becomes a legally enforceable and fully negotiable instrument of debt. When the terms of the note are satisfied, the debt is discharged. If the terms of the note are not met, the lender may choose to sue to collect on the note or to foreclose.

A note need not be tied to a mortgage or a deed of trust. A note used as a debt instrument without any related collateral is called an *unsecured note*. Unsecured notes are used by banks and other lenders to extend short-term personal loans.

A note is a **negotiable instrument** like a check or a bank draft. The lender who holds the note is called the *payee* and may transfer the right to receive payment to a third party by signing the instrument over (that is, by assigning it) to the third party or by delivering the instrument to the third party.

Interest

Interest is a charge for the use of money. Interest may be due at either the end or the beginning of each payment period. Payment made at the beginning of each period is *payment in advance*. Payment made at the end of a period is *payment in arrears*. Whether interest is charged in advance or in arrears is specified in the note. This distinction is important if the property is sold before the debt is repaid in full. Most mortgages have interest in arrears.

Usury

Charging interest in excess of the maximum rate allowed by law is called **usury**. To protect consumers from unscrupulous lenders, many states have enacted laws limiting the interest rate that may be charged on loans. In some states, the legal maximum rate is a fixed amount. In others, it is a floating interest rate that is adjusted up or down at specific intervals based on a certain economic standard such as the prime lending rate or the rate of return on government bonds.

Whichever approach is taken, lenders are penalized for making usurious loans. In some states, a lender that makes a usurious loan is permitted to collect the borrowed money but only at the legal rate of interest. In others, a usurious lender may lose the right to collect any interest or may lose the entire amount of the loan in addition to the interest.

Technically, there is no legal limit specifically imposed by Illinois on the rate of interest that a lender may charge a borrower when the loan is secured by real estate.

There is, however, exemption from these state laws. Residential first mortgage loans made by federally chartered institutions, or loans made by lenders insured or guaranteed by federal agencies, are exempt from state interest regulations, and consequently are subject to federal limits.

Included in the federal law's definition of "residential loans" are loans for purchasing houses, condominiums, manufactured housing, and loans to buy stock in a cooperative. The overall effect in Illinois is to apply federal usury limits to many if not most residential loans, thereby protecting the consumer.

Loan Origination Fee

The processing of a mortgage application is called *loan origination*. When a mortgage loan is originated, a **loan origination fee** is charged by most lenders to cover the expenses involved in generating the loan. These include the loan officer's salary, paperwork, and the lender's other costs of doing business. While a loan origination fee serves a different purpose from discount points, both increase the lender's yield. Therefore, the federal government treats the fee like discount points. It is included in the annual percentage rate, and the IRS lets a buyer deduct the loan origination fee.

Discount Points

A lender may sell a mortgage to investors. However, the interest rate that a lender charges the borrower for a loan might be less than the yield (true rate of return) an investor demands. To make up the difference, the lender charges the borrower **discount points**. The number of points charged depends on the difference between the interest rate and the required investor yield and how long the lender expects it will take the borrower to pay off the loan.

For the borrowers, one discount point equals 1% of the loan amount and is charged as prepaid interest at the closing. For example, three discount points charged on a $100,000 loan would be $3,000 ($100,000 × 3%, or 0.03). If a house sells for $100,000 and the borrower seeks an $80,000 loan, each point would be $800. In some cases, however, the points in a new acquisition may be paid in cash at closing rather than being financed as part of the total loan amount.

EXAMPLE

To determine how many points are charged on a loan, divide the total dollar amount of the points by the amount of the loan. For example, if the loan amount is $350,000 and the charge for points is $9,275, how many points are being charged?

$9,275 ÷ $350,000 = 0.0265 or 2.65% or 2.65 points

Prepayment

Most mortgage loans are paid in installments over a long period. As a result, the total interest paid by the borrower may add up to more than the principal amount of the loan. That does not come as a surprise to the lender; the total amount of accrued interest is carefully calculated during the origination phase to determine the profitability of each loan. If the borrower repays the loan before the end of the term, the lender collects less than the anticipated interest. For this reason, some mortgage notes contain a prepayment clause, which requires that the borrower pay a **prepayment penalty** against the unearned portion of the interest for any payments made ahead of schedule.

The penalty may be as little as 1% of the balance due at the time of prepayment or as much as all the interest due for the first 10 years of the loan. Some lenders allow the borrower to pay off a certain percentage of the original loan without paying a penalty. However, if the loan is paid off in full, the borrower may be charged a percentage of the principal paid in excess of that allowance. Note that lenders may not charge prepayment penalties on mortgage loans insured or guaranteed by the federal government or on those loans that have been sold to Fannie Mae or Freddie Mac.

Lenders in Illinois are prohibited from charging a borrower a prepayment penalty on a fixed-rate loan secured by residential real estate when the loan's interest rate is greater than 8% per year. However, they can charge a prepayment penalty on an adjustable-rate loan.

MORTGAGE DOCUMENT OR DEED OF TRUST

As previously stated, a note does need to be tied to either a mortgage or a deed of trust. In Illinois, the note used to obtain money to purchase real property is usually secured by a mortgage.

The mortgage document or deed of trust clearly establishes that the property is security for a debt, identifies the lender and the borrower, and includes an accurate legal description of the property. Both the mortgage document and deed of trust incorporate the terms of the note by reference. They should be signed by all parties who have an interest in the real estate. Common provisions of both instruments are discussed here.

Deed of Trust

In some situations, lenders may prefer to use a three-party instrument called a **deed of trust** (also called a *trust deed*), rather than a mortgage. A deed of trust conveys naked title or bare legal title—that is, title without the right of possession. The deed is given as security for the loan to a third party, called the trustee. The trustee holds title on behalf of the lender, who is called the **beneficiary**. The beneficiary is the holder of the note. The conveyance establishes the actions that the trustee may take if the *trustor* (borrower) defaults under any of the deed of trust terms (Figure 15.1 and Figure 15.2 compare mortgages and deeds of trust). In states where a deed of trust is generally preferred, foreclosure procedures for default are usually simpler and faster than for mortgage loans.

Figure 15.1: Mortgages

Mortgage—Two Parties

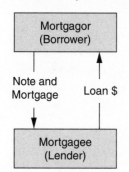
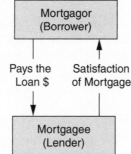

Figure 15.2: Deeds of Trust

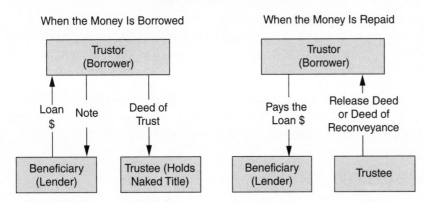

Deed of Trust—Three Parties

In Illinois, a deed of trust is treated like a mortgage and is subject to the same rules including foreclosure. The trustor (borrower) in a deed of trust holds the title to the real estate.

Duties of the Mortgagor or Trustor

The borrower is required to fulfill certain obligations created by the mortgage or deed of trust. These usually include

- payment of the debt in accordance with the terms of the note;

- payment of all real estate taxes on the property given as security;

- maintenance of adequate insurance to protect the lender if the property is destroyed or damaged by fire, windstorm, or other hazard;

- maintenance of the property in good repair at all times; and

- receipt of lender authorization before making any major alterations on the property.

Failure to meet any of these obligations can result in a borrower's default. The loan documents may, however, provide for a grace period (such as 30 days) during which the borrower can meet the obligation and cure the default. If the borrower does not do so, the lender has the right to foreclose on the mortgage or deed of trust and collect on the note.

MORTGAGE CLAUSES AND PROVISIONS

Acceleration Clause

The mortgage or deed of trust typically includes an **acceleration clause** to assist the lender in foreclosure. If a borrower defaults, the lender has the right to "accelerate the maturity of the debt." This means the lender may declare the entire debt due and payable immediately. Without an acceleration clause, the lender would have to sue the borrower every time a payment was overdue.

When all mortgage loan payments have been made and the note has been paid in full, the borrower will want the public record to show that the debt has been satisfied and that the lender is divested of all rights conveyed under the mortgage. By the provisions of the *defeasance clause* in most mortgage documents, the lender is required to execute a **satisfaction of mortgage** (also called a *release of mortgage* or *mortgage discharge*) when the note has been fully paid. This document returns to the borrower all interest in the real estate originally conveyed to the lender. Entering this release in the public record shows that the mortgage lien has been removed from the property.

If a mortgage has been assigned by a recorded assignment, the release must be executed by the assignee or mortgagee.

When a real estate loan secured by a deed of trust has been completely repaid, the beneficiary must make a written request that the trustee convey the property back to the grantor. The trustee executes and delivers a **release deed** (also called a *deed of reconveyance*) to the trustor. The release deed conveys the same rights and powers that the trustee was given under the deed of trust. The release deed should be acknowledged and recorded in the public records of the county in which the property is located.

Any mortgagee, or his assignees or agents, who fails to deliver a release to the mortgagor or the grantor of a deed of trust within one month after full payment and satisfaction will be liable to pay the mortgagor or grantor a $200 penalty. The release also must state the following on its face in bold letters:

> **FOR THE PROTECTION OF THE OWNER, THIS RELEASE SHALL BE FILED WITH THE RECORDER OR THE REGISTRAR OF TITLES IN WHOSE OFFICE THE MORTGAGE OR DEED OF TRUST WAS FILED.**

It is then the mortgagor's responsibility to record the release.

Alienation Clause

The lender may want to prevent a future purchaser of the property from being able to assume the loan, particularly if the original interest rate is low. For this reason, some lenders include an **alienation clause** (also called a *resale clause*, *due-on-sale clause*, or *call clause*) in the note. An alienation clause provides that when the property is sold, the lender may either declare the entire debt due immediately or permit the buyer to assume the loan at the current market interest rate.

Other clauses in a mortgage or deed of trust enable the lender to take care of the property in the event of the borrower's negligence or default. If the borrower does not pay taxes or insurance premiums or fails to make necessary repairs on the property, the lender may step in and do so. The lender has the power to protect the security (the real estate). Any money advanced by the lender to cure a default may be either added to the unpaid debt or declared immediately due from the borrower.

Assignment of the Mortgage

Without changing the provisions of a contract, a note may be sold to a third party, such as an investor or another mortgage company. The original mortgagee endorses the note to the third party and executes an assignment of mortgage. The assignee becomes the new owner of the debt and security instrument. When the debt is paid in full (or satisfied), the assignee is required to execute the *satisfaction* (or release) of the security instrument.

Tax and Insurance Reserves

Many lenders require that borrowers provide a reserve fund to meet future real estate taxes and property insurance premiums. This fund is called an **escrow account** (also called an *impound account* or *trust account*). When the mortgage or deed of trust loan is made, the borrower starts the reserve by depositing funds to cover the amount of unpaid real estate taxes. If a new insurance policy has just been purchased, the insurance premium reserve will be started with the deposit of one-twelfth of the insurance premium liability. The borrower's monthly loan payments will include principal, interest, tax, and insurance (PITI). Other costs such as private mortgage insurance premiums (PMI), flood insurance, or homeowners association dues may also be included.

Illinois law prescribes additional guidelines that must be followed by lenders who require escrow accounts for mortgage loans on single-family, owner-occupied residential properties. The Mortgage Tax Escrow Act (765 ILCS 915/) provides that except during the first year of the loan, a lender may not require an escrow accumulation of more than 150% of the previous year's real estate taxes. Lenders must give borrowers written notice of the act's provisions at closing.

The Mortgage Escrow Account Act (765 ILCS 910/) states that when the principal loan balance has been reduced to 65% of its original amount, borrowers may terminate their escrow account. The latter does not apply to loans insured, guaranteed, supplemented, or assisted by the state of Illinois or agencies of the federal government such as FHA and VA.

Also, borrowers have the right to pledge an interest-bearing deposit in an amount sufficient to cover the entire amount of anticipated future tax bills and insurance premiums instead of establishing an escrow account.

Flood Insurance Reserves

The National Flood Insurance Reform Act of 1994 imposes certain mandatory obligations on lenders and loan servicers to set aside (escrow) funds for flood insurance on new loans. The act also applies to any loan still outstanding on September 23, 1994. This means that if a lender or servicer discovers that a secured property is in a flood hazard area, it must notify the borrower. The borrower then has 45 days to purchase flood insurance. If the borrower fails to procure flood insurance, the lender must purchase the insurance on the borrower's behalf. The cost of the insurance may be charged to the borrower.

Assignment of Rents

If the property involved includes rental units, the borrower may provide for rents to be assigned to the lender in the event of the borrower's default. The assignment may be included in the mortgage or deed of trust, or it may be a separate document. In either case, the assignment should clearly indicate that the borrower intends to assign the rents, not merely pledge them as security for the loan. In title-theory states, lenders are automatically entitled to any rents if the borrower defaults.

Buying Property "Subject to" or "Assuming" Existing Financing

When a person purchases real estate that is subject to an outstanding mortgage or deed of trust, the buyer may take the property in one of two ways. The property may be purchased *subject to* the mortgage or the buyer may *assume* the mortgage or deed of trust and agree to pay the debt. This technical distinction becomes important if the buyer defaults and the mortgage or deed of trust is foreclosed.

When the property is sold subject to the mortgage, the buyer is not personally obligated to pay the debt in full. The buyer takes title to the real estate knowing that he must make payments on the existing loan. Upon default, the lender forecloses and the property is sold by court order to pay the debt. If the sale does not pay off the entire debt, the purchaser is not liable for the difference. In some circumstances, however, the original seller might continue to be liable.

EXAMPLE

A man owns an investment rental property that is mortgaged. For health reasons, he wants to sell the property to the woman who has been managing the property and who also wants to use the rental property as an investment. The owner sells the property to the woman subject to the mortgage. In the sale, the buyer takes title and assumes responsibilities for the loan, but after two months she can no longer make payments on the loan. There is a foreclosure sale and because the owner sold the property subject to the mortgage, he (not the buyer) is personally liable if proceeds from the foreclosure sale do not meet the obligations.

In contrast, a buyer who purchases the property and assumes the seller's debt becomes personally obligated for the payment of the entire debt, and the seller (original mortgagor) is still liable until the mortgagee releases the seller. This release generally occurs when the buyer establishes a seasoned payment history (a stable and consistent history of payments under the terms of the loan). If the mortgage is foreclosed and the court sale does not bring enough money to pay the debt in full, a deficiency judgment against the assumer and the original borrower may be obtained for the unpaid balance of the note. If the lender has released the original borrower, only the assumer is liable.

If a seller wants to be completely free of the original mortgage loan, the seller(s), buyer(s), and lender must execute a **novation** agreement in writing. The novation makes the buyer solely responsible for any default on the loan. The original borrower (seller) is freed of any liability for the loan.

The existence of a lien does not prevent the transfer of property; however, when a secured loan is assumed, the mortgagee or beneficiary must approve the assumption and any release of liability of the original mortgagor or trustor. Because a loan may not be assumed without lender approval, the lending institution would require the assumer to qualify financially, and many lending institutions charge a transfer fee to cover the costs of changing the records. This charge can be paid by either the buyer or the seller.

Recording a Mortgage or Deed of Trust

The mortgage document or deed of trust must be recorded in the recorder's office of the county in which the real estate is located. Recording gives constructive notice to the world of the borrower's obligations. Recording also establishes the lien's priority.

Priority of a Mortgage or Deed of Trust

Priority of mortgages and other liens normally is determined by the order in which they were recorded. A mortgage or deed of trust on land that has no prior mortgage lien is a *first mortgage* or *deed of trust*. If the owner later executes another loan for additional funds, the new loan becomes a *second mortgage* or *deed of trust* (also called a *junior lien*) when it is recorded. The second lien is subject to the first lien; the first has prior claim to the value of the land pledged as security. Because second loans represent greater risk to the lender, they are usually issued at higher interest rates.

The priority of mortgage or deed of trust liens may be changed by a *subordination agreement*, in which the first lender subordinates its lien to that of the second lender. To be valid, such an agreement must be signed by both lenders.

PROVISIONS OF LAND CONTRACTS AND OTHER OWNER FINANCING

Real estate can be purchased under a land contract. Real estate is usually sold on contract for specific financial reasons. For example, mortgage financing may be unavailable to a borrower for some reason. High interest rates may make borrowing too expensive, or the purchaser may not have a sufficient down payment to cover the difference between a mortgage loan and the selling price.

Under a **land contract** (also called a *contract for deed* or *installment contract*), the buyer (called the *vendee*) agrees to make a down payment and a monthly loan payment that includes interest and principal directly to the seller. The payment also may include real estate tax and insurance reserves. The seller (called the *vendor*) retains legal title to the property during the contract term, and the buyer is granted *equitable title* and possession. At the end of the loan term, the seller delivers clear title. In the event the seller fails to deliver clear title, the buyer (vendee) would file a vendee's lien. The contract usually permits the seller to evict the buyer in the event of default. In that case, the seller may keep any money the buyer has already paid. If, however, the buyer has 20% equity in the property and a contract in excess of five years, judicial foreclosure would be necessary.

While land contracts or owner financing can occur with residential or commercial properties, they are more common with unimproved acreage and farmland sales. Sometimes the seller is the primary lender, and at other times, the seller may be in a secondary position. In either case, the sellers would want to secure their interest either by the use of a deed, note and mortgage, deed of trust, or perhaps the use of a contract for deed instrument.

Predatory Lending and Mortgage Fraud

Predatory lending is any lending practice that imposes unfair or abusive loan terms on a borrower. It is also any practice that through deception, coercion, exploitation, or unscrupulous actions convinces a borrower to accept unfair terms on a loan that a borrower doesn't need, doesn't want, or can't afford.

Predatory loans have caused many families to lose their homes. Mortgagors, unable to repay the debt, often face foreclosure. Not only is the mortgagor affected, but the neighborhood is also affected as homes fall into disrepair and property values decrease as homes are abandoned.

Subprime loans are often made to individuals with bad credit histories. The high up-front fees and higher interest rates usually set up the mortgagor for failure from the start. Equifax, a credit reporting company, considers an individual with a credit score below 650 as a candidate for a subprime loan.

As a licensee, it's important to be able to refer our clients to lenders and mortgage brokers or mortgage bankers who will look out for the best interests of our clients. As a fiduciary, it is the lender's responsibility to act loyally on behalf of their and our client.

Another area of concern is mortgage fraud. According to CoreLogic, a company specializing in data analytics, in 2018, one out of every 109 mortgage applications showed signs of fraud. The Federal Bureau of Investigation considers mortgage fraud as a subcategory of financial institution fraud (FIF). Mortgage fraud is characterized by some type of material misstatement, misrepresentation, or mission in relation to a mortgage loan that is then relied upon by a lender.

There are two distinct areas for mortgage fraud. The first is fraud for profit, in which an individual or individuals use the lending process to steal cash and equity from homeowners and lenders. Fraud for profit usually involves collusion of industry insiders such as bank officers, appraisers, mortgage brokers, attorneys, loan originators, and other industry professionals.

The second area of mortgage fraud is fraud for housing, which involves the illegal actions of a borrower to take, acquire, or maintain ownership of a property. Though the list of fraudulent activities is long, this type of fraud can be as simple as falsifying employment records or pay stubs, buying into other people's bank accounts or credit scores (known as "asset rental"), or lying about occupancy to obtain a cheaper interest rate.

A licensee who becomes aware that a client or customer is perpetrating fraud should probably contact the lender. Receipt of commission from a transaction as a result of mortgage fraud could be construed as complicit behavior.

Mortgage Law

Though fundamentally the relationship between a mortgagor and a mortgagee is contractual, there are certain legal doctrines at play as well. These doctrines of property law, known as *theories*, spell out basic interests that the mortgagor and mortgagee have in the property.

In **title theory** states, the mortgagor actually gives *legal title* to the mortgagee (or some other designated individual) and retains **equitable title**. Legal title is returned to the mortgagor when the debt is paid in full (or some other obligation is performed). In theory, the lender actually owns the property until the debt is paid. The lender allows the borrower all the usual rights of ownership, such as possession and use. Because the lender holds legal title, the lender has the right to immediate possession of the real estate and rents from the mortgaged property if the mortgagor defaults.

In **lien theory** states, the mortgagor/borrower holds both legal and equitable title. The mortgagee/lender simply has a lien on the property as security for the mortgage debt. The mortgage is nothing more than collateral for the loan. If the mortgagor defaults, the mortgagee must go through a formal *foreclosure* proceeding to obtain legal title. The property is offered for sale, and sale proceeds are used to pay all or part of the remaining debt. In some states, a defaulting mortgagor may redeem the property during a certain period after the sale. A borrower who fails to redeem the property during that time loses the property irrevocably.

A number of states have adopted an **intermediate mortgage theory** based on the principles of title-theory states but still requiring the mortgagee to formally foreclose to obtain legal title.

Illinois does not adhere strictly to either the title or lien theory. As a result, Illinois often is called an intermediate mortgage theory state. Mortgages and deeds of trust in Illinois convey only qualified title to the lender as security for the loan during the existence of the debt. The mortgagor/borrower remains the owner of the mortgaged property for all beneficial purposes, subject to the lien created by the mortgage or deed of trust. The qualified title held by the lender is subject to the **defeasance clause**, which stipulates that such title must be fully reconveyed, or released back, to the mortgagor at the time the debt is repaid in full.

In reality, the differences between the parties' rights in a lien-theory state and those in a title-theory state are more technical than actual. A typical procedure before any foreclosure is to accelerate the loan based on the original agreement made with the borrower. This means asking for the loan to be paid in full based on the borrower's having broken the original promise to repay with regular payments.

FORECLOSURE

Borrowers who default on mortgage payments force lenders to exercise their rights, via the acceleration clause, to foreclose against properties used as security for their loans. **Foreclosure** is a legal procedure in which property pledged as security for a loan is sold to satisfy the debt. The foreclosure procedure brings the rights of the parties and all junior lienholders to a conclusion. It passes title either to the person holding the mortgage document or deed of trust or to a third party who purchases the realty at a *foreclosure sale*.

Methods of Foreclosure

There are three general types of foreclosure proceedings—nonjudicial, judicial, and strict foreclosure. The specific provisions and procedures for each vary from state to state.

Nonjudicial Foreclosure

Some states allow **nonjudicial foreclosure** procedures to be used when the security instrument contains a *power-of-sale clause*. In nonjudicial foreclosure, no court action is required.

Judicial Foreclosure

Judicial foreclosure allows the property to be sold by court order after the mortgagee has given sufficient public notice. When a borrower defaults, the lender may accelerate the due date of the remaining principal balance, along with all overdue interest, penalties, and administrative costs. The lender's attorney then can file a suit to foreclose the lien. After presentation of the facts in court, the property is ordered sold. A public sale is advertised and held, and the real estate is sold to the highest bidder.

By statute, mortgage foreclosures may be brought about only through a court proceeding. As a result, Illinois is classified as a *judicial foreclosure state*. Under the Illinois Mortgage Foreclosure Law (735 ILCS 5/), the term *mortgage* includes

- deeds of trust,

- installment contracts payable over a period in excess of five years (when the unpaid balance is less than 80% of the purchase price),

- certain collateral assignments of the beneficial interest in land trusts used as security for lenders, and

- traditional mortgage instruments.

Strict Foreclosure

Although judicial foreclosure is the prevalent practice, it is still possible in some states for a lender to acquire mortgaged property through a **strict foreclosure** process. In this process, appropriate notice must first be given to the delinquent borrower. Then, once the proper papers have been prepared and recorded, the court establishes a deadline by which the balance of the defaulted debt must be paid in full. If the borrower does not pay off the loan by that date, the court simply awards full legal title to the lender. No sale takes place.

Deed in Lieu of Foreclosure

As an alternative to foreclosure, a lender may accept a **deed in lieu of foreclosure** from the borrower. This is sometimes called a *friendly foreclosure* because it is carried out by mutual agreement rather than by lawsuit. The major disadvantage of the "deed in lieu" is that the mortgagee takes the real estate subject to all junior liens. In a foreclosure action, all junior liens are eliminated. Also, by accepting a deed in lieu of foreclosure, the lender usually loses any rights pertaining to FHA or private mortgage insurance or VA guarantees. Finally, a deed in lieu of foreclosure is still considered an adverse element in the borrower's credit history.

Redemption

Illinois has an **equitable right of redemption** which allows the borrower to pay the lender the amount in default plus costs and thereby extinguish the debt. This right begins after the notice but before the foreclosure sale.

In Illinois, a mortgagor in default who wishes to exercise the equitable right of redemption to avoid loss of the mortgaged real estate may do so for a period of seven months after the date of service on the mortgagor or after first publication date, whichever is later. This time period can currently be shortened to as little as 30 days after a judgment is entered if the property has been abandoned or is vacant. When a property is redeemed in this way, the foreclosure sale does not occur. Otherwise, the foreclosure sale is held as soon as possible after the equitable right of redemption expires.

The mortgagor generally has a right to remain in possession of the property from the time of service of summons until the entry of a judgment of foreclosure. After judgment and through the 30th day after confirmation of the sale, the mortgagor can still retain possession but may be required to pay rent to the holder of the certificate of sale. Thirty-one days after judgment, the mortgagor must have vacated the property or be subject to eviction. The owner of the certificate of sale receives a quitclaim deed, in this situation called a **sheriff's deed**, and gains the right to possession.

Illinois also offers a **statutory right of reinstatement**. This option is applicable when the defaulting mortgagor wishes to cure the default and reinstate the loan as though no acceleration had occurred. The mortgagor has the right to exercise this statutory right for a period of 90 days after service of summons or publication date. At the lender's discretion, expressed through an attorney, the right of reinstatement may be extended to run as long as the equitable right of redemption.

The reinstatement right usually may be exercised only once every five years. After reinstatement occurs, the suit must be dismissed by the lender, and the mortgage loan remains in effect just as before (see 735 ILCS 5/15).

When a default is not cured by redemption or reinstatement, the entry of a decree of foreclosure will lead to a *judicial sale* of the property, usually called a **sheriff's sale**. Each defendant to the suit must be given written personal notice of the sale, and public notice of the sale must be published in a newspaper of general circulation. The successful bidder at the sale receives a **certificate of sale**, not a deed. Only after the sale is confirmed by the court will the certificate holder receive a sheriff's deed. See Figure 15.3.

Figure 15.3: Statutory Right of Reinstatement

Statutory right of reinstatement / catch-up on your payments and late fees / once every five years

Date of Service   90 days   Foreclosure Sale

7 months

Equitable right of redemption / pay everything back!

Deficiency Judgment

The foreclosure sale may not produce enough cash to pay the loan balance in full after deducting expenses and accrued unpaid interest. In this case, where permitted by law, the mortgagee may be entitled to a *personal judgment* against the borrower for the unpaid balance. Such a judgment is a **deficiency judgment**. It may also be obtained against any endorsers or guarantors of the note and against any owners of the mortgaged property who assumed the debt by written agreement. However, if any money remains from the foreclosure sale after paying the debt and any other liens (such as a second mortgage or mechanic's lien), expenses, and interest, these proceeds are paid to the borrower.

Short Sales

A *short sale* is the process by which a lender accepts less than the amount owed on the property. A short sale most often occurs when the owner/borrower is unable to make the mortgage payments and cannot sell the house for what is owed on the property. The lender agrees to accept less because the lender may lose more money by acquiring the property through a foreclosure process and then holding the property until another buyer is found.

The lender, however, may reserve the right to file suit to acquire the missing amount, called a deficiency. Where the deficiency amount is forgiven in the short sale, the IRS may consider this amount to be taxable income for the borrower. For specific details, be sure to consult a competent tax advisor.

As a practical matter, lenders often take their time in determining whether or not to agree to a short sale. Licensees working with short sales should expect the process to be long and tedious and to handle issues not usually present in a standard sales agreement.

Bankruptcy and Foreclosure

Any discussion a licensee has with a consumer over foreclosure and bankruptcy should involve the licensee's advice to the consumer to seek legal advice. Foreclosure laws and procedures are complicated. Bankruptcy will not relieve the mortgagor of the necessity of paying the mortgage, but it might give some breathing space. Any filing for bankruptcy most likely happens shortly after the receipt of the foreclosure notice and before the actual foreclosure sale.

In a filing of either a Chapter 13 or Chapter 7 bankruptcy, the court should automatically issue an order for relief that includes an automatic stay, which directs creditors to immediately cease their collection activities. In a Chapter 7 bankruptcy, the sale will be postponed, typically for three to four months, while the bankruptcy is pending. However, the lender can ask the court for a motion to lift the automatic stay, which will allow the sale to proceed. If the lender is successful, the mortgagor will not be granted the extra three to four months.

A Chapter 13 bankruptcy allows the mortgagor to pay off the "arrearage" (late unpaid payments) over the length of the Chapter 13 repayment plan, five years in most cases. However, the current mortgage payments will still need to be met, so the mortgagor will need enough income to make those payments in addition to the added expense of the arrearage. As long as all the payments are made, the mortgagor will avoid foreclosure and keep the home.

SUMMARY

Loans secured by a mortgage or deed of trust provide the principal sources of financing for real estate operations. Mortgage loans involve a borrower (the mortgagor) and a lender (the mortgagee). Deed of trust loans involve a third-party "manager" (the trustee), in addition to a borrower (the trustor) and a lender (the beneficiary). Often the trustee/manager and the beneficiary in this type of loan have close interaction.

After a lending institution has received, investigated, and approved a loan application, it issues a commitment to make the mortgage loan. The borrower is required to execute a note agreeing to repay the debt and to execute a mortgage or deed of trust placing a lien on the real estate to secure the note. The security instrument is recorded to give constructive notice to the world of the lender's interest.

The mortgage document or deed of trust secures the debt and sets forth the obligations of the borrower and the rights of the lender. Full payment of the note by its terms entitles the borrower to a satisfaction, or release, which is recorded to clear the lien from the public records. Default by the borrower may result in acceleration of payments, a foreclosure sale, and, after the redemption period (if provided by state law), loss of title.

Lenders may accept a deed in lieu of foreclosure from the borrower instead of pursuing a formal foreclosure. This does not eliminate junior liens and is still an adverse element in the borrower's credit history.

Another alternative to foreclosure is the short sale. A short sale occurs when the lender agrees to accept less than the outstanding loan balance when the property is sold. The lender must agree to accept the lesser amount and may or may not forgive the resulting deficiency.

 Illinois is an intermediate mortgage theory state. There is no state-imposed usury limit in Illinois on the rate that may be charged for a loan secured by real estate and made by private lenders. However, federal anti-usury laws supersede state laws on first-time residential mortgages and on federally insured or guaranteed loans. The Mortgage Escrow Account Act gives borrowers certain protections by limiting the size of escrow accounts and permitting alternatives to escrow.

Illinois is also classified as a judicial foreclosure state. There is no statutory right of redemption in Illinois, but there is equitable right of redemption and statutory right of reinstatement. When property is purchased at a sheriff's sale, the successful bidder receives a certificate of sale until the sale is confirmed by a court. After confirmation, the certificate holder receives a quitclaim deed, which in this situation is also called a sheriff's deed.

UNIT 15 QUIZ

1. A charge of three discount points on a $120,000 loan equals
   A. $450.
   B. $4,500.
   C. $3,600.
   D. $116,400.

2. A prospective buyer needs to borrow money to buy a house. The buyer applies for and obtains a real estate loan from a mortgage company. The buyer then signs a note and a mortgage. In this example, the buyer is the
   A. beneficiary.
   B. mortgagee.
   C. mortgagor.
   D. vendor.

3. A prospective buyer needs to borrow money to buy a house. The buyer applies for and obtains a real estate loan from a mortgage company. The buyer then signs a note and a mortgage. In this example, the mortgage company is the
   A. mortgagor.
   B. beneficiary.
   C. vendor.
   D. mortgagee.

4. The borrower under a deed of trust is called the
   A. trustee.
   B. trustor.
   C. beneficiary.
   D. vendee.

5. In a land contract, the vendee
   A. is not responsible for the real estate taxes on the property.
   B. does not pay interest and principal.
   C. obtains legal title at closing.
   D. has possession during the term of the contract.

6. A borrower has defaulted on a loan. Which of these *BEST* describes the rights of the lender in this situation?
   A. The acceleration clause in the note gives the lender the right to have all future installments due and payable immediately on default.
   B. The escalation clause in the note allows the lender to collect all future interest due on the loan should a buyer default.
   C. The defeasance clause in the note stipulates that the lender may begin foreclosure proceedings to collect the remaining mortgage balance.
   D. The alienation clause in the note allows the lender to convey the mortgage to a buyer at the foreclosure sale.

7. After a mortgagor makes final payment to the mortgagee, the mortgagee would give the mortgagor a
   A. release deed.
   B. deed of trust.
   C. satisfaction of mortgage.
   D. mortgage estoppel.

8. Under a typical land contract, when does the vendor give the deed to the vendee?
   A. At the closing
   B. When the contract is fulfilled and all payments have been made
   C. When the contract for deed is approved by the parties
   D. After the first year's real estate taxes are paid

9. If a borrower must pay $2,700 for points on a $90,000 loan, how many points is the lender charging for this loan?
   A. 3
   B. 2
   C. 5
   D. 6

10. Pledging property for a loan without giving up possession of the property itself is called
    A. defeasance.
    B. alienation.
    C. novation.
    D. hypothecation.

11. Although the homeowners have located a buyer for their home, the buyer's offer is less than what the homeowners owe. In this situation, if the lender agrees to accept an amount less than owed, the lender has agreed to a
    A. short sale.
    B. friendly foreclosure.
    C. deed in lieu of foreclosure.
    D. waiver of redemption.

12. Discount points on a mortgage are computed as a percentage of the
    A. selling price.
    B. closing costs.
    C. down payment.
    D. loan amount.

13. In Illinois, mortgage foreclosures may be obtained only through a court proceeding. This means Illinois is characterized as a
    A. judicial foreclosure state.
    B. strict foreclosure state.
    C. foreclosure-by-lawsuit state.
    D. intermediate mortgage theory state.

14. In Illinois, when may a mortgagor in default exercise the right of reinstatement?
    A. At any time before the foreclosure sale
    B. Up to six months after the foreclosure sale
    C. Up to 90 days after service of summons
    D. Up to 90 days after the payments become delinquent but before summons

15. In Illinois, when must a release be delivered to a mortgagor or trustor once the mortgage or deed of trust has been fully satisfied?
    A. Within 48 hours of full payment and satisfaction
    B. Within one month after full payment and satisfaction
    C. Within five business days after full payment and satisfaction
    D. Within 90 days after full payment and satisfaction

16. The successful bidder at a foreclosure sale in Illinois immediately receives a
    A. sheriff's deed.
    B. certificate of sale.
    C. deed of foreclosure.
    D. certificate of foreclosure.

17. According to the Mortgage Escrow Account Act, an individual who has owned his home for 12 years and reduced his mortgage balance to 65% of its original amount may
    A. receive a 50% rebate from the lender on his escrow account.
    B. earn the statutory interest rate on his escrow account deposit.
    C. terminate his escrow account.
    D. obtain a second loan with only a token down payment.

18. What is the Illinois usury ceiling for loans secured by real property?
    A. 8%
    B. None of these
    C. 9½%
    D. A fluctuating rate based on the quarterly federal reserve rate

19. Which of these is included in the definition of *mortgage* contained in the Illinois Mortgage Foreclosure Law?
    A. Installment contracts payable over at least five years, with a 20% down payment
    B. Installment contracts payable over a maximum of five years
    C. Assignments of beneficial interests in living trusts
    D. Deeds in trust

20. Which of these describes the theory of the mortgagor/mortgagee relationship in Illinois?
    A. Title theory
    B. Lien theory
    C. Conventional theory
    D. Intermediate mortgage theory

UNIT 16

Real Estate Financing: Practice

LEARNING OBJECTIVES

When you have completed this unit, you will be able to accomplish the following.

> Identify the types of institutions in the primary and secondary mortgage markets.
> Distinguish among different financing techniques.
> Explain the requirements and qualifications for conventional, FHA, and VA loan programs.
> Describe the various types of financing available to real estate purchasers and the role of government financing regulations.

KEY TERMS

adjustable-rate mortgage (ARM)
amortized loan
balloon payment
blanket loan
buydown
certificate of reasonable value (CRV)
Community Reinvestment Act (CRA)
construction loan
conventional loan
Equal Credit Opportunity Act (ECOA)
Fannie Mae
Federal Reserve System (the Fed)
FHA loan

Freddie Mac
Ginnie Mae
growing equity mortgage (GEM)
home equity loan
loan-to-value (LTV) ratio
mortgage insurance premium (MIP)
mortgage loan originator (MLO)
open-end loan
package loan
primary mortgage market
private mortgage insurance (PMI)
purchase money mortgage (PMM)

Real Estate Settlement Procedures Act (RESPA)
reverse mortgage
secondary mortgage market
Secure and Fair Enforcement for Mortgage Licensing Act of 2008 (SAFE Act)
straight loan
trigger terms
TRID (TILA RESPA Integrated Disclosure rule)
Truth in Lending Act (TILA)
VA loan
wraparound loan

OVERVIEW

Most real estate transactions require some form of financing. The challenge for today's real estate licensees is to maintain a working knowledge of the various financing options. By understanding financing techniques and payment options, real estate licensees can be valuable participants in helping buyers reach their real estate goals.

THE REAL ESTATE FINANCING MARKET

Before turning to the specific types of mortgage options available to consumers, it is important to have a clear understanding of the bigger picture: the market in which those mortgages exist. The real estate financing market has the following three basic components:

- Government influences (primarily the Federal Reserve System, but also the Federal Home Loan Banks and the Office of the Comptroller of the Currency)
- The primary mortgage market
- The secondary mortgage market

Under the umbrella of the financial policies set by the Federal Reserve System, the primary mortgage market originates loans that are bought, sold, and traded in the secondary mortgage market.

Increasing reserve requirements raises rates:

- Decreases money flow
- Slows economy and purchases
- Slows inflation

Decreasing reserve requirements lowers rates:

- Increases money for loans
- Stimulates market
- Increases inflation

The Federal Reserve System

The Federal Reserve System (the Fed) maintains sound credit conditions, helps counteract inflationary and deflationary trends, and creates a favorable economic climate. The Fed divides the country into 12 Federal Reserve Districts, each served by a Federal Reserve Bank. All nationally chartered banks must join the Fed and purchase stock in its district reserve banks. The Fed regulates the flow of money and interest rates in the marketplace through its member banks by controlling reserve requirements and discount rates.

Reserve Requirements

The Fed requires that each member bank keep a certain level of assets on hand as reserve funds. These reserves are unavailable for loans or any other use. This requirement not only protects customer deposits but also provides a means of manipulating the flow of cash in the money market.

The higher the reserve requirement, the less money the lender has to lend; therefore, the interest rate will climb. The inverse is that the reserve requirements are lowered. There are more available funds for lending and interest rates drop.

Discount Rate

Federal Reserve member banks borrow money from the district reserve banks in order to expand their lending operations. The discount rate is the rate charged by the Fed when it lends money to its member banks. The *prime rate* is the short-term interest rate charged to a bank's largest, most creditworthy customers. If the Fed raises the discount rate, the prime rate will undoubtably increase. If the Fed lowers the discount rate, the prime rate will lower.

Additional Practices

The Fed also has the ability to increase or decrease the supply of money in the market through the purchase and sale of securities. By selling securities, the Fed takes money off the market, and the cost of money should increase. By purchasing those securities back, the Fed attempts to place more funds into the marketplace and drive the cost of money down.

The Primary Mortgage Market

The **primary mortgage market** is made up of the lenders that originate mortgage loans. These lenders make money available directly to borrowers and make their income from finance charges and charging interest.

In addition to the income directly related to loans, some lenders derive income from *servicing* loans for other mortgage lenders or the investors who have purchased the loans. Servicing loans involves such activities as

- collecting payments (including insurance and taxes),
- accounting,
- bookkeeping,
- preparing insurance and tax records,
- processing payments of taxes and insurance, and
- following up on loan payment and delinquency.

Some of the major lenders in the primary market include the following:

- *Thrifts, savings associations, and commercial banks.* These institutions are called fiduciary lenders because of their fiduciary obligations to protect and preserve their depositors' funds.

- *Insurance companies.* Insurance companies accumulate large sums of money from the premiums paid by their policyholders. While part of this money is held in reserve to satisfy claims and cover operating expenses, much of it is free to be invested in profit-earning enterprises such as long-term real estate loans.

- *Credit unions.* Credit unions are cooperative organizations whose members place money in savings accounts. In the past, credit unions made only short-term consumer and home improvement loans. Now, they routinely originate longer-term first and second mortgage and deed of trust loans.

- *Pension funds.* Pension funds usually have large amounts of money available for investment. Because of the comparatively high yields and low risks offered by mortgages, pension funds have begun to participate actively in financing real estate projects. Most real estate activities for pension funds are handled through mortgage bankers and mortgage brokers.

- *Endowment funds.* Many commercial banks and mortgage bankers handle investments for endowment funds. The endowments of hospitals, universities, colleges, charitable foundations, and other institutions provide a good source of financing for low-risk commercial and industrial properties.

- *Investment group financing.* Large real estate projects, such as highrise apartment buildings, office complexes, and shopping centers, are often financed as joint ventures through group financing arrangements like syndicates, limited partnerships, and real estate investment trusts.

- *Mortgage banking companies.* Mortgage banking companies originate mortgage loans with money belonging to insurance companies, pension funds, and individuals with funds of their own. They make real estate loans with the intention of selling them to investors and receiving a fee for servicing the loans.

- *Mortgage brokers.* Mortgage brokers are not lenders. They are intermediaries who bring borrowers and lenders together. Mortgage brokers locate potential borrowers, process preliminary loan applications, and submit the applications to lenders for final approval. They do not service loans once they are made.

The federal **Secure and Fair Enforcement for Mortgage Licensing Act of 2008 (SAFE Act)** requires that each individual state must license and register **mortgage loan originators (MLOs)**. An MLO is anyone who, for compensation or expectation of compensation, takes a residential mortgage loan by phone or in person.

IN PRACTICE

A growing number of consumers apply for mortgage loans online. Many major lenders' websites offer information to potential borrowers regarding their current loan programs and requirements. In addition, online brokerage or matchmaking organizations link lenders with potential borrowers. Some borrowers prefer the internet for its convenience in shopping for the best rates and terms, accessing a wide variety of loan programs, and speeding up the loan approval process.

The Secondary Mortgage Market

In addition to the primary mortgage market where loans are originated, there is a **secondary mortgage market**. In the secondary market, various agencies purchase existing mortgages from banks and savings associations and assemble those mortgages into packages called *blocks* or *pools*. Securities that represent shares in these pooled mortgages are then sold to investors or other agencies (see Figure 16.1). The secondary mortgage market allows for the resupply of funds for lending to the primary mortgage market.

Figure 16.1: Secondary Mortgage Market

Institution	Secondary Market Function
Fannie Mae	Conventional, VA, FHA loans
Freddie Mac	Mostly conventional loans
Ginnie Mae	Special assistance loans

Fannie Mae

The Federal National Mortgage Association, usually called **Fannie Mae**, is a government-sponsored enterprise that provides a secondary market for mortgage loans, dealing in conventional, Federal Housing Administration (FHA), and Department of Veterans Affairs (VA) loans. Fannie Mae buys a pool of mortgages from a lender, and that pool may then be used as collateral for *mortgage-backed securities* that are sold on the global market. The Fannie Mae loan limits shown in Figure 16.2 define loans that are conforming.

Figure 16.2: Fannie Mae/Freddie Mac Conforming Loan Limits (2020)

Dwelling Size	Loan Limit
One-family unit	$510,400
Two-family unit	$653,550
Three-family unit	$789,950
Four-family unit	$981,700

Maximum loan limits are 50% higher in Alaska, Guam, Hawaii, the U.S. Virgin Islands, and for other certain high-cost areas.

Ginnie Mae

The Government National Mortgage Association, usually called **Ginnie Mae**, administers special-assistance programs and guarantees mortgage backed securities using FHA and VA loans as collateral. The Ginnie Mae *pass-through certificate* is a security interest in a pool of mortgages that provides for a monthly pass-through of principal and interest payments directly to the certificate holder. Such certificates are guaranteed by Ginnie Mae.

Ginnie Mae is a wholly owned government corporation within the Department of Housing and Urban Development (HUD).

Freddie Mac

Like Fannie Mae, the Federal Home Loan Mortgage Corporation, usually called **Freddie Mac**, is a government-sponsored enterprise that provides a secondary market primarily for conventional loans.

Many lenders use the standardized forms and follow the guidelines issued by Fannie Mae and Freddie Mac. In fact, the use of such forms is mandatory for lenders wishing to sell mortgages in the agencies' secondary mortgage market. The standardized documents include loan applications, credit reports, and appraisal forms.

FINANCING TECHNIQUES

Real estate financing comes in a wide variety of forms. Different payment plans alternately tend to gain and lose favor with lenders and borrowers as the cost and availability of mortgage money fluctuates. While the payment plans described in the following sections are commonly called *mortgages*, they are really loans secured by either a mortgage or a deed of trust.

Straight Loans

A **straight loan** (also called an *interest-only loan* or *term loan*) is a nonamortized loan that essentially divides the loan into two amounts to be paid off separately. The borrower makes periodic payments of interest only, followed by the payment of the principal in full at the end of the term.

Amortized Loans

Unlike a straight loan payment, the payment in an **amortized loan** (also called a *direct reduction loan*) partially pays off both principal and interest. Most mortgage and deed of trust loans are amortized loans. Regular periodic payments are made over a term of years, generally 15 or 30 years, and at the end of the term, the full amount of the principal and all interest due is reduced to zero.

> **MATH CONCEPTS Interest And Principal Credited From Amortized Payments**
>
> Lenders charge borrowers a certain percentage of the principal as interest for each year a debt is outstanding. The amount of interest due on any one payment date is calculated by computing the total yearly interest (based on the unpaid balance) and dividing that figure by the number of payments made each year.
>
> For example, assume the current outstanding balance of a loan is $70,000. The interest rate is 7.5% per year, and the monthly payment is $489.30. Based on these facts, the interest and principal due on the next payment are computed as shown:
>
> $70,000 loan balance × 0.075 annual interest rate = $5,250 annual interest
>
> $5,250 annual interest ÷ 12 months = $437.50 monthly interest
>
> $489.30 monthly payment − $437.50 monthly interest = $51.80 monthly principal
>
> $70,000 loan balance − $51.80 monthly principal = $69,948.20

This process is followed with each payment over the term of the loan. The same calculations are made each month, starting with the declining new balance figure from the previous month.

The most frequently used plan is the *fully amortized loan* (also called a *level-payment loan*). Under such a plan, the mortgagor pays a constant amount, usually monthly. The lender credits each payment first to the interest due, then to the principal amount of the loan. As a result, while each payment remains the same, the portion applied to repayment of the principal grows, and the interest due declines as the unpaid balance of the loan is reduced (see Figure 16.3). If the borrower pays additional amounts that are applied directly to the principal, the loan will amortize more quickly. This benefits the borrower because she will pay less interest if the principal is paid off before the end of its term.

Figure 16.3: Level-Payment Amortized Loan

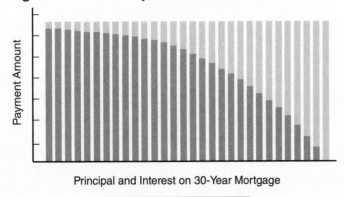

Principal and Interest on 30-Year Mortgage

Principal   Interest

In Figure 16.4, the effect of the term can be seen on the amortized payment of a $100,000 mortgage paid at 5% interest. What is of most concern to a home buyer is their ability to make the monthly payment fit within their PITI, now and in the future. There are many variables at play including the amount of the loan, the interest rate, and the term.

Figure 16.4: Effect of Term on Amortized Payments

10 years	15 years	25 years	30 years
$1,066.66	$790.79	$584.59	$536.82

Adjustable-Rate Mortgages (ARMs)

Adjustable-rate mortgages (ARMs) generally originate at one rate of interest, then fluctuate up or down during the loan term, based on some objective economic indicator. Because the interest rate on ARMs may change, the mortgagor's loan repayments also may change. Details of how and when the interest rate will change are included in the note. Common components of an ARM include the following:

- The *index* is an undeterminable economic indicator that is used to adjust the interest rate in the loan. Most indexes are tied to U.S. Treasury securities.

- The interest rate is usually the index rate plus a premium, called the *margin*. The margin represents the lender's cost of doing business.

- *Rate caps* limit the amount the interest rate may change. Most ARMs have two types of rate caps—periodic and aggregate. A *periodic rate cap* limits the amount the rate may increase at any one time. An *aggregate rate cap* limits the amount the rate may increase over the entire life of the loan.

- The mortgagor is protected from unaffordable individual payments by the *payment cap*, which sets a maximum amount for payments.

- The *adjustment period* establishes how often the rate may be changed, whether it is monthly, quarterly, or annually.

- Lenders may offer a *conversion option*, which permits the mortgagor to convert from an adjustable-rate to a fixed-rate loan at certain intervals during the life of the mortgage.

Figure 16.5 illustrates the effect interest rate fluctuations and periodic caps have on an adjustable-rate mortgage. Obviously, without rate caps and payment caps, a single mortgage's interest rate could fluctuate wildly over several adjustment periods, depending on the behavior of the index to which it is tied. In Figure 16.5, the borrower's rate changes from a low of 5.9% to a high of 9.5%. Such unpredictability makes personal financial planning difficult. On the other hand, if the loan had a periodic rate cap of 7.5%, the borrower's rate would never go above that level, regardless of the index's behavior. Similarly, a lender would want a floor to keep the rate from falling below a certain rate (here, 6.5%). The shaded area in the figure shows how caps and floors protect against dramatic changes in interest rates.

Figure 16.5: Adjustable-Rate Mortgage Graph

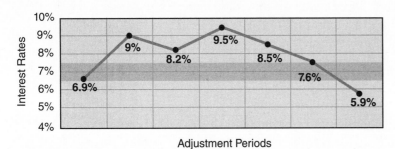

Balloon Payment Loans

When the periodic payments are not enough to fully amortize the loan by the time the final payment is due, the final payment is larger than the others—this is called a **balloon payment**. A balloon loan is a *partially amortized loan* because principal is still owed at the end of the term. It is frequently assumed that if payments are made promptly, the lender will extend the balloon payment for another limited term. The lender, however, is not legally obligated to grant this extension and can require payment in full when the note is due.

Growing Equity Mortgages (GEMs)

A **growing equity mortgage (GEM)** (also called a *rapid-payoff mortgage*) uses a fixed interest rate, but payments of principal are increased according to an index or a schedule. Thus, the total payment increases, and the loan is paid off more quickly. A GEM is most frequently used when the borrower's income is expected to keep pace with the increasing loan payments.

Reverse Mortgages

A **reverse mortgage** allows people 62 or older to borrow money against the equity they have built in their home. Reverse mortgages are the opposite of conventional mortgages in that the homeowner's equity diminishes as the loan amount increases. The money may be used for any purpose, and the borrowers may opt to receive the money in a lump sum, fixed monthly payments, an open line of credit, or other options. The borrower is charged a fixed rate of interest, and no payments are due until the property is sold or the borrower defaults, moves, or dies. Though reverse mortgages have been available for decades, they have become more widespread as people live longer and need more money. The FHA Home Equity Conversion Mortgage (HECM) is one of the more common reverse mortgages.

Nonrecourse Loans

A *nonrecourse loan* is one in which the borrower is not held personally responsible for the loan. The lender has no recourse against the borrower personally in the event of a default. Nonrecourse loans are common in those situations in which the lender is highly confident that the value of the property involved is itself sufficient security. Nonrecourse loans are more common in commercial and investment real estate transactions than in residential situations.

LOAN PROGRAMS

Mortgage loans are generally classified based on their **loan-to-value (LTV) ratios**. The LTV is the ratio of debt to value of the property (the sale price or the appraisal value, whichever is less). The lower the ratio of debt to value, the higher the down payment by the borrower. For the lender, the higher down payment means a more secure loan, which minimizes the lender's risk.

> **MATH CONCEPTS Determining LTV Ratios**
>
> Mortgage amount ÷ appraised value of the property = LTV ratio
>
> If a property has an appraised value of $100,000, with a loan of $90,000, the LTV ratio is 90%:
>
> $90,000 ÷ $100,000 = 90%

Debt-To-Income Ratios and Qualified Mortgages

A home purchased at a price of 350,000 ($70,000 down) on a 30-year loan at 6% interest will ultimately cost the consumer more than $590,000.

Mortgage terms and payment plans are the two biggest factors to consider when deciding whether to own or rent a home. To determine whether a prospective buyer can afford a certain purchase, most lenders use automated underwriting and credit scoring. In addition, the Consumer Financial Protection Bureau (CFPB) has issued rules regarding home mortgages in an attempt to protect consumers from getting in over their head. In order for a loan to be eligible for purchase on the secondary market by a government-sponsored enterprise (Fannie Mae or Freddie Mac), it must be a "qualified mortgage," which requires a debt-to-income ratio of 43%. The payments on all debts—total housing plus any long-term debts (anything taking more than 10 months to pay off) such as car payments, student loans, or other mortgages—cannot exceed 43% of the buyer's gross monthly income. Expenses such as insurance premiums, utilities, and routine medical care are not included in the 43% figure but are considered to be covered by the remaining 57% of the buyer's monthly income. (As of this writing, the director of the CFPB has sent a letter to Congress requesting the removal of the 43% requirement. As always, consult with a lender about what may or may not be required for financing.)

Conventional Loans

Conventional loans are viewed as the most secure loans because their LTV ratios are often lowest. Usually, the ratio is 80% of the value of the property or less because the borrower makes a down payment of at least 20%. The security for the loan is provided solely by the mortgage; the payment of the debt rests on the ability of the borrower to pay. In making such a loan, the lender relies primarily on its appraisal of the property. Information from credit reports that indicates the reliability of the prospective borrower is also important. No additional insurance or guarantee on the loan is necessary to protect the lender's interest. The government is not involved in conventional loans.

Lenders can set criteria by which a borrower and the collateral are evaluated to qualify for a loan. Today, the secondary mortgage market has a significant impact on borrower qualifications, standards for the collateral, and documentation procedures followed by lenders. Loans must meet strict criteria to be sold to Fannie Mae and Freddie Mac. Lenders still can be flexible in their lending decisions, but they may not be able to sell unusual loans in the secondary market.

Importance of Credit Scores

The creditworthiness of buyers is a key element in qualifying for a conventional loan. Underwriters consider several factors known about the applicant (e.g., credit scores and payment history) before determining whether to make the loan. Today, with the exception of FHA loans and a few nonconforming loans, the interest rate available to borrowers is largely based on credit scores, which range from 300 to 850. The higher the credit score, the lower the risk to the lender. Lenders offer these borrowers lower interest rates and may permit a smaller down payment. Lenders almost always require a higher interest rate and/or a larger down payment for those with lower scores. Today, the FHA is the best source for a mortgage loan for a borrower with a lower credit score.

Importance of Credit History

In addition to credit scores, underwriters consider from two to seven years of a potential borrower's repayment history, especially for rent and/or mortgage loans. A payment is considered late if it is more than 30 days past due. Underwriters especially look for bankruptcies, judgments, and foreclosures. Loan underwriters may make exceptions if the applicant can show specific reasons for the late payments (e.g., a death, divorce, or medical reasons). Applicants who are consistently more than 30 days late for rent or mortgage payments will most likely be ineligible for VA and FHA loans and other loans that are sold to Fannie Mae and Freddie Mac.

Private Mortgage Insurance

One way a borrower can obtain a mortgage loan with a lower down payment is by obtaining **private mortgage insurance (PMI)**. In a PMI program, the borrower purchases an insurance policy that provides the lender with funds in the event the borrower defaults on the loan. This allows the lender to assume more risk so that the LTV ratio is higher than for other conventional loans. The borrower purchases insurance from a private mortgage insurance company as additional security to insure the lender against borrower default. LTV ratios of up to 95% of the appraised value of the property may be possible with mortgage insurance; although this percentage may change with shifting economic climates and corresponding lending practices.

PMI protects the top 20 to 30% of the loan against borrower default. The borrower pays a monthly fee, which can be financed in with the loan, while the insurance is in force. Because only a portion of the loan is insured, the lender must allow the borrower to terminate the coverage once the loan is repaid to a certain level.

Under the Homeowners Protection Act of 1998, PMI must terminate automatically when the borrower reaches a 22% equity position based on the original value of the property at the time the loan was originated with no allowance for appreciation or depreciation if the loan was written after July 29, 1999, and the borrower is current on mortgage payments.

FHA-Insured Loans

The Federal Housing Administration (FHA), which operates under HUD, neither builds homes nor lends money. The common term **FHA loan** refers to a loan that is insured by the agency. The FHA insurance provides security to the lender in addition to the real estate. As with PMI, the FHA insures lenders against loss from borrower default. FHA loans must be made by FHA-approved lending institutions. (FHA qualifying ratios are 31% and 43%.)

The 203(b) fixed-rate loan is a popular FHA home loan, especially among first-time homebuyers. As of 2013, the 203(b) FHA loan will finance up to 97% of the borrower's loan. Other types of FHA loans are available, including one-year adjustable-rate mortgages, home improvement and rehabilitation loans, and loans for the purchase of condominiums. Specific standards for condominium complexes and the ratio of owner-occupants to renters must be met for a loan on a condominium unit to be financed through FHA insurance programs.

The borrower is charged a **mortgage insurance premium (MIP)** for all FHA loans. The *up-front premium* is charged at closing and can be financed into the mortgage loan.

The lender of an FHA-insured loan may charge discount points in addition to a loan origination fee. The payment of points is a matter of negotiation between the seller and the buyer.

VA-Guaranteed Loans

The Department of Veterans Affairs (VA) is authorized to guarantee loans to purchase or construct homes for eligible veterans and their spouses (including unremarried spouses of veterans whose deaths were service-related). Like the FHA loan, the **VA loan** is something of a misnomer. The VA does not normally lend money; rather, it guarantees loans made by lending institutions approved by the agency. (VA loans have only one ratio, the back end ratio at 41%.)

Specific service requirements must be satisfied before an individual is eligible for a VA loan, and to determine what portion of a mortgage loan the VA will guarantee, the veteran must apply for a certificate of eligibility. A VA loan guarantee is tied to the current conforming loan limit for Fannie Mae and Freddie Mac. Lenders will typically loan four times the guarantee (for example, a conforming loan of $424,100 ÷ 4 = $106,025 VA guarantee).

The VA also issues a **certificate of reasonable value (CRV)** for the property being purchased. The CRV states the property's current market value based on a VA-approved appraisal and places a ceiling on the amount of a VA loan allowed for the property. If the purchase price is greater than the amount cited in the CRV, the veteran may pay the difference in cash.

Agricultural Loan Programs

The Farm Service Agency (FSA) is an agency of the U.S. Department of Agriculture. The FSA offers programs to help families purchase or operate family farms. Through the Rural Housing and Community Development Service (RHCDS), it also provides loans to help families purchase or improve single-family homes in rural areas. FSA loan programs fall into two categories: guaranteed loans, made and serviced by private lenders and guaranteed for a specific percentage by the FSA, and loans made directly by the FSA.

The Federal Agricultural Mortgage Corporation, usually called Farmer Mac, is another government-sponsored enterprise that operates similarly to Fannie Mae and Freddie Mac but in the context of agricultural loans. It was created to improve the availability of long-term credit at stable interest rates to America's farmers, ranchers, and rural homeowners, businesses, and communities. Farmer Mac pools or bundles agricultural loans from lenders for sale as mortgage-backed securities.

OTHER FINANCING TECHNIQUES

A variety of other financing techniques exist to satisfy the diverse needs of individual borrowers.

Purchase-Money Mortgages

A **purchase money mortgage (PMM)** is a note and mortgage created at the time of purchase when the seller agrees to finance all or part of the purchase price and consists of a first or junior lien, depending on whether prior mortgage liens exist. Often called seller financing or owner financing, a PMM is often used when the buyer does not qualify for a typical lender loan. The buyer/borrower executes a note and mortgage at the time of purchase and the seller records the mortgage against the property. Payments are made to the seller, according to the terms of the note. If the buyer stops making payments, the seller has recourse to foreclose on the property.

EXAMPLE

A man wants to buy a farm for $200,000. He has a $40,000 down payment and agrees to assume an existing mortgage of $80,000. Because the buyer might not qualify for a new mortgage under the circumstances, the owner agrees to take back a purchase-money second mortgage in the amount of $80,000. At the closing, the buyer will execute a mortgage and note in favor of the owner, who will convey title to the buyer.

Package Loans

A **package loan** includes real and personal property. Package loans usually include furniture, drapes, kitchen range, refrigerator, dishwasher, washer, dryer, freezer, and other appliances as part of the sales price of the home.

Blanket Loans

A **blanket loan** covers more than one parcel or lot. It is usually used to finance subdivision developments. However, it can be used to finance the purchase of improved properties or to consolidate loans as well. A blanket loan usually includes a *partial release clause*, which permits the borrower to obtain the release of any one lot or parcel from the lien by repaying a certain amount of the loan. The lender issues a partial release for each parcel released from the mortgage lien. The release form includes a provision that the lien will continue to cover all other unreleased lots.

Wraparound Loans

A **wraparound loan** enables a borrower with an existing mortgage or deed of trust loan to obtain additional financing from a second lender without paying off the first loan. The second lender gives the borrower a new, increased loan at a higher interest rate and assumes payment of the existing loan. The total amount of the new loan includes the existing loan as well as the additional loan taken out by the borrower. The borrower makes payments to the new lender based on the total amount, and the new lender in turn makes payments on the original loan out of the borrowers' payments.

A wraparound mortgage can be used to refinance real property or finance the purchase of real property.

Open-End Loans

An **open-end loan** secures a note executed by the borrower to the lender. It also secures any future advances of funds made by the lender to the borrower. The interest rate on the initial amount borrowed is fixed, but interest on future advances may be charged at the market rate in effect. An open-end loan is often a less costly alternative to a home improvement loan. It allows the borrower to "open" the mortgage or deed of trust to increase the debt to its original amount, or the amount stated in the note, after the debt has been reduced by payments over a period of time. The mortgage usually states a maximum amount that can be secured, the terms and conditions under which the loan can be opened, and the provisions for repayment.

Construction Loans

A **construction loan** (also called *interim financing*) is made to finance the construction of improvements on real estate such as homes, apartments, and office buildings. The lender commits to the full amount of the loan but disburses the funds in payments called *draws* during construction. Draws are made to the developer or general contractor for that part of the construction work that has been completed since the previous payment. Before each payment, the lender has the right to inspect the work. The general contractor must provide the lender with adequate waivers that release all mechanic's lien rights for the work covered by the payment.

Construction loans are generally short-term (interim) financing. The borrower pays interest only on the monies that have actually been disbursed. The borrower is expected to arrange for a permanent loan (also called an *end loan* or *take-out loan*), which will repay or take out the construction financing lender when the work is completed.

Buydowns

A **buydown** is a way to temporarily (or permanently) lower the initial interest rate on a mortgage or deed of trust loan. Perhaps a homebuilder wishes to stimulate sales by offering a lower-than-market rate, or a first-time residential buyer may have trouble qualifying for a loan at the prevailing rates. In any case, a lump sum is paid in cash to the lender at the closing. The payment offsets (and so reduces) the interest rate and monthly payments during the mortgage's first few years.

Home Equity Loans

Home equity loans provide a source of funds using the equity built up in a home. The original mortgage loan remains in place, and the home equity loan is junior to the original lien. It is an alternative to refinancing and can be used for a variety of financial needs, such as to

- finance the purchase of expensive items;
- consolidate existing installment loans on credit card debt; and
- pay medical, education, home improvement, or other expenses.

A home equity loan can be taken out as a fixed loan amount or as a home equity line of credit (HELOC). With a HELOC, lenders extend a line of credit that borrowers can use at will. Borrowers receive their money by checks sent to them, deposits made into checking or savings accounts, or a book of drafts they can use up to their credit limits.

FINANCING LEGISLATION

The federal government regulates the lending practices of mortgage lenders through the Truth in Lending Act, the Equal Credit Opportunity Act, the Community Reinvestment Act, the Real Estate Settlement Procedures Act and the TILA and RESPA Integrated Disclosure Rule (TRID).

Truth in Lending Act (TILA)

The **Truth in Lending Act (TILA)**, often called *Regulation Z*, requires that credit institutions inform borrowers of all finance charges and the true interest rate before a loan is completed. Because of TILA, borrowers can compare the costs of various lenders and avoid the uninformed use of credit. Regardless of the loan amount, TILA applies when a credit transaction is secured by a residence. The regulation does not apply to business or commercial loans or to agricultural loans of any amount.

In the case of many consumer credit transactions covered by TILA, the borrower has three days in which to rescind the transaction by merely notifying the lender. However, this right of rescission does not apply to owner-occupied residential purchase money, first mortgage, or deed of trust loans. It does, however, apply to refinancing a home mortgage or to a home equity loan.

Advertising

TILA provides strict regulation of real estate advertisements in all media that refer to mortgage financing terms. General phrases like "flexible terms available" may be used, but if details are given, they must comply with the act. The APR—which is calculated based on all charges rather than the interest rate alone—must be stated.

Advertisements for buydowns or reduced-rate mortgages must show both the limited term to which the interest rate applies and the annual percentage rate. If a variable-rate mortgage is advertised, the advertisement must include

- the number and timing of payments,
- the amount of the largest and smallest payments, and
- a statement of the fact that the actual payments will vary between these two extremes.

Specific credit terms, such as *down payment, monthly payment, dollar amount of the finance charge*, or *term of the loan*, are called **trigger terms**. These terms may not be advertised unless the advertisement includes the following information:

- Cash price
- Required down payment
- Number, amounts, and due dates of all payments
- Annual percentage rate
- Total of all payments to be made over the term of the mortgage (unless the advertised credit refers to a first mortgage or deed of trust to finance the acquisition of a dwelling)

TILA provides severe financial penalties for noncompliance.

TRID and the Loan Estimate (LE)

The Loan Estimate shows the consumer the amount of money borrowed, the interest rate, the amount of interest paid, the number of payments, the individual amount of those payments, any associated costs for the loan, estimate of closing costs, and an estimate of the cash needed to close.

The LE must be delivered or placed in the mail no later than the third business day after receiving the consumer's "application." "Application" is defined as when the lender has received the following information regarding the loan:

- Address of the property
- Loan amount
- Income of the borrower
- Contract price for the property
- Social Security Number of the borrower

Equal Credit Opportunity Act (ECOA)

The **Equal Credit Opportunity Act (ECOA)** prohibits lenders and others who grant or arrange credit to consumers from discriminating against credit applicants on the basis of

- race,
- color,
- religion,
- national origin,
- sex,
- marital status,
- age (provided the applicant is of legal age), or
- dependence on public assistance.

Furthermore, lenders and other creditors must inform all rejected credit applicants of the principal reasons for the denial or termination of credit. The notice must be provided in writing within 30 days. ECOA also provides that a borrower is entitled to a copy of the appraisal report if the borrower paid for the appraisal.

Community Reinvestment Act (CRA)

Community reinvestment refers to the responsibility of financial institutions to help meet their communities' needs for low-income and moderate-income housing. Under the **Community Reinvestment Act (CRA)**, financial institutions are expected to meet the deposit and credit needs of their communities; participate and invest in local community development and rehabilitation projects; and participate in loan programs for housing, small businesses, and small farms.

Financial institutions are periodically reviewed by one of three federal financial supervisory agencies: the Office of the Comptroller of the Currency, the Federal Reserve's Board of Governors, or the FDIC. Financial institutions must post a public notice that their community reinvestment activities are subject to federal review, and they must make the results of these reviews public.

Real Estate Settlement Procedures Act (RESPA)

The **Real Estate Settlement Procedures Act (RESPA)** applies to any residential real estate transaction involving a new first mortgage loan. RESPA is designed to ensure that buyer and seller are fully informed of all settlement costs.

SUMMARY

The federal government affects real estate financing money and interest rates through the Fed's discount rate and reserve requirements; it also participates in the secondary mortgage market. The secondary market purchases and holds the loans as investments.

Loans commonly available today include fully amortized and straight loans as well as adjustable-rate mortgages (ARMs), growing equity mortgages (GEMS), balloon payment mortgages, and reverse mortgages.

Many mortgage and deed of trust loan programs exist, including conventional loans, those insured by the FHA or private mortgage insurance companies, or those guaranteed by the VA. FHA and VA loans must meet certain requirements for the borrower to obtain the benefits of government backing; it is this backing that induces the lender to lend its funds at the good rates that FHA and VA purchasers typically enjoy. The interest rates for these loans are often lower than those charged for conventional loans, and other requirements may be less stringent.

The Farm Service Agency (FSA) is part of the Department of Agriculture and provides programs to help families purchase or operate family farms, including the Rural Housing and Community Development Service (RHCDS) and Farmer Mac.

Other types of real estate financing include seller-financed purchase money mortgages or deeds of trust, blanket mortgages, package mortgages, wraparound mortgages, open-end mortgages, construction loans, and home equity loans.

The Truth in Lending Act requires that lenders inform prospective borrowers of all finance charges involved in a loan if real estate is the security. TRID requires the issuance of the Loan Estimate (LE) to the borrower as the vehicle to inform the borrower of the terms of the loan. Severe penalties are provided for noncompliance. The federal Equal Credit Opportunity Act prohibits creditors from discriminating against credit applicants on the basis of race, color, religion, national origin, sex, marital status, age, or dependence on public assistance. The Real Estate Settlement Procedures Act requires that lenders inform both buyers and sellers of all fees and charges required for the settlement or closing of residential real estate transactions.

UNIT 16 QUIZ

1. A buyer purchased a residence for $195,000. She made a down payment of $25,000 and agreed to assume the seller's existing mortgage, which had a current balance of $123,000. The buyer financed the remaining $47,000 of the purchase price by executing a mortgage and note to the seller. This type of loan by which the seller becomes the mortgagee is called a
   A. purchase money mortgage.
   B. wraparound mortgage.
   C. package mortgage.
   D. balloon note.

2. A buyer purchased a new residence for $175,000. He made a down payment of $15,000 and obtained a $160,000 mortgage loan. The builder of the house paid the lender 3% of the loan balance for the first year and 2% for the second year. This represented a total savings for the buyer of $8,000. What type of mortgage arrangement is this?
   A. Wraparound
   B. Buydown
   C. Package
   D. Blanket

3. Which of these is *NOT* a participant in the secondary market?
   A. Fannie Mae
   B. Ginnie Mae
   C. Freddie Mac
   D. Credit unions

4. A buyer purchased a home for cash 30 years ago. Today, the buyer receives monthly checks from a mortgage lender that supplement her income. The buyer *MOST* likely has obtained
   A. a shared-appreciation mortgage.
   B. an adjustable-rate mortgage.
   C. a reverse mortgage.
   D. an overriding deed of trust.

5. Which characteristic of a fixed-rate home loan that is amortized according to the original payment schedule is *TRUE*?
   A. The loan cannot be sold in the secondary market.
   B. The monthly payment amount will fluctuate each month.
   C. The interest rate change may be based on an index.
   D. The amount of interest to be paid is predetermined.

6. When the Fed raises its discount rate, which is likely to happen?
   A. The buyer's points will decrease.
   B. Mortgage money will become plentiful.
   C. Interest rates will rise.
   D. The percentage of ARMs will decrease.

7. In a loan that requires periodic payments that do not fully amortize the loan balance by the final payment, which term *BEST* describes the final payment?
   A. Adjustment
   B. Acceleration
   C. Variable
   D. Balloon

8. A developer received a loan that covers five parcels of real estate and provides for the release of the mortgage lien on each parcel when certain payments are made on the loan. This type of loan arrangement is called a
   A. purchase money loan.
   B. package loan.
   C. blanket loan.
   D. wraparound loan.

9. Funds for FHA loans are usually provided by
   A. the Federal Housing Administration.
   B. the Federal Reserve System.
   C. the seller.
   D. qualified lenders.

10. A home is purchased using a fixed-rate, fully amortized mortgage loan. Which statement regarding this mortgage is *TRUE*?
    A. Each mortgage payment amount is the same.
    B. A balloon payment will be made at the end of the loan.
    C. Each mortgage payment reduces the principal by the same amount.
    D. The principal amount in each payment is greater than the interest amount.

11. Which of these *BEST* defines the secondary market?
    A. Lenders who deal exclusively in second mortgages
    B. Where loans are bought and sold after they have been originated
    C. The major lender of residential mortgages and deeds of trust
    D. The major lender of FHA and VA loans

12. The primary activity of Freddie Mac is to
    A. guarantee mortgages with the full faith and credit of the federal government.
    B. act in tandem with Ginnie Mae to provide special assistance in times of tight money.
    C. buy and pool blocks of conventional mortgages.
    D. buy and sell VA and FHA mortgages.

13. A borrower obtains a $100,000 mortgage loan for 30 years at 7.5% interest. If the monthly payments of $902.77 are credited first to interest and then to principal, what will be the balance of the principal after the borrower makes the first payment?
    A. $99,097.32
    B. $99,772.00
    C. $100,000.00
    D. $99,722.23

14. A buyer borrowed $85,000 to be repaid in monthly installments of $823.76 at 11.5% annual interest. How much of the buyer's first-month payment was applied to reducing the principal amount of the loan?
    A. $8.15
    B. $91.80
    C. $9.18
    D. $814.58

15. If a lender agrees to make a loan based on an 80% LTV ratio, what is the amount of the loan if the property appraises for $114,500 and the sales price is $116,900?
    A. $91,600
    B. $83,200
    C. $91,300
    D. $92,900

16. A borrower wants to negotiate a $113,000 loan. Which of these loan terms would he need to accept to pay the least amount of interest over the life of the loan?
    A. 7% amortized over 30 years
    B. 8% amortized over 20 years
    C. 10% amortized over 25 years
    D. 9% amortized over 15 years

17. Which of these is the difference between the market value and any mortgages the borrower has on the property?
    A. Equitable interest
    B. Equitable title
    C. Equity
    D. Equitable lien

18. Which law requires that all advertising that references mortgage financing terms contain certain disclosures?
    A. Equal Credit Opportunity Act
    B. Truth in Lending Act
    C. Community Reinvestment Act
    D. Fair Housing Act

19. Which statement is *TRUE* regarding the Truth in Lending Act (TILA)?
    A. If a borrower is refinancing, TILA states that the borrower has five days to rescind the transaction by merely notifying the lender.
    B. Finance charges that must be disclosed include loan fees, service charges, and discount points.
    C. If an advertisement discloses the interest rate, then it has met truth-in-lending requirements.
    D. For the purposes of TILA, a creditor is a person who extends consumer credit more than five times each year.

20. In order to assist prospective buyers who lacked a down payment on their property, a married couple agreed to "take back paper" at the closing for a part of the purchase price. The document *MOST* likely used would be a
    A. reverse annuity mortgage.
    B. package mortgage.
    C. shared appreciation mortgage.
    D. purchase money mortgage.

UNIT
17

Leases

LEARNING OBJECTIVES

When you have completed this unit, you will be able to accomplish the following.

> Identify the four types of leasehold estates.
> Describe the requirements and general conditions of a valid lease.
> Distinguish the various types of leases.
> Explain the rights of landlords and tenants in an eviction proceeding and the effect of protenant legislation and civil rights laws on the landlord-tenant relationship.

KEY TERMS

actual eviction	gross lease	net lease
assignment	ground lease	nondisturbance clause
cash rent	holdover tenancy	percentage lease
constructive eviction	implied warranty of	rental-finding service
estate at sufferance	habitability	reversionary right
estate at will	lease	right of first refusal
estate for years	leasehold estate	security deposit
estate from period to	lease purchase	sharecropping
period	month-to-month tenancy	sublease

OVERVIEW

There are millions of renters in the United States. Although some owners manage their own properties (a real estate license is not required to do so), many are professionally managed. In Illinois, property management requires a real estate license, and an individual real estate licensee must perform property management services under the supervision of the sponsoring broker. Licensees should be aware of their local rental market in order to better assist buyers who may not qualify to buy their own property, to locate an appropriate property for an investor-buyer, or to manage their own portfolios. In any case, real estate licensees should be aware of leases, management agreements, landlord-tenant issues, and more.

LEASING REAL ESTATE

A **lease** is a contract between an owner of real estate (the *lessor*) and a tenant (the *lessee*). It is a contract to transfer the lessor's rights to exclusive possession and use of the property to the tenant for a specified period. The lease establishes the length of time the contract is to run, the amount the lessee is to pay for use of the property, and other rights and obligations of the parties. The landlord retains a **reversionary right** to possession after the lease term expires. The lessor's interest is called a *leased fee estate plus reversionary right*.

The statute of frauds in Illinois requires that lease agreements be in writing to be enforceable if they are for more than one year. The written rule also applies to leases for one year or less that will not be performed within one year of the contract date. Verbal leases for one year or less that can be performed within a year of their making are enforceable. Written leases should be signed by both lessor and lessee.

LEASEHOLD ESTATES

A tenant's right to possess real estate for the term of the lease is called a **leasehold estate** (also called a *less-than-freehold estate*). A leasehold is generally considered personal property. Just as there are several types of freehold (ownership) estates, there are different kinds of leasehold estates (see Figure 17.1).

Figure 17.1: Leasehold Estates Illustration

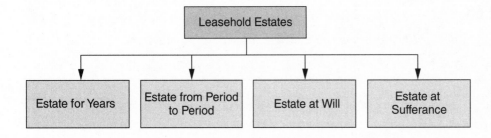

Estate for Years

Tenancy for years = any definite period

An **estate for years** (also called a *tenancy for years* or *fixed-term tenancy*) is a leasehold estate that continues for a definite period of time. That period may be years, months, weeks, or even days. An estate for years always has specific beginning and ending dates.

When the estate expires, the lessee is required to vacate the premises and surrender possession to the lessor. No notice is required to terminate the estate for years because the lease agreement states a specific expiration date. When the expiration date comes, the lease expires, and the tenant's rights are extinguished.

If both parties agree, the estate for years may be terminated before the expiration date. Otherwise, neither party may terminate without showing that the lease agreement has been breached. Any extension of the tenancy requires that a new contract be negotiated.

As is characteristic of all leases, a tenancy for years gives the lessee the right to occupy and use the leased property according to the terms and covenants contained in the lease agreement. It must be remembered that a lessee has the right to use the premises for the entire lease term. That right is unaffected by the original lessor's death or sale of the property unless the lease states otherwise. If the original lease provides for an option to renew, no further negotiation is required; the tenant merely exercises his option.

Estate from Period to Period

Estate from period to period = indefinite term; automatically renewing

An estate from period to period (or *periodic tenancy*) is created when the landlord and the tenant enter into an agreement for an indefinite time—that is, the lease does not contain a specific expiration date. Such a tenancy is created for a specific payment period—for example, month to month, week to week, or year to year—but continues indefinitely until proper notice of termination is given. Rent is payable at definite intervals. An estate from period to period is characterized by continuity because it is automatically renewable under the original terms of the agreement until one of the parties gives notice to terminate. In effect, the payment and acceptance of rent extend the lease for another period. A month-to-month tenancy, for example, is created when a tenant takes possession with no definite termination date and pays monthly rent.

An estate from period to period also might be created when a tenant with an estate for years remains in possession (estate at sufferance) after the lease term expires. If the landlord accepts the rent and no new lease agreement is made, a **holdover tenancy** is created. The landlord's acceptance of the rent is usually considered conclusive proof of acceptance of the holdover tenancy. Some leases stipulate that in the absence of a renewal agreement, a tenant who holds over does so as a month-to-month tenant.

In Illinois, a holdover tenancy created in such a fashion becomes an estate from period to period based on the original term.

To terminate an estate from period to period, either the landlord or the tenant must give proper notice. The form and timing of the notice are usually established by state statute. Normally, the notice must be given one period in advance; that is, to terminate an estate from week to week, one week's notice is required, and to terminate an estate from month to month, one month's notice is required. For an estate from year to year, however, the requirements vary from two to six months' notice.

The following notices are required by Illinois statute:

- *Tenancy from year to year.* At least 60 days' written notice is required at any time within the four-month period before the last 60 days of the lease period.

- *Tenancy from month to month.* In any periodic estate having a term of less than year to year but greater than week to week, 30 days' written notice is required.

- *Tenancy from week to week.* Seven days' written notice is required.

- *Farm tenancies from year to year.* Parties must give at least four months' written notice to terminate and may do so only at the end of the period. To vacate March 1, farm tenancy notice must be given by November 1.

Estate at Will

Estate at will = indefinite term; possession with landlord's consent

An estate at will (also called a *tenancy at will*) gives the tenant the right to possess property with the landlord's consent for an unspecified or uncertain term. An estate at will is a tenancy of indefinite duration; it continues until it is terminated by either party giving proper notice. An estate at will may be created by express agreement or by operation of law and is automatically terminated by the death of either the landlord or the tenant. During the existence of an estate at will, the tenant has all the rights and obligations of a lessor-lessee relationship, including the duty to pay rent at regular intervals.

As a practical matter, an estate at will is rarely used in a written agreement and is viewed skeptically by the courts. It is usually interpreted as an estate from period to period, with the period being defined by the interval of rental payments.

Estate at Sufferance

Estate at sufferance = tenant's previously lawful possession continued without landlord's consent

An estate at sufferance (also called a ***tenancy at sufferance***) arises when a tenant who lawfully possessed real property continues in possession of the premises without the landlord's consent after the rights expire (a holdover). This estate can arise when a tenant for years fails to surrender possession at the lease's expiration and continues until the landlord completes the eviction process. An estate at sufferance also can occur by operation of law when a borrower continues in possession after a foreclosure sale and beyond the redemption period's expiration.

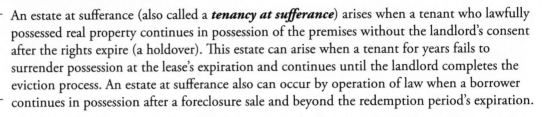

Under Illinois law, a tenancy at sufferance arises when a tenant remains in possession after the term of the lease expires. A landlord has a choice to evict the tenant as a trespasser or treat the tenant as a holdover tenant. If treating the tenant as a holdover tenant, the landlord is entitled to charge double rent (735 ILCS 5/9-202). Note that the word "entitled" is key. The landlord is entitled to seek double the rent through civil action.

LEASE AGREEMENTS

Most states require no special wording to establish the landlord-tenant relationship. The lease may be written, oral, or implied, depending on the circumstances and the requirements of the statute of frauds. The law of the state where the real estate is located must be followed to ensure the validity of the lease.

Requirements of a Valid Lease

A lease is a form of contract. To be valid, a lease must meet essentially the same requirements as any other contract. They are as follows:

- *Capacity to contract.* The parties must have the legal capacity to contract.
- *Legal objectives.* The objectives of the lease must be legal.
- *Offer and acceptance.* The parties must reach a mutual agreement on all the terms of the contract.
- *Consideration.* The lease must be supported by valid consideration. Rent is the normal consideration given for the right to occupy the leased premises. However, the payment of rent is not essential as long as consideration was granted in creating the lease itself. Sometimes, for example, this consideration is labor performed on the property. Because a lease is a contract, it is not subject to subsequent changes in terms unless these changes are executed in the same manner as the original lease.

The leased premises should be clearly described. The legal description of the real estate should be used if the lease covers land, such as a ground lease. If the lease is for a part of a building, such as an apartment, the space itself or the apartment designation should be described specifically. If supplemental space is to be included, the lease should clearly identify it. Leases are available from organizations such as the Chicago Association of REALTORS®.

IN PRACTICE

Preprinted lease agreements are usually better suited to residential leases. Commercial leases are generally more complex, have different legal requirements, and may include complicated calculations of rent and maintenance costs. Letters of intent are often prepared in advance of a commercial lease by the licensees representing the respective parties (see Figure 17.2). This letter of intent generally sets forth the basic agreement between the parties that both parties' attorneys can then use to prepare the lease from. Commercial leases and complex residential leases should only be drafted by a licensed attorney.

Figure 17.2: Sample Letter of Intent

February 16, 2017

Mr. Robert Smith, Broker
The Smith Group
123 Appleton Way
Tinseltown, Illinois 12345

RE: Parkway Ventures

Dear Mr. Smith:

On behalf of ABC Development, we are pleased to present the following Letter of Intent to Parkway Ventures (referred to hereafter as Tenant) for your review and analysis.

BUILDING:	Mitchell Towers
LANDLORD:	ABC Development owners and operators of Mitchell Towers since 2000.
PREMISES:	Suite 1000, approximately 950 rentable square feet.
LEASE TERM:	Two years (2 years).
RENT & LEASE COMMENCEMENT:	April 1, 2017, or upon substantial completion. Rent shall escalate on every 12-month anniversary.
GROSS RENTAL RATE:	$19.00 per rentable square foot.
GROSS RENTAL RATE ESCALATION:	The gross rental rate shall escalate by $0.50 annually per year cumulative commencing Year 2 of the lease term.
SECURITY DEPOSIT:	Tenant shall provide 1 month's gross rent at the time of lease execution.
REAL ESTATE TAXES & OPERATING EXPENSES:	Tenant shall pay its proportionate share of annual real estate taxes and annual operating expenses in excess of a 2017 base year. Current operating and tax estimates for the 2017 year are $12.00. The 2016 actual operating and taxes were $11.60.
ELECTRICITY:	The premises are separately metered for lights and outlets. Tenant shall receive a monthly electricity invoice from the building.
TENANT IMPROVEMENT:	Tenant shall accept the premises in "AS IS" condition. Tenant shall be responsible for all phone and data work.
AMENITIES:	The building is equipped with many amenities including but not limited to fiber optics, indoor parking, and a conference center.
AFTER-HOURS HVAC SUPPLEMENTAL SYSTEM:	Landlord currently provides heating, ventilation, and air-conditioning (HVAC) during regular business hours, which is from 6:00 am to 6:00 pm weekdays and from 6:00 am to 2:00 pm on Saturdays. HVAC required at times other than these mentioned shall be provided at an extra cost to the tenant.
SECURITY:	Landlord provides 24-hour manned security 365 days per year.
JANITORIAL:	The building provides office cleaning by a professional cleaning company five nights per week. The building shall provide cleaning to the levels provided in Class "A" properties.
TELECOMMUNICATIONS FACILITIES:	Landlord shall allow Tenant the right to choose its own telephone and data vendor and will allow said vendor reasonable access to the Tenant premises.
LEASE COMMISSION:	Landlord recognizes that Tenant is represented by The Smith Group, a real estate company. In addition, Landlord shall not be subject to any outside claim presented by any other "real estate company" on this transaction. Tenant shall indemnify Landlord from any such claim. A separate leasing commission agreement shall be executed as part of this transaction at the appropriate time.
CONFIDENTIALITY:	The information contained herein is for the express purpose of consummating a lease transaction with Tenant.
EXPIRATION:	This Lease proposal shall be null and void in the event that the Landlord has not entered into a lease with Tenant within thirty (30) days from the date hereof.
EXCULPATION:	This Letter of Intent is non-binding and is subject to prior leasing, the approval of Landlord, and the mutual execution and delivery of a fully executed lease satisfactory to both Landlord and Tenant. This Letter of Intent shall supersede previous Letters of Intent submitted.

Best Regards,
John Doe
ABC Development

Possession of Premises

The lessor, as the owner of the real estate, is usually bound by the implied covenant of quiet enjoyment—the presumed promise by the lessor that the lessee may take possession of the premises. The landlord further guarantees that he will not interfere in the tenant's possession or use of the property.

The lease may allow the landlord to enter the property to perform maintenance, to make repairs, or for other stated purposes. The tenant's permission is usually required.

Use of Premises

A lessor may restrict a lessee's use of the premises through provisions included in the lease. *Use restrictions* are particularly common in leases for stores or commercial space. For example, a lease may provide that the leased premises are to be used "only as a real estate office and for no other purpose." In the absence of such clear limitations, a lessee may use the premises for any lawful purpose.

Term of Lease

The term of a lease is the period for which the lease will run. It should be stated precisely, including the beginning and ending dates, together with a statement of the total period of the lease. For example, a lease might run "for a term of 30 years beginning June 1, 2017, and ending May 31, 2047." A perpetual lease for an inordinate amount of time or an indefinite term will usually be ruled invalid. However, if the language of the lease and the surrounding circumstances clearly indicate that the parties intended such a term, the lease will be binding on the parties. Some states prohibit leases that run for 100 years or more.

Security Deposit

Most leases require that the tenant provide some form of **security deposit** to be held by the landlord during the lease term. If the tenant defaults on payment of rent or damages the premises, the lessor may keep all or part of the deposit to compensate for the loss.

Other safeguards against nonpayment of rent may include an advance rental payment, contracting for a lien on the tenant's property, or requiring that the tenant have a third person guarantee payment.

Landlords who receive security deposits on residential leases of units in properties containing five or more units may not withhold any part of a security deposit as compensation for property damage unless they give the tenant an itemized statement listing the alleged damage. This statement must be delivered within 30 days of the date on which the premises are vacated. If the statement is not furnished, the landlord must return the entire security deposit within 45 days of the premises being vacated. Any landlord who is found by a court to have failed to comply with this requirement, or who has done so in bad faith, must pay the tenant double the security deposit due plus court costs and attorney's fees.

Illinois lessees are entitled to receive annual interest on their security deposits. As of 2016, the rate of interest on security deposits under rental agreements in Chicago is 0.01%. Landlords who receive security deposits on residential leases of units in properties of 25 or more units, on deposits held for more than six months, are required to pay interest from the date of the deposit at a rate equal to the interest paid on a minimum deposit passbook savings account of the state's largest commercial bank (measured by total assets) with its main banking facilities located in Illinois. Any landlord who is found by a court to have willfully withheld interest on a tenant's security deposit must pay the tenant an amount equal to the security deposit plus the tenant's court costs and attorney's fees. Note that Chicago security deposit rules and rates for residential landlords differ under the Residential Landlord and Tenant Ordinance.

IN PRACTICE

A lease should specify whether a payment is a security deposit or an advance rental. If it is a security deposit, the tenant is usually not entitled to apply it to the final month's rent. If it is an advance rental, the landlord must treat it as income for tax purposes.

Improvements

Neither the landlord nor the tenant is required to make any improvements to the leased property. The tenant may, however, make improvements with the landlord's permission. In most residential properties, any alterations become the property of the landlord. However, many commercial leases permit tenants to install trade fixtures (articles attached to a rental space that are required by tenants to conduct their businesses). Trade fixtures may be removed before the lease expires, provided the tenant restores the premises to their previous condition, with allowance for the wear and tear of normal use.

Accessibility

The federal Fair Housing Act makes it illegal to discriminate against prospective tenants on the basis of physical disability. Tenants with disabilities must be permitted to make reasonable modifications to a property at their own expense. However, if the modifications would interfere with a future tenant's use, the landlord may require that the premises be restored to their original condition at the end of the lease term at the tenant's expense.

IN PRACTICE

The Americans with Disabilities Act (ADA) applies to commercial, nonresidential property in which public goods or services are provided. The ADA requires that such properties either be free of architectural barriers or provide reasonable accommodations for persons with disabilities.

Maintenance of Premises

Lessors of residential property are required to maintain dwelling units in a habitable condition. Landlords must make any necessary repairs to common areas such as hallways, stairs, and elevators, and they must maintain safety features such as fire sprinklers and smoke alarms. The tenant does not have to make any repairs but must return the premises in the same condition they were received, with allowances for ordinary wear and tear. Lessees of commercial and industrial properties, however, usually maintain the premises and are often responsible for making their own repairs.

The Illinois Supreme Court first confirmed the concept of an **implied warranty of habitability** in residential tenancies in 1972. Since then, Illinois courts have repeatedly confirmed and amplified the warranty. A landlord must deliver and maintain throughout the duration of the lease any residential leasehold free from defects that would render the use of the dwelling "unsafe or unsanitary" and unfit for human occupancy. Nothing may be present on the premises that could seriously endanger the life, health, or safety of the tenant.

The conditions that violate the implied warranty of habitability vary depending on the state and jurisdiction where the premises are located. Generally, a landlord can be in violation by failing to

■ provide access to drinkable water and hot water, heat during cold weather, working electricity, a smoke detector, and a working bathroom and toilet;

■ remediate rodent or insect infestations; or

■ correct building code violations.

A tenant must give the landlord notice of a defect and reasonable time in which to cure it. As a remedy, the tenant may choose to

■ move out and terminate the lease if repairs are not made within a reasonable time (known as constructive eviction),

■ stay and repair the problem and deduct the repair costs from the next month's rent (repair costs cannot exceed one month's rent), or

■ sue for any damages resulting from the defective condition.

Destruction of Premises

The obligation to pay rent for damaged or destroyed premises differs depending on the type of property and the lease. Usually, residential tenants are permitted to reduce their rent payments in proportion to the amount of space they are unable to use. Likewise, tenants who lease only part of a building, such as office or commercial space, generally are not required to continue to pay rent after the leased premises are destroyed. In fact, in some states, if the property was destroyed as a result of the landlord's negligence, the tenant can recover damages.

On the other hand, tenants who have constructed buildings on leased land, often agricultural or industrial land, are still obligated for the payment of rent if the improvements are damaged or destroyed. If the buildings are destroyed, these tenants must turn to their insurance companies to deal with their loss of the improvement.

Assignment and Subleasing

Lease **assignment** occurs when a tenant transfers all of his leasehold interests to another person. The new tenant is legally obligated for all the promises the original tenant made in the lease.

On the other hand, when a tenant transfers less than all the leasehold interests by leasing them to a new tenant, the original tenant has **subleased** (or *sublet*) the property. The original tenant remains responsible for rent being paid by the new tenant and for any damage done to the rental during the lease term. The new tenant is responsible only to the original tenant to pay the rent due. Most leases prohibit a lessee from assignment or subleasing without the lessor's consent. This permits the lessor to retain control over the occupancy of the leased premises. As a rule, the lessor must not unreasonably withhold consent. The sublessor's (original lessee's) interest in the real estate is called a *sandwich lease* (see Figure 17.3). In both assignments and subleases, details of the new arrangement should be in writing.

Figure 17.3: Assignment vs. Subletting

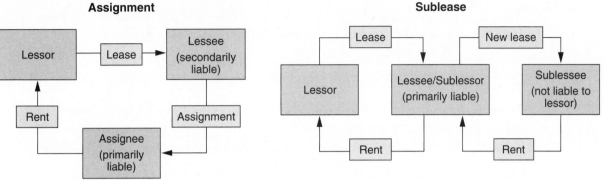

Recording a Lease

It is usually unnecessary to record a lease; although most states do allow a lease to be recorded in the county in which the property is located. Leases of three years or longer often are recorded as a matter of course, and some states require that long-term leases be recorded, especially when the lessee intends to mortgage the leasehold interest.

In some states, only a memorandum of lease is filed. A *memorandum of lease* gives notice of the interest but does not disclose the terms of the lease. Only the names of the parties and a description of the property are included.

Creditors of the property owner and purchasers who do not have actual notice of a leasehold interest are considered to have legal notice of a lease if the lease, or a memorandum of it, is recorded with the recorder or registrar of the county in which the property is located.

Nondisturbance Clause

A **nondisturbance clause** is a mortgage clause stating that in the event that the mortgagee forecloses on the mortgagor-lessor's building, the mortgagee agrees not to terminate the tenancies of lessees who pay their rent.

Options

A lease may contain an *option* that grants the lessee the privilege of renewing the lease (called a *renewal option*). However, the lessee must give notice of his intention to exercise the option. Some leases grant the lessee the option to purchase the leased premises (called a *purchase option*). This option normally allows the tenant the right to purchase the property at a predetermined price within a certain period, possibly the lease term. The lease might also contain a **right of first refusal** clause, allowing the tenant the opportunity to buy the property before the owner accepts an offer from another party.

IN PRACTICE

All of these general statements concerning provisions of a lease are controlled by the actual terms of the agreement and state law. Great care must be exercised in reading the entire lease document before signing it because every clause in the lease has an economic and legal impact on either the landlord or the tenant. While preprinted lease forms are available, they are not necessarily suitable for every situation. When complicated lease situations arise, legal counsel should be sought.

BASIC TYPES OF LEASES

There are three basic types of leases: gross lease, net lease, and percentage lease. The type of lease that exists depends on the manner in which rent is determined.

Gross Lease

Gross lease = lessee pays basic rent.

In a **gross lease**, the tenant pays a fixed rent and the landlord pays all taxes, assessments, insurance, maintenance and utilities connected with the property (usually called property charges or operating expenses). This is the typical rent structure involved in apartment rentals.

Net Lease

Net lease = lessee pays basic rent plus all or some property charges

In a **net lease**, the tenant pays all or some of the operating expenses in addition to the rent. The monthly rental constitutes net income for the landlord after operating costs have been paid. Leases for commercial or industrial buildings and the land on which they are located are usually net leases.

In a *triple-net lease* (also called a *net-net-net lease*), the tenant pays all operating and other expenses in addition to rent. These expenses include taxes, assessments, insurance, maintenance, utilities, and other charges related to the premises.

Percentage Lease

Percentage lease = lessee pays basic rent plus percent of gross sales (may pay property charges)

A gross lease or a net lease may be a **percentage lease**. In a percentage lease, the rent is based on a minimum fixed rental fee plus a percentage of the gross income generated by the tenant doing business on the leased property. This type of lease is usually used for retail businesses and restaurants. The percentage charged is negotiable and varies depending on the nature of the business, the location of the property, and general economic conditions.

> **MATH CONCEPTS   Calculating Rents**
>
> Percentage leases call for a minimum monthly rent payment plus payment of a percentage of the tenant's gross sales income exceeding a stated annual amount. For example, a lease might require minimum rent of $1,300 per month, plus 5% of the business's sales exceeding $160,000 (known as the Breakpoint). On an annual sales volume of $250,000, the annual rent is calculated as follows:
>
> $1,300 per month × 12 months = $15,600
>
> $250,000 − $160,000 = $90,000
>
> $90,000 × 0.05 (5%) = $4,500
>
> $15,600 base rent + $4,500 percentage rent = $20,100 total annual rent

OTHER LEASE ARRANGEMENTS

Variable Lease

Several types of leases allow for increases in the rental charges during the lease period. One of these is the *graduated lease*, which provides for specified rent increases at set future dates. Another is the *index lease*, which allows rent to be increased or decreased periodically, based on changes in the consumer price index or some other economic indicator.

Ground Lease

When a landowner leases unimproved land to a tenant who agrees to erect a building on the land, the lease is usually called a **ground lease**. Ground leases usually involve separate ownership of the land and buildings. These leases must be for a long enough term to make the transaction desirable to the tenant investing in the building, and often run for terms of 50 to 99 years. Ground leases are generally net leases—the lessee must pay rent on the ground as well as real estate taxes, insurance, maintenance, and utilities.

Lease Purchase

A **lease purchase** is used when a tenant wants to purchase the property but is unable to do so. Perhaps the tenant cannot obtain favorable financing or clear title, or the tax consequences of a current purchase would be unfavorable. In this arrangement, the purchase agreement is the primary consideration, and the lease is secondary. Part of the periodic rent is applied toward the purchase price of the property until that price is reduced to an amount for which the tenant can obtain financing or purchase the property outright, depending on the terms of the lease-purchase agreement.

Sale-and-Leaseback Arrangement

In a *sale-and-leaseback arrangement*, the owners of property sell the property and then lease it back again for an agreed period. A sale-and-leaseback is often used when extra capital is needed on a construction project. The original owners pull out their equity to use on other projects and reduce their taxable income when they pay rent to the new owner. The new owner now has a reliable source of rental income for an extended time.

Agricultural Lease

Agricultural landowners often lease their land to tenant farmers, who provide the labor to produce and bring in a crop. A landowner can be paid by a tenant in one of two ways: as an agreed-on rental amount in cash in advance (**cash rent**), or as a percentage of the profits or losses from the sale of the crop when it is sold (**sharecropping**).

DISCHARGE OF LEASES

As with any contract, a lease is discharged when the contract terminates. Termination can occur when all parties have fully performed their obligations under the agreement, or when the parties agree to cancel the lease. For example, if the tenant offers to surrender the leasehold interest and the landlord accepts the tenant's offer, the lease is terminated.

A tenant who simply abandons leased property remains liable for compliance with the terms of the lease—including payment of rent. If the landlord intends to sue for unpaid rent, most states require an attempt to mitigate damages by attempting to re-rent the premises in order to limit the amount owed by the defaulting tenant.

The lease generally does not terminate if the parties die or if the property is sold. There are two exceptions to this general rule:

- A lease from the owner of a *life estate* ends when the tenant's life ends.
- The death of either party terminates a *tenancy at will*.

In all other cases, the heirs of a deceased landlord are bound by the terms of existing leases.

If leased real estate is sold or otherwise conveyed, the new landlord takes the property subject to the rights of the tenants. A lease agreement may, however, contain language that permits a new landlord to terminate existing leases. Such a clause, commonly called a *sale clause*, requires that the tenants be given some period of notice before the termination. A tenancy may also be terminated by operation of law, as in a bankruptcy or condemnation proceeding.

Breach of Lease

When a tenant breaches any lease provision, the landlord may sue the tenant to obtain a judgment to cover past-due rent, damages to the premises, or other defaults. Likewise, when a landlord breaches any lease provision, the tenant is entitled to certain remedies. The rights and responsibilities of the landlord-tenant relationship are governed primarily by state law.

If a tenant defaults on the payment of rent, the landlord has two options:

■ The landlord may elect to serve the tenant with five days' written notice, demanding payment of the delinquent rent within five days after the notice is received. If the tenant fails to pay the rent, the landlord may terminate the lease automatically and sue for possession without further notice. If the tenant pays the past-due rent, the lease continues in full force.

■ Alternatively (and in cases in which the tenant's breach is other than by nonpayment of rent), the landlord may terminate the tenancy by serving the tenant with 10 days' written notice, including a demand for possession. After the 10-day period expires, the landlord may sue for possession without further notice, even if the default is cured.

Landlord's Remedies—Actual Eviction

When a tenant breaches a lease or improperly retains leased premises, the landlord may regain possession through a legal process called **actual eviction**. The landlord must serve notice on the tenant before commencing the lawsuit.

In Illinois, a landlord seeking actual eviction of a tenant must file an action called a *forcible entry and detainer*. It can be used when a tenancy has expired by default, by its terms, by operation of law, or by proper notice. The suit should be filed in the circuit court of the county in which the property is located.

If the court rules in favor of the landlord, a *judgment for possession* (and money damages) will be entered, and an *order of possession* will be issued by the clerk of the court. The tenant must then leave peaceably, removing all of his property from the premises. Traditionally, however, if a residential tenant personally appears in court and the landlord prevails, the court will delay issuing the order for a reasonable time to allow the tenant to find alternative housing.

When a tenant refuses to vacate peaceably after a judgment for possession has been entered, the landlord must deliver the order to the sheriff, who will forcibly evict the tenant. The landlord then has the right to re-enter and regain possession of the property.

Until a judgment for possession is issued, the landlord must be careful not to harass the tenant in any manner, such as locking the tenant out of the property, impounding the tenant's possessions, or disconnecting the utilities (such as electricity and natural gas). Illinois landlords have no right to self-help; that is, they may not forcibly remove a tenant without following the proper legal procedures.

FAIR HOUSING AND CIVIL RIGHTS LAWS

Fair housing and civil rights laws affect landlords and tenants just as they do sellers and purchasers. All persons must have access to housing of their choice without any differentiation in the terms and conditions because of their race, color, religion, familial status, disability, or gender. State and local municipalities may have their own fair housing laws that add protected classes such as age and sexual orientation. Withholding an apartment that is available for rent, segregating certain persons in separate sections of an apartment complex or parts of a building, and charging different amounts for rent or security deposits to persons in the protected classes all constitute violations of the law.

The Illinois Human Rights Act extends the list of protected classes for Illinois "to secure for all individuals within Illinois the freedom from discrimination against any individual because of his or her race, color, religion, sex, national origin, ancestry, age, order of protection status, marital status, physical or mental disability, military status, sexual orientation, or unfavorable discharge from military service in connection with employment, real estate transactions, access to financial credit, and the availability of public accommodations" (775 ILCS 5/1-102(a)).

Also, many municipalities have local ordinances expanding protected classes. Licensees should be familiar with these local laws. For example, source of income is a protected class in the city of Chicago and all of Cook County, and refusing to rent to a Section 8 voucher holder is discrimination.

ENVIRONMENTAL HAZARDS AND RENTERS

The Residential Lead-Based Paint Hazard Reduction Act, also called Title X, focused more strongly on disclosure and REALTOR® liability. This federal law supersedes any state laws that are not as strong. Real estate licensees leasing properties built before 1978 must ensure that landlords disclose any possible lead-based paint or related hazards. This disclosure form must be completed even in the case of an oral lease agreement. Once an offer for lease is received, the licensee representing the lessor (landlord) must ensure that the landlord provides the following to the tenant:

- The EPA-approved pamphlet Protect Your Family From Lead In Your Home
- Any known information concerning the presence of lead-based paint or related hazards in the property (landlords of multiunit buildings must include information about common areas and other units when the information was obtained via a building-wide evaluation)
- A "Lead Warning Statement" in or attached to the contract

The Lead Poisoning Prevention Act (410 ILCS 45/) requires that the owner of any residential building cited by the state as a lead-paint hazard give prospective tenants written notice of the danger unless the owners have a certificate of compliance. This act is bolstered in its scope by the federal legislation noted earlier. When a mitigation order is issued to an owner of a building containing lead hazards, the owner has 90 days to eliminate the hazard in a manner prescribed by state law, or 30 days if occupied by a child under age six or by a pregnant woman.

Illinois also has a Radon Awareness Act which requires landlords to disclose any knowledge of Radon gas on the premises. Radon is a naturally occurring odorless and colorless gas, the second leading cause of lung cancer in the United States. The disclosure is only required for dwelling units below the third story above ground level.

REGULATION OF THE RENTAL INDUSTRY

Rental-Finding Services

Because of the nationwide demand for rental housing, there has been a rapid growth in the rental-finding service industry. A **rental-finding service** is any business that finds, attempts to find, or offers to find for any person for consideration a unit of rental real estate or a lessee for a unit of rental real estate not owned or leased by the business.

Rental-finding services are required to enter into written contracts with the parties for whom their services are to be performed. The contract must clearly disclose

- the term of the contract;
- the total amount to be paid for the services;
- the service's policy regarding the refunding of fees paid in advance, and the conditions under which refunds may or may not be paid (printed in a larger typeface than the rest of the contract);
- the type of rental unit, geographic area, and price range the prospective tenant desires;
- a detailed statement of the services to be performed;
- a statement that the contract will be void, and all fees paid in advance will be refunded, if the information provided regarding possible rental units available is not current or accurate (that is, if a rental unit is listed that has not been available for more than two days); and
- a disclosure that information regarding possible rental units may be up to two days old.

Regarding any individual rental unit, a prospective tenant must be provided with

- the name, address, and telephone number of the owner;
- a description of the unit, monthly rent, and security deposit required;
- a description of the utilities available and included in the rent;
- the occupancy date and lease term;
- a statement describing the source of the information; and
- any other information the prospective tenant may reasonably be expected to need.

A rental-finding service may not list or advertise any rental unit without the express written authority of the unit's owner or agent.

A real estate licensee who violates any of these conditions may be construed to have demonstrated incompetence and may be subject to appropriate disciplinary measures.

Any person or business entity that operates a rental-finding service in Illinois must obtain a real estate license and comply with all provisions of the Real Estate License Act of 2000. General-circulation newspapers that advertise rental property and listing contracts between owners or lessors of real estate and registrants are exempt from this requirement.

Residential Leasing Agents

Sections 5-5 through 5-10 of the Real Estate License Act of 2000 provide for a limited-scope license for individuals who wish to engage solely in activities related to the leasing of residential real property. For example, the following activities would appropriately fall under this limited license, if the licensee did not engage in any other real estate activities (such as marketing single-family homes):

- Leasing or renting residential real property
- Collecting rent for residential real property
- Attempting, offering, or negotiating to lease, rent, or collect rent for the use of residential real property

The Act establishes specific qualifications and educational requirements for residential leasing agents, including a written examination.

Referral Fees

Section 5-20 of the Real Estate License Act of 2000 allows landlords to pay a referral fee to tenants. A resident tenant of a unit who refers a prospective tenant for a unit in the same building or complex may be paid a referral fee if he

- refers no more than three prospective lessees in any 12-month period;
- receives compensation of no more than $5,000 or the equivalent of two month's rent, whichever is less, in any 12-month period; and
- limits his activities to referring prospective lessees to the owner (or the owner's agent) and does not show units, discuss lease terms, or otherwise participate in the negotiation of a lease.

SUMMARY

A lease is an agreement that grants one person the right to use the property of another in return for consideration.

A leasehold estate that runs for a specific length of time creates an estate for years; one that runs for an indefinite period creates an estate from period to period (e.g., year to year or month to month). An estate at will runs as long as the landlord permits. An estate at sufferance is possession without the consent of the landlord. A leasehold estate is classified as a personal property interest.

The requirements of a valid lease include capacity to contract, a legal objective, offer and acceptance, and consideration. In addition, state statutes of frauds generally require that any lease that will not be completed within one year of the date of its making must be in writing to be enforceable in court. Most leases also include clauses relating to rights and obligations of the landlord and tenant, such as the appropriate use of the premises, subletting, judgments, maintenance of the premises, and termination of the lease period.

A lease may be terminated by the expiration of the lease period, the mutual agreement of the parties, or a breach of the lease by either the landlord or tenant. In most cases, neither the death of the tenant nor the landlord's sale of the rental property terminates a lease.

If a tenant defaults on any lease provision, the landlord may sue for a money judgment, actual eviction, or both. If the premises have become uninhabitable due to the landlord's negligence or failure to correct conditions within a reasonable time, the tenant may have the remedy of constructive eviction—that is, the right to abandon the premises and refuse to pay rent until the premises are repaired.

The rental industry is highly regulated. Fair housing and civil rights laws protect the rights of tenants, and landlords should familiarize themselves with these laws.

Sections 5-5 through 5-10 of the Real Estate License Act of 2000 provide for a limited-scope license for individuals who wish to engage solely in activities related to the leasing of residential real property. Article 5 contains particulars on the residential leasing agent license.

The Illinois Human Rights Act defines fair housing as including freedom from discrimination against an individual because of race, color, religion, sex, national origin, ancestry, age, marital status, physical or mental disability, familial status, military status, unfavorable discharge from military service, or sexual orientation and order of protection status in connection with employment, real estate transactions, access to financial credit, and the availability of public accommodations.

The Frauds Act (740 ILCS 80/) requires that leases for more than one year or that those cannot be performed within one year be in writing to be enforceable. Oral leases for less than one year are enforceable. Illinois law establishes specific notice requirements for termination of leases and for the withholding or payment of interest on security deposits. Federal lead-based-paint laws are strictly enforced in Illinois. Even a short oral lease requires that a lead-paint disclosure be supplied.

UNIT 17 QUIZ

1. A ground lease is usually
   A. long term.
   B. short term.
   C. for 100 years or longer.
   D. a gross lease.

2. A tenant enters into a commercial lease that requires a monthly rent based on a minimum set amount plus an additional amount determined by the tenant's gross receipts exceeding $5,000. This type of lease is called a
   A. standard lease.
   B. gross lease.
   C. net lease.
   D. percentage lease.

3. If a tenant moved out of a rented store building because access to the building was blocked as a result of the landlord's negligence, the
   A. tenant would have no legal recourse against the landlord.
   B. tenant would be entitled to recover damages from the landlord.
   C. landlord would be liable for the rent until the expiration date of the lease.
   D. landlord would have to provide substitute space.

4. A tenant signs a lease that includes a schedule of rent increases on specific dates over the course of the lease term. What type of lease has the tenant signed?
   A. Percentage
   B. Net
   C. Graduated
   D. Index

5. A tenant still has five months remaining on a one-year apartment lease. When the tenant moves to another city, she transfers possession of the apartment to a friend for the entire remaining term of the lease. The friend pays rent directly to the tenant. In this situation, the tenant has become
   A. an assignor.
   B. a sublessee.
   C. a lessor.
   D. a sublessor.

6. A tenant's lease has expired. The tenant has neither vacated the premises nor negotiated a renewal lease, and the landlord has declared that she does not want the tenant to remain in the building. This form of possession is called
   A. an estate for years.
   B. a periodic estate.
   C. an estate at will.
   D. an estate at sufferance.

7. A tenant's tenancy for years will expire in two weeks. The tenant plans to move to a larger apartment across town when the current tenancy expires. What must the tenant do to terminate this agreement?
   A. The tenant needs to do nothing; the agreement will terminate automatically.
   B. The tenant must give the landlord two weeks' prior notice.
   C. The tenant must give the landlord one week's prior notice.
   D. The agreement will terminate only after the tenant signs a lease for the new apartment.

8. When a tenant holds possession of a landlord's property without a current lease agreement and without the landlord's approval, the
   A. tenant is maintaining a gross lease.
   B. landlord can file suit for possession.
   C. tenant has no obligation to pay rent.
   D. landlord may be subject to a constructive eviction.

9. Under the negotiated terms of a particular residential lease, the landlord is required to maintain the water heater. If a tenant is unable to get hot water because of a faulty water heater that the landlord has failed to repair after repeated notification, which remedy would be available to the tenant?
   A. Suing the landlord for damages
   B. Being refunded back rent by the landlord
   C. Abandoning the premises under constructive eviction
   D. Assigning the lease agreement

10. A person has a one-year leasehold interest in a house. The interest automatically renews itself at the end of each year. The person's interest is called a tenancy
    A. for years.
    B. at will.
    C. from period to period.
    D. at sufferance.

11. What is rent?
    A. Contractual consideration to a third party
    B. All monies paid by the lessor to the lessee
    C. Total balance owed under the terms of a lease
    D. Consideration for the use of real property

12. A net lease is
    A. an agreement in which the tenant pays a fixed rent and the landlord pays all taxes, insurance, and other charges on the property.
    B. a lease in which the tenant pays the landlord a percentage of the monthly profits derived from the tenant's commercial use of the property.
    C. a lease in which the tenant pays rent plus maintenance and property charges.
    D. a lease-purchase agreement in which the landlord agrees to apply part of the monthly rent toward the ultimate purchase price of the property.

13. A commercial lease calls for a minimum rent of $1,200 per month plus 4% of the annual gross business exceeding $150,000. If the total rent paid at the end of one year was $19,200, how much business did the tenant do during the year?
    A. $159,800
    B. $250,200
    C. $270,000
    D. $279,200

14. In Illinois, which of these statements is *TRUE* regarding a lease for more than one year?
    A. The lease must include a provision for interest to be paid on all security deposits.
    B. The lease must be recorded to give actual notice of the resident tenant's right of possession.
    C. The lease may be terminated only by written notice to the tenant, even if it contains a definite expiration date.
    D. The lease must be in writing and signed to be enforceable in court.

15. A tenant rents an apartment in a 100-unit highrise in a Chicago suburb for $900 per month. The tenant decides to move when she learns that her rent will be raised by 25% at the expiration of her one-year lease. When she moved in, the tenant deposited $1,200 as a security deposit. How will the interest paid on the tenant's deposit be determined?
    A. The interest paid should be based on the prime rate as of December 31 of the calendar year preceding the rental agreement.
    B. The interest paid should be 5% per year, from the date of deposit.
    C. The interest rate should be computed at a rate equal to that paid on a minimum deposit passbook savings account at the state's largest commercial bank.
    D. Under these facts, the tenant is not entitled to receive interest on her security deposit.

16. How many days' advance notice is required to terminate a month-to-month tenancy in Illinois?
    A. 5
    B. 15
    C. 60
    D. 30

17. A landlord who owns a 20-unit apartment building in Decatur, Illinois, has held a tenant's security deposit for three months. The tenant, who is on a month-to-month lease, informs the landlord that he will be vacating the apartment in 30 days. Based on these facts, which of these statements is *TRUE*?
    A. The landlord must pay the tenant four months' interest on the security deposit.
    B. The tenant is entitled to three months' interest on the security deposit.
    C. The landlord owes the tenant no interest on the security deposit.
    D. If the tenant vacates the premises in these circumstances, the landlord is entitled to retain the security deposit as statutory damages.

18. A tenant has a one-year lease on an apartment. If the tenant fails to pay his rent when it is due, the landlord may
    A. terminate the tenant's lease without notice when the rent is more than 10 days past due.
    B. serve notice on the tenant to pay the delinquent rent within five days.
    C. hire a moving company to remove the tenant's furniture and personal property from the premises.
    D. serve notice on the tenant to pay the rent within five days and proceed with a suit for possession regardless of whether or not the tenant pays the past-due rent.

19. In Illinois, a landlord must give a tenant at least 60 days' written notice to terminate which of these tenancies?
    A. Tenancy from year to year
    B. Tenancy at will
    C. Tenancy for years
    D. Tenancy at sufferance

20. Before entering into a service relationship with a prospective tenant, a rental-finding service must provide the prospective tenant with a written contract that discloses what information?
    A. A statement that information about rental units may be up to two days old
    B. The total amount to be paid over the lease term
    C. A statement that the contract will be invalid if information about a rental unit is provided when the unit has been unavailable for more than five days
    D. A copy of the brokerage agreement between the owner and the rental-finding service

UNIT 18

Property Management

LEARNING OBJECTIVES

When you have completed this unit, you will be able to accomplish the following.

> Identify the basic elements of a management agreement.
> Describe a property manager's functions.
> Explain risk management and the role of environmental regulations and the Americans with Disabilities Act in the property manager's job.

KEY TERMS

Americans with Disabilities Act (ADA)	multiperil policy	tenant improvements
management agreement	property manager	workers' compensation acts
management plan	risk management	
	surety bonds	

THE PROPERTY MANAGER

Property management involves the leasing, managing, marketing, and overall maintenance of real estate owned by others. Basic management duties include budgeting, setting rental rates, selecting tenants, collecting rent, maintaining the property, complying with legal requirements, and providing periodic financial and operational reports to the owner. Property management is one of the fastest-growing areas of real estate, and many mortgage lenders require that investors hire a professional property manager to manage their properties.

Property management is a complex and specialized field, requiring property managers to wear many hats. It is not unusual for a property manager to be a market analyst, leasing agent, accountant, advertising specialist, and maintenance person—all in the same day. In addition, the property manager frequently interacts with other professionals, including lawyers, environmental engineers, and accountants.

The **property manager** carries out the goals of the property owner by making sure the property earns income. Achieving this goal involves numerous responsibilities: the physical property must be maintained in good condition; suitable tenants must be found; rent must be collected; and employees must be hired and supervised. The property manager is also responsible for budgeting and controlling expenses, keeping proper accounts, and making periodic reports to the owner. In all of these activities, the manager's primary goal is to operate and maintain the physical property in such a way as to preserve and enhance the owner's capital investment.

The property manager has an agency relationship with the owner, which involves greater authority and discretion over management decisions than an employee would have. A property manager or an owner may employ building managers to supervise the daily operations of a building. In some cases, these individuals are residents of the building they supervise.

> A property manager
> - maintains the owner's investment and
> - ensures that the property produces income.

Specialized Opportunities

Specialization in the field of property management has opened a range of new opportunities. In addition to residential properties, well-trained specialists may manage shopping centers, commercial buildings, and industrial parks. The following are other areas of specialization.

Community Association Management

The prevalence of homeowners and condominium associations, combined with complex planning and development codes, have placed new demands on property managers. Working as part of a team, these property managers assist in providing a comprehensive array of services to volunteer boards. Many states now require at least a real estate license or an association management license for those who specialize in managing community associations.

The Community Association Manager Licensing and Disciplinary Act (225 ILCS 427/) was created to regulate community association managers, to ensure that managers are qualified to engage in community association management, and to enforce high standards of professional conduct by those licensed. Anyone acting under this license cannot perform any activities for which a real estate broker's license is required under the Real Estate License Act of 2000. Likewise, a real estate licensee may not perform community association activities without that license.

Asset Management

Asset managers monitor a portfolio of properties similar to a securities portfolio by analyzing the performance of the properties and making recommendations to the owners of the properties. Real property asset management helps clients decide what type of real estate to invest in (commercial or residential), which property is best to purchase, the best financial sources for a real estate purchase, and when to dispose of property.

Corporate Property Management

Corporate property managers manage properties for corporations that invest in real estate. Because these corporations may not deal primarily in real estate, they may not be knowledgeable about property management. Hiring a corporate property manager allows the corporation to invest in real estate without having the specialized knowledge of property management. Property management agreements must be in writing. In Illinois, property management requires a real estate license and an individual real estate licensee must perform property management services under the supervision of a sponsoring broker.

THE MANAGEMENT PLAN AND AGREEMENT

The Management Plan

Property management begins with a management plan prepared by the property manager. A **management plan** outlines the details of the owner's objectives for the property, as well as what the property manager expects to accomplish and how, including all financial objectives. In preparing a management plan, a property manager analyzes three factors: the owner's objectives, the regional and neighborhood market, and the specific property. Occupancy, absorption rates, and new starts are critical indicators. The plan also includes a budgetary section listing sources of revenue and anticipated expenses. While the management plan is a document for the present, it is forward-looking in determining the feasibility of a property owner's long-term goals for a specific property.

The Management Agreement

The first step in taking over the management of any property is to enter into a **management agreement** with the owner. This agreement creates a general agency relationship between the owner and the property manager. It defines the duties and responsibilities of each party. It is also a guide used in operating the property as well as a reference in case of future disputes between the owner and property manager.

Like any other contract involving real estate, the management agreement should be in writing. It should include the following elements:

- *Description of the property.* This should include both the property's street address and legal description.

- *Time period the agreement covers.* This should include specific provisions for termination.

- *Definition of the management's responsibilities.* All the manager's duties should be specifically stated in the contract.

- *Statement of the owner's purpose.* The owner should clearly state what the manager is to accomplish. One owner may want to maximize net income, while another may want to increase the capital value of the investment. Long-term goals are often key.

- *Extent of the manager's authority.* This provision should state what authority the manager is to have in matters such as hiring, firing, and supervising employees; fixing rental rates for space; and making expenditures and authorizing repairs. Repairs that exceed a certain expense limit may require the owner's written approval.

- *Reporting.* The frequency and detail of the manager's periodic reports on operations and financial position should be agreed on. These reports serve as a means for the owner to monitor the manager's work and operational trends; they form a basis for shaping management policy.

- *Management fee.* The fee may be based on a percentage of gross or net income, a fixed fee, or some combination of these factors. Management fees are subject to the same antitrust laws as sales commissions and cannot be standardized in the marketplace (e.g., price-fixing). The fee must be negotiated between the property manager and the principal.

- *Allocation of costs.* The agreement should state which of the property manager's expenses (i.e., office rent, office help, telephone, advertising, and association fees) will be paid by the manager and which costs will be paid by the owner.

- *Equal opportunity statement.* Residential property management agreements should include a statement that the property will be shown, rented, and otherwise made available to all persons protected by state or federal law.

MATH CONCEPTS Rental Commissions

Residential property managers often earn commissions when they find new tenants for a property. Rental commissions usually are based on the annual rent from a property. For example, if an apartment unit rents for $1,200 per month and the commission payable is 8%, the commission is calculated as follows:

$1,200 per month × 12 months = $14,400

$14,400 × 0.08 (8%) = $1,152

PROPERTY MANAGER'S RESPONSIBILITIES

Financial Reports

One of the property manager's primary responsibilities is maintaining financial reports, including an operating budget, cash flow report, profit and loss statement, and budget comparison statement.

Operating Budget

An operating budget is the projection of income and expenses for the operation of a property over a one-year period. This budget is based on anticipated revenues and expenses and serves as a guide for the property's anticipated financial performance.

Once a property manager has managed a property for a length of time, an operating budget may be developed based on the results of the profit and loss statement in comparison to the original budget (actual versus projected). After making the comparison, a new operating budget is prepared for a new period in the future.

Income

Income includes gross rents collected, delinquent rental payments, vending, late fees, and storage charges. Any losses from uncollected rental payments or evictions are deducted from the total gross to arrive at the total adjusted income.

In some properties, there is space that is not income producing, such as the property manager's office. The rental value of the property that is not producing income is subtracted from the gross rental income to equal the gross collectible, or billable, rental income.

Expenses

Fixed and variable expenses include administrative costs (including building personnel), operating expenses, and maintenance costs. Fixed expenses that remain constant and do not change include employee wages, utilities, and other basic operating costs. Variable expenses may be recurring or nonrecurring and can include capital improvements, building repairs, and landscaping.

Cash Flow Report

A cash flow report is a monthly statement that details the financial status of the property. Sources of income and expenses are noted, as well as net operating income and net cash flow. The cash flow report is the most important financial report because it provides a picture of the property's current financial status.

The formula for arriving at cash flow is as follows:

Gross rental income + other income – losses incurred = total income

Total income – operating expenses = net operating income before debt service (e.g., mortgage payments)

Net operating income before debt service – debt service – reserves = cash flow

Profit and Loss Statement

A profit and loss statement is a financial picture of revenues and expenses used to determine whether the business has made money or suffered a loss. It may be prepared monthly, quarterly, semiannually, or annually. The statement is created from the monthly cash flow reports and does not include itemized information.

Budget Comparison Statement

The budget comparison statement compares the actual results with the original budget, often giving either percentages or a numerical variance of actual versus projected income and expenses. Budget comparisons are especially helpful in identifying trends in order to help with future budget planning.

Renting the Property

Effective rental of the property is essential to ensure the long-term financial health of the property. Property managers sometimes employ leasing agents to assist with this aspect of property management.

Setting Rental Rates

Rental rates are influenced primarily by supply and demand. The property manager should conduct a detailed survey of the competitive space available in the neighborhood, emphasizing similar properties. In establishing rental rates, the property manager has four long-term considerations:

■ The rental income must be sufficient to cover the property's fixed charges and operating expenses.

■ The rental income must provide a fair return on the owner's investment.

■ The rental rate should be in line with prevailing rates in comparable buildings in the area. It may be slightly higher or slightly lower, depending on the strength of the property.

■ The current vacancy rate in the property is a good indicator of how much of a rent increase is advisable. A building with a low vacancy rate is a better candidate for an increase than one with a high vacancy rate.

A rental rate for residential space is usually stated as the monthly rate per unit. Commercial leases—including office, retail, and industrial space rentals—are usually stated according to either annual or monthly rates per square foot.

MATH CONCEPTS   Calculating Annual Rent Per Square Foot

1. Determine the total square footage of the rental premises (generally floor space only).

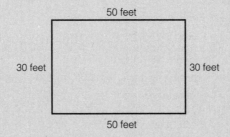

50 feet × 30 feet = 1,500 square feet

2. Find the total annual rent.

$1,850 per month × 12 months = $22,200 per year

3. Divide the total annual rent by the total square feet to determine the annual rate per square foot.

$22,200 per year ÷ 1,500 square feet = $14.80 per square foot

---

An elevated level of vacancy may indicate poor management or a defective or undesirable property. On the other hand, a high occupancy rate may mean that rental rates are too low. Whenever the occupancy level of an apartment or office building exceeds 95%, the property manager should investigate the rental market to determine whether a rent increase is warranted.

Selecting Tenants

Proper selection is the first step in establishing and maintaining sound, long-term relationships with tenants. The property manager should be sure that the premises are suitable for a tenant in terms of size, location, and amenities and that the tenant is able to pay for the space.

A commercial tenant's business should be compatible with the building and the other tenants. The property manager must consider how all tenants mesh. The types of businesses or services should be complementary, and the introduction of competitors (sometimes precluded in the lease) should be undertaken only with care. This not only pleases existing tenants but helps diversify the owner's investment and increases the likelihood of profitability.

The residential property manager must always comply with fair housing laws in selecting tenants. Although fair housing laws do not apply to commercial properties, commercial property managers need to be aware of federal, state, and local antidiscrimination and equal opportunity laws that may govern industrial or retail properties.

Collecting Rents

A property manager should accept only those tenants who can be expected to meet their financial obligations. In addition to contacting credit bureaus, the selection process involves calling financial references and, if possible, interviewing the former landlord.

The terms of rental payment should be spelled out in the lease agreement, including

- time and place of payment,
- provisions and penalties for late payment and returned checks, and
- provisions for cancellation and damages in case of nonpayment.

The property manager should establish a firm and consistent collection plan. The plan should include a system of notices and records that complies with state and local law.

Every attempt must be made to collect rent without resorting to legal action. Legal action is costly and time-consuming and does not contribute to good tenant relations. When it is unavoidable, legal action must be taken in cooperation with the property owner's or management firm's legal counsel.

In Illinois, an individual business entity with a broker license can assist the public in sales or leasing transactions involving all types of real property. However, only a managing broker license allows someone to supervise or sponsor other licensees and to collect compensation for brokerage services.

Specific legal procedures must be followed in taking legal action against a tenant. In addition, Illinois law has specific provisions regarding the maintenance and payment of interest on security deposits. Property managers (who must have broker or managing broker licenses) must put security deposits in a special escrow account, in the same way that real estate licensees must handle earnest money. Please note that real estate broker licenses may be issued to individuals or legal entities such as corporations, partnerships, and limited liabilities companies. An individual business entity with a broker license can assist the public in sales or leasing transactions involving all types of real property. However, a broker license does not allow someone to supervise or sponsor other licensees. A broker license also does not allow someone to collect compensation for brokerage services directly from the public or from other sponsoring brokers. All brokers must collect all compensation for brokerage services through their sponsor. Managing brokers are the only real estate licensees who are allowed to supervisor other licenses. Unlike brokers and managing brokers, residential leasing agents can only engage in activities directly associated with residential leasing. Residential leasing agents cannot perform these activities if the property being leased is commercial property. The security deposits must be deposited in the escrow account by the next business day after a lease is signed, and this must be recorded in the journal and ledger. This escrow account is a non-interest-bearing account unless the property is residential with 25 or more units, in which case interest must be paid to the tenants.

Maintaining Good Relations With Tenants

The ultimate success of a property manager depends on the ability of the manager to maintain good relations with tenants. Dissatisfied tenants eventually vacate the property. A high tenant turnover rate results in greater advertising and redecorating expenses as well as lowered profits from rents. Regular newsletters or posted memoranda help keep tenants informed and involved. Maintenance and service requests must be attended to promptly, and all lease terms and building rules must be enforced consistently and fairly. A good manager is tactful and decisive and acts to the benefit of both owner and occupants.

Maintaining the Property

One of the property manager's most important functions is the supervision of property maintenance. To maintain the property efficiently, the property manager must be able to assess the building's needs and how best to meet them. A property manager must learn to balance services provided with their costs; that is, to satisfy tenants' needs while minimizing operating expenses.

A primary maintenance objective is to protect the physical integrity of the property over the long term. For example, preserving the property by repainting the exterior or replacing the heating system helps decrease long-term maintenance costs. Keeping the property in good condition involves the following four types of maintenance:

- Preventive maintenance (periodic or seasonal)
- Repair or corrective maintenance (as needed)
- Routine maintenance (daily or ordinary)
- Tenant improvements

Preventive maintenance includes regularly scheduled activities such as painting and seasonal servicing of appliances and systems. Preventive maintenance preserves the long-range value and physical integrity of the building. This is both the most critical and the most neglected maintenance responsibility. Failure to perform preventive maintenance invariably leads to greater expense in other areas of maintenance.

Corrective maintenance involves the actual repairs that keep the building's equipment, utilities, and amenities functioning. Repairing a boiler, fixing a leaky faucet, or mending a broken air-conditioning unit are acts of corrective maintenance.

A property manager must also supervise *routine maintenance* of the building. Routine maintenance includes such day-to-day duties as cleaning common areas, performing minor carpentry and plumbing adjustments, and providing regularly scheduled upkeep of landscaping. Good routine maintenance is similar to good preventive maintenance—both head off problems before they become expensive.

A commercial or industrial property manager often is called on to make **tenant improvements**—alterations to the interior of the building to meet a tenant's particular space needs. Such construction alterations range from simply repainting or recarpeting to completely gutting the interior and redesigning the space by erecting new walls, adding partitions, and revamping electrical systems. In new construction especially, the interiors are usually left incomplete so that they can be adapted to the needs of individual tenants. One matter that must be clarified is which improvements will be considered *trade fixtures* (personal property belonging to the tenant) and which will belong to the real estate's owner.

Modernization or renovation of buildings that have become functionally obsolete and thus unsuited to today's building needs is also important. The renovation of a building often enhances marketability and potential income.

REGULATIONS

Handling Environmental Concerns

Property managers must be able to respond to a variety of environmental problems because they have become increasingly important issues. Managers may manage structures containing asbestos or radon or be called on to arrange an environmental audit of a property. Managers must see that any hazardous wastes produced by their employers or tenants are properly disposed of. Even nonhazardous waste of an office building must be controlled to avoid violation of laws requiring segregation and recycling of types of wastes. Of course, property managers may want to provide recycling opportunities for tenants even if not required by law to do so.

Air quality issues are a key concern for those involved in property management and design. Building-related illness (BRI) and sick building syndrome (SBS) are illnesses that are more prevalent today because of energy and efficiency standards used in construction that make buildings more airtight with less ventilation. SBS is more typical in an office building.

Americans With Disabilities Act

The **Americans with Disabilities Act (ADA)** has had a significant impact on the responsibilities of the property manager, both in building amenities and in employment issues.

Title I of the ADA provides for the employment of qualified job applicants regardless of their disability. Any employer with 15 or more employees must adopt nondiscriminatory employment procedures. In addition, employers must make reasonable accommodations to enable individuals with disabilities to perform essential job functions.

Property managers must also be familiar with Title III of the ADA, which prohibits discrimination in commercial properties and public accommodations. The ADA requires that property managers ensure that people with disabilities have full and equal access to facilities and services. The property manager typically is responsible for determining whether a building meets the ADA's accessibility requirements. The property manager must also prepare and execute a plan for restructuring or retrofitting a building that is not in compliance. ADA experts and architectural designers may need to be consulted.

To protect owners of existing structures from the massive expense of extensive remodeling, the ADA recommends *reasonably achievable accommodations* to provide access to the facilities and services. New construction and remodeling, however, must meet higher standards because new design costs less than retrofitting. An unexpected benefit to new owners is that many of the accessible design features and accommodations benefit everyone.

Existing barriers must be removed when this can be accomplished in a readily achievable manner—that is, with relatively little difficulty and at relatively low cost. The following are typical examples of readily achievable modifications:

- Ramping or removing an obstacle from an otherwise accessible entrance
- Lowering wall-mounted public telephones
- Adding raised letters and Braille markings on elevator buttons
- Installing auditory signals in elevators
- Reversing the direction in which doors open (for wheelchair accessibility)
- Providing doors that have mechanisms that will open and close the doors automatically

Alternative methods can be used to provide reasonable accommodations if extensive restructuring is impractical or if retrofitting is unduly expensive. For example, installing a cup dispenser at a water fountain that is too high for an individual in a wheelchair may be more practical than installing a lower unit.

IN PRACTICE

Federal, state, and local laws may provide additional requirements for accommodating people with disabilities. Real estate licensees should be aware of the full range of laws to ensure that their practices are in compliance.

RISK MANAGEMENT

Enormous monetary losses can result from certain unexpected or catastrophic events. As a result, one of the most critical areas of responsibility for a property manager is risk management. **Risk management** involves answering the question "What happens if something goes wrong?"

The perils of any risk must be evaluated in terms of options. In considering the possibility of a loss, the property manager must decide whether it is better to

- avoid risk by removing the source of risk (for example, a swimming pool may pose an unacceptable risk if a day care center is located in the building);

- control risk by preparing for an emergency before it happens (e.g., by installing sprinklers, fire doors, and security systems);

- transfer risk to another party (such as by taking out an insurance policy); or

- retain risk by deciding that the chances of the event occurring are too small to justify the expense of any other response (an alternative might be to take out an insurance policy with a large deductible, which is usually considerably less expensive).

Security of Tenants

The physical safety of tenants of the leased premises is an important issue for property managers and owners. Court decisions across country have held owners and their agents responsible for physical harm that was inflicted on tenants by intruders. These decisions have prompted property managers and owners to think about how to protect tenants and secure apartments from intruders.

Insurance

Insurance is one way to protect against losses. Many types of insurance are available. An insurance audit should be performed by a competent, reliable insurance agent who is familiar with insurance issues for the type of property involved. The audit will indicate areas in which greater or lesser coverage is recommended and will highlight particular risks. The final decision, however, must be made by the property owner.

Some common types of coverage available to income property owners and managers include the following:

- *Fire and hazard.* Fire insurance policies provide coverage against direct loss or damage to property from a fire on the premises. Standard fire coverage can be extended to include other hazards such as windstorm, hail, smoke damage, or civil insurrection.

- *Consequential loss, use, and occupancy.* Consequential loss insurance covers the results, or consequences, of a disaster. Consequential loss can include the loss of rent or revenue to a business that occurs if the business's property cannot be used.

- *Contents and personal property.* This type of insurance covers building contents and personal property during periods when they are not actually located on the business premises.

■ *Liability*. Liability insurance covers the risks an owner assumes whenever the public enters the building. A claim paid under this coverage is used for medical expenses by a person who is injured in the building as a result of the owner's negligence. Claims for those hurt in the course of their employment are covered by state laws called **workers' compensation acts**. A building owner who is an employer must obtain a workers' compensation policy from a private insurance company.

■ *Casualty*. Casualty insurance policies include coverage against theft, burglary, vandalism, and machinery damage as well as health and accident insurance. Casualty policies are usually written on specific risks, such as theft, rather than being all-inclusive.

■ *Surety bonds*. **Surety bonds** cover an owner against financial losses resulting from an employee's criminal acts or negligence while performing assigned duties.

Many insurance companies offer **multiperil policies** for apartment and commercial buildings. These policies offer a "package" of standard commercial coverage, such as fire, hazard, liability, and casualty. Special coverage for earthquakes and floods is also available.

Insurance for the personal property of tenants is also available to tenants. Many tenants do not realize that if a property burns, their personal property is usually not covered by the landlord's policy.

In Illinois, the policy type tenants should ask for is HO-4, designed specifically to cover renters' personal property.

Claims

Two possible methods can be used to determine the amount of a claim under an insurance policy. One is the *depreciated cash value* (also called the *actual cash value*) of the damaged property. That is, the property is not insured for what it would cost to replace it but rather for what it was originally worth, less the depreciation in value that results from use and the passage of time. The other method is *current replacement cost*. In this sort of policy, the building or property is insured for what it would cost to rebuild or replace it today. When purchasing insurance, a manager must decide whether a property should be insured at full replacement cost or at a depreciated cost. Full replacement cost coverage is generally more expensive than depreciated cost.

THE PROPERTY MANAGEMENT PROFESSION

Most metropolitan areas have local associations of building and property owners and managers that are affiliates of regional and national associations. These professional organizations provide information and contacts for all aspects of property management. Well-known associations include the following:

■ Building Owners and Managers Association International (BOMA): commercial real estate

■ Building Owners and Managers Institute International (BOMI): education programs for commercial property and facility management industries

■ Community Associations Institute (CAI): homeowners associations, condominiums, and other planned communities

■ Institute of Real Estate Management (IREM): multifamily and commercial real estate designation

■ International Council of Shopping Centers (ICSC): shopping centers worldwide

- ■ National Apartment Association (NAA): multifamily housing industry
- ■ National Association of Home Builders (NAHB): all aspects of home building
- ■ National Association of Residential Property Managers (NARPM): single-family and small residential properties

SUMMARY

Property management is a specialized service provided to owners of income-producing properties. The owner's managerial function may be delegated to an individual or a firm with particular expertise in the field. The property manager, as agent of the owner, becomes the administrator of the project and assumes the executive functions required for the care and operation of the property.

A management agreement establishes the agency relationship between owner and manager. It must be prepared carefully to define and authorize the manager's duties and responsibilities, and it should be in writing.

Projected expenses, the manager's analysis of the building's condition, and local rent patterns form the basis for determining rental rates for the property. Once a rent schedule is established, the property manager is responsible for soliciting financially responsible tenants whose needs are suited to the available space. The manager collects rents, maintains the building, hires necessary employees, pays taxes for the building, and deals with tenant problems.

Maintenance includes safeguarding the physical integrity of the property and performing routine cleaning and repairs. It also includes making tenant improvements, such as adapting the interior space and overall design of the property to suit tenants' needs.

The manager is expected to secure adequate insurance coverage for the premises. Fire and hazard insurance cover the property and fixtures against catastrophes. Consequential loss, use, and occupancy insurance protect the owner against revenue losses. Casualty insurance provides coverage against losses such as theft, vandalism, and destruction of machinery. The property manager should also secure public liability insurance to insure the owner against claims made by people injured on the premises. Workers' compensation policies cover the claims of employees injured on the job.

Increasing needs for safety and security awareness, knowledge of environmental issues, and concern for the federal and state fair housing laws round out the potpourri of issues that a property manager must often address.

 Property managers must be licensed real estate brokers or managing brokers. Resident managers are exempt under certain circumstances.

Community association managers are regulated under the Community Association Manager Licensing and Disciplinary Act.

UNIT 18 QUIZ

1. Which type of insurance coverage insures an employer against *MOST* claims for job-related injuries?
   A. Consequential loss
   B. Workers' compensation
   C. Casualty
   D. Surety bond

2. Residential leases are usually expressed as
   A. an annual or monthly rate per square foot.
   B. a percentage of total space available.
   C. an annual rate per room.
   D. a monthly rate per unit.

3. Avoid, control, transfer, or retain are the four alternative techniques of
   A. tenant relations.
   B. acquiring insurance.
   C. risk management.
   D. property management.

4. From a management point of view, apartment building occupancy that reaches as high as 98% would tend to indicate that
   A. the building is poorly managed.
   B. the building has reached its maximum potential.
   C. rent could be raised.
   D. the building is a desirable place to live.

5. A guest slips on an icy stair at an apartment building and is hospitalized. A claim against the building owner for medical expenses may be paid under which of these policies held by the owner?
   A. Workers' compensation
   B. Liability
   C. Casualty
   D. Fire and hazard

6. When a property manager is establishing a budget for the building, what should be included as an operating expense?
   A. Utilities
   B. Replacement reserves
   C. Debt service
   D. Depreciation

7. A property manager is offered a choice of three insurance policies with different deductibles. If the property manager selects the policy with the highest deductible, which risk management technique is being used?
   A. Avoiding risk
   B. Retaining risk
   C. Controlling risk
   D. Transferring risk

8. Contaminated groundwater, toxic fumes from paint and carpeting, and lack of proper ventilation are all examples of
   A. issues beyond the scope of a property manager's job description.
   B. problems faced only in newly constructed properties.
   C. environmental concerns that a property manager may have to address.
   D. issues that arise under the Americans with Disabilities Act.

9. Tenant improvements are
   A. always construed to be fixtures.
   B. removable by the tenant.
   C. paid for by the landlord.
   D. adaptations of space to suit tenants' needs.

10. When a manager develops an operating budget, which of these is considered a variable expense?
    A. Employee wages
    B. Utilities
    C. Building repairs
    D. Basic operating costs

11. In *MOST* market areas, rents are determined by
    A. supply-and-demand factors.
    B. the local apartment owners' association.
    C. HUD's annually published rental guidelines.
    D. a tenants' union.

12. A highrise apartment building burns to the ground. What type of insurance covers the landlord against the resulting loss of rent?
    A. Fire and hazard
    B. Liability
    C. Casualty
    D. Consequential loss, use, and occupancy

13. A property manager hires a full-time maintenance person. While repairing a faucet in one of the apartments, the maintenance person steals a television set, and the tenant sues the owner. The property manager could protect the owner against this type of loss by purchasing
    A. a surety bond.
    B. liability insurance.
    C. workers' compensation insurance.
    D. casualty insurance.

14. Which of these might indicate that rents are too low?
    A. A poorly maintained building
    B. High building occupancy
    C. Many For Lease signs in the area
    D. High tenant turnover rates

15. A property manager repairs a malfunctioning boiler in the building. This is classified as which type of maintenance?
    A. Preventive
    B. Routine
    C. Corrective
    D. Construction

16. A property manager who enters into a management agreement with an owner is usually a
    A. special agent.
    B. universal agent.
    C. general agent.
    D. designated agent.

17. Which law requires removing existing barriers when readily achievable in public buildings and adding Braille markings to elevator buttons?
    A. Fair Housing Act
    B. Americans with Disabilities Act
    C. Equal Credit Opportunity Act
    D. Regulation Z

18. Which action by a property manager is a breach of her fiduciary relationship to the owner?
    A. Generating a high net operating income by maintaining the property
    B. Maintaining good relations with the tenants
    C. Checking the credit history of minority applicants only
    D. Scrutinizing property expenses

19. A property manager's total compensation consists of a monthly salary, a 12% commission based on annual rental for each vacant unit the property manager fills, and the free use of one of the apartments as the property manager's personal primary residence. Based on these facts, is the property manager required by Illinois law to obtain a real estate broker or managing broker license?
    A. Yes. Any person who is compensated for performing real estate activities for a commission must have a broker or managing broker license, regardless of any other form of compensation.
    B. Yes. Because the property manager's compensation is based in part on recruiting new tenants rather than simply collecting rents, the property manager must have a broker or managing broker license.
    C. No. Property managers are not required to have real estate licenses in Illinois.
    D. No. Persons acting as resident managers, who live in the managed property, are specifically exempt from the general licensing requirements.

20. The property manager of a small, 20-unit apartment building requires a security deposit. In this case, the property manager
    A. must pay interest on the security deposit.
    B. is not required to deposit the security deposit into an escrow account.
    C. is not required to pay interest on the security deposit.
    D. may deposit the security deposit into the general operating fund.

Real Estate Appraisal

LEARNING OBJECTIVES

When you have completed this unit, you will be able to accomplish the following.

› Identify the different types and basic principles of value.
› Describe the three basic valuation approaches used by appraisers.
› Explain the steps in the appraisal process.

KEY TERMS

anticipation
appraisal
appraiser
assemblage
broker's price opinion
  (BPO)
capitalization rate
change
comparative market
  analysis
competition
conformity
contribution
cost approach
depreciation
economic life
external obsolescence

functional obsolescence
gross income multiplier
  (GIM)
gross rent multiplier
  (GRM)
highest and best use
income approach
index method
law of increasing returns
law of diminishing returns
market value
net operating income
  (NOI)
physical deterioration
plottage
progression
quantity-survey method

reconciliation
regression
replacement cost
reproduction cost
sales comparison
  approach
square-foot method
straight-line method
substitution
supply and demand
*Uniform Standards of
  Professional Appraisal
  Practice (USPAP)*
unit-in-place method
value

OVERVIEW

Appraisal is a distinct area of specialization within the world of real estate professionals. Appraisal provides a clearer understanding about the market's response to a subject property. Real estate licensees must be aware of the fundamental principles of valuation in order to complete an accurate and effective comparative market analysis (CMA) that assists seller clients in arriving at a reasonable asking price and buyer clients in making appropriate offers based on current market conditions. Furthermore, knowledge of the appraisal process allows the licensee to recognize an unacceptable appraisal.

APPRAISING

Appraisal is the act or process of developing an opinion of value. An appraisal report is the written or oral communication of an appraisal. Typically, appraisal reports for lenders, for example, are written in a uniform format. An **appraiser** is a person trained to provide valuation services competently in an impartial and objective manner, according to the appraisal process. Appraising is a professional service, which is usually performed for a fee.

Regulation of Appraisal Activities

Title XI of the federal Financial Institutions Reform, Recovery, and Enforcement Act of 1989 (FIRREA) requires that appraisals used in connection with a federally related transaction be performed by someone who is state certified or licensed. A *federally related transaction* is any real estate–related financial transaction in which a federal financial institution or regulatory agency engages in, contracts for, or regulates and requires the services of an appraiser. This includes transactions involving the sale, lease, purchase, investment, or exchange of real property. It also includes the interests in property, or the financing, refinancing, or the use of real property as security for a loan or an investment, including mortgage-backed securities.

Federal law requires that appraisers be licensed or certified according to individual state law. State qualifications must conform to the federal requirements that, in turn, follow the criteria for certification established by the Appraiser Qualifications Board (AQB) of the Appraisal Foundation. The Appraisal Foundation is a national body composed of representatives of some of the major appraisal and related organizations. Appraisers are also expected to follow the ***Uniform Standards of Professional Appraisal Practice (USPAP)*** established by the Foundation's Appraisal Standards Board.

The Real Estate Appraiser Licensing Act of 2002 (225 ILCS 458/), as amended in 2009, provides for mandatory licensure with limited exceptions of Illinois appraisers.

Illinois recognizes the following three categories of appraisers:

- *Associate real estate trainee appraiser.* Entry level appraiser; all reports must be cosigned by a state-certified residential real estate appraiser or state-certified general real estate appraiser.

- *Certified residential real estate appraiser.* Qualified to appraise residential property of one unit to four units without regard to transaction value or complexity, but with restrictions in accordance with Title XI, *USPAP,* and criteria established by the AQB. Certified residential real estate appraisers may also appraise other types of real property having a transaction value of less than $250,000.

- *Certified general real estate appraiser.* Qualified to appraise all types of real property without restrictions as to the scope of practice subject to *USPAP* requirements.

An appraisal report prepared by an appraiser recognized under the act must identify on the report, by name, the individual who ordered or originated the appraisal assignment. The appraiser must retain the original copy of all contracts engaging his services as an appraiser and all appraisal reports, including any supporting data used to develop the appraisal report, for a period of not less than five years, or two years after the final disposition of any judicial proceeding in which testimony was given, whichever is longer. In addition, the appraiser must retain contracts, logs, and appraisal reports used in meeting prelicense experience requirements for a period of five years.

The Real Estate Appraiser Licensing Act of 2002 established a fee structure and disciplinary and enforcement mechanism for appraisers. Associate real estate trainee and certification candidates also must meet strict competency, education, examination, and experience requirements. The appraisal profession itself maintains rigorous standards requiring all Illinois associate trainees to become certified residential appraisers within two years of initial licensure. An individual appraiser may not use the titles "state-certified" or "associate real estate trainee appraiser" unless actually recognized as such by the state.

Comparative Market Analysis

A comparative market analysis (CMA) is distinctly different from an appraisal report offered by a licensed appraiser and should reflect that difference as per 225 ILCS 454/10-45. An appraisal is based on an analysis of properties that have actually sold, as well as competitive listings. The CMA, in contrast, features properties similar to the subject property in size, location, and amenities and is based on

- recently closed properties (solds),
- properties currently on the market (competition for the subject property), and
- properties that did not sell (expired listings in the area).

Remember the importance of historical and expired sales. They provide a snapshot of what price consumers were willing to pay and what they were not for comparable properties. This data can be used to support a CMA.

Broker's Price Opinion (BPO)

A **broker's price opinion (BPO)** is a less-expensive alternative of valuating properties often used by lenders working with home equity lines, refinancing, portfolio management, foreclosures, loss mitigation, and collections. Both Fannie Mae and Freddie Mac provide forms that are used by real estate licensees who perform BPOs for a fee. Although some BPOs are more extensive and include information about the neighborhood and interior analysis, many are simply "drive-bys" that verify the existence of the property, along with a listing of comparable sales. A BPO should not be confused with an appraisal, which consists of more in-depth analysis of gathered information and which may be performed only by a licensed appraiser. A BPO cannot be used if the matter involves a federally related transaction that requires an appraisal and/or the transaction occurs in a state that requires an appraiser's license.

Remember, when you communicate a value to a customer or client, back it up with data and statistics that are easy for the client or customer to understand and that support your conclusion.

VALUE

MEMORY TIP

For the four char-
acteristics of value,
remember DUST:

◾ Demand

◾ Utility

◾ Scarcity

◾ Transferability

To have **value** in the real estate market—that is, to have monetary worth based on desirability—a property must have the following four characteristics:

◾ *Demand*. The need or desire for possession or ownership backed by the financial means to satisfy that need

◾ *Utility*. The property's usefulness for its intended purposes

◾ *Scarcity*. A finite supply

◾ *Transferability*. The relative ease with which ownership rights are transferred from one person to another

Market Value

The goal of an appraiser is to express an opinion of market value. The **market value** of real estate is the most probable price that a property should bring in a fair sale (also known as "an arm's length transaction"). This definition makes three assumptions. First, it presumes a competitive and open market. Second, the buyer and the seller are both assumed to be acting prudently and knowledgeably. Third, market value depends on the price not being affected by unusual circumstances.

The following are essential factors in rendering an opinion of value:

◾ The most probable price is not the average or highest price.

◾ The buyer and the seller must be unrelated and acting without undue pressure.

◾ Both buyer and seller must be well informed about the property's use and potential, including both its defects and its advantages.

◾ A reasonable time must be allowed for exposure in the open market.

◾ Payment must be made in cash or its equivalent.

◾ The price must represent a normal consideration for the property sold, unaffected by special financing amounts or terms, services, fees, costs, or credits incurred in the market transaction.

Market Value Versus Market Price

Market value is a
reasonable opinion
of a property's value.

Market price is the
actual selling price
of a property.

Cost may not equal
either market value
or market price.

Market value is an opinion of value based on an analysis of data. The data may include not only an analysis of comparable sales but also an analysis of potential income, expenses, and replacement costs (less any depreciation). *Market price*, on the other hand, is what a property actually sells for—its sales price. Market price is a historical fact.

Market Value Versus Cost

An important distinction can be made between market value and cost. One of the most common misconceptions about valuing property is that cost represents market value. Cost and market value may be the same; in fact, when the improvements on a property are new, cost and value are likely to be equal. But more often, cost does not equal market value. For example, a homeowner may install a swimming pool for a cost of $15,000, though the cost of the improvement may not add $15,000 to the value of the property.

Basic Principles of Value

A number of economic principles can affect the value of real estate.

Anticipation

According to the principle of **anticipation**, value is created by the expectation that certain events will occur. Value can increase or decrease in anticipation of some future benefit or detriment. For example, the value of a house may be affected if rumors circulate that an adjacent property may be converted to commercial use in the near future.

Change

The principle of **change** relates to the economic and social forces that affect value. The competent appraiser will understand the economic and social forces that impact a market: growth, stability, decline, or restoration.

Competition

Competition is the interaction of supply and demand. Excess profits tend to attract competition. For example, the success of a retail store may cause investors to open similar stores in the area. This tends to mean less profit for all the stores concerned unless the purchasing power in the area increases substantially.

Conformity

The principle of **conformity** means that maximum value is created when a property is in harmony with its surroundings. Maximum value is realized if the use of land conforms to existing neighborhood standards. In single-family residential neighborhoods, for example, buildings should be similar in design, construction, size, and age. This is called *homogeneity*.

Contribution

Under the principle of **contribution**, the value of any part of a property is measured by its effect on the value of the whole. Installing a swimming pool, greenhouse, or tennis court may not add value to the property equal to the cost, but remodeling an outdated kitchen or bathroom might.

Highest and Best Use

The most profitable single use to which a property may be put, or the use that is most likely to be in demand in the near future, is the property's **highest and best use**. The use must be

- legally permitted,
- physically possible,
- economically or financially feasible, and
- the most profitable or maximally productive.

The tests of highest and best use are considered sequentially. The tests of legally permissible and physically possible may be performed in either order, but they must be applied before the tests of financial feasibility and maximum productivity. The highest and best use of a site can change with social, political, and economic forces. For example, a parking lot in a busy downtown area may not maximize the land's profitability to the same extent an office building would. Highest and best use is discussed in every appraisal.

Increasing and Diminishing Returns

The addition of more improvements to land and structures increases total value only to the asset's maximum value. Beyond that point, additional improvements no longer affect a property's value. As long as money spent on improvements produces an increase in income or value, the **law of increasing returns** applies. At the point where additional improvements do not increase income or value, the **law of diminishing returns** applies. No matter how much money is spent on the property, the property's value will not keep pace with the expenditures. A remodeled kitchen or bathroom might increase the value of a house; adding restaurant-quality appliances and gold faucets, however, would be a cost that the owner probably would not be able to recover.

Plottage

The principle of **plottage** holds that merging or consolidating adjacent lots into a single, larger one produces a greater total land value than the sum of the two sites valued separately. For example, two adjacent lots valued at $35,000 each might have a combined value of $90,000 if consolidated. The process of merging two separately owned lots under one owner is called **assemblage**. Plottage is the amount that value is increased by successful assemblage.

Regression and Progression

In general, the worth of a better-quality property is adversely affected by the presence of a lesser-quality property; this is called the principle of **regression**. Thus, in a neighborhood of modest homes, a structure that is larger, better maintained, or more luxurious would tend to be valued in the same range as the less-lavish homes. Conversely, under the principle of **progression**, the value of a modest home would be higher if it were located among larger, fancier properties.

Substitution

Under the principle of **substitution**, the maximum value of a property tends to be set by how much it would cost to purchase an equally desirable and valuable substitute property. Substitution is the foundation of the sales comparison approach.

Supply and Demand

The principle of **supply and demand** holds that the value of a property depends on the number of properties available in the marketplace—the supply of the product. When supply increases, value decreases and when demand increases, value increases.

THE THREE APPROACHES TO VALUE

To arrive at an accurate opinion of value, appraisers traditionally use three basic valuation techniques: the *sales comparison approach*, the *cost approach*, and *the income approach*. The three methods serve as checks against each other. Using them narrows the range within which the final estimate of value falls. Each method addresses a specific type of property.

The Sales Comparison Approach

In the **sales comparison approach**, an estimate of value is obtained by comparing the property being appraised (the subject property) with recently sold comparable properties (properties similar to the subject, called *comps*). Because no two parcels of real estate are exactly alike, each comparable property must be analyzed for differences and similarities between it and the subject property. This approach is a good example of the principle of substitution, discussed previously. The elements of comparison for which adjustments must be made include the following:

- *Financing concessions.* The financing terms must be considered, including adjustments for differences such as mortgage loan terms and owner financing.

- *Market conditions.* Interest rates, supply and demand, and other economic indicators must be analyzed.

- *Conditions of sale.* Adjustments must be made for motivational factors that would affect the sale, such as foreclosure, a sale between family members, or some nonmonetary incentive.

- *Market conditions since the date of sale.* An adjustment must be made if economic changes occur between the date of sale of the comparable property and the date of the appraisal.

- *Location or area preference.* Similar properties might differ in price from neighborhood to neighborhood or even between locations within the same neighborhood.

- *Physical features and amenities.* Physical features, such as the structure's age, size, and condition, may require adjustments.

EXAMPLE

Two condos in the same neighborhood, one that sold and one that is the subject of an appraisal, are very similar. The comp sold for $145,000 and has a garage valued at $9,000. The subject property has no garage, but it has a fireplace valued at $5,000. What is the indicated value of the subject property?

$145,000	The comp sale price
– 9,000	The Comp is Better, Subtract—CBS
+ 5,000	The Comp is Poorer, Add—CPA
$141,000	The indicated value of the subject property

The sales comparison approach is considered the most reliable of the three approaches in appraising single-family homes, where the intangible benefits might be difficult to measure otherwise. Most appraisals include a minimum of three comparable sales reflective of the subject property. Whenever possible, the comparables should be recent sales (less than six months), close by, and as similar as possible to the subject property. An example of the sales comparison approach is shown in Figure 19.1.

Figure 19.1: Sales Comparison Approach to Value Example

	Subject Property	Comparable Properties A	B	C
Sales price		$260,000	$252,000	$265,000
Financing concessions	none	none	none	none
Date of sale		current	current	current
Location	good	same	poorer+6,500	same
Age	6 years	same	same	same
Size of lot	60' × 135'	same	same	larger –5,000
Landscaping	good	same	same	same
Construction	brick	same	same	same
Style	ranch	same	same	same
No. of rooms	6	same	same	same
No. of bedrooms	3	same	poorer +500	same
No. of baths	1½	same	same	better –500
Sq. ft. of living space	1,500	same	same	better –1,000
Other space (basement)	full basement	same	same	same
Condition—exterior	average	better –1,500	poorer +1,000	better –1,500
Condition—interior	good	same	same	better –500
Garage	2-car attached	same	same	same
Other improvements	none	none	none	none
Net adjustments		–1,500	+8,000	–8,500
Adjusted value		$258,500	$260,000	$256,500

Note that the value of a feature that is present in the subject but not in the comparable property is *added* to the sales price of the comparable. Likewise, the value of a feature that is present in the comparable but not in the subject property is *subtracted.* A good way to remember this is: CBS stands for "comp better subtract" and CPA stands for "comp poorer add." The adjusted sales prices of the comparables represent the probable range of value of the subject property. From this range, a single market value estimate can be selected.

The Cost Approach

The **cost approach** to value also is based on the principle of substitution. The cost approach consists of five steps:

1. Estimate the value of the land as though it were vacant and available to be put to its highest and best use.

2. Estimate the current cost of constructing the buildings and improvements.

3. Estimate the amount of accrued depreciation resulting from the property's physical deterioration, functional obsolescence, and external obsolescence.

4. Deduct the accrued depreciation (step 3) from the current construction cost (step 2).

5. Add the estimated land value (step 1) to the depreciated cost of the building and site improvements (step 4) to arrive at the total property value.

EXAMPLE

Current cost of construction = $185,000

Accrued depreciation = $30,000

Value of the land = $55,000

($185,000 – $30,000) + 55,000 = $210,000

In this example, the total property value is $210,000.

There are two ways to look at the construction cost of a building for appraisal purposes: reproduction cost and replacement cost. **Reproduction cost** is the construction cost at current prices of an exact duplicate of the subject improvement, including both the benefits and the drawbacks of the property. **Replacement cost** is the cost to construct an improvement similar to the subject property using current construction methods and materials but not necessarily an exact duplicate. Replacement cost is more frequently used in appraising older structures because it eliminates obsolete features and takes advantage of current construction materials and techniques.

Figure 19.2 shows an example of the cost approach to value, applied to the same property as in Figure 19.1.

Figure 19.2: Cost Approach to Value Example

Subject Property

Land valuation: Size 60' × 135' @ $450 per front foot	=	$ 27,000
Plus site improvements: driveway, walks, landscaping, etc.	=	8,000
Total		$ 35,000

Building valuation: replacement cost

1,500 sq. ft. @ $85 per sq. ft. =	$127,500	
Less depreciation:		
Physical depreciation		
Curable		
(items of deferred maintenance)		
exterior painting	-$4,000	
Incurable (structural deterioration)	-$9,750	
Functional obsolescence	-$2,000	
External obsolescence	0	
Total depreciation	-$15,750	

Depreciated value of building	$111,750
Indicated value by cost approach	$146,750

MATH CONCEPTS   Cost Approach Basics

(cost NEW – depreciation) + land = value of property

Reproduction or replacement cost (NEW)	$500,000
Age	5 years
Full economic life	40 years
Land valuation	$50,000
Yearly depreciation amount ($500,000 ÷ 40 years)	$12,500
Full loss (5 years × $12,500 per year)	$62,500
Depreciated value of the structure ($500,000 – $62,500)	$437,500
Total property value ($437,000 + $50,000)	$487,000

Determining Reproduction or Replacement Cost New

An appraiser using the cost approach computes the reproduction or replacement cost of a building using one of the following four methods:

- *Square-foot method.* The cost per square foot of a recently built comparable structure is multiplied by the number of square feet (using exterior dimensions) in the subject building. This is the most common and easiest method of cost estimation. Figure 19.2 uses the **square-foot method** (also called the *comparison method*). For some properties, the cost per cubic foot of a recently built comparable structure is multiplied by the number of cubic feet in the subject structure.

- *Unit-in-place method.* In the **unit-in-place method** (also known as the segregated cost method), the replacement cost of a structure is estimated based on the construction cost per unit of measure of individual building components, including material, labor, overhead, and builder's profit. Most components are measured in square feet; although items such as plumbing fixtures are estimated by cost. The sum of the components is the cost of the new structure.

- *Quantity-survey method.* In the **quantity-survey method**, the quantity and quality of all materials (e.g., lumber, brick, and plaster) and the labor are estimated on a unit cost basis. These factors are added to indirect costs (e.g., building permit, survey, payroll, taxes, and builder's profit) to arrive at the total cost of the structure. This method is detailed and time-consuming, but is the most accurate method of appraising new construction.

- *Index method.* In the **index method**, a factor representing the percentage increase of construction costs up to the present time is applied to the original cost of the subject property. Because it fails to take into account individual property variables, this method is useful only as a check of the estimate reached by one of the other methods.

Depreciation

In a real estate appraisal, **depreciation** is a loss in value due to any cause compared with today's cost of replacement. It refers to a condition that adversely affects the value of an improvement to real property. Land does not depreciate—it retains its value indefinitely, except in such rare cases as downzoned urban parcels, improperly developed land, or misused farmland. Depreciation is the result of a negative condition that affects real property.

Depreciation is considered *curable* or *incurable*, depending on the contribution of the expenditure to the value of the property. For appraisal purposes, depreciation is divided into the following three classes, according to its cause:

- *Physical deterioration.* In **physical deterioration**, a *curable* item is one in need of repair, such as painting (deferred maintenance), that is economically feasible and would result in an increase in value equal to or exceeding the cost. An item is *incurable* if it is a defect caused by physical wear and tear if its correction would not be economically feasible or contribute a comparable value to the building, such as a crack in the foundation. The cost of a major repair may not warrant the financial investment.

- *Functional obsolescence.* **Functional obsolescence** means a loss in value from the market's response to the item. Outmoded or unacceptable physical or design features that are no longer considered desirable by purchasers are considered curable. Such features could be replaced or redesigned at a cost that would be offset by the anticipated increase in ultimate value. Outmoded plumbing, for example, is usually easily replaced. Room function may be redefined at no cost if the basic room layout allows for it. A bedroom adjacent to a kitchen, for example, may be converted to a family room. Gold-plated plumbing fixtures in a modestly priced tract home is an example of functionally superadequate obsolescence. Incurable obsolescence includes undesirable physical or design features that cannot be easily remedied because the cost of the cure would be greater than its resulting increase in value. For example, an office building that cannot be economically air-conditioned suffers from incurable functional obsolescence if the cost of adding air-conditioning is greater than its contribution to the building's value.

- *External obsolescence.* **External obsolescence** (previously known as economic or environmental obsolescence) is the loss in value caused by factors outside a property. These factors can be zoning, environmental, social, or economic forces. In this case, the depreciation is always incurable; the loss in value cannot be reversed by spending money on the property. For example, proximity to a polluting factory or a deteriorating neighborhood is a factor that could not be cured by the owner of the subject property. However, if the polluting factory is shut down, the loss in value may possibly be reversed.

The easiest but least precise way to determine depreciation is the **straight-line method** (also called the *economic age-life method*). Depreciation is assumed to occur at an even rate over a structure's **economic life**—the period during which it is expected to remain useful for its original intended purpose. The property's cost is divided by the number of years of its expected economic life to derive the amount of annual depreciation.

EXAMPLE

A $300,000 property may have a land value of $75,000 and an improvement value of $225,000. If the improvement is expected to last 60 years, the annual straight-line depreciation would be $3,750 ($225,000 ÷ 60 years). Such depreciation can be calculated as an annual dollar amount or as a percentage of a property's improvements.

The cost approach is most helpful in the appraisal of newer or special-purpose buildings such as schools, churches or places of worship, and public buildings. Such properties are difficult to appraise using other methods because there are seldom enough local sales to use as comparables and because the properties do not ordinarily generate income.

Much of the functional obsolescence and all of the external obsolescence can be evaluated only by considering the actions of buyers in the marketplace.

The Income Approach

The **income approach** to value is based on the present value of the rights to future income. It assumes that the income generated by a property will determine the property's value. The income approach is used for valuation of income-producing properties such as apartment buildings, office buildings, and shopping centers. In estimating value using the income approach, an appraiser must take five steps, illustrated in Figure 19.3.

Figure 19.3: Income Capitalization Approach to Value Example

Potential gross annual income	$60,000
Market rent (100% capacity)	
Income from other sources (vending machines and pay phones)	+600
	$60,600
Less vacancy and collection losses (estimated) @ 4%	−2,424
Effective gross income	$58,176
Expenses:	
Real estate taxes	$9,000
Insurance	1,000
Heat	2,500
Maintenance	6,400
Utilities, electricity, water, gas	800
Repairs	1,200
Decorating	1,400
Replacement of equipment	800
Legal and accounting	600
Advertising	300
Management	3,000
Total	$27,000
Annual net operating income	$31,176

Capitalization rate = 10% (overall rate)

Capitalization of annual net income: $31,176 ÷ 0.10 = $311,760

Income value by income approach = $311,760

1. Estimate annual potential gross income. An estimate of economic rental income must be made based on market studies. Current rental income may not reflect the current market rental rates, especially in the case of short-term leases or leases about to terminate. Potential income includes other income to the property from such sources as operating expense reimbursements from tenants, vending machines, parking fees, and laundry machines, for example.

2. Deduct an appropriate allowance for vacancy and rent loss, based on the appraiser's experience, and arrive at effective gross income.

3. Deduct the annual operating expenses, enumerated in , from the effective gross income to arrive at the annual **net operating income (NOI)**. Management costs are always included, even if the current owner manages the property. Mortgage payments (principal and interest) are debt service and not considered operating expenses. Capital expenditures are not considered expenses; however, an allowance can be calculated representing the annual usage of each major capital item. This allowance is called *reserves for replacement* or *replacement reserves*.

4. Estimate the price a typical investor would pay for the income produced by this particular type and class of property. This is done by estimating the rate of return (or yield) that an investor will demand for the investment of capital in this type of building. This rate of return is called the overall **capitalization rate** (or *cap rate*) and is determined by comparing the relationship of NOI to the sales prices of similar properties that have sold in the current market. For example, a comparable property that is producing an annual net income of $15,000 is sold for $187,500. The capitalization rate is $15,000 divided by $187,500, or 8%. If other comparable properties sold at prices that yielded substantially the same rate, it may be concluded that 8% is the market rate that the appraiser should apply to the subject property.

5. Apply the market-derived capitalization rate to the property's annual NOI to arrive at the estimate of the property's value.

With the appropriate capitalization rate and the projected annual NOI, the appraiser can obtain an indication of value by the income approach.

This formula and its variations are important in dealing with income property:

> Income ÷ rate = value
>
> Income ÷ value = rate
>
> Value × rate = income

These formulas may be illustrated graphically as:

Annual net operating income ÷ capitalization rate = value

EXAMPLE

$72,000 income ÷ 9% capitalization rate = $800,000 value, or

$72,000 income ÷ 8% capitalization rate = $900,000 value

Note the relationship between rate and value: As the rate goes down, the value increases.

Gross Rent or Gross Income Multipliers

If a buyer is interested in purchasing a one-to-four-unit residential rental property, the **gross rent multiplier (GRM)** would be used for the appraisal value. If the buyer is interested in purchasing five or more units, a commercial **gross income multiplier (GIM)** is often used in the appraisal process.

Because single-family residences usually produce only rental incomes, the GRM is used. This relates a sales price to monthly rental income. However, commercial and industrial properties generate income from many other sources (rent, concessions, operating expense reimbursements from tenants, escalation clause income, and so forth), and they are valued using their annual income from all sources.

The formulas are as follows:

For five or more residential units, commercial, or industrial property:

Sales price ÷ gross annual income = gross income multiplier (GIM)

For one to four residential units:

Sales price ÷ gross monthly rent = gross rent multiplier (GRM)

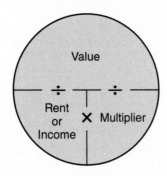

EXAMPLE

If a home recently sold for $382,000 and its monthly rental income was $2,650, the GRM for the property would be computed as follows:

$382,000 ÷ $2,650 = 144.15 GRM

To establish an accurate GRM, an appraiser must have recent sales and rental data from at least four properties that are similar to the subject property. The resulting GRM then can be applied to the estimated fair market rental of the subject property to arrive at its market value. The formula is:

Rental income × GRM = estimated market value

Figure 19.4 shows some examples of GRM comparisons.

Figure 19.4: Gross Rent Multiplier Table

Comparable No.	Sales Price	Monthly Rent	GRM
1	$280,000	$1,800	155.55
2	243,000	1,350	180.00
3	287,000	2,000	143.50
4	262,500	1,675	156.72
Subject	?	1,750	?

Note that, based on an analysis of these comparisons, comparables 2 and 3 show extremes. Based on monthly rent between comparables 1 and 4, a GRM of 156.72 seems reasonable for homes in this area. In the opinion of an appraiser, the estimated value of the subject property would be $1,750 × 156.72, or $274,260.

Reconciliation

When the three approaches to value are applied to the same property, they normally produce three separate indications of value (for example, compare Figure 19.1 and Figure 19.2). **Reconciliation** is the act of analyzing and effectively weighing the findings from the three approaches. In reconciliation, an appraiser explains not only the appropriateness of each approach but also the relative reliability of the data within each approach in line with the type of value. The appraiser should also explain how the data reflect the market functions.

The process of reconciliation is not taking the average of the three estimates of value. An average implies that the data and logic applied in each of the approaches are equally valid and reliable and should therefore be given equal weight. In fact, however, certain approaches are more valid and reliable with some kinds of properties than with others.

EXAMPLE

In appraising a home, the income approach is rarely valid, and the cost approach is of limited value unless the home is relatively new. Therefore, the sales comparison approach is usually given greatest weight in valuing single-family residences. In the appraisal of income or investment property, the income approach normally is given the greatest weight. In the appraisal of churches or places of worship, libraries, theaters, museums, schools, and other special-use properties where little or no income or sales revenue is generated, the cost approach usually is assigned the greatest weight. From this analysis, or reconciliation, a single estimate of market value is produced.

THE APPRAISAL PROCESS

Although appraising is not an exact or a precise science, the key to an accurate appraisal lies in the methodical collection and analysis of data. The appraisal process is an orderly set of procedures used to collect and analyze data to arrive at an ultimate value conclusion. The data are divided into the following two basic classes:

■ General data, which covers the nation, region, city, and neighborhood. Of particular importance is the neighborhood, where an appraiser finds the physical, economic, social, and political influences that directly affect the value and potential of the subject property.

■ Specific data, which covers details of the subject property as well as comparative data relating to costs, sales, and income and expenses of properties similar to and competitive with the subject property.

Figure 19.5 outlines the steps an appraiser takes in carrying out an appraisal assignment.

Figure 19.5: The Appraisal Process

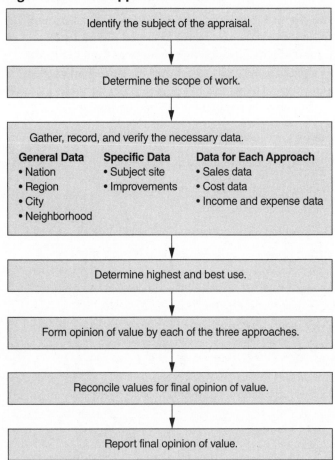

Once the approaches have been reconciled and an opinion of value has been reached, the appraiser prepares a report for the client. The report should

- identify the real estate and real property interest being appraised;

- identify the client and any other intended users;

- state the type and definition of value and cite the source of the definition;

- state the purpose and intended use of the appraisal;

- state the effective date of the opinions of value and the date of the report;

- state the extent of the process of collecting, confirming, and reporting the data (this is called scope of work);

- list all assumptions and limiting conditions that affect the analysis, opinion, and conclusions of value;

- describe the information considered, the appraisal procedures followed, and the reasoning that supports the report's conclusions (if an approach was excluded, the report should explain why);

- summarize the scope of work used to develop the appraisal;

- state the use of the real estate existing as of the date of value and the use of the real estate reflected in the appraisal;

■ describe (if necessary or appropriate) the appraiser's opinion of the highest and best use of the real estate;

■ clearly and conspicuously

– state all extraordinary assumptions and hypothetical conditions, and

– state that their use might have affected the assignment results;

■ describe any additional information that may be appropriate to show compliance with the specific guidelines established in the *USPAP* or to clearly identify and explain any departures from these guidelines; and

■ include signed certification, as required by the *USPAP*.

The Uniform Residential Appraisal Report is the form required by many government agencies (see Figure 19.6). It illustrates the types of detailed information required of an appraisal of residential property.

IN PRACTICE

While the appraiser does not determine value, neither is value determined by what the seller wants to get, what the buyer wants to pay, or what the real estate licensee recommends. The appraiser, relying on experience and expertise in valuation theories, develops a supportable and objective report called an appraisal that verifies the value indicated by the market. Sellers and real estate licensees may not agree with the appraiser's value and may argue that it is lower than they think that it should be. However, because most appraisals are ordered by lenders who base their loan on this value, the appraiser must be able to back up the appraisal report with quantifiable conclusions. Significantly, sales contracts may also be contingent upon the property appraising to sales price.

Figure 19.6: General Business Cycle

Uniform Residential Appraisal Report — File #

The purpose of this summary appraisal report is to provide the lender/client with an accurate, and adequately supported, opinion of the market value of the subject property.

SUBJECT

- Property Address — City — State — Zip Code
- Borrower — Owner of Public Record — County
- Legal Description
- Assessor's Parcel # — Tax Year — R.E. Taxes $
- Neighborhood Name — Map Reference — Census Tract
- Occupant ☐ Owner ☐ Tenant ☐ Vacant — Special Assessments $ — ☐ PUD — HOA $ ☐ per year ☐ per month
- Property Rights Appraised ☐ Fee Simple ☐ Leasehold ☐ Other (describe)
- Assignment Type ☐ Purchase Transaction ☐ Refinance Transaction ☐ Other (describe)
- Lender/Client — Address
- Is the subject property currently offered for sale or has it been offered for sale in the twelve months prior to the effective date of this appraisal? ☐ Yes ☐ No
- Report data source(s) used, offering price(s), and date(s).

CONTRACT

- I ☐ did ☐ did not analyze the contract for sale for the subject purchase transaction. Explain the results of the analysis of the contract for sale or why the analysis was not performed.
- Contract Price $ — Date of Contract — Is the property seller the owner of public record? ☐ Yes ☐ No — Data Source(s)
- Is there any financial assistance (loan charges, sale concessions, gift or downpayment assistance, etc.) to be paid by any party on behalf of the borrower? ☐ Yes ☐ No
- If Yes, report the total dollar amount and describe the items to be paid.

NEIGHBORHOOD

Note: Race and the racial composition of the neighborhood are not appraisal factors.

Neighborhood Characteristics	One-Unit Housing Trends	One-Unit Housing	Present Land Use %
Location ☐ Urban ☐ Suburban ☐ Rural	Property Values ☐ Increasing ☐ Stable ☐ Declining	PRICE AGE	One-Unit %
Built-Up ☐ Over 75% ☐ 25–75% ☐ Under 25%	Demand/Supply ☐ Shortage ☐ In Balance ☐ Over Supply	$ (000) (yrs)	2-4 Unit %
Growth ☐ Rapid ☐ Stable ☐ Slow	Marketing Time ☐ Under 3 mths ☐ 3–6 mths ☐ Over 6 mths	Low	Multi-Family %
Neighborhood Boundaries		High	Commercial %
		Pred.	Other %

- Neighborhood Description
- Market Conditions (including support for the above conclusions)

SITE

- Dimensions — Area — Shape — View
- Specific Zoning Classification — Zoning Description
- Zoning Compliance ☐ Legal ☐ Legal Nonconforming (Grandfathered Use) ☐ No Zoning ☐ Illegal (describe)
- Is the highest and best use of the subject property as improved (or as proposed per plans and specifications) the present use? ☐ Yes ☐ No If No, describe

Utilities	Public	Other (describe)		Public	Other (describe)	Off-site Improvements—Type	Public	Private
Electricity	☐	☐	Water	☐	☐	Street	☐	☐
Gas	☐	☐	Sanitary Sewer	☐	☐	Alley	☐	☐

- FEMA Special Flood Hazard Area ☐ Yes ☐ No FEMA Flood Zone — FEMA Map # — FEMA Map Date
- Are the utilities and off-site improvements typical for the market area? ☐ Yes ☐ No If No, describe
- Are there any adverse site conditions or external factors (easements, encroachments, environmental conditions, land uses, etc.)? ☐ Yes ☐ No If Yes, describe

IMPROVEMENTS

General Description	Foundation	Exterior Description materials/condition	Interior materials/condition
Units ☐ One ☐ One with Accessory Unit	☐ Concrete Slab ☐ Crawl Space	Foundation Walls	Floors
# of Stories	☐ Full Basement ☐ Partial Basement	Exterior Walls	Walls
Type ☐ Det. ☐ Att. ☐ S-Det./End Unit	Basement Area sq. ft.	Roof Surface	Trim/Finish
☐ Existing ☐ Proposed ☐ Under Const.	Basement Finish %	Gutters & Downspouts	Bath Floor
Design (Style)	☐ Outside Entry/Exit ☐ Sump Pump	Window Type	Bath Wainscot
Year Built	Evidence of ☐ Infestation	Storm Sash/Insulated	Car Storage ☐ None
Effective Age (Yrs)	☐ Dampness ☐ Settlement	Screens	☐ Driveway # of Cars
Attic ☐ None	Heating ☐ FWA ☐ HWBB ☐ Radiant	Amenities ☐ Woodstove(s) #	Driveway Surface
☐ Drop Stair ☐ Stairs	☐ Other Fuel	☐ Fireplace(s) # ☐ Fence	☐ Garage # of Cars
☐ Floor ☐ Scuttle	Cooling ☐ Central Air Conditioning	☐ Patio/Deck ☐ Porch	☐ Carport # of Cars
☐ Finished ☐ Heated	☐ Individual ☐ Other	☐ Pool ☐ Other	☐ Att. ☐ Det. ☐ Built-in

- Appliances ☐ Refrigerator ☐ Range/Oven ☐ Dishwasher ☐ Disposal ☐ Microwave ☐ Washer/Dryer ☐ Other (describe)
- Finished area **above** grade contains: Rooms Bedrooms Bath(s) Square Feet of Gross Living Area Above Grade
- Additional features (special energy efficient items, etc.)
- Describe the condition of the property (including needed repairs, deterioration, renovations, remodeling, etc.).
- Are there any physical deficiencies or adverse conditions that affect the livability, soundness, or structural integrity of the property? ☐ Yes ☐ No If Yes, describe
- Does the property generally conform to the neighborhood (functional utility, style, condition, use, construction, etc.)? ☐ Yes ☐ No If No, describe

Figure 19.6: General Business Cycle (continued)

Uniform Residential Appraisal Report
File #

There are _____ comparable properties currently offered for sale in the subject neighborhood ranging in price from $ _____ to $ _____.
There are _____ comparable sales in the subject neighborhood within the past twelve months ranging in sale price from $ _____ to $ _____.

FEATURE	SUBJECT	COMPARABLE SALE # 1		COMPARABLE SALE # 2		COMPARABLE SALE # 3	
Address							
Proximity to Subject							
Sale Price	$		$		$		$
Sale Price/Gross Liv. Area	$ sq. ft.	$ sq. ft.		$ sq. ft.		$ sq. ft.	
Data Source(s)							
Verification Source(s)							
VALUE ADJUSTMENTS	DESCRIPTION	DESCRIPTION	+(-) $ Adjustment	DESCRIPTION	+(-) $ Adjustment	DESCRIPTION	+(-) $ Adjustment
Sale or Financing Concessions							
Date of Sale/Time							
Location							
Leasehold/Fee Simple							
Site							
View							
Design (Style)							
Quality of Construction							
Actual Age							
Condition							
Above Grade Room Count	Total Bdrms. Baths	Total Bdrms. Baths		Total Bdrms. Baths		Total Bdrms. Baths	
Gross Living Area	sq. ft.	sq. ft.		sq. ft.		sq. ft.	
Basement & Finished Rooms Below Grade							
Functional Utility							
Heating/Cooling							
Energy Efficient Items							
Garage/Carport							
Porch/Patio/Deck							
Net Adjustment (Total)		☐ + ☐ -	$	☐ + ☐ -	$	☐ + ☐ -	$
Adjusted Sale Price of Comparables		Net Adj. % Gross Adj. %	$	Net Adj. % Gross Adj. %	$	Net Adj. % Gross Adj. %	$

I ☐ did ☐ did not research the sale or transfer history of the subject property and comparable sales. If not, explain

My research ☐ did ☐ did not reveal any prior sales or transfers of the subject property for the three years prior to the effective date of this appraisal.
Data source(s)
My research ☐ did ☐ did not reveal any prior sales or transfers of the comparable sales for the year prior to the date of sale of the comparable sale.
Data source(s)
Report the results of the research and analysis of the prior sale or transfer history of the subject property and comparable sales (report additional prior sales on page 3).

ITEM	SUBJECT	COMPARABLE SALE # 1	COMPARABLE SALE # 2	COMPARABLE SALE # 3
Date of Prior Sale/Transfer				
Price of Prior Sale/Transfer				
Data Source(s)				
Effective Date of Data Source(s)				

Analysis of prior sale or transfer history of the subject property and comparable sales

Summary of Sales Comparison Approach

Indicated Value by Sales Comparison Approach $

Indicated Value by: Sales Comparison Approach $ **Cost Approach (if developed)** $ **Income Approach (if developed)** $

This appraisal is made ☐ "as is", ☐ subject to completion per plans and specifications on the basis of a hypothetical condition that the improvements have been completed, ☐ subject to the following repairs or alterations on the basis of a hypothetical condition that the repairs or alterations have been completed, or ☐ subject to the following required inspection based on the extraordinary assumption that the condition or deficiency does not require alteration or repair:

Based on a complete visual inspection of the interior and exterior areas of the subject property, defined scope of work, statement of assumptions and limiting conditions, and appraiser's certification, my (our) opinion of the market value, as defined, of the real property that is the subject of this report is $ _____ , as of _____ , which is the date of inspection and the effective date of this appraisal.

Freddie Mac Form 70   March 2005   Page 2 of 6   Fannie Mae Form 1004   March 2005

Figure 19.6: General Business Cycle (continued)

Uniform Residential Appraisal Report   File #

SAMPLE

COST APPROACH TO VALUE (not required by Fannie Mae)

Provide adequate information for the lender/client to replicate the below cost figures and calculations.

Support for the opinion of site value (summary of comparable land sales or other methods for estimating site value)

ESTIMATED ☐ REPRODUCTION OR ☐ REPLACEMENT COST NEW	OPINION OF SITE VALUE .... = $			
Source of cost data	Dwelling	Sq. Ft. @ $	.... = $	
Quality rating from cost service Effective date of cost data		Sq. Ft. @ $	.... = $	
Comments on Cost Approach (gross living area calculations, depreciation, etc.)				
	Garage/Carport	Sq. Ft. @ $	.... = $	
	Total Estimate of Cost-New		.... = $	
	Less Physical	Functional	External	
	Depreciation			= $( )
	Depreciated Cost of Improvements.................................... = $			
	"As-is" Value of Site Improvements.................................... = $			
Estimated Remaining Economic Life (HUD and VA only) Years	Indicated Value By Cost Approach .... = $			

INCOME APPROACH TO VALUE (not required by Fannie Mae)

Estimated Monthly Market Rent $ X Gross Rent Multiplier   = $ Indicated Value by Income Approach

Summary of Income Approach (including support for market rent and GRM)

PROJECT INFORMATION FOR PUDs (if applicable)

Is the developer/builder in control of the Homeowners' Association (HOA)? ☐ Yes ☐ No   Unit type(s) ☐ Detached ☐ Attached

Provide the following information for PUDs ONLY if the developer/builder is in control of the HOA and the subject property is an attached dwelling unit.

Legal name of project

Total number of phases   Total number of units   Total number of units sold

Total number of units rented   Total number of units for sale   Data source(s)

Was the project created by the conversion of an existing building(s) into a PUD? ☐ Yes ☐ No   If Yes, date of conversion

Does the project contain any multi-dwelling units? ☐ Yes ☐ No   Data source(s)

Are the units, common elements, and recreation facilities complete? ☐ Yes ☐ No   If No, describe the status of completion.

Are the common elements leased to or by the Homeowners' Association? ☐ Yes ☐ No   If Yes, describe the rental terms and options.

Describe common elements and recreational facilities

ADDITIONAL COMMENTS

COST APPROACH

INCOME

PUD INFORMATION

Figure 19.6: General Business Cycle (continued)

Uniform Residential Appraisal Report   File #

This report form is designed to report an appraisal of a one-unit property or a one-unit property with an accessory unit; including a unit in a planned unit development (PUD). This report form is not designed to report an appraisal of a manufactured home or a unit in a condominium or cooperative project.

This appraisal report is subject to the following scope of work, intended use, intended user, definition of market value, statement of assumptions and limiting conditions, and certifications. Modifications, additions, or deletions to the intended use, intended user, definition of market value, or assumptions and limiting conditions are not permitted. The appraiser may expand the scope of work to include any additional research or analysis necessary based on the complexity of this appraisal assignment. Modifications or deletions to the certifications are also not permitted. However, additional certifications that do not constitute material alterations to this appraisal report, such as those required by law or those related to the appraiser's continuing education or membership in an appraisal organization, are permitted.

SCOPE OF WORK: The scope of work for this appraisal is defined by the complexity of this appraisal assignment and the reporting requirements of this appraisal report form, including the following definition of market value, statement of assumptions and limiting conditions, and certifications. The appraiser must, at a minimum: (1) perform a complete visual inspection of the interior and exterior areas of the subject property, (2) inspect the neighborhood, (3) inspect each of the comparable sales from at least the street, (4) research, verify, and analyze data from reliable public and/or private sources, and (5) report his or her analysis, opinions, and conclusions in this appraisal report.

INTENDED USE: The intended use of this appraisal report is for the lender/client to evaluate the property that is the subject of this appraisal for a mortgage finance transaction.

INTENDED USER: The intended user of this appraisal report is the lender/client.

DEFINITION OF MARKET VALUE: The most probable price which a property should bring in a competitive and open market under all conditions requisite to a fair sale, the buyer and seller, each acting prudently, knowledgeably and assuming the price is not affected by undue stimulus. Implicit in this definition is the consummation of a sale as of a specified date and the passing of title from seller to buyer under conditions whereby: (1) buyer and seller are typically motivated; (2) both parties are well informed or well advised, and each acting in what he or she considers his or her own best interest; (3) a reasonable time is allowed for exposure in the open market; (4) payment is made in terms of cash in U. S. dollars or in terms of financial arrangements comparable thereto; and (5) the price represents the normal consideration for the property sold unaffected by special or creative financing or sales concessions* granted by anyone associated with the sale.

*Adjustments to the comparables must be made for special or creative financing or sales concessions. No adjustments are necessary for those costs which are normally paid by sellers as a result of tradition or law in a market area; these costs are readily identifiable since the seller pays these costs in virtually all sales transactions. Special or creative financing adjustments can be made to the comparable property by comparisons to financing terms offered by a third party institutional lender that is not already involved in the property or transaction. Any adjustment should not be calculated on a mechanical dollar for dollar cost of the financing or concession but the dollar amount of any adjustment should approximate the market's reaction to the financing or concessions based on the appraiser's judgment.

STATEMENT OF ASSUMPTIONS AND LIMITING CONDITIONS: The appraiser's certification in this report is subject to the following assumptions and limiting conditions:

1. The appraiser will not be responsible for matters of a legal nature that affect either the property being appraised or the title to it, except for information that he or she became aware of during the research involved in performing this appraisal. The appraiser assumes that the title is good and marketable and will not render any opinions about the title.

2. The appraiser has provided a sketch in this appraisal report to show the approximate dimensions of the improvements. The sketch is included only to assist the reader in visualizing the property and understanding the appraiser's determination of its size.

3. The appraiser has examined the available flood maps that are provided by the Federal Emergency Management Agency (or other data sources) and has noted in this appraisal report whether any portion of the subject site is located in an identified Special Flood Hazard Area. Because the appraiser is not a surveyor, he or she makes no guarantees, express or implied, regarding this determination.

4. The appraiser will not give testimony or appear in court because he or she made an appraisal of the property in question, unless specific arrangements to do so have been made beforehand, or as otherwise required by law.

5. The appraiser has noted in this appraisal report any adverse conditions (such as needed repairs, deterioration, the presence of hazardous wastes, toxic substances, etc.) observed during the inspection of the subject property or that he or she became aware of during the research involved in performing this appraisal. Unless otherwise stated in this appraisal report, the appraiser has no knowledge of any hidden or unapparent physical deficiencies or adverse conditions of the property (such as, but not limited to, needed repairs, deterioration, the presence of hazardous wastes, toxic substances, adverse environmental conditions, etc.) that would make the property less valuable, and has assumed that there are no such conditions and makes no guarantees or warranties, express or implied. The appraiser will not be responsible for any such conditions that do exist or for any engineering or testing that might be required to discover whether such conditions exist. Because the appraiser is not an expert in the field of environmental hazards, this appraisal report must not be considered as an environmental assessment of the property.

6. The appraiser has based his or her appraisal report and valuation conclusion for an appraisal that is subject to satisfactory completion, repairs, or alterations on the assumption that the completion, repairs, or alterations of the subject property will be performed in a professional manner.

Unit 19

Figure 19.6: General Business Cycle (continued)

Uniform Residential Appraisal Report   File

APPRAISER'S CERTIFICATION: The Appraiser certifies and agrees that:

1. I have, at a minimum, developed and reported this appraisal in accordance with the scope of work requirements stated in this appraisal report.

2. I performed a complete visual inspection of the interior and exterior areas of the subject property. I reported the condition of the improvements in factual, specific terms. I identified and reported the physical deficiencies that could affect the livability, soundness, or structural integrity of the property.

3. I performed this appraisal in accordance with the requirements of the Uniform Standards of Professional Appraisal Practice that were adopted and promulgated by the Appraisal Standards Board of The Appraisal Foundation and that were in place at the time this appraisal report was prepared.

4. I developed my opinion of the market value of the real property that is the subject of this report based on the sales comparison approach to value. I have adequate comparable market data to develop a reliable sales comparison approach for this appraisal assignment. I further certify that I considered the cost and income approaches to value but did not develop them, unless otherwise indicated in this report.

5. I researched, verified, analyzed, and reported on any current agreement for sale for the subject property, any offering for sale of the subject property in the twelve months prior to the effective date of this appraisal, and the prior sales of the subject property for a minimum of three years prior to the effective date of this appraisal, unless otherwise indicated in this report.

6. I researched, verified, analyzed, and reported on the prior sales of the comparable sales for a minimum of one year prior to the date of sale of the comparable sale, unless otherwise indicated in this report.

7. I selected and used comparable sales that are locationally, physically, and functionally the most similar to the subject property.

8. I have not used comparable sales that were the result of combining a land sale with the contract purchase price of a home that has been built or will be built on the land.

9. I have reported adjustments to the comparable sales that reflect the market's reaction to the differences between the subject property and the comparable sales.

10. I verified, from a disinterested source, all information in this report that was provided by parties who have a financial interest in the sale or financing of the subject property.

11. I have knowledge and experience in appraising this type of property in this market area.

12. I am aware of, and have access to, the necessary and appropriate public and private data sources, such as multiple listing services, tax assessment records, public land records and other such data sources for the area in which the property is located.

13. I obtained the information, estimates, and opinions furnished by other parties and expressed in this appraisal report from reliable sources that I believe to be true and correct.

14. I have taken into consideration the factors that have an impact on value with respect to the subject neighborhood, subject property, and the proximity of the subject property to adverse influences in the development of my opinion of market value. I have noted in this appraisal report any adverse conditions (such as, but not limited to, needed repairs, deterioration, the presence of hazardous wastes, toxic substances, adverse environmental conditions, etc.) observed during the inspection of the subject property or that I became aware of during the research involved in performing this appraisal. I have considered these adverse conditions in my analysis of the property value, and have reported on the effect of the conditions on the value and marketability of the subject property.

15. I have not knowingly withheld any significant information from this appraisal report and, to the best of my knowledge, all statements and information in this appraisal report are true and correct.

16. I stated in this appraisal report my own personal, unbiased, and professional analysis, opinions, and conclusions, which are subject only to the assumptions and limiting conditions in this appraisal report.

17. I have no present or prospective interest in the property that is the subject of this report, and I have no present or prospective personal interest or bias with respect to the participants in the transaction. I did not base, either partially or completely, my analysis and/or opinion of market value in this appraisal report on the race, color, religion, sex, age, marital status, handicap, familial status, or national origin of either the prospective owners or occupants of the subject property or of the present owners or occupants of the properties in the vicinity of the subject property or on any other basis prohibited by law.

18. My employment and/or compensation for performing this appraisal or any future or anticipated appraisals was not conditioned on any agreement or understanding, written or otherwise, that I would report (or present analysis supporting) a predetermined specific value, a predetermined minimum value, a range or direction in value, a value that favors the cause of any party, or the attainment of a specific result or occurrence of a specific subsequent event (such as approval of a pending mortgage loan application).

19. I personally prepared all conclusions and opinions about the real estate that were set forth in this appraisal report. If I relied on significant real property appraisal assistance from any individual or individuals in the performance of this appraisal or the preparation of this appraisal report, I have named such individual(s) and disclosed the specific tasks performed in this appraisal report. I certify that any individual so named is qualified to perform the tasks. I have not authorized anyone to make a change to any item in this appraisal report; therefore, any change made to this appraisal is unauthorized and I will take no responsibility for it.

20. I identified the lender/client in this appraisal report who is the individual, organization, or agent for the organization that ordered and will receive this appraisal report.

Figure 19.6: General Business Cycle (continued)

Uniform Residential Appraisal Report   File

21. The lender/client may disclose or distribute this appraisal report to: the borrower; another lender at the request of the borrower; the mortgagee or its successors and assigns; mortgage insurers; government sponsored enterprises; other secondary market participants; data collection or reporting services; professional appraisal organizations; any department, agency, or instrumentality of the United States; and any state, the District of Columbia, or other jurisdictions; without having to obtain the appraiser's or supervisory appraiser's (if applicable) consent. Such consent must be obtained before this appraisal report may be disclosed or distributed to any other party (including, but not limited to, the public through advertising, public relations, news, sales, or other media).

22. I am aware that any disclosure or distribution of this appraisal report by me or the lender/client may be subject to certain laws and regulations. Further, I am also subject to the provisions of the Uniform Standards of Professional Appraisal Practice that pertain to disclosure or distribution by me.

23. The borrower, another lender at the request of the borrower, the mortgagee or its successors and assigns, mortgage insurers, government sponsored enterprises, and other secondary market participants may rely on this appraisal report as part of any mortgage finance transaction that involves any one or more of these parties.

24. If this appraisal report was transmitted as an "electronic record" containing my "electronic signature," as those terms are defined in applicable federal and/or state laws (excluding audio and video recordings), or a facsimile transmission of this appraisal report containing a copy or representation of my signature, the appraisal report shall be as effective, enforceable and valid as if a paper version of this appraisal report were delivered containing my original hand written signature.

25. Any intentional or negligent misrepresentation(s) contained in this appraisal report may result in civil liability and/or criminal penalties including, but not limited to, fine or imprisonment or both under the provisions of Title 18, United States Code, Section 1001, et seq., or similar state laws.

SUPERVISORY APPRAISER'S CERTIFICATION: The Supervisory Appraiser certifies and agrees that:

1. I directly supervised the appraiser for this appraisal assignment, have read the appraisal report, and agree with the appraiser's analysis, opinions, statements, conclusions, and the appraiser's certification.

2. I accept full responsibility for the contents of this appraisal report including, but not limited to, the appraiser's analysis, opinions, statements, conclusions, and the appraiser's certification.

3. The appraiser identified in this appraisal report is either a sub-contractor or an employee of the supervisory appraiser (or the appraisal firm), is qualified to perform this appraisal, and is acceptable to perform this appraisal under the applicable state law.

4. This appraisal report complies with the Uniform Standards of Professional Appraisal Practice that were adopted and promulgated by the Appraisal Standards Board of The Appraisal Foundation and that were in place at the time this appraisal report was prepared.

5. If this appraisal report was transmitted as an "electronic record" containing my "electronic signature," as those terms are defined in applicable federal and/or state laws (excluding audio and video recordings), or a facsimile transmission of this appraisal report containing a copy or representation of my signature, the appraisal report shall be as effective, enforceable and valid as if a paper version of this appraisal report were delivered containing my original hand written signature.

SAMPLE

APPRAISER	SUPERVISORY APPRAISER (ONLY IF REQUIRED)
Signature_____	Signature_____
Name _____	Name _____
Company Name _____	Company Name _____
Company Address_____	Company Address_____
Telephone Number _____	Telephone Number _____
Email Address_____	Email Address_____
Date of Signature and Report_____	Date of Signature _____
Effective Date of Appraisal _____	State Certification #_____
State Certification #_____	or State License #_____
or State License #_____	State _____
or Other (describe)_____ State #_____	Expiration Date of Certification or License _____
State _____	
Expiration Date of Certification or License _____	SUBJECT PROPERTY
ADDRESS OF PROPERTY APPRAISED	☐ Did not inspect subject property
_____	☐ Did inspect exterior of subject property from street
_____	Date of Inspection _____
APPRAISED VALUE OF SUBJECT PROPERTY $_____	☐ Did inspect interior and exterior of subject property
LENDER/CLIENT	Date of Inspection _____
Name _____	
Company Name _____	COMPARABLE SALES
Company Address_____	☐ Did not inspect exterior of comparable sales from street
_____	☐ Did inspect exterior of comparable sales from street
Email Address_____	Date of Inspection _____

Unit 19

SUMMARY

An appraisal is an estimate or opinion of value based on supportable evidence and appraisal methods, defined by the *Uniform Standards of Appraisal Practice (USPAP)*. An appraiser must be state-licensed or certified for an appraisal performed as part of a federally related transaction.

Real estate licensees also compile data. A comparative market analysis (CMA) is a report of market statistics that assists consumers in the listing and buying process, but it is not an appraisal. A broker's price opinion (BPO) may be used in a non-federally related transaction: home equity lines, refinancing, portfolio management loss mitigation, and collections.

Basic to appraising are certain underlying economic principles, such as highest and best use, substitution, supply and demand, conformity, anticipation, increasing and diminishing returns, regression, progression, plottage, contribution, competition, and change.

Value is created by demand, utility, scarcity, and transferability of property (DUST). Market value is the most probable price that property should bring in a fair sale, but market value is not necessarily the same as price paid or cost to construct.

A sales comparison approach makes use of sales of properties comparable (called comps) to the property that is the subject of the appraisal by adding or subtracting the value of a feature present or absent in the subject property versus the comparable.

The cost approach estimates current reproduction or replacement cost of constructing building and other property improvements using the square-foot method, the unit-in-place method, the quantity-survey method, or the index method. The cost approach also estimates accrued depreciation using the straight-line method (economic age-life method) or by estimating items of physical deterioration, functional obsolescence, or external obsolescence.

The income approach is based on the present value of the right to future income and uses the following five steps:

1. Estimate annual potential gross income

2. Deduct allowance for vacancy and rent loss to find effective gross income

3. Deduct annual operating expenses to find net operating income (NOI)

4. Estimate rate of return (capitalization rate or cap rate) for subject analyzing capitalization rates of similar properties

5. Derive estimate of subject's market value by applying capitalization rate to annual NOI: net operating income ÷ capitalization rate = value

The gross rent multiplier (GRM) may be used to estimate the value of single-family residential rental properties; a gross income multiplier (GIM), based on gross annual income from all sources, may be used for larger residential and commercial properties.

The Real Estate Appraiser Licensing Act of 2002, as amended in 2009, requires mandatory licensure, with limited exceptions, of Illinois appraisers. Only individuals (not corporations, partnerships, firms, or groups) may be certified as appraisers or act as associate real estate trainee appraisers.

UNIT 19 QUIZ

1. Which of these appraisal methods uses a rate of investment return?
   A. Income approach
   B. Sales comparison approach
   C. Cost approach
   D. Gross income multiplier method

2. The characteristics of value include
   A. progression.
   B. anticipation.
   C. scarcity.
   D. balance.

3. Two adjacent vacant lots are each worth $50,000. However, if they are sold as a single lot, the combined parcel is worth $120,000. What principle does this illustrate?
   A. Substitution
   B. Regression
   C. Progression
   D. Plottage

4. The amount of money a property commands in the marketplace is its
   A. intrinsic value.
   B. subjective value.
   C. market value.
   D. book value.

5. A homeowner constructs an eight-bedroom brick house with a tennis court, greenhouse, and indoor pool in a neighborhood of modest two- and three-bedroom frame houses on narrow lots. The value of this house is likely to be affected by what principle?
   A. Progression
   B. Assemblage
   C. Change
   D. Regression

6. A homeowner constructs an eight-bedroom brick house with a tennis court, greenhouse, and indoor pool in a neighborhood of modest two- and three-bedroom frame houses on narrow lots. The owners of the lesser-valued houses in the neighborhood may find that the values of their homes are affected by what principle?
   A. Increasing returns
   B. Progression
   C. Competition
   D. Regression

7. For appraisal purposes, depreciation is *NOT* caused by
   A. accelerated capitalization.
   B. functional obsolescence.
   C. physical deterioration.
   D. external obsolescence.

8. The term *reconciliation* refers to
   A. loss of value due to any cause.
   B. analyzing the results obtained by the different approaches to value to determine a final estimate of value.
   C. separating the value of the land from the total value of the property to compute depreciation.
   D. the process by which an appraiser determines the highest and best use for a parcel of land.

9. If a property's annual net income is $24,000 and it is valued at $300,000, what is its capitalization rate?
   A. 10.5%
   B. 12.5%
   C. 15%
   D. 8%

10. Certain figures must be determined by an appraiser before value can be computed by the income approach. Which of these is *NOT* used by an appraiser applying the income approach to value?
    A. Annual net operating income
    B. Capitalization rate
    C. Accrued depreciation
    D. Annual gross income

11. An appraiser who is asked to determine the value of an existing strip shopping center would probably give the *MOST* weight to which approach to value?
    A. Cost approach
    B. Income approach
    C. Sales comparison approach
    D. Index method

12. The market value of a parcel of real estate is
    A. an estimate of its future benefits.
    B. an estimate of the most probable price it should bring.
    C. the amount of money paid for the property.
    D. its value without improvements.

13. Capitalization is the process by which annual net operating income is used to
    A. determine cost.
    B. estimate value.
    C. establish depreciation.
    D. determine potential tax value.

14. From the reproduction or replacement cost of a building, the appraiser deducts depreciation, which represents
    A. the remaining economic life of the building.
    B. remodeling costs to increase rentals.
    C. loss of value due to any cause.
    D. costs to modernize the building.

15. The effective gross annual income from a property is $112,000. Total expenses for this year are $53,700. What capitalization rate was used to obtain a valuation of $542,325?
    A. 9.75%
    B. 10.25%
    C. 10.75%
    D. 10.5%

16. Which factor is important in comparing properties under the sales comparison approach to value?
    A. Active listings
    B. Date of sale
    C. Property rent roll
    D. Depreciation

17. A building was purchased five years ago for $240,000. It currently has an estimated remaining useful life of 60 years. What is the property's total depreciation to date?
    A. $14,364
    B. $20,000
    C. $18,462
    D. $54,000

18. Which of these is the act of analyzing and effectively weighing the findings from the three approaches to appraisal?
    A. Reconciliation
    B. Reintegration
    C. Benefit analysis
    D. Appraisal analysis

19. The appraised value of a residence with four bedrooms and one bathroom would probably be reduced because of
    A. functional obsolescence.
    B. external obsolescence.
    C. curable physical deterioration.
    D. incurable physical deterioration.

20. An individual wants to be an appraiser in the northwest suburbs of Chicago. While she is willing to appraise residential properties, her real interest is in appraising commercial properties. If she wants to be qualified to conduct appraisals under FIRREA, this individual must
    A. become a certified general real estate appraiser.
    B. become an associate real estate trainee appraiser.
    C. become a certified residential real estate appraiser.
    D. do nothing because individuals who wish to conduct appraisals under FIRREA must receive federal appraisal certification rather than state licensing.

UNIT
20

Land Use Controls and Property Development

LEARNING OBJECTIVES

When you have completed this unit, you will be able to accomplish the following.

› Describe how a comprehensive plan influences local real estate development.
› Distinguish the function and characteristics of building codes and zoning ordinances.
› Explain the various issues involved in subdivision.
› Identify the various types of public and private land-use controls.

KEY TERMS

buffer zone	developer	restrictive covenants
building code	enabling acts	subdivider
comprehensive plan	Interstate Land Sales Full	subdivision
conditional-use permit	Disclosure Act of 1968	variance
covenants, conditions,	laches	zoning ordinance
and restrictions (CC&Rs)	nonconforming use	
density zoning	plat map	

OVERVIEW

Broad though they may be, the rights of real estate ownership are not absolute. Land use is regulated by public and private restrictions and through the public ownership of land by federal, state, and local governments.

The government encourages private ownership of land, but this does not always mean that owners can do whatever they want with their properties. It is necessary for a certain amount of land to be owned by the government for such uses as municipal buildings, state government buildings, schools, and military bases. Government ownership may also serve the public interest through urban renewal efforts, public housing, and streets and highways. Often, the only way to ensure that enough land is set aside for recreational and conservation purposes is through direct government ownership in the form of national and state parks and forest preserves.

The states' *police power* is their inherent authority to create regulations needed to protect the public health, safety, and welfare. Through **enabling acts**, states delegate to counties and local municipalities the authority to enact ordinances in keeping with general laws. The increasing demands placed on finite natural resources have made it necessary for cities, towns, and villages to increase their limitations on the private use of real estate. There are now controls over noise, air, and water pollution as well as population density.

Article VII of the Constitution of the State of Illinois allows for *home-rule* units of government. Any municipality with a population in excess of 25,000 and any county that has a chief executive officer elected by the people are automatically home-rule units. However, a home-rule unit may elect by referendum not to be one. On the other hand, a municipality of fewer than 25,000 people may elect by referendum to become a home-rule unit of government. Townships are not allowed to be home-rule units.

Constitutionally, a home-rule unit of government may exercise any power and perform any function pertaining to its government, including the exercise of police power by way of laws that control the use of land. Home-rule units also have greater freedom to enforce their laws, including the power to jail offenders for up to six months. Non-home-rule units derive their authority to pass land-use controls from the state government through enabling statutes.

Occasionally, the laws of one unit of government conflict with another's. If any ordinance of a home rule county conflicts with any ordinance of a home rule municipality, the municipal ordinance prevails. Township zoning ordinances must give way to county zoning ordinances, and townships are not empowered to pass subdivision controls or building codes.

THE COMPREHENSIVE PLAN

Local governments, municipalities, and counties establish development goals by creating a comprehensive plan. The **comprehensive plan** (also called the *master plan*) is not a regulatory document but rather a guide to planning for change rather than reacting to proposals. The comprehensive plan is usually long term—20 years or longer—and often includes (1) a general plan that can be revised and updated more frequently, (2) plans for specific areas, and (3) strategic plans. Systematic planning for orderly growth consists of the following basic elements:

- Land use—that is, a determination of how much land may be proposed for residence, industry, business, agriculture, traffic and transit facilities, utilities, community facilities, parks and recreational facilities, floodplains, and areas of special hazards

- Housing needs of present and anticipated residents, including rehabilitation of declining neighborhoods as well as new residential developments

- Movement of people and goods, including highways and public transit, parking facilities, and pedestrian and bikeway systems

- Community facilities and utilities such as schools, libraries, hospitals, recreational facilities, fire and police stations, water resources, sewage and waste treatment and disposal, storm drainage, and flood management

- Energy conservation to reduce energy consumption and promote the use of renewable energy sources

The preparation of a comprehensive plan involves surveys, studies, and analyses of housing, demographic, and economic characteristics and trends. A given municipality's planning activities may be coordinated with other government bodies and private interests to achieve orderly growth and development.

ZONING

Zoning is a regulatory tool that helps communities regulate and control how land is used. **Zoning ordinances** are local laws that implement the comprehensive plan and regulate and control the use of land and structures within designated land-use districts. If the comprehensive or master plan is the big picture, zoning makes up the details of that picture.

No nationwide or statewide zoning ordinances exist. Rather, zoning powers are conferred on municipal governments by state enabling acts. State and federal governments may, however, regulate land use through special legislation, such as scenic easements, coastal management, and environmental laws.

Zoning affects

- permitted uses of each parcel of land,
- lot sizes,
- types of permissible structures,
- building heights,
- setbacks (the minimum distance away from streets or sidewalks that structures may be built),
- style and appearance of structures,
- density (the ratio of land area to structure area), and
- protection of natural resources.

Zoning ordinances cannot be static; they must remain flexible to meet the changing needs of society.

EXAMPLE

Many factories and warehouses sit empty due to changing economic conditions. Some cities have begun changing the zoning ordinances for such properties to permit new residential or commercial developments in areas once zoned strictly for heavy industrial use. Coupled with tax incentives, these changes attract developers back into these cities. Simple zoning changes can help revitalize whole neighborhoods in big cities.

Zoning Objectives

Land is divided into zones. The zones are identified by a coding system that outlines how the land may be used according to the code. Common zoning classifications include "C" for commercial, "R" for residential, and "A" for agricultural. These land-use areas are further divided into subclasses. For example, residential areas may be subdivided to provide for detached single-family dwellings, semi-detached structures containing not more than four dwelling units, walk-up apartments, highrise apartments, and so forth.

A planned unit development (PUD) is a development where land is set aside for mixed-use purposes, such as residential, commercial, and public areas. Zoning regulations may be modified for PUDs.

To meet both the growing demand for a variety of housing types and the need for innovative residential and nonresidential development, municipalities often adopt ordinances for subdivisions and planned residential developments. Some municipalities also use buffer zones to ease transition from one use to another. A **buffer zone** is typically a strip of land separating land dedicated to one use from land dedicated to another use. For example, landscaped parks and playgrounds and hiking trails are used to screen residential areas from nonresidential zones. Also, many municipalities use certain types of zoning to focus on special land-use objectives. These include

- *bulk zoning* (also called *density zoning*) to control density and avoid overcrowding by imposing restrictions such as setbacks and maximum building heights, and requiring a specified percentage of open area or by restricting new construction projects;
- *aesthetic zoning* to specify certain types of architecture for new buildings; and
- *incentive zoning* to ensure that certain uses are incorporated into developments, such as requiring the street floor of an office building to house retail establishments.

Constitutional Issues and Zoning Ordinances

Zoning can be a highly controversial issue and often raises questions of constitutional law. The government provides *public hearings* for citizens to discuss zoning ordinances before they are enacted.

Any land-use legislation that is destructive, unreasonable, arbitrary, or confiscatory is usually considered void. Furthermore, zoning ordinances must not violate the various provisions of the state's constitution. Commonly applied tests in determining the validity of ordinances require that

- power be exercised in a reasonable manner;
- provisions be clear and specific;
- ordinances be nondiscriminatory;
- ordinances promote public health, safety, and general welfare under the police power concept; and
- ordinances apply to all property in a similar manner.

It is sometimes very difficult to determine what level of compensation is fair in any particular situation. The compensation may be negotiated between the owner and the government, or the owner may seek a court judgment setting the amount.

Zoning Permits

Compliance with zoning can be monitored by requiring that property owners obtain permits before they begin any development. A permit will not be issued unless a proposed development conforms to the permitted zoning, among other requirements. Zoning permits are usually required before building permits can be issued.

Zoning Hearing Board

Zoning hearing boards (also called *zoning boards of appeal*) have been established in most communities to hear complaints about the effects a zoning ordinance may have on specific parcels of property. Petitions for variances or exceptions to the zoning law may be presented to these boards.

Nonconforming Use

Frequently, a lot or an improvement does not conform to the zoning law because it existed before the enactment or amendment of the zoning ordinance. Such a **nonconforming use** may be allowed to continue legally as long as it complies with the regulations governing nonconformities in the local ordinance or until the improvement is destroyed or torn down or the current use is abandoned. If the nonconforming use is allowed to continue indefinitely, it is grandfathered into the new zoning.

Real estate licensees should never assume, nor allow their clients to assume, that the existing nonconforming use will be allowed to continue. Buyers should verify with the local zoning authorities the conditions under which the use is allowed to remain or whether changes are permitted.

 EXAMPLE

Under a city's old zoning ordinances, a grocery store was located within a commercial zone. When the zoning map was changed to accommodate an increased need for residential housing, the grocery store was grandfathered into the new zoning; that is, it was allowed to continue its successful operations even though it did not fit the new zoning rules.

Conditional-Use Permits and Variances

Once a plan or zoning ordinance is enacted, property owners and developers know what they can and cannot do on their property. However, they may want to propose changes to the existing zoning in order to use their property somewhat differently. Generally these owners may appeal for either a conditional-use permit or a variance to allow a use that does not meet current zoning requirements.

> Conditional-use permits allow nonconforming but related land uses.
>
> Variances permit prohibited land uses to avoid undue hardship.

A **conditional-use permit** (or *special-use permit*) is usually granted to a property owner to allow a special use of property, defined as an allowable conditional use, within that zone, such as a day care center in a residential district. For a conditional-use permit to be appropriate, the intended use must meet certain standards set by the municipality.

A **variance** (also called an *exception*), on the other hand, provides relief if zoning regulations deprive an owner of the reasonable use of the property. To qualify for a variance, the owner must demonstrate the unique circumstances that make the variance necessary. In addition, the owner must prove that she is harmed and burdened by the regulations. Any such variance is said to "run with the land," meaning the exception is passed on to any later owners after a change has been made.

Both conditional-use permits and variances are issued by zoning boards only after public hearings. The neighbors of a proposed use must be given an opportunity to voice their opinions.

A property owner also can seek a complete change in the zoning classification of a parcel of real estate by obtaining an amendment to the district map or a zoning ordinance for that area, but this is significantly more involved and requires approval by the community's governing body.

BUILDING CODES AND CERTIFICATES OF OCCUPANCY

Most municipalities have enacted ordinances called **building codes** to specify construction standards that must be met when repairing or erecting buildings. Building codes set the requirements for kinds of materials and standards of workmanship, sanitary equipment, electrical wiring, fire prevention, and similar issues. In addition to adhering to building codes, a property owner who wants to build a structure or alter or repair an existing building usually must obtain a *building permit*. Through the permit requirement, municipal officials are made aware of new construction or alterations and can verify compliance with building codes and zoning ordinances. Inspectors will closely examine the plans and conduct periodic inspections of the work. Once the completed structure has been inspected and found satisfactory, the municipal inspector issues a *certificate of occupancy* (also called an *occupancy permit*).

If a building has been converted from another use to residential use or a new home has been constructed, the municipal inspector must ensure that the construction complies with relevant ordinances and codes. A certificate of occupancy indicating that the property is suitable for habitation by meeting certain safety and health standards must be issued before anyone moves in and often before a lender will allow closing.

If the construction of a building or an alteration violates a deed restriction, the issuance of a building permit will not cure this violation. A building permit is merely evidence of the applicant's compliance with municipal regulations.

Similarly, communities with historic districts, or communities that are interested in maintaining a particular "look" or character, may have aesthetic ordinances. These laws require that all new construction or restorations be approved by a special board. The board ensures that the new structures will "blend in" with existing building styles. Owners of existing properties may need to obtain approval to have their homes painted or remodeled.

IN PRACTICE

Planning, zoning, and restricting the use of real estate is extremely technical, and the interpretation of the law is not always clear. Questions concerning any of these subjects in relation to real estate transactions should be referred to legal counsel. Furthermore, landowners should be aware of the costs for various permits.

SUBDIVISION

Most communities have adopted **subdivision** and land development ordinances as part of their comprehensive plans. An ordinance includes provisions for submitting and processing *subdivision plats*. A major advantage of subdivision ordinances is that they encourage flexibility, economy, and ingenuity in the use of land. A **subdivider** is a person who buys undeveloped acreage and divides it into smaller lots for sale to individuals or developers or for the subdivider's own use. A **developer** (who also may be a subdivider) improves the land, constructs homes or other buildings on the lots, and sells them. In a new residential subdivision, developers usually pay the costs to provide new water, sewer, streets, curbs, and sidewalks. Developing is generally a much more extensive activity than subdividing.

Regulation of Land Development

Just as no national zoning ordinance exists, no uniform planning and land development legislation affects the entire country. Laws governing subdividing and land planning are controlled by the state and local governing bodies where the land is located.

Land Development Plan

Before the actual subdividing can begin, the subdivider must go through the process of land development planning. The plan must comply with the municipality's comprehensive plan. Although comprehensive plans and zoning ordinances are not necessarily inflexible, a plan that requires them to be changed will be subject to more complicated review by municipal government officials.

Plats

From the land development and subdivision plans, the subdivider draws plats. A **plat map** is a detailed map that illustrates the geographic boundaries of individual lots. It shows the blocks, sections, streets, public easements, and monuments in the prospective subdivision. A plat also may include engineering data and restrictive covenants. The plats must be approved by the municipality before they can be recorded. Once a plat is properly recorded, it may be used as an adequate legal description of real property.

Subdivision Plans

Most subdivisions are laid out by use of lots and blocks. An area of land is designated as a block, and the area making up this block is divided into lots. A subdivider usually determines the size as well as the location of individual lots, and this issue must be considered carefully because the maximum or minimum lot size is regulated by local ordinances.

Furthermore, the land itself must be studied, usually in cooperation with a surveyor, so that the subdivision takes advantage of natural drainage and land contours. In addition, a percolation test of the soil is done to determine the ability of the ground to absorb and drain water. This information helps to determine the suitability of a site for certain kinds of development and for the installation of septic tanks or injection wells for sewage treatment plants. A subdivider registering a development with the U.S. Department of Housing and Urban Development (HUD) must include a percolation report in the application. A subdivider should provide for utility easements, as well as easements for water and sewer mains.

One negative aspect of subdivision development is the potential for increased tax burdens on all residents, both inside and outside the subdivision. To protect local taxpayers against the costs of a heightened demand for public services, many local governments strictly regulate nearly all aspects of subdivision development and may impose impact fees. *Impact fees* are charges made in advance to cover anticipated expenses involving offsite capital improvements such as water and sewer facilities expansion, additional roads, and school expansions.

Subdivision Density

Zoning ordinances typically establish special **density zoning** (also called *bulk zoning*) ordinances for certain subdivisions, which restrict the average maximum number of houses per acre that may be built within a particular subdivision. For example, a typical zoning restriction may set the minimum lot area on which a subdivider can build a single-family housing unit at 10,000 square feet. This means that the subdivider can build four houses per acre. In such cases, the subdivider may choose to cluster building lots to achieve an open effect. Regardless of lot size or number of units, the subdivider will be consistent with the ordinance as long as the average number of units in the development remains at or below the maximum density. This average is called *gross density*.

PRIVATE LAND-USE CONTROLS

Not all restrictions on the use of land are imposed by government bodies. Certain restrictions to control and maintain the desirable quality and character of a property or subdivision may be created by private entities, including the property owners themselves. These restrictions are separate from and in addition to the land-use controls exercised by the government. However, no private restriction can violate a local, state, or federal law.

Restrictive Covenants

Restrictive covenants are limitations to the use of property imposed by a past owner or the current owner and are binding on future grantees.

On the other hand, **covenants, conditions, and restrictions (CC&Rs)** are private rules set up by the developer that set standards for all the parcels within the defined subdivision. The developer's restrictions may be imposed through a covenant in the deed or by a separate recorded declaration. CC&Rs typically govern the type, height, and size of buildings that individual owners can erect, as well as land use, architectural style, construction methods, setbacks, and square footage. CC&Rs are enforced by the homeowners association.

Restrictive covenants cannot be used for illegal purposes, such as for the exclusion of members of certain races, nationalities, or religions.

Private land-use controls may be more restrictive of an owner's use than the local zoning ordinances. The rule is that the more restrictive of the two takes precedence.

Private restrictions can be enforced in court when one lot owner applies to the court for an injunction to prevent a neighboring lot owner from violating the recorded restrictions. The court injunction will direct the violator to stop or remove the violation. The court retains the power to punish the violator for failing to obey. If adjoining lot owners stand idly by while a violation is committed, they can lose the right to an injunction by their inaction. The court might claim their right was lost through **laches**, the legal principle that a right may be lost through undue delay or failure to assert it.

Any restrictive covenant that forbids or restricts conveyance, encumbrance, occupancy, or lease on the basis of race, color, religion, or national origin is void. Exceptions to this section of the Illinois Human Rights Act are allowed for religious and charitable organizations.

Homeowners Association Regulations

Because a condominium (condo) unit is often described as a "fee simple estate with a tenancy in common interest," the oversight and the management of the common interests is under the authority of the condo board representing the interests of the entire association. How units are used, even modified, is controlled by the condo declaration, bylaws, and regulations. While it is the initial condo developer's responsibility to create the condo declaration, it is the association's board of directors that drafts the bylaws and regulations. Issues ranging from fines and fees to unit improvements are usually addressed in these documents.

REGULATION OF LAND SALES

Just as the sale and use of property within a state are controlled by state and local governments, the sale of property in one state to buyers in another is subject to strict federal and state regulations.

Interstate Land Sales Full Disclosure Act

The U.S. Congress created the federal **Interstate Land Sales Full Disclosure Act of 1968** to facilitate regulation of interstate land sales and to protect consumers from fraud and abuse in the sale or lease of land. The act required land developers to register subdivisions of 100 or more nonexempt lots with HUD and to provide each purchaser with a disclosure document called a property report. The property report contains relevant information about the subdivision and must be delivered to each purchaser before the signing of the contract or agreement.

The report must disclose specific information about the land, including

- the type of title being transferred to the buyer,
- the number of homes currently occupied on the site,
- the availability of recreation facilities,
- the distance to nearby communities,
- utility services and charges, and
- soil conditions and foundation or construction problems.

Under the act, the purchaser has the right to revoke any contract to purchase a regulated lot until midnight on the seventh day after the contract was signed. If the purchaser or lessee does not receive a copy of the property report before signing the purchase contract or lease, she may bring an action to void the contract within two years after signing it.

The act provides a number of exceptions. For example, it does not apply to subdivisions consisting of fewer than 25 lots or to those in which the lots are of 20 acres or more. Lots offered for sale solely to developers also are exempt from the act's requirements, as are lots on which buildings exist or where a seller is obligated to construct a building within two years. Misrepresentation or failure to comply with the act's requirements subjects a seller to criminal penalties (fines and imprisonment) as well as to civil damages.

SUMMARY

Land use is controlled and regulated through public restrictions, private (or nongovernmental) restrictions, and direct public ownership of land.

The police power of the state is the state's authority to create regulations to protect the public health, safety, and welfare. State enabling acts allow the power to enact laws authorized by the state's police power to be passed down to municipalities and other local governing authorities. Such regulations must be exercised in a reasonable manner, meaning they must be clear and specific, nondiscriminatory, and applied to all property in a similar manner.

Land may be taken for public use through the government's right of eminent domain or the process of condemnation. The owner must be given just (fair) compensation.

A comprehensive plan (also called a master plan) sets forth the development goals and objectives for the community. Zoning ordinances are local laws implementing the land uses designated in the comprehensive plan and typically cover issues such as permitted uses, lot sizes, types of structures, building heights, setbacks, style and appearance of structures, density, and protection of natural resources. Zoning classifies property by uses and types, such as commercial, industrial, residential, agricultural, and planned unit developments (PUDs).

Other ways in which zoning is used include

■ buffer zones separating residential from nonresidential areas,

■ bulk zoning to control density,

■ aesthetic zoning to specify certain types of architecture for new buildings, and

■ incentive zoning to ensure certain uses are incorporated into developments.

Zoning is enforced through the use of permits, and an individual case may be considered by a zoning hearing board (also called a zoning board of appeals), which may decide to allow a nonconforming use to continue, grant a variance from a zoning ordinance to permit a prohibited land use to avoid undue hardship, or grant a conditional-use (special-use permit).

Building codes specify standards for construction, plumbing, sewers, electrical wiring, and fire prevention equipment. A certificate of occupancy (occupancy permit) is issued upon satisfactory completion of work for which the permit was issued.

Subdivision and land development regulations are adopted to maintain control of the development of expanding community areas so that growth is harmonious with community standards.

A subdivider buys undeveloped acreage, divides it into smaller parcels, and develops or sells it. A developer builds homes on the lots and sells them through the developer's own sales organization or through local real estate brokerage firms. City planners and land developers work together to plan whole communities that are later incorporated into cities, towns, or villages.

Land development must comply with the master plans adopted by counties, cities, villages, or towns. This may entail approval of land-use plans by local planning committees or commissioners.

The process of subdivision includes dividing the tract of land into lots and blocks and providing for utility easements, as well as laying out street patterns and widths. A subdivider generally must record a completed plat of subdivision (including the necessary approvals from public officials) in the county where the land is located. Subdividers usually place restrictions on the use of all lots in a subdivision as a general plan for the benefit of all future owners.

Private land-use controls are exercised by owners through deed restrictions and restrictive covenants. These private restrictions may be enforced by obtaining a court injunction to stop a violator.

The Constitution of the State of Illinois provides for certain units of government to exercise home rule authority. When a county's ordinance conflicts with a municipality's, the municipal ordinance prevails.

The Illinois Human Rights Act prohibits restrictive covenants that discriminate on the basis of race, color, religion, or national origin.

UNIT 20 QUIZ

1. A subdivision declaration reads, "No property within this subdivision may be further subdivided for sale or otherwise, and no property may be used for any purpose other than single-family housing." This is an example of
   A. an illegal reverter clause.
   B. R-1 zoning.
   C. a conditional-use clause.
   D. a restrictive covenant.

2. A landowner who wants to use property in a manner prohibited by a local zoning ordinance but which would benefit the community can apply for
   A. a prescriptive easement.
   B. an occupancy permit.
   C. a conditional-use permit.
   D. a property dedication.

3. What is NOT included in public land-use controls?
   A. Subdivision regulations
   B. Restrictive covenants
   C. Environmental protection laws
   D. Comprehensive plan specifications

4. Under its zoning authority, what may a town legally regulate?
   A. Building ownership
   B. Business ownership
   C. Enabling acts
   D. The number of buildings

5. The purpose of a building permit is to
   A. ensure compliance with municipal regulations.
   B. assert a deed's restrictive covenant.
   C. maintain municipal control over inverse condemnation.
   D. show compliance with restrictive covenants.

6. Zoning powers are conferred on municipal governments
   A. through the master plan.
   B. by state enabling acts.
   C. by popular local vote.
   D. through city charters.

7. A town enacts a new zoning code. Under the new code, commercial buildings are not permitted within 1,000 feet of the lake. A commercial building that is permitted to continue in its former use even though it is built on the lakeshore is an example of
   A. variance.
   B. special use.
   C. adverse possession.
   D. nonconforming use.

8. To determine whether a location can be put to future use as a retail store, one would examine the
   A. building code.
   B. zoning ordinance.
   C. list of permitted nonconforming uses.
   D. housing code.

9. Which of these is NOT a legal deed restriction?
   A. The types of buildings that may be constructed
   B. The activities that are not to be conducted at the site
   C. The allowable ethnic origins of purchasers
   D. The minimum size of buildings to be constructed

10. A restriction in a seller's deed may be enforced by
    A. the zoning board of appeal.
    B. the city building commission.
    C. a court injunction.
    D. the state legislature.

11. A man owns a large tract of land. After an adequate study of all the relevant facts, the man legally divides the land into 30 lots suitable for the construction of residences. In this situation, the man is acting as
    A. a developer.
    B. a land planner.
    C. a subdivider.
    D. an urban planner.

12. A map illustrating the sizes and locations of streets and lots in a subdivision is called a
    A. plat.
    B. gridiron plan.
    C. survey.
    D. property report.

13. In one city, developers are limited by law to constructing no more than an average of three houses per acre in any subdivision. What does this restriction regulate?
    A. Clustering
    B. Out-lots
    C. Covenants
    D. Gross density

14. Common zoning classifications include
    A. "C" for commercial, "R" for residential, and "A" for agricultural.
    B. "P" for planned, "B" for buffer-zoned, and "C" for commercial.
    C. "A" for agricultural, "C" for comprehensive, and "S" for subdivided.
    D. "R" for residential, "D" for density zoned, and "A" for agricultural.

15. Permitted land uses, housing projections, transportation issues, and objectives for implementing future controlled development would all be found in a community's
    A. zoning ordinance.
    B. enabling act.
    C. comprehensive plan.
    D. land-control law.

16. Which of these *BEST* defines the term *planned unit development (PUD)*?
    A. A development where land is set aside for mixed-use purposes, such as residential, commercial, and public areas
    B. A development established entirely by inverse condemnation
    C. A planned area where a nonconforming use is never allowed
    D. A development registered with the U.S. Department of Housing and Urban Development

17. Under the federal law designed to protect the public from fraudulent interstate land sales, a developer involved in interstate land sales of 100 or more lots must
    A. provide each purchaser with a printed report disclosing details of the property.
    B. pay the prospective buyer's expenses to see the property involved.
    C. provide preferential financing.
    D. allow a 30-day cancellation period.

18. Which of these statements *BEST* describes enabling statutes in Illinois?
    A. They make all counties, cities, and villages subject to Illinois state zoning laws.
    B. They require all Illinois counties, cities, and villages to adopt the requirements of the federal municipal planning commission.
    C. They set environmental controls on current land use.
    D. They grant counties, cities, and villages the power to make and enforce local zoning ordinances.

19. A man wants the city zoned to prohibit all fast food restaurants. Which of these is his *BEST* course of action?
    A. Persuade the town government to change the local zoning laws
    B. Petition the Illinois legislature to amend the state zoning laws
    C. File suit to force the city to conform with existing Illinois zoning laws
    D. Ask HUD to force the city to zone against fast food restaurants under its Fifth Amendment powers

20. A zoning law passed by a village conflicts with an existing county zoning law. Both the village and the county are home-rule units of government. In this situation, which of these statements is *TRUE*?
    A. The village's law will prevail because municipal ordinances supersede county ordinances under the Illinois constitution.
    B. Under the Illinois constitution, the county law will prevail because its zoning laws affect a larger geographic area.
    C. The Illinois constitution provides that a conflict between the laws of two home-rule units must be resolved in the appropriate circuit court.
    D. Whichever law is most restrictive will prevail, unless the issue involves a constitutional question, in which case the law least restrictive of private property rights will supersede the more restrictive law.

UNIT
21

> ## Fair Housing and Ethical Practices

LEARNING OBJECTIVES

When you have completed this unit, you will be able to accomplish the following.

> Describe fair housing laws, including protected classes under these laws, and exemptions to the laws.
> Explain how fair housing laws address a variety of discriminatory practices and regulate real estate advertising.

KEY TERMS

Americans with Disabilities Act (ADA)	code of ethics	redlining
	ethics	steering
blockbusting	Fair Housing Act	

OVERVIEW

Licensees and their clients and customers today reflect the changing diversity in American society: those for whom English is a second language, people from a wide range of cultural backgrounds, people of various age and religious preferences, and people with disabilities, to name just a few. Although some differences are protected by state and federal laws, others are not. Understanding and working to uphold principles of equal opportunity is critical to creating and maintaining a diverse, vibrant, and ultimately profitable real estate market for everyone.

EQUAL OPPORTUNITY IN HOUSING

The civil rights laws governing the real estate industry ensure that everyone has the opportunity to live where they choose. Federal, state, and local fair housing or equal opportunity laws affect every phase of a real estate transaction, from listing to closing. Despite the legal framework created by legislatures and the Supreme Court to preserve the constitutional rights of all citizens, discriminatory attitudes have not been eliminated. Real estate licensees must eliminate actions or words that further discrimination (or the appearance of discrimination) if they wish to conduct an ethical and legal business. Similarly, any discriminatory attitudes of property owners or property seekers must be addressed by the licensee if these attitudes affect compliance with fair housing laws.

Working with clients who may have discriminatory attitudes is difficult, and the pressure to avoid offending a client can be intense. However, ethics and the law demand that licensees comply with fair housing laws. Failure to comply with fair housing laws is both a civil and a criminal violation and constitutes grounds for disciplinary action against a licensee.

The Real Estate License Act of 2000 and the general rules require that licensees fully adhere to the principles of equal housing opportunity. A licensee is prohibited from taking any listing or participating in any transaction in which the property owner seeks to discriminate based on race, color, ancestry, religion, national origin, sex, handicap, or familial status. Breaking fair housing laws in Illinois is a criminal act and grounds for discipline. Violating provisions or restrictions of the Act or the rules can result in suspension, nonrenewal, or revocation of the violator's license or censure, reprimand, or fine imposed by IDFPR.

The Act requires that when a judgment in either a civil or criminal proceeding has been made against a licensee for illegally discriminating, his license must be suspended or revoked unless an appeal is active. If there has already been an order by an administrative agency finding discrimination by a licensee, the board must penalize the licensee.

Many cities and villages in Illinois have their own fair housing laws, many of which are stricter than state or federal laws. These laws are enforced on the local level and may take precedence over federal laws when the local law has been ruled substantially equivalent to the federal statute. Licensees should be familiar with local regulations, as well as with state and federal law.

FAIR HOUSING ACT

The Fair Housing Act prohibits discrimination based on
■ race,
■ color,
■ religion,
■ sex,
■ national origin,
■ disability, and
■ familial status.

The Civil Rights Act of 1866 prohibited discrimination in housing based on race or color. Title VIII of the Civil Rights Act of 1968, usually called the **Fair Housing Act**, prohibits discrimination in housing based on race, color, religion, and national origin. In the years since, other laws have been passed that expand the classes protected by the Fair Housing Act (see Figure 21.1). The Department of Housing and Urban Development (HUD) administers the Fair Housing Act. HUD has established rules and regulations that further interpret fair housing practices. In addition, HUD distributes the equal housing opportunity poster (see Figure 21.2), which declares that the office in which it is displayed promises to adhere to the Fair Housing Act and pledges support for affirmative marketing and advertising programs. The fair housing poster should be displayed in every real estate office.

Figure 21.1: Federal and State Fair Housing Laws

Legislation	Race	Color	Religion	National Origin	Sex	Disability	Familial Status	Age	Marital Status
Civil Rights Act of 1866	■	■							
Title VIII of the Fair Housing Act of 1968	■	■	■	■					
Housing and Community Development Act of 1974	■	■	■	■	■				
Fair Housing Amendments Act of 1988	■	■	■	■	■	■	■		
Illinois Human Rights Act*	■	■	■	■	■	■	■	■	■

*The Illinois Human Rights Act specifies both "physical and mental" disability. It also adds as a protected class: age, ancestry, military status, unfavorable military discharge, sexual orientation, and order of protection status as it impacts employment, real estate transactions, financial credit, or availability of public accommodations.

IN PRACTICE

When HUD investigates a licensee for discriminatory practices, it may consider failure to prominently display the equal housing opportunity poster in the licensee's place of business as evidence of discrimination.

Figure 21.2: Equal Opportunity Housing Poster

U. S. Department of Housing and Urban Development

EQUAL HOUSING OPPORTUNITY

We Do Business in Accordance With the Federal Fair Housing Law

(The Fair Housing Amendments Act of 1988)

It is illegal to Discriminate Against Any Person Because of Race, Color, Religion, Sex, Handicap, Familial Status, or National Origin

---

■ In the sale or rental of housing or residential lots

■ In advertising the sale or rental of housing

■ In the financing of housing

■ In the provision of real estate brokerage services

■ In the appraisal of housing

■ Blockbusting is also illegal

Anyone who feels he or she has been discriminated against may file a complaint of housing discrimination:
    1-800-669-9777 (Toll Free)
    1-800-927-9275 (TTY)

U.S. Department of Housing and Urban Development
Assistant Secretary for Fair Housing and Equal Opportunity
Washington, D.C. 20410

Previous editions are obsolete

form HUD-928.1 (2/2003)

Figure 21.3 lists examples of various fair housing restrictions.

Figure 21.3: Fair Housing Restrictions

Prohibited by the Fair Housing Act	Example
Refusing to sell, rent, or negotiate the sale or rental of housing as a means of discriminating	An apartment building has several vacant units. When an Asian family asks to see one of the units, the owner tells them to go away.
Changing terms, conditions, or services for different individuals as a means of discriminating	A landlord tells a Roman Catholic prospective tenant that the rent for a duplex is $600 per month. However, when talking with the other tenants, the prospective tenant learns that all the Lutherans in the complex pay only $525 per month.
Advertising any discriminatory preference or limitation in housing or making any inquiry or reference that is discriminatory in nature	A real estate licensee places the following advertisement in a newspaper: "Just listed! Perfect home for white family, near excellent parochial school!"
Representing that a property is not available for sale or rent when in fact it is	A man who uses a wheelchair is told that the house he wants to rent is no longer available. The next day, however, the "For Rent" sign is still in the window.
Profiting by inducing property owners to sell or rent on the basis of the prospective entry into the neighborhood of persons of a protected class	A real estate licensee sends brochures to homeowners in the predominantly white Ridgewood neighborhood. The brochures, which feature the licensee's past success selling homes, include photos of racial minorities, population statistics, and the caption "The Changing Face of Ridgewood."
Altering the terms or conditions of a home loan, or denying a loan, as a means of discrimination	A lender requires a divorced mother of two young children to pay for a credit report. In addition, her father must cosign her application. After talking to a single male friend, the woman learns that he was not required to do either of those things, despite his lower income and poor credit history.
Denying membership or participation in a multiple listing service, a real estate organization, or another facility related to the sale or rental of housing as a means of discrimination	The county real estate association meets weekly to discuss available properties and buyers. None of the county's black or female licensees is allowed to be a member of the association.

Definitions

HUD's regulations provide specific definitions that clarify the scope of the Fair Housing Act.

Housing

Housing is a dwelling that includes any building or part of a building designed for occupancy as a residence by one or more families. This includes a single-family house, a condominium, a cooperative, and manufactured housing, as well as vacant land on which any of these structures will be built.

Familial Status

Familial status refers to the presence of one or more individuals who have not reached the age of 18 and who live with either a parent or a guardian. In effect, the familial status reference means that the act's protections extend to families with children. The term includes a woman who is pregnant. Unless a property qualifies as housing for older persons, all properties must be made available to families with children under the same terms and conditions as anyone else. It is illegal to advertise properties as being for "adults only" or to indicate a preferred number of children. Occupancy standards (the number of persons permitted to reside in a property) must be based on objective factors such as sanitation or safety.

Disability

A *disability* is a physical or mental impairment. It is unlawful to discriminate against prospective buyers or tenants on the basis of such disability.

Landlords must make reasonable accommodations to existing policies, practices, or services to permit persons with disabilities to have equal enjoyment of the premises. For example, it is reasonable for a landlord to permit service animals (such as guide dogs) in a normally "no pets" building or to provide designated parking spaces for persons with disabilities.

The Department of Housing and Urban Development (HUD) clearly states that "an assistance animal is an animal that works, provides assistance, or performs tasks for the benefit of a person with a disability or that provides emotional support that alleviates one or more identified effects of a person's disability. An assistance animal is not a pet. Furthermore, individuals with a disability may ask to keep an assistance animal as a reasonable accommodation to a housing provider's pet restrictions. Housing providers cannot refuse to make reasonable accommodations in rules, policies, practices, or services when such accommodations may be necessary to afford a person with a disability the equal opportunity to use and enjoy a dwelling (see HUD.gov).

Persons with disabilities must also be permitted to make reasonable modifications to the premises at their own expense. Such modifications might include lowering door handles or installing bath rails for a person in a wheelchair. Failure to permit reasonable modification constitutes discrimination. However, the law recognizes that certain reasonable modifications might make a rental property undesirable to the general population. In such a case, the landlord is allowed to require that the property be restored to its previous condition when the lease period ends.

The landlord may not increase the customarily required security deposit for persons with disabilities. However, where it is necessary in order to ensure with reasonable certainty that funds will be available to pay for the restorations at the end of the tenancy, the landlord may negotiate as part of such a restoration agreement a provision requiring that the tenant pay into an interest-bearing escrow account, over a reasonable period, a reasonable amount of money not to exceed the cost of the restorations. The interest in the account accrues to the benefit of the tenant. A landlord may condition permission for a modification on the renter providing a reasonable description of the proposed modifications, as well as reasonable assurances that the work will be done in a workmanlike manner and that any required building permits will be obtained.

In newly constructed multifamily buildings with an elevator and four or more units, public and common areas must be accessible to persons with disabilities, and doors and hallways must be wide enough for wheelchairs. The entrance to each unit must be accessible, as well as the light switches, electrical outlets, thermostats, and other environmental controls. People in wheelchairs should be able to use the kitchen and the bathrooms; bathroom walls should be reinforced to accommodate later installation of grab bars. Ground-floor units must meet these requirements in buildings that do not have an elevator. Licensees should be aware that state and local laws may require stricter standards.

Exemptions to the Fair Housing Act

There is never an exemption regarding race. However, regarding other classes and under certain conditions, the Fair Housing Act exempts

- owner-occupied buildings with no more than four units,

- single-family housing sold or rented without the use of a real state licensee, and

- housing operated by organizations and private clubs that limit occupancy to members.

The sale or rental of a single-family home is exempt when

- the home is owned by an individual who does not own more than three such homes at one time (and who does not sell more than one every two years),

- a real estate licensee is not involved in the transaction, and

- discriminatory advertising is not used.

The rental of rooms or units is exempt in an owner-occupied one- to four-family dwelling.

Note that dwelling units owned by religious organizations may be restricted to people of the same religion if membership in the organization is not restricted on the basis of race, color, or national origin. A private club that is not open to the public may restrict the rental or occupancy of lodgings that it owns to its members as long as the lodgings are not operated commercially.

Housing for Older Persons

While the Fair Housing Act protects families with children, certain properties can be restricted to occupancy by elderly persons. Housing intended for persons 62 or older or housing occupied by at least one person 55 or older (where 80% of the units are occupied by individuals 55 or older) is exempt from the familial status protection.

In 1995, Congress passed the Housing for Older Persons Act (HOPA), which repealed the requirement that 55-and-older housing have "significant facilities and services" designed for seniors. HOPA still requires that at least 80% of occupied units have one person age 55 or older living there. The act prohibits the awarding of monetary damages against those who, in good faith, reasonably believed that property designated as housing for older persons was exempt from familial status provisions of the Fair Housing Act.

Americans With Disabilities Act

Although the **Americans with Disabilities Act (ADA)** is not a housing or credit law, it still has a significant effect on the real estate industry. The ADA addresses the rights of persons with disabilities in employment and public accommodations. Real estate licensees are often employers, and real estate brokerage offices are public spaces. The ADA's goal is to enable persons with disabilities to become part of the economic and social mainstream of society.

Title I of the ADA requires that employers make *reasonable accommodations* that enable an individual with a disability to perform essential job functions. Reasonable accommodations include making the work site accessible, restructuring a job, providing part-time or flexible work schedules, and modifying equipment used on the job. The provisions of ADA apply to any employer with 15 or more employees.

Title III of the ADA requires that persons with disabilities have full accessibility to businesses, goods, and public services. While the federal civil rights laws have traditionally been seen as focused on residential housing, business and commercial real estate are fully covered by Title III. Because persons with disabilities have the right to full and equal access to businesses and public services under the ADA, building owners and managers must ensure that any obstacle restricting this right is eliminated. The *2010 ADA Standards for Accessible Design* contains detailed specifications for designing parking spaces, curb ramps, elevators, drinking fountains, toilet facilities, and directional signs to ensure maximum accessibility.

ADA and the Fair Housing Act

Some properties are subject to both the ADA and the Fair Housing Act. For example, in an apartment complex, the rental office is a place of public accommodation. As such, it is covered by the ADA and must be accessible to persons with disabilities at the owner's expense. Individual rental units are covered by the Fair Housing Act. A tenant who wishes to modify the unit to make it accessible would be responsible for the cost.

IN PRACTICE

Real estate licensees need a general knowledge of the ADA's provisions. It is necessary for a licensee's workplace and employment policies to comply with the law. Amendments to the ADA are periodically introduced in the U.S. Congress, and it is important to be aware of changes in the law. Also, licensees who are building managers must ensure that properties are legally accessible. However, ADA compliance questions may also arise regarding a client's property. Unless the licensee is a qualified ADA expert, it is best to advise commercial clients to seek the services of an attorney or a consultant who specializes in ADA issues.

Reporting Violations

The Fair Housing Act is administered by the Office of Fair Housing and Equal Opportunity (FHEO) under the direction of the secretary of HUD. Any aggrieved person who believes illegal discrimination has occurred may file a complaint with HUD within one year of the alleged act. HUD may also initiate its own complaint.

FAIR HOUSING VIOLATIONS

Blockbusting

Blockbusting (also called *panic peddling or panic selling*) is the act of encouraging people to sell or rent their homes by claiming that the entry of a protected class of people into the neighborhood will have some sort of negative impact on property values. Any message, however subtle or accidental, that property should be sold or rented because the neighborhood is "undergoing changes" is considered blockbusting. It is illegal to suggest that the presence of certain persons will cause property values to decline, crime or antisocial behavior to increase, or the quality of schools to suffer.

Steering

Steering is the channeling of homeseekers to particular neighborhoods. It also includes discouraging potential buyers or renters from considering certain areas. In either case, it is an illegal limitation of a purchaser's options. In the rental process, steering occurs when the landlord puts members of a protected class on a certain floor or in a certain building.

Another form of steering occurs when the landlord tells a member of a protected class that no vacancy exists when, in fact, there is a vacancy. Many cases of steering are subtle, motivated by assumptions or perceptions about a homebuyer's preferences, and are frequently based on some stereotype. A licensee should never assume that prospective buyers "expect" to be directed to certain neighborhoods or properties. Steering anyone is illegal, and any licensees who engage in steering subject themselves (and the brokerage firm) to a civil lawsuit.

The Real Estate License Act of 2000 expressly prohibits

> influencing or attempting to influence, by any words or acts, a prospective seller, purchaser, occupant, landlord, or tenant of real estate, in connection with viewing, buying, or leasing real estate, so as to promote or tend to promote the continuance or maintenance of racially and religiously segregated housing or so as to retard, obstruct, or discourage racially integrated housing on or in any street, block, neighborhood, or community. (225 ILCS 454/20-20(a)(30))

Advertising

Advertisements of property for sale or rent may not include language indicating a preference or limitation. No exception to this rule exists, regardless of subtle or "accidental" wordings. However, an advertisement that is gender specific, such as "female roommate sought," is allowed as long as the advertiser seeks to share living quarters with someone of the same gender. The media used for promoting property or real estate services must not target any one population to the exclusion of others. The use of media that targets only certain groups based on, for example, language or geography, is also viewed as being potentially discriminatory. For example, limiting advertising to a cable television channel viewed mostly by one demographic group might be construed as discriminatory. The best rule is never to advertise using only one group of narrowly focused media. Running ads in several locales or in general-circulation media as a standard rule is good practice.

Positive language in the ads, too, may be a factor in determining the legitimacy of a discrimination charge. Many licensees choose to run a small version of the equal housing opportunity symbol in all the materials that represent them, along with the words "equal housing opportunity" underneath. Repeating the HUD poster statement, "We do business in accordance with the federal Fair Housing Law" may go a long way toward assisting a licensee whose integrity on such issues is ever incorrectly questioned. The fair housing symbol signals to the world that one is open for business to anyone who is of age and financially able to purchase real estate.

Those who prepare appraisals or any statements of valuation—whether they are formal or informal, oral or written (including a comparative market analysis)—may consider any normal qualifying factors that affect value. However, race, color, religion, national origin, sex, disability, and familial status may not be considered.

Redlining

Disparate Treatment – Actions seek to discriminate.

Disparate Impact – The effect of one's actions are discriminatory.

Redlining is the practice of refusing to make mortgage loans or issue insurance policies in specific areas for reasons other than the applicant's financial qualifications. Redlining refers to literally or figuratively drawing a line around particular areas. Redlining is often based on racial grounds rather than on any real objection to an applicant's creditworthiness. A lending institution can, however, refuse a loan solely on sound, documentable financial grounds.

Intent and Effect

Owners and licensees must examine their activities and policies carefully to determine whether they unintentionally appear to engage in discriminatory actions. Whenever policies or practices result in unequal treatment of persons in a protected class, they are considered discriminatory, regardless of intent. This "effects test" is applied by regulatory agencies to determine whether discrimination has occurred. There are two different principles under which one may be charged:

Disparate Treatment is when one's actions are specifically discriminatory, as in a rental sign that states, "We do not rent to Cavemen." The only population affected are Cavemen.

Disparate Impact is when the effect of one's actions are discriminatory. Now the rental sign states, "We do not rent to individuals who wear Mastodon clothing." While not specifically mentioning a population, the impact of the restriction really only effects one segment of the population.

The Illinois Human Rights Act

The Real Estate License Act of 2000 prohibits any action that constitutes a violation of the Illinois Human Rights Act. This is true regardless of whether a complaint has been filed with or adjudicated by the Illinois Human Rights Commission. The Illinois Human Rights Act includes some prohibitions that also are specifically addressed by the Real Estate License Act of 2000.

Under the Illinois Human Rights Act, it is a civil rights violation for any licensee to engage in any of the following acts of discrimination based on race, color, religion, national origin, ancestry, age (40+), sex, marital status, physical or mental disability, military service or unfavorable discharge from military service, familial status, or sexual orientation and order of protection status in connection with employment, real estate transactions, access to financial credit, and the availability of public accommodations:

- Refuse to engage in a real estate transaction with a person
- Alter the terms, conditions, or privileges of a real estate transaction
- Refuse to receive or fail to transmit an offer
- Refuse to negotiate
- Represent that real property is not available for inspection, sale, rental, or lease when in fact it is available; or fail to bring a property listing to an individual's attention; or refuse to permit him to inspect real estate
- Publicize, through any means or use, an application form that indicates an intent to engage in unlawful discrimination
- Offer, solicit, accept, use, or retain a listing of real property with knowledge that unlawful discrimination is intended

It is a civil rights violation for the owner or agent of any housing accommodation to engage in any of the following discriminatory acts against children:

- Require, as a condition to the rental of a housing accommodation, that the prospective tenant will not have one or more children younger than 18 residing in his family at the time the application for rental is made

■ Insert a condition in any lease that terminates the lease if one or more children younger than age 18 are ever in the family occupying the housing

■ Any agreement or lease that contains a condition such as "the above is legally void as to that condition"; the lease itself remains in force, but the clause is void and unenforceable

It is also a civil rights violation in Illinois to discriminate against any person who is blind, hearing impaired, or physically disabled in the terms, conditions, or privileges of sale or rental property. Similarly, it is a civil rights violation to refuse to sell or rent to a prospective buyer or tenant because he has a service animal. Neither may a seller or a landlord require the inclusion of any additional charge in a lease, rental agreement, or contract of purchase or sale because a person who is blind, hearing-impaired, or physically disabled has a service animal. Of course, the tenant may be liable for any actual damage done to the premises by the animal.

Exemptions

The following individuals, property types, and transactions are exempt from the anti-discriminatory provisions of the Illinois Human Rights Act:

■ Private owners of single-family homes if (1) they own fewer than three single-family homes (including beneficial interests), (2) they were (or a member of their family was) the last current resident of the home, (3) the home was sold without the use of a real estate licensee, and (4) the home was sold without the use of discriminatory advertising

■ Apartment buildings for not more than four families living independently of each other, if the owner resides in one of the housing accommodations

■ Private rooms in a private home occupied by an owner or owner's family member

■ Reasonable local, state, or federal restrictions regarding the maximum number of occupants permitted to occupy a dwelling

■ A religious organization, association, or society (or any nonprofit institution or organization operated, controlled, or supervised by or in conjunction with a religious organization, association, or society) may limit the sale, rental, or occupancy of dwellings owned or operated by it (for other than commercial reasons) to persons of the same religion or give preference to persons of the same religion. This exemption is limited; it does not apply if membership in the religion is restricted on account of race, color, or national origin.

■ Restricting the rental of rooms in a housing accommodation to persons of one sex

■ Appraisers may take into consideration any factors other than those based on unlawful discrimination or familial status in furnishing appraisals

■ Individuals who have been convicted by any court of illegally manufacturing or distributing controlled substances

■ Housing for older persons on the basis of familial status. "Housing for older persons" means housing that is intended for and occupied solely by persons 62 years of age or older, or intended and operated for occupancy by persons 55 years of age or older and at least 80% of the occupied units are occupied by at least one person who is 55 or older

■ A child sex offender who owns residential real estate, in which the offender lives and rents, is exempt from renting a unit in that property to a person who is the parent or guardian of a child or children under 18 years of age (P.A. 95-42, eff. 8-10-07; 95-820, eff. 1-1-09)

Threats or Acts of Violence

It is possible that licensees may find themselves the targets of threats, verbal abuse, or intimidation merely for complying with fair housing laws. In such a case, the victim should report the incident immediately to law enforcement officials. The federal Fair Housing Act not only protects the rights of those who seek the benefits of the open housing law but also protects owners and licensees who aid or encourage the enjoyment of open housing rights.

IMPLICATIONS FOR REAL ESTATE LICENSEES

Licensees are a community's real estate experts. Along with the privilege of profiting from real estate transactions comes the social and legal responsibility to ensure that everyone's civil rights are protected. Establishing relationships with community and fair housing groups to discuss common concerns and develop solutions to problems is a constructive activity.

All parties deserve the same standard of service. Every future homeowner has the right to expect fair and equal treatment, with property showings based only on stated needs and financial capability. A good test is to answer the question, "Are we providing this service for everyone?" If an act is not performed consistently, or if an act affects individuals in a less-than-standard way, it could be construed as discriminatory. Standardized inventories of property listings, standardized criteria for financial qualification, and written documentation of activities and conversations (especially if the licensee senses a client wishes to act in a discriminatory way) are three effective means of self-protection for licensees. The consequences for anyone who violates the law are serious. In addition to the financial penalties, the livelihood of licensees who violate the law will be in danger if their license is suspended or revoked. That the offense was unintentional is no defense. Licensees must scrutinize their practices with care and not fall victim to clients or customers who maneuver to discriminate.

Beyond being the law, fair housing is good business. It ensures the greatest number of properties are available for sale and for rent and ensures the largest possible pool of potential purchasers and tenants.

PROFESSIONAL ETHICS

Compliance with the law is not always enough to achieve a standard of professional conduct. Licensees must make sure to conduct themselves not just legally but also ethically.

Ethics refers to a high moral system of principles, rules, and standards that are based on personal values. The ethical system of a profession establishes guidelines that reach to the higher principles of what is "right." Those principles may exist apart from the law. Professional ethics in business usually focus on two main aspects of the profession:

- They establish standards for integrity and competence in dealing with consumers of an industry's services.
- They define a code of conduct for relations within the industry and among its professionals.

Codes of Ethics

One way that many organizations address ethics within their industry is by adopting specific, written codes of ethics. A **code of ethics** is a written system of standards for professional, values-based conduct. The code contains statements designed to advise, guide, and regulate job behavior. To be effective, a code of ethics must be specific by creating rules that either prohibit or encourage certain behaviors. By including sanctions for violators, a code of ethics becomes more effective.

The National Association of REALTORS® (NAR) adopted a code of conduct for its members in 1913. This code, called the *Code of Ethics and Standards of Practice*, establishes strict professional standards for all REALTORS®. While not all licensees are REALTORS®, the *Code of Ethics and Standards of Practice* has proved helpful because it contains practical applications of business ethics.

Many other professional organizations in the real estate industry have codes of ethics as well. In addition, many state real estate commissions are required by law to establish codes or canons of ethical behavior for their states' licensees.

SUMMARY

Federal regulations regarding equal opportunity in housing are contained principally in the Fair Housing Act, which prohibits discrimination on the basis of race, color, religion, sex, disability, familial status, or national origin in the sale, rental, or financing of residential property. Discriminatory actions include refusing to deal with an individual or a specific group, changing any terms of a real estate or loan transaction, changing the services offered for any individual or group, creating statements or advertisements that indicate discriminatory restrictions, or otherwise attempting to make a dwelling unavailable to any person or group because of race, color, religion, sex, disability, familial status, or national origin. The law also prohibits steering, blockbusting, and redlining.

Complaints under the Fair Housing Act may be reported to and investigated by the Department of Housing and Urban Development (HUD).

A real estate business is only as good as its reputation. Real estate licensees can maintain good reputations by demonstrating good business ability and adhering to ethical standards of business practices. Many licensees subscribe to a code of ethics as members of professional real estate organizations, such as the National Association of REALTORS®.

Licensees in Illinois are required by various statutes and the Real Estate License Act of 2000 to adhere to all principles of equal opportunity in housing. Failure to comply with state and federal equal housing laws is grounds for license revocation in addition to other civil or criminal penalties.

The Illinois Human Rights Act amplifies federal legislation for Illinois. It bars discrimination on the basis of race, color, religion, national origin, ancestry, age (40+), sex, marital status, physical and mental disability, military service, unfavorable military discharge, familial status, sexual orientation, and order of protection status.

UNIT 21 QUIZ

1. Under the Fair Housing Act, which action is legally permitted?
   A. Restricting occupancy in an apartment complex to senior citizens, if qualified and registered as housing for seniors
   B. Altering the terms of a loan to discriminate against a member of a minority group
   C. Refusing to rent an apartment to an individual because of his physical disability
   D. Telling a minority individual that an apartment has been rented when in fact it has not

2. Encouraging people to sell or rent their homes by claiming that entry of a protected class of people into the neighborhood will have a negative impact on property values constitutes
   A. steering.
   B. blockbusting.
   C. a violation of the ADA.
   D. redlining.

3. The federal Fair Housing Act prohibits discrimination in housing based on
   A. sex.
   B. all of these.
   C. disability or familial status.
   D. race, color, religion, or national origin.

4. During a listing presentation, a real estate licensee said to the seller, who owned two residential properties, "I hear a family of those people are moving in, and you'd better put your house on the market before values drop!" Has the licensee violated any fair housing law?
   A. Yes, the licensee is guilty of steering.
   B. Yes, the licensee is guilty of blockbusting.
   C. No because the seller owns fewer than three houses.
   D. No because the licensee does not intend to publicly advertise the property.

5. A licensee entered into a buyer agency agreement with Japanese man. The licensee showed him only properties where it was obvious that other Japanese people lived. Has the licensee violated any fair housing law?
   A. Yes, the licensee is guilty of blockbusting.
   B. No because a Japanese buyer would want to live in a Japanese neighborhood.
   C. No because as a buyer agent, it is the licensee's responsibility to make decisions for the buyer.
   D. Yes, the licensee is guilty of steering.

6. A lender's refusal to lend money to potential homeowners attempting to purchase properties located in predominantly African-American neighborhoods is called
   A. blockbusting.
   B. steering.
   C. prequalifying.
   D. redlining.

7. Which of these is *NOT* permitted under the federal Fair Housing Act?
   A. The owner of a 20-unit residential apartment building rents to white men only.
   B. An expensive club in Chicago rents rooms only to members who are graduates of a particular university.
   C. A Catholic convent refuses to furnish housing for a Jewish man.
   D. An owner refuses to rent the other side of her duplex to a family with children.

8. As an office policy, a sponsoring broker requires that sponsored licensees show prospective buyers from racial or ethnic minority groups only properties that are in certain areas of town where few members of their groups currently live. The sponsoring broker prepares a map illustrating the appropriate neighborhoods for each racial or ethnic group. Through this policy, the sponsoring broker hopes to achieve racial balance in residential housing. Which of these statements is *TRUE* regarding the sponsoring broker's policy?
   A. Because the effect of the sponsoring broker's policy is discriminatory, it constitutes illegal steering regardless of his intentions.
   B. While the sponsoring broker's policy may appear to constitute blockbusting, application of the effects test proves its legality.
   C. The sponsoring broker's policy clearly shows the intent to discriminate.
   D. While the sponsoring broker's policy may appear to constitute steering, application of the intent test proves its legality.

9. If a seller refuses to sell her home to a buyer on the basis of that buyer's race, what law is violated?
   A. ADA
   B. Fair Steering Act
   C. Fair Advertising Act
   D. Fair Housing Act

10. A Lithuanian American real estate broker offers a special discount to Lithuanian American clients. This practice is
   A. legal in certain circumstances.
   B. legal but ill-advised.
   C. an example of steering.
   D. illegal.

11. Under the Americans with Disabilities Act (ADA), which of these is *TRUE*?
   A. The ADA requires that employers make reasonable accommodations that enable a person with a disability to perform essential job functions.
   B. Business and commercial real estate are exempt from the ADA.
   C. The provisions of the ADA do not apply to employers with fewer than 50 employees.
   D. The ADA does not apply to public buildings.

12. After a broker takes a listing of a residence, the owners specify that they will not sell their home to any Asian family. The broker should
   A. explain to the owner that the instruction violates federal law and that the broker cannot comply with it.
   B. advertise the property exclusively in Asian-language newspapers.
   C. abide by the principal's directions despite the fact that they conflict with the fair housing laws.
   D. require that the owner sign a separate legal document stating the additional instruction as an amendment to the listing agreement.

13. Which of these is *TRUE* pursuant to the Fair Housing Act?
   A. A landlord may unilaterally increase her customarily required security deposit if the tenant is disabled.
   B. Good intentions are always a defense to allegations of a Fair Housing Act violation.
   C. Landlords must make reasonable accommodations to existing policies or practices to permit disabled persons to have equal enjoyment of the premises.
   D. Steering is not illegal if it is based on the licensee's reasonable expectations.

14. A real estate licensee tells a single man with two small children that homes for sale in a condominium complex are available only to married couples with no children. Which statement is *TRUE*?
   A. Because a single-parent family can be disruptive if the parent provides little supervision of the children, the condominium is permitted to discriminate against the family under the principle of rational basis.
   B. The man may file a complaint alleging discrimination on the basis of familial status.
   C. Condominium complexes are exempt from the fair housing laws and can therefore restrict children.
   D. Restrictive covenants in a condominium take precedence over the fair housing laws.

15. The following ad appeared in the newspaper: "For sale: 4 BR brick home; Redwood School District; excellent Elm Street location; next door to St. John's Church and right on the bus line. Move-in condition; priced to sell." Which of these statements is *TRUE*?
    A. The ad is appropriate.
    B. Fair housing laws do not apply to newspaper advertising.
    C. The ad should not mention St. John's Church.
    D. The ad should state that the property is available to families with children.

16. A landlord rented an apartment to a person with a disability, and the tenant wants to make certain changes to the unit to accommodate her disability. Which of these does *NOT* constitute a reasonable modification?
    A. Widen the doorways
    B. Lower the kitchen cabinets
    C. Install a dog run for service animals in the lobby
    D. Lower the light switches

17. Which of these is legal?
    A. Negotiating with a person with a disability to establish an escrow account for the cost to restore a property after it has been modified
    B. Charging a family with children a higher security deposit than those with no children
    C. Picturing only white people in a brochure as the "happy residents" in a housing community
    D. Refusing to sell a house to a person who has a history of mental illness

18. Which of these is *TRUE* pursuant to the Illinois Human Rights Act?
    A. Tenants can never be held liable for any damages to the premises caused by a service animal.
    B. It is not a civil rights violation to discriminate against a person who is blind.
    C. It is not a civil rights violation to discriminate against a person who is hearing impaired.
    D. It is a civil rights violation to refuse to sell or rent because the prospective buyer or tenant has a service animal.

19. When a landlord rented an apartment in his six-unit building to a young couple, he didn't notice that the woman was pregnant. After the baby was born, the landlord canceled their lease, citing the lease's no-children clause. Which of these statements is *TRUE*?
    A. The landlord is acting legally under an exemption to the Illinois Human Rights Act.
    B. The landlord must give the tenants 60 days in which to find a new apartment.
    C. The landlord is violating the Illinois Human Rights Act regarding the exclusion of children.
    D. The landlord may refuse to rent to families with children only if he lives in the building.

20. A woman owns two multiunit apartment buildings: a two-flat on Oak Street and a 12-unit building on Main Street. She lives in an apartment in the Main Street property. Which of her properties, if any, is exempt from the Illinois Human Rights Act?
    A. Neither property
    B. The Oak Street property only
    C. The Main Street property only
    D. Both properties

UNIT
22

Environmental Issues and the Real Estate Transaction

LEARNING OBJECTIVES

When you have completed this unit, you will be able to accomplish the following.

› Describe the warning signs, characteristics, causes, and solutions for the various environmental hazards most commonly found in real estate transactions.
› Identify the basic environmental hazards a real estate agent should be aware of in order to protect her client's interests.
› Explain the fundamental liability issues arising under environmental protection laws.

KEY TERMS

asbestos	encapsulation	Superfund Amendments
brownfield	formaldehyde	and Reauthorization Act
capping	groundwater	(SARA)
carbon monoxide (CO)	innocent landowner	underground storage tank
Comprehensive	immunity	(UST)
Environmental	landfill	water table
Response,	lead	
Compensation, and	mold	
Liability Act (CERCLA)	radon	

OVERVIEW

Most states, including Illinois, recognize the need to balance commercial use of land with the need to preserve vital resources and to protect our air, water, and soil. A growing number of homebuyers base their decisions in part on the desire for fresh air, clean water, and outdoor recreational opportunities. Preservation of a state's environment both enhances the quality of life and helps strengthen property values. Preventing environmental problems and cleaning up existent pollutants revitalizes the land while creating greater opportunities for responsible development.

HAZARDOUS SUBSTANCES

Because no one wants to live in a toxic environment, pollution and hazardous substances in the environment can affect the desirability and market value of entire neighborhoods and towns. When showing properties, each possible living structure should be studied with an eye to red flags that may suggest environmental problems.

The Illinois Environmental Protection Agency (IEPA) is charged with maintaining and enhancing the state's air, land, and water quality through education, inspection, regulation, enforcement, recycling, and prevention activities. The Pollution Control Board and Hazardous Materials Advisory Board are two of the many bodies created to assist the IEPA in specific areas. Most Illinois environmental regulations are required by statute to be identical in substance to environmental protection regulations established by the U.S. Environmental Protection Agency (EPA).

Health issues based on environmental hazards are real estate issues. It is important that licensees are aware of local environmental issues and practice proper disclosure, encouraging buyer clients to seek outside expertise for testing and information whenever appropriate. Licensees must also encourage their seller clients to make full, honest disclosures and help any buyer clients locate authoritative information about hazardous substances. Licensees are expected to be aware of environmental issues and to ensure that the safety interests of all parties involved in real estate transactions are protected. Licensees should be familiar with state and federal environmental laws and the regulatory agencies that enforce them.

Asbestos

Asbestos insulation can create airborne contaminants that may result in respiratory diseases.

Asbestos is a fire-resistant mineral that was once used extensively as insulation and to strengthen other building materials. Asbestos was found in most construction, including residential. On July 12, 1989, EPA issued a final rule banning most asbestos-containing products. In 1991, this regulation was overturned by the Fifth Circuit Court of Appeals in New Orleans. As a result of the Court's decision, the following specific asbestos-containing products remain banned: flooring felt, rollboard, and corrugated, commercial, or specialty paper. In addition, the regulation continues to ban the use of asbestos in products that have not historically contained asbestos, otherwise referred to as "new uses" of asbestos. The EPA estimates that, even today, about 20% of the nation's commercial and public buildings have asbestos-containing materials (ACMs).

Asbestos was used to cover pipes, ducts, and heating and hot water units. Its fire-resistant properties made it a popular material for use in floor tile, exterior siding, roofing products, linoleum flooring materials, joint compounds, wallboard material, backing, and mastics. Though some ACMs are easy to identify (e.g., insulation around heating and water pipes), identifying asbestos may be more difficult when it is behind walls or under floors.

Asbestos is highly friable, meaning that as it ages, asbestos fibers break down easily into tiny filaments and particles. This makes asbestos especially harmful when it is disturbed or exposed and becomes airborne, as often occurs during renovation or remodeling. Those who inhale asbestos fibers often develop serious and deadly respiratory diseases decades later. While federal regulations establish guidelines for owners of public and commercial buildings to test for ACMs, there are no guidelines regarding the presence of asbestos in residential properties.

Because improper removal may further contaminate the air within the structure, asbestos removal requires state-licensed technicians and specially sealed environments. The waste generated must be disposed of at a licensed facility, which further adds to the cost of removal. **Encapsulation**, or the sealing off of disintegrating asbestos, is an alternate method of asbestos control that may be preferable to removal in certain circumstances. However, an owner must periodically monitor the condition of the encapsulated asbestos to make sure it is not disintegrating.

Only a certified asbestos inspector should perform an asbestos inspection of a structure to identify which building materials may contain asbestos. The inspector can also provide recommendations and estimate costs associated with remediation. It is vital that a buyer knows where asbestos-containing materials are located so that they are not disturbed during any repair, remodeling, demolition, or even routine use. Appraisers also should be aware of the possible presence of asbestos.

More information on asbestos-related issues is available from the EPA.

Lead-Based Paint and Other Lead Hazards

Lead from paint or other sources can result in damage to the brain, nervous system, kidneys, and blood. Children younger than six are particularly vulnerable.

Lead was used as a pigment and drying agent in alkyd oil-based paint. Lead-based paint may be on any interior or exterior surface, but it is particularly common on doors, windows, and other woodwork. The federal government estimates that lead is present in about 75% of all private housing built before 1978, or approximately 57 million homes, ranging from low-income apartments to million-dollar mansions.

Children younger than six are the most vulnerable to damage from excessive lead levels. Elevated levels of lead in children cause learning disabilities, developmental delays, reduced height, and poor hearing, and the effects are generally irreversible. Excessive exposure in adults can induce anemia and hypertension, trigger gallbladder problems, and cause reproductive problems in both men and women.

Lead dust can be ingested from the hands by a crawling infant, inhaled by any occupant of a structure, or ingested from the water supply because of lead pipes or lead solder. Soil and groundwater may be contaminated by everything from lead plumbing in leaking landfills to discarded skeets and bullets from an old shooting range. High levels of lead have been found in soil located near waste-to-energy incinerators, as well as along roadways over 40 years old due to the former prevalence of lead in gasoline. While the EPA states that 50–400 parts per million is a natural level for lead in the soil, at these aforementioned sites, it is likely much higher.

The federal Lead-Based Paint Hazard Reduction Act of 1992 (LBPHRA) requires disclosure of the presence of any known lead-based paint hazards to potential buyers or renters. The law, however, does not expressly require that anyone test for the presence of lead-based paint.

LBPHRA requires the following from sellers and landlords of residential dwellings built before 1978:

- Sellers, lessors, and renovators must disclose any knowledge of lead-based paint hazards. Sellers must make such disclosures before execution of a contract for sale. Sales contracts must include a completed disclosure form about lead-based paint (see Figure 22.1).

- Any lease must disclose known information on lead-based paint and hazards before the lease takes effect.

- Buyers have up to 10 days to conduct a risk assessment or an inspection for the presence of lead-based paint hazards.

- Licensees must provide buyers and lessees with *Protect Your Family from Lead in Your Home*, a pamphlet created by the EPA, HUD, and the U.S. Consumer Product Safety Commission.

- Renovators must give homeowners the *Protect Your Family from Lead in Your Home* pamphlet before starting any renovation work.

- Anyone paid to perform work that disturbs paint in housing and child-occupied facilities must be trained and certified in the EPA's lead-based work practices. This includes residential rental property owners/managers, general contractors, and special trade contractors (e.g., painters, plumbers, carpenters, and electricians). The Renovation, Repair, and Painting (RRP) program involves pre-renovation education. This education includes distribution of the pamphlet *Renovate Right: Important Lead Hazard Information for Families, Child Care Providers, and Schools* to the property owners before work commences.

- Licensees must ensure that all parties comply with LBPHRA's disclosure requirements (licensees should use EPA-written disclosure forms rather than creating their own forms).

LBPHRA applies to housing built before 1978 with the following six exceptions:

- Property sold at foreclosure, although the disclosure must be made at resale time

- Rental property that is certified "lead-based paint free" by an inspector who is certified under a federal program or federally authorized state certification program

- Property leased for 100 days or less, with no lease renewal or extension

- Renewals of existing leases if disclosure was made at the time of the initial lease

- Units with no bedrooms or with no separation between sleeping and living areas

- Housing for the elderly or disabled if children under the age of six are not expected to live there

There is considerable controversy about practical approaches for handling the presence of lead-based paint. Removal or encapsulation is sometimes used. Federal law requires that only licensed lead inspectors, abatement contractors, risk assessors, abatement project designers, and abatement workers may deal with the removal or encapsulation of lead in a structure.

Anyone who performs lead abatement or mitigation activities without a license is guilty of a Class A misdemeanor. The Department of Public Health (DPH) oversees the qualifying, training, and licensing of lead abatement contractors and lead abatement workers in Illinois.

The Illinois Lead Poisoning Prevention Act (410 ILCS 45/) requires that physicians screen children younger than six years old for lead poisoning when the child lives in an area considered by the state to be at "high risk" for lead exposure. High-risk areas include slum and blighted housing; proximity to highway or heavy local traffic; proximity to a lead-using or lead-generating industry; and incidence of elevated blood lead levels, poverty, and the number of young children in the area.

When a child is diagnosed as having an elevated level of lead in her bloodstream, the physician must report the condition to the DPH. After notification, the DPH may inspect the child's residence for the existence of exposed lead-bearing substances (including dust, paint, and lead pipes). If the inspection identifies a lead hazard, the property owner is required to mitigate the condition within 90 days (30 days if a child under six or a pregnant woman is at risk). Licensed lead abatement contractors must be used for lead removal. The owner will receive a certificate of compliance once the DPH is satisfied that the lead hazard has been removed.

Figure 22.1: Disclosure of Information and Acknowledgment—Lead-Based Paint and/or Lead-Based Paint Hazards

ILLINOIS REALTORS®
DISCLOSURE OF INFORMATION AND ACKNOWLEDGEMENT
LEAD-BASED PAINT AND/OR LEAD-BASED PAINT HAZARDS

Lead Warning Statement

Every purchaser of any interest in residential real property on which a residential dwelling was built prior to 1978 is notified that such property may present exposure to lead from lead-based paint that may place young children at risk of developing lead poisoning. Lead poisoning in young children may produce permanent neurological damage, including learning disabilities, reduced intelligence quotient, behavioral problems, and impaired memory. Lead poisoning also poses a particular risk to pregnant women. The seller of any interest in residential real property is required to provide the buyer with any information on lead-based paint hazards from risk assessments or inspections in the seller's possession and notify the buyer of any known lead-based paint hazards. A risk assessment or inspection for possible lead-based paint hazards is recommended prior to purchase.

Property Address: _____

Seller's Disclosure (initial)

_____ (a) Presence of lead-based paint and/or lead-based paint hazards (check one below):

     ☐ Known lead-based paint and/or lead-based paint hazards are present in the housing (explain):

        _____

        _____

     ☐ Seller has no knowledge of lead-based paint and/or lead-based paint hazards in the housing.

_____ (b) Records and Reports available to the seller (check one below):

     ☐ Seller has provided the purchaser with all available records and reports pertaining to lead-based paint and/or lead-based paint hazards in the housing (list documents below): _____

        _____

     ☐ Seller has no reports or records pertaining to lead-based paint and/or lead-based paint hazards in the housing.

Purchaser's Acknowledgment (initial)

_____ (c) Purchaser has received copies of all information listed above.

_____ (d) Purchaser has received the pamphlet *Protect Your Family From Lead in Your Home*.

_____ (e) Purchaser has (check one below):

     ☐ Received a 10-day opportunity (or mutually agreed upon period) to conduct a risk assessment or inspection of the presence of lead-based paint or lead-based paint hazards; or

     ☐ Waived the opportunity to conduct a risk assessment or inspection for the presence of lead-based paint and/or lead-based paint hazards.

Agent's Acknowledgment (initial)

_____ (f) Agent has informed the seller of the seller's obligations under 42 U.S.C. 4852d and is aware of his/her responsibility to ensure compliance.

Certification of Accuracy

The following parties have reviewed the information above and certify to the best of their knowledge, that the information they have provided is true and accurate.

Seller _____ Date _____   Purchaser _____ Date _____

Seller _____ Date _____   Purchaser _____ Date _____

Agent _____ Date _____   Agent _____ Date _____

(This disclosure form should be attached to the Contract to Purchase) FORM 420 (7/28/16)
COPYRIGHT ILLINOIS REALTORS®. Reprinted with permission.

An owner who has received a lead mitigation notice must provide any prospective lessees for the affected unit with a written notice of the existence of an identified lead hazard. In addition, all owners of residential buildings or units must give current and prospective lessees information on the potential health hazards posed by lead and a copy of an informational brochure.

Radon

Radon is a naturally occurring gas that is a cause of lung cancer.

Radon is a naturally occurring, colorless, odorless, tasteless, radioactive gas produced by the decay of other radioactive substances. Radon is measured in picocuries (a unit of radiation) contained in a liter of air (i.e., pCi/L). Radon is found in every state and territory, with outdoor radon levels averaging 0.4 pCi/L. Fans and thermal "stack effects" (i.e., rising hot air drawing cooler air in from the ground through cracks in basement and foundation walls) pulls radon into buildings.

According to the American Cancer Society, radon is a "Class A" known human carcinogen, meaning that it is known to cause cancer in humans. According to the American Lung Association, radon is the second-leading cause of lung cancer in the United States. The potential for developing lung cancer from radon exposure is a function of the extent and length of that exposure.

Because neither the EPA nor current scientific consensus has established a threshold safe level of radon exposure, the EPA suggests an "action" level of 4 pCi/L. Mitigation consists of removing the radon before it seeps into the house. A fan is installed in a pipe running from the basement to the attic to draw the radon up and out. Radon mitigation is less expensive when the system is installed during construction.

Because about 7% of homes probably need mitigation, licensees should discuss radon concerns with their buyers. Licensees can direct buyers to the EPA website for the pamphlet *A Citizen's Guide to Radon* and for additional information about testing and mitigation methods.

The Illinois Radon Awareness Act (420 ILCS 46/) requires a seller to provide to buyers and tenants, before the buyer is obligated under any contract to purchase residential real property, a Disclosure of Information on Radon Hazards (see Figure 22.2) along with the pamphlet *Radon Testing Guidelines for Real Estate Transaction*," stating that the property may present the potential for exposure to radon. Radon disclosure is also required if a previous tenant tested and found radon levels over 4 pCi/L.

In short, the act requires a separate disclosure document for radon to be included in most residential real estate transactions. The disclosure document

- has a radon warning statement advising buyers that the home may pose a threat to their health if it has elevated levels of radon and that all homes should be tested for radon;

- requires that a seller provide an Illinois Emergency Management Agency (IEMA)-approved pamphlet about general radon information to a buyer and disclose all information along with any available documentation of the radon levels in the home;

- requires that real estate agents sign the disclosure to confirm that sellers have been made aware of their obligations;

- requires that all parties involved sign the disclosure acknowledging the transfer of the above information; and

- requires that sellers disclose that they have no knowledge of elevated radon concentrations or that prior elevated radon concentrations have been mitigated or remediated.

Figure 22.2: Disclosure of Information on Radon Hazards

ILLINOIS REALTORS®
DISCLOSURE OF INFORMATION ON RADON HAZARDS
(For Residential Real Property Sales or Purchases)

Radon Warning Statement

Every buyer of any interest in residential real property is notified that the property may present exposure to dangerous levels of indoor radon gas that may place the occupants at risk of developing radon-induced lung cancer. Radon, a Class-A human carcinogen, is the leading cause of lung cancer in non-smokers and the second leading cause overall. The seller of any interest in residential real property is required to provide the buyer with any information on radon test results of the dwelling showing elevated levels of radon in the seller's possession.

The Illinois Emergency Management Agency (IEMA) strongly recommends ALL homebuyers have an indoor radon test performed prior to purchase or taking occupancy, and mitigated if elevated levels are found. Elevated radon concentrations can easily be reduced by a qualified, licensed radon mitigator.

Seller's Disclosure (initial each of the following which applies)

_____ (a) Elevated radon concentrations (above EPA or IEMA recommended Radon Action Level) are known to be present within the dwelling. (Explain).

_____ (b) Seller has provided the purchaser with the most current records and reports pertaining to elevated radon concentrations within the dwelling.

_____ (c) Seller either has no knowledge of elevated radon concentrations in the dwelling or prior elevated radon concentrations have been mitigated or remediated.

_____ (d) Seller has no records or reports pertaining to elevated radon concentrations within the dwelling.

Purchaser's Acknowledgment (initial each of the following which applies)

_____ (e) Purchaser has received copies of all information listed above.

_____ (f) Purchaser has received the IEMA approved Radon Disclosure Pamphlet.

Agent's Acknowledgement (initial IF APPLICABLE)

_____ (g) Agent has informed the seller of the seller's obligations under Illinois law.

Certification of Accuracy

The following parties have reviewed the information above and each party certifies, to the best of his or her knowledge, that the information he or she has provided is true and accurate.

Seller _____ **Date** _____

Seller _____ **Date** _____

Purchaser _____ **Date** _____

Purchaser _____ **Date** _____

Agent _____ **Date** _____

Agent _____ **Date** _____

Property Address: _____

City, State, Zip Code: _____

FORM 422 (7/28/16) COPYRIGHT ILLINOIS REALTORS®. Reprinted with permission.   1/1

The act does not require that all homes in a real estate transaction be tested or that the home be mitigated if the test results are elevated. It also does not apply to the transfer of any residential dwelling unit located three stories (or higher) above ground level in any structure.

If any of the required disclosures occur after the buyer has made an offer to purchase the residential real property, the seller must complete the required disclosure activities before accepting the buyer's offer and allow the buyer an opportunity to review the information and possibly amend the offer.

The provisions of this act do not apply to

- transfers pursuant to court order;

- transfers from a mortgagor to a mortgagee by deed in lieu of foreclosure or consent judgment, transfer by judicial deed issued pursuant to a foreclosure sale, transfer by a collateral assignment of a beneficial interest of a land trust, or a transfer by a mortgagee or a successor in interest to the mortgagee's secured position;

- transfers by a fiduciary in the course of the administration of a decedent's estate, guardianship, conservatorship, or trust;

- transfers from one co-owner to one or more other co-owners;

- transfers pursuant to testate or intestate succession;

- transfers made to a spouse or to a person or persons in the lineal line of consanguinity of one or more of the sellers;

- transfers from an entity that has taken title to residential real property from a seller for the purpose of assisting in the relocation of the seller, so long as the entity makes available to all prospective buyers a copy of the disclosure form furnished to the entity by the seller;

- transfers to or from any governmental entity; and

- transfers of any residential dwelling unit located three stories (or higher) above ground level in any structure.

Formaldehyde

Formaldehyde is a chemical that is a suspected carcinogen.

Formaldehyde is a colorless chemical with a strong, pronounced odor. It was used widely in the manufacture of building materials and household products because of its preservative characteristics. Often emitted as a gas, formaldehyde is one of the most common and problematic volatile organic compounds (VOCs) and is one of the few indoor air pollutants that can be measured. Formaldehyde was listed as a hazardous air pollutant in the Clean Air Act Amendments of 1990.

Formaldehyde is classified as a probable human carcinogen. Furthermore, it may trigger respiratory problems, as well as eye and skin irritations, in 10 to 20% of the population. It is a major contributor to sick building syndrome (SBS) in commercial properties.

The largest source of formaldehyde in any building is likely to be the off-gassing from pressed-wood products made from using adhesives that contain urea-formaldehyde (UF) resins. Pressed-wood products include particleboard, hardwood plywood paneling, and medium-density fiberboard. It is also used in carpeting and ceiling tiles. Since 1985, HUD has regulated the use of plywood and particleboard so that they conform to specified formaldehyde-emission levels in the construction of prefabricated homes and manufactured housing (mobile homes).

Carbon Monoxide

Carbon monoxide is a by-product of fuel combustion that may result in death in poorly ventilated areas.

Carbon monoxide (CO) is a colorless, odorless gas that occurs due to incomplete combustion as a by-product of burning such fuels as wood, oil, and natural gas. Furnaces, water heaters, space heaters, fireplaces, and wood stoves all produce CO as a natural result of combustion. When these appliances function properly and are properly ventilated, CO emissions are not a problem. However, when improper ventilation or equipment malfunctions permit large quantities of CO to be released into a residence or commercial structure, it poses a significant health hazard. The effects of CO are compounded by the fact that it is so difficult to detect. CO is quickly absorbed by the body, where it inhibits the blood's ability to transport oxygen and results in dizziness and nausea. As the concentrations of CO increase, the symptoms become more severe. More than 300 deaths from CO poisoning occur each year, with thousands of others requiring hospital emergency room care.

CO detectors are available, and their use is mandatory in some areas. Annual maintenance of heating systems also helps avoid CO exposure.

Illinois requires that all residences be equipped with working CO detectors. Detectors must be located within 15 feet of all bedrooms.

Mold

Mold can infest homes and may produce toxins that cause allergic reactions and asthma attacks.

Mold can be found almost anywhere and can grow on almost any organic substance, so long as moisture, oxygen, and an organic food source are present. Some molds can cause serious health problems, including allergic reactions and asthma attacks, and some molds are known to produce potent toxins and/or irritants.

Moisture feeds mold growth. If a moisture problem is not discovered or addressed, mold growth can eventually destroy what it is growing on. Some moisture problems in homes and buildings have been directly linked to construction practices, resulting in buildings that are too tightly sealed, preventing adequate ventilation. Building materials, such as drywall, may not allow moisture to escape properly. The material used in drywall wicks moisture to the glue and paper (food sources for molds). Vinyl wallpaper and exterior insulation finish systems (EIFS) (also called *synthetic stucco*) do not allow moisture to escape. Other moisture problems include roof leaks, unvented combustion appliances, and landscaping or gutters that direct water to the building.

The EPA provides guidelines for the remediation and/or cleanup of mold and moisture problems in schools and commercial buildings.

IN PRACTICE

HUD now requires mold disclosure on all HUD sales contracts.

ADDITIONAL ENVIRONMENTAL HAZARDS

Groundwater Protection

Groundwater is the water that exists under the earth's surface within the tiny spaces or crevices in geological formations. Groundwater forms the **water table**, the natural level at which the ground is saturated. The water table may be several hundred feet underground or near the surface. When the earth's natural filtering systems are inadequate to ensure the availability of pure water, any contamination of underground water threatens the supply of pure, clean water for private wells or public water systems. If groundwater is not protected from contamination, the earth's natural filtering systems may be inadequate to ensure the availability of pure water. Numerous state and federal laws have been enacted to preserve and protect the water supply, led by the Safe Drinking Water Act (SDWA). The SDWA authorizes the EPA to set national health-based standards for drinking water. Later amendments strengthened the law by increasing source water protection, operator training, and funding for water system improvements and public information. For example, the EPA now requires that water suppliers report any health risk situation within 24 hours instead of the 72 hours mandated in the past.

Water can be contaminated from a number of sources. Runoff from waste disposal sites, leaking underground storage tanks, and pesticides and herbicides are some of the main culprits. Because water flows naturally, contamination can spread far from its source. Once contamination has been identified, its source can usually be eliminated, and the water may eventually be made clean. However, the process can be time-consuming and expensive.

Many property disclosure forms require sellers to identify the property's water source, such as well water, municipal water supply, or some other source. Anything other than a municipal water supply should be tested. Also, sellers are generally required to identify the type of septic system because an incorrectly placed or poorly functioning system can contaminate the water source.

IN PRACTICE

Real estate licensees should educate their sellers about full disclosure concerning a property's water supply and septic systems. Buyers should be educated about potential groundwater contamination sources both on and off a property. Licensees should always recommend testing the water supply when it is not part of a municipal source.

Underground Storage Tanks

Underground storage tanks (USTs) are commonly found on sites where petroleum products are used or where gas stations and auto repair shops are located. They also may be found in a number of other commercial and industrial establishments—including printing and chemical plants, wood treatment plants, paper mills, paint manufacturers, dry cleaners, and food-processing plants—for storing chemicals or process wastes. In residential areas, they are used to store heating oil.

Some tanks are currently in use, but many are long forgotten. Licensees should be particularly alert to the presence of fill pipes, vent lines, stained soil, and fumes or odors, any of which may indicate the presence of a UST.

State and federal laws impose strict requirements on landowners to detect and correct leaks in an effort to protect the groundwater. The federal UST program is regulated by the EPA. The regulations apply to tanks that contain hazardous substances or liquid petroleum products and that store at least 10% of their volume underground. UST owners are required to register their tanks and adhere to strict technical and administrative requirements.

Owners are also required to demonstrate that they have sufficient financial resources to cover any damage that might result from leaks.

The following types of tanks are among those that are exempt from the federal regulations:

■ Tanks that hold less than 110 gallons

- Farm and residential tanks that hold 1,100 gallons or less of motor fuel used for noncommercial purposes
- Tanks that store heating oil burned on the premises
- Tanks on or above the floor of underground areas such as basements or tunnels
- Septic tanks and systems for collecting stormwater and wastewater

The Leaking Underground Storage Tank section of the IEPA governs the detection, identification, monitoring, mitigation, and removal of buried underground storage tanks (particularly those containing petroleum products). The program is authorized to disburse money from a special fund to assist property owners in complying with mandatory remediation activities.

Waste Disposal Sites

Federal, state, and local regulations govern the location, construction, content, and maintenance of landfill sites built to accommodate the vast quantities of garbage produced every day in America. A **landfill** is an enormous hole, either excavated for the purpose of waste disposal or left over from surface mining operations. The hole is lined with clay or a synthetic liner to prevent leakage of waste material into the water supply. A system of underground drainage pipes permits the monitoring of leaks and leaching. Waste is laid on the liner at the bottom of the excavation, and a layer of topsoil is then compacted onto the waste. The layering procedure is repeated until the landfill is full, with the layers mounded up, sometimes as high as several hundred feet.

Capping is the process of laying two to four feet of soil over the top of the site and then planting grass on it to enhance the landfill's aesthetic value and prevent erosion. A ventilation pipe runs from the landfill's base through the cap to vent off accumulated natural gases created by the decomposing waste. Test wells around landfill operations are installed to constantly monitor the groundwater in the surrounding area, and soil analyses test for contamination.

Capped landfills have been used as parks and golf courses. Rapid suburban growth has resulted in many housing developments and office campuses being built on landfill sites. Most newer landfill sites are well documented, but the locations of many older landfill sites are no longer known.

Special hazardous waste disposal sites contain radioactive waste from nuclear power plants, toxic chemicals, and waste materials produced by medical, scientific, and industrial processes. These disposal sites are usually limited to extremely remote locations, well away from populated areas or farmland. Hazardous and radioactive waste disposal sites are subject to strict state and federal regulation to prevent the escape of toxic substances.

Brownfields

Brownfields are defunct, derelict, or abandoned commercial or industrial sites, many of which are suspected to contain toxic wastes. According to the U.S. General Accounting Office, several hundred thousand brownfields plague communities as eyesores and potentially dangerous and hazardous properties, often contributing to the decline of surrounding urban property values.

ENVIRONMENTAL PROTECTION

CERCLA

The **Comprehensive Environmental Response, Compensation, and Liability Act (CERCLA)**, commonly called the *Superfund*, was enacted in 1980. It established a fund of $9 billion to clean up uncontrolled hazardous waste sites and to respond to spills. It created a process for identifying potentially responsible parties (PRPs) and ordering them to take responsibility for the cleanup action. CERCLA is administered and enforced by the EPA.

Liability Under CERCLA

Liability under CERCLA is considered strict, joint and several, and retroactive. Strict liability means that the owner is responsible to the injured party without excuse. Joint and several liability means that each of the individual owners is personally responsible for the total damages. If only one of the owners is financially able to handle the total damages, that owner must pay the total and collect the proportionate shares from the other owners whenever possible. Retroactive liability means that the liability is not limited to the current owner but includes people who have owned the site in the past.

Superfund Amendments and Reauthorization Act

In 1986, the U.S. Congress amended CERCLA with the **Superfund Amendments and Reauthorization Act (SARA)**. The amended statute contains stronger cleanup standards for contaminated sites and five times the funding of the original Superfund, which expired in September 1985.

The amended act also sought to clarify the obligations of lenders. The amendments created a concept called **innocent landowner immunity**—it was recognized that in certain cases, a landowner in the chain of ownership was completely innocent of all wrongdoing and therefore should not be held liable. The innocent landowner immunity clause established the criteria by which to judge whether a person or a business could be exempted from liability. The criteria included the following:

- The pollution was caused by a third party.
- The property was acquired after the fact.
- The landowner had no actual or constructive knowledge of the damage.
- Due care was exercised when the property was purchased (the landowner made a reasonable search, called an *environmental site assessment*) to determine that no damage to the property existed.
- Reasonable precautions were taken in the exercise of ownership rights.

The most serious problems associated with value involve the presence of undisclosed landfills and hazardous waste sites. Licensees can encourage buyers to consult www.epa.gov/superfund/sites/index.htm to determine whether a property of interest is located near a Superfund site. Buyers should also speak with neighbors. Many buyers of commercial and industrial properties hire an environmental engineer to conduct detailed studies before closing. In other words, the parties should do everything possible to avoid surprises.

LIABILITY OF REAL ESTATE LICENSEES

Real estate licensees can avoid liability with environmental issues by

■ becoming familiar with common environmental problems in their area,

■ looking for signs of environmental contamination,

■ advising (and including as a contingency) an environmental audit if contamination is expected, and

■ not giving specific opinions on environmental issues.

Real estate licensees and all others involved in a real estate transaction must be aware of their potential liability under state and federal environmental laws.

Sellers often carry the most legal liability exposure. Innocent landowners might be held responsible, even though they did not know about the presence of environmental hazards. Purchasers may be held liable, even if they didn't cause the contamination. Lenders may end up owning worthless assets if owners default on the loans rather than undertaking expensive cleanup efforts. Real estate licensees could be held liable for improper disclosure; therefore, it is necessary to be aware of the potential environmental risks from neighboring properties such as gas stations, manufacturing plants, or even funeral homes.

Discovery of Environmental Hazards

Real estate licensees are not expected to have the technical expertise necessary to discover the presence of environmental hazards. However, because they are presumed by the public to have special knowledge about real estate, licensees must be aware both of possible hazards and of where to seek professional help.

The most appropriate people on whom a real estate licensee can rely for sound environmental information are scientific or technical experts. Environmental auditors (also called *environmental assessors*) are scientific or technical experts who can provide the most comprehensive studies. Developers and purchasers of commercial and industrial properties often rely on an environmental assessment that includes the property's history of use, a current-use review, and an investigation into the existence of reported or known contamination sources in the subject area that may affect the property. Testing of soil, water, air, and structures can be conducted, if warranted.

Not only do environmental experts detect environmental problems, they can usually offer guidance about how best to resolve the conditions. Although environmental audits or assessments may occur at any stage in a transaction, they are most frequently a contingency that must be satisfied before closing.

ENVIRONMENTAL SITE ASSESSMENTS

An environmental site assessment is often performed on a property to show that due care was exercised in determining whether any environmental impairments exist. The assessment can help prevent parties from becoming involved in contaminated property and work as a defense to liability. It is often requested by a lending institution, developer, or a potential buyer. The assessment is commonly performed in phases, such as Phase 1 or Phase 2. A Phase 1 environmental report is requested first to determine whether any potential environmental problems exist at or near the subject property that may cause impairment. Additional phases are performed as warranted and requested.

Another test that is often performed is a **percolation test**. Most often associated with septic tank use, a percolation test is used to determine the absorption rate of the soil around a septic tank.

There are no federal regulations that define what an environmental assessment must include. However, one of the most accepted industry standards is provided by the American Society for Testing Materials International.

A federally funded project requires that an *environmental impact statement (EIS)* be performed. These statements detail the impact the project will have on the environment. They can include information about air quality, noise, public health and safety, energy consumption, population density, wildlife, vegetation, and need for sewer and water facilities. Increasingly, these statements are also being required for private development.

SUMMARY

Environmental issues are important to real estate licensees because they have an impact on clients. They may affect real estate transactions by raising issues of health risks or cleanup costs. Some of the principal environmental toxins include asbestos, lead, radon, urea-formaldehyde insulation, formaldehyde gas, and mold.

Asbestos is a mineral composed of fibers that have fireproofing and insulating qualities, and it is a health hazard when those fibers break down and are inhaled. Encapsulation and professional removal are two methods of eliminating its harmful effects.

Lead is found in paint dust, paint chips, and lead pipes, and also may be present in soil or groundwater. Eating or ingesting the chips or dust of lead paint (or drinking water that has passed through lead pipes) can lead to serious health problems, especially mental diminishment and kidney difficulties. Children younger than six are particularly vulnerable to its effects. Painting over lead paint is of some use, but it is best to have paint removed by a qualified professional if children are present. Lead pipes should be replaced. Licensees should be aware of the significance of 1978 for lead.

Radon is an odorless, tasteless, radioactive gas produced by the natural decay of radioactive substances in the ground and is found throughout the United States. According to the American Lung Association, radon gas is the second-leading cause of lung cancer in the United States. Testing for radon in buildings is not a federal requirement.

Water pollutants, many from gasoline, can often be filtered out if they are identified. The source of the problem—such as leaking pipes or underground storage tanks—should always be addressed and, ideally, removed.

Mold can be found anywhere and can grow on almost any organic substance, as long as moisture, oxygen, and an organic food source are present. If a moisture problem is not discovered or addressed, mold growth can gradually destroy what it is growing on.

Improperly constructed or maintained landfills may also present a danger to groundwater that exists under the earth's surface.

Licensees and their clients should be aware and on the watch for any possible environmental contamination sources.

The Illinois Radon Awareness Act requires sellers to provide buyers of residential real estate the IEMA pamphlet *Radon Testing Guidelines for Real Estate Transactions*, along with the Illinois Disclosure of Information on Radon Hazards form stating that the property may present the potential for exposure to radon. A seller is not required to test or mitigate if test results are elevated.

UNIT 22 QUIZ

1. Asbestos is *MOST* dangerous when it
   A. is used as insulation.
   B. gets wet.
   C. crumbles and becomes airborne.
   D. is wrapped around heating and water pipes.

2. The term *encapsulation* refers to the
   A. process of sealing a landfill with three to four feet of topsoil.
   B. way in which asbestos insulation is applied to pipes and wiring systems.
   C. way in which asbestos becomes airborne.
   D. method of sealing disintegrating asbestos.

3. A real estate licensee showed a pre-World War I house to a prospective buyer. The buyer has two toddlers and is worried about potential health hazards. Which of these is *TRUE*?
   A. There is a risk that urea-foam insulation was used in the original construction.
   B. The licensee is authorized to inspect for lead and remove any lead risks.
   C. Removal of lead-based paint and asbestos hazards is covered by standard title insurance policies.
   D. Because the house was built before 1978, lead-based paint is likely present.

4. Which of these is *TRUE* regarding asbestos?
   A. The removal of asbestos can cause further contamination of a building.
   B. Asbestos causes health problems only when it is eaten.
   C. The level of asbestos in a building is affected by weather conditions.
   D. HUD requires all asbestos-containing materials to be removed from all residential buildings.

5. Which of these *BEST* describes the water table?
   A. Level at which underground storage tanks may be safely buried
   B. Natural level at which the ground is saturated
   C. Measuring device used by specialists to measure groundwater contamination
   D. Always underground

6. Radon poses the greatest potential health risk to humans when it is
   A. contained in insulation material used in residential properties during the 1970s.
   B. found in high concentrations in unimproved land.
   C. trapped and concentrates in inadequately ventilated areas.
   D. emitted by malfunctioning or inadequately ventilated appliances.

7. Which of these describes the process of creating a landfill site?
   A. Waste is liquefied, treated, and pumped through pipes to "tombs" under the water table.
   B. Waste is compacted and sealed into a container and then placed in a "tomb" designed to last several thousand years.
   C. Waste is buried in an underground concrete vault.
   D. Waste and topsoil are layered in a pit, mounded up, and then covered with dirt and plants.

8. Liability under CERCLA is
   A. limited to the owner of record.
   B. joint and several and retroactive, but not strict.
   C. voluntary.
   D. strict, joint and several, and retroactive.

9. Which of these has *NOT* been proven to pose health hazards?
   A. Asbestos fibers
   B. Carbon monoxide
   C. Electromagnetic fields
   D. Lead-based paint

10. Which of these environmental hazards poses a risk due to particles or fibers in the air?
    A. Carbon monoxide
    B. Radon
    C. UFFI
    D. Asbestos

11. The Residential Lead-Based Paint Hazard Reduction Act establishes procedures for disclosing the presence of lead in
    A. residential properties built before 1978.
    B. all residential properties offered for sale.
    C. new residential construction only.
    D. residential properties built before 1990.

12. Which of these is *NOT* exempt from disclosure regulations of the Residential Lead-Based Paint Hazard Reduction Act?
    A. Studio apartments where the living area is not separated from the sleeping area
    B. Senior-citizen housing
    C. A duplex built before 1978
    D. Residences for the disabled

13. The segment of the population most likely to obtain lead poisoning from paint is
    A. the elderly.
    B. teenagers.
    C. all of these.
    D. children.

14. Mold and mildew found in the home fall into which category of pollutants?
    A. Pesticides
    B. Biological
    C. Formaldehyde
    D. Hazardous waste

15. Which of these is *FALSE* about underground water contamination?
    A. It is a minor problem in the United States.
    B. Any contamination of underground water can threaten the supply of pure, clean water from private wells and public water systems.
    C. Protective state and federal laws concerning water supply have been enacted.
    D. Real estate licensees need to be aware of potential contamination sources.

16. In regulations regarding lead-based paint, HUD requires that
    A. homeowners test for its presence.
    B. known paint hazards be disclosed.
    C. paint be removed from surfaces before selling.
    D. only licensed contractors deal with its removal.

17. A method of sealing off disintegrating asbestos is called
    A. encapsulation.
    B. capping.
    C. containment.
    D. contamination closure.

18. The agency primarily responsible for protecting Illinois's natural resources against pollution and other hazards is the
    A. Pollution Control Board of Illinois (PCB).
    B. Illinois Department of Environmental Affairs (IDEA).
    C. Illinois Department of Environmental Regulation (IDER).
    D. Illinois Environmental Protection Agency (IEPA).

19. Environmental regulations in Illinois are
    A. all more stringent than federal regulations.
    B. less restrictive than federal regulations.
    C. substantially equivalent to federal regulations.
    D. not subject to federal regulations.

20. Which are exempt from radon disclosure under the Illinois Radon Awareness Act?
    A. Residential rentals, if radon has been detected and remediated in the past
    B. Properties with six or more units
    C. Transfers between neighbors
    D. Transfers between co-owners

UNIT 23

Closing the Real Estate Transaction

LEARNING OBJECTIVES

When you have completed this unit, you will be able to accomplish the following.

> Identify the issues of particular interest to the buyer and the seller as a real estate transaction closes.
> Describe the procedures involved in face-to-face closings from those in escrow closings.
> Describe legislation related to closing.
> Describe the steps involved in preparing a closing statement.
> Explain the general rules for prorating.

KEY TERMS

accrued item	credit	proration
affiliated business arrangement (ABA)	debit	Real Estate Settlement Procedures Act (RESPA)
	escrow	
closing	Loan Estimate (LE)	TILA-RESPA Integrated Disclosure Rule (TRID)
Closing Disclosure (CD)	prepaid item	

OVERVIEW

A real estate **closing** is the culmination of many efforts—finding clients, negotiating offers, solving problems, coordinating inspections, and much more. At the closing, title to the real estate is transferred in exchange for payment of the purchase price. It's also a complicated time because until closing preparations begin, the licensee's relationship is primarily with the buyer or the seller. During the closing period, new players come on the scene: appraisers, inspectors, loan officers, insurance agents, and lawyers. Negotiations continue, sometimes right up until the property is finally transferred. A thorough knowledge of the process is the best defense against the risk of a transaction failing.

PRECLOSING PROCEDURES

Closing involves two major events. First, the promises made in the sales contract are fulfilled; second, the mortgage funds are distributed to the buyer. Before the property changes hands, however, important issues must be resolved. Many real estate licensees maintain lists of events that must take place before the actual closing in order to avoid surprises that might lead to delays. Each party—buyer and seller—has specific concerns that must be addressed.

Buyer's Issues

Both buyers and their lenders must be sure that the seller can deliver the title that was promised in the purchase agreement and that the property is now in essentially the same condition it was in when the buyers and the sellers agreed to the sale. This involves inspecting

- the title evidence;
- the seller's deed;
- any documents demonstrating the removal of undesired liens and encumbrances;
- the survey;
- the results of any required inspections, such as termite or structural inspections, or required repairs; and
- any leases, if tenants reside on the premises.

IN PRACTICE
Although the *For Your Protection: Get a Home Inspection* pamphlet is required only for FHA loans, the information is valuable for all buyers. The pamphlet emphasizes the difference between an appraisal and a home inspection.

Final Property Inspection

In the real estate contract, the buyer usually reserves the right to make a *final inspection* (also called a *walk-through*) shortly before the closing takes place. Accompanied by the licensee, the buyer verifies that necessary repairs have been made, that the property has been well maintained, that all fixtures are in place, and that no unauthorized removal or alteration of any part of the improvements has taken place. It is not an opportunity to reopen negotiations.

Survey

A *survey* provides information about the exact location and size of the property. The sales contract specifies who will pay for the survey. Typically, the survey indicates the location of all buildings, driveways, fences, and other improvements located on the premises. Any improvements located on adjoining property that may encroach on the premises being bought also will be noted. The survey should set out, in full, any existing easements and encroachments. Whether or not the sales contract calls for a survey, lenders frequently require one.

IN PRACTICE
Relying on old surveys is not a good idea; the property should be resurveyed by a competent surveyor, whether or not the title company or lender requires it. A current survey confirms that the property purchased is exactly what the buyer wants.

Seller's Issues

Naturally, the seller's main interest is to receive payment for the property. Sellers want to be sure that the buyer has obtained the necessary financing and has sufficient funds to complete the sale. Sellers will also want to be certain that they have complied with all the buyer's requirements so the transaction will be completed.

Both parties will want to inspect the closing statement to make sure that all monies involved in the transaction have been accounted for properly. The parties may be accompanied by their attorneys.

IN PRACTICE

Licensees may discuss with clients the approximate expenses involved in closing at the time the listing agreement or buyer agency agreement is entered into but not later than the time when the sales contract is signed.

Title Procedures

Both the buyer and the buyer's lender will want assurance that the seller's title complies with the requirements of the sales contract. Additionally, lenders require title insurance in the event any "clouds" on the title (encumbrances on the real estate or claims on the title) should come up during the course of ownership. The title insurance is not issued until it is clear that such encumbrances from the past are unlikely. A major goal of title procedures is for the new owner to obtain a clear and valid "owner's title policy." Such a policy comes as close as any document can to providing evidence of ownership of a property that is unencumbered by any past liens or potential claims.

As a first step toward a new owner's title policy, before closing and establishment of the new owner's title, the seller is usually required to produce a current abstract of title or title commitment from the title insurance company. When an abstract of title is used, the purchaser's attorney examines it and issues an opinion of title. This opinion, like the title commitment, is a statement of the status of the seller's title. It discloses all liens, encumbrances, easements, conditions, or restrictions that appear on the record and to which the seller's title is subject.

On the date when the sale is actually completed (the date of delivery of the deed), the buyer has a title commitment or an abstract that was issued several days or weeks before the closing. For this reason, there usually are two searches of the public records. The first shows the status of the seller's title on the date of the first search. Usually, the seller pays for this search. The second search, called a *bring-down*, is made after the closing and is generally paid for by the purchaser. The abstract should be reviewed before closing to resolve any problems that might cause delays or threaten the transaction.

As part of this later search, the seller may be required to execute an *affidavit of title*—a sworn statement in which the seller assures the title insurance company (and the buyer) that there have been no judgments, bankruptcies, or divorces involving the seller since the date of the title examination. The affidavit promises that no unrecorded deeds or contracts have been made, no repairs or improvements have gone unpaid, and no defects in the title have arisen that the seller knows of. The seller also affirms that he is in possession of the premises. In some areas, this form is required before the title insurance company will issue an owner's policy to the buyer. The affidavit gives the title insurance company the right to sue the seller if his statements in the affidavit are incorrect.

Pursuant to the 2010 "Good Funds" amendment to the Title Insurance Act, the title insurance agent or independent escrowee acting as the closing agent may not make disbursements at closing when the amounts held for disbursement include funds from any single party in excess of $50,000, unless those funds (called *good funds*)

- are wired funds unconditionally held by and credited to the closing agent;
- are in the form of a check issued by the state of Illinois, the United States, or a political subdivision of Illinois or the United States;
- are in the form of a check drawn on the fiduciary account of another title insurance company or title insurance agent so long as there are reasonable grounds to believe the funds are available to back the check; or
- have been received by the closing agent and are finally settled and credited to the account of the closing agent.

The restrictions for amounts less than $50,000 are much less stringent. For example, if a party to the transaction brings funds to the table for closing, the good funds would include a personal check not exceeding $5,000 as long as there are reasonable grounds to believe that sufficient funds are available to back the check. Cash monies up to $49,999.99 can be provided at closing by a party and be considered good funds. Also, cashier's checks or certified checks drawn on or issued by a financial institution chartered by any state in the United States up to $49,999.99 will be considered good funds.

- It's always best to check with the title company to see in what form they will allow funds to appear at closing. They are often reluctant to take personal checks of any amount.

A subsequent amendment to the Title Insurance Act clarified that money coming from a brokerage need not be wire transferred unless it is greater than $50,000.

Whether the purchaser pays cash or obtains a new loan to purchase the property, the seller's existing loan is paid in full and satisfied on record. The exact amount required to pay the existing loan is provided in a current payoff statement from the lender, effective on the date of closing. This payoff statement (or *estoppel certificate* or *certificate of no defense*) notes the unpaid amount of principal, the interest due through the date of payment, the fee for issuing the certificate of satisfaction or release deed, credits (if any) for tax and insurance reserves, and the amount of any prepayment penalties. Once the borrower has executed the estoppel certificate, the borrower cannot thereafter claim that he did not owe the amount indicated in the payoff or estoppel certificate. The same procedure would be followed for any other liens that must be released before the buyer takes title.

In a transaction in which the buyer assumes the seller's existing mortgage loan, the buyer will want to know the exact balance of the loan as of the closing date. In some areas, it is customary for the buyer to obtain a mortgage reduction certificate from the lender that certifies the amount owed on the mortgage loan, the interest rate, and the last interest payment made.

In some areas, real estate sales transactions customarily are closed through an escrow. In these areas, the escrow instructions usually provide for an extended coverage policy to be issued to the buyer as of the date of closing. The seller has no need to execute an affidavit of title.

IN PRACTICE

Licensees often assist in pre-closing arrangements as part of their service to customers. In some states, licensees are required to advise the parties of the approximate expenses involved in closing when a real estate sales contract is signed. In other states, licensees have a statutory duty to coordinate and supervise closing activities. Aside from state laws on this issue, a licensee without a specific role in the closing may still be the person with the most knowledge about the transaction. Because of this, many licensees feel it is part of their fiduciary duty to be present at a face-to-face closing.

CONDUCTING THE CLOSING

Closing is known by many names. For example, in some areas, closing is called *settlement and transfer*. In other parts of the country, the parties to the transaction sit around a single table and exchange copies of documents, a process called passing papers ("We passed papers on the new house Wednesday morning"). In other regions, the buyer and the seller may never meet at all; the paperwork is handled by an escrow agent in a process called *closing escrow* ("We'll close escrow on our house next week"). Whether the closing occurs face to face or through escrow, the main concerns are that the buyer receives marketable title and the seller receives the purchase price.

In Illinois, the closing statement is customarily prepared by the seller's attorney. Although real estate licensees are prohibited from completing formal closing statements as a result of the Illinois Supreme Court's decision in *Chicago Bar Association, et al., v. Quinlan and Tyson, Inc.*, estimated statements are often needed when preparing a comparative market analysis (CMA), when filling out an offer for a buyer, or when presenting an offer to a seller. For this reason, licensees must understand the preparation of a closing statement, which includes the expenses and prorations of costs to close the transaction.

Face-to-Face Closing

In a face-to-face closing, the parties meet face to face.

Face-to-face closings may be held at a number of locations, including the offices of the title company, the lending institution, an attorney for one of the parties, the broker, the county recorder, or the escrow company. Those attending a closing may include

- the buyer or the buyer's duly authorized agent;

- the seller or the seller's duly authorized agent;

- the real estate licensees (both the buyer's and the seller's agents);

- the seller's and the buyer's attorneys;

- representatives of the lending institutions involved with the buyer's new mortgage loan, the buyer's assumption of the seller's existing loan, or the seller's payoff of an existing loan; and

- a representative of the title insurance company.

Unit 23

Closing Agent or Closing Officer

A closing agent may be a representative of the title company, the lender, the real estate broker, or the buyer's or the seller's attorney. Some title companies and law firms employ paralegal assistants who conduct closings for their firms.

The closing agent orders and reviews the title insurance policy or title certificate, surveys, property insurance policies, and other items. After reviewing the agreement of sale (purchase agreement), the agent prepares a closing statement indicating the division of income and expenses between the parties. Finally, the time and place of closing must be arranged.

The Exchange

When the parties are satisfied that everything is in order, the exchange is made. The seller delivers the signed deed to the buyer, who accepts it. All pertinent documents are then recorded in the correct order to ensure continuity of title. The buyer's new mortgage or deed of trust must be recorded after the deed because the buyer cannot pledge the property as security for the loan until he owns it.

Closing in Escrow

In an escrow closing, a third party coordinates the closing activities on behalf of the buyer and seller.

Although a few states prohibit transactions that are closed in escrow, escrow closings are used to some extent in most states.

An **escrow** is a method of closing in which a disinterested third party is authorized to act as escrow agent and to coordinate the closing activities. The escrow agent (also called the *escrow holder*) may be an attorney, a title company, a trust company, an escrow company, or the escrow department of a lending institution. Many real estate firms offer escrow services. However, a real estate licensee cannot be a disinterested party in a transaction from which he expects to collect a commission. Because the escrow agent is placed in a position of great trust, many states have laws regulating escrow agents and limiting who may serve in this capacity.

Escrow Procedure

When a transaction will close in escrow, the buyer and the seller execute escrow instructions to the escrow agent after the sales contract is signed. One party selects an escrow agent. Which party selects the agent is determined either by negotiation or by state law. Once the contract is signed, the broker turns over the earnest money to the escrow agent, who deposits it in a special trust, or escrow, account.

Buyer and seller deposit all pertinent documents and other items with the escrow agent before the specified date of closing.

The seller usually deposits

- the deed conveying the property to the buyer,
- title evidence (abstract and attorney's opinion of title, certificate of title, title insurance, or Torrens certificate),
- existing hazard insurance policies,
- a letter or mortgage reduction certificate from the lender stating the exact principal remaining (if the buyer assumes the seller's loan),

- affidavits of title (if required),

- a payoff statement (if the seller's loan is to be paid off),

- bill of sale,

- survey,

- transfer tax declarations,

- paid water bill, and

- other instruments or documents necessary to clear the title or to complete the transaction.

The buyer deposits

- the balance of the cash needed to complete the purchase, usually via wire transfer or in the form of a certified check;

- loan documents (if the buyer secures a new loan);

- proof of hazard insurance and flood insurance (if required); and

- other necessary documents, such as inspection reports required by the lender.

The escrow agent has the authority to examine the title evidence. When marketable title is shown in the name of the buyer and all other conditions of the escrow agreement have been met, the agent is authorized to disburse the purchase price to the seller, less all charges and expenses. The agent then records the deed and mortgage or deed of trust (if a new loan has been obtained by the purchaser).

If the escrow agent's examination of the title discloses liens, a portion of the purchase price can be withheld from the seller. The withheld portion is used to pay the liens to clear the title.

If the seller cannot clear the title, or if for any reason the sale cannot be consummated, the escrow instructions usually provide that the parties be returned to their former statuses as if no sale occurred. The escrow agent reconveys title to the seller and returns the purchase money to the buyer. If the seller dies before the closing date but after having given a signed deed to the escrow agent, the closing still may proceed, with the escrow agent transferring title to the buyer and turning the purchase price over to the seller's estate.

IRS Reporting Requirements

Certain real estate closings must be reported to the Internal Revenue Service (IRS) on Form 1099-S. The affected properties include sales or exchanges of

- land (improved or unimproved), including air space;

- an inherently permanent structure, including any residential, commercial, or industrial building;

- a condominium unit and its appurtenant fixtures and common elements (including land); or

- shares in a cooperative housing corporation.

Information to be reported includes the sales price, the amount of property tax reimbursement credited to the seller, and the seller's Social Security number. If the closing agent does not notify the IRS, the responsibility for filing the form falls on the mortgage lender; however, the real estate licensees or the parties to the transaction ultimately could be held liable.

Unit 23

Licensee's Role at Closing

Real estate licensees are not authorized to give legal advice or otherwise engage in the practice of law. A licensee's job is essentially finished as soon as the sales contract is signed. After the contract is signed, the attorneys take over. Even so, a licensee's service generally continues all the way through closing because it is in the licensee's best interest that the transactions move successfully and smoothly to a conclusion. This may mean actively arranging for title evidence, surveys, appraisals, and inspections or repairs for structural conditions, water supplies, sewage facilities, or toxic substances.

Lender's Interest at Closing

Whether a buyer obtains new financing or assumes the seller's existing loan, the lender wants to protect its security interest in the property. The lender has an interest in making sure that the buyer gets good, marketable title and that tax and insurance payments are maintained. Lenders want their mortgage lien to have priority over other liens. They also want to ensure that insurance is kept up to date in case property is damaged or destroyed. Therefore, lenders may require a survey, a pest control or another inspection report, or a certificate of occupancy (for a newly constructed building). In order to ensure that the buyer takes good and marketable title at closing, lenders generally require a mortgagee's title insurance policy.

LEGISLATION RELATED TO CLOSING

The **Real Estate Settlement Procedures Act (RESPA)** is a federal law that requires certain disclosures about the mortgage and settlement process and prohibits certain practices that increase the cost of settlement services, such as "kickbacks" and referral fees. The Consumer Financial Protection Bureau (CFPB) issued the **TILA-RESPA Integrated Disclosure rule (TRID)** to implement provisions of the Dodd-Frank Act intended to combine and clarify financing disclosures to consumers.

RESPA

RESPA regulations apply to first-lien residential mortgage loans made to finance the purchases of one- to four-family homes, cooperatives, and condominiums, for either investment or occupancy, as well as second or subordinate liens for home equity loans when a purchase is financed by a federally related mortgage loan. Federally related loans are those made by banks, savings and loan associations, or other lenders whose deposits are insured by federal agencies; loans insured by the FHA and guaranteed by the VA; loans administered by HUD; and loans intended to be sold by the lenders to Fannie Mae, Ginnie Mae, or Freddie Mac.

RESPA does not apply to the following settlements:

- Loans on large properties (i.e., more than 25 acres)
- Loans for business or agricultural purposes
- Construction loans or other temporary financing
- Vacant land (unless a dwelling will be placed on the lot within two years)
- A transaction financed solely by a purchase money mortgage taken back by the seller
- An installment contract (contract for deed)
- A buyer's assumption of a seller's existing loan (If the terms of the assumed loan are modified, or if the lender charges more than $50 for the assumption, the transaction is subject to RESPA regulations.)

RESPA prohibits certain practices that increase the cost of settlement services:

- Section 8 prohibits kickbacks and fee-splitting for referrals of settlement services and unearned fees for services not actually performed. These settlement services include activities such as mortgage loans, title searches, title insurance, attorney services, surveys, credit reports, and appraisals. Violations are subject to criminal and civil penalties, including fines up to $10,000 and/or imprisonment up to one year. Consumers may privately pursue a violator in court; the violator may be liable for an amount up to three times the amount of the charge paid for the service.

- Section 9 prohibits home sellers from requiring that homebuyers buy title insurance from a particular company. Buyers may sue the seller for such a violation; violators are liable for up to three times the amount of all charges paid for the title insurance.

- Section 10 prohibits lenders from requiring excessive escrow account deposits, money set aside to pay taxes, hazard insurance, and other charges related to the property.

IN PRACTICE

Although RESPA's requirements are aimed primarily at lenders, real estate licensees fall under RESPA when they refer buyers to particular lenders, title companies, attorneys, or other providers of settlement services. Licensees who offer computerized loan origination (CLO) are also subject to regulation. Remember that buyers have the right to select their own providers of settlement services.

Affiliated Business Arrangements

To streamline the settlement process, a real estate firm, title insurance company, mortgage broker, home inspection company, or even a moving company may agree to offer a package of services to consumers, a system called an **affiliated business arrangement (ABA)**. RESPA permits an ABA as long as a consumer is clearly informed of the relationship among the service providers; that participation is not required; that other providers are available; and that the only thing of value received by one business entity from others, in addition to permitted payments for services provided, is a return on ownership interest or franchise relationship.

Fees must be reasonably related to the value of the services provided and not be fees exchanged among the affiliated companies simply for referring business to one another. This referral-fee prohibition may be a particularly important issue for licensees who offer computerized loan origination (CLO) services to their clients and customers. CLOs that provide services to consumers may charge for the services provided, but those fees must be disclosed on the CD. While a borrower's ability to comparison shop for a loan may be enhanced by a CLO, the range of choices must not be limited. Consumers must be informed of the availability and costs of other lenders (see Figure 23.1).

TILA-RESPA Integrated Disclosure Rule (TRID)

In 2010, federal legislation known as the Dodd-Frank Wall Street Reform and Consumer Protection Act (Dodd-Frank) created the TILA-RESPA Integrated Disclosure rule is a consumer protection ruling that gives more transparency to the loan process. It does not apply to cash transactions.

Scope

The TRID rule applies to most closed-end consumer credit transactions secured by real property. Credit extended to certain trusts for tax or estate planning purpose is not exempt from the TRID rule. However, some specific categories of loans are excluded from the rule. Specifically, the TRID rule does not apply to HELOCs, reverse mortgages, mortgages secured by a mobile home or by a dwelling that is not attached to real property. The rule also does not apply to loans made by a person or entity that makes five or fewer mortgages in a calendar year.

Figure 23.1: Affiliated Business Arrangement Disclosure

Affiliated Business Arrangement Disclosure

This is to give you notice that _____ (referring party) has a business relationship with ____ _____ as a loan originator/solicitor. Because of this relationship, this referral may provide (referring party) a financial or other benefit.

[A.] Set forth below is the estimated charge or range of charges for the settlement services listed.

You are **NOT** required to use the listed provider as a condition for settlement of your loan on, or purchase, sale, or refinance of, the subject property. **THERE ARE FREQUENTLY OTHER SETTLEMENT SERVICE PROVIDERS AVAILABLE WITH SIMILAR SERVICES. YOU ARE FREE TO SHOP AROUND TO DETERMINE THAT YOU ARE RECEIVING THE BEST SERVICES AND THE BEST RATE FOR THESE SERVICES.**

[provider] [charge or range of charges]

_____

_____

[B.] Set forth below is the estimated charge or range of charges for the settlement services of an attorney, credit reporting agency, or real estate appraiser that we, as your lender, will require you to use, as a condition of your loan on this property, to represent our interests in the transaction.

[provider and settlement service] [charge or range of charges]

_____

_____

ACKNOWLEDGMENT:

I/we have read this disclosure form, and understand that _____ (referring party) is referring me/us to purchase from the above-described settlement service provider and may receive a financial or other benefit as the result of this referral.

Borrower's Signature   Date

_____

Borrower's Signature   Date

_____

The Disclosures

TRID is composed of two main disclosures: The Loan Estimate (LE) and the Closing Disclosure (CD).

- The Loan Estimate shows the consumer the amount of money borrowed, the interest rate, the amount of interest paid, the number of payments, the individual amount of those payments, any associated costs for the loan, an estimate of closing costs, and an estimate of the cash needed to close.

- The Closing Disclosure again shows the loan terms and charges but also shows the costs associated with closing and the cash needed to close. It is the document, which accounts for all debits and credits, that is distributed to participants at the closing.

Timeframe for Disclosures

The Loan Estimate must be delivered or placed in the mail by the lender, no later than the third business day after the lender receives the consumer's application. The Closing Disclosure must be provided to the consumer for review at least three business days prior to consummation. From start to finish, there must be at least a seven business day period from the lender's sending of the LE to the consummation of the loan.

■ "Application" means when the lender has received the following information regarding the loan: address of the property, loan amount, income of the borrower, contract value of the property, name of the borrower, and the Social Security number of the borrower. When the lender is in receipt of all SIX items, she must deliver the LE to the borrower within three business days.

■ "Intent to Proceed" – after the borrower receives the LE and they intend to use the mortgage product, they must provide the lender with an "Intent to Proceed" which the lender is then required to document.

■ "Consummation" means the date that the borrower and lender are contractually obligated to each other. The borrower has three business days to review the CD prior to consummation. (NOTE: consummation is not closing. Consummation is the date that the lender and borrower are obligated through the signing of the mortgage documents. Closing is the date of the transfer of title. The date of consummation and closing might very well be the same but not necessarily.)

■ "Business Day" is a day on which the creditor's offices are open to the public for carrying out substantially all of its business functions. "Business day" means all calendar days except Sundays and legal public holidays.

Closing may occur any time after consummation as long any of the following does not occur: no change to the APR of more than 1/8% (.125), no change of the loan product, or no addition of a prepayment penalty. If there is any change, then a new CD is required and a new three-day waiting period is instituted.

Scope and Effect on the Licensee

TRID deals with the relationship between the lender and the borrower; therefore one might assume that the licensee need only have a cursory knowledge of the rule. However, because the loan and home buying process is often overwhelming for buyers, agents should stay in touch with them and help them manage the timelines and proper notifications (see Figure 23.2).

Figure 23.2: Time Frame for Closing (Without Complications)

Sunday	Monday	Tuesday	Wednesday	Thursday	Friday	Saturday
1	2 Application is received.	3	4	5 Last day to send the LE.	6	7
8	9 If LE was mailed on the 5th, it is considered received. Lender must be notified of "Intent to Proceed."	10 CD must be delivered and received to close on the 13th.	11	12	13 Earliest closing date – 7 days after initial delivery of the LE on the 5th.	14

Inside the Loan Estimate (LE)

The first disclosure the lender is required to give under TRID is the Loan Estimate (see Figure 23.3).

Inside the Closing Disclosure (CD)

The CD gives a full accounting of all credits and debits at closing. It also, for comparison purposes, gives a reiteration of the figures provided in the LE. It details any important clauses contained in the mortgage regarding assumption of the loan, pay on demand, late payments, negative amortization, partial repayment, the security used as collateral, any escrow accounts, and contact information for the participants of the transaction (see Figure 23.4).

Mortgage Servicing Disclosure Statement

The Mortgage Servicing Disclosure Statement tells the borrower whether the lender intends to service the loan or to transfer it to another lender. It will also provide information about resolving complaints.

Figure 23.3: The Loan Estimate (LE)

FICUS BANK
4321 Random Boulevard • Somecity, ST 12340

Save this Loan Estimate to compare with your Closing Disclosure.

Loan Estimate

DATE ISSUED	2/15/2013	**LOAN TERM**	30 years
APPLICANTS	Michael Jones and Mary Stone	**PURPOSE**	Purchase
	123 Anywhere Street	**PRODUCT**	Fixed Rate
	Anytown, ST 12345	**LOAN TYPE**	☒ Conventional ☐FHA ☐VA ☐_____
PROPERTY	456 Somewhere Avenue	**LOAN ID #**	123456789
	Anytown, ST 12345	**RATE LOCK**	☐ NO ☒ YES, until 4/16/2013 at 5:00 p.m. EDT
SALE PRICE	$180,000		

*Before closing, your interest rate, points, and lender credits can change unless you lock the interest rate. All other estimated closing costs expire on **3/4/2013** at 5:00 p.m. EDT*

Loan Terms

		Can this amount increase after closing?
Loan Amount	$162,000	**NO**
Interest Rate	3.875%	**NO**
Monthly Principal & Interest *See Projected Payments below for your Estimated Total Monthly Payment*	$761.78	**NO**
		Does the loan have these features?
Prepayment Penalty		**YES** • **As high as $3,240** if you pay off the loan during the first 2 years
Balloon Payment		**NO**

Projected Payments

Payment Calculation	Years 1-7	Years 8-30
Principal & Interest	$761.78	$761.78
Mortgage Insurance	+ 82	+ —
Estimated Escrow *Amount can increase over time*	+ 206	+ 206
Estimated Total Monthly Payment	$1,050	$968

		This estimate includes	In escrow?
Estimated Taxes, Insurance & Assessments *Amount can increase over time*	**$206** a month	☒ Property Taxes ☒ Homeowner's Insurance ☐ Other: *See Section G on page 2 for escrowed property costs. You must pay for other property costs separately.*	YES YES

Costs at Closing

Estimated Closing Costs	$8,054	Includes $5,672 in Loan Costs + $2,382 in Other Costs – $0 in Lender Credits. *See page 2 for details.*
Estimated Cash to Close	$16,054	Includes Closing Costs. *See Calculating Cash to Close on page 2 for details.*

Visit **www.consumerfinance.gov/mortgage-estimate** for general information and tools.

Figure 23.3: The Loan Estimate (LE) (continued)

Closing Cost Details

Loan Costs

A. Origination Charges	$1,802
.25 % of Loan Amount (Points)	$405
Application Fee	$300
Underwriting Fee	$1,097

B. Services You Cannot Shop For	$672
Appraisal Fee	$405
Credit Report Fee	$30
Flood Determination Fee	$20
Flood Monitoring Fee	$32
Tax Monitoring Fee	$75
Tax Status Research Fee	$110

C. Services You Can Shop For	$3,198
Pest Inspection Fee	$135
Survey Fee	$65
Title – Insurance Binder	$700
Title – Lender's Title Policy	$535
Title – Settlement Agent Fee	$502
Title – Title Search	$1,261

D. TOTAL LOAN COSTS (A + B + C)	$5,672

Other Costs

E. Taxes and Other Government Fees	$85
Recording Fees and Other Taxes	$85
Transfer Taxes	

F. Prepaids	$867
Homeowner's Insurance Premium (6 months)	$605
Mortgage Insurance Premium (months)	
Prepaid Interest ($17.44 per day for 15 days @ 3.875%)	$262
Property Taxes (months)	

G. Initial Escrow Payment at Closing			$413
Homeowner's Insurance	$100.83 per month for 2 mo.		$202
Mortgage Insurance	per month for mo.		
Property Taxes	$105.30 per month for 2 mo.		$211

H. Other	$1,017
Title – Owner's Title Policy (optional)	$1,017

I. TOTAL OTHER COSTS (E + F + G + H)	$2,382

J. TOTAL CLOSING COSTS	$8,054
D + I	$8,054
Lender Credits	

Calculating Cash to Close

Total Closing Costs (J)	$8,054
Closing Costs Financed (Paid from your Loan Amount)	$0
Down Payment/Funds from Borrower	$18,000
Deposit	– $10,000
Funds for Borrower	$0
Seller Credits	$0
Adjustments and Other Credits	$0
Estimated Cash to Close	$16,054

Figure 23.3: The Loan Estimate (LE) (continued)

Additional Information About This Loan

LENDER	Ficus Bank	**MORTGAGE BROKER**
NMLS/__ LICENSE ID		**NMLS/__ LICENSE ID**
LOAN OFFICER	Joe Smith	**LOAN OFFICER**
NMLS/__ LICENSE ID	12345	**NMLS/__ LICENSE ID**
EMAIL	joesmith@ficusbank.com	**EMAIL**
PHONE	123-456-7890	**PHONE**

Comparisons — Use these measures to compare this loan with other loans.

In 5 Years	$56,582	Total you will have paid in principal, interest, mortgage insurance, and loan costs.
	$15,773	Principal you will have paid off.
Annual Percentage Rate (APR)	4.274%	Your costs over the loan term expressed as a rate. This is not your interest rate.
Total Interest Percentage (TIP)	69.45%	The total amount of interest that you will pay over the loan term as a percentage of your loan amount.

Other Considerations

Appraisal — We may order an appraisal to determine the property's value and charge you for this appraisal. We will promptly give you a copy of any appraisal, even if your loan does not close. You can pay for an additional appraisal for your own use at your own cost.

Assumption — If you sell or transfer this property to another person, we
☐ will allow, under certain conditions, this person to assume this loan on the original terms.
☒ will not allow assumption of this loan on the original terms.

Homeowner's Insurance — This loan requires homeowner's insurance on the property, which you may obtain from a company of your choice that we find acceptable.

Late Payment — If your payment is more than *15* days late, we will charge a late fee of *5% of the monthly principal and interest payment.*

Refinance — Refinancing this loan will depend on your future financial situation, the property value, and market conditions. You may not be able to refinance this loan.

Servicing — We intend
☐ to service your loan. If so, you will make your payments to us.
☒ to transfer servicing of your loan.

Confirm Receipt

By signing, you are only confirming that you have received this form. You do not have to accept this loan because you have signed or received this form.

_____   _____   _____   _____
Applicant Signature   Date   Co-Applicant Signature   Date

Figure 23.4: The Closing Disclosure (CD)

Closing Disclosure

This form is a statement of final loan terms and closing costs. Compare this document with your Loan Estimate.

Closing Information

Date Issued	4/15/2013
Closing Date	4/15/2013
Disbursement Date	4/15/2013
Settlement Agent	Epsilon Title Co.
File #	12-3456
Property	456 Somewhere Ave
	Anytown, ST 12345
Sale Price	$180,000

Transaction Information

Borrower	Michael Jones and Mary Stone
	123 Anywhere Street
	Anytown, ST 12345
Seller	Steve Cole and Amy Doe
	321 Somewhere Drive
	Anytown, ST 12345
Lender	Ficus Bank

Loan Information

Loan Term	30 years
Purpose	Purchase
Product	Fixed Rate
Loan Type	☒ Conventional ☐ FHA
	☐ VA ☐ _____
Loan ID #	123456789
MIC #	000654321

Loan Terms

		Can this amount increase after closing?
Loan Amount	$162,000	NO
Interest Rate	3.875%	NO
Monthly Principal & Interest *See Projected Payments below for your Estimated Total Monthly Payment*	$761.78	NO
		Does the loan have these features?
Prepayment Penalty		YES • **As high as $3,240** if you pay off the loan during the first 2 years
Balloon Payment		NO

Projected Payments

Payment Calculation	Years 1-7	Years 8-30
Principal & Interest	$761.78	$761.78
Mortgage Insurance	+ 82.35	+ —
Estimated Escrow *Amount can increase over time*	+ 206.13	+ 206.13
Estimated Total Monthly Payment	**$1,050.26**	**$967.91**

		This estimate includes	In escrow?
Estimated Taxes, Insurance & Assessments *Amount can increase over time* *See page 4 for details*	$356.13 a month	☒ Property Taxes ☒ Homeowner's Insurance ☒ Other: Homeowner's Association Dues *See Escrow Account on page 4 for details. You must pay for other property costs separately.*	YES YES NO

Costs at Closing

Closing Costs	$9,712.10	Includes $4,694.05 in Loan Costs + $5,018.05 in Other Costs – $0 in Lender Credits. *See page 2 for details.*
Cash to Close	$14,147.26	Includes Closing Costs. *See Calculating Cash to Close on page 3 for details.*

Figure 23.4: The Closing Disclosure (CD) (continued)

Closing Cost Details

Loan Costs	Borrower-Paid		Seller-Paid		Paid by Others
	At Closing	Before Closing	At Closing	Before Closing	
A. Origination Charges	**$1,802.00**				
01 0.25 % of Loan Amount (Points)	$405.00				
02 Application Fee	$300.00				
03 Underwriting Fee	$1,097.00				
04					
05					
06					
07					
08					
B. Services Borrower Did Not Shop For	**$236.55**				
01 Appraisal Fee to John Smith Appraisers Inc.					$405.00
02 Credit Report Fee to Information Inc.		$29.80			
03 Flood Determination Fee to Info Co.	$20.00				
04 Flood Monitoring Fee to Info Co.	$31.75				
05 Tax Monitoring Fee to Info Co.	$75.00				
06 Tax Status Research Fee to Info Co.	$80.00				
07					
08					
09					
10					
C. Services Borrower Did Shop For	**$2,655.50**				
01 Pest Inspection Fee to Pests Co.	$120.50				
02 Survey Fee to Surveys Co.	$85.00				
03 Title – Insurance Binder to Epsilon Title Co.	$650.00				
04 Title – Lender's Title Insurance to Epsilon Title Co.	$500.00				
05 Title – Settlement Agent Fee to Epsilon Title Co.	$500.00				
06 Title – Title Search to Epsilon Title Co.	$800.00				
07					
08					
D. TOTAL LOAN COSTS (Borrower-Paid)	**$4,694.05**				
Loan Costs Subtotals (A + B + C)	$4,664.25	$29.80			

Other Costs	Borrower-Paid		Seller-Paid		Paid by Others
E. Taxes and Other Government Fees	**$85.00**				
01 Recording Fees Deed: $40.00 Mortgage: $45.00	$85.00				
02 Transfer Tax to Any State			$950.00		
F. Prepaids	**$2,120.80**				
01 Homeowner's Insurance Premium (12 mo.) to Insurance Co.	$1,209.96				
02 Mortgage Insurance Premium (mo.)					
03 Prepaid Interest ($17.44 per day from 4/15/13 to 5/1/13)	$279.04				
04 Property Taxes (6 mo.) to Any County USA	$631.80				
05					
G. Initial Escrow Payment at Closing	**$412.25**				
01 Homeowner's Insurance $100.83 per month for 2 mo.	$201.66				
02 Mortgage Insurance per month for mo.					
03 Property Taxes $105.30 per month for 2 mo.	$210.60				
04					
05					
06					
07					
08 Aggregate Adjustment	– 0.01				
H. Other	**$2,400.00**				
01 HOA Capital Contribution to HOA Acre Inc.	$500.00				
02 HOA Processing Fee to HOA Acre Inc.	$150.00				
03 Home Inspection Fee to Engineers Inc.	$750.00			$750.00	
04 Home Warranty Fee to XYZ Warranty Inc.			$450.00		
05 Real Estate Commission to Alpha Real Estate Broker			$5,700.00		
06 Real Estate Commission to Omega Real Estate Broker			$5,700.00		
07 Title – Owner's Title Insurance (optional) to Epsilon Title Co.	$1,000.00				
08					
I. TOTAL OTHER COSTS (Borrower-Paid)	**$5,018.05**				
Other Costs Subtotals (E + F + G + H)	$5,018.05				

	Borrower-Paid		Seller-Paid		Paid by Others
J. TOTAL CLOSING COSTS (Borrower-Paid)	**$9,712.10**				
Closing Costs Subtotals (D + I)	$9,682.30	$29.80	$12,800.00	$750.00	$405.00
Lender Credits					

Figure 23.4: The Closing Disclosure (CD) (continued)

Calculating Cash to Close

Use this table to see what has changed from your Loan Estimate.

	Loan Estimate	Final	Did this change?
Total Closing Costs (J)	$8,054.00	$9,712.10	YES • See **Total Loan Costs (D)** and **Total Other Costs (I)**
Closing Costs Paid Before Closing	$0	− $29.80	YES • You paid these Closing Costs **before closing**
Closing Costs Financed (Paid from your Loan Amount)	$0	$0	NO
Down Payment/Funds from Borrower	$18,000.00	$18,000.00	NO
Deposit	− $10,000.00	− $10,000.00	NO
Funds for Borrower	$0	$0	NO
Seller Credits	$0	− $2,500.00	YES • See Seller Credits in **Section L**
Adjustments and Other Credits	$0	− $1,035.04	YES • See details in **Sections K and L**
Cash to Close	$16,054.00	$14,147.26	

Summaries of Transactions

Use this table to see a summary of your transaction.

BORROWER'S TRANSACTION

K. Due from Borrower at Closing	$189,762.30
01 Sale Price of Property	$180,000.00
02 Sale Price of Any Personal Property Included in Sale	
03 Closing Costs Paid at Closing (J)	$9,682.30
04	
Adjustments	
05	
06	
07	
Adjustments for Items Paid by Seller in Advance	
08 City/Town Taxes to	
09 County Taxes to	
10 Assessments to	
11 HOA Dues 4/15/13 to 4/30/13	$80.00
12	
13	
14	
15	

L. Paid Already by or on Behalf of Borrower at Closing	$175,615.04
01 Deposit	$10,000.00
02 Loan Amount	$162,000.00
03 Existing Loan(s) Assumed or Taken Subject to	
04	
05 Seller Credit	$2,500.00
Other Credits	
06 Rebate from Epsilon Title Co.	$750.00
07	
Adjustments	
08	
09	
10	
11	
Adjustments for Items Unpaid by Seller	
12 City/Town Taxes 1/1/13 to 4/14/13	$365.04
13 County Taxes to	
14 Assessments to	
15	
16	
17	

CALCULATION	
Total Due from Borrower at Closing (K)	$189,762.30
Total Paid Already by or on Behalf of Borrower at Closing (L)	− $175,615.04
Cash to Close ☒ From ☐ To Borrower	**$14,147.26**

SELLER'S TRANSACTION

M. Due to Seller at Closing	$180,080.00
01 Sale Price of Property	$180,000.00
02 Sale Price of Any Personal Property Included in Sale	
03	
04	
05	
06	
07	
08	
Adjustments for Items Paid by Seller in Advance	
09 City/Town Taxes to	
10 County Taxes to	
11 Assessments to	
12 HOA Dues 4/15/13 to 4/30/13	$80.00
13	
14	
15	
16	

N. Due from Seller at Closing	$115,665.04
01 Excess Deposit	
02 Closing Costs Paid at Closing (J)	$12,800.00
03 Existing Loan(s) Assumed or Taken Subject to	
04 Payoff of First Mortgage Loan	$100,000.00
05 Payoff of Second Mortgage Loan	
06	
07	
08 Seller Credit	$2,500.00
09	
10	
11	
12	
13	
Adjustments for Items Unpaid by Seller	
14 City/Town Taxes 1/1/13 to 4/14/13	$365.04
15 County Taxes to	
16 Assessments to	
17	
18	
19	

CALCULATION	
Total Due to Seller at Closing (M)	$180,080.00
Total Due from Seller at Closing (N)	− $115,665.04
Cash ☐ From ☒ To Seller	**$64,414.96**

Figure 23.4: The Closing Disclosure (CD) (continued)

Additional Information About This Loan

Loan Disclosures

Assumption
If you sell or transfer this property to another person, your lender
☐ will allow, under certain conditions, this person to assume this loan on the original terms.
☒ will not allow assumption of this loan on the original terms.

Demand Feature
Your loan
☐ has a demand feature, which permits your lender to require early repayment of the loan. You should review your note for details.
☒ does not have a demand feature.

Late Payment
If your payment is more than *15* days late, your lender will charge a late fee of *5% of the monthly principal and interest payment.*

Negative Amortization (Increase in Loan Amount)
Under your loan terms, you
☐ are scheduled to make monthly payments that do not pay all of the interest due that month. As a result, your loan amount will increase (negatively amortize), and your loan amount will likely become larger than your original loan amount. Increases in your loan amount lower the equity you have in this property.
☐ may have monthly payments that do not pay all of the interest due that month. If you do, your loan amount will increase (negatively amortize), and, as a result, your loan amount may become larger than your original loan amount. Increases in your loan amount lower the equity you have in this property.
☒ do not have a negative amortization feature.

Partial Payments
Your lender
☒ may accept payments that are less than the full amount due (partial payments) and apply them to your loan.
☐ may hold them in a separate account until you pay the rest of the payment, and then apply the full payment to your loan.
☐ does not accept any partial payments.
If this loan is sold, your new lender may have a different policy.

Security Interest
You are granting a security interest in
456 Somewhere Ave., Anytown, ST 12345

You may lose this property if you do not make your payments or satisfy other obligations for this loan.

Escrow Account
For now, your loan
☒ will have an escrow account (also called an "impound" or "trust" account) to pay the property costs listed below. Without an escrow account, you would pay them directly, possibly in one or two large payments a year. Your lender may be liable for penalties and interest for failing to make a payment.

Escrow		
Escrowed Property Costs over Year 1	$2,473.56	Estimated total amount over year 1 for your escrowed property costs: *Homeowner's Insurance Property Taxes*
Non-Escrowed Property Costs over Year 1	$1,800.00	Estimated total amount over year 1 for your non-escrowed property costs: *Homeowner's Association Dues* You may have other property costs.
Initial Escrow Payment	$412.25	A cushion for the escrow account you pay at closing. See Section G on page 2.
Monthly Escrow Payment	$206.13	The amount included in your total monthly payment.

☐ will not have an escrow account because ☐ you declined it ☐ your lender does not offer one. You must directly pay your property costs, such as taxes and homeowner's insurance. Contact your lender to ask if your loan can have an escrow account.

No Escrow		
Estimated Property Costs over Year 1		Estimated total amount over year 1. You must pay these costs directly, possibly in one or two large payments a year.
Escrow Waiver Fee		

In the future,
Your property costs may change and, as a result, your escrow payment may change. You may be able to cancel your escrow account, but if you do, you must pay your property costs directly. If you fail to pay your property taxes, your state or local government may (1) impose fines and penalties or (2) place a tax lien on this property. If you fail to pay any of your property costs, your lender may (1) add the amounts to your loan balance, (2) add an escrow account to your loan, or (3) require you to pay for property insurance that the lender buys on your behalf, which likely would cost more and provide fewer benefits than what you could buy on your own.

Figure 23.4: The Closing Disclosure (CD) (continued)

Loan Calculations

Total of Payments. Total you will have paid after you make all payments of principal, interest, mortgage insurance, and loan costs, as scheduled.	$285,803.36
Finance Charge. The dollar amount the loan will cost you.	$118,830.27
Amount Financed. The loan amount available after paying your upfront finance charge.	$162,000.00
Annual Percentage Rate (APR). Your costs over the loan term expressed as a rate. This is not your interest rate.	4.174%
Total Interest Percentage (TIP). The total amount of interest that you will pay over the loan term as a percentage of your loan amount.	69.46%

 Questions? If you have questions about the loan terms or costs on this form, use the contact information below. To get more information or make a complaint, contact the Consumer Financial Protection Bureau at **www.consumerfinance.gov/mortgage-closing**

Other Disclosures

Appraisal
If the property was appraised for your loan, your lender is required to give you a copy at no additional cost at least 3 days before closing. If you have not yet received it, please contact your lender at the information listed below.

Contract Details
See your note and security instrument for information about
• what happens if you fail to make your payments,
• what is a default on the loan,
• situations in which your lender can require early repayment of the loan, and
• the rules for making payments before they are due.

Liability after Foreclosure
If your lender forecloses on this property and the foreclosure does not cover the amount of unpaid balance on this loan,

☒ state law may protect you from liability for the unpaid balance. If you refinance or take on any additional debt on this property, you may lose this protection and have to pay any debt remaining even after foreclosure. You may want to consult a lawyer for more information.

☐ state law does not protect you from liability for the unpaid balance.

Refinance
Refinancing this loan will depend on your future financial situation, the property value, and market conditions. You may not be able to refinance this loan.

Tax Deductions
If you borrow more than this property is worth, the interest on the loan amount above this property's fair market value is not deductible from your federal income taxes. You should consult a tax advisor for more information.

Contact Information

	Lender	Mortgage Broker	Real Estate Broker (B)	Real Estate Broker (S)	Settlement Agent
Name	Ficus Bank		Omega Real Estate Broker Inc.	Alpha Real Estate Broker Co.	Epsilon Title Co.
Address	4321 Random Blvd. Somecity, ST 12340		789 Local Lane Sometown, ST 12345	987 Suburb Ct. Someplace, ST 12340	123 Commerce Pl. Somecity, ST 12344
NMLS ID					
ST License ID			Z765416	Z61456	Z61616
Contact	Joe Smith		Samuel Green	Joseph Cain	Sarah Arnold
Contact NMLS ID	12345				
Contact ST License ID			P16415	P51461	PT1234
Email	joesmith@ficusbank.com		sam@omegare.biz	joe@alphare.biz	sarah@epsilontitle.com
Phone	123-456-7890		123-555-1717	321-555-7171	987-555-4321

Confirm Receipt

By signing, you are only confirming that you have received this form. You do not have to accept this loan because you have signed or received this form.

Applicant Signature	Date	Co-Applicant Signature	Date

THE CLOSING STATEMENT

A debit is an amount an individual owes.

A credit is an amount that an individual is owed.

The completion of a closing statement, now realized in the CD, involves an accounting of the parties' debits and credits. A debit is an amount that a party owes and must pay at closing. A credit is an amount entered in a person's favor—an amount that has already been paid, an amount being reimbursed, or an amount the buyer promises to pay in the form of a loan.

To determine the amount a buyer needs at closing, the buyer's debits are totaled. Any expenses and prorated amounts for items prepaid by the seller are added to the purchase price. The buyer's credits are then totaled. These include the earnest money (already paid), the balance of the loan the buyer obtains or assumes, and the seller's share of any prorated items the buyer will pay in the future (see Figure 23.5). Finally, the total of the buyer's credits is subtracted from the total debits to arrive at the actual amount of cash the buyer must bring to closing. The buyer usually wires this amount or brings a cashier's or certified check.

Figure 23.5: Credits and Debits

Item	Credit to Buyer	Debit to Buyer	Credit to Seller	Debit to Seller	Prorated
Principal amount of new mortgage	■				
Payoff of existing mortgage				■	
Unpaid principal balance if assumed mortgage	■			■	
Accrued interest on existing assumed mortgage	■			■	■
Tenant's security deposit	■			■	
Purchase-money mortgage	■			■	
Unpaid water and other utility bills	■			■	■
Buyer's earnest money	■			■	
Selling price of property		■	■		
Fuel oil on hand (valued at current market price)		■	■		■
Prepaid insurance and tax reserve for mortgage assumed by buyer		■	■		■
Refund to seller of prepaid water charges and similar utility expenses		■	■		■
Accrued general real estate taxes	■			■	■

Note that this table is based on generally applicable practices; closing practices may differ from state to state.

A similar procedure is followed to determine how much money the seller actually will receive. The seller's debits and credits are each totaled. The credits include the purchase price plus the buyer's share of any prorated items that the seller has prepaid. The seller's debits include expenses, the seller's share of prorated items to be paid later by the buyer, and the balance of any mortgage loan or other lien that the seller pays off. Finally, the total of the seller's debits is subtracted from the total credits to arrive at the amount the seller will receive.

Broker's Commission

The responsibility for paying the broker's commission will have been determined by previous agreement. If the broker is the agent for the seller, the seller normally is responsible for paying the commission. If an agency agreement exists between a broker and the buyer, or if two agents are involved (one for the seller and one for the buyer), the commission may be distributed as an expense between both parties or according to some other arrangement.

Attorney's Fees

If either party's attorney will be paid from the closing proceeds, that party will be charged with the expense in the closing statement. This expense may include fees for the preparation or review of documents or for representing the parties at settlement.

Recording Expenses

The seller usually pays for recording charges (filing fees) necessary to clear all defects and furnish the purchaser with a marketable title. Items customarily charged to the seller include the recording of release deeds or satisfaction of mortgages, quitclaim deeds, affidavits, and satisfaction of mechanics' liens. The buyer pays for recording charges that arise from the actual transfer of title. Such items usually include recording the deed that conveys title to the purchaser and a mortgage or deed of trust executed by the buyer.

Transfer Tax

Most states require some form of transfer tax, conveyance fee, or tax stamps on real estate conveyances. This expense is most often borne by the seller; although customs vary. In addition, many cities and local municipalities charge transfer taxes. Responsibility for these charges varies according to local practice.

In Illinois, state and county transfer taxes are usually paid by the seller in accordance with most sales contracts. Some local ordinances establish additional municipal transfer taxes that are to be paid for by the seller, the buyer, or both.

Title Expenses

Responsibility for title expenses varies according to local custom. In most areas, the seller is required to furnish evidence of good title and pay for the title search. If the buyer's attorney inspects the evidence or if the buyer purchases a title insurance policy, the buyer is charged for the expense.

Because the seller usually is required by the contract to furnish evidence of good title, the seller customarily pays for the owner's title insurance policy. The buyer customarily pays for the lender's policy, which ensures that the lender has a valid first lien.

Loan Fees

For a new loan, the lender generally charges an origination fee and possibly discount points if the borrower wants a below-market interest rate. These lender charges for taking, underwriting, and processing the loan application, including points and origination fees, may not increase before closing. If there is a change, the lender has three business days to revise the LE. If the buyer assumes the seller's existing financing, the buyer may be required to pay an assumption fee. Also, under the terms of some mortgage loans, the seller may be required to pay a prepayment charge or penalty for paying off the mortgage loan before its due date.

Tax Reserves and Insurance Reserves (Escrow or Impound Accounts)

Most mortgage lenders require that borrowers provide reserve funds or escrow accounts to pay future real estate taxes and insurance premiums. A borrower starts the account at closing by depositing funds to cover at least the amount of unpaid real estate taxes from the date of lien to the end of the current month (the buyer receives a credit from the seller at closing for any unpaid taxes). Afterward, an amount equal to one month's portion of the estimated taxes is included in the borrower's monthly mortgage payment.

The borrower is responsible for maintaining adequate fire or hazard insurance as a condition of the mortgage loan. The first year's premium is generally paid in full at closing, and an amount equal to one month's premium is paid after that. The borrower's monthly loan payment includes the principal and interest on the loan, plus one-twelfth of the estimated taxes and insurance (PITI). The taxes and insurance are held by the lender in the escrow or impound account until the bills are due.

IN PRACTICE

RESPA permits lenders to maintain a cushion equal to one-sixth of the total estimated amount of annual taxes and insurance. However, if state law or mortgage documents allow for a smaller cushion, the lesser amount prevails.

Appraisal Fees

The purchaser usually pays the appraisal fees. When the buyer obtains a mortgage, it is customary for the lender to require an appraisal, and the buyer bears the cost. If the fee is paid at the time of the loan application, it is reflected on the closing statement as already having been paid.

Survey Fees

The purchaser who obtains new mortgage financing customarily pays the survey fees. The sales contract may require the seller to furnish a survey.

Normally, there is no formal survey done in property sales. Instead, the dimensions, boundaries, etc. are taken from the deed. If the buyer needs a survey for some reason (e.g. if it's a large lot, and the mortgage company wants a survey as well as an appraisal), the buyer would pay or it is negotiated at the time of the contract.

Additional Fees

An FHA borrower owes a lump sum for payment of the mortgage insurance premium (MIP) if it is not financed as part of the loan. A VA mortgagor pays a funding fee directly to the VA at closing. If a conventional loan carries private mortgage insurance, the buyer prepays one year's insurance premium at closing.

Accounting for Expenses

Expenses paid out of the closing proceeds are debited only to the party making the payment. Occasionally an expense item, such as an escrow fee, a settlement fee, or a transfer tax, may be shared by the buyer and the seller. In this case, each party is debited for its share of the expense.

Buyer Down Payment and Closing Costs

Traditionally, at closing, the purchase price is paid from various funding sources. The two main components for the buyer's purchase price are the down payment and the mortgage. The mortgage funds will be supplied by the lender. The down payment is usually composed of the earnest money and any additional money that the buyer needs to meet the total cost of the purchase.

For instance, a purchase of $100,000, if financed with an 80% loan ($80,000), is still short $20,000. That remaining $20,000 could consist of $5,000 in earnest money transfer and the remaining $15,000, which the buyer would bring to closing.

Of course, there are additional costs that the buyer must pay at closing. The buyer will be expected to pay for certain transfer taxes, if applicable, title charges, attorney's fees, et cetera. These charges can range from 2% of the sales price to as much as 7% of the sales price. Sometimes, it is more; sometimes, it is less. A couple of days before closing, the buyer's attorney will often notify the buyer of these additional charges and instruct the buyer to bring additional funds on top of the remaining purchase price.

In the earlier example, if the additional charges to the buyer are $3,000, the buyer would now have to bring $18,000 to closing. This is known as "cash to close." This amount comprises the remaining $15,000 for the down payment and the additional $3,000 of closing expenses.

Not only does the buyer have closing costs, but the seller also does. Unless the property is selling short, the seller's closing costs will all be subtracted from the sales price at closing. Again, the amount of closing costs will vary depending on the terms of the transaction and the location of the property. Seller closing costs can also fit into a wide range from 1% to 5% of the sales price.

> **MATH CONCEPTS**
>
> $100,000 purchase price
> – *$80,000 mortgage (supplied by lender)*
> – $5,000 earnest money (supplied by escrow agent)
> $15,000 remaining down payment (supplied by buyer)
> + $3,000 buyer's closing charges (paid by buyer)
> $18,000 Total Cash to Close From Buyer

PRORATIONS

Accrued items are buyer credits.

Prepaid items are seller credits.

Most closings involve the division of financial responsibility between the buyer and the seller for such items as loan interest, taxes, rents, fuel, and utility bills. These allowances are called **prorations**. Prorations are necessary to ensure that expenses are divided fairly between the seller and the buyer. For example, the seller may owe current taxes that have not been billed; the buyer would want this settled at the closing. Where taxes must be paid in advance, the seller is entitled to a rebate at the closing. If the buyer assumes the seller's existing mortgage or deed of trust, the seller usually owes the buyer an allowance for accrued interest through the date of closing.

Accrued items, such as water bills, Illinois real estate taxes, and interest on an assumed mortgage that is paid in arrears, are expenses to be prorated that are owed by the seller but later will be paid by the buyer. The seller therefore pays for these items by giving the buyer credits for them at closing.

Prepaid items, such as fuel oil in a tank, are expenses to be prorated that have been prepaid by the seller but not fully used up. They are therefore credits to the seller.

The Arithmetic of Prorating

Accurate prorating involves four considerations:

- The nature of the item being prorated
- Whether it is an accrued item that requires the determination of an earned amount
- Whether it is a prepaid item that requires the determination of an unearned amount (that is, a refund to the seller)
- What arithmetic must be used

The computation of a proration involves identifying a yearly charge for the item to be prorated and then dividing by 12 to determine a monthly charge for the item. It is usually also necessary to identify a daily charge for the item by dividing the monthly charge by the number of days in the month. These smaller portions are then multiplied by the number of months or days in the prorated period to determine the accrued or unearned amount that will be figured in the settlement.

When you prorate, the number of days may be calculated using a *statutory year* (also called a *banker's year*) or a *calendar year*. A statutory year contains 12 months with 30 days in each month, for a total of 360 days. A calendar year contains 12 months with 28 to 31 days in each month for a total of 365 days. The total number of days in a calendar leap year is 366.

In a proration problem, you will be told whether to prorate *through* the day of closing or *to* the day of closing. This is very important when calculating the days owed. When prorating through the day of closing, the seller is responsible for the day of closing. When prorating to the day of closing, the buyer is responsible for the day of closing.

A third method, the *statutory month variation*, is also acceptable in Illinois. In this method, the yearly charge is divided by 12 to determine a monthly amount. The monthly charge then is divided by the actual number of days in the month in which the closing occurs. This final number is the daily charge for that month.

The final proration figure will vary slightly, depending on which computation method is used. The final figure also varies according to the number of decimal places to which the division is carried. All the computations in this unit are computed by carrying the division to three decimal places. The third decimal place is rounded off to cents only after the final proration figure is determined.

Accrued Items

When the real estate tax is levied for the calendar year and is payable during that year or in the following year, the accrued portion is for the period from January 1 through the date of closing. If the current tax bill has not yet been issued, the parties must agree on an estimated amount based on the previous year's bill and any known changes in assessment or tax levy for the current year.

Sample Proration Calculation

Assume a sale is to be closed on September 17. Current real estate taxes of $1,200 are to be prorated. A 360-day year is used. The accrued period, then, is 8 months and 17 days. First determine the prorated cost of the real estate tax per month and day:

$1,200 ÷ 12 months = $100 per month
$100 ÷ 30 days = $3.333 per day

Next, multiply these figures by the accrued period and add the totals to determine the prorated real estate tax:

$100 × 8 months = $800
$3.333 × 17 days = $56.661
$800 + $56.661 = $856.661, or $856.66

Thus, the accrued real estate tax for 8 months and 17 days is $856.66 (rounded off to two decimal places after the final computation). This amount represents the seller's accrued earned tax. It will be a credit to the buyer and a debit to the seller on the closing statement.

To compute this proration using the actual number of days in the accrued period, the following method is used: The accrued period from January 1 to September 17 runs 260 days (January's 31 days plus February's 28 days and so on, plus the 17 days of September).

$1,200 tax bill ÷ 365 days = $3.288 per day
$3.288 × 260 days = $854.88

While these examples show proration as of the date of settlement, the agreement of sale may require otherwise. For example, a buyer's possession date may not coincide with the settlement date, in which case the parties could prorate according to the date of possession.

Prepaid Items

A tax proration could be a prepaid item in some locations. Because real estate taxes may be paid in the early part of the year, a tax proration calculated for a closing that takes place later in the year must reflect that the seller has already paid the tax. For example, in the preceding problem, suppose that all taxes had been paid. The buyer, then, would have to reimburse the seller; the proration would be credited to the seller and debited to the buyer.

In figuring the tax proration, it is necessary to ascertain the number of future days, months, and years for which taxes have been paid. Using the Statutory method, the formula commonly used for this purpose is as follows:

	Years	Months	Days
Taxes paid to (Dec. 31, end of tax year)	201X	12	30 (statutory)
Date of closing (Sept. 17, 201X)	201X	−9	−17
Period for which tax must be returned		3	13 to seller (in "prepay" locale)

With this formula (using the statutory-month method), we can find the amount the buyer will reimburse the seller for the portion of the real estate tax already paid for time the buyer will live in the house. The prepaid period, as determined using the formula for prepaid items, is 3 months and 13 days.

3 months	×	$100 per month	=	$300
13 days	×	$3.333 per day	=	$43.329
$300	+	$43.329	=	$343.329, or $343.33

$343.33 is credited to the seller and debited to the buyer.

In Illinois (and some other states), taxes are paid in arrears (2014 is paid in 2015) and the roles reverse (buyer credit, seller debit), but the math is essentially the same.

Sample Prepaid Item Calculation

One example of a prepaid item is a water bill. Assume that the water is billed in advance by the city without using a meter. The six months' billing is $60 for the period ending October 31. The sale is to be closed on August 3. Because the water bill is paid to October 31, the prepaid time must be computed. Using a 30-day basis, the time is the 27 days left in August plus 2 full months: $60 ÷ 6 = $10 per month. For one day, divide $10 by 30, which equals $0.333 per day. The prepaid period is 2 months and 27 days, so

27 days	×	$0.333 per day	=	$8.991
2 months	×	$10		=	$20
$8.991	+	$20		=	$28.991, or $28.99

This is a prepaid item; it is credited to the seller and debited to the buyer on the closing statement.

To figure this based on the actual days in the month of closing, the following process would be used:

$10 per month	÷	31 days in August	=	$0.323 per day
		August 4 through August 31	=	28 days
28 days	×	$0.323		=	$9.044
2 months	×	$10		=	$20
$9.044	+	$20		=	$29.044, or $29.04

General Rules for Prorating

The rules or customs governing the computation of prorations for the closing of a real estate sale vary greatly from state to state. The following are some general guidelines for preparing the closing statement:

- In most states, the seller owns the property on the day of closing, and prorations or apportionments usually are made to and including the day of closing. In a few states, however, it is provided specifically that the buyer owns the property on the closing date. In that case, adjustments are made as of the day preceding the day on which title is closed.

- Mortgage interest, general real estate taxes, water taxes, insurance premiums, and similar expenses usually are computed by using 360 days in a year and 30 days in a month (a statutory year). However, the rules in some areas provide for computing prorations on the basis of the actual number of days in the calendar month of closing. The agreement of sale should specify which method will be used.

■ Accrued or prepaid general real estate taxes usually are prorated at the closing. When the amount of the current real estate tax cannot be determined definitely, the proration is usually based on the last obtainable tax bill.

■ Special assessments for municipal improvements such as sewers, water mains, or streets usually are paid in annual installments over several years, with annual interest charged on the outstanding balance of future installments. The seller normally pays the current installment, and the buyer assumes all future installments. The special assessment installment generally is not prorated at the closing. A buyer may insist that the seller allow the buyer a credit for the seller's share of the interest to the closing date. The agreement of sale may address the manner in which special assessments will be handled at settlement.

■ Rents are usually adjusted on the basis of the actual number of days in the month of closing. It is customary for the seller to receive the rents for the day of closing and to pay all expenses for that day. If any rents for the current month are uncollected when the sale is closed, the buyer often agrees by a separate letter to collect the rents if possible and remit the pro rata share to the seller.

■ Security deposits made by tenants to cover the last month's rent of the lease or to cover the cost of repairing damage caused by the tenant generally are transferred by the seller to the buyer.

Real Estate Taxes

Proration of real estate taxes varies, depending on how the taxes are paid in the area where the real estate is located. In some states, real estate taxes are paid in advance; that is, if the tax year runs from January 1 to December 31, taxes for the coming year are due on January 1. In this case, the seller, who has prepaid a year's taxes, should be reimbursed for the portion of the year remaining after the buyer takes ownership of the property. In other areas, taxes are paid in arrears on December 31 for the year just ended. In this case, the buyer should be credited by the seller for the time the seller occupied the property. Sometimes, taxes are due during the tax year, partly in arrears and partly in advance; sometimes they are payable in installments. It gets even more complicated if city, state, school, and other property taxes start their tax years in different months. Whatever the case may be in a particular transaction, the licensee should understand how the taxes will be prorated.

Taxes in Illinois are paid in arrears. The buyer must be credited for any taxes that still will be paid in the future for time in the "past" (i.e., up until closing) when the seller occupied the property. If an unpaid installment based on last year has been billed, this specific amount is credited to the buyer and debited to the seller. The buyer must be credited with the current year's taxes to time of closing because those taxes will not be paid until next year (again by the buyer/new owner). Consequently, the seller is debited accordingly, to the date of close, and a proration (and often a tax estimate based on last year's tax) is necessary for this latter figure.

The following formula may be used in Illinois:

> Last annual tax bill ÷ 360 × number of days from January 1 to closing date = tax proration (the amount seller owes buyer)

Mortgage Loan Interest

The interest is paid in arrears on almost every mortgage loan, so buyer and seller must understand that the mortgage payment due on June 1, for example, includes interest due for the month of May. Thus, the buyer who assumes a mortgage on May 31 and makes the June payment pays for the time the seller occupied the property and should be credited with a month's interest. On the other hand, the buyer who places a new mortgage loan on May 31 may be pleasantly surprised to hear that he will not need to make a mortgage payment until a month later.

The terms of some assumed mortgage loans provide that interest is charged at the beginning of the month (in advance); without this provision, interest is always charged at the end of the month (in arrears). When the interest on the existing mortgage to be assumed by the buyer is charged at the beginning of the month, the *unearned portion* (that is, the part that is prepaid from the date of closing to the end of the month) must be credited to the seller and debited to the buyer. When the mortgage interest is charged at the end of the month, the *earned portion* of the mortgage interest through the date of closing is an accrued expense, debited to the seller and credited to the buyer.

SUMMARY

Closing a real estate sale involves both title procedures and financial matters. The clients' real estate agents are often present at the closing to see that the sale is actually concluded, to lend support to valued clients, and to account for the earnest money deposit (which has normally been held in escrow by the real estate office).

Closings must be reported to the IRS on Form 1099-S.

The Consumer Financial Protection Bureau (CFPB) implements the rule known as TRID, which is a combination of disclosures associated with the Truth In Lending Act (TILA) and the Real Estate Settlement Procedures Act (RESPA). The two main disclosures are the Loan Estimate which details all aspects of the loan and an estimate of closing costs and the Closing Disclosure which is a full accounting of funds at closing and additional information regarding the mortgage. Both documents have strict timeframes for issuance.

RESPA requires disclosure of all settlement costs when a residential real estate purchase is financed by a federally related mortgage loan.

Though the TRID Closing Disclosure is a document that details information for the borrower, because of its thoroughness of accounting and the necessity of a final accounting document at closing, the CFPB allows the CD to be used by all parties at closing.

The CD lists the sales price, earnest money deposit, and all adjustments and prorations due between buyer and seller. It shows the net amount due the seller at closing. The buyer reimburses the seller for prepaid items like taxes or unused fuel oil. The seller credits the buyer for bills the seller owes, but the buyer will have to pay accrued items such as unpaid water bills.

State and county transfer taxes are usually paid by the seller, who also customarily pays for the owner's title insurance policy. The buyer usually pays for the lender's title insurance policy.

Illinois permits proration by the statutory month variation method.

Real estate taxes in Illinois are paid in arrears; that is, in the year after they become a lien.

UNIT 23 QUIZ

1. All encumbrances and liens shown on the report of title (other than those waived or agreed to by the purchaser and listed in the contract) must be removed so that the title can be delivered free and clear. The removal of such encumbrances is the duty of the
   A. seller.
   B. buyer.
   C. broker.
   D. title company.

2. Legal title passes from seller to buyer
   A. on the date of execution of the deed.
   B. when the deed is delivered and accepted.
   C. when the closing statement has been signed.
   D. when the deed is placed in escrow.

3. Which of these would a lender generally require at the time of closing?
   A. Market value appraisal
   B. Application
   C. Title insurance
   D. Credit report

4. The Closing Disclosure (CD) may be used to illustrate all settlement charges for
   A. every real estate transaction.
   B. transactions financed by VA and FHA loans only.
   C. all transactions involving commercial property.
   D. residential transactions financed by federally related mortgage loans.

5. The principal amount of a purchaser's new mortgage loan is a
   A. credit to the seller.
   B. debit to the seller.
   C. credit to the buyer.
   D. debit to the buyer.

6. The earnest money left on deposit with the seller's real estate broker is a
   A. credit to the seller.
   B. credit to the buyer.
   C. balancing factor.
   D. debit to the buyer.

7. If a seller collected rent of $1,400 payable in advance, from an attic tenant on April 1, which of these is *TRUE* at the closing on April 15?
   A. Seller owes buyer $700.
   B. Buyer owes seller $700.
   C. Seller owes buyer $1,400.
   D. Buyer owes seller $1,400.

8. Security deposits are listed on a closing statement as a credit to the
   A. seller.
   B. lender.
   C. buyer.
   D. broker.

9. A building was purchased for $285,000 with 10% down and a loan for the balance. If the lender charged the buyer two discount points, how much cash did the buyer need to come up with at closing if the buyer incurred no other costs?
   A. $28,500
   B. $30,200
   C. $31,700
   D. $33,630

10. A buyer of a $300,000 home has paid $22,000 as earnest money and has a loan commitment for 70% of the purchase price. How much more cash does the buyer need to bring to the closing, provided the buyer has no closing costs?
    A. $68,000
    B. $30,000
    C. $58,000
    D. $61,600

11. At closing, the listing broker's commission usually is shown as a
    A. credit to the seller.
    B. credit to the buyer.
    C. debit to the buyer.
    D. debit to the seller.

12. At the closing of a real estate transaction, the person performing the settlement gave the buyer a credit for certain accrued items. These items were
    A. bills relating to the property that will have to be paid by the buyer.
    B. bills relating to the property that have already been paid by the seller.
    C. all the seller's real estate bills.
    D. all the buyer's real estate bills.

13. The purpose of TRID is to
    A. make sure buyers do not borrow more than they can repay.
    B. make real estate licensees more responsive to buyers' needs.
    C. establish standard escrow and appraisal procedures.
    D. give more transparency to the loan process.

14. The document that provides borrowers with general information about their loan is the
    A. mortgage disclosure statement.
    B. Loan Estimate.
    C. Good Faith Estimate (GFE).
    D. closing statement.

15. Consummation may occur how many days after the issuance of the Closing Disclosure?
    A. Seven business days
    B. Three business days
    C. Three business days after closing
    D. Three business days before consummation

16. Under TRID, if the APR increases by.125 percent, how many business days does the lender have to reissue another LE?
    A. Two
    B. Three
    C. Four
    D. Five

17. If the annual real estate taxes on a property were $2,129 last year, what would be the per diem amount for prorations this year using the actual-number-of-days method?
    A. $5.83
    B. $4.90
    C. $5.86
    D. $5.98

18. In Illinois, which party customarily prepares the closing statement?
    A. Seller's attorney
    B. Buyer's attorney
    C. Listing broker
    D. Seller's lender

19. Which of these formulas *BEST* expresses the statutory month variation method of calculating a daily prorated charge for an annual prepaid expense?
    A. (Total charge ÷ 12) ÷ actual days in month of closing = daily prorated charge
    B. (Total charge ÷ 360) × 12 = daily prorated charge
    C. (Total charge ÷ 360) × actual days in month of closing = daily prorated charge
    D. (Total charge ÷ 365 = y) (y ÷ 12) × actual days in closing month = daily prorated charge

20. In Illinois, which party usually pays the state and county transfer taxes?
    A. Buyer
    B. Buyer pays state taxes; seller pays county and municipal taxes
    C. Whichever party is specified in the local ordinance
    D. Seller

Real Estate Mathematics

LEARNING OBJECTIVE

When you have completed this unit, you will be able to accomplish the following.

› Perform math calculations to determine interest and the value of income-producing properties.

KEY TERMS

frontage
interest

net operating income
(NOI)

perimeter

OVERVIEW

Math is an integral part of the real estate profession. The amount and complexity of the math you encounter will vary, depending on your chosen area of real estate. Calculators and computers are great time-savers, but licensees still need a solid, basic knowledge of math.

Some people are comfortable with math, while others experience anxiety and stress. Study, review, and practice will help you overcome stress and anxiety. With practice and review, your confidence and ability in real estate math will grow.

This review covers the basics of real estate math, as well as the math problems you will most likely find on your real estate licensing examination.

FRACTIONS, DECIMALS, AND PERCENTAGES

A fraction has two parts: the numerator (the number above the line) and the denominator (the number below the line) (see Figure 24.1). The denominator shows the full number of equal parts in the whole. The numerator shows how many of those equal parts are identified. In the example, the whole or total has been divided into eight equal parts, and you have seven of those equal parts.

Figure 24.1: Parts of a Fraction

7	Numerator	(Top Number)
8	Denominator	(Bottom Number)

A decimal is a number that uses a decimal point followed by digits as a way of showing values less than one (for example, 3.25, meaning three complete units and one-quarter of a unit). To convert a fraction to a decimal, divide the numerator by the denominator. For example:

$7/8 = 7 \div 8 = 0.875$

$11/8 = 11 \div 8 = 1.375$

Percent (%) means per hundred or per hundred parts. The whole or total always represents 100%.

75% = 75 parts of 100 parts = $75 \div 100 = 0.75 = 3/4$

20% = 120 parts of 100 parts = $120 \div 100 = 1.2 = 1 1/5$

To convert a percentage to a decimal, move the decimal two places to the left and drop the % sign.

12.5% = $12.5 \div 100 = 0.125$

20% = $2 \div 100 = 0.20$ or 0.2

Conversely, to convert a decimal to a percentage, move the decimal two places to the right and add the % sign.

0.0875 = 8.75%

0.9 = 90%

Some fractions are commonly expressed as their decimal equivalents, and vice versa:

$1/10 = 0.100 = 10\%$

$1/8 = 0.125 = 12.5\%$ or $12 1/2\%$

$1/6 = 0.167 = 16.7\%$ or $16 2/3\%$

$1/5 = 0.20 = 20\%$

$1/4 = 0.25 = 25\%$

$1/3 = 0.333 = 33.3\%$ or $33 1/3\%$

$3/8 = 0.375 = 37.5\%$ or $37 1/2\%$

$2/5 = 0.40 = 40\%$

$1/2 = 0.50 = 50\%$

$3/5 = 0.60 = 60\%$

$5/8 = 0.625 = 62.5\%$ or $62 1/2\%$

$2/3 = 0.667 = 66.7\%$ or $66 2/3\%$

¾ = 0.75 = 75%

⅘ = 0.80 = 80%

⅞ = 0.875 = 87.5% or 87½%

The following three formulas are important for solving all percentage problems:

Total × rate = part

Part ÷ rate = total

Part ÷ total = rate

To easily remember these formulas,

- ■ multiply when part is unknown,
- ■ divide when part is known, and
- ■ when you divide, always enter part into the calculator first.

EXAMPLE

A house and lot are priced at $235,000. The lot alone is valued at $54,000. The lot's value is what percentage of the total value?

> Part ÷ total = rate
>
> $54,000 ÷ $235,000 = 0.229 = 23% (rounded)

EXAMPLE

A broker charges 5.5% commission. What is her commission on the sale of a property for $190,000?

> Total × rate = part
>
> $190,000 × 5.5% = $10,450

AREA

Real estate professionals often need to determine a property's floor or ground area. The **perimeter** of an object or a parcel is the sum of the length of all of its sides. The area within the perimeter is floor or ground space and is usually expressed in square units or acres.

The term *per front foot* refers to a lot's frontage. **Frontage** is the length of a property along a street or waterfront. If two unlabeled dimensions are given for a parcel of land, the first dimension is the frontage.

Irregularly shaped property can be measured easily by a nonsurveyor only if its dimensions can be translated into rectangles and triangles. If possible, break the property into smaller units (rectangles and triangles), measure each individually, and then add them together to find the total area.

Squares and Rectangles

Squares and rectangles are four-sided objects. All four sides of a square are the same length. Opposite sides of a rectangle are the same lengths; therefore, all squares are also rectangles. The equation to determine the area of a rectangle is:

Length × width = area

MATH TIP

When two dimensions are given, assume it to be a rectangle unless told otherwise.

Twelve inches (12") = 1 foot (1')

Three feet = 1 yard

EXAMPLE

How many square feet are in a room 15 feet 6 inches by 30 feet 9 inches? The inches must be converted to feet to complete the computation.

6" ÷ 12 = 0.5' + 15' = 15.5' wide

9" ÷ 12 = 0.75' + 30' = 30.75' long

30.75' × 15.5' = 476.625 square feet

Triangles

A triangle is a three-sided figure. The formula used to determine the area of a triangle is

½ base × height = area

Or

base × height ÷ 2 = area

EXAMPLE

What is the area of a triangular parcel of land that is 400 feet wide and 200 feet deep?

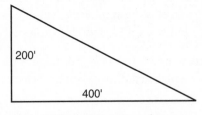

400' × 200' ÷ 2 = 40,000 sq. ft.

Computing Construction Costs

There are several different ways to estimate building construction costs. The most basic is the square-foot method, which uses the area of the building.

Most homes and commercial buildings have a cost per square foot. This cost may vary from region to region and can depend on the quality of construction materials used, but experience and industry averages provide fairly accurate figures.

EXAMPLE

A contractor has been asked to estimate the cost to build a new house. The home's living area is 1,783 square feet with a 500-square-foot garage. In this region, homes typically cost $110 per square foot to build, though garage space only costs $60 because the ceiling and interior walls can be left unfinished. What is the estimated cost of constructing this house?

1,783 sq. ft. × $110 = $196,130

500 sq. ft. × $60 = $30,000

$196,130 + $30,000 = $226,130

FINANCE PROBLEMS

Interest

Interest is the cost of using money. The amount of interest paid is determined by the agreed annual interest rate, the amount of money borrowed (loan amount) or the amount of money still owed (loan balance), and the period of time the money is held. When a lender grants a loan for real estate, the loan-to-value (LTV) ratio is the percentage of the sales price or appraised value (whichever is less) that the lender is willing to lend.

Interest on a loan secured by real estate is typically simple interest based on a specified annual return. For example, a 4.5% annual interest payment on a loan of $180,000 is $180,000 × 0.045, or $8,100. As a monthly payment, the interest is $8,100 ÷ 12, or $675. Interest is always calculated on the remaining principal balance.

> **MATH TIP**
> Use 360-day years and 30-day months unless instructed to do otherwise.

The formulas for computing real estate loan interest payments are as follows:

Principal × rate × time = interest

Interest ÷ rate × time = principal

Interest ÷ principal × time = rate

Interest ÷ principal × rate = time

The principal is the unpaid balance of the loan. The rate is the percentage rate of interest to be paid. The time is the length of the period for which interest is to be paid.

EXAMPLE

A home equity loan with a 4.5% interest rate has a remaining balance of $123,000. What is the monthly interest?

Principal × rate × time = interest

$123,000 × 0.045 × $\frac{1}{12}$ = $461.25

Interest rate tables and loan amortization calculators, which can be found online, can be used to shortcut some of the steps involved in computing monthly payments of principal and interest. Such tables and calculators can be used to determine interest payments. They also can be used to tell the potential investor how much of the principal balance must be paid to pay down the loan balance over a given number of payments, called amortization.

Value for Income-Producing Properties

When appraising income-producing property, the value is estimated by using the annual **net operating income (NOI)** and the current market rate of return or capitalization rate. Annual scheduled gross income is adjusted for vacancies and credit losses to arrive at the annual effective gross income. The annual operating expenses are deducted from the annual effective gross income to arrive at the annual NOI.

Vacancy/credit loss is usually expressed as a percentage of the scheduled gross.

Scheduled gross income – vacancies and credit losses = effective gross income

Effective gross income – annual operating expenses = NOI

NOI ÷ rate of return = value

NOI ÷ value = rate of return

Value × rate of return = NOI

EXAMPLE

An office building produces $132,600 annual gross income. If the annual expenses are $30,600 and the appraiser estimates the value using an 8.5% rate of return, what is the estimated value?

$132,600 annual gross income – $30,600 annual expenses = $102,000 NOI

$102,000 ÷ 8.5% = $1,200,000 value

These formulas also can be used to calculate either the return on investment (ROI) for real estate investing or the monthly NOI. The total becomes original cost or investment instead of value.

EXAMPLE

A man invests $335,000 in a property that should produce a 9% rate of return. What monthly NOI will he receive?

$335,000 × 9% (0.09) = $30,150

$30,150 NOI ÷ 12 months = $2,512.50 monthly NOI

SUMMARY

Real estate practice does not typically require complex mathematics, though licensees should be familiar with the some basic concepts and formulas. With a foundation in calculating areas, interest, and amortization, you should be comfortable with most necessary computations.

UNIT 24 QUIZ

1. A 100-foot-by-125-foot lot sold for $125,000. What was the price per front foot?
   A. $1,250
   B. $10
   C. $556
   D. $1,000

2. If the savings and loan gives you a 90% loan on a house valued at $88,500, how much additional cash must you produce as a down payment if you have already paid $4,500 in earnest money?
   A. $4,350
   B. $3,500
   C. $4,000
   D. $8,850

3. What would you pay for a building producing $11,250 annual net income and showing a minimum rate of return of 9%?
   A. $101,250
   B. $122,625
   C. $125,000
   D. $123,626

4. Your monthly rent is $525. What is your rent as a percentage of an annual income of $21,000?
   A. 25%
   B. 30%
   C. 33%
   D. 40%

5. Two sponsoring brokers evenly split the 6% commission on a $73,000 home. The selling broker was paid 70% of his sponsoring broker's share. The listing broker was paid 30% of her sponsoring broker's share. How much did the listing broker receive?
   A. $1,314
   B. $1,533
   C. $4,380
   D. $657

6. Find the number of square feet in a lot with a frontage of 75 feet 6 inches and a depth of 140 feet 9 inches.
   A. 216.25
   B. 10,652.04
   C. 25,510.81
   D. 10,626.63

7. You attempt to appraise a 28-unit apartment house, employing the income approach. Each unit rents for $775 per month, an amount that seems consistent with similar rental units in the vicinity. For the past five years, the annual expenses of operation have averaged $82,460. The complex has maintained a consistent vacancy rate of 5%. A potential investor is only interested if the return is 9.5%. What value would you arrive at using these variables?
   A. $868,000
   B. $1,873,100
   C. $2,741,100
   D. $1,736,000

8. The buyer has agreed to pay $175,000 in sales price, 2.5 loan discount points, and a 1% origination fee. If the buyer receives a 90% loan-to-value ratio, how much will the buyer owe at closing for points and the origination fee?
   A. $5,512.50
   B. $1,575.00
   C. $3,937.50
   D. $6,125.00

9. Calculate eight months' interest on a $5,000 interest-only loan at 9.5%.
   A. $39.58
   B. $316.67
   C. $237.50
   D. $475.00

10. An office building produces $68,580 annual net operating income. What price would you pay for this property to show a minimum return of 12% on your investment?
   A. $489,857
   B. $685,800
   C. $571,500
   D. $768,096

11. A man earns $20,000 per year and can qualify for a monthly PITI payment equal to 25% of his monthly salary. If the annual tax and insurance is $678.24, what loan amount will he will qualify for if the monthly PI payment factor is $10.29 per $1,000 of loan amount?
   A. $35,000
   B. $40,500
   C. $43,000
   D. $66,000

12. What percentage of profit would you make if you paid $10,500 for a lot, built a home on the lot that cost $93,000, and then sold the lot and house together for $134,550?
   A. 30%
   B. 13%
   C. 23%
   D. 45%

13. A buyer pays $2,500 each for four parcels of land. He subdivides them into six parcels and sells each of the six parcels for $1,950. What was the buyer's percentage of profit?
   A. 14.5%
   B. 52%
   C. 17%
   D. 78%

14. A woman earns an annual income of $60,000, and her husband earns $2,400 per month. How much can the couple pay monthly for their total housing payment if the lender uses a 28% qualifying ratio?
   A. $2,072
   B. $672
   C. $1,400
   D. $2,352

15. A buyer is granted a 90% loan of $340,500. How much will her monthly principal and interest payment be, using a loan payment factor of $7.16 per $1,000 of loan?
   A. $2,194.18
   B. $3,064.50
   C. $2,437.98
   D. $4,755.59

PRACTICE ILLINOIS REAL ESTATE LICENSING EXAMS

Modern Real Estate Practice in Illinois is designed to prepare you for a career in real estate. However, before you can become a broker, managing broker, residential leasing agent, or an instructor, you must, under Illinois law, obtain a license. Passing the real estate licensing exam plays a large part in determining your eligibility to become licensed. The exam is designed to test your knowledge of real estate laws, principles, and practices.

The state exam is currently prepared and administered by AMP, Applied Measurement Professionals, Inc. a division of PSI Services, LLC, an independent testing company under the sanction of the Illinois Department of Financial and Professional Regulation (IDFPR). The Illinois *Candidate Handbook* is available at PSI/AMP's website (www.goamp.com) and contains detailed information about the licensing exam, including fees, scheduling, and locations. The *Candidate Handbook* also contains current, in-depth topic outlines.

WHAT TO EXPECT FROM THE EXAM

Illinois broker, managing broker, residential leasing agent, and instructor candidates are given separate exams. Questions for the exams involve two broad areas: knowledge of material and application of knowledge in the real estate professions.

The rules for taking the exam are set by IDFPR and the PSI/AMP testing service and are detailed in the *Candidate Handbook*. The state exam must be completed within the allotted time. PSI/AMP provides computer monitors, each equipped with a clock that shows you exactly how much time you have remaining to complete the exam. Once the test begins, you are not allowed to leave the test site until you have completed the exam. Guessing is not penalized; be sure to answer every question.

You must pass both the national and state sections of the exam with a 75% to qualify for your real estate license. They are administered and scored separately. Candidates who pass only one portion must retake and pass the other portion within one year of passing the first portion. Failure to do so will result in having to take the entire exam again.

Candidates are allowed up to four attempts to pass the exam. After the fourth attempt, you are required to retake the education coursework. Candidates also must not let their coursework lapse for more than two years before taking the exam or they will need to retake the education coursework.

Broker Exam

The broker exam consists of 100 questions on national real estate topics and 40 questions on Illinois-specific real estate topics. The questions are multiple choice, with four answer choices for each question. Broker candidates are expected to solve basic problems in real estate mathematics related to such topics as commissions, interest, prorations, and square footage; at least 10% of the questions involve some sort of mathematical calculation.

Content Outlines

The *Candidate Handbook* includes outlines of the subject areas that are tested on the national and state sections of the test and the approximate number of questions coming from each area. These outlines are an important study tool for preparing to take your exam.

MULTIPLE-CHOICE QUESTIONS: TEST-TAKING STRATEGIES

There are many different ways to prepare for and take multiple-choice exams. While no one can tell you which method will work best for you, it's always a good idea to think about what you're going to do before you do it. In any case, there is no secret formula: the only sure way to improve your odds of a correct answer is to study and learn the material.

Always remember that a multiple-choice question always gives you the correct answer. You don't have to remember how words are spelled, and you don't have to try to guess what the question is about. The answer is always there right in front of you.

The key to success in taking multiple-choice exams is actually twofold:

- Know the correct answer. Go to class, pay attention, take good notes, and study the material.

- If you don't know the correct answer, carefully analyze the questions and answers and make a reasonable guess. Even if you don't know the answer, you will probably know which answers are clearly wrong and which ones are more likely than the others to be right.

If you can eliminate one answer as wrong, you have improved your odds of "guessing correctly" from 25% to 33%. If you can eliminate two wrong answers, you have a 50% shot at a correct guess. Of course, if you can eliminate three wrong answers, your chance of a correct response is 100%.

Multiple-Choice Question Structure

A multiple-choice question has a basic structure. It starts with the stem: the text of the question that sets up the need for an answer. The stem may be an incomplete statement that is finished by the correct answer or it may be a story problem or hypothetical example about which you will be asked a question. It may be a math problem in which you are given basic information and asked to solve a mathematical calculation, such as the amount of commission or capital gain.

The stem is always followed by options: four possible answers to the question. Depending on the structure and content of the stem, the options may be single words or numbers, phrases, or complete sentences. Three of the options are distractors: incorrect answers intended to distract you from the correct choice. The fourth option is the correct answer.

Reading a Multiple-Choice Question

Here are three suggestions for how to read a multiple-choice test question:

■ *The traditional method.* Read the question through from start to finish and then read the options. When you get to the correct answer, mark it and move on. This method works best for short questions, such as those that require completion or simply defining a term. For longer, more complicated questions or those that are not quite so clear, however, you may miss important information.

■ *The focus method.* As we've seen, multiple-choice questions have different parts. In longer math or story-type questions, the last line of the stem contains the question's focus: the basic issue the item asks you to address. That is, the question is always in the last line of the stem. In the focus method, when you come to a longer item, read the last line of the stem first. This will clue you in to what the question is about. Then go back and read the stem from beginning to end; while you are reading the complicated facts or math elements, you know what to look for. You can watch for important items and disregard unnecessary information.

■ *The upside-down method.* This technique takes the focus method one step further. Here, you do just what the name implies: you start reading the question from the bottom up. By reading the four options first, you know exactly what to focus on. For example, a question might include several dollar values in the stem, leading you to believe you're going to have to do a math calculation. You'll be trying to recall all the equations you've memorized, only to find at the end of the stem that you're only expected to define a term.

TAKING THE PRACTICE EXAMS

The following three practice exams have been designed to help test your knowledge in preparation for the actual licensing exam.

The first two exams consist of 150 questions: 90 questions on general, national real estate principles and 60 questions covering Illinois-specific law and practice. Note that proration calculations are based on a 30-day month unless otherwise specified.

The third practice exam consists of 50 Illinois-specific questions, with emphasis on the Illinois Real Estate License Act of 2000.

PRACTICE EXAM ONE

1. Which of these is a lien on real estate?
   A. Recorded easement
   B. Recorded mortgage
   C. Encroachment
   D. Deed restriction

2. A sales contract was signed under duress. Which of these describes this contract?
   A. Voidable
   B. Breached
   C. Discharged
   D. Void

3. A sponsoring broker receives a check for earnest money from a buyer and deposits the money in the sponsoring broker's personal interest-bearing checking account over the weekend. This action exposes the sponsoring broker to a charge of
   A. commingling.
   B. novation.
   C. subrogation.
   D. accretion.

4. A borrower takes out a mortgage loan that requires monthly payments of $875.70 for 20 years and a final payment of $24,095. This is what type of loan?
   A. Wraparound
   B. Accelerated
   C. Balloon
   D. Variable

5. When demand for a commodity decreases and supply increases,
   A. price is not affected.
   B. price tends to rise.
   C. price tends to fall.
   D. the market becomes stagnant.

6. A broker signs a contract with a buyer. Under the contract, the broker agrees to help the buyer find a suitable property and to represent the buyer in negotiations with the seller. Although the buyer may not sign an agreement with any other broker, she may look for properties on her own. The broker is entitled to payment only if the broker locates the property that is purchased. What kind of agreement has this broker signed?
   A. Exclusive buyer agency agreement
   B. Exclusive-agency buyer agency agreement
   C. Open buyer agency agreement
   D. Option contract

7. A man conveys property to a woman by delivering a deed. The deed contains five covenants. This is *MOST* likely a
   A. warranty deed.
   B. quitclaim deed.
   C. grant deed.
   D. deed in trust.

8. A real estate licensee does not show non-Asian clients any properties in several traditionally Asian neighborhoods. She bases this practice on the need to preserve the valuable cultural integrity of Asian immigrant communities. Which of these statements is *TRUE?*
   A. The licensee's policy is steering and violates the fair housing laws regardless of her motivation.
   B. Because the licensee is not attempting to restrict the rights of any single minority group, the practice does not constitute steering.
   C. The licensee's policy is steering, but it does not violate the fair housing laws because she is motivated by cultural preservation, not by exclusion or discrimination.
   D. The licensee's policy has the effect, but not the intent, of steering.

9. A grandmother grants a life estate to her grandson and stipulates that on the grandson's death, the title to the property will pass to her son-in-law. This second estate is called
   A. a remainder.
   B. a reversion.
   C. an estate at sufferance.
   D. an estate for years.

10. Which of these is *TRUE* concerning a property held in joint tenancy?
    A. A maximum of two people can own the real estate.
    B. The fractional interests of the owners can be different.
    C. Additional owners may be added later.
    D. There is always the right of survivorship.

11. A real estate licensee has a written contract with his sponsoring broker that specifies that he will not be treated as an employee. The licensee's entire income is from sales commissions rather than an hourly wage. For federal income tax purposes, the licensee is considered
    A. a real estate assistant.
    B. an employee.
    C. a subagent.
    D. an independent contractor.

12. The states in which the lender holds title to mortgaged real estate are called
    A. title-theory states.
    B. lien-theory states.
    C. statutory title states.
    D. strict title forfeiture states.

13. The form of tenancy that expires on a specific date is a
    A. joint tenancy.
    B. tenancy for years.
    C. tenancy in common.
    D. tenancy by the entirety.

14. A suburban home that lacks indoor plumbing suffers from
    A. functional obsolescence.
    B. curable physical deterioration.
    C. incurable physical deterioration.
    D. external obsolescence.

15. If a developer wants to build a commercial building closer to the street than is permitted by the local zoning ordinance because the shape of the lot makes a standard setback impossible, the developer should seek a
    A. variance.
    B. nonconforming use permit.
    C. conditional use permit.
    D. density zoning permit.

16. A licensee showed an owner-occupied property that had window screens, custom venetian blinds, and a wall bed to a buyer. The owner accepted the buyer's offer. What may the seller remove before closing?
    A. All of the identified items because they are trade fixtures
    B. Only the venetian blinds as personal property
    C. Only the wall bed because it is real property
    D. None of these identified items

17. A real estate broker specializes in helping both buyers and sellers fill in the blanks and negotiate the terms of the contract. Because the broker is an agent of both parties, he may not disclose either party's confidential information to the other. The broker is acting as
    A. a buyer's agent.
    B. a seller's agent.
    C. a transactional broker.
    D. a dual agent.

18. The portion of the value of an owner's property that exceeds the amount of the owner's mortgage debt is called
    A. equality.
    B. escrow.
    C. surplus.
    D. equity.

19. A buyer has an 80/20 LTV and a $5,000 earnest money deposit which will be used at closing to cover part of the down payment. If the purchase price of the home is $250,000, how much additional funds must the seller bring to complete the down payment?
    A. $45,000
    B. $50,000
    C. $75,000
    D. $20,000

20. Police powers include
    A. deed restrictions.
    B. zoning.
    C. restrictive covenants.
    D. taxation.

21. A seller wants to net $165,000 from the sale of her house after paying the sponsoring broker's fee of 5%. The seller's gross sales price will be
    A. $155,750.
    B. $156,750.
    C. $173,248.
    D. $173,684.

22. How many square feet are in three acres?
    A. 43,560
    B. 130,680
    C. 156,840
    D. 27,878,400

23. A purchaser obtains financing from a local savings association to purchase a condominium unit. In this situation, which of these *BEST* describes the purchaser?
    A. Vendor
    B. Mortgagor
    C. Grantor
    D. Lessor

24. The current value of a property is $240,000. The property is assessed at 40% of its current value for real estate tax purposes with an equalization factor of 1.5 applied to the assessed value. If the tax rate is $4 per $100 of assessed valuation, what is the amount of tax due on the property?
    A. $2,500
    B. $3,840
    C. $5,760
    D. $214,400

25. A building was sold for $360,000, with the purchaser putting 10% down and obtaining a loan for the balance. The lending institution charged a 1% loan origination fee. What was the total cash used for the purchase?
    A. $3,240
    B. $6,500
    C. $39,240
    D. $39,600

26. Several brokerage firms were accused of violating antitrust laws. Of the following, they were *MOST* likely accused of
    A. not having an equal housing opportunity sign in an office window.
    B. undisclosed dual agencies.
    C. price-fixing.
    D. dealing in unlicensed exchange services.

27. A capitalization rate is the
    A. amount determined by the gross rent multiplier.
    B. rate of return a property will produce on the owner's investment.
    C. mathematical value determined by a sales price.
    D. rate at which the amount of depreciation in a property is measured.

28. The National Do Not Call Registry provides that
    A. licensees may never contact consumers without written authorization.
    B. consumers with whom a licensee has had a business relationship can be contacted for up to 12 months after termination of that relationship.
    C. licensees may not contact previous customers who are on the registry.
    D. consumers who have made an inquiry to a licensee may be contacted up to three months later.

29. If a house was sold for $140,000 and the buyer obtained an FHA-insured mortgage loan for $133,700, how much money would the buyer pay in discount points if the lender charged two points?
    A. $495
    B. $2,674
    C. $2,800
    D. $3,800

30. The commission rate is 7¾% on a sale of $250,000. What is the dollar amount of the commission?
    A. $17,500
    B. $19,375
    C. $20,425
    D. $22,925

31. A buyer makes an offer on a property and the seller accepts. Three weeks later, the buyer announces that "the deal's off" and refuses to go through with the sale. If the seller is entitled to keep the buyer's earnest money deposit, it is *MOST* likely because the sales contract contains
    A. a liquidated damages clause.
    B. a contingent damages clause.
    C. an actual damages clause.
    D. a revocation clause.

32. Until the land contract is paid in full, what is the status of the purchaser's interest in the property?
    A. Purchaser holds legal title to the premises.
    B. Purchaser has no legal interest in the property.
    C. Purchaser possesses a legal life estate in the premises.
    D. Purchaser has equitable title in the property.

33. Three years after signing a five-year lease, business A outgrew its rental space. Business A would like business B to take on the responsibility of the lease for the remaining two years. B can do this through
    A. an assignment.
    B. a novation.
    C. a substitution.
    D. a rescission.

34. An ownership interest that permits multiple purchasers to buy interests in the same piece of real estate is a
    A. leasehold.
    B. time-share.
    C. condominium.
    D. cooperative.

35. For an offer to purchase real estate to become a sales contract, whose signature is necessary?
    A. Buyer's only
    B. Buyer's and seller's
    C. Seller's only
    D. Seller's and seller's broker's

36. A borrower just made the final payment on a mortgage loan. Regardless of this fact, the records will still show a lien on the mortgaged property until
    A. a satisfaction of the mortgage document is recorded.
    B. a reconveyance of the mortgage document is delivered to the mortgage holder.
    C. a novation of the mortgage document takes place.
    D. an estoppel of the mortgage document is filed with the clerk of the county in which the mortgagee is located.

37. If the annual net income from a commercial property is $22,000 and the capitalization rate is 8%, what is the value of the property using the income approach?
    A. $176,000
    B. $183,000
    C. $200,000
    D. $275,000

38. A sponsoring broker enters into a listing agreement with a seller in which the seller will receive $120,000 from the sale of a vacant lot and the sponsoring broker will receive any sale proceeds exceeding that amount. This is what type of listing?
    A. Exclusive agency
    B. Net
    C. Exclusive right to sell
    D. Multiple

39. An individual sold her house and moved into a cooperative apartment. Under the cooperative form of ownership, the individual will
    A. become a shareholder in the corporation.
    B. not lose her apartment if she pays her share of the expenses.
    C. have to take out a new mortgage loan on her unit.
    D. receive a fixed-term lease for her unit.

40. A defect or a cloud on title to property may be cured by
    A. obtaining proof of satisfaction from all appropriate parties.
    B. bringing an action to register the title.
    C. paying cash for the property at the settlement.
    D. bringing an action to repudiate the title.

41. A buyer signed an exclusive-agency buyer agency agreement with a sponsoring broker. If the buyer finds a suitable property with no assistance from any licensee, the sponsoring broker is entitled to
    A. full compensation from the buyer, regardless of who found the property.
    B. full compensation from the seller.
    C. partial compensation as generally required under this type of agreement.
    D. no compensation under the terms of this type of agreement.

42. Under the terms of a net lease, a commercial tenant usually would be responsible for paying
    A. principle debt service.
    B. real estate taxes.
    C. income tax payments.
    D. mortgage interest expense.

43. The Fair Housing Act of 1968 prohibits discrimination based on
    A. familial status.
    B. sexual orientation.
    C. race.
    D. public assistance income.

44. If a borrower must pay $6,000 for points on a $150,000 loan, how many points is the lender charging for this loan?
    A. 3
    B. 4
    C. 5
    D. 6

45. What is the difference between a general lien and a specific lien?
    A. A general lien cannot be enforced in court, while a specific lien can.
    B. A specific lien is held by only one person, while a general lien must be held by two or more people.
    C. A general lien is a lien against personal property, while a specific lien is a lien against real estate.
    D. A specific lien is a lien against a certain parcel of real estate, while a general lien covers all of a debtor's property.

46. In an option to purchase real estate, which of these statements is *TRUE* of the optionee?
    A. The optionee must purchase the property but may do so at any time within the option period.
    B. The optionee is limited to a refund of the option consideration if the option is exercised.
    C. The optionee cannot obtain third-party financing on the property until after the option has expired.
    D. The optionee has no obligation to purchase the property during the option period.

47. In 2004, an owner constructed a building that was eight stories high. In 2014, the municipality changed the zoning ordinance and prohibited buildings taller than six stories. Which of these statements is *TRUE* regarding the existing eight-story building?
    A. The building must be demolished.
    B. The building is a conditional use.
    C. The building is a nonconforming use.
    D. The owner must obtain a variance.

48. How many acres are there in the N½ of the SW¼ and the NE¼ of the SE¼ of a section?
    A. 20
    B. 40
    C. 80
    D. 120

49. A home is the smallest in a neighborhood of large, expensive houses. The effect of the other houses on the value of this particular home is called
    A. regression.
    B. progression.
    C. substitution.
    D. contribution.

50. What kind of lien is created as a result of a judgment, estate or inheritance taxes, the decedent's debts, or unpaid federal income taxes?
    A. Specific
    B. General
    C. Voluntary
    D. Equitable

51. A broker received a deposit along with a written offer from a buyer. The offer stated: "The offeror will leave this offer open for the seller's acceptance for a period of 10 days." On the fifth day, and before acceptance by the seller, the offeror notified the broker that the offer was withdrawn and demanded the return of the deposit. Under these circumstances, the offeror
    A. cannot withdraw the offer; it must be held open for the full 10-day period, as promised.
    B. has the right to withdraw the offer and secure the return of the deposit any time before being notified of the seller's acceptance.
    C. can withdraw the offer, and the seller and the broker will each retain one-half of the forfeited deposit.
    D. can withdraw the offer, and the broker is legally entitled to declare the deposit forfeited and retain all of it in lieu of the lost commission.

52. A man and a woman own property as joint tenants. The woman sells her interest to another woman. What is the relationship between the man and the second woman regarding the property?
    A. Joint tenants
    B. Tenants in common
    C. Tenants by the entirety
    D. No relationship exists because the first woman cannot sell her joint tenancy interest

53. A property owner and a tenant verbally enter into a six-month lease. If the tenant defaults, the property owner may
    A. not bring a court action because six-month leases must be in writing under the parol evidence rule.
    B. not bring a court action because the statute of frauds governs six-month leases.
    C. bring a court action because six-month leases need not be in writing to be enforceable.
    D. bring a court action because the statute of limitations does not apply to oral leases, regardless of their term.

54. On Monday, a woman offers to sell her vacant lot to a man for $35,000. On Tuesday, the man counteroffers to buy the lot for $25,500. On Friday, the man withdraws his counteroffer and accepts the woman's original price of $35,000. Under these circumstances,
    A. a valid agreement exists because the man accepted the woman's offer exactly as it was made, regardless of the fact that it was not accepted immediately.
    B. a valid agreement exists because the man accepted before the woman advised him that the offer was withdrawn.
    C. no valid agreement exists because the woman's offer was not accepted within 72 hours of its having been made.
    D. no valid agreement exists because the man's counteroffer canceled the woman's original offer and, once rejected, it cannot be re-accepted.

55. A property owner's neighbors use her driveway to reach their garage, which is on their property. The property owner's attorney explains that the neighbors have an easement appurtenant that gives them the right to use her driveway. The property owner's property is the
    A. dominant tenement.
    B. servient tenement.
    C. prescriptive tenement.
    D. appurtenant tenement.

56. What action returns the parties to a contract to their original positions, before the contract, including the return of any deposit?
    A. Cancellation
    B. Substitution
    C. Rescission
    D. Subordination

57. A deed conveys ownership to the grantee "as long as the existing building is not torn down." What type of estate does this deed create?
    A. Determinable fee estate
    B. Fee simple absolute estate
    C. Nondestructible estate
    D. Life estate pur autre vie, with the measuring life being that of the building

58. Taxes levied on a property owner to pay for installation of sidewalks or sewers are called
    A. ad valorem taxes.
    B. general assessments.
    C. special assessments.
    D. special excise taxes.

59. What do local zoning ordinances regulate?
    A. Environmental penalties
    B. Deed restrictions
    C. Restrictive covenants
    D. Permitted land uses

60. A sponsoring broker took a listing and later discovered that a court had previously declared the client incompetent. At this point, the status of the listing is
    A. unaffected because the sponsoring broker acted in good faith as the owner's agent.
    B. of no value to the sponsoring broker because the contract is void.
    C. the basis for recovery of a commission from the client's guardian or trustee if the sponsoring broker produces a buyer.
    D. on hold and may be renegotiated between the broker and the client, based on the new information.

61. A borrower defaulted on his home mortgage loan payments, and the lender obtained a court order to foreclose on the property. At the foreclosure sale, the property sold for $164,000; the unpaid balance on the loan at the time of foreclosure was $178,000. What must the lender do to recover the $14,000 that the borrower still owes?
    A. Sue for specific performance
    B. Sue for damages
    C. Seek a deficiency judgment
    D. Seek a judgment by default

62. Which of these is exempt from the federal Fair Housing Act of 1968?
    A. The sale of a listed, owner-occupied single-family home when the listing broker does not advertise the property
    B. The refusal to rent an apartment to a physically disabled person
    C. An owner-occupied building with no more than four units
    D. The restriction of noncommercial housing where a certified statement has not been filed with the government

63. When compared with a 30-year payment period, taking out a loan with a 20-year payment results in
    A. lower equity buildup.
    B. greater impound requirements.
    C. lower monthly payments.
    D. higher monthly payments.

64. A licensee arrives to present a purchase offer to an older man, who is seriously ill, and finds the man's son and daughter-in-law also present. The son and daughter-in-law urge the man to accept the offer, even though it is much less than the asking price for the property. If the man accepts the offer, the man may later claim that
    A. the licensee improperly presented an offer that was less than the asking price.
    B. the licensee's failure to protect the man from the son and daughter-in-law constituted a violation of the licensee's fiduciary duties.
    C. the man's rights under the ADA have been violated by the son and daughter-in-law.
    D. the man was under undue influence from the son and daughter-in-law, so the contract is voidable.

65. A deed of conveyance contained only the following guarantee: "This property was not encumbered during the time the grantor owned it except as noted in this deed." What type of deed did the grantor give to the grantee?
    A. General warranty
    B. Special warranty
    C. Bargain and sale
    D. Quitclaim

66. An unmarried couple owns a parcel of real estate. Each owns an undivided interest, with the man owning one-third and the woman owning two-thirds. The form of ownership under which the couple owns their property is
A. severalty.
B. joint tenancy.
C. tenancy at will.
D. tenancy in common.

67. A man agrees to purchase a house for $84,500. He pays $2,000 as earnest money and obtains a new mortgage loan for $67,600. The purchase contract provides for a March 15 settlement. He and the sellers prorate the present year's real estate taxes of $1,880.96, which have been prepaid. The man has additional closing costs of $1,250, and the sellers have other closing costs of $850. Using the actual number of days method, how much cash must the man bring to the settlement?
A. $16,389
B. $17,650
C. $17,840
D. $19,639

68. A broker advertised a house he had listed for sale at the price of $247,900. An African American couple saw the house and were interested in it. When the prospects asked the broker the price of the house, the broker told the prospects $253,000. Under the federal Fair Housing Act of 1968, such a statement is
A. legal because the law requires only that the African American be given the opportunity to buy the house.
B. legal because the representation was made by the broker and not directly by the owner.
C. illegal because the difference in the offering price and the quoted price was greater than 10%.
D. illegal because the terms of the potential sale were changed for the couple.

69. An owner placed her farm in a trust, naming herself as the beneficiary. When the owner died, her will directed the trustee to sell the farm and distribute the proceeds of the sale to her heirs. The trustee sold the farm in accordance with the will. What type of deed was delivered at settlement?
A. Trustee's deed
B. Trustor's deed
C. Deed in trust
D. Reconveyance deed

70. An appraiser has been hired to prepare an appraisal report of a property for loan purposes. The property is an elegant old mansion that is now leased out as a restaurant. To which approach to value should the appraiser probably give the greatest weight when making this appraisal?
A. Income
B. Sales comparison
C. Replacement cost
D. Reproduction cost

71. An applicant applies for a mortgage, and the loan officer suggests that she might consider a term mortgage loan. Which of these statements *BEST* explains what the loan officer means?
A. All the interest is paid at the end of the term.
B. The debt is partially amortized over the life of the loan.
C. The length of the term is limited by state law.
D. The entire principal amount is due at the end of the term.

72. A condominium community offers a swimming pool, tennis courts, and a biking trail. These facilities are *MOST* likely owned by the
A. condominium board.
B. corporation in which the unit owners hold stock.
C. unit owners in the form of proportional divided interests.
D. unit owners in the form of percentage undivided interests.

73. On a closing statement in a typical real estate transaction, the buyer's earnest money deposit is reflected as a
A. credit to the buyer and a debit to the seller.
B. credit to the seller and a debit to the buyer.
C. credit to both the buyer and the seller.
D. debit to the buyer only.

74. Prepaid insurance and tax reserves, in which the buyer assumes the mortgage, will appear on a typical closing statement as a
A. credit to the buyer and a debit to the seller.
B. credit to the seller only.
C. debit to the seller only.
D. debit to the buyer and a credit to the seller.

75. Real property can become personal property by the process called
    A. attachment.
    B. severance.
    C. hypothecation.
    D. accretion.

76. Property owners give a neighbor permission to park a camper in their yard for a few weeks. The property owners do not charge rent for the use of the yard. The property owners have given the neighbor
    A. an easement.
    B. an estate for years.
    C. a license.
    D. a permissive encroachment.

77. A tenant's lease has expired, but the tenant has not vacated the premises or negotiated a renewal lease. The landlord has declared that the tenant is not to remain in the building. This situation is an example of
    A. an estate for years.
    B. an estate from year to year.
    C. tenancy at will.
    D. tenancy at sufferance.

78. A property owner signs a listing agreement with a sponsoring broker. A second broker obtains a buyer for the house, and the sponsoring broker does not receive a commission. The sponsoring broker does not sue the seller. The listing agreement between the seller and the sponsoring broker was most likely
    A. an exclusive right to sell agreement.
    B. an open agreement.
    C. an exclusive agency agreement.
    D. a dual agency agreement.

79. A sponsoring broker established the following office policy: "All listings taken by any licensee associated with this real estate brokerage must include compensation based on a 5% commission. No lower commission rate is acceptable." If the sponsoring broker attempts to impose this uniform commission requirement, which of these statements is *TRUE*?
    A. A homeowner may sue the sponsoring broker for violating the antitrust law's prohibition against price-fixing.
    B. The licensees associated with the brokerage will not be bound by the requirement and may negotiate any commission rate they choose.
    C. The sponsoring broker must present the uniform commission policy to the local professional association for approval.
    D. The sponsoring broker may, as a matter of office policy, legally set the minimum commission rate acceptable for the firm.

80. Because the owner of an apartment building failed to perform routine maintenance, the apartment building's central heating system broke down in the fall. The owner neglected to have the heating system repaired, and a tenant had no heat in her apartment for the first six weeks of winter. Although eight months remained on the tenant's lease, she moved out of the apartment and refused to pay any rent. If the owner sues to recover the outstanding rent, which of the following would be the tenant's *BEST* defense?
    A. Because the tenant lived in the apartment for more than 25% of the lease term, she was entitled to move out at any time without penalty.
    B. The tenant was entitled to vacate the premises because the landlord's failure to repair the heating system constituted abandonment.
    C. Because the apartment was made uninhabitable, the landlord's actions constituted actual eviction.
    D. The landlord's actions constituted constructive eviction.

81. A buyer purchased a parcel of land and immediately sold the mineral rights to an oil company. The buyer gave up his
    A. air rights.
    B. surface rights.
    C. subsurface rights.
    D. occupancy rights.

82. A developer built a six-story structure. Several years later, an ordinance was passed in that area banning any building six stories or higher. This building is a
    A. nonconforming use.
    B. situation in which the structure would have to be demolished.
    C. conditional use.
    D. violation of the zoning laws.

83. What is the maximum capital gains tax exclusion allowable for a married couple, filing jointly, who have lived in their home for the past 3½ years?
    A. $100,000
    B. $250,000
    C. $500,000
    D. $750,000

84. Statements by a real estate licensee that somewhat exaggerate the intangibles of a property without committing fraud are called
    A. polishing.
    B. puffing.
    C. prospecting.
    D. marketing.

85. When planning a subdivision, a developer should determine the kinds of land uses to be involved and the amounts of land to be allocated to each use by considering
    A. which are the most profitable types of buildings to construct.
    B. what he considers an ideal development.
    C. the comprehensive plan of the local government.
    D. the customs of the area and what other developers have already done.

86. Which of these is *TRUE* regarding condominiums?
    A. If a unit owner does not pay the monthly maintenance fee, the entire community will be foreclosed.
    B. The covenants and restrictions define the responsibilities of the owners and declare how the homeowners association will operate the condo community.
    C. If one unit owner defaults on property taxes, those taxes will be owed by the remaining unit owners.
    D. A condominium unit may be mortgaged like any other parcel of real estate.

87. Which of these is a legal practice?
    A. To refuse to sell, rent, or negotiate with a person because of race
    B. As a property manager, to check the credit of females only
    C. To display the equal housing opportunity poster
    D. To refuse to let persons with a disability, at their expense, modify a dwelling

88. Which of these is a voidable contract?
    A. A contract with no contingencies
    B. A contract entered into on a legal holiday
    C. A contract that has not been recorded with the recorder of deeds
    D. A contract entered into by a minor

89. An owner entered into a three-month listing agreement with a sponsoring broker. Last week, the owner also entered into the same three-month listing agreement with two separate brokers. The owner has negotiated
    A. exclusive-right-to-sell listings.
    B. exclusive agency listings.
    C. open listings.
    D. net listings.

90. An appraiser was contracted to determine the value of a large apartment building for a potential investor client. Which appraisal method is the *MOST* useful for this type of property?
    A. Comparative market analysis
    B. The square foot method
    C. Income approach
    D. Cost approach

In Illinois

91. A large manufacturing company agrees to relocate to an economically depressed neighborhood of Chicago if the city can provide suitable property. The property needed is a large vacant lot owned by an investment partnership that refuses to sell. If the City of Chicago wants to relieve unemployment in the neighborhood and improve commercial conditions in the city by bringing in the manufacturer, what can the city legally do?
    A. Nothing; private real property is exempt from the power of eminent domain.
    B. Obtain title to the property by escheat through the provisions of Article I, Section 15, of the Illinois Constitution.
    C. Immediately obtain title through tacking.
    D. Exercise the right of eminent domain through a condemnation proceeding.

92. Illinois law requires that a preprinted offer to purchase that is intended to become a binding contract have which of these headings?
    A. Real Estate Sales Contract
    B. Offer to Purchase
    C. Standard Purchase Offer and Contract
    D. Purchase Offer Form

93. In 1971, a developer conveyed a motel and restaurant to an investor "on condition that no liquor is ever served on the property." The conveyance provided that if liquor were served on this property, ownership would revert to the developer. In 2014, the investor sold the motel and restaurant to his son. Based on these facts, which statement is *TRUE*?
    A. The sale of the motel and restaurant in 2014 extinguished the developer's right of reverter.
    B. Both the developer's right of reverter and the condition expired by operation of Illinois statute in 2000; the investor is free to sell the motel and restaurant without condition.
    C. While the condition continues forever, the developer's right of reverter expires after 40 years.
    D. Both the condition and the developer's right of reverter automatically expired in 2005.

94. A couple is married and both are Illinois residents. If their principal residence, with a mortgage of $50,000, is foreclosed on and sold for $165,000, how much money will be left over to satisfy any unsecured debt?
    A. Nothing
    B. $85,000
    C. $100,000
    D. $115,000

95. Which of these statements in a deed would establish a valid tenancy by the entirety in Illinois?
    A. "To A and B, a lawfully married couple, as tenants by the entirety"
    B. "To A and B, husband and wife, not as joint tenants or tenants in common but as tenants by the entirety"
    C. "To A and B jointly, as married tenants by the entirety"
    D. "To A and B as tenants by the entirety in accordance with Illinois law"

96. An ownership arrangement in which the purchaser receives a fee simple ownership in real property for longer than three years but the right to actually use the property for a specific period of less than one year (on a recurring basis) is a
    A. time-share use.
    B. time-share estate.
    C. public offering statement.
    D. membership camp.

97. Which of these would be required to be surveyed and have a plat recorded under the Illinois Plat Act?
    A. An owner divides a 30-acre parcel into five equal lots.
    B. An owner divides a 20-acre parcel into five equal lots.
    C. An owner conveys a single 20-acre parcel.
    D. An owner divides a single 20-acre parcel into two 6-acre lots and an 8-acre lot.

98. The general datum plane referred to by surveyors throughout Illinois is the
    A. Chicago City Datum.
    B. New York Harbor Datum.
    C. North American Vertical Datum.
    D. Centralia Datum.

99. While the identity of the beneficiary of a land trust is not usually disclosed without the beneficiary's written permission, under what conditions may the trustee be compelled to do so?
    A. When the information is demanded by the Illinois Department of Revenue
    B. During the discovery process of a lawsuit or criminal action not involving the property
    C. When a private request is filed in the public records office
    D. When applying to a state agency for a license or permit affecting the property

100. An owner paid the first installment of her Illinois general real estate tax on July 1. The amount due was $2,380. If the county assessor issued the owner's bill 30 days before the penalty date of June 1, does the owner owe any penalty?
    A. No; the penalty date for the payment of all Illinois general real estate taxes is September 1.
    B. Yes; the owner will have to pay $35.70 as a penalty in addition to the real estate tax owed.
    C. No; the assessor is required by statute to issue tax bills 60 days before any penalty date.
    D. Yes; the owner will have to pay $71.40 as a penalty in addition to the real estate tax owed.

101. A judgment issued by an Illinois court is a
    A. general, involuntary legal lien on all of a debtor's real property and an equitable, specific lien on the debtor's personal property.
    B. general, involuntary, equitable lien on both real and personal property owned by the debtor.
    C. specific lien on the debtor's real and personal property, effective for a nonrenewable period of five years.
    D. general, involuntary, equitable lien on both real and personal property, effective for renewable five-year periods.

102. A man owned property in Peoria before his marriage. The wife has no ownership interest in the property. The owner and his wife live in Chicago, and a tenant occupies the house in Peoria. If the owner wants to sell the property, who is required by law to sign the listing agreement?
    A. Both the owner and his wife because they are a married couple
    B. The owner only because he and his wife do not live in the house
    C. The owner and the tenant as tenant in possession
    D. The owner, his wife, and the tenant

103. A common item appearing in an Illinois listing agreement is
    A. a statement that the property must be shown only to certain prospective buyers because of race, color, religion, national origin, sex, handicap, or familial status.
    B. the time duration of the listing.
    C. the complete legal description of the property being sold.
    D. the proposed net sales price of the property.

104. In Illinois, which agency is responsible for licensing leasing agents?
    A. Division of Real Estate
    B. Department of Financial Institutions
    C. Illinois Department of Financial and Professional Regulation
    D. Department of Insurance Registration

105. In Illinois, when a sponsoring broker is taking a listing and asks the seller to complete a disclosure of property conditions,
    A. the disclosures are optional, and the seller may avoid liability by refusing to make any disclosures about the condition of the property.
    B. the standard disclosures cover a narrow range of structural conditions only.
    C. the sponsoring broker should give the seller advice regarding which property conditions to disclose and which to ignore.
    D. seller disclosure of known property conditions is required by Illinois statute.

106. How long must a claimant hold adverse, exclusive, continuous, and uninterrupted use of a property under claim of right in Illinois in order to obtain a prescriptive easement in Illinois?
    A. 10 years
    B. 17 years
    C. 20 years
    D. 30 years

107. An Illinois real estate licensee is the listing agent for a home. After one month of the three-month listing passes without any offers on the property, the licensee becomes concerned. At the time the listing agreement was signed, the licensee and the sellers orally agreed that if no offers were received after one month, the price of the property would be reduced by 10%. Because the sellers are out of town, the licensee crosses out the old listing price, writes in the new one, and then updates the information on the multiple listing service. Three days later, a prospective buyer comes into the listing licensee's office to make an offer on the property. Based on these facts, which of these statements is *TRUE*?
    A. Illinois licensees are prohibited by law from making any addition to, deletion from, or other alteration of a written listing agreement without the written consent of the principal.
    B. Although Illinois law usually prohibits altering a written listing agreement, the listing licensee acted properly in this situation because the sellers were out of town.
    C. Changing the listing price of a property is a matter of professional discretion, and Illinois licensees are permitted to make alterations to only that aspect of a listing agreement without the written consent of the principal.
    D. Although Illinois law usually prohibits altering a written listing agreement, the listing licensee acted properly in this situation because of the prior oral agreement with the sellers.

108. A sponsoring broker signs a listing agreement with a seller. The agreement contains the following clause: "If the property has not been sold after three months from the date of this signing, this agreement will automatically continue for additional three-month periods thereafter until the property is sold." Based on these facts, which of these statements is *TRUE*?
    A. The agreement is legal under Illinois law because it contains a reference to a specific time limit.
    B. This agreement is illegal in Illinois.
    C. Illinois law will automatically apply a statutory six-month listing period to this open listing.
    D. This agreement is legal under Illinois law because the time periods are for less than six months each.

109. Under a land contract in Illinois, what type of title does the purchaser have until the "final" closing when the obligation to seller is paid in full?
    A. Equitable title
    B. Full legal title
    C. Land title
    D. No title

110. How are members of the Illinois Real Estate Administration and Disciplinary Board selected?
    A. Appointed by the governor
    B. Appointed by the commissioner of real estate
    C. Elected by licensees
    D. Elected in statewide elections every six years

111. What is the advantage of seeking an injunction against a licensee who is violating the Real Estate License Act of 2000?
    A. The statute of limitations no longer applies.
    B. When the injunction is granted, it doubles the penalty for violations of the Act.
    C. It increases the offense to a felony.
    D. It stops the violation from continuing.

112. An Illinois licensee's license may be suspended or revoked for which of the following actions?
    A. Giving earnest money to his or her sponsoring broker rather than depositing it directly
    B. Being declared mentally incompetent
    C. Disclosing agency
    D. Displaying a For Sale sign on a property with the owner's consent

113. In Illinois, which of these is a required element of a valid deed?
    A. Specifically identified grantee
    B. Notarization of grantees' signature
    C. Hold harmless clause
    D. Name of the lender

114. An approximately straight line (except for corrections) connecting Rockford and Cairo is the
    A. Second Principal Meridian.
    B. Third Principal Meridian.
    C. Fourth Principal Meridian.
    D. Centralia Base Line.

115. A sponsoring broker received an earnest money deposit along with a sales contract from a buyer. Under Illinois law, what must the sponsoring broker do with the money?
    A. Open a special, separate escrow account that will contain funds for this transaction only, separate from funds received in any other transaction.
    B. Deposit the money in an existing special noninterest-bearing escrow account in which all earnest money received from buyers may be held at the same time.
    C. Immediately (or by the next business day) commingle the funds by depositing the earnest money in his personal interest-bearing checking or savings account.
    D. Hold the earnest money deposit in a secure place in his real estate brokerage office until the offer is accepted.

116. *Chicago Bar Association, et al. v. Quinlan and Tyson, Inc.*, established what principle in Illinois real estate law?
    A. Real estate sponsoring brokers must establish a special escrow account for earnest money deposits.
    B. The seller must bear any losses that occur before title to property passes or before the buyer takes possession.
    C. Real estate licensees may only fill in blanks and make appropriate deletions on preprinted standard form contracts.
    D. Once a contract is signed, a real estate licensee may not make any additions, deletions, or insertions without the written consent of the parties.

117. Under Illinois law, what is the statutory usury ceiling on loans secured by real estate?
    A. 10%
    B. 15%
    C. 22%
    D. No limit

118. A real estate licensee is aware that certain areas of the city are particularly unfriendly to members of certain minority groups. For these groups' own protection, the licensee shows members of such groups homes for sale only in "friendly" neighborhoods into which members of their minority group have moved in the past. Based on these facts, which of these statements is *TRUE*?
    A. The Real Estate License Act of 2000 does not prohibit the licensee's actions because the licensee is being protective rather than discriminatory.
    B. The critical element in this type of activity is profit motive; if the licensee's actions are not driven by increased profits, the licensee will not be subject to discipline under the Real Estate License Act of 2000.
    C. While the licensee's actions are clearly prohibited by Illinois statute, the Real Estate License Act of 2000 does not address blockbusting or steering.
    D. The licensee's actions are expressly prohibited by the Real Estate License Act of 2000.

119. The sale price of the property is $250,000. What is the Illinois state transfer tax on this transaction?
    A. $125
    B. $250
    C. $500
    D. $1,250

120. IDFPR may *NOT*
    A. conduct license examinations.
    B. issue and renew licenses.
    C. impose jail time on persons who violate license law.
    D. collect fees from applicants and licensees.

121. In Illinois, how must the real property transfer tax be paid?
    A. By personal check, made out to the Illinois Department of Revenue
    B. By certified check, made out to the Illinois Housing Development Authority
    C. By purchasing transfer tax stamps from the county recorder or appropriate local authority
    D. In monthly payments to the lender during the first five years of ownership

122. In Illinois, which property is totally exempt from paying general real estate taxes?
    A. Retirement housing for the elderly
    B. Properties financed with FHA funds
    C. Private schools
    D. Housing owned by a disabled veteran

123. A landlord has a "no pets" policy in his apartment building. If a visually impaired person wants to rent an apartment from the landlord, but owns a guide dog, which of these statements is *TRUE*?
    A. If the landlord's "no pets" policy is applied uniformly, in a nondiscriminatory manner, it may be legally applied to the guide dog as well.
    B. The Illinois Human Rights Act specifically prohibits the landlord from refusing to rent the apartment to the visually impaired person on the basis of the landlord's "no pets" policy.
    C. Under the Illinois Human Rights Act, the landlord may not discriminate against the visually impaired person on the basis of a "no pets" policy, but the landlord may require the tenant to pay an additional damage fee.
    D. The Illinois Human Rights Act does not address the issue of guide, hearing, or support dogs.

124. Real property was conveyed for $185,000. What amount will have to be paid in county transfer tax?
    A. $37.00
    B. $92.50
    C. $185.00
    D. $1,850.00

125. Which of these statements is *TRUE* of an Illinois county having fewer than 60,000 residents?
    A. The recorder of deeds must be elected.
    B. Deeds are recorded by the elected recorder of deeds in the nearest county having a population over 60,000.
    C. The city clerk of the largest population center acts as recorder of deeds.
    D. The county clerk also serves as recorder of deeds.

126. Which is a requirement for a deed to be recorded in Illinois?
    A. The name of the grantee typed or printed below the grantee's signature
    B. Payment of required tax stamps
    C. A blank page for use by the recorder
    D. The name, address, and age of the grantee

127. The purpose of the Real Estate Recovery Fund is to
    A. permit licensees to reestablish their businesses after a natural or financial disaster.
    B. reward consumers for identifying licensees who are engaged in violations of the real estate license law or other wrongful acts.
    C. compensate individuals who suffer losses due to the wrongful acts of a licensee.
    D. pay for the court costs and legal fees required to defend licensees against accusations of wrongdoing.

128. Which activity requires a real estate license?
    A. An MLS providing listing information to members
    B. A resident manager who collects rent on behalf of a building owner
    C. A service that, for a fee, matches individuals who want to buy and sell properties
    D. An executor selling a decedent's building

129. In Illinois, if the buyer of a property is a licensed broker,
    A. the buyer does not need to disclose this fact.
    B. this must be disclosed after closing.
    C. the buyer must only disclose if asked.
    D. this must be disclosed in writing to the parties to the transaction.

130. What is the name of the act that requires that Illinois developers file statements of record with HUD before they offer unimproved lots for sale in interstate commerce via telephone?
    A. HUD Registration Act
    B. Interstate Land Sales Full Disclosure Act
    C. Interstate Undeveloped Land Act
    D. NAFA

131. In Illinois, if an owner defaults on a mortgage loan and the property is ordered sold at a foreclosure sale, the owner may redeem the property
    A. before the sale, under the statutory right of redemption.
    B. before the sale, under the equitable right of redemption.
    C. after the sale, under the statutory right of redemption.
    D. after the sale, under the statutory right of reinstatement.

132. For three days, a man watched from his kitchen window as a small construction crew built an attractive gazebo in his backyard. The man had not contracted with anyone to build a gazebo and in fact had never given much thought to having one. But the man liked what he saw. When the contractor presented the man with a bill for the work, the man refused to pay, pointing out that he'd never signed a contract to have the work done. Can the contractor impose a mechanic's lien on the man's property under Illinois law?
    A. No; in Illinois, a mechanic's lien attaches on the date the contract is signed or the work is ordered, and neither event occurred here.
    B. No; the man cannot be forced to pay for the contractor's mistake.
    C. Yes; if a landowner knows of work being done on the property and does not object or disclaim responsibility, a mechanic's lien may be created.
    D. Yes; the man should have mailed a notice of nonresponsibility to the contractor's main place of business.

133. A woman's property in Peoria has an assessed value of $175,000. The local tax rate is 3%, and no equalization factor is used. If the tax was levied in April 2011, the woman had to pay
    A. $2,625 on January 1, 2012.
    B. $2,625 on June 1, 2012.
    C. $2,625 on September 1, 2011.
    D. $5,250 on June 1, 2011.

134. In Illinois, real estate licensees may
    A. complete a bill of sale after a sales contract has been signed.
    B. fill in blanks on preprinted form contracts customarily used in their community.
    C. suggest additional language to be added to a preprinted sales contract by a buyer or a seller.
    D. explain the legal significance of specific preprinted contract clauses to a buyer or a seller.

135. For which of the following acts is IDFPR required to suspend or revoke a licensee's license?
    A. Failing to perform as promised in a guaranteed sales plan
    B. Having been found liable in a civil trial for illegal discrimination
    C. Commingling others' money or property with the licensee's own
    D. Failing to provide information requested by IDFPR within 30 days of the request as part of a complaint or audit procedure

136. Three weeks before a man begins his Illinois real estate prelicense class, he offers to help his neighbor sell her house. The neighbor agrees to pay him a 5% commission. An offer is accepted while the man is taking the class and closes the day before the man passes the examination and receives his real estate license. The neighbor refuses to pay the man the agreed commission. Can the man sue to recover payment?
    A. Yes; because the man was formally enrolled in a course of study intended to result in a real estate license at the time an offer was procured and accepted, the commission agreement is binding.
    B. No; in Illinois, a real estate licensee must be sponsored by a broker who has a permanent office in affiliate licenses are displayed in order to collect a commission from a seller.
    C. Yes; while the statute of frauds forbids recovery on an oral agreement for the conveyance of real property, Illinois law permits enforcement of an oral commission contract under these facts.
    D. No; Illinois law prohibits lawsuits to collect commissions unless the injured party is a real estate licensee, and the license was in effect before the agreement was reached.

137. An Illinois real estate licensee may lawfully collect compensation from
    A. either a buyer or a seller.
    B. a sponsoring broker only.
    C. any party to the transaction or the party's representative.
    D. a licensed real estate broker only.

138. A woman has a mortgage loan secured by real property. Under recent law, the woman may terminate the loan's escrow account when the remaining balance is equal to or less than what percentage of the original amount?
    A. 35%
    B. 50%
    C. 65%
    D. 75%

139. Three people decide to form a partnership to buy and sell real estate. One partner plans to specialize in residential real estate, the second in commercial real estate, and the third does not plan to list, sell, or rent, but to supervise the office décor and plan holiday parties. Under these facts, which of the general partners needs to be licensed for the partnership to qualify for a broker's license in Illinois?
    A. None; under Illinois law, a partnership is an independent entity that may obtain a managing broker's license regardless of the status of any individual partner.
    B. Either of the two who are listing and selling, depending on whether the partnership's emphasis will be residential or commercial properties, must be licensed.
    C. All general partners in a general partnership must hold a broker or managing broker license.
    D. All three partners must be licensed real estate managing brokers.

140. Regarding mortgages, Illinois is most accurately described as
    A. an intermediate mortgage theory state.
    B. a lien-theory state.
    C. a title-theory state.
    D. an equitable-theory state.

141. Which of these is legal in Illinois?
    A. Offering finder's fees to consumers
    B. Giving referral fees to other licensees
    C. Using a lottery to convey the property
    D. Indicating a "standard commission" when asked

142. Regarding security deposits, what difference is there between requirements for the landlord of a three-unit apartment building and the landlord of a 30-unit apartment building?
    A. Both landlords must give tenants an itemized statement of alleged damages before they can withhold any part of the security deposit as compensation.
    B. Only the landlord of the 30-unit building is required to pay interest on security deposits.
    C. Only the landlord of the three-unit building is required to give tenants an itemized statement of alleged damages before any part of the security deposit may be withheld as compensation.
    D. Both landlords are required to pay interest on security deposits at a rate linked to minimum deposit passbook savings accounts at Illinois's largest commercial bank.

143. How many members are on the Illinois Real Estate Administration and Disciplinary Board?
    A. 6 members
    B. 8 members
    C. 9 members
    D. 15 members

144. In Illinois, how much written notice is a landlord required to give a tenant to pay overdue rent before terminating the lease, when the tenant is in default only for failing to pay rent on time?
    A. 0 days
    B. 3 days
    C. 5 days
    D. 10 days

145. In Illinois, if a home rule county has an ordinance that conflicts with that of a home rule city, whose ordinance will prevail?
    A. The county's ordinance
    B. The city's ordinance
    C. The relevant township ordinance
    D. None of these

146. A nonpossessory interest in real property is also called
    A. an encumbrance.
    B. a leasehold estate.
    C. a license.
    D. a servient tenement.

147. When a broker is representing her client, she is *MOST* likely acting as
    A. a universal agent.
    B. an ostensible agent.
    C. a special agent.
    D. a dual agent.

148. Which lien has priority in a foreclosure sale?
    A. First lien recorded
    B. Mechanics or materialmen who file a timely notice after commencing work on the property
    C. Delinquent property taxes
    D. Mortgagee or original lender

149. The individual appointed to the position of real estate coordinator
    A. may not have held a real estate license in the past.
    B. has their license put into inactive status for the duration of the appointment.
    C. must hold an active real estate license.
    D. must sign a statement that she will not pursue real estate activities that require a license during the appointment.

150. What is the penalty if a person is convicted of practicing real estate without first obtaining a real estate license?
    A. Fine of up to $5,000 and/or up to six months imprisonment
    B. Fine up to $10,000 but no prison
    C. Up to $25,000 for each offense
    D. Minimum of six months but no more than one year imprisonment

PRACTICE EXAM TWO

1. A landlord sold an apartment building so that a freeway can be built. The tenant's lease has expired, but the landlord permits him to stay in the apartment until the building is torn down. The tenant continues to pay the rent as prescribed in the lease. What kind of tenancy does the tenant have?
   A. Holdover tenancy
   B. Month-to-month tenancy
   C. Tenancy at sufferance
   D. Tenancy at will

2. The owner of a house wants to fence the yard for her dog. When the fence is erected, the fencing materials are converted to real estate by
   A. severance.
   B. subrogation.
   C. adaptation.
   D. attachment.

3. A man wants to sell his house as quickly as possible and believes that the best way to do this is to have several brokers compete against one another for the commission. The man's listing agreements with four different brokers specifically promise that if one of them finds a buyer for his property, the man will be obligated to pay a commission to that broker. What type of agreement has the man entered into?
   A. Executed
   B. Discharged
   C. Unilateral
   D. Bilateral

4. In some states, by paying the debt after a foreclosure sale, a borrower has the right to regain the property under the principle of
   A. novation.
   B. redemption.
   C. reversion.
   D. recovery.

5. A balloon loan is
   A. a straight loan.
   B. a term loan.
   C. a partially amortized loan.
   D. an illegal loan.

6. An investor hires a real estate licensee to locate suitable properties for investment purposes. When the licensee finds a property that the investor might be interested in buying, she is careful to find out as much as possible about the property's owners and why their property is on the market. The licensee's efforts to keep the investor informed of all facts that could affect a transaction is the common-law duty of
   A. care.
   B. truth.
   C. obedience.
   D. disclosure.

7. A parcel of vacant land 80 feet wide and 200 feet deep was sold for $200 per front foot. How much money would a broker receive for her 60% share in the 10% commission?
   A. $640
   B. $960
   C. $1,600
   D. $2,400

8. Which situation violates the federal Fair Housing Act of 1968?
   A. The refusal of a property manager to rent an apartment to a Catholic couple who is not otherwise qualified
   B. The general policy of a loan company to grant home improvement loans to qualified individuals living in transitional neighborhoods
   C. A widowed woman's insistence on renting her spare bedroom only to another widowed woman
   D. The intentional neglect of a broker to show an Asian family any property listings in all-white neighborhoods

9. A seller sold a 2-acre parcel for $1.50 per square foot. What was the total sales price?
   A. $65,340
   B. $87,120
   C. $130,680
   D. $174,240

10. A condo was purchased for $125,000. It appraised for $120,500 and previously sold for $118,250. Based on these facts, if the purchaser applies for an 80% mortgage, what amount of the loan will the purchaser receive?
    A. $94,600
    B. $96,400
    C. $100,000
    D. $106,750

11. A buyer and a seller both sign a purchase contract. What kind of title interest, if any, does the buyer have in the property at this point?
    A. Legal
    B. Equitable
    C. Defeasible
    D. None of these

12. Which of these federal laws requires that finance charges be stated as an annual percentage rate?
    A. Truth in Lending Act
    B. Real Estate Settlement Procedures Act (RESPA)
    C. Equal Credit Opportunity Act (ECOA)
    D. Federal Fair Housing Act

13. A seller signed a 90-day listing agreement with a sponsoring broker. Two weeks later, the seller was killed in an accident. What is the present status of the listing?
    A. The listing agreement is binding on the seller's estate for the remainder of the 90 days.
    B. Because the seller's intention to sell was clearly defined, the listing agreement is still in effect and the sponsoring broker may proceed to market the property on behalf of the seller's estate.
    C. The listing agreement is binding on the seller's estate only if the sponsoring broker can produce an offer to purchase the property within the remainder of the listing period.
    D. The listing agreement terminated automatically when the seller died.

14. A woman conveys ownership of an office building to a nursing home. The nursing home agrees that the rental income will pay for the expenses of caring for the woman's parents. When the woman's parents die, ownership of the office building will revert to the woman. The estate held by the nursing home is a
    A. remainder life estate.
    B. legal life estate.
    C. life estate pur autre vie.
    D. temporary leasehold estate.

15. A purchaser signs a buyer's brokerage agreement under which the licensee will help the purchaser find a three-bedroom house in the $285,000 to $300,000 price range. A seller comes into the licensee's office and signs a listing agreement to sell the seller's two-bedroom condominium for $170,000. Based on these facts, which of these statements is *TRUE*?
    A. The purchaser is the licensee's client; the seller is the licensee's customer.
    B. The purchaser is the licensee's customer; the seller is the licensee's client.
    C. While both the purchaser and the seller are clients, the licensee owes the fiduciary duties of an agent only to the seller.
    D. Because both the purchaser and the seller are the licensee's clients, the licensee owes the fiduciary duties of an agent to both.

16. In a township of 36 sections, which of these statements is *TRUE*?
    A. Section 31 lies to the east of Section 32.
    B. Section 18 is by law set aside for school purposes.
    C. Section 6 lies in the northeast corner of the township.
    D. Section 16 lies to the north of Section 21.

17. A lawyer represented the seller in a transaction. Her client informed her that he did not want to recite the actual consideration that was paid for the house. Based on these instructions, the lawyer
    A. must inform her client that only the actual price of the real estate may appear on the deed.
    B. may prepare a deed that shows only nominal consideration of $10.
    C. should inform the seller that either the full price should be stated in the deed or all references to consideration should be removed from it.
    D. may show a price on the deed other than the actual price, provided that the variance is not greater than 10% of the purchase price.

18. A sponsoring broker obtained a listing agreement to act as the listing agent in the sale of the client's home. When a buyer was found for the property, all agreements were signed. As an agent for the seller, the sponsoring broker is responsible for
    A. completing the buyer's loan application.
    B. making sure that the buyer receives copies of all documents the seller is required to deliver to the buyer.
    C. ensuring that the buyer is qualified for the new mortgage loan.
    D. scheduling the buyer's inspection of the property.

19. What is a real estate broker's share of the commission when the sales price of a property is $195,000 and the broker is entitled to 65% of the 7.5% commission?
    A. $950.63
    B. $8,872.50
    C. $9,506.25
    D. $95,062.50

20. If an appraiser is estimating the value of a property using the cost approach, which of these describes what the appraiser should do?
    A. Estimate the replacement cost of the improvements
    B. Deduct the depreciation of the land and buildings
    C. Determine the original cost and adjust for depreciation
    D. Review the sales prices of comparable properties

21. Three business days before the closing of a real estate loan transaction, a mortgage loan originator must provide the borrower with the Closing Disclosure (CD). This disclosure is in keeping with which of the following?
    A. Equal Credit Opportunity Act (ECOA)
    B. Truth in Lending Act
    C. TRID
    D. Fair Housing Act

22. The landlord of an apartment building neglected to repair the building's plumbing system. As a result, the apartments did not receive water, as provided by the leases. If a tenant's unit becomes uninhabitable, which of the following would *MOST* likely result?
    A. Suit for possession
    B. Claim of constructive eviction
    C. Tenancy at sufferance
    D. Suit for negligence

23. A man conveys a life estate to his sister. Under the terms of the man's conveyance, the property will pass to his niece upon his sister's death. Which of these *BEST* describes the niece's interest in the property during the sister's lifetime?
    A. Remainder
    B. Reversion
    C. Life estate pur autre vie
    D. Redemption

24. On a settlement statement, prorations for real estate taxes paid in arrears are shown as a
    A. credit to the seller and a debit to the buyer.
    B. debit to the seller and a credit to the buyer.
    C. credit to both the seller and the buyer.
    D. debit to both the seller and the buyer.

25. What type of lease establishes a rental payment and requires that the lessor pay for the taxes, insurance, and maintenance on the property?
    A. Percentage
    B. Gross
    C. Expense only
    D. Net

26. A conventional loan was closed on July 1 for $57,200 at 13.5% interest amortized over 25 years at $666.75 per month. On September 1, what would the principal amount be after the monthly payment was made?
    A. $56,533.25
    B. $56,556.50
    C. $57,065.35
    D. $57,176.75

27. In the preceding question, what would the interest portion of the payment be?
    A. $610.65
    B. $620.25
    C. $643.50
    D. $666.75

28. When a seller listed her home with a broker for $190,000, the seller told the broker, "I have to sell quickly because of a job transfer. If necessary, I can accept a price as low as $175,000." The broker then told a prospective buyer to offer $180,000 "because the seller is desperate to sell." The seller accepted the buyer's offer. Based on these facts, the broker
    A. did not violate his agency relationship with the seller because the broker did not reveal the seller's lowest acceptable price.
    B. violated his agency relationship with the seller.
    C. acted properly to obtain a quick offer on the seller's property, in accordance with the seller's instructions.
    D. violated his duties toward the buyer by failing to disclose that the seller would accept a lower price than the buyer offered.

29. Which of these *BEST* describes the capitalization rate under the income approach to estimating the value of real estate?
    A. Rate at which a property increases in value
    B. Rate of return a property earns as an investment
    C. Rate of capital required to keep a property operating most efficiently
    D. Maximum rate of return allowed by law on an investment

30. On a settlement statement, the cost of the lender's title insurance policy required for a new loan is usually shown as a
    A. credit to the seller.
    B. credit to the buyer.
    C. debit to the seller.
    D. debit to the buyer.

31. An FHA-insured loan for $57,500 at 8.5% for 30 years was closed on July 17, 2013. The first monthly payment is due on September 1. Because interest is paid monthly in arrears, what was the amount of the interest adjustment the buyer owes at the settlement, using the statutory month variation method?
    A. $183.96
    B. $230.80
    C. $407.29
    D. $4,887.50

32. A seller received an opinion of value from his listing agent of $255,000 for his property. He sold the property for $249,000. Which of the following is *TRUE*?
    A. $255,000 is the market price.
    B. $249,000 is the market price.
    C. $249,000 is the market value.
    D. The market value cannot be determined.

33. A woman has a contract to paint her brother's garage door for $1,200. Before starting the project, the woman has a skiing accident and breaks both arms. She asks a friend to take over the job. The friend paints the brother's garage door, and the brother pays the friend $1,200 for the work. This scenario is an example of
    A. assignment.
    B. acceptance.
    C. novation.
    D. revocation.

34. When searching the public record regarding title to a specific property, what is the researcher *MOST* likely to find?
    A. Encroachments
    B. Rights of parties in possession
    C. Inaccurate survey
    D. Judgments

35. A rectangular lot is worth $193,600. This value is the equivalent of $4.40 per square foot. If one lot dimension is 200 feet, what is the other dimension?
    A. 110 feet
    B. 220 feet
    C. 400 feet
    D. 880 feet

36. A sponsoring broker listed a seller's property at an 8% commission rate. After the property was sold and the settlement had taken place, the seller discovered that the broker had been listing similar properties at 6% commission rates. Based on this information alone, which of these statements is *TRUE*?
   A. The broker has done nothing wrong because a commission rate is always negotiable between the parties.
   B. If the broker inflated the usual commission rate for the area, the broker may be subject to discipline by the state real estate commission.
   C. The seller is entitled to rescind the transaction based on the principle of lack of reality of consent.
   D. The seller is entitled to a refund from the broker of 2% of the commission.

37. A woman has six months remaining on her apartment lease. Her monthly rent is $1,875. The woman moves out of the apartment, and her friend moves in. The friend pays the woman a monthly rental of $1,700, and the woman continues paying the full rental amount under her lease to the landlord. When the woman's lease term expires, her friend will either move out or sign a new lease with the landlord. This is an example of
   A. assignment.
   B. subletting.
   C. rescission and renewal.
   D. surrender.

38. One broker asked another, "Will I have to prove that I was the procuring cause if my seller sells the property himself?" The other broker answers, "No, not if you have an
   A. "option listing."
   B. "open listing."
   C. "exclusive-agency listing."
   D. "exclusive-right-to-sell listing."

39. The capitalization rate on a property reflects which of these factors?
   A. Risk of the investment
   B. Replacement cost of the improvements
   C. Real estate taxes
   D. Debt service

40. A woman just learned that the city would like to tear down three homes across the street and build a new multi-unit apartment building in their place. She wants to sell her home now, before the value decreases. This is an example of
   A. competition.
   B. conformity.
   C. anticipation.
   D. contribution.

41. A person who dies without having made a will is said to be
   A. a testate.
   B. a testator.
   C. in probate.
   D. intestate.

42. A farmer owns the W½ of the NW¼ of the NW¼ of Section 22. The remainder of the large NW¼ can be purchased for $300 per acre. Owning the remainder of the NW¼ of Section 22 would cost the farmer
   A. $6,000.
   B. $12,000.
   C. $42,000.
   D. $48,000.

43. In a standard sales contract, several words were crossed out or inserted by the parties. To eliminate future controversy as to whether the changes were made before or after the contract was signed, the usual procedure is to
   A. write a letter to each party listing the changes.
   B. have each party write a letter to the other approving the changes.
   C. redraw the entire contract.
   D. have both parties initial or sign in the margin near each change.

44. The manager of an apartment building receives an 8½% commission for each new tenant that he signs, based on the unit's annualized rent. In one year, the manager signed five new tenants. Three of the apartments rented for $795 per month; one rented for $900 per month; and one rented for $1,200 per month. What was the total amount of the manager's new-tenant commissions for that year?
   A. $381.23
   B. $2,952.90
   C. $3,685.47
   D. $4,574.70

45. The monthly rent on a warehouse is $1.85 per square foot. Assuming the warehouse is 36 feet by 200 feet, what is the total monthly rent?
   A. $370
   B. $7,200
   C. $13,320
   D. $16,552

46. A veteran wishes to refinance his home with a VA-guaranteed loan. The lender is willing, but insists on 3½ discount points. In this situation, the veteran can
   A. refinance with a VA loan, provided the lender charges no discount points.
   B. refinance with a VA loan, provided the lender charges no more than two discount points.
   C. be required to pay a maximum of 1% of the loan as an origination fee.
   D. proceed with the refinance loan and pay the discount points.

47. A father owns two properties. He conveys one property to his daughter with no restrictions; the daughter holds all rights to this property forever. The man then conveys the second property to his son "so long as no real estate licensee ever sets foot on the property." If a licensee visits the second property, ownership will revert to the father. Based on these two conveyances, which of these statements is *TRUE*?
   A. The daughter holds the first property in fee simple; the son holds the second property in fee simple determinable.
   B. The daughter holds the first property in fee simple absolute; the son holds the second property in fee simple defeasible, subject to a condition subsequent.
   C. The son may not transfer ownership of the second property without his father's permission.
   D. The father has retained a right of reentry regarding the second property.

48. A real estate transaction had a closing date of November 15. The seller, who was responsible for costs up to and including the date of settlement, paid the property taxes of $1,116 for the calendar year. On the closing statement, the buyer would be
   A. debited $139.50.
   B. debited $976.50.
   C. credited $139.50.
   D. credited $976.50.

49. An agreement that ends all future lessor-lessee obligations under a lease is called
   A. an assumption.
   B. a surrender.
   C. a novation.
   D. a breach.

50. A man buys a house for $234,500. He makes a $25,000 cash down payment and takes out a $209,500 mortgage for 30 years. The lot value is $80,000. If the man wants to depreciate the property over a period of 27½ years, how much will the annual depreciation amount be, using the straight-line method?
   A. $3,818.18
   B. $4,709.09
   C. $5,618.18
   D. $8,527.27

51. A property manager leased a store for three years. The first year, the store's rent was $1,000 per month, and the rent was to increase 10% per year thereafter. The manager received a 7% commission for the first year, 5% for the second year, and 3% for the balance of the lease. The total commission earned by the property manager was
   A. $840.
   B. $1,613.
   C. $1,936.
   D. $2,785.

52. Against a recorded deed from the owner of record, the party with the weakest position is a
   A. person with a prior unrecorded deed who is not in possession.
   B. person in possession with a prior unrecorded deed.
   C. tenant in possession with nine months remaining on the lease.
   D. painter who is half-finished painting the house at the time of the sale and who has not yet been paid.

53. An individual bought a home in 2014 for $346,000. Three years later, he sold the home for $374,800 and moved into an apartment. What amount of this transaction is taxable?
   A. $11,320
   B. $16,980
   C. $28,800
   D. None of it

54. A man moved into an abandoned home and installed new cabinets in the kitchen. When the owner discovered the occupancy, the owner had the man ejected. What is the status of the kitchen cabinets?
    A. The man has no right to the cabinets.
    B. The cabinets remain because they are trade fixtures.
    C. Although the cabinets stay, the man is entitled to the value of the improvements.
    D. The man can keep the cabinets if they can be removed without damaging the real estate.

55. A man, his nephew, and his niece are joint tenants. The man sells his interest to his sister, and then his nephew dies. As a result, which of these statements is *TRUE*?
    A. The nephew's heirs are joint tenants with the man and his sister.
    B. The nephew's heirs and the man are joint tenants, but the sister is a tenant in common.
    C. The man is a tenant in common with his sister's and nephew's heirs.
    D. The man's niece and the man's sister are tenants in common.

56. In a settlement statement, the selling price *ALWAYS* is
    A. a debit to the buyer.
    B. a debit to the seller.
    C. a credit to the buyer.
    D. greater than the loan amount.

57. The state wants to acquire a strip of farmland to build a highway. Does the state have the right to acquire privately owned land for public use?
    A. Yes; the state's right is called condemnation.
    B. Yes; the state's right is called eminent domain.
    C. Yes; the state's right is called escheat.
    D. No; under the U.S. Constitution, state or federal governments may never acquire private property.

58. A woman's estate was distributed according to her will as follows: 54% to her husband, 18% to her children, 16% to her grandchildren, and the remainder to her college. The college received $79,000. How much did the woman's children receive?
    A. $105,333
    B. $118,500
    C. $355,500
    D. $658,333

59. Which of these is an example of external obsolescence?
    A. Numerous pillars supporting the ceiling in a store
    B. Leaks in the roof of a warehouse, making the premises unusable and therefore unrentable
    C. Coal cellar in a house with central heating
    D. Vacant, abandoned, and run-down buildings in an area

60. Which of these phrases, when placed in a print advertisement, would comply with the requirements of the Truth in Lending Act?
    A. "12% interest"
    B. "12% rate"
    C. "12% annual interest"
    D. "12% annual percentage rate"

61. If an office building lease does not prohibit assignment or subletting, under what conditions, if any, may the tenant assign the space?
    A. Only to an associated corporation
    B. Only with any rent increase being split with the owner.
    C. After hiring legal counsel to obtain full rights to the lease.
    D. Freely

62. The Equal Credit Opportunity Act makes it illegal for lenders to refuse credit to or otherwise discriminate against
    A. a parent of twins who receives public assistance and who cannot afford the monthly mortgage payments.
    B. a new homebuyer who does not have a favorable credit history.
    C. a single person who receives public assistance.
    D. an unemployed person with no job prospects and no identifiable source of income.

63. When a woman died, a deed was found in her desk drawer. While the deed had never been recorded, it was signed, dated, and acknowledged. The deed gave the woman's house to a local charity. The woman's will, however, provided as follows: "I leave all of the real and personal property that I own to my beloved nephew." In this situation, the house *MOST* likely will go to the
    A. charity because acknowledgment creates a presumption of delivery.
    B. charity because the woman's intent was clear from the deed.
    C. nephew because the woman still owned the house when she died.
    D. nephew because the deed had not been recorded.

64. If a woman takes out a $90,000 loan at 7½% interest to be repaid at the end of 15 years with interest only paid annually, what is the total interest that the woman will pay over the life of the loan?
    A. $10,125
    B. $80,000
    C. $101,250
    D. $180,000

65. Jason, a listing agent, is sitting an open house for his client. Jessica, enters the open house and likes it. She begins to ask questions about how much she should offer and best negotiation tactics. Jason is happy to answer all of her questions. In this situation, which of the following is *TRUE?*
    A. Jason is acting as an undisclosed dual agent.
    B. As long as Jason has given Jessica a Disclosure of No Agency, he should be fine.
    C. Since Jessica verbally said she'd like help, Jason should answer all her questions.
    D. Jason should do what's necessary to make the deal happen.

66. To net the owner $90,000 after a 6% commission is paid, the selling price would have to be
    A. $95,400.
    B. $95,745.
    C. $95,906.
    D. $96,000.

67. Which of these would *MOST* likely be legal under the provisions of the Civil Rights Act of 1968?
    A. A lender refuses to make loans in areas in which more than 25% of the population is Hispanic.
    B. A private country club development ties home ownership to club membership, but due to local demographics, all club members are white.
    C. A church excludes African Americans from membership and rents its nonprofit housing to church members only.
    D. A licensee directs prospective buyers away from areas where they are likely to feel uncomfortable because of their race.

68. It is discovered after a sale that the purchased land parcel is 10% smaller than the owner represented it to be. The broker who transmitted the information concerning size of the parcel to the buyer is
    A. not liable as long as he only repeated the seller's data which he knew to be misrepresented.
    B. not liable if the misrepresentation was unintentional.
    C. not liable if the buyer actually inspected what she was getting.
    D. liable if he knew or should have known of the discrepancy.

69. On a residential lot 70 feet square, the side yard building setbacks are 10 feet, the front yard setback is 25 feet, and the rear yard setback is 20 feet. The maximum possible size for a single-story structure is how many square feet?
    A. 1,000
    B. 1,200
    C. 1,250
    D. 4,900

70. Which of the following is a purpose of the Real Estate Settlement Procedures Act (RESPA)?
    A. To ensure that there have been no hidden payments between service providers
    B. To make real estate brokers more responsive to buyers' needs
    C. To require use of a particular title insurance company
    D. To allow lenders to charge for services that were not performed

71. The rescission provisions of the Truth in Lending Act apply to which transactions?
    A. Agricultural loans
    B. Construction lending
    C. Business financing
    D. Consumer credit

72. A property has a net income of $30,000. An appraiser decides to use a 12% capitalization rate rather than a 10% rate on this property. What is the result of using the higher capitalization rate?
    A. 2% increase in the appraised value
    B. $50,000 increase in the appraised value
    C. $50,000 decrease in the appraised value
    D. No change in the appraised value

73. The section of a purchase contract that provides for the buyer to forfeit any earnest money if the buyer fails to complete the purchase is called the provision for
    A. liquidated damages.
    B. punitive damages.
    C. hypothecation.
    D. subordination.

74. In one commercial building, the tenant intends to start a health food shop using her life savings. In an identical adjacent building is a showroom leased to a major national retailing chain. Both tenants have long-term leases with identical rents. Which of these statements is *TRUE*?
    A. If the values of the buildings were the same before the leases, the values will be the same after the leases.
    B. An appraiser would most likely use a higher capitalization rate for the store leased to the national retailing chain.
    C. The most accurate appraisal method an appraiser could use would be the sales comparison approach to value.
    D. The building with the health food shop will probably appraise for less than the other building.

75. A builder wants to offer financial assistance to prospective buyers but does not want to lower the price of the homes. Instead the builder agrees to pay a lump sum in cash to the lender at closing so that the buyers will enjoy a lower interest rate. What type of loan is this?
    A. Equity
    B. Participation
    C. Open-end
    D. Buydown

76. A $100,000 loan at 12% could be amortized with monthly payments of $1,200.22 on a 15-year basis or payments of $1,028.63 on a 30-year basis. The 30-year loan results in total payments of what percent of the 15-year loan's total payments?
    A. 146%
    B. 158%
    C. 171%
    D. 228%

77. According to a broker's comparative market analysis (CMA), a property is worth $125,000. The homeowner bought the property for $90,000 and added $50,000 in improvements, for a total of $140,000. The property sold for $122,500. Which of these amounts represents the property's market price?
    A. $90,000
    B. $122,500
    C. $125,000
    D. $140,000

78. What will be the amount of tax payable where the property's assessed value is $85,000 and the tax rate is 4% in a community in which an equalization factor of 110% is used?
    A. $2,337.50
    B. $3,090.91
    C. $3,700.40
    D. $3,740.00

79. In a settlement statement, how will a proration of prepaid water, gas, and electric charges be reflected?
    A. Debit to the seller and a credit to the buyer
    B. Debit to the buyer and a credit to the seller
    C. Debit to the buyer only
    D. Credit to the seller only

80. An apartment manager decides not to purchase flood insurance. Instead, the manager installs raised platforms in the basement storage areas and has the furnace placed on eight-inch legs. This form of risk management is called
    A. avoiding the risk.
    B. controlling the risk.
    C. retaining the risk.
    D. transferring the risk.

81. A real estate broker was responsible for a chain of events that resulted in the sale of one of his client's properties. The broker is legally called the
    A. initiating factor.
    B. procuring cause.
    C. responsible party.
    D. compensable cause.

82. A characteristic of real estate licensees who are independent contractors is that they commonly receive
    A. more than 50% of income in the form of a monthly salary or hourly wage.
    B. company-provided health insurance and other benefits.
    C. reimbursement for documented travel and business expenses.
    D. more than 90% of income based on sales production.

83. In the cost approach to value, the appraiser makes use of the
    A. owner's original cost of the building.
    B. estimated current replacement cost of the building.
    C. sales prices of similar buildings in the area.
    D. assessed value of the building.

84. A buyer enters into an exclusive-agency buyer agency agreement with a real estate broker. Based on these facts, which of these statements is *TRUE*?
    A. The buyer is obligated to pay the broker's compensation regardless of who finds a suitable property.
    B. If the buyer finds a suitable property without the broker's assistance, she is under no obligation to pay the broker.
    C. The buyer may enter into other, similar agreements with other brokers.
    D. If the buyer finds a suitable property without the broker's assistance, the buyer will have to pay the broker's compensation.

85. Which of these is *TRUE* of a comparative market analysis (CMA)?
    A. A CMA is the same as an appraisal.
    B. A sponsoring broker, not an affiliate, is required to prepare a CMA.
    C. A certified real estate appraiser prepares a CMA.
    D. A CMA contains a compilation of other similar properties that have sold.

86. An owner sells his fourplex. Regarding this situation, which of these is *TRUE*?
    A. The tenants may void their leases.
    B. The lender may void the leases.
    C. The current leases must be honored by the new landlord.
    D. The current leases may be discharged by the previous landlord.

87. When appraising a single-family home, an appraiser considers which of these in determining the value of a property?
    A. Racial demographics
    B. Date sold
    C. Properties located within a 10-mile radius
    D. Pending property sales

88. Under TRID, a lender must extend the closing how many business days if the APR is increased by more than.125% before closing?
    A. Three
    B. Two
    C. Five
    D. Seven

89. One general rule of the federal do-not-call regulations is that
    A. states must maintain separate do-no-call lists.
    B. the national registry must be searched once a year.
    C. real estate offices are exempt from the laws because they are not telemarketers.
    D. it is illegal to make an unsolicited phone call to a number listed on the national registry.

90. Federal regulations on unsolicited email
    A. require commercial emails to include a physical address for the sender.
    B. require prior permission of recipients in order to send email to them.
    C. require that email lists be scrubbed every 31 days.
    D. exempt phone calls to individuals with whom the office has a prior business relationship.

In Illinois

91. A transaction is closing on May 2 in a non-leap year. Which of these is the proration of an annual charge of $560, using the statutory variation method?
    A. $188.78
    B. $189.68
    C. $190.78
    D. $191.98

92. Under Illinois law, what is the statutory ceiling on the prepayment penalty a lender may charge on loans secured by real estate that bear more than 8% annual interest?
    A. 1%
    B. 3%
    C. 8%
    D. None

93. A tenant agrees to rent an apartment for nine months under a verbal agreement with the landlord. If the tenant defaults, the landlord may
    A. not bring court action because of parol evidence rule.
    B. not bring court action because of the statute of frauds.
    C. bring a court action because one-year leases need not be in writing to be enforced.
    D. bring a court action because the statute of limitations does not apply to verbal leases.

94. What principle of landlord-tenant relations was established by the Illinois Supreme Court in 1972?
    A. Interest payments required on all security deposits
    B. Landlord damages for a tenant's failure to vacate the premises
    C. Implied warranty of habitability in residential tenancies
    D. Landlord may forcibly remove a tenant without court action under the doctrine of "self-help"

95. In Illinois, if a landlord purposely fails to maintain an apartment building's furnace and plumbing, what option is available to a tenant whose apartment is without heat and water during the first three months of winter?
    A. Suit for constructive eviction
    B. Suit for actual eviction
    C. Suit for forcible detainer
    D. Suit for negligent default

96. A woman pays $1,250 per month for her apartment. If she refers three new tenants to the building's owner during the year, how much is she entitled to receive under the Real Estate License Act of 2000 if the landlord's normal referral fee is $500 per new tenant?
    A. Nothing, unless she is a licensed real estate broker, managing broker, or rental-finding agent
    B. $1,000
    C. $1,250
    D. $1,500

97. Which of these properties are exempt from paying real estate taxes?
    A. Apartment complexes
    B. Industrial parks
    C. Shopping centers
    D. Educational institutions

98. Which of these is *TRUE* pursuant to the Illinois Human Rights Act?
    A. It is a civil rights violation to require, as a condition to the rental of an apartment, that the prospective tenant not have any children under 18 residing in her family at the time the rental application is made.
    B. It is legal to refuse to rent to a tenant because she has a service animal.
    C. It is legal to refuse to sell to a prospective purchaser because she has a service animal.
    D. It is legal to refuse to rent to a blind person if the landlord states safety concerns as the rationale for the refusal.

99. The Illinois Human Rights Act specifically exempts
    A. gender-based discrimination in housing intended for multigender occupancy.
    B. religious organizations giving preference in housing to nonmembers.
    C. a five-unit apartment building with a resident property manager living in one of the units.
    D. a three-unit apartment building with the owner living in one of the units.

100. Many of the residents of the landlord's apartment building are elderly, and some are in poor health. To ensure that they are not disturbed, the landlord politely declines to rent units to families or individuals who have young children. However, the landlord provides such persons with a printed list of nearby apartment buildings that welcome children. Based on these facts, which of these statements is *TRUE*?
    A. By providing a printed list of alternative comparable housing, the landlord is in full compliance with the Illinois Human Rights Act.
    B. Because the landlord's primary intent is to protect existing tenants' quality of life, and not to discriminate against prospective tenants who have young children, the Illinois Human Rights Act does not apply to this situation.
    C. The landlord's policy violates the Illinois Human Rights Act.
    D. While the landlord's policy, as stated, violates the Illinois Human Rights Act, he could add a "no children" provision to leases offered to new tenants and avoid violating the act.

101. What is the relationship between the Illinois agency statutes and the common law of agency?
    A. Illinois agency statutes supersede the common law of agency in Illinois.
    B. Illinois agency statutes and the common law of agency both govern agency relationships in Illinois.
    C. Agency statutes are simply an administrative codification of the common law of agency.
    D. The Illinois agency statutes govern managing broker's relationships with clients, while the common law of agency applies to broker relationships.

102. In regards to advertising, which of the following is *TRUE* in Illinois?
    A. The name of the sponsoring broker need not appear.
    B. The licensee's license number must appear in all advertisements.
    C. The name of the sponsoring broker must be in the same or larger font size than that of the licensee.
    D. As part of the name, team names may include the word *associates*.

103. A real estate sponsoring broker commonly names individual sponsored licensees in her brokerage office as the exclusive agents of certain clients, leaving the other sponsored licensees free to represent other parties in a transaction. Which of these statements is *TRUE* regarding this practice?
    A. Because it is a common office practice, it is permitted as an exception to the general statutory prohibition against such arrangements.
    B. Illinois agency law specifically permits designated agency arrangements such as this.
    C. This is an example of designated agency, which is an illegal relationship under Illinois agency law.
    D. The sponsoring broker will be considered an undisclosed dual agent under these facts and will be in violation of Illinois law.

104. A sponsoring broker decides to "sweeten" an MLS listing for a property by making a blanket offer of subagency. Is the sponsoring broker's action acceptable?
    A. Yes because Illinois law permits the creation of subagency relationships only through multiple listing services.
    B. Yes because a subagency relationship may be created by either a blanket offer in an MLS or through a specific agreement between parties.
    C. No because subagency is illegal under Article 15 of the Real Estate License Act of 2000.
    D. No because subagency relationships may not be offered through an MLS in Illinois.

105. A broker represents the seller in a transaction. When prospective buyers ask to look at the property, the broker must
    A. tell them that they must first enter into a buyer representation agreement with another licensee.
    B. clearly disclose in writing that the broker represents the seller's interests.
    C. inform them that if a transaction results, a dual agency may be the best course of action.
    D. show them the property without making any disclosures about the broker's relationship with the seller because the best time to close is at contract signing.

106. Several years ago, a unit in a condominium community was the site of a brutal and highly publicized murder. The unit was sold to an elderly woman who contracted the AIDS virus in a blood transfusion and died in the unit last year. What are the disclosure responsibilities to prospective purchasers of this unit?
    A. Agents must disclose both the murder and the AIDS-related death.
    B. Agents are specifically required to disclose the AIDS death and may (at seller discretion) disclose the murder.
    C. Agents are specifically prohibited by federal law from disclosing AIDS.
    D. Agents must not disclose the murder but should disclose the AIDS-related death.

107. The required amount of continuing education for an Illinois broker is
    A. 6 hours per year.
    B. 12 hours every year.
    C. 12 hours per renewal period.
    D. waived by examination.

108. Illegal discrimination might result in which of these actions?
    A. Loss of license
    B. Unlimited civil fines by the Department
    C. Reduced errors and omissions insurance premiums
    D. None of these

109. Sam, an active licensee, spends his days at Acme Real Estate solely answering the phone and processing closing documents.
    A. Sam is exempt from continuing education requirements.
    B. Processing closing documents is a licensed activity.
    C. He must have a written employment agreement with the sponsoring broker.
    D. Though licensed for the last two years, since Sam doesn't transact business, he will not be able to obtain a managing broker's license.

110. A buyer wants to have a clause included in the sales contract under which the seller offers assurances that no one has died in the home. Which of these statements is *TRUE* in Illinois?
    A. The licensee may include the clause because such standard disclosures are in general usage.
    B. Only the buyer or a licensed attorney may prepare the clause for inclusion in the sales contract.
    C. In Illinois, licensees are permitted to add additional clauses to blank form contracts, such as the clause described here, that do not directly involve the conveyance of title to real property.
    D. Under Illinois law, a clause such as the one described here is not permitted and any contract containing such a clause will be void.

111. A broker lists the seller's home. Under the terms of the agreement, when the property sells, the seller will receive a guaranteed $75,000. Any amount left over after the seller's $75,000 will constitute the broker's compensation. Based on these facts, which of these statements is *TRUE* in Illinois?
    A. This type of arrangement, called a guaranteed sales agreement, is illegal in Illinois, and the broker will be disciplined for entering into it.
    B. This type of arrangement, called a net listing, is illegal in Illinois, and the broker will be disciplined for entering into it.
    C. This is an example of a guaranteed sales agreement, which is permissible in Illinois if the broker provides the seller with the necessary disclosures.
    D. This is an example of a net listing, which is discouraged (but not illegal) in Illinois.

112. In Illinois, which of these in a listing agreement would result in the suspension or revocation of a licensee's license to practice real estate?
    A. A specified commission rate
    B. No specific termination date
    C. No broker protection clause
    D. A specific termination date

113. Under Illinois law, which disclosure must be included in an exclusive listing agreement?
    A. Anticipated seller closing costs
    B. Tax identification number
    C. Seller's net return
    D. Minimum services language

114. A married couple lives in Springfield, Illinois. The wife is the owner of their home. If the couple decides to sell their home and move to Wisconsin, who is required to sign the listing agreement?
    A. Both the husband and the wife must sign the listing.
    B. Because the wife is the sole owner of their home, she is the only party legally required to sign the listing.
    C. Because the husband and the wife are married, the signature of either spouse is legally sufficient.
    D. The husband is required to sign the listing only if the wife plans to use the capital gains exclusion.

115. From what source do Illinois local units of government receive their powers of eminent domain?
    A. A grant of authority signed by the governor
    B. Article 5 of the U.S. Constitution
    C. The Illinois Statehood Charter of 1818 and the Code of Administrative Procedure
    D. The Illinois Constitution and Code of Civil Procedure

116. A person dies without leaving a will. If the deceased owns real property in Illinois and has no heirs, what will happen to her real property?
    A. The deceased's real property will be taken by the county in which it is located under the power of eminent domain.
    B. Ownership of the deceased's real property will go to the state of Illinois through escheat.
    C. The deceased's property will escheat to the county in which it is located.
    D. The deceased's property will escheat to the county in which she last resided before her death.

117. Is there any limitation on an original grantor's right of reverter in Illinois?
    A. Yes; both an original grantor's right of reverter and the enforceability of the underlying condition expire by law after 20 years.
    B. Yes; the original grantor's right of reverter continues for 40 years; although the underlying condition remains enforceable.
    C. Yes; both the original grantor's right of reverter and the underlying condition automatically expire after 99 years.
    D. No; under Illinois law, there is no limitation on an original grantor's future interest.

118. Which of these is available to a surviving spouse in Illinois?
    A. Homestead
    B. Dower
    C. Curtesy
    D. A marital easement

119. How much of an estate of homestead is an individual entitled to in Illinois?
    A. $3,250
    B. $5,000
    C. $10,000
    D. $15,000

120. Which of these conducts is cause for discipline under the Real Estate License Act of 2000?
    A. Using misleading or untruthful advertising
    B. Violating the Illinois Human Rights Act
    C. Encouraging homeowners to sell when minorities move into the neighborhood
    D. All of these

121. Real property locations in Illinois are described by their geographic relation to
    A. the Fifth Principal Meridian.
    B. a government check.
    C. correction line F.
    D. the second, third, and fourth principal meridians.

122. How often is the assessed valuation of all real estate in Illinois adjusted by county authorities?
    A. Quarterly
    B. Annually
    C. Biennially
    D. Every three years

123. An Illinois resident was born on March 6, 2011. When will this person become of legal age?
    A. March 6, 2029
    B. March 7, 2029
    C. March 6, 2032
    D. March 7, 2032

124. If a minor enters into a contract in Illinois, what is the statutory period within which the minor may legally void the contract after reaching the age of majority?
    A. The statutory period is 6 months.
    B. The statutory period is 1 year.
    C. After the minor reaches the age of majority, the contract is binding.
    D. There is no statutory period.

125. Which of these is essential to the validity of a deed in Illinois?
    A. A seal (or the word *seal*)
    B. Acknowledgment
    C. Granting clause
    D. Recording

126. In Illinois, the amount of consideration used to determine transfer taxes must be shown on the
    A. Recording Form.
    B. Real Estate Declaration of Transfer.
    C. Blue Sheet.
    D. Tax Code Sheet.

127. How far back does a normal Illinois title search go?
    A. 15 years
    B. 40 years
    C. 75 years
    D. 125 years

128. Which of these are exempt from the provisions of the Real Estate License Act of 2000?
    A. Property owners who sell or lease property on behalf of others because they are familiar with the process
    B. Individual who is employed as a resident property manager
    C. Individual who engages in fee-based management services
    D. Individual involved in the business of selling equitable title to property more than twice in any 12-month periodr

129. Which of these is a requirement for obtaining an Illinois broker's license?
    A. Having successfully completed 45 hours of approved real estate courses
    B. Being at least 17 years of age
    C. Being of good moral character
    D. Having been actively engaged as a licensed broker for at least five years

130. A person who successfully completed her Illinois real estate education requirement on November 1, 2020, may take the state license exam no later than
    A. October 31, 2023
    B. December 31, 2023.
    C. October 31, 2022.
    D. November 1, 2024.

131. What is the expiration date of every broker's license in Illinois?
    A. The broker's birthday, every other year
    B. April 30 of each even-numbered year
    C. May 31 of each odd-numbered year
    D. Every other anniversary date of the individual broker's license

132. An Illinois sponsoring broker wants to open a branch office in a neighboring town. The sponsoring broker applies for a branch office license and gives the branch a name that clearly identifies its relationship with his main office. The sponsoring broker names a licensed Illinois residential leasing agent, as the designated managing broker. In this situation, will the sponsoring broker receive approval for the branch office?
    A. Yes; the sponsoring broker has fully complied with the requirements of the Real Estate License Act of 2000.
    B. No; under the Real Estate License Act of 2000, sponsoring brokers cannot have branch offices in more than one municipality.
    C. No; branch office management requires a special license.
    D. No; the manager of a branch office must hold a managing broker's license.

133. A licensee could tell that a prospective buyer would probably not make an offer if she knew the previous occupant of a property had died from complications related to AIDS and did not disclose that fact. An Illinois real estate broker set up a micro brokerage real estate services outlet in a convenience store by placing a desk at the end of the snack food aisle. A managing broker waited outside an AMP testing facility and handed out brochures to prospective licensees on their way in to take the real estate exam, encouraging them to apply for a job at his office. Which, if any, of these individuals is subject to disciplinary action for violating the Real Estate License Act of 2000?
    A. The licensee only
    B. The managing broker only
    C. All three licensed individuals
    D. Only the two brokers

134. Which of these is grounds for a disciplinary action?
    A. Being convicted of a felony in Illinois
    B. Advertising in a magazine that the broker is a member of the Chicago Association of REALTORS® when the broker is not
    C. Depositing escrow money into a personal account
    D. All of these

135. A licensee engaged in activities that constitute violations of the Illinois Human Rights Act, including blockbusting and discrimination on the basis of disability. The licensee also cashed a $25,000 earnest money check from a prospective buyer and used the proceeds to buy a new car. Despite rigorous management and oversight, the licensee's sponsoring broker was completely unaware of all of these activities. When the licensee's violations are brought to IDFPR's attention, which of these statements is *TRUE*?
    A. The sponsoring broker will probably not have his license revoked as a result of the licensee's violations.
    B. The licensee's sponsoring broker will be required to pay any fine imposed against the licensee out of his own personal funds.
    C. The licensee's violations are legally the responsibility of the sponsoring broker, who will be subject to the same disciplinary action as the licensee, regardless of whether he knew the violations had occurred.
    D. The licensee's sponsoring broker will be held liable for the Human Rights Act violations only.

136. A broker is convicted of a crime involving fraud in Wisconsin on November 9. On February 1 of the following year, the Wisconsin licensing agency notifies IDFPR of the conviction. Based on this information, which of these is *TRUE*?
    A. The broker should have called IDFPR first.
    B. IDFPR may refuse to renew the broker's license based on his Wisconsin conviction for a crime involving fraud.
    C. Because the conviction was not in Illinois, no discipline will occur.
    D. A conviction due to fraud does not constitute a violation of the Real Estate License Act of 2000.

137. Which of these accurately describes the review process for a final administrative decision of IDFPR?
    A. The accused may appeal a final administrative decision of IDFPR directly to the Illinois Supreme Court.
    B. The accused may petition the circuit court of the county in which the accused resides. The circuit court's decision may be appealed directly to the Illinois Supreme Court.
    C. The accused may petition the circuit court of the county in which the property involved in the transaction that gave rise to the violation is located. The circuit court's decision may be appealed directly to the federal district court.
    D. The accused may request a rehearing by IDFPR, but administrative decisions may not be appealed to any court.

138. Which of these is required to adopt a company policy manual?
    A. Sole proprietorship with no other sponsored licensees
    B. Self-sponsored broker with no sponsored licensees
    C. Brokerage company with sponsored licensees
    D. None of these

139. Every Illinois broker who applies for renewal of a license must successfully complete how many hours of continuing education courses in each two-year license renewal period?
    A. 6
    B. 8
    C. 9
    D. 12

140. Regarding mortgage theory, Illinois is usually described as
    A. a title-theory state.
    B. a lien-theory state.
    C. an intermediate mortgage-theory state.
    D. a security-theory state.

141. Twenty years ago, a man obtained a 30-year mortgage loan to purchase a home. The interest rate on the loan was 9.275%. Today, the man is prepared to pay off the loan early. Based on these facts, which of these statements is *TRUE* in Illinois?
    A. The man's lender is entitled by statute to charge the man a prepayment penalty equal to one year's interest on the current balance of the loan.
    B. The man's lender is permitted by Illinois statute to charge the man a prepayment penalty of no more than 8% of the current outstanding balance of the loan.
    C. Illinois does not take an official statutory position on the issue of prepayment penalties.
    D. Because the man's interest rate is greater than 8%, the lender may not charge a prepayment penalty under Illinois law.

142. In Illinois, if a landlord wants to terminate a year-to-year tenancy, how much notice must the tenant receive?
    A. 7 days
    B. 30 days
    C. 60 days
    D. 4 months

143. In Illinois, which of these is *TRUE* of an individual who wishes to engage only in the leasing of residential real property?
    A. The individual must obtain a broker's license and be employed by a broker who specializes in residential leases.
    B. The individual may obtain a certified leasing-agent designation by passing a test.
    C. The individual may obtain a residential leasing-agent license by completing 15 hours of instruction and passing a written examination.
    D. The individual may engage in residential leasing activities without obtaining a license or other certification.

144. In Illinois, which of these must be disclosed?
    A. Stigmatized property
    B. Dual agency
    C. Registered sex offenders
    D. Single agency

145. If an annual charge of $560 is prorated in October using the statutory variation method, which of these will be the resulting daily charge?
    A. $1.51
    B. $1.53
    C. $1.54
    D. $1.56

146. In Illinois, the closing statement is customarily prepared by the
    A. buyer's attorney.
    B. buyer's broker.
    C. seller's broker.
    D. seller's attorney.

147. Zoning ordinances may regulate
    A. water usage.
    B. deed restrictions.
    C. restrictive covenants.
    D. density.

148. Which of these is *TRUE* regarding option contracts?
    A. An option contract is classified as a unilateral contract.
    B. An option contract that has been exercised is classified as a bilateral contract.
    C. The option money may not be applied toward the purchase price.
    D. The seller is the optionee, and the buyer is the optionor.

149. Grounds for discipline under the Real Estate License Act of 2000 include
    A. disclosing dual agency.
    B. representing a broker other than the sponsoring broker.
    C. advertising the sponsoring broker's name in the advertisement.
    D. maintaining an escrow account to hold earnest money deposits.

150. Which of these will terminate a listing contract?
    A. Only the seller agreeing to cancel because it is a unilateral decision of the client.
    B. The foreclosure of the neighbor's property will terminate the contract.
    C. The death of the seller will terminate the contract.
    D. There is no cancellation provision in listing contracts.

PRACTICE EXAM THREE

1. Under the Real Estate License Act of 2000, which of these could work in a limited way indefinitely without a specific license?
   A. Transaction manager hired by a sponsored broker
   B. Residential leasing agent hired by a property management company
   C. Residential leasing agent working independently
   D. Broker working independently

2. The number of hours of continuing education that can be taken in one day
   A. is not regulated by the law.
   B. can be up to 12 hours.
   C. cannot be more than nine hours.
   D. cannot be more than 6 hours.

3. Why is early discussion of agency so important under the Real Estate License Act of 2000?
   A. Working with a consumer may now be construed as an implied agency if nothing else has been stated.
   B. Working with a consumer may compel the consumer to pay a commission, whether a written agreement exists or not.
   C. If nothing is stated, subagency may be in effect.
   D. If nothing is stated, a minimum hourly fee may be demanded after the fact.

4. Prelicense courses will have to be retaken if a license has been expired for more than
   A. 6 months.
   B. 1 year.
   C. 18 months.
   D. 2 years.

5. Under the Real Estate License Act of 2000, a buyer to whom a licensee is showing houses under a buyer-brokerage agreement is considered to be
   A. without a formal relationship.
   B. a customer.
   C. a client.
   D. a possible client.

6. Which of these statements could an Illinois buyer's agent appropriately make to a buyer client?
   A. "Here are the CMAs. I think they suggest the highest range you should pay is about $110,000–$120,000, but that's up to you."
   B. "The listing agent said the floors underneath the carpet are oak. Isn't that great?"
   C. "I know this neighborhood. Don't worry about radon."
   D. "There really isn't any way to get a list of released sex offenders' addresses in Illinois."

7. Employment agreements with a sponsoring broker must cover at *LEAST*
   A. supervision, duties, referral fees, and MLS requirements.
   B. referral fees, commission splits, and cooperation with other brokers.
   C. supervision, duties, compensation, and termination.
   D. salary and benefits agreed on.

8. Who needs to disclose material facts related to a transaction in Illinois?
   A. Listing agent
   B. Buyer's agent
   C. Sellers
   D. All of these, if they have material information

9. What is *TRUE* of licensees under the Real Estate License Act of 2000?
   A. Whenever the company name does appear, it must be in letters the same size or larger than the sponsored broker's name.
   B. Social media accounts are not covered by the Act.
   C. They are usually paid directly by the person who selected them and with whom they work most closely.
   D. They need an employment agreement with the sponsoring broker and must be paid by the sponsoring broker.

10. What is *TRUE* about real estate advertising in Illinois under the Real Estate License Act of 2000?
    A. The company name must appear in a print ad for houses.
    B. Whenever the company name does appear, it must be in letters larger than the sponsored broker's name.
    C. Links on a broker's real estate website must routinely be approved by IDFPR.
    D. The company name is usually not needed on a website.

11. Which of these does *NOT* need to be disclosed in Illinois?
    A. To a buyer: the fact that the seller is also a client
    B. To a seller's agent: the fact that the buyer client qualifies for the purchase price with only $5,000 to spare
    C. To a customer who is just starting to work with the licensee: he is a customer, but that agency is possible and may very quickly be presumed in Illinois if nothing else is said
    D. To a buyer client: the fact that the licensee holds a 1.1% interest in a property he wants to buy

12. Who may pay compensation to a broker in Illinois?
    A. Listing agent in the office
    B. Sponsoring broker
    C. Title company
    D. Mortgage company

13. Which of these may be offered to an Illinois licensee for referring business to a lawyer or loan officer?
    A. A weekend in Peoria
    B. A small stereo
    C. A cash amount less than $200
    D. None of these

14. For which of these could a licensee be late in Illinois without affecting license renewal?
    A. Student loans
    B. Illinois income tax
    C. Child support
    D. Mortgage payment

15. Under the Real Estate License Act of 2000, when the license of any sponsoring broker is suspended or revoked, what is *TRUE* regarding sponsored licensees' agreements with that sponsoring broker?
    A. They expire on the date of suspension.
    B. Each licensee has 10 days in which to find another sponsoring broker.
    C. A licensee can continue to work through the suspension.
    D. The licensee has 30 days in which to finish all deals.

16. Which of these licensee statements is *NOT* appropriate in Illinois?
    A. Licensee answering a call-in customer's question: "The standard commission is 6%."
    B. Listing agent to buyer's agent: "List price is $200,000, but my seller will probably sell for about $195,000."
    C. Buyers' agent to listing agent: "My buyers need to buy this weekend, so I think we can get this deal together."
    D. All of these.

17. When a broker passes the license examination
    A. they should apply for their license through the IDFPR portal.
    B. they have their sponsoring broker fill out the required paperwork.
    C. they receive their license from the testing center.
    D. they have to take the post-license course before securing their license.

18. What should a buyer's agent check first if a buyer indicates he does *NOT* want to buy a home in a floodplain?
    A. The listings in the MLS computer
    B. Floodplain maps for the area.
    C. The seller's disclosure form for a given home
    D. House addresses available through FEMA

19. What is the guideline for when agency should be disclosed in Illinois?
    A. No later than 48 hours after meeting a customer
    B. No later than 72 hours after meeting a customer
    C. As early as possible
    D. During negotiations

20. Which of these is *TRUE* concerning dual agency in Illinois?
    A. Dual agency is never allowed.
    B. Dual agency need not be disclosed.
    C. Dual agency is permitted so long as the buyer and the seller are informed and consent to the representation of both in writing.
    D. Dual agency is permissible so long as a transactional arbitrator is brought in to facilitate the transaction.

21. Under the Real Estate License Act of 2000, what must be in writing?
    A. Grantee's signature on the deed
    B. All listings
    C. Exclusive-agency and exclusive-right-to-sell listings
    D. Agency between a buyer and a broker

22. A broker placed the following order with the telephone company: "List my name in the directory under the heading Real Estate as 'John Smith, Real Estate Broker, Residential Property is My Specialty.'" The broker is also required to include
    A. his license number.
    B. the expiration date of his license.
    C. his street address.
    D. the name of his employing (sponsoring) broker.

23. Who designates a sponsored broker in Illinois to act as a designated agent?
    A. The state
    B. The seller or the buyer
    C. The broker himself, in signing a client agreement
    D. The sponsoring broker

24. Actions being brought against licensees under Article 15 (Agency Relationships) of the Real Estate License Act of 2000 must be taken
    A. within five years after the facts become known.
    B. within one year after the facts become known.
    C. any time after the closing if negligence can be proven.
    D. within six months after closing.

25. Under the Real Estate License Act of 2000, which of these statements is *TRUE*?
    A. The person with whom a licensee works is always a customer if nothing else is said.
    B. The person with whom a licensee works is a client if nothing else is said.
    C. The person who works with buyers who do not want client status is called their agent.
    D. A client becomes a client only when the agency agreement is signed.

26. Who pays a licensed residential leasing agent?
    A. The owner of the properties being rented
    B. The tenant
    C. The sponsoring broker
    D. The previous tenant

27. How long may an individual work as a residential leasing agent without a license in Illinois, provided the agent is working to obtain a license and has a proper sponsor?
    A. 30 days
    B. 90 days
    C. 120 days
    D. 130 days

28. An Illinois licensee has listed a property whose owner had AIDS. The licensee should
    A. note that the owner had AIDS at the bottom of the disclosure sheet, per federal law.
    B. note that the owner had AIDS at the bottom of the disclosure sheet, per state law.
    C. do what seems right; there is no specific obligation to disclose, but if the agent feels it is best for all parties, the agent may do so.
    D. not mention this to anyone, unless the owner directs the agent to do so.

29. Which of these is *TRUE* about residential leasing agents in Illinois?
    A. Residential leasing agents in Illinois may operate independently as long they are approved by IDFPR.
    B. While residential leasing agents are not licensed, a test indicating basic competence must be passed to work as a residential leasing agent.
    C. Residential leasing agents must have a sponsoring broker.
    D. Residential leasing agents may work without a license for 130 days if properly supervised.

30. A buyer's agent is showing properties to a young mother of three children whose safety is paramount to her. Which of these is *NOT* appropriate?
    A. The agent tells the mother she can check addresses of convicted but released sex offenders online.
    B. The agent decides to show only certain neighborhoods.
    C. The licensee checks properties surrounding an interesting subject property carefully for any signs of oil leaks, USTs, formaldehyde odors, gas odors, bogs, or fire/explosion hazards.
    D. The buyer's agent recommends radon testing, carbon monoxide detectors, and water testing.

31. Under the Real Estate License Act of 2000, which of the following is not identified as compensation?
    A. Cash.
    B. Lottery ticket.
    C. Raffle drawing.
    D. A "thank you".

32. How much do local (city or town) tax stamps in Illinois cost?
    A. $1.50 per $1,000
    B. $2.00 per $500
    C. Vary by street
    D. Vary by town

33. In Illinois, if a sponsored broker leaves one firm to go to another, the broker's listings
    A. automatically go with the agent.
    B. stay with the sponsoring broker unless the employment agreement stipulates otherwise.
    C. are canceled.
    D. are left to the discretion of the sellers.

34. A licensee must have the owners' written consent to advertise their house
    A. in a newspaper.
    B. by putting up a yard sign.
    C. online.
    D. in all of these ways.

35. In Illinois, which type of deed becomes null and void after one year if it is not recorded?
    A. General warranty deed
    B. Special warranty deed
    C. Bargain and sale deed
    D. Tax deed

36. An expired real estate license may be renewed in Illinois for
    A. one year.
    B. two years.
    C. three years.
    D. five years.

37. Which of these escrow records must be kept by a broker?
    A. Journal
    B. Ledger
    C. Monthly reconciliation statements
    D. All of these

38. The principal to whom a real estate agent gives advice and counsel is a
    A. subagent.
    B. customer.
    C. client.
    D. fiduciary.

39. The Real Estate Recovery Fund was
    A. established to provide a means of compensating people who have been harmed by a licensee's negligence.
    B. created to provide licensees with errors and omissions insurance.
    C. established to provide up to $100,000 for losses.
    D. created to recover escrow losses.

40. The *MOST* important purpose of the Real Estate License Act of 2000 is to
    A. protect the public.
    B. protect the real estate industry from fraudulent practices.
    C. regulate real estate businesses.
    D. regulate real estate practitioners.

41. Real estate licensees in Illinois must disclose
    A. minor problems in the neighborhood of which they have knowledge.
    B. designated agency.
    C. special compensation found outside the scope of their agency relationship.
    D. all of these.

42. Which appraisal licensing category allows an appraiser to appraise residential property of one unit to four units without regard to transaction value or complexity?
    A. Associate trainee real estate appraiser
    B. Certified residential appraiser
    C. Certified general real estate appraiser
    D. None of these

43. Escrow records must be maintained for at *LEAST*
    A. 3 years.
    B. 5 years.
    C. 7 years.
    D. 10 years.

44. Illinois recognizes which of the following estates?
    A. Homestead
    B. Curtesy
    C. Dower
    D. Community property

45. In Illinois, in order to be eligible for a homestead estate, an owner must
    A. file an eligibility form with the state agency.
    B. have an equity interest in the property.
    C. be married.
    D. reside in the property.

46. What is the composition of the Real Estate Administration and Disciplinary Board?
    A. Six members elected by the public
    B. Eight members elected by local associations of REALTORS®
    C. Eight members appointed by the director
    D. Fifteen members appointed by the governor

47. When does a residential leasing agent's license expire?
    A. On the date it was first acquired, every two years
    B. On July 31 of each even-numbered year
    C. On April 30 of each odd-numbered year
    D. On January 1, every third year

48. Which of these may *NOT* be offered to consumers in Illinois?
    A. Coupons to the local grocery store if they list
    B. Discounts on commission if they list
    C. A new television if they buy
    D. A finder's fee for referring client prospects

49. Which of these would *NOT* happen for offenses noted in the Real Estate License Act of 2000?
    A. $5,000 fine
    B. $25,000 fine
    C. License revoked
    D. Commissions seized

50. An unlicensed individual who engages in activities for which a real estate license is required is subject to which of these penalties?
    A. A fine not to exceed $1,000
    B. A fine not to exceed $5,000 and one-year imprisonment
    C. A civil penalty of $25,000 per count in addition to possible other penalties stipulated by law
    D. A civil penalty not to exceed $25,000 and a mandatory prison term not to exceed five years

ANSWER KEY

The following are the correct answers for the unit quiz questions and practice exams. In parentheses following the correct answers are references to the pages where the question topics are discussed or explained.

Questions that involve math are marked with an asterisk (*); suggested calculations for these questions are on pages 525–527.

If you answer a question incorrectly, go back and restudy the material until you understand the correct answer.

Unit 1 Quiz Answers	Unit 2 Quiz Answers	Unit 3 Quiz Answers
1. **C (2)**	1. **C (12–13)**	1. **A (27)**
2. **B (6)**	2. **B (18)**	2. **B (27–28)**
3. **D (6)**	3. **D (14)**	3. **A (27)**
4. **C (7)**	4. **C (16)**	4. **C (26)**
5. **A (2)**	5. **D (15)**	5. **A (26)**
6. **D (4)**	6. **C (13)**	6. **A (26)**
7. **B (7)**	7. **C (18)**	7. **A (28)**
8. **C (3)**	8. **A (14)**	8. **A (28)**
9. **D (4)**	9. **A (17)**	9. **D (29)**
10. **A (5)**	10. **C (17)**	10. **C (28)**
11. **C (6)**	11. **B (16)**	11. **D (27)**
12. **B (2)**	12. **A (18)**	12. **C (26)**
13. **C (6)**	13. **D (13)**	13. **A (27–28)**
14. **A (5)**	14. **D (12)**	14. **D (27–28)**
15. **D (7)**	15. **A (15)**	15. **C (26)**
16. **D (7)**	16. **B (13)**	16. **A (27)**
17. **B (3)**	17. **D (15)**	17. **D (28)**
18. **C (6)**	18. **C (18)**	18. **C (29)**
19. **B (2)**	19. **B (14)**	19. **B (29)**
20. **B (7)**	20. **C (16)**	20. **A (27)**

Unit 4 Quiz Answers

1. D (36)
2. A (50)
3. B (38)
4. C (54)
5. A (50)
6. A (49)
7. B (36)
8. A (37)
9. B (38)
10. C (54)
11. A (37)
12. B (38)
13. D (45)
14. A (53)
15. C (46)
16. D (37)
17. A (38)
18. A (54)
19. B (54)
20. C (50)

Unit 5 Quiz Answers

1. A (77)
2. C (67)
3. A (78)
4. D (77)
5. D (80)
6. C (77)
7. A (67)
8. B (81)
9. B (80)
10. B (80)
11. C (82)
12. D (83)
13. C (82)
14. A (67)
15. B (67)
16. D (66)
17. A (77)
18. B (78)
19. B (67)
20. B (82)

Unit 6 Quiz Answers

1. B (89)
2. C (90–91)
3. A (114)
4. C (90)
5. C (96–97)
6. A (91)
7. A (90–91)
8. D (93)
9. A (89)
10. B (96–97)
11. C (104)
12. C (93–94)
13. A (96–97)
14. C (96–97)
15. B (91)

16. C (106)
17. C (91–92)
18. D (112)
19. C (106)
20. A (90)

Unit 7 Quiz Answers

1. B (122)
2. C (125)
3. D (125)
4. B (130)
5. C (124)
6. B (131)
7. A (133)
8. A (122)
9. B (125)
10. A (130)
11. B (128)
12. C (127)
13. D (133)
14. D (129)
15. B (132)
16. C (128)
17. B (132)
18. C (131–132)
19. A (123)
20. D (131)

Unit 8 Quiz Answers

1. B (141)
2. C (140–141)

3. **A (140–141)**

4. **D (145)**

5. **C (150)**

6. **A (151)**

7. **D (140)**

8. **A (141)**

9. **C (143)**

10. **A (141–142)**

11. **C (150)**

12. **B (141, 143)**

13. **A (142)**

14. **A (141)**

15. **D (145–146)**

16. **A (143)**

17. **C (147)**

18. **B (140–141)**

19. **C (142)**

20. **B (149)**

Unit 9 Quiz Answers

1. **C (164–165)**

2. **A (164)**

3. **A (158)**

4. **B (162)**

5. **D (162)**

6. **A (162)**

7. **D (162)**

8. **C (163)**

9. **A (159)**

10. **C (163)**

11. **D (163)**

12. **A (163)**

13. **B (163)**

14. **C (163)**

15. **D (162)**

16. **B (163)**

17. **A (159–160)**

18. **C (166)**

19. **D (166)**

20. **A (166)**

Unit 10 Quiz Answers

1. **C (174)**

2. **C (175)**

3. **D (176)**

4. **D (174)**

5. **C (175)**

6. **A (178)**

7. **C (176)**

8. **A (182)**

9. **D (178)**

10. **C (182)**

11. **A (183)**

12. **B (181)**

13. **A (182)**

14. **D (182)**

15. **C (176)**

16. **A (176)**

17. **B (178)**

18. **B (175)**

19. **A (181)**

20. **B (179)**

Unit 11 Quiz Answers

1. **B (191)**

2. **C (196)**

3. **D (192)**

4. **D (193)**

5. **A (198)**

6. **D (199)**

7. **B (216)**

8. **D (217)**

9. **B (202)**

10. **A (218)**

11. **C (192)**

12. **C (193)**

13. **D (193)**

14. **A (193)**

15. **B (218)**

16. **A (199)**

17. **C (202)**

18. **A (197–200)**

19. **D (199)**

20. **A (218)**

Unit 12 Quiz Answers

1. **B (226)**

2. **A (226)**

3. **C (226)**

4. **D (228)**

5. **B (229–231)**

6. **C (229)**

7. **D (230)**

8. **C (228)**

9. **B (228)**

10. **D (234)**

11. **A (233)**

12. **A (229)**

13. **B (235)**

14. **D (235)**

15. **B (234)**

16. **C (235)**

17. **B (231–232)**

18. **A (231)**

19. **C (235)**

20. **A (235)**

Unit 13 Quiz Answers

1. **C (242)**

2. **D (242)**

3. **B (244)**

4. **C (243)**

5. **D (245)**

6. **A (244)**

7. **D (244)**

8. **B (244)**

9. **A (245)**

10. **C (245)**

11. **B (244)**

12. **A (247)**

13. **D (247)**

14. **C (246–247)**

15. **D (246)**

16. **B (243)**

17. **A (242)**

18. **C (242)**

19. **A (242)**

20. **A (242)**

Unit 14 Quiz Answers

1. **B (254–255, 260)**

2. **C (257)**

3. **D (264)**

4. **C (264)**

5. **A (280)**

6. **C (281)**

7. **A (263)**

8. **D (271–272)**

9. **A (267)**

10. **C (277)**

11. **A (254–255)**

12. **D (276)**

13. **A (282)**

14. **B (274)**

15. **D (276)**

16. **A (273)**

17. **C (264)**

18. **C (260)**

19. **A (281)**

20. **D (271–272)**

Unit 15 Quiz Answers

1. **C (290)**

2. **C (291–292)**

3. **D (291–292)**

4. **B (291–292)**

5. **D (296)**

6. **A (298–299)**

7. **C (292)**

8. **B (296)**

9. **A (290)**

10. **D (288)**

11. **A (300)**

12. **D (290)**

13. **A (298–299)**

14. **C (299–300)**

15. **B (293)**

16. **B (300)**

17. **C (294)**

18. **B (289)**

19. **A (298–299)**

20. **D (298–299)**

Unit 16 Quiz Answers

1. **A (316)**

2. **B (317)**

3. **D (307–308)**

4. **C (312)**

5. **D (310)**

6. **C (306)**

7. **D (312)**

8. C (316)

9. D (314–315)

10. A (310)

11. B (308)

12. C (309)

13. D (310)

14. C (310)

15. A (313)

16. D (311)

17. C (27, 31)

18. B (318)

19. B (318)

20. D (316)

Unit 17 Quiz Answers

1. A (335)

2. D (334)

3. B (332)

4. C (334)

5. D (332–333)

6. D (328)

7. A (326)

8. B (326)

9. C (332)

10. C (327)

11. D (328)

12. C (334)

13. C (334)

14. D (326)

15. C (330)

16. D (327)

17. C (330–331)

18. B (336)

19. A (327)

20. A (338)

Unit 18 Quiz Answers

1. B (355)

2. D (350)

3. C (354)

4. C (350)

5. B (355)

6. A (349)

7. B (354)

8. C (352–353)

9. D (352)

10. C (349)

11. A (349)

12. D (354–355)

13. A (355)

14. B (349–350)

15. C (352)

16. C (347)

17. B (353)

18. C (350–351)

19. D (351, 356)

20. C (351)

Unit 19 Quiz Answers

1. A (370)

2. C (362)

3. D (364)

4. C (362)

5. D (364)

6. B (364)

7. A (369)

8. B (373)

9. D (371)

10. C (366–367)

11. B (370)

12. B (362)

13. B (370–371)

14. C (368)

15. C (371)

16. B (365)

17. C (368–369)

18. A (373)

19. A (369)

20. A (360–361)

Unit 20 Quiz Answers

1. D (392)

2. C (389)

3. B (392)

4. D (387)

5. A (390)

6. B (387)

7. D (389)

8. B (387)

9. C (390–392)

10. C (392)

11. **C (390)**

12. **A (391)**

13. **D (391)**

14. **A (387)**

15. **C (386)**

16. **A (387)**

17. **A (393)**

18. **D (386)**

19. **A (387)**

20. **A (386)**

Unit 21 Quiz Answers

1. **A (405)**

2. **B (406)**

3. **B (400)**

4. **B (406)**

5. **D (406–407)**

6. **D (407)**

7. **A (403)**

8. **A (408)**

9. **D (400)**

10. **D (407)**

11. **A (405–406)**

12. **A (403)**

13. **C (401, 405)**

14. **B (403–404)**

15. **C (407)**

16. **C (404)**

17. **A (404)**

18. **D (408–409)**

19. **C (408–409)**

20. **A (408–409)**

Unit 22 Quiz Answers

1. **C (416)**

2. **D (416–417)**

3. **D (417)**

4. **A (416–417)**

5. **B (423)**

6. **C (420)**

7. **D (425)**

8. **D (425)**

9. **C (416, 417, 423)**

10. **D (416)**

11. **A (417)**

12. **C (417)**

13. **D (417)**

14. **B (423)**

15. **A (424–425)**

16. **B (417–418)**

17. **A (416–417)**

18. **D (416)**

19. **C (416)**

20. **D (420)**

Unit 23 Quiz Answers

1. **A (433)**

2. **B (436)**

3. **C (438)**

4. **D (440–442)**

5. **C (451)**

6. **B (451)**

7. **A (456–457)**

8. **C (451)**

9. **D (452–454)**

10. **A (454)**

11. **D (451)**

12. **A (454)**

13. **D (439–440)**

14. **B (440)**

15. **B (441)**

16. **B (441)**

17. **A (458)**

18. **A (435)**

19. **A (455)**

20. **D (452)**

Unit 24 Quiz Answers

1. **A   The answer is $1,250.**

   $125,000 sales price ÷ 100 front feet = $1,250 per front foot

2. **A   The answer is $4,350.**

   100% value – 90% LTV = 10% down payment

   $88,500 × 10% (0.10) = $8,850 down payment

   $8,850 down payment – $4,500 earnest money = $4,350 due at closing

3. **C   The answer is $125,000.**

   $11,250 annual net income ÷ 9% (0.09) = $125,000 price

4. **B** **The answer is 30%.**

   $525 monthly rent × 12 months = $6,300 annual rent

   $6,300 annual rent ÷ $21,000 annual income = 0.30 or 30%

5. **D** **The answer is $657.**

   $73,000 sales price × 6% (0.06) = $4,380 full commission

   $4,380 full commission ÷ 2 sponsoring brokers = $2,190 sponsoring broker's share of the commission

   $2,190 sponsoring broker's share of the commission × 30% (0.30) = $657 listing broker's commission

6. **D** **The answer is 10,626.63.**

   6" ÷ 12 = 0.5' + 75' = 75.5' frontage

   9" ÷ 12 = 0.75' + 140' = 140.75' depth 140.75' × 75.5' = 10,626.63 square feet

7. **D** **The answer is $1,736,000.**

   $775 monthly rent × 28 units × 12 months = $260,400 annual scheduled gross income

   $260,400 annual scheduled gross income − 5% vacancy rate = $247,380 annual effective gross income

   $247,380 annual effective gross income − $82,460 annual expenses = $164,920 annual net operating income

   $164,920 annual net income ÷ 9.5% (0.095) = $1,736,000 value

8. **A** **The answer is $5,512.50.**

   2.5 points loan discount + 1 point origination fee = 3.5 points

   $175,000 loan × 90% or (0.90) = $157,500 sales price

   $157,500 loan × 3.5% (0.035) = $5,512.50 for points and origination fee

9. **B** **The answer is $316.67.**

   $5,000 loan × 9.5% (0.095) = $475 annual interest

   $475 annual interest ÷ 12 months × 8 months = $316.67 interest

10. **C** **The answer is $571,500.**

    $68,580 annual net operating income ÷ 12% (0.12) = $571,500 price

11. **A** **The answer is $35,000.**

    $20,000 annual salary ÷ 12 months = $1,666.67 monthly salary; $1,666.67 monthly salary × 25% = $416.67 monthly PITI payment

    $678.24 annual taxes and insurance ÷ 12 months = $56.52 monthly taxes and insurance

    $416.67 monthly PITI payment − $56.52 monthly TI = $360.15 monthly PI payment

    $360.15 monthly PI payment ÷ $10.29 × $1,000 = $35,000 loan

12. **A** **The answer is 30%.**

    $10,500 cost of lot + $93,000 cost of home = $103,500 total cost

    $134,550 sales price − $103,500 total cost = $31,050 profit

    $31,050 profit ÷ $103,500 total cost = 0.3 or 30%

13. **C** **The answer is 17%.**

    $2,500 cost × 4 parcels = $10,000 total cost

    $1,950 sales price × 6 parcels = $11,700 sales price

    $11,700 sales price − $10,000 cost = $1,700 profit

    $1,700 profit ÷ $10,000 cost = 0.17 or 17% profit

14. **A** **The answer is $2,072.**

    $60,000 annual salary ÷ 12 months = $5,000 wife's monthly salary + 2,400 husband's monthly salary = $7,400 total monthly salary

    $7,400 total monthly salary × 28% (0.28) = $2,072 monthly payment

15. **C** **The answer is $2,437.98.**

    $340,500 loan ÷ $1,000 × $7.16 = $2,437.98 monthly principal and interest payment

Practice Exam One Answers

1. **B (174)**

2. **A (196)**

3. **A (40)**

4. **C (312)**

5. **C (6)**

6. **B (106–107)**

7. **A (230)**

8. **A (406)**

9. **A (127)**

10. **D (141)**

11. **D (67)**

12. **A (297)**

13. **B (326)**

14. **A (369)**

15. **A (389)**

16. **D (17–18)**

17. **D (53–54)**

18. **D (27)**

19. **A (313)**

20. **B (122)**

21. **D (96–97)**

22. **B (163)**

23. **B (288)**

24. **C (178)**

25. **C (290)**

26. **C (80–81)**

27. **B (371)**

28. **D (82)**

29. **B (290)**

30. **B (80)**

31. **A (198)**

32. **D (216)**

33. **A (332–333)**

34. **B (151)**

35. **B (192)**

36. **A (292)**

37. **D (370–371)**

38. **B (91)**

39. **A (150–151)**

40. **A (244)**

41. **D (106–107)**

42. **B (334)**

43. **C (400)**

44. **B (290)**

45. **D (174)**

46. **D (218)**

47. **C (389)**

48. **D (163)**

49. **B (364)**

50. **B (174)**

51. **B (193–194)**

52. **B (140)**

53. **C (328)**

54. **D (194)**

55. **B (130)**

56. **C (198)**

57. **A (125)**

58. **C (181)**

59. **D (387)**

60. **B (196)**

61. **C (300)**

62. **C (405)**

63. **D (310–311)**

64. **B (37–40)**

65. **B (230)**

66. **D (140)**

67. **B (456)**

68. **D (403)**

69. **A (231)**

70. **A (370)**

71. **D (309)**

72. **D (148–150)**

73. **A (451)**

74. **D (451)**

75. **B (17)**

76. **C (132)**

77. **D (328)**

78. **B (91)**

79. **D (77–78)**

80. **D (332)**

81. **C (13)**

82. **A (389)**

83. **C (28)**

84. **B (45)**

85. **C (386)**

86. **D (148–149)**

87. **C (400–402)**

88. **D (196)**

89. **C (91)**

90. **C (370)**

91. **D (122)**

92. **A (200)**

93. **C (126)**

94. **B (298–300)**

95. **B (143–144)**

96. **B (151)**

97. **B (167)**

98. **C (168)**

99. **D (146)**

100. **D (180–181)**

101. **B (183)**

102. **B (144)**

103. **C (103)**

104. **C (251–252)**

105. **D (39–40)**

106. **C (132)**

107. **A (199–200)**

108. **B (106)**

109. **A (216)**

110. **A (253)**

111.D (281)

112.B (275–277)

113.A (226)

114.B (160)

115.B (216)

116.C (199)

117.D (289)

118.D (275–276)

119.B (231)

120.C (275–277)

121.C (231)

122.C (176–177)

123.B (408–410)

124.B (231)

125.D (242)

126.B (242–243)

127.C (281)

128.C (254–255)

129.D (270)

130.B (393)

131.B (299)

132.C (182)

133.B (178)

134.B (199)

135.B (275–277)

136.D (282)

137.B (77)

138.C (394)

139.C (146–147)

140.A (297)

141.B (274)

142.B (330)

143.D (253)

144.C (336)

145.B (386)

146.A (128)

147.C (50)

148.C (175)

149.B (253)

150.C (257)

Practice Exam Two Answers

1. D (327)

2. D (18)

3. C (191)

4. B (299)

5. C (312)

6. D (39–40)

7. B (80)

8. D (403)

9. C (162)

10. B (313)

11. B (216)

12. A (318)

13. D (114)

14. C (127)

15. D (38)

16. D (162)

17. B (227)

18. B (39)

19. C (80)

20. A (365)

21. C (439–440)

22. B (336)

23. A (127)

24. B (451)

25. B (335)

26. D (308)

27. C (308)

28. B (39)

29. B (371)

30. D (451)

31. A (452)

32. B (362)

33. A (197)

34. D (241)

35. B (466)

36. A (77)

37. B (332)

38. D (90–91)

39. A (371)

40. C (363)

41. D (234–235)

42. C (163)

43. D (197)

44. D (348)

45. C (466)

46. D (315)

47. A (122–124)

48. A (451)

49. B (335)

50. **C (369)**

51. **C (348)**

52. **A (243–244)**

53. **D (27–28)**

54. **A (331)**

55. **D (140–141)**

56. **A (451)**

57. **B (122)**

58. **B (464–465)**

59. **D (369)**

60. **D (319)**

61. **D (332)**

62. **C (319)**

63. **C (235)**

64. **C (308)**

65. **A (54)**

66. **B (96)**

67. **B (403)**

68. **D (270–271)**

69. **C (464–465)**

70. **A (444)**

71. **D (313)**

72. **C (371)**

73. **A (217)**

74. **D (370–372)**

75. **D (317)**

76. **C (308)**

77. **B (361)**

78. **D (178)**

79. **B (451)**

80. **B (352–353)**

81. **B (77)**

82. **D (67)**

83. **B (365)**

84. **B (106–107)**

85. **D (93–94)**

86. **C (335)**

87. **B (363–362)**

88. **A (441)**

89. **D (82–83)**

90. **A (83–84)**

91. **B (452)**

92. **D (291)**

93. **C (326–327)**

94. **C (332)**

95. **A (332)**

96. **D (256)**

97. **D (181)**

98. **A (407)**

99. **D (407)**

100. **C (406)**

101. **A (35)**

102. **C (272)**

103. **B (50–54)**

104. **D (268–269)**

105. **B (96)**

106. **C (270)**

107. **C (80)**

108. **A (274)**

109. **C (268)**

110. **D (47)**

111. **D (90)**

112. **B (106)**

113. **D (90)**

114. **A (144)**

115. **D (117)**

116. **C (122)**

117. **B (124)**

118. **A (128)**

119. **D (128–129)**

120. **D (274)**

121. **D (159–160)**

122. **B (178)**

123. **A (193)**

124. **D (194)**

125. **C (226)**

126. **B (231–232)**

127. **B (244)**

128. **B (257)**

129. **C (258)**

130. **C (258)**

131. **B (262–263)**

132. **D (263)**

133. **D (274)**

134. **D (274)**

135. **A (275–276)**

136. **B (274)**

137. **B (275)**

138. **C (70)**

139. **D (264)**

140. C (291–292)

141. D (288)

142. C (327)

143. C (271–272)

144. B (54)

145. A (452)

146. D (435)

147. D (386)

148. A (218)

149. B (274)

150. C (114)

Practice Exam Three Answers

1. A (80)
2. B (264)
3. A (49)
4. D (258)
5. C (36–37)
6. A (45)
7. C (67)
8. D (37)
9. D (67)
10. A (271–272)
11. B (39)
12. B (77)
13. D (444)
14. D (275–276)
15. A (68)
16. D (76)
17. A (260–261)
18. C (102–106)

19. C (268–269)
20. C (268–269)
21. C (90)
22. D (270)
23. D (50)
24. A (270, 282)
25. B (47)
26. C (77)
27. C (271–272)
28. D (47)
29. C (268)
30. B (406–407)
31. D (77)
32. D (231–232)
33. B (90–91)
34. D (103)
35. D (180)
36. B (262–263)
37. D (271–272)
38. C (36–37)
39. A (281)
40. A (247)
41. B (272)
42. B (360–361)
43. B (271)
44. A (128–129)
45. D (128–129)
46. D (253)
47. B (262–263)
48. D (268)

49. D (274)
50. C (257)

Math Calculations

Unit 3

14. $9,500 + $800 + $1,000
= $11,300

Unit 5

9. $8,200 ÷ 0.06 = $136,666.67

10. $2,520 × 2 = $5,040 ÷
$72,000 = 0.07 or 7%

Unit 6

5. $12,925 ÷ $235,000 = 0.055
or 5.5%

10. 0.065 × 0.40 = 0.026
$9,750 ÷ 0.026 = $375,000

13. $153,500 × 0.06 × 0.40
= $3,684

14. $387,000 × 0.055 = $21,285
$387,000 − $21,285
= $365,715

Unit 9

8. 43,560 × $2.15 = $93,654

12. 4.5 × 43,560 = 196,020
$78,400 ÷ 196,020 = 0.40
150 × 100 = 15,000
0.40 × 15,000 = $6,000

13. 10 × 43,560 − 26,000 ÷ 5,000
= 81.92, rounded to 81

14. 400 × 640 ÷ 2 = 128,000
÷ 43,560 = 2.94

Unit 10

6. $160,000 × 0.75 × 0.040
= $4,800

9. $47,250 × 1.25 × 0.025
= $1,477

Unit 15

1. $120,000 × 0.03 = $3,600

9. $2,700 ÷ $90,000 = 0.03 or 3 points

Unit 16

13. $100,000 × 0.075 = $7,500 ÷ 12 = $625 interest

$902.77 − $625.00 = $277.77

$100,000 − $277.77 = $99,722.23

14. $85,000 × 0.115 = 9,775 ÷ 12 = $814.58

$823.76 − $814.58 = $9.18

15. $114,500 × 0.80 = $91,600

Unit 17

13. $1,200 × 12 = $14,400

$19,200 − 14,400 = 4,800 ÷ 0.04 = $120,000

$120,000 + 150,000 = $270,000

Unit 19

9. $24,000 ÷ $300,000 = 0.08 or 8%

15. $112,000 − $53,700 ÷ $542,000 = 10.75%

17. $240,000 ÷ 65 × 5 = $18,462

Unit 23

9. $285,000 × 0.10 = $28,500

$285,000 − $28,500 = $256,500

$256,500 × 0.02 = $5,130 + $28,500 = $33,630

10. $300,000 × 0.30 = $90,000

$90,000 − $22,000 = $68,000

17. $2,129 ÷ 365 = $5.83

Practice Exam One

19. $250,000 × 0.2 − $5,000 = $45,000

21. $165,000 ÷ 0.95 = $173,684

22.   3 × 43,560 = 130,680 sq. ft.

24. $240,000 × 0.40 × 1.5 × 0.04 = $5,760

25. $360,000 × 0.90 = $324,000 × 0.01 = $3,240

$360,000 × 0.10 = $36,000 + $3,240 = $39,240

29. $133,700 × 0.02 = $2,674

30. $250,000 × 0.0775 = $19,375

37. $22,000 ÷ 0.08 = $275,000

44. $6,000 ÷ $150,000 = 0.04 or 4 points

48.   2 × 4 = 8. 640 ÷ 8 = 80

4 × 4 = 16. 640 ÷ 16 = 40

80 + 40 = 120 acres

67.   Count the actual number of days from March 16 through December 31: 291 days.

$1,880.96 ÷ 365 = $5.153 × 291 = $1,500

$84,500 − 67,600 = $16,900 down − $2,000 paid = $14,900

$14,900 + 1,500 + 1,250 = $17,650

94. $165,000 + 50,000 − $30,000 (their total homestead) = $185,000

119. $250,000 ÷ $500 = 500 × $0.50 = $250

124. $185,000 ÷ $500 = 370 × $0.25 = $92.50

133. $175,000 × 0.030 ÷ 2 = $2,625 on June 1

Practice Exam Two

7.   80' × $200 = $16,000 × 0.10 × 0.60 = $960

9.   2 × 43,560 = 87,120 sq. ft.

87,120 × $1.50 = $130,680

10. $120,500 × 0.80 = $96,400

19. $195,000 × 0.075 × 0.65 = $9,506.25

26. $57,200 × 0.135 = $7,722 ÷ 12 = $643.50

$666.75 − 643.50 = $23.25

$57,200 − 23.25 = $57,176.75

27. $57,200 × 0.135 = $7,722 ÷ 12 = $643.50

31. $57,500 × 0.085 = $4,887.50 ÷ 12 = 407.29

407.29 ÷ 31 = 13.14384

13.1384 × 14 = 183.93

The bank will add interest on the day of closing.

32. $142,500 × 1.27 = $180,975

35. $193,600 ÷ $4.40 = 44,000 sq. ft. ÷ 200' = 220 ft

40. $142,000 − 18,000 = $124,000 value of building ÷ 3l.5 years = $3,936.51

$3,936.51 × 7 years = $27,556 depreciation

$142,000 − 27,556 = $114,444

42.   2 × 4 × 4 = 32

640 ÷ 32 = 20 acres that he owns.

He wants to own 160 acres. 160 − 20 = 140 acres × $300 = $42,000

44. $795 × 3 = $2,385

$2,385 + 1,200 + 900 = $4,485 × 12 = $53,820 × 0.085 = $4,574.70

45.   36 ft × 200 ft = 7,200 sq. ft.

7,200 × $1.85 = $13,320

48.   45 days to the end of the year.

$1,116 ÷ 360 = $3.10 × 45 days = $139.50

50. $234,500 − 80,000 = $154,500 value of building ÷ 27.5 = $5,618.18

51. $1,000 × 12 × 0.07 = $840

$1,100 × 12 × 0.05 = 660

$1,210 × 12 × 0.03 = 435.60

$840 + 660 + 435.60 = $1,936

58.   54% + 18% + 16% = 88%

100% − 88% = 12% to the college

$79,000 ÷ 0.12 = $658,333 × 0.18 = $118,500

64. $90,000 × 0.075 = $6,750 × 15 = $101,250

66. $90,000 ÷ 0.94 = $95,745

69.   Subtract front setback 25' and rear setback 20' from 70': 70' − 45' = 25'

Subtract side setback 10' and side setback 10' from 70': 70' − 20' = 50'

50' × 25' = 1,250 sq. ft.

72. $30,000 ÷ 0.10 = $300,000

$30,000 ÷ 0.12 = $250,000

$300,000 − 250,000 = $50,000

76. $1,200.22 × 12 × 15 = $216,040

$1,028.63 × 12 × 30 = $370,307

$370,307 ÷ 216,040 = 1.71 or 171%

78. $85,000 × 1.10 × 0.040 = $3,740

91.   January 1 to May 2 is 4 months and 2 days

$560 ÷ 12 = $46.667 × 4 months = $186.667

$46.667 ÷ 31 × 2 days = $3.011

$186.667 + 3.011 = $189.68

145. $560 ÷ 12 ÷ 31 = $1.505 or $1.51

GLOSSARY

abstract of title   The condensed history of a title to a particular parcel of real estate, consisting of a summary of the original grant and all subsequent conveyances and encumbrances affecting the property and a certification by the abstractor that the history is complete and accurate.

acceleration clause   The clause in a mortgage or deed of trust that can be enforced to make the entire debt due immediately if the borrower defaults on an installment payment or other covenant.

accession   Acquiring title to additions or improvements to real property as a result of the annexation of fixtures.

accretion   The increase or addition of land by the deposit of sand or soil washed up naturally from a river, lake, or sea.

accrued item   On a closing statement, items of expense that are incurred but not yet payable, such as interest on a mortgage loan or taxes on real property.

acknowledgment   A formal declaration made before a duly authorized officer, usually a notary public, by a person who has signed a document.

Act   The Real Estate License Act of 2000.

actual eviction   The legal process that results in the tenants being physically removed from the leased premises.

actual notice   Express information or fact; that which is known; direct knowledge.

addendum   Any provision added to an existing contract without altering the content of the original; it must be signed by all parties.

address of record   The designated address recorded by the Department in the applicant's or licensee's application file or license file as maintained by the Department.

adjustable-rate mortgage (ARM)   A loan characterized by a fluctuating interest rate, usually one tied to a bank or savings and loan association cost-of-funds index.

adverse possession   The actual, open, notorious, hostile, and continuous possession of another's land under a claim of right. Possession for a statutory period may be a means of acquiring title.

affidavit of title   A written statement, made under oath by a seller or grantor of real property and acknowledged by a notary public, in which the grantor (1) identifies himself and indicates marital status, (2) certifies that since the examination of the title on the date of the contract no defects have occurred in the title, and (3) certifies that he is in possession of the property (if applicable).

affiliated business arrangement (ABA)   A system under which, to streamline the settlement process, a real estate firm, title insurance company, mortgage broker, home inspection company, or even a moving company may agree to offer a package of services to consumers.

affiliated business disclosure   A disclosure that a company or individual referring settlement services has either an affiliate relationship with or a direct or beneficial ownership interest of more than 1% in a provider of settlement services and who then refers business to that provider or in some way influences the selection of that provider.

agency   The relationship between a principal and an agent wherein the agent is authorized to represent the principal in certain transactions.

agency coupled with an interest   An agency relationship in which the agent is given an estate or interest in the subject of the agency (the property).

agent   One who acts or has the power to act for another. A fiduciary relationship is created under the law of agency when a property owner, as the principal, executes a listing agreement or management contract authorizing a licensed sponsoring broker to be his agent.

air lot   A designated airspace over a piece of land. An air lot, like surface property, may be transferred.

air rights   The right to use the open space above a property, usually allowing the surface to be used for another purpose.

alienation   The act of transferring property to another. See also voluntary alienation and involuntary alienation.

alienation clause   The clause in a mortgage or deed of trust that states that the balance of the secured debt becomes immediately due and payable at the lender's option if the property is sold by the borrower. In effect, this clause prevents the borrower from assigning the debt without the lender's approval.

allodial system   A system of land ownership in which land is held free and clear of any rent or service due to the government; commonly contrasted to the feudal system. Land is held under the allodial system in the United States.

amendment   A change to an existing contract.

American Land Title Association (ALTA) policy   A title insurance policy that protects the interest in a collateral property of a mortgage lender who originates a new real estate loan.

Americans with Disabilities Act (ADA)   Legislation that prohibits discrimination against the physically or mentally impaired as it relates to employment opportunities and public accommodations.

amortized loan   A loan in which the principal as well as the interest is payable in monthly or other periodic installments over the term of the loan.

annexation   Method of converting personal property into real property (e.g., using cement, stones, and sand to build a sidewalk).

annual percentage rate (APR)   The relationship of the total finance charges associated with a loan. This must be disclosed to borrowers by lenders under the Truth in Lending Act.

anticipation   The appraisal principle holding that value can increase or decrease based on the expectation of some future benefit or detriment produced by the property.

antitrust laws   Laws designed to preserve the free enterprise of the open marketplace by making illegal certain private conspiracies and combinations formed to minimize competition. Most violations of antitrust laws in the real estate business involve either price-fixing or allocation of customers or markets (real estate companies agreeing to limit their areas of trade or dealing to certain areas or properties).

applicant   Any person, as defined by the Act, who applies to the Department for a valid license as a managing broker, broker, or residential leasing agent.

appraisal   An estimate of the quantity, quality, or value of something. The process through which conclusions of property value are obtained; also refers to the report that sets forth the process of estimation and conclusion of value.

appraiser   An independent person trained to provide an unbiased opinion of value in an impartial and objective manner according to the appraisal process.

appreciation   An increase in the worth or value of a property due to economic or related causes, which may prove to be either temporary or permanent; opposite of depreciation.

appropriation   The way a taxing body actually authorizes the expenditure of funds and provides for the sources of the funding.

appurtenance   A right, privilege, or improvement belonging to, and passing with, the land.

appurtenant easement   An easement that is annexed to the ownership of one parcel and allows the owner the use of the neighbor's land.

asbestos   A mineral once in insulation and other materials that can cause respiratory diseases.

assemblage   The combining of two or more adjoining lots into one larger tract to increase their total value.

assessment   The imposition of a tax, charge, or levy, usually according to established rates.

assignment   The transfer in writing of interest in a bond, mortgage, lease, or other instrument.

assumption of mortgage   Acquiring title to property on which there is an existing mortgage and agreeing to be personally liable for the terms and conditions of the mortgage, including payments.

attachment   The act of taking a person's property into legal custody by writ or other judicial order to hold it available for application to that person's debt to a creditor.

attorney's opinion of title   An abstract of title that an attorney has examined and has certified to be, in his opinion, an accurate statement of the facts concerning the property ownership.

automated underwriting   Software that permits lenders to expedite the loan approval process and reduce lending costs.

automatic extension   A clause in a listing agreement stating that the agreement will continue automatically for a certain period of time after its expiration date. In many states, use of this clause is discouraged or prohibited.

avulsion   The sudden tearing away of land, as by earthquake, flood, volcanic action, or the sudden change in the course of a stream.

balance   The appraisal principle stating that the greatest value in a property will occur when the type and size of the improvements are proportional to each other as well as to the land.

balloon payment   A final payment of a mortgage loan that is considerably larger than the required periodic payments because the loan amount was not fully amortized.

bargain and sale deed   A deed that carries with it no warranties against liens or other encumbrances but does imply that the grantor has the right to convey title. The grantor may add warranties to the deed at his discretion.

base line   The main imaginary line running east and west and crossing a principal meridian at a definite point, used by surveyors for reference in locating and describing land under the rectangular (government) survey system of legal description.

basis   The financial interest that the Internal Revenue Service attributes to an owner of an investment property for the purpose of determining annual depreciation and gain or loss on the sale of the asset. If a property was acquired by purchase, the owner's basis is the cost of the property plus the value of any capital expenditures for improvements to the property, minus any depreciation allowable or actually taken. This new basis is called the adjusted basis.

benchmark   A permanent reference mark or point established for use by surveyors in measuring differences in elevation.

beneficiary   (1) The person for whom a trust operates or on whose behalf the income from a trust estate is drawn. (2) A lender in a deed of trust loan transaction. Also called a legatee.

bequest   A gift of personal property under a will. Also called a legacy.

bilateral contract   A contract by which all parties to the instrument are legally bound to act as prescribed.

bill of sale   A legal document that transfers personal property.

binder   An agreement that may accompany an earnest money deposit for the purchase of real property as evidence of the purchaser's good faith and intent to complete the transaction.

blanket loan   A mortgage covering more than one parcel of real estate, providing for each parcel's partial release from the mortgage lien on repayment of a definite portion of the debt.

blind ad   An advertisement whereby the sponsoring broker's name is not identified in the advertisement.

blockbusting   The illegal practice of inducing homeowners to sell their properties by making representations regarding the entry or prospective entry of persons of a particular race or national origin into the neighborhood.

Board   The Real Estate Administration and Disciplinary Board of the Department as created by Section 25-10 of the Act.

boot   Money or property given to make up any difference in value or equity between two properties in an exchange.

branch office   A secondary place of business apart from the principal or main office from which real estate business is conducted. A branch office must be run by a licensed managing broker working on behalf of the sponsoring broker.

branch office license   In Illinois, a separate license that must be obtained for each branch office a sponsoring broker wishes to establish.

breach of contract   Violation of any terms or conditions in a contract without legal excuse; for example, failure to make a payment when it is due.

broker   One who acts as an intermediary on behalf of others for a fee or commission.

broker's price opinion (BPO)   A less-expensive alternative of valuating properties often used by lenders working with home equity lines, refinancing, portfolio management, loss mitigation, and collections. Many BPOs simply consist of a "drive by" that verifies the existence of the property, along with a listing of comparable sales.

brokerage   The bringing together of parties interested in making a real estate transaction.

brokerage agreement   A written or oral agreement between a sponsoring broker and a consumer for licensed activities to be provided to a consumer in return for compensation or the right to receive compensation from another. They may constitute either a bilateral or unilateral agreement between the sponsoring broker and the sponsoring broker's client depending upon the content of the brokerage agreement. All exclusive brokerage agreements must be in writing.

brownfield   Defunct, derelict, or abandoned commercial or industrial sites; many have toxic wastes.

Brownfields Legislation   Provides federal funding to states and localities to clean up brownfields sites.

buffer zone   A strip of land, usually used as a park or designated for a similar use, separating land dedicated to one use from land dedicated to another use (e.g., residential from commercial).

building code   An ordinance that specifies minimum standards of construction for buildings to protect public safety and health.

building permit   Written governmental permission for the construction, alteration, or demolition of an improvement, showing compliance with building codes and zoning ordinances.

bundle of legal rights   The concept of land ownership that includes ownership of all legal rights to the land—for example, possession, control within the law, and enjoyment.

buydown   A financing technique used to reduce the monthly payments for the first few years of a loan. Funds in the form of discount points are given to the lender by the builder or the seller to buy down or lower the effective interest rate paid by the buyer, thus reducing the monthly payments for a set time.

buyer agency agreement   A principal-agent relationship in which the sponsoring broker is the agent for the buyer, with fiduciary responsibilities to the buyer.

CAN-SPAM Act of 2003   Establishes requirements for commercial email, spells out penalties for email senders, and gives consumers the right to have emailers stop sending emails to them.

capital gain   Profit earned from the sale of an asset.

capitalization   A mathematical process for estimating the value of a property using a proper rate of return on the investment and the annual net operating income expected to be produced by the property. The formula is expressed as net income ÷ rate = value.

capitalization rate   The rate of return a property will produce on the owner's investment.

capping   The process of laying two to four feet of soil over the top of a landfill and then planting grass on it to enhance the landfill's aesthetic value and prevent erosion.

carbon monoxide (CO)   A colorless, odorless gas that occurs due to incomplete combustion as a by-product of burning such fuels as wood, oil, and natural gas. Improperly ventilated CO can lead to death.

cash flow   The net spendable income from an investment, determined by deducting all operating and fixed expenses from the gross income. When expenses exceed income, a negative cash flow results.

cash rent   In an agricultural lease, the amount of money given as rent to the landowner at the outset of the lease, as opposed to sharecropping.

caveat emptor   A Latin phrase meaning "let the buyer beware."

certificate of occupancy   A permit issued by the appropriate local governing body to establish that the property is suitable for habitation by meeting certain safety and health standards. Also called an occupancy permit.

certificate of reasonable value (CRV)   A form indicating the appraised value of a property being financed with a VA loan.

certificate of sale   The document generally given to the purchaser of delinquent property taxes at a tax foreclosure sale.

certificate of title   A statement of opinion on the status of the title to a parcel of real property based on an examination of specified public records.

chain of title   The succession of conveyances, from some accepted starting point, whereby the present holder of real property derives title.

change   The appraisal principle that holds that no physical or economic condition remains constant.

chattel   Items of personal property, including such tangibles as chairs, tables, clothing, money, bonds, and bank accounts. Chattels include trade fixtures.

client   A person who is being represented by a licensee; the principal.

closing   The point at which ownership of a property is transferred in exchange for the selling price.

Closing Disclosure (CD)   A lender's disclosure required by TRID which shows all the costs of closing, in addition to, the costs of the loan, and a comparison from the Loan Estimate with actual costs. The CD must be issued 3 business days before consummation of the loan.

closing statement   A detailed cash accounting of a real estate transaction showing all cash received, all charges and credits made, and all cash paid out in the transaction.

cloud on title   Any document, claim, unreleased lien, or encumbrance that may impair the title to real property or make the title doubtful; usually revealed by a title search and removed by either a quitclaim deed or suit to quiet title.

code of ethics   A written system of standards for ethical conduct.

codicil A supplement or an addition to a will, executed with the same formalities as a will, that normally does not revoke the entire will.

coinsurance clause A clause in insurance policies covering real property requiring that the policyholder maintain fire insurance coverage generally equal to at least 80% of the property's actual replacement cost.

collateral Something having value that is given to secure repayment of a debt.

commingling The illegal act by a real estate licensee of mingling client or customer funds with the licensee's personal funds.

commission Payment to a licensee for services rendered, such as in the sale or purchase of real property; usually a percentage of the selling price of the property.

common elements Parts of a property that are necessary or convenient to the existence, maintenance, and safety of a condominium or are normally in common use by all of the condominium residents. Each condominium owner has an undivided ownership interest in the common elements.

common law The body of law based on custom, usage, and court decisions.

common law of agency The traditional law governing the principal-agent relationship, superseded by statute in Illinois.

Community Association Manager Licensing and Disciplinary Act Legislation created to provide for the regulation of managers of community association management and provide for high standards of professional conduct by those licensed. Anyone acting under this license cannot perform any activities for which a real estate managing broker's license is required under the Real Estate License Act of 2000.

community property A system of property ownership based on the theory that each spouse has an equal interest in the property acquired by the efforts of either spouse during marriage.

Community Reinvestment Act (CRA) Under the act, financial institutions are expected to meet the deposit and credit needs of their communities; participate and invest in local community development and rehabilitation projects; and participate in loan programs for housing, small businesses, and small farms.

comparable A property used in an appraisal report that is substantially equivalent to the subject property.

comparative market analysis (CMA) A comparison of the prices of recently sold homes that are similar to a listing seller's home in terms of location, style, and amenities.

compensation The valuable consideration given by one person or entity to another person or entity in exchange for the performance of some activity or service.

competition The appraisal principle stating that excess profits generate competition.

Comprehensive Environmental Response, Compensation, and Liability Act (CERCLA) A federal law administered by the Environmental Protection Agency that establishes a process for identifying parties responsible for creating hazardous waste sites, forcing liable parties to clean up toxic sites, bringing legal action against responsible parties, and funding the abatement of toxic sites. Also see Superfund.

comprehensive plan A detailed plan to guide the long-term physical development of a particular area.

condemnation A judicial or administrative proceeding to exercise the power of eminent domain, through which a government agency takes private property for public use and compensates the owner.

conditional-use permit Written governmental permission allowing a use inconsistent with zoning but necessary for the common good, such as locating an emergency medical facility in a predominantly residential area.

condominium The absolute ownership of a unit in a multiunit building based on a legal description of the airspace the unit actually occupies, plus an undivided interest in the ownership of the common elements, which are owned jointly with the other condominium unit owners.

confession of judgment clause Permits judgment to be entered against a debtor without the creditor's having to institute legal proceedings.

confidential information Information given by a client to a licensee during the term of a brokerage agreement that the client requests (in writing or verbally) the licensee keep in confidence; relates to the client's negotiating position; or could do damage to the client's negotiating position if disclosed.

conformity The appraisal principle holding that the greater the similarity among properties in an area, the better they will hold their value.

consideration (1) That received by the grantor in exchange for his deed. (2) Something of value that induces a person to enter into a contract.

construction loan A short-term loan usually made during the construction phase of a building project.

constructive eviction Actions of a landlord that so materially disturb or impair a tenant's enjoyment of the leased premises that the tenant is effectively forced to move out and terminate the lease without liability for any further rent.

constructive notice Notice given to the world by recorded documents. All people are charged with knowledge of such documents and their contents, whether or not they have actually examined them. Possession of property is also considered constructive notice that the person in possession has an interest in the property.

consumer A person or entity seeking or receiving licensed activities.

contemporaneous offers When a buyer's agent is acting as designated agent for more than one prospective buyer who the designated agent has reason to believe is making or preparing to make contemporaneous offers to purchase the property located at a specific address, the buyers have the option of being referred to another designated agent who will serve as the agent of the buyer.

contingency A provision in a contract that requires a certain act to be done or a certain event to occur before the contract becomes binding.

contract A legally enforceable promise or set of promises that must be performed and for which, if a breach of the promise occurs, the law provides a remedy. See also unilateral contract and bilateral contract.

contribution The appraisal principle that states that the value of any component of a property is what it gives to the value of the whole or what its absence detracts from that value.

conventional life estate Created intentionally by the owner. It may be established either by deed at the time the ownership is transferred during the owner's life or by a provision of the owner's will after the owner's death.

conventional loan A loan that requires no government insurance or guarantee.

conversion The wrongful appropriation of property belonging to another (i.e. earnest money); also, the process of changing a property's status from rental to condominium.

conveyance Any document that transfers title to real property. The term is also used in describing the act of transferring.

cooperative A residential multiunit building whose title is held by a trust or a corporation that is owned by and operated for the benefit of persons living within the building, who are the beneficial owners of the trust or stockholders of the corporation, each possessing a proprietary lease.

cooperative commission In Illinois, an arrangement whereby both the buyer's and the seller's real estate agents are paid by the seller.

Coordinator The Coordinator of Real Estate created in Section 25-15 of the Act.

co-ownership Ownership held by two or more persons.

corporation An entity created by operation of law, whose rights of doing business are essentially the same as those of an individual. The entity has continuous existence until it is dissolved according to legal procedures.

correction line Provisions in the rectangular survey (government survey) system made to compensate for the curvature of the earth's surface. Every fourth township line (at 24-mile intervals) is used as a correction line on which the intervals between the north and south range lines are remeasured and corrected to a full six miles.

cost approach The process of estimating the value of a property by adding to the estimated land value the appraiser's estimate of the reproduction or replacement cost of the building, less depreciation.

counteroffer A new offer made in response to an offer received. It has the effect of rejecting the original offer, which cannot be accepted thereafter unless revived by the offeror.

covenant A written agreement between two or more parties in which a party or parties pledge to perform or not perform specified acts regarding property; usually found in such real estate documents as deeds, mortgages, leases, and contracts for deed.

covenants, conditions, and restrictions (CC&Rs) Private rules set up by the developer that set standards for all the parcels within a defined subdivision.

covenant of quiet enjoyment The covenant implied by law by which a landlord guarantees that a tenant may take possession of leased premises and that the landlord will not interfere in the tenant's possession or use of the property.

credit On a closing statement, an amount entered in a person's favor—either an amount the party has paid or an amount for which the party must be reimbursed.

credit hour   Fifty minutes of instruction in course work that meets the requirements set forth in rules adopted by the Department.

curtesy   A life estate, usually a fractional interest, given by some states to the surviving husband in real estate owned by his deceased wife. Most states have abolished curtesy.

customer   A consumer who is not being represented by the licensee, but for whom the licensee is performing ministerial acts.

datum   A horizontal plane from which heights and depths are measured.

debit   On a closing statement, an amount charged; that is, an amount that the debited party must pay.

decedent   A person who has died.

dedication   The voluntary transfer of private property by its owner to the public for some public use, such as for streets or schools.

deed   A written instrument that, when executed and delivered, conveys title to or an interest in real estate.

deed in lieu of foreclosure   A deed given by the mortgagor to the mortgagee when the mortgagor is in default under the terms of the mortgage. This is a way for the mortgagor to avoid foreclosure.

deed in trust   An instrument that grants a trustee under a land trust full power to sell, mortgage, and subdivide a parcel of real estate. The beneficiary controls the trustee's use of these powers under the provisions of the trust agreement.

deed of trust   An instrument used to create a mortgage lien by which the borrower conveys title to a trustee, who holds it as security for the benefit of the note holder (the lender). Also called a trust deed.

deed restrictions   Clauses in a deed limiting the future uses of the property.

default   The nonperformance of a duty, whether arising under a contract or otherwise; failure to meet an obligation when due.

defeasance clause   A clause used in leases and mortgages that cancels a specified right upon the occurrence of a certain condition, such as cancellation of a mortgage on repayment of the mortgage loan.

deficiency judgment   A personal judgment levied against the borrower when a foreclosure sale does not produce sufficient funds to pay the mortgage debt in full.

density zoning   Zoning ordinances that restrict the maximum average number of houses per acre that may be built within a particular area, generally a subdivision.

Department of Housing and Urban Development (HUD)   Government agency that administers the Fair Housing Act, governs RESPA, and provides standardized forms.

depreciation   (1) In appraisal, a loss of value in property due to any cause, including physical deterioration, functional obsolescence, and external obsolescence. (2) In real estate investment, an expense deduction for tax purposes taken over the period of ownership of income property.

descent   Acquisition of an estate by inheritance in which an heir succeeds to the property by operation of law.

designated agency   A contractual relationship between a sponsoring broker and a client in which one of more licensees associated with, or employed by, the broker are designated as an agent of the client.

designated agent   A licensee authorized by a sponsoring broker to act as the agent for a specific principal in a particular transaction.

designated managing broker   Managing broker appointed by the sponsoring broker to have supervisory responsibilities and who is registered with the Department.

developer   One who attempts to put land to its most profitable use through the construction of improvements.

devise   A gift of real property by will. The donor is the devisor, and the recipient is the devisee.

discount point   A unit of measurement used for various loan charges; one point equals 1% of the amount of the loan.

discount rate   The interest rate set by the Federal Reserve that member banks are charged when they borrow money through the Fed.

Division of Real Estate   A division of IDFPR responsible for safeguarding the public by enforcing professional licensure.

doctrine of prior appropriation   The right to use any water, with the exception of limited domestic use, is controlled by the state rather than by the landowner adjacent to the water.

dominant tenement   A property that includes in its ownership the appurtenant right to use an easement over another person's property for a specific purpose.

dower   The legal right or interest, recognized in some states, that a wife acquires in the property her husband held or acquired during their marriage. During the husband's lifetime, the right is only a possibility of an interest; on his death, it can become an interest in land.

dual agency   Representing both parties to a transaction. In Illinois, this is illegal unless both parties agree to it in writing.

due-on-sale clause A provision in the mortgage stating that the entire balance of the note is immediately due and payable if the mortgagor transfers (sells) the property.

duress Unlawful constraint or action exercised on a person whereby the person is forced to perform an act against his will. A contract entered into under duress is voidable.

earnest money Money deposited by a buyer under the terms of a contract. It may be forfeited if the buyer defaults but applied to the purchase price if the sale is closed.

easement A right to use the land of another for a specific purpose, such as for a right-of-way or utilities.

easement by condemnation An easement created by the government or government agency that has exercised its right under eminent domain.

easement by necessity An easement allowed by law as necessary for the full enjoyment of a parcel of real estate; for example, a right of ingress and egress over a grantor's land.

easement by prescription An easement acquired by continuous, open, and hostile use of the property for the period of time prescribed by state law.

easement in gross An easement that is not created for the benefit of any land owned by the owner of the easement but that attaches personally to the easement owner. For example, a right granted by Eleanor Franks to Joe Fish to use a portion of her property for the rest of his life would be an easement in gross.

economic life The number of years during which an improvement will add value to the land.

education provider A school licensed by the Department offering courses in pre-license, post-license, or continuing education required by the Act.

electronic means of proctoring A methodology providing assurance that the person taking a test and completing the answers to questions is the person seeking licensure or credit for continuing education and is doing so without the aid of a third party or other device.

emblements Growing crops, such as corn, that are produced annually through labor and industry. Also called fructus industriales.

eminent domain The right of a government or municipal quasi-public body to acquire property for public use through a court action called condemnation, in which the court decides that the use is a public use and determines the compensation to be paid to the owner.

employee Someone who works as a direct employee of an employer and has employee status. The employer is obligated to withhold income taxes and Social Security taxes from the compensation of employees.

employment contract A document evidencing formal employment between employer and employee or between principal and agent. In the real estate business, this generally takes the form of a listing agreement or management agreement.

enabling acts State legislation that confers zoning powers on municipal governments.

encapsulation A method of controlling environmental contamination by sealing off a dangerous substance.

encroachment A building or some portion of it (for example, a wall or fence) that extends beyond the land of the owner and illegally intrudes on some land of an adjoining owner or a street or alley.

encumbrance Anything (for example, a mortgage, tax, or judgment lien; an easement; a restriction on the use of the land) that may diminish the value or use and enjoyment of a property.

Equal Credit Opportunity Act (ECOA) The federal law that prohibits discrimination in the extension of credit because of race, color, religion, national origin, sex, age, or marital status.

equalization factor A factor (number) by which the assessed value of a property is multiplied to arrive at a value for the property that is in line with statewide tax assessments. The ad valorem tax is based on this adjusted value.

equitable lien A lien that arises out of common law.

equitable right of redemption The right of a defaulted property owner to recover the property before its sale by paying the appropriate fees and charges.

equitable title The interest held by a vendee under a contract for deed or an installment contract; the equitable right to obtain absolute ownership to property when legal title is held in another's name.

equity The interest or value that an owner has in property over and above any indebtedness.

Equity in Eminent Domain Act Legislation that provides protections for private property owners when government seeks to acquire land for economic development projects.

erosion   The gradual wearing away of land by water, wind, and general weather conditions; the diminishing of property by the elements.

errors and omissions (E&O) insurance   Business liability insurance that helps protect real estate professionals, individuals, or companies from bearing the full cost of the defense for lawsuits relating to an error or omission in providing covered professional services.

escheat   The reversion of property to the state or county in cases where a decedent dies intestate without heirs capable of inheriting, or when the property is abandoned.

escrow   The closing of a transaction through a third party called an escrow agent, or escrowee, who receives certain funds and documents to be delivered on the performance of certain conditions outlined in the escrow instructions.

escrow account   The trust account established by a sponsoring broker under the provisions of the license law for the purpose of holding funds on behalf of the sponsoring broker's principal or some other person until the consummation or termination of a transaction. Also called a trust account.

escrow moneys   All moneys, promissory notes, or any other type or manner of legal tender or financial consideration deposited with any person for the benefit of the parties to the transaction.

estate at sufferance   The tenancy of a lessee who lawfully comes into possession of a landlord's real estate but who continues to occupy the premises improperly after his lease rights have expired. Also called a tenancy at sufferance.

estate at will   An estate that gives the lessee the right to possession until the estate is terminated by either party; the term of this estate is indefinite. Also called a tenancy at will.

estate for years   An interest for a certain, exact period in property leased for a specified consideration. Also called a tenancy for years.

estate from period to period   An interest in leased property that continues from period to period—week to week, month to month, or year to year. Also called a tenancy from period to period.

estate in land   The degree, quantity, nature, and extent of interest a person has in real property.

estate taxes   Federal taxes on a decedent's real and personal property.

estoppel   Method of creating an agency relationship in which someone states incorrectly that another person is his agent, and a third person relies on that representation.

estoppel certificate   A document in which a borrower certifies the amount owed on a mortgage loan and the rate of interest.

ethics   The systems of moral principles and rules that become standards for professional conduct.

eviction   A legal process to oust a person from possession of real estate.

evidence of title   Proof of ownership of property; commonly a certificate of title, an abstract of title with lawyer's opinion, title insurance, or a Torrens registration certificate.

exclusive-agency listing   A listing contract under which the owner appoints a broker as his exclusive agent for a designated period of time to sell the property on the owner's stated terms for a commission. The owner reserves the right to sell without paying anyone a commission if he sells to a prospect who has not been introduced or claimed by the sponsoring broker.

exclusive brokerage agreement   A written brokerage agreement that provides that the sponsoring broker has the sole right, through one or more sponsored licensees, to act as the exclusive agent or representative of the client and that meets the requirements of Section 15-75 of the Act.

exclusive right-to-sell listing   A listing contract under which the owner appoints a designated broker as his exclusive agent for a designated period to sell the property on the owner's stated terms. The owner agrees to pay the designated broker a commission when the property is sold, whether by the designated broker, the owner, or another broker.

executed contract   A contract in which all parties have fulfilled their promises and thus performed the contract.

execution   (1) The signing and delivery of an instrument. (2) A legal order directing an official to enforce a judgment against the property of a debtor.

executory contract   A contract under which something remains to be done by one or more of the parties.

express agency   An agency relationship based on a formal agreement between the parties.

express agreement   An oral or written contract in which the parties state the contract's terms and express their intentions in words. Also called an express contract.

external obsolescence   Reduction in a property's value caused by outside factors (those that are off the property).

Fair Housing Act   The federal law that prohibits discrimination in housing based on race, color, religion, sex, handicap, familial status, and national origin.

Fannie Mae   A quasi-government agency established to purchase any kind of mortgage loans in the secondary mortgage market from the primary lenders.

Federal Deposit Insurance Corporation (FDIC)   An independent federal agency that insures the deposits in commercial banks.

Federal Reserve System (the Fed)   The country's central banking system, which controls the nation's monetary policy by regulating the supply of money and interest rates.

fee simple absolute   The maximum possible estate or right of ownership of real property, continuing forever.

fee simple defeasible   An estate in which the holder has a fee simple title that may be divested on the occurrence or nonoccurrence of a specified event. There are two categories of defeasible fee estates: fee simple on condition precedent (also called fee simple determinable) and fee simple on condition subsequent.

FHA loan   A loan insured by the Federal Housing Administration and made by an approved lender in accordance with the FHA's regulations.

fiduciary   One in whom trust and confidence is placed, such as a broker employed under the terms of a listing contract or buyer agency agreement.

fiduciary duties   Certain duties owed by a real estate licensee to a principal, including the duties of care, obedience, loyalty, disclosure, accounting, and confidentiality.

fiduciary standard   A legal standard that holds a licensee to the highest ethical standards that the law provides.

Financial Institutions Reform, Recovery, and Enforcement Act of 1989 (FIRREA)   Enacted in response to the savings and loan crisis of the 1980s, this act restructured the savings and loan association regulatory system.

fiscal policy   The government's policy in regard to taxation and spending programs. The balance between these two areas determines the amount of money the government will withdraw from or feed into the economy, which can counter economic peaks and slumps.

fixture   An item of personal property that has been converted to real property by being permanently affixed to the realty.

foreclosure   The legal procedure whereby property used as security for a debt is sold to satisfy the debt in the event of default in payment of the mortgage note or default of other terms in the mortgage document. The foreclosure procedure brings the rights of all parties to a conclusion and passes the title in the mortgaged property to either the holder of the mortgage or a third party, who may purchase the realty at the foreclosure sale, free of all encumbrances affecting the property subsequent to the mortgage.

formaldehyde   A colorless chemical with a strong, pronounced odor. It is classified as a possible human carcinogen.

fractional section   A parcel of land less than 160 acres, usually found at the edge of a rectangular survey.

fraud   Deception intended to cause a person to give up property or a lawful right.

Freddie Mac   A corporation established to purchase primarily conventional mortgage loans in the secondary mortgage market.

freehold estate   An estate in land in which ownership is for an indeterminate length of time, in contrast to a leasehold estate.

frontage   The length of a property along a street or waterfront.

functional obsolescence   A loss of value to an improvement to real estate arising from functional problems, often caused by age or poor design.

future interest   A person's present right to an interest in real property that will not result in possession or enjoyment until sometime in the future, such as a reversion or right of reentry.

gain   Investment result of more money than originally paid.

gap   A defect in the chain of title of a particular parcel of real estate; a missing document or conveyance that raises doubt as to the present ownership of the land.

general agency   The relationship of a broker, managing broker, or leasing agent with a sponsoring broker.

general agent   One who is authorized by a principal to represent the principal in a specific range of matters.

general lien   The right of a creditor to have all of a debtor's property (both real and personal) sold to satisfy a debt.

general partnership   A typical form of joint venture in which each general partner shares in the administration, profits, and losses of the operation.

general real estate tax   A tax levied according to value, generally used to refer to real estate tax. Also called an ad valorem tax.

general warranty deed   A deed in which the grantor fully warrants good clear title to the premises. Used in most real estate deed transfers, a general warranty deed offers the greatest protection of any deed.

Ginnie Mae   A government agency that plays an important role in the secondary mortgage market. It sells mortgage-backed securities that are backed by pools of FHA and VA loans.

government check   The 24-mile-square parcels composed of 16 townships in the rectangular survey system of legal description.

government lot   Fractional sections in the rectangular survey system that are less than one quarter-section in area.

grantee   A person who receives a conveyance of real property from a grantor.

granting clause   Words in a deed of conveyance that state the grantor's intention to convey the property at the present time. This clause is generally worded as "convey and warrant"; "grant"; "grant, bargain, and sell"; or the like.

grantor   The person transferring title to or an interest in real property to a grantee.

gratuitous agency   An agency that exists even if no fee is involved.

gross income multiplier (GIM)   A figure used as a multiplier of the gross annual income of a property to produce an estimate of the property's value.

gross lease   A lease of property according to which a landlord pays all property charges regularly incurred through ownership, such as repairs, taxes, insurance, and operating expenses. Most residential leases are gross leases.

gross rent multiplier (GRM)   The figure used as a multiplier of the gross monthly income of a property to produce an estimate of the property's value.

ground lease   A lease of land only, on which the tenant usually owns a building or is required to build as specified in the lease. Such leases are usually long-term net leases; the tenant's rights and obligations continue until the lease expires or is terminated through default.

groundwater   The water that exists under the earth's surface within the tiny spaces or crevices in geological formations.

group boycotting   Two or more businesses conspiring against another business, or agreeing to withhold their patronage, in order to reduce competition.

growing-equity mortgage (GEM)   A loan in which the monthly payments increase annually, with the increased amount being used to directly reduce the principal balance outstanding and thus shorten the overall term of the loan.

guaranteed sales plan   Any real estate purchase or sales plan in which a sponsoring broker enters into an unconditional written contract with a seller, promising to purchase the seller's property for a specified price, if the property has not sold within an agreed period of time on terms acceptable to seller.

heir   One who might inherit or succeed to an interest in land under the state law of descent when the owner dies without leaving a valid will.

highest and best use   The possible use of a property that would produce the greatest net income and thereby develop the highest value.

holdover tenancy   A tenancy whereby a lessee retains possession of leased property after the lease has expired and the landlord, by continuing to accept rent, agrees to the tenant's continued occupancy as defined by state law.

home equity loan   A loan under which a property owner uses his residence as collateral and can then draw funds up to a prearranged amount against the property. Also called a line of credit.

Home Mortgage Disclosure Act   Requires that all institutional mortgage lenders with assets in excess of $36 million and with one or more offices in a given geographic area make annual reports.

homeowners insurance policy   A standardized package insurance policy that covers a residential real estate owner against financial loss from fire, theft, public liability, and other common risks.

homestead   Land that is owned and occupied as the family home. In many states, a portion of the area or value of this land is protected or exempt from judgments for debts.

hypothecation   To pledge property as security for an obligation or loan without giving up possession of it.

Illinois Department of Financial and Professional Regulation (IDFPR)   The entity responsible for administering and enforcing the Illinois Real Estate License Act of 2000.

Illinois Human Rights Act   Legislation that prohibits discrimination on the basis of race, color, religion, sex, national origin, ancestry, familial status, physical or mental disability, age, marital status, unfavorable military discharge, sexual orientation, and order of protection status.

Illinois Radon Awareness Act   Legislation that requires a seller to provide to a buyer, before the buyer is obligated under any contract to purchase residential real property, a disclosure of information on radon hazards and the pamphlet Radon Testing Guidelines for Real Estate Transactions stating that the property may present the potential for exposure to radon.

implied agency   Agency, intentional or otherwise, created by action or deed.

implied contract   A contract under which the agreement of the parties is demonstrated by their acts and conduct.

implied warranty of habitability   A theory in landlord/tenant law in which the landlord renting residential property implies that the property is habitable and fit for its intended use.

improvement   (1) Any structure, usually privately owned, erected on a site to enhance the value of the property—for example, building a fence or a driveway. (2) A publicly owned structure added to or benefiting land, such as a curb, sidewalk, street, or sewer.

inactive   A status of licensure where the licensee holds a current license under this Act, but the licensee is prohibited from engaging in licensed activities because the licensee is unsponsored or the license of the sponsoring broker with whom the licensee is associated or by whom he or she is employed is currently expired, revoked, suspended, or otherwise rendered invalid under the Act.

income approach   The process of estimating the value of an income-producing property through capitalization of the annual net income expected to be produced by the property during its remaining useful life.

independent contractor   Someone who is retained to perform a certain act but who is subject to the control and direction of another only as to the end result and not as to the way in which the act is performed. Unlike an employee, an independent contractor pays for all expenses, Social Security, and income taxes, and receives no employee benefits. Most real estate brokers are independent contractors.

index method   The appraisal method of estimating building costs by multiplying the original cost of the property by a percentage factor to adjust for current construction costs.

inflation   The gradual reduction of the purchasing power of the dollar, usually related directly to the increases in the money supply by the federal government.

informed written consent   Consent given by a client that allows a licensee to act as a dual agent.

inheritance taxes   State-imposed taxes on a decedent's real and personal property.

innocent landowner immunity   A clause of the Superfund Amendments and Reauthorization Act that establishes the criteria by which to judge whether a person or business could be exempted from environmental liability.

interest   A charge made by a lender for the use of money.

intermediate mortgage theory   Theory based on the principles of title theory states but still requiring the mortgagee to formally foreclose to obtain legal title.

Interstate Land Sales Full Disclosure Act of 1968   Federal law that regulates the sale of certain real estate in interstate commerce.

intestate   The condition of a property owner who dies without leaving a valid will. Title to the property will pass to the decedent's heirs as provided in the state law of descent.

investment   Money directed toward the purchase, improvement, and development of an asset in expectation of income or profits.

involuntary alienation   The act of transferring property to another through eminent domain or adverse possession.

involuntary lien   A lien placed on property without the consent of the property owner.

joint tenancy   Ownership of real estate between two or more parties who have been named in one conveyance as joint tenants. Upon the death of a joint tenant, the decedent's interest passes to the surviving joint tenant or tenants by the right of survivorship.

joint venture   The joining of two or more people to conduct a specific business enterprise. A joint venture is similar to a partnership in that it must be created by agreement between the parties to share in the losses and profits of the venture. It is unlike a partnership in that the venture is for one specific project only, rather than for a continuing business relationship.

judgment   The formal decision of a court on the respective rights and claims of the parties to an action or suit. After a judgment has been entered and recorded with the county recorder, it usually becomes a general lien on the property of the defendant.

judicial foreclosure   Type of foreclosure that allows the property to be sold by court order after the lender has given sufficient public notice to the defaulting borrower.

junior lien   An obligation, such as a second mortgage, that is subordinate in right or lien priority to an existing lien on the same realty.

Junk Fax Prevention Act of 2005   A federal law under which unsolicited fax advertisements and solicitations may only be sent to persons with whom the sender has an established business relationship.

laches   An equitable doctrine used by courts to bar a legal claim or prevent the assertion of a right because of undue delay or failure to assert the claim or right.

land   The earth's surface, extending downward to the center of the earth and upward infinitely into space, including things permanently attached by nature, such as trees and water.

land contract   A contract for the sale of real estate whereby the purchase price is paid in periodic installments by the purchaser, who is in possession of the property even though title is retained by the seller until all payments are received in full. Also called a contract for deed or an articles of agreement for warranty deed.

landfill   An enormous hole, either excavated for the purpose of waste disposal or left over from surface mining operations.

latent defect   A hidden structural defect that could not be discovered by ordinary inspection and that threatens the property's soundness or the safety of its inhabitants. Some states impose on sellers and licensees a duty to inspect for and disclose latent defects.

law of diminishing returns   Law that applies when at the point where additional improvements do not increase income or value.

law of increasing returns   Law that applies as long as money being spent on improvements produces an increase in income or value.

lead   Used as a pigment and drying agent in alkyd oil-based paint in about 75% of housing built before 1978. An elevated level of lead in the body can cause serious damage to the brain, kidneys, nervous system, and red blood cells. Children under the age of six are most vulnerable.

Lead-Based Paint Hazard Reduction Act   Persons selling or leasing residential housing constructed before 1978 must disclose the presence of known lead-based paint and provide purchasers or tenants with any relevant records or reports.

leads   The name or names of a potential buyer, seller, lessor, lessee, or client of a licensee.

lease   A written or oral contract between a landlord (the lessor) and a tenant (the lessee) that transfers the right to exclusive possession and use of the landlord's real property to the lessee for a specified period of time and for a stated consideration (rent). By state law, leases for longer than a certain period of time (generally one year) must be in writing to be enforceable.

lease purchase   The purchase of real property, the consummation of which is preceded by a lease, usually long term. Typically done for tax or financing purposes.

leasehold estate   A tenant's right to occupy real estate during the term of a lease, generally considered to be a personal property interest.

legal description   A description of a specific parcel of real estate complete enough for an independent surveyor to locate and identify it.

legally competent parties   People who are recognized by law as being able to contract with others; those of legal age and sound mind.

levy   To assess; to seize or collect. To levy a tax is to assess a property and set the rate of taxation. To levy an execution is to officially seize the property of a person to satisfy an obligation.

liability coverage   Insurance that covers injuries or losses sustained within the home.

license   (1) A privilege or right granted to a person by a state to operate as a real estate broker, managing broker, or leasing agent. (2) The revocable permission for a temporary use of land—a personal right that cannot be sold.

licensed activities   Those activities listed in the definition of "broker" under this Section of the Act.

licensee   Any person, as defined in this Section of the Act, who holds a valid unexpired license as a managing broker, broker, or residential leasing agent.

lien   A right given by law to certain creditors to have their debts paid out of the property of a defaulting debtor, usually by means of a court sale.

lien theory   Some states interpret a mortgage as being purely a lien on real property. The mortgagee thus has no right of possession but must foreclose the lien and sell the property if the mortgagor defaults.

lien waiver   Collected by the landowner from each contractor and subcontractor to create a continuing record that all lien claimants have released their lien rights.

life estate   An interest in real or personal property that is limited in duration to the lifetime of its owner or some other designated person or persons.

life tenant   A person in possession of a life estate.

limited liability company (LLC)   A business structure that combines the most attractive features of limited partnerships and corporations. The members of an LLC enjoy the limited liability offered by a corporate form of ownership and the tax advantages of a partnership.

limited partnership   A business arrangement whereby the operation is administered by one or more general partners and funded, by and large, by limited or silent partners who are, by law, responsible for losses only to the extent of their investments.

liquidated damages   An amount predetermined by the parties to a contract as the total compensation to an injured party should the other party breach the contract.

lis pendens   A recorded legal document giving constructive notice that an action affecting a particular property has been filed in either a state or federal court.

listing agreement   A contract between an owner (as principal) and a real estate sponsoring broker (as agent) by which the sponsoring broker is employed as agent to find a buyer for the owner's real estate on the owner's terms, for which service the owner agrees to pay a commission.

listing broker   The sponsoring broker in a multiple listing situation from whose office a listing agreement is initiated, as opposed to the cooperating sponsoring broker, from whose office negotiations leading up to a sale are initiated. The listing sponsoring broker and the cooperating sponsoring broker may be the same person.

listing presentation   Any communication, written or oral and by any means or media, between a managing broker or broker and a consumer in which the licensee is attempting to secure a brokerage agreement with the consumer to market the consumer's real estate for sale or lease.

littoral rights   (1) A landowner's claim to use water in large navigable lakes and oceans adjacent to her property. (2) The ownership rights to land bordering these bodies of water up to the high-water mark.

Loan Estimate (LE)   A lender's disclosure showing all associated costs of the mortgage, including the APR, number of payments, amount of all payments, amount of all interest to be paid, and any pertinent clauses. The LE must be generated three business days after application.

loan origination fee   A fee charged to the borrower by the lender for making a mortgage loan. The fee is usually computed as a percentage of the loan amount.

loan-to-value (LTV) ratio   The relationship between the amount of the mortgage loan and the value of the real estate being pledged as collateral.

lot-and-block system   A method of describing real property that identifies a parcel of land by reference to lot and block numbers within a subdivision, as specified on a recorded subdivision plat. Also called the recorded plat system.

management agreement   A contract between the owner of income property and a management firm or individual property manager that outlines the scope of the manager's authority.

management plan   A highly detailed plan that lays out the owner's objectives with the property, as well as what the property manager wants to accomplish and how, including all budgetary information.

managing broker   A broker who has supervisory responsibilities for licensees in one or, in the case of a multi-office company, more than one office and who has been appointed as such by the sponsoring broker.

manufactured housing   Dwellings that are built offsite and trucked to a building lot where they are installed or assembled.

marital property   All property acquired after the date of marriage for the duration of the marriage, except by gift or will.

market   A place where goods can be bought and sold and a price established.

market price   The price a property actually sells for. Also called sales price.

market value   The most probable price that property would bring in an arm's-length transaction under normal conditions on the open market.

marketable title   Good or clear title, reasonably free from the risk of litigation over possible defects.

material fact   Any fact that, if known, might reasonably be expected to affect the course of events.

mechanic's lien   A statutory lien created in favor of contractors, laborers, and materialmen who have performed work or furnished materials in the erection or repair of a building.

medium of advertising   Any method of communication intended to influence the general public to use or purchase a particular good or service or real estate, including, but not limited to, print, electronic, social media, and digital forums.

meridian   One of a set of imaginary lines running north and south and crossing a base line at a definite point, used in the rectangular survey system of property description.

metes-and-bounds method   A legal description of a parcel of land that begins at a well-marked point and follows the boundaries, using directions and distances around the tract, back to the point of beginning.

minimum services   A provision of the Real Estate License Act of 2000 that requires licensees to perform a minimum level of service to clients.

ministerial acts   In Illinois, acts that a licensee may perform for a consumer that are informative and do not constitute active representation.

minor   Someone who has not reached the age of majority and therefore does not have legal capacity to transfer title to real property.

mold   Fungi that grows in the form of multicellular filaments called hyphae. Some mold can cause disease, and others play a role in biodegradation or the production of antibiotics and enzymes.

monetary policy   Governmental regulation of the amount of money in circulation through such institutions as the Federal Reserve Board.

month-to-month tenancy   A periodic tenancy under which the tenant rents for one month at a time. In the absence of a rental agreement (oral or written), a tenancy is generally considered to be month to month.

monument   A fixed natural or artificial object used to establish real estate boundaries for a metes-and-bounds description.

mortgage   (1) A conditional transfer or pledge of real estate as security for the payment of a debt. (2) The document creating a mortgage lien.

mortgage banker   Mortgage loan companies that originate, service, and sell loans to investors.

mortgage broker   An agent of a lender who brings the lender and borrower together. The broker receives a fee for this service.

mortgage insurance premium (MIP)   An up-front premium charged at closing for all FHA loans.

mortgage lien   A lien or charge on the property of a mortgagor that secures the underlying debt obligations.

mortgage loan originator (MLO)   Anyone who, for compensation or expectation of compensation, takes a residential mortgage loan by phone or in person.

mortgagee   A lender in a mortgage loan transaction.

mortgagor   A borrower in a mortgage loan transaction.

multiperil policy   Insurance policies that offer protection from a range of potential perils, such as those of a fire, hazard, public liability, and casualty.

multiple listing clause   A provision in an exclusive listing for the authority and obligation on the part of the listing broker to distribute the listing to other brokers in the multiple listing organization.

multiple listing service (MLS)   A marketing organization composed of member brokers who agree to share their listing agreements with one another in the hope of procuring ready, willing, and able buyers for their properties more quickly than they could on their own. Most MLSs accept exclusive-right-to-sell or exclusive-agency listings from their member brokers.

mutual assent   A meeting of the minds between parties.

National Do Not Call Registry   A registry managed by the Federal Trade Commission that lists the phone numbers of consumers who have indicated their preference to limit the telemarketing calls they receive.

Nationwide Mortgage Licensing System (NMLS)   Mortgage loan originators (MLOs) in Illinois are required to register in this system.

negligent misrepresentation   Occurs when the broker should have known that a statement about a material fact was false.

negotiable instrument   A written promise or order to pay a specific sum of money that may be transferred by endorsement or delivery. The transferee then has the original payee's right to payment.

net lease   A lease requiring that the tenant pay not only rent but also costs incurred in maintaining the property, including taxes, insurance, utilities, and repairs.

net listing   A listing based on the net price the seller will receive if the property is sold. Under a net listing the sponsoring broker can offer the property for sale at the highest price obtainable to increase the commission. This type of listing is legal in Illinois, though it is discouraged.

net operating income (NOI)   The income projected for an income-producing property after deducting losses for vacancy, collection, and operating expenses.

nonconforming use   A use of property that is permitted to continue after a zoning ordinance prohibiting it has been established for the area.

nondisturbance clause   A mortgage clause stating that the mortgagee agrees not to terminate the tenancies of the lessees in the event the mortgagee forecloses on the mortgagor-lessor's building.

nonjudicial foreclosure   Some states allow nonjudicial foreclosure procedures to be used when the security instrument contains a power-of-sale clause. In this case, no court action is required.

nonmarital property   Any property in possession prior to marriage.

novation   Substituting a new obligation for an old one or substituting new parties to an existing obligation.

obsolescence   The loss of value due to factors that are outmoded or less useful. Obsolescence may be functional or economic.

offer and acceptance   Two essential components of a valid contract; a "meeting of the minds."

office   A broker's place of business where the general public is invited to transact business and where records may be maintained and licenses displayed, whether or not it is the broker's principal place of business.

open buyer agency agreement   An agreement that permits the buyer to enter into multiple agreements with an unlimited number of sponsoring brokers, and the sponsoring broker receives compensation only if she locates the property the buyer ultimately purchases. Also called a nonexclusive buyer agency agreement.

open listing   A listing contract under which the sponsoring broker's commission is contingent on the sponsoring broker producing a ready, willing, and able buyer before the property is sold by the seller or another sponsoring broker.

open-end loan   A mortgage loan that is expandable by increments up to a maximum dollar amount, the full loan being secured by the same original mortgage.

option   An agreement to keep open for a set period an offer to sell or purchase property.

option listing   Listing with a provision that gives the listing sponsoring broker the right to purchase the listed property.

package loan   A real estate loan used to finance the purchase of both real property and personal property, such as in the purchase of a new home that includes carpeting, window coverings, and major appliances.

partition suit   The division of cotenants' interests in real property when the parties do not all voluntarily agree to terminate the co-ownership; takes place through court procedures.

partnership   An association of two or more individuals who carry on a continuing business for profit as co-owners. Under the law, a partnership is regarded as a group of individuals rather than as a single entity. See also general partnership and limited partnership.

party wall   A wall that is located on or at a boundary line between two adjoining parcels of land and is used or intended to be used by the owners of both properties.

payment cap   The limit on the amount the monthly payment can be increased on an adjustable-rate mortgage when the interest rate is adjusted.

percentage lease   A lease, commonly used for commercial property, whose rental is based on the tenant's gross sales at the premises; it usually stipulates a base monthly rental plus a percentage of any gross sales above a certain amount.

percolation test   A test of the soil to determine if it will absorb and drain water adequately to use a septic system for sewage disposal.

perimeter   The length of an area's outer boundary.

person   Individuals, entities, corporations, limited liability companies, registered limited liability partnerships, foreign and domestic partnerships, and other business entities, except that when the context otherwise requires, the term may refer to a single individual or other described entity.

personal property   Items, called chattels, that do not fit into the definition of real property; movable objects. Also called personalty.

physical deterioration   A reduction in a property's value resulting from a decline in physical condition; can be caused by action of the elements or by ordinary wear and tear.

PITI Acronym for principle, interest, taxes, and insurance—expenses that comprise an owner's monthly payment.

planned unit development (PUD) Planned combination of diverse land uses, such as housing, recreation, and shopping, in one contained development or subdivision.

plat map A map of a town, section, or subdivision indicating the location and boundaries of individual properties. Also called a subdivision plat.

plottage The increase in value or utility resulting from the consolidation (assemblage) of two or more adjacent lots into one larger lot.

point of beginning (POB) In a metes-and-bounds legal description, the starting point of the survey, situated in one corner of the parcel. All metes-and-bounds descriptions must follow the boundaries of the parcel back to the point of beginning.

police power The government's right to impose laws, statutes, and ordinances, including zoning ordinances and building codes, to protect the public health, safety, and welfare.

power of attorney A written instrument authorizing a person, the attorney-in-fact, to act as agent for another person to the extent indicated in the instrument.

prepaid item On a closing statement, items that have been paid in advance by the seller, such as insurance premiums and some real estate taxes, for which she must be reimbursed by the buyer.

prepayment penalty A charge imposed on a borrower who pays off the loan principal early. This penalty compensates the lender for interest and other charges that would otherwise be lost.

price-fixing Real estate companies conspiring to set fixed compensation rates.

primary mortgage market The mortgage market in which loans are originated, consisting of lenders such as commercial banks, savings and loan associations, and mutual savings banks.

principal (1) A sum loaned or employed as a fund or an investment, as distinguished from its income or profits. (2) The original amount (as in a loan) of the total due and payable at a certain date. (3) A main party to a transaction—the person for whom the agent works.

principal meridian The main imaginary line running north and south and crossing a base line at a definite point, used by surveyors for reference in locating and describing land under the rectangular (government) survey system of legal description.

prior appropriation A concept of water ownership in which the landowner's right to use available water is based on a government-administered permit system.

priority The order of position or time. The priority of liens is generally determined by the chronological order in which the lien documents are recorded; tax liens, however, have priority even over previously recorded liens.

private mortgage insurance (PMI) Insurance provided by a private carrier that protects a lender against a loss in the event of a foreclosure and deficiency.

probate A legal process by which a court determines who will inherit a decedent's property and what the estate's assets and liabilities are.

proctor Any person, including, but not limited to, an instructor, who has a written agreement to administer examinations fairly and impartially with a licensed education provider.

procuring cause The chain of events, without abandonment or estrangement, which leads to a sale on the seller's terms. Under an open listing, the sponsoring broker who is the procuring cause of the sale receives the commission.

professional real estate services Services that require a person to have an Illinois real estate license in order to perform those services on behalf of clients, customers, and consumers.

progression An appraisal principle that states that, between dissimilar properties, the value of the lesser-quality property is favorably affected by the presence of the better-quality property.

promissory note A financing instrument that states the terms of the underlying obligation is signed by its maker and is negotiable (transferable to a third party).

property management agreement An agreement between the property owner and sponsoring broker. It sets forth the nature of the relationship between the two parties. The agreement covers such items as time period, property manager's responsibilities, extent of property manager's authority, compensation, and reporting to name a few.

property manager Someone who manages real estate for another person for compensation. Duties include collecting rents, maintaining the property, and keeping up all accounting.

property report   The mandatory federal and state documents compiled by subdividers and developers to provide potential purchasers with facts about a property before their purchase.

proprietary lease   A lease given by the corporation that owns a cooperative apartment building to the shareholder for the shareholder's right as a tenant to an individual apartment.

proration   Expenses, either prepaid or paid in arrears, that are divided or distributed between buyer and seller at the closing.

protected class   Any group of people designated as such by federal or state law. It currently includes ethnic minorities, women, religious groups, persons with handicaps, and others.

puffing   Exaggerated or superlative comments or opinions.

pur autre vie   "For the life of another." A life estate pur autre vie is a life estate that is measured by the life of a person other than the grantee.

purchase money mortgage (PMM)   A note secured by a mortgage or deed of trust given by a buyer, as borrower, to a seller, as lender, as part of the purchase price of the real estate.

quantity-survey method   The appraisal method of estimating building costs by calculating the cost of all of the physical components in the improvements, adding the cost to assemble them and then including the indirect costs associated with such construction.

quick-take   A summary proceeding permitted by Illinois law in which a plaintiff/condemnor may obtain immediate fee simple title to real property, including the rights of possession and use.

quiet title   A court action to remove a cloud on the title.

quitclaim deed   A conveyance by which the grantor transfers whatever interest she has in the real estate, without warranties or obligations.

radon   A naturally occurring gas that is suspected of causing lung cancer.

range   A strip of land six miles wide, extending north and south and numbered east and west according to its distance from the principal meridian in the rectangular (government) survey system of legal description.

rate cap   The limit on the amount the interest rate can be increased at each adjustment period in an adjustable-rate loan. The cap also may set the maximum interest rate that can be charged during the life of the loan.

ready, willing, and able buyer   One who is prepared to buy property on the seller's terms and is ready to take positive steps to consummate the transaction.

real estate   Land; a portion of the earth's surface extending downward to the center of the earth and upward infinitely into space, including all things permanently attached to it, whether naturally or artificially.

Real Estate Administration and Disciplinary Board   Illinois regulatory body tasked with maintaining standards of professional conduct, discipline, and examination.

real estate investment trust (REIT)   Trust ownership of real estate by a group of individuals who purchase certificates of ownership in the trust, which in turn invests the money in real property and distributes the profits back to the investors free of corporate income tax.

Real Estate License Act 2000 (the Act)   State law enacted to protect the public from fraud, dishonesty, and incompetence in the purchase and sale of real estate. It was amended in 2011.

real estate licensee   The point of contact between two or more people in negotiating the sale, purchase, or rental of property.

Real Estate Recovery Fund   A fund established to cover claims of aggrieved parties who have suffered monetary damage through the actions of a real estate licensee.

Real Estate Research and Education Fund   A fund maintained by the Illinois State Treasury for research and education at state institutions of higher education or other organizations for research and the advancement of education in the real estate industry.

Real Estate Settlement Procedures Act (RESPA)   The federal law that requires certain disclosures to consumers about mortgage loan settlements. The law also prohibits the payment or receipt of kickbacks and certain kinds of referral fees.

real property   The interests, benefits, and rights inherent in real estate ownership.

REALTOR®   A registered trademark term reserved for the sole use of active members of the National Association of REALTORS®.

reconciliation   The final step in the appraisal process, in which the appraiser combines the estimates of value received from the sales comparison, cost, and income approaches to arrive at a final estimate of market value for the subject property.

recording   The act of entering or recording documents affecting or conveying interests in real estate in the recorder's office established in each county. Until it is recorded, a deed or mortgage ordinarily is not effective against subsequent purchasers or mortgagees.

rectangular survey system   System established in 1785 by the federal government, providing for surveying and describing land by reference to principal meridians and base lines. Also called the government survey system.

redemption   The right of a defaulted property owner to recover her property by curing the default.

redemption period   A period of time established by state law during which a property owner has the right to redeem her real estate from a foreclosure or tax sale by paying the sales price, interest, and costs. Many states do not have mortgage redemption laws.

redlining   The illegal practice of a lending institution denying loans or restricting their number for certain areas of a community.

reduction certificate   The document signed by a lender indicating the amount required to pay a loan balance in full and satisfy the debt; used in the settlement process to protect both the seller's and the buyer's interests. Also called a payoff statement.

regression   An appraisal principle stating that, between dissimilar properties, the value of the better-quality property is affected adversely by the presence of the lesser-quality property.

regular employee   A person working an average of 20 hours per week for a person or entity who would be considered as an employee under the Internal Revenue Service rules for classifying workers.

reinstatement   The activation of a suspended, revoked, or inoperative license.

release deed   A document, also called a deed of reconveyance, that transfers all rights given a trustee under a deed of trust loan back to the grantor after the loan has been fully repaid.

remainder interest   The remnant of an estate that has been conveyed to take effect and be enjoyed after the termination of a prior estate, such as when an owner conveys a life estate to one party and the remainder to another.

renewal period   The period beginning 90 days prior to the expiration date of a license.

rent   A fixed, periodic payment made by a tenant of a property to the owner for possession and use, usually by prior agreement of the parties.

rent schedule   A statement of proposed rental rates, determined by the owner or the property manager or both, based on a building's estimated expenses, market supply and demand, and the owner's long-range goals for the property.

rental-finding service   Any business that finds, attempts to find, or offers to find for any person for consideration a unit of rental real estate or a lessee for a unit of rental real estate not owned or leased by the business.

replacement cost   The construction cost at current prices of a property that is not necessarily an exact duplicate of the subject property but serves the same purpose or function as the original.

reproduction cost   The construction cost at current prices of an exact duplicate of the subject property.

residential leasing agent   A person who is employed by a broker to engage in licensed activities limited to leasing residential real estate who has obtained a license as provided for in Section 5-5 of the Act.

restrictive covenants   A clause in a deed that limits the way the real estate ownership may be used.

reverse mortgage   A loan under which the homeowner receives monthly payments based on her accumulated equity rather than a lump sum. The loan must be repaid at a prearranged date or on the death of the owner or the sale of the property.

reversionary interest   The remnant of an estate that the grantor holds after granting a life estate to another person.

reversionary right   The return of the rights of possession and quiet enjoyment to the lessor at the expiration of a lease.

right of first refusal   A clause allowing the tenant the opportunity to buy the property before the owner accepts an offer from another party.

right of survivorship   The right by which, upon the death of a joint tenant, the decedent's interest passes to the surviving joint tenant or tenants by the right of survivorship.

right-of-way   The right given by one landowner to another to pass over the land, construct a roadway, or use as a pathway, without actually transferring ownership.

riparian rights   An owner's rights in land that borders on or includes a stream, river, or lake. These rights include access to and use of the water.

risk management   Evaluation and selection of appropriate property and other insurance.

rules and regulations   Real estate licensing authority orders that govern licensees' activities; they usually have the same force and effect as statutory law.

sale-leaseback arrangement   A transaction in which an owner sells her improved property and, as part of the same transaction, signs a long-term lease to remain in possession of the premises.

sales comparison approach   The process of estimating the value of a property by examining and comparing actual sales of comparable properties.

satisfaction of mortgage   A document acknowledging the payment of a mortgage debt.

secondary mortgage market   A market for the purchase and sale of existing mortgages, designed to provide greater liquidity for mortgages.

Secretary   The Secretary of the Department of Financial and Professional Regulation, or a person authorized by the Secretary to act in the Secretary's stead.

section   A portion of a township under the rectangular (government) survey system. A township is divided into 36 sections, numbered 1 through 36. A section is a square with mile-long sides and an area of one square mile, or 640 acres.

Secure and Fair Enforcement for Mortgage Licensing Act of 2008 (SAFE Act)   Act requires that each individual state must license and register mortgage loan originators (MLOs).

security deposit   A payment by a tenant, held by the landlord during the lease term and kept (wholly or partially) on default or destruction of the premises by the tenant.

seisin   Possession of real property under claim of freehold estate (fee simple).

separate property   Under community property law, property owned solely by either spouse before the marriage, acquired by gift or inheritance after the marriage, or purchased with separate funds after the marriage.

servient tenement   Land on which an easement exists in favor of an adjacent property (called a dominant estate). Also called a servient estate.

setback   The amount of space local zoning regulations require between a lot line and a building line.

severalty   Ownership of real property by one person only. Also called sole ownership.

severance   Changing an item of real estate to personal property by detaching it from the land; for example, cutting down a tree.

sharecropping   In an agricultural lease, the agreement between the landowner and the tenant farmer to split the crop or the profit from its sale.

sheriff's deed   In Illinois, a specialized quitclaim deed issued to the purchaser of a foreclosed home, the owner of which exercises the equitable right of redemption.

sheriff's sale   Occurs when a default is not cured by redemption or reinstatement and a decree of foreclosure is entered.

short sale   A sale of real estate in which the sale proceeds fall short of the balance owed on the property's mortgage loan.

single agency   The representation of a single principal.

situs   The personal preference of people for one area over another.

Small Business Liability Relief and Brownfields Revitalization Act   Provides funds to assess and clean up brownfields, clarifies liability protections, and provides tax incentives toward enhancing state and tribal response programs.

special agent   One who is authorized by a principal to perform a single act or transaction; a real estate broker is usually a special agent authorized to find a ready, willing, and able buyer for a particular property.

special assessment   A tax or levy customarily imposed against only those specific parcels of real estate that will benefit from a proposed public improvement like a street or sewer.

special warranty deed   A deed in which the grantor warrants, or guarantees, the title only against defects arising during the period of her tenure and ownership of the property and not against defects existing before that time.

specific lien   A lien affecting or attaching only to a certain, specific parcel of land or piece of property.

specific performance   A legal action to compel a party to carry out the terms of a contract.

sponsoring broker   The broker who is sponsoring a licensed broker, managing broker, or leasing agent.

sponsorship   That a sponsoring broker has certified to the Department that a managing broker, broker, or residential leasing agent named thereon is employed by or associated by written agreement with the sponsoring broker and the Department has registered the sponsorship, as provided for in Section 5-40 of the Act.

square-foot method   The appraisal method of estimating building costs by multiplying the number of square feet in the improvements being appraised by the cost per square foot for recently constructed similar improvements.

statute of frauds   The part of a state law that requires that certain instruments, such as deeds, real estate sales contracts, and certain leases, be in writing to be legally enforceable.

statute of limitations   That law pertaining to the period within which certain actions must be brought to court.

statutory lien   A lien imposed on property by statute (for example, a tax lien).

statutory right of redemption   The right of a defaulted property owner to recover the property after its sale by paying the appropriate fees and charges.

statutory right of reinstatement   In Illinois, an option available when the defaulting mortgagor wishes to cure the default and reinstate the loan as if no acceleration had occurred.

steering   The illegal practice of channeling prospective homebuyers to particular areas, either to maintain the homogeneity of an area or to change the character of an area, which limits their choices of where they can live.

stigmatized property   A property that has acquired an undesirable reputation due to an event that occurred on or near it, such as violent crime, gang-related activity, illness, or personal tragedy.

straight loan   A loan in which only interest is paid during the term of the loan, with the entire principal amount due with the final interest payment. Also called a term loan.

straight-line method   A method of calculating depreciation for tax purposes, computed by dividing the adjusted basis of a property by the estimated number of years of remaining useful life.

strict foreclosure   A way for a lender to acquire mortgaged property as an alternative to judicial foreclosure.

subagent   One who is employed by a person already acting as an agent.

subdivider   One who buys undeveloped land, divides it into smaller, usable lots, and sells the lots to potential users.

subdivision   A tract of land divided by the owner, called the subdivider, into blocks, building lots, and streets according to a recorded subdivision plat, which must comply with local ordinances and regulations.

sublease   The leasing of premises by a lessee to a third party for part of the lessee's remaining term. See also assignment.

subordination agreement   A written agreement between holders of liens on a property that changes the priority of mortgage, judgment, and other liens under certain circumstances.

subrogation   The substitution of one creditor for another, with the substituted person succeeding to the legal rights and claims of the original claimant. Subrogation is used by title insurers to acquire from the injured party rights to sue to recover any claims the insurers have paid.

substantive contact   Dialogue between a licensee and a consumer that moves to consumer's motives, objectives, financial qualifications, and other confidential information that, if disclosed, could harm the consumer's bargaining position.

substantive contact   Dialogue between a licensee and a consumer that moves to consumer's motives, objectives, financial qualifications, and other confidential information that, if disclosed, could harm the consumer's bargaining position

substitution   An appraisal principle stating that the maximum value of a property tends to be set by the cost of purchasing an equally desirable and valuable substitute property, assuming that no costly delay is encountered in making the substitution.

subsurface rights   Ownership rights in a parcel of real estate to the water, minerals, gas, oil, and so forth that lie beneath the surface of the property.

suit for specific performance   A court action in which the defaulting party is sued to perform under the terms and conditions agreed to in the contract.

suit to quiet title   A court action intended to establish or settle the title to a particular property, especially when there is a cloud on the title.

Superfund   Popular name of the hazardous-waste cleanup fund established by CERCLA.

Superfund Amendments and Reauthorization Act (SARA)   An amendatory statute that contains stronger cleanup standards for contaminated sites, increased funding for Superfund, and clarifications of lender liability and innocent landowner immunity. See also Comprehensive Environmental Response, Compensation, and Liability Act (CERCLA).

supply and demand   The appraisal principle that follows the interrelationship of the supply of and demand for real estate. Because appraising is based on economic concepts, this principle recognizes that real property is subject to the influences of the marketplace, as is any other commodity.

surety bond   An agreement by an insurance or bonding company to be responsible for certain possible defaults, debts, or obligations contracted for by an insured party. In the real estate business, a surety bond is generally used to ensure that a particular project will be completed at a certain date or that a contract will be performed as stated.

surface rights   Ownership rights in a parcel of real estate that are limited to the surface of the property and do not include the air above it (air rights) or the minerals below the surface (subsurface rights).

survey   The process by which boundaries are measured and land areas are determined; the onsite measurement of lot lines, dimensions, and position of a house on a lot, including the determination of any existing encroachments or easements.

syndicate   A combination of people or firms formed to accomplish a business venture of mutual interest by pooling resources. In a real estate investment syndicate, the parties own and/or develop property, with the main profit generally arising from the sale of the property.

tacking   Adding or combining successive periods of continuous occupation of real property by adverse possessors. This concept enables someone who has not been in possession for the entire statutory period to establish a claim of adverse possession.

tax deed   An instrument given to a purchaser after the expiration of the redemption rights. See also certificate of sale.

tax lien   A charge against property, created by operation of law. Tax liens and assessments take priority over all other liens.

tax sale   A court-ordered sale of real property to raise money to cover delinquent taxes.

taxation   The process by which a government or municipal quasi-public body raises monies to fund its operation.

team   Any two or more licensees who work together to provide real estate brokerage services, represent themselves to the public as being part of a team or group, are identified by a team name that is different than their sponsoring broker's name, and together are supervised by the same managing broker and sponsored by the same sponsoring broker.

tenancy by the entirety   The spousal joint ownership of the principal residence acquired during marriage. Upon the death of one spouse, the survivor becomes the owner of the property.

tenancy in common   A form of co-ownership by which each owner holds an undivided fractional interest in real property as if she were sole owner. Each individual owner has the right to partition. Unlike joint tenants, tenants in common have right of inheritance.

tenant   One who holds or possesses lands or tenements by any kind of right or title.

tenant improvements   Alterations to the interior of a building to meet the functional demands of the tenant.

testate   Having made and left a valid will.

testator   A person who has made a valid will.

tie-in agreement   An agreement to sell one product only if the buyer purchases another product as well. The sale of the first product is "tied" to the purchase of a second product. Also called a tying agreement.

TILA-RESPA Integrated Disclosure Rule (TRID)   Rule that implements provisions of the Dodd-Frank Act intended to combine and clarify financing disclosures to consumers.

time is of the essence   A phrase in a contract that requires the performance of a certain act within a stated period of time.

time-share   A form of ownership interest that may include an estate interest in property and that allows use of the property for a fixed or variable time period.

time-share estate   A fee simple interest in a time-share property.

time-share use   A right of occupancy in a time-share property, less than a fee simple interest.

title   (1) The right to or ownership of land. (2) The evidence of ownership of land.

title insurance   A policy insuring the owner or mortgagee against loss by reason of defects in the title to a parcel of real estate, other than encumbrances, defects, and matters specifically excluded by the policy.

title search   The examination of public records relating to real estate to determine the current state of the ownership.

title theory   Some states interpret a mortgage to mean that the lender is the owner of mortgaged land. On full payment of the mortgage debt, the borrower becomes the landowner.

town house   A type of residential dwelling with two floors that is connected to one or more dwellings by a common wall or walls. Title to the unit and lot vest in the owner who shares a fractional interest with other owners for the common areas.

township   The principal unit of the rectangular (government) survey system. A township is a square with six-mile sides and an area of 36 square miles.

township line   The lines in a rectangular survey system that run east and west, parallel to the base line six miles apart.

township tier   Township lines that form strips of land and are designated by consecutive numbers north or south of the base line.

trade fixture   An article installed by a tenant under the terms of a lease and removable by the tenant before the lease expires.

transfer tax   Tax stamps required to be affixed to a deed by state and/or local law.

trigger terms   Specific credit terms that may not be advertised unless the advertisement includes other detailed information.

trust   A fiduciary arrangement whereby property is conveyed to a person or institution, called a trustee, to be held and administered on behalf of another person, called a beneficiary. The one who conveys the trust is called the trustor.

trustee   The individual or entity entrusted to main the trust or the holder of bare legal title in a deed of trust loan transaction.

trustee's deed   A deed executed by a trustee conveying land held in a trust.

trustor   The creator of the trust or the borrower in a deed of trust loan transaction.

Truth in Lending Act (TILA)   Federal legislation that allows the government to regulate the lending practices of mortgage lenders. Often called Regulation Z.

unauthorized practice of law   The act of engaging in the practice of law without authorization to practice law pursuant to state law.

underground storage tank (UST)   Commonly found on sites where petroleum products are used or where gas stations and auto repair shops are located. In residential areas, tanks are used to store heating oil. Over time, neglected tanks may leak hazardous substances into the environment.

unenforceable contract   A contract that has all the elements of a valid contract, yet neither party can sue the other to force performance of it.

Uniform Probate Code   Federal legislation that gives the surviving spouse the right to take an elective share on the death of the other spouse.

Uniform Standards of Professional Appraisal Practice (USPAP)   A set of standards that details information required of an appraisal of residential property. The Uniform Residential Appraisal Report is required by many government agencies.

Uniform Vendor and Purchaser Risk Act   States that the seller bears any loss that occurs before the title passes or the buyer takes possession.

unilateral contract   A one-sided contract wherein one party makes a promise so as to induce a second party to do something. The second party is not legally bound to perform; however, if the second party does comply, the first party is obligated to keep the promise.

unit-in-place method   The appraisal method of estimating building costs by calculating the costs of all the physical components in the structure, with the cost of each item including its proper installation, connection, and so forth. Also called the segregated cost method.

unity of ownership   The four unities traditionally needed to create a joint tenancy—unity of title, time, interest, and possession.

universal agent   A person empowered to do anything the principal could do personally.

unsecured debt   Any type of debt or general obligation that is not collateralized by a lien on specific assets of the borrower in the case of bankruptcy or liquidation.

usury   Charging interest at a higher rate than the maximum rate established by state law.

VA loan   A mortgage loan on approved property made to a qualified veteran by an authorized lender and guaranteed by the Department of Veterans Affairs to limit the lender's possible loss.

valid contract   A contract that complies with all the essentials of a contract and is binding and enforceable on all parties to it.

value   The power of a good or service to command other goods in exchange for the present worth of future rights to its income or amenities.

variance   Permission obtained from zoning authorities to build a structure or conduct a use that is expressly prohibited by the current zoning laws; an exception from the zoning ordinances.

vendee   A buyer, usually under the terms of a land contract.

vendor   A seller, usually under the terms of a land contract.

void contract   A contract that has no legal force or effect because it does not meet the essential elements of a contract.

voidable contract   A contract that seems to be valid on the surface but may be rejected or disaffirmed by one or both of the parties.

voluntary alienation   The act of voluntarily transferring property to another, such as by gift or sale.

voluntary lien   A lien placed on property with the knowledge and consent of the property owner.

walk-through   The final property inspection by the buyer, a few days before closing, to ensure that the property is in the same condition that it was in at the time the sales contract was written.

waste   An improper use or an abuse of a property by a possessor who holds less than fee ownership, such as a tenant, life tenant, mortgagor, or vendee. Such waste ordinarily impairs the value of the land or the interest of the person holding the title or the reversionary rights.

water table   The natural level at which the ground is saturated.

will   A written document, properly witnessed, providing for the transfer of title to property owned by the deceased, called the testator.

workers' compensation acts   Laws that require an employer to obtain insurance coverage to protect her employees who are injured in the course of their employment.

wraparound loan   A method of refinancing in which the new mortgage is placed in a secondary, or subordinate, position; the new mortgage includes both the unpaid principal balance of the first mortgage and whatever additional sums are advanced by the lender.

writ of attachment   To prevent a debtor from conveying title to such previously unsecured real estate while a court suit is being decided, a creditor may seek a writ of attachment, by which the court retains custody of the property until the suit concludes.

zoning ordinance   An exercise of police power by a municipality to regulate and control the character and use of property.

INDEX